The Bhagavadgītā

The Bhagavadgītā

A Sublime Hymn of Yoga
Composed by the Ancient Seer Vyāsa

Translation from Sanskrit by
Nataraja Guru

With Explanatory Dialogue by
Nitya Chaitanya Yati

DK
PRINTWORLD
Publishers of Indian Traditions

Cataloging in Publication Data — DK
[Courtesy: D.K. Agencies (P) Ltd. <docinfo@dkagencies.com>]

Bhagavadgītā.
The Bhagavadgītā : a sublime hymn of yoga composed by the ancient Seer Vyāsa / translation from Sanskrit by Nataraja Guru ; with explanatory dialogue by Nitya Chaitanya Yati. – Third revised edition.
pages cm
English and Sanskrit (Sanskrit in Devanagari and roman).
Includes index.
ISBN 9788124611418

1. Bhagavadgītā – Commentaries. 2. Hinduism – Sacred books. 3. Yoga. I. Nataraja Guru, 1895-1973, translator. II. Nityacaitanya Yati, 1924-1999, writer of added commentary. III. Bhagavadgītā. English. IV. Title.

LCC BL1138.64.E5 2022 | DDC 294.5924047 23

ISBN 978-81-246-1141-8
First Published, 1981
Second edition published in 1993
Third revised edition published in 2022

Printed and published by:
D.K. Printworld (P) Ltd.
Regd. Office: "Vedaśrī", F-395 Sudershan Park
(Metro Station: ESI Hospital), New Delhi - 110015
Phones: (011) 2545 3975; 2546 6019
e-mail: indology@dkprintworld.com
Web: www.dkprintworld.com

To
Nataraja Guru

Sañjaya said:

By the grace of Vyāsa I heard this supreme
and most secret Yoga spoken by Kṛṣṇa Himself,
the Lord of Yoga, as immediately given to my senses.

Oh King! as I remember and remember this marvellous
and sacred dialogue between Keśava and Arjuna,
I rejoice over and over again.

As I remember and remember the most marvellous
form of Hari, great is my astonishment, Oh King!
and I rejoice over and over again.

Where there is Kṛṣṇa, the Lord of Yoga,
where there is Pārtha, the Archer,
there will be prosperity, victory, progress,
and well-established justice: such is my belief.

– Chapter XVIII, verses 75-78

Contents

Preface to the Third Edition

WITH the publication of the third edition of Guru Nitya Chaitanya Yati's commentary on the *Bhagavad Gītā* we reflect on the events that have led to this occasion. First, it was Nataraja Guru who boldly wrote his revolutionary commentary to explain the enigmas and obscurities untouched by earlier commentators, both from the West and the East. His translation and commentary is noted for the lucid manner in which the intention of the author, the sage-bard Vyasa, is presented. Later, while teaching the *Bhagavad Gītā* to a growing number of students in the US, Nitya Chaitanya Yati wrote his own commentary based on the translation by Nataraja Guru. He writes in the Preface to the First Edition: "I used my classes as an opportunity to give a fresh commentary on the verses. I would never have ventured to do so if I had not had the privilege of being both initiated and guided by the Guru himself in the "triple system" of the *Brahma Sūtra*s, the *Upaniṣad*s and the *Bhagavad Gītā*". He grounded his commentary on scientific psychology to tackle the problems of the modern mind. Thus the perennial wisdom of the *Gītā* is now accessible to the contemporary generation, and its relevance is evident from the high demand, which has prompted the publication of a new edition. This revised edition has a few improvements vis-à-vis the earlier editions of 1981 and 1993. There are original Sanskrit *śloka*s, latest diacritical transliteration, an updated index, a redesigned format and a new cover design. Many people, too numerous to mention by name, have contributed their valuable time and resources in this endeavour. To all of them we extend our heartfelt gratitude.

Narayana Gurukula and D.K. Printworld together have also brought out Nataraja Guru's translation and commentary: *The Bhagavad Gītā, A Sublime Hymn of Dialectics Composed by the Antique Sage-Bard Vyasa,* as well as Guru Muni Narayana Prasad's *Life's Pilgrimage through the Gītā,* both of which have evoked an avid interest among readers.

We highly appreciate the keen interest of the management of D.K. Printworld and their team for their readiness, enthusiasm and hard work in bringing out the third edition. We look forward to future editions which will nourish the spiritual aspirations of generations to come all across the globe!

Vyasa Prasad

Preface to the Second Edition

In the 1970s, I was invited to teach the *Bhagavadgītā* in the United States at Portland State University and the First Methodist Church in Portland, Oregon. At that time, my Guru's *Bhagavadgītā* translation and commentary, on which I had been relying heavily, was out of print. The need arose for me to give my own interpretation to my students who were growing in numbers. So I used my classes as an opportunity to give a fresh commentary on the verses. I would never have ventured to do so if I had not had the privilege of being both initiated and guided by the Guru himself in the "triple system" of the *Brahmasūtras*, the Upaniṣads, and the *Bhagavadgītā*.

In an original, easy to understand format, the commentary divides each of the *Gītā*'s eighteen chapters into three sections: the first elucidating the basic concepts involved; the second including Sanskrit text in Roman script along with the English meaning of each word or phrase and Nataraja Guru's lucid and revolutionary English translation; and the third carrying our explanatory notes and comments in the form of an assumed dialogue between a teacher and student.

The first edition, which appeared in 1981, was very well received by the public and, in a short time, the edition was sold out and has been unavailable for several years.

Our several centers of the Gurukula around the globe and other discerning readers have been putting pressure on me to bring out a new edition of my commentary and D.K. Printworld (P) Ltd. has agreed to do so. That is the immediate prompting for bringing out the present edition.

Our friends from the United States, Nancy Yeilding and Scott Teitsworth, volunteered to help in getting another edition with their moral support and I thought it a good augury to have a second edition.

Nitya Chaitanya Yati

Preface to the First Edition

In 1970, when I visited the United States of America, I was invited to give a talk on the *Bhagavad Gita* to the Theosophical Society in Portland, Oregon. This marked the beginning of a chain of events leading to my return to Portland in 1971, there to teach the *Gita* at Portland State University, through the faculty of Arts and Letters.

Though the *Gita* has been translated and commented upon by a number of highly accredited scholars of both the East and the West, I preferred to use the commentary of my own teacher, Nataraja Guru. Unfortunately, when I was due to teach at Portland State University, the Guru's commentary on the *Gita* was out of print. I had no alternative but to write the present book based on the Guru's translation and commentary, and to use it in teaching my students. I would never have ventured to do so if I had not had the privilege of being both initiated and guided by the Guru himself in the "triple system" of the *Brahma Sutras*, the *Upanishads* and the *Bhagavad Gita*. I can never adequately express my devotion and gratitude to my Guru for the Grace he ever showers upon me. With his permission, I have transposed many pages from his book into the present one as part of the dialogue between the teacher and the student, which are not specially marked or documented by any footnote.

Each chapter is divided into three sections. The first is a general introduction to the concepts dealt with. The second section contains the Sanskrit text in transliteration, the English meaning of each word or phrase, and a translation rendered by Nataraja Guru. The third section contains our explanatory notes in the form of an assumed dialogue between a teacher and his student. The present book was prepared by a dedicated team of helpers. One person who untiringly assisted me from the start, by taking down dictation, typing out the draft and editing it meticulously was my friend Anne Lafreniere. In preparing the final transcript, I also had the assistance of Peter Oppenheimer, Eva Looney and Nancy Yeilding. The word-by-word translation of the Sanskrit text was prepared by Sathya Thevi Chelliah. The typescript was examined by A.K. Pavithran and edited by John Goodman. The final transcript was made by Richard S. Teitsworth. This preface is to express my gratitude to these and many other friends, not mentioned here by name.

Nitya Chaitanya Yati

Foreword

STUDENTS OF THE *Bhagavadgītā* the world over will welcome the appearance of this commentary by Guru Nitya Chaitanya Yati.

As spiritual leader of the Narayana Gurukula Movement, Nitya is the continuator of the Vedāntin thought of Śaṅkara, Narayana Guru and Nataraja Guru. However, he confounds any such categorization, as does the present volume.

Because of its character as a book of universal wisdom, the *Bhagavadgītā* can be used as the scriptural support for many doctrinal points of view – religious sects, philosophical schools of thought, and even social theory. Nitya's interpretation, however, is not in support of any "school" or doctrine whatever.

The significant clue to his view of the *Gītā* is found in the form he has chosen to give his commentary: that of a dialogue between Teacher and Student. The *Gītā* itself is in the form of a *saṁvāda* between Kṛṣṇa and Arjuna, and in choosing the same structure for his comments, Nitya very clearly indicates his intention. His commentary is not directed to philosophers and scholars, but to every individual human being regardless of culture, who ponders the nature of his own relation to the Divine.

Arjuna's purely human predicament on the battlefield of the Kurus is often viewed by philosophers as a mere fictional setting within which the lofty wisdom of the *Gītā* is expounded. But in choosing such a setting, Vyāsa unequivocably establishes the practical intention of the *Gītā*. It is the human predicament which evokes the *Gītā*, and it is the predicament of daily life that the *Gītā* resolves.

In his commentary, Nitya never loses sight of this orientation. The illuminative dialogue between Teacher and Student is the clear reflection of thousands of such dialogues between Nitya and his disciples all over the world.

Whether in India, Southeast Asia, Australia, Europe or the Americas, his relationship with his students is always the same. He never preaches doctrine; he does not espouse particular philosophical views; he utterly eschews any appearance of authority. Always he is the dear and compassionate friend, the humorous and unfailing guide in time of troubles.

It is as such a friend and guide that he appears here. Not to philosophize, but to help; not to pontificate, but to clarify.

This is not to say that the reader will find this commentary either "popular" or easy. Nitya's deep compassion is accompanied by a powerful and profound intellect. The reader will find his own intelligence and understanding challenged at every turn. But he will find his own efforts repaid a thousandfold. In this volume Guru Nitya has established a bridge between the Divine Wisdom of the *Bhagavadgītā* and you – whoever you are, wherever you may be, whatever your condition. Accept this gift with gratitude and delight as from a dear friend.

AUṀ TAT SAT

Vashon Island, USA DON BERRY

Guide to Sanskrit Pronunciation

VOWELS

a	pronounced like the u in "but"
ā	like the a in "far"
i	like the e in "me"
ī	a longer sound, like the ee in "beet"
u	like the o in "to"
ū	a longer sound, like the oo in "pool"
ṛ	like the ri in "rig" (very short)
e	like the a in "gate"
ai	like the i in "high"
o	like the o in "note"
au	like the ou in "loud"

The Sanskrit alphabet has a beautiful structure. As the Sanskrit alphabet distinguishes more sounds than the English alphabet, it is useful to look at this structure to learn the correct pronunciation of the consonants. This will help to clarify the two main problems for the English speaker: aspiration and "the point of contact" (*sparśa*). For convenience we will use the vowel *a* (pronounced like the u in "but"), to make the consonants articulable syllables. Read across from left to right.

CONSONANTS

ka	*kha*	*ga*	*gha*	*ṅa*
ca	*cha*	*ja*	*jha*	*ña*
ṭa	*ṭha*	*ḍa*	*ḍha*	*ṇa*
ta	*tha*	*da*	*dha*	*na*
pa	*pha*	*ba*	*bha*	*ma*
ya	*ra*	*la*	*va*	
śa	*ṣa*	*sa*		
ha				

The first five groups of five consonants are arranged by points of contact in the vocal apparatus, proceeding from back to front. The points of contact are the velum, the soft palate, the hard palate, the teeth, and the lips, respectively. At the end of each series is a nasal sound made at that point of contact.

The second and fourth consonants in each of these first five series are aspirated. All the other consonants are unaspirated, with the exceptions of *śa*, *ṣa*, *sa* and *ha*. To determine whether you aspirate a particular consonant, place your hand in front of your mouth. If you can feel your breath on your hand, that consonant is being aspirated. It is normal for English speakers to aspirate the *k*, c, *t*, and *p* when these consonants come at the beginning of a word, but Sanskrit words could start either with an unaspirated syllable, like *ka*, or an aspirated syllable, like *kha*.

Pronounce the consonants as follows:

k as in "skip", *kh* like the *k* in "kiss", *g* as in "go" (always "hard"), *ṅ* like the ng in "sing", *c* like the ch in "eschew" (never a "k" or "s"), *ch* slightly harder, as in "much", *j* as in"jam ", *ñ* as a gentle ny sound, like then *ñ* in the Spanish "Señor". The series starting with *ṭa* and the series starting with *ta* are distinguished by the respective position of the tongue in each series. The English "t" and "d" is often pronounced somewhere between the two positions. In the first (*ṭa*) series the tongue should be curled back further toward the roof of the mouth. In the second (*ta*) series the tip of the tongue should protrude slightly between the teeth. These sounds are characteristically "flatter" and less resonant than the preceding series. Go a little more gently than the usual English "t's" and "d's". Pronounce the *ṭ* and *t* as in "storm" (observing the different points of contact), the *ṭh* and *th* like the t in "tie" (not like the th in "think"), make the *ḍ*, *d*, *ṇ*, and *n* sounds as in English, but carefully observing the different points of contact. Pronounce *p* as in "spin", *ph* like the p in "pin" (not like the ph in "phase"), *b* as in "bear", *m as* in "my".

Note the nasals (*ṅ*, *ñ*, *ṇ*, *n*, *m*) go naturally with the corresponding consonants in the series they are in. Thus in the English words "hanker" and "anger" the "n" is pronounced like the Sanskrit *ṅ*, or as the ng in"sing". It is natural for "n" to precede "t" and "d" in words, as in "hunter" and "hinder". And it is natural for "m" to precede "p" and "b", as in "limp" and "lumber". The symbol here transliterated as *ṁ* is not technically a separate letter, and it is pronounced as the nasal appropriate to the consonant that immediately follows it. Thus, it is pronounced like the letter *ṅ* in the names *Śaṅkara* and *Sāṁkhya*, like the letter *ñ* in the name *Sañjaya*, like the n in *saṁnyāsa*, and as m in *saṁbhavāmi* and *saṁyamya*. (It stands for the letter *m* not only when it precedes the consonants in the series beginning with *pa*, but also when it precedes any of the consonants which follow *ma* in the Sanskrit alphabet, and when it comes at the end of u word.)

Pronounce *y* as in "yes", *r* softly, something like the r in "drama", *l* as in "love", *v* with just the slightest contact between the upper teeth and the lower lip (greater than that used for the w in "wile", and less than that used for the v in "vile"). Pronounce *ś* as a gentle sy sound, like the sh in "shove", *ṣ* with the tongue slightly further back, and slightly more aspirated, like the sh in "fish", *s* as in "so", *h* fully aspirated, as in "hope".

The symbol often found at the end of words and transliterated as *ḥ* is slightly aspirated, and echoes the vowel that just precedes it. It is always a very short sound, and so for the vowels *a* and *ai* the echo will be *i*, while for *o* and *au* it will be *u*. Examples: *devaḥ* pronounced as *devaha*, *devāḥ* pronounced as *devāha*, *devaiḥ* pronounced as *devaihi*. In all of these the very last syllable is extremely short.

There is really no English equivalent for the consonants *gh*, *jh*, *ḍh*, *dh*, and *bh*. Some rough approximations are: *gh* as in "loghouse" *jh* as in "hedgehog" (hejhog), *dh* as in "adhere", *ḍh* is the same aspirated *d* with the tongue further back on the palate, *bh* as in "abhor". They are not to be pronounced as two separate sounds, despite the form in which they are transliterated. These letters must be given the same strong aspiration that the letters "k", "c", "t", and "p" are given at the beginning of English words.

By carefully examining their position in the Sanskrit alphabet and saying the letters in order, you can get a feeling for their correct pronunciation. Any speaker of a modern Indian language could give assistance in learning to pronounce the letters of the Sanskrit alphabet, as words such as *dharma* (the first word in the *Gītā*) are in their vocabularies.

Introduction to the Bhagavadgītā

TEACHER: Let me introduce the Gītā to you.

STUDENT: *What is the Gītā?*

Do you know the Mahābhārata?

I suppose Bhārata *is the Sanskrit name of India. What is Mahābhārata?*

Mahā means great. Mahābhārata is "Greater India". In ancient days the term Mahābhārata referred to a state of mind, or a culture that was lived not within the limit of the political or geographical unit called "India". It covered a vast area stretching from the Pacific Islands in the Far East to the Mediterranean in the West, in which region the Hindu–Buddhistic culture exerted a great influence in the arts, literature, and socio-political thought, although politically it was never under a single monarch at any time. Our reference, however, is not to that "Greater India" but to an epic called the *Mahābhārata* which reflects the life and ideals of the people who lived in India around 1000 BCE. It is not the usual story of a single hero and a few other characters. It is a great saga, singing the heroic deeds and thoughts of hundreds of heroes and heroines, and highlighting all aspects of human life. The *Mahābhārata* does not treat any human value as irrelevant or insignificant. In its composition there are themes both beautiful and ugly; it contains side-splitting comedies as well as blood-curdling tragedies. In fact, nothing of the rich legacy of India's ancient tradition is left out of this great epic. We can easily call it an encyclopedia of psychological types and a compendium of Upaniṣadic thoughts and ideals.

Who wrote this epic?

It is believed that Kr̥ṣṇa Dvaipāyana Vyāsa composed the *Mahābhārata.* There are other great works attributed to Vyāsa, such as the *Vedāntasūtras* and the *Pātañjala Sūtra Bhāṣya*. We do not know whether both these Vyāsas are the same person. Like the term "Pope", names such as Vyāsa, Vasiṣṭha, Nārada, and Kaśyapa, often mentioned in the archaic literature of India, were not personal names but spiritual appellations vested on the succeeding heads of the respective hierarchies. Therefore we cannot say whether the *Mahābhārata* and other works were written by the same Vyāsa or a number of Vyāsas. All that we can surmise is that it was written by a certain Vyāsa. The name Vyāsa literally means a compiler or editor.

How is Vyāsa related to the Gītā?

In Vyāsa's *Mahābhārata* there is a section called Bhīṣmaparva. In it there is a sub-section consisting of seven hundred verses beginning with verse 830. This sub-section is called the Bhagavadgītā.

I know that Gītā means a song and Bhagavān *means the Lord. Is the Bhagavadgītā a musical composition of the Lord?*

No, it is called a song in a very special sense. The spiritual quest of man can bring him great agony. If in his plight of anguish he turns to the Gītā, he can derive from it consolation and solace and he will have the feeling that he is listening to a divine song straight from the lips of the Lord himself. Only in that sense is the Gītā called the "Song of the Lord". The Gītā is a song in the sense in which Plato means the rapture of higher intuition by his expression "the hymn of dialectics". When a man does not know what his innate tendencies are, what his natural talents are, and what his basic drive is, he is likely to miss his mark in life. For such a person the rediscovery of his true Self brings to him a joy he has never experienced before. The Gītā helps one to rediscover his real Self, so he will naturally look upon it as a Song of songs as well as a Book of books.

Could we say that the Bhagavadgītā is the sermon of the Lord?

It is, of course, a sermon of the Lord. Apart from being a sermon, it also reveals the nature of the Lord. It teaches man's true identity with the Lord. Thus it is a song of the Lord, about the Lord and by the Lord. It is in this sense it is called the Bhagavadgītā.

Is the Gītā a holy book?

Many people look upon it as an object of worship. Some carry it with them as a talisman, others touch it to ward off evil. These are very crude and childish ways of expressing appreciation for the Gītā. Actually the Gītā teaches us to go beyond the idea of the holy and the unholy, so it is not right to look upon the Gītā as a holy book. You should evaluate it as a book of great wisdom, and approach it in the right manner.

What do you mean by the right manner?

If you want to understand, appreciate, and critically evaluate a book, you should first be qualified to read it. This is called, in Sanskrit, having *adhikāra* (competency). Second, you should know with what subject the book is dealing. In other words, you should know the epistemology of the book.

In Sanskrit the subject matter is called *viṣaya*. Third, you should know the method employed in the book to arrive at its conclusive teaching. The methodology adopted in a book is called its *sambandha*. Fourth, you should know the purpose of the book, and how you are going to be benefited by its study. In Sanskrit this is called the *prayojana* of the book, its axiology. Thus, if you are competent to read a book with reference to its epistemology, methodology, and axiology, you would make a correct evaluation of it. Only in that case can you claim to have the right kind of appreciation.

Am I qualified to study the Gītā?

If you are already a knower of the Absolute, like the great sage Śuka who had no personal identity, and if you are always in a state of absolute merger with the Supreme, there is no need for you to learn the Gītā. On the other hand, if your mind is full of external pursuits, and if you are always tormented by unquenchable passions and have no love for truth, you need not bother to study the Gītā. Wait until you become disillusioned and badly want to know who you are. If, however, you do not come under either of these categories, you must be thirsting for truth. If you love truth and want to seek it, there is nothing like the Gītā to guide you. If you are convinced that there is something beyond the world of the senses, and if you have a thirst for such a joy that is not limited to the perishable, the Gītā can surely help you to find it in your own Self.

Great! That suits me. What is the subject matter of the Gītā?

In one word we can describe it as *brahma-vidyā* (Science of the Absolute). By Absolute we mean here that supreme knowledge which is Self-founded and by which alone everything exists and everything is known. Until you realize this truth, you know only relative factors. One who feels the pangs of life and does not know how to get out of them is called a *viṣādī*. *Viṣāda* means the sadness generated by conflict. Conflict arises out of paradoxical situations, and life bristles with paradoxes. The enigmas and paradoxes of life can be resolved only by knowing the Absolute.

The Bhagavadgītā, in a very comprehensive manner, deals with the riddles of life. In the first chapter is presented a typical seeker confronted by a grave enigma which he cannot get over by mere ratiocination. A carping seeker, questioning everything in a state of agony, is called a *pūrvapakṣin* (an anterior skeptic). The whole of the first chapter and the first nine verses of the second chapter consist of the presentation of the anterior skeptic, Arjuna.

The second chapter explains the stand of the wisdom teacher, Kṛṣṇa. In contrast to the notions of a skeptic who is in conflict, the wise one always sees the omnipresence of the Absolute as the true foundation of everything, and as the indwelling spirit in everyone. Knowing the Absolute as one's own imperishable Self is described in the second chapter as Sāṁkhya–Yoga.

A man who is afflicted by world-consciousness, even after realizing that he is none other than the Absolute, will find it hard to keep away from the necessary demands of his biological and psychological urges. It is these urges that necessitate action. Hence it is necessary to discuss the implications of action in the context of wisdom. The third chapter of Gītā, therefore, describes how action can be unitively treated so that it will not bind the agent to the consequent result.

What is unitive action?

That will be explained later. Brute action is to be differentiated from action guided by wisdom. Comprehensive knowledge and unitive action are counterparts of a situation. Each has its own discipline and is to be understood separately. The secret of being wise and also acting accordingly is taught in the fourth chapter called Jñāna-Yoga.

The fifth chapter is Karma-Saṁnyāsa-Yoga. In this chapter it is shown how the necessary aspects of life can be unitively treated. Finding peace in one's own Self and sharing it with others is made the chief goal of life; and following the dictates of the Absolute in every situation is treated as most natural to the realized person.

The sixth chapter is called Dhyāna-Yoga. This chapter describes Yoga more as a discipline than a philosophical vision. It is described as a *sādhana* (discipline undergone to achieve a specific attainment), and not as a *darśana* (a truth to be visualized). In this chapter it is taught how the self is raised by the higher Self, and how the lower self can be fully established in the higher Self. The self finding its natural repose in the Self is described as a true state of Yoga.

What is the higher Self?

It is the same as God. The seventh chapter is Jñāna-Vijñāna-Yoga. In it all values are categorized in terms of the physical (*ādhibhautika*), the divine (*ādhidaivika*), and the sacrificial (*ādhiyājñika*). These are graded and arranged in such a manner that one value complements the other. This chapter also teaches how the Self can be related to the non-Self without conflict.

The eighth chapter is called Akṣara-Brahman-Yoga. To contemplate the benign qualities of the Supreme Lord of one's own Self is the highest form of devotion. Devotion verticalizes the mind and action horizontalizes it. To fight an enemy with valour and strategic tact is undoubtedly a horizontalized attitude of the mind. In spite of the conflicting nature of these two attitudes — fighting and contemplation — Arjuna is taught in this chapter how he can contemplate the Lord as his own Self and also fight. The dialectical secret by which one can cancel out pairs of opposites is presented in this chapter.

The ninth chapter is called Rājavidyā-Rājaguhya-Yoga.

Guhya *means secrect. Does this chapter deal with anything esoteric or occult? Is it open to all?*

There is nothing esoteric about it. No discipline can be termed scientific (*śāstra*), unless it is open and universal, both in its scope and application. The Gītā presents a Science of the Absolute. It does not withhold from anyone any secret whatsoever.

Then in what sense is this chapter a secret?

Einstein's Theory of Relativity can remain a secret to those who do not know higher mathematics and advanced physics. As in the study of physics, there is a methodical way in which the Gītā works out its lessons. Each chapter leads to the next, and we come to its conclusive teaching in the ninth chapter. To be able to grasp the full implications of the secrets of the Gītā, the student should be disciplined in its special methodology, the dialectical way of reasoning (*yoga-mīmāṁsā*).

The type of reasoning we commonly employ is linear. When we argue from a general principle to a specific conclusion, or inductively hypothesize a general notion, our reason conforms to the pattern of linear thinking. On the other hand, when we cognize the polarization of counterparts that belong to a dialectical situation, and arrive at a unitive or integrated notion cancelling out the elements of contradiction in the opposing pairs, we are employing dialectical reasoning. In this chapter our mind is lifted to the loftiest heights of sublimity, and hence this is called the chapter of the supreme secret. This chapter is introductory to the tenth, which narrates the cosmic structure of the universe in terms of divine values.

Does each chapter deal with a separate topic? Has the Gītā any inner coordination?

Truth is many-faceted, and innumerable are the possible angles of vision. Each angle permits us only a relative vision. However, each vision has its own structural secrets and functional participation with the whole. Hence it is necessary to have a separate chapter to provide each comprehensive vision with a suitable frame of reference consistent with an overall scheme of correlation. The eighteen chapters of the Gītā are not disjunctly designed. Each chapter is structurally related to its adjacent chapters, and is intended to be complementary to them. The eighteen chapters are arranged as spokes on the hub of *brahma-vidyā* (Science of the Absolute). The method employed in each chapter has, in common with the rest, the goal of the realization of the Self through Yoga. Further, we see that the conclusive teaching given at the close of the ninth chapter is again repeated in the closing chapter. This again shows that the Gītā has a consistent teaching, which can undoubtedly be described as one-pointed devotion (*ekāntika bhakti*).

Instead of giving the conclusive teaching only in the last chapter, why is it given in the ninth as well as the eighteenth chapter?

The author of the Gītā has in his mind a structural design of his work. He uses the first half of the book to discuss fundamentals and pure principles. The second half is for applied philosophy. It is in this second half that he gives the diagnostic and symptomatic analysis of personality, which one can apply to oneself to discern one's *svadharma*. *Svadharma* is the Sanskrit term for the characteristic foundation of individual personality. Both the pure teaching of the first half and the applied teaching of the second half lead to the same teaching that one should live always in the adoration of the Absolute, feeling one's identity with the Absolute in thought, word and deed. We now go on to the second half of the book.

Our true being is the Self (*ātman*). *Ātman* is described as *sat-cit-ānanda*. *Sat* means existence, *cit* is subsistence, and *ānanda* is the value-factor. Actual presences or value-factors belonging to the universe are described in this chapter as aspects of the Absolute with which we can relate ourselves. The difference between the values presented in the previous chapter and this one is negligible. Comparatively, the values given in the ninth chapter are more conceptual. This justifies the title, "Unitive Recognition of Positive Values" (Vibhūti-Yoga), for the tenth chapter.

Why is ānanda *translated as value? If ātman is the same as the Absolute, all experiences should come within its scope. Pain, suffering, disease, poverty, and death are not at all blissful or enjoyable. Is not* ānanda *the opposite of misery?*

We can catalogue a long list of evil items, but we cannot assign the cause of these to an agency outside the pale of the Absolute. That is why we don't want to translate *ānanda* as bliss. The term we use here is "value". Items of pleasure can be arranged in terms of qualitative or quantitative units of values of an ascending or descending order. We are counting positive values when we go from indifference to the highest state of bliss. We descend in the value-scale when we go from the highest bliss to the zero point. If we go any further from the zero point we will advance in the opposite direction, which should be counted as negative values. Thus, pain and pleasure, irrespective of their accompanying modes of affectivity, come under the scale of values, positive or negative.

Earlier you said that from the tenth chapter onward we come to the application of the teachings given in the first nine chapters. The tenth chapter also appears to be theoretical rather than being applied.

In the tenth chapter we only just enter the second half of the book. Here, Kṛṣṇa has to prepare the mind of Arjuna to receive an experience which is very unusual and difficult to comprehend in its entirety, or to appreciate without sufficient instruction. Thus the tenth chapter actually marks the beginning of applied *yoga* in the Science of the Absolute.

How does Arjuna experience the cosmic structure of values?

The eleventh chapter is the "Unitive Vision of the Absolute". In Sanskrit this is called Viśvarūpa-Darśana-Yoga. We get empirical certitude by direct perception. The Absolute and spiritual values cannot be directly perceived, but they can be intuitively visualized. Spiritual vision also is direct. While direct perception in Sanskrit is called *pratyakṣa* (seen by the eye), spiritual vision is called *aparokṣa* (not perceived by another). Arjuna gets a direct vision of the Absolute with the aid of an inner eye of spiritual vision with which he was blessed by his Guru, Śrī Kṛṣṇa. The mere description of the Absolute gives only a theoretical understanding and intellectual appreciation. It should be followed by one's own direct experience. This chapter is devoted to the description of Arjuna's direct experience.

The twelfth chapter is named Bhakti-Yoga. We may translate it as "Unitive Devotion and Contemplation". The term *bhakti* is used here in a very specific sense. It is not just an emotional attachment or an enchantment that one feels towards the Divine. *Bhakti*, in Vedānta, means "continuous contemplation of one's own true nature as the Absolute". A true model of *bhakti* (devotion), and of a *bhakta* (devotee), is given in this chapter.

The thirteenth chapter is Kṣetra-Kṣetrajña-Vibhāga-Yoga. *Kṣetra* means "the field", *kṣetrajña* is "the knower of the field". In Bhakti-Yoga we learn that it is the Divine that dwells in every being. This chapter enables us to differentiate the Self from the non-Self. It is translated as "The Unitive Understanding of the Distinction between the Actual and the Perceptual".

Does everybody experience devotion the same way?

Peter differs from Paul. The fourteenth chapter deals with personality variations based on *guṇa*. It is entitled Guṇatraya-Vibhāga-Yoga. *Guṇa* means "a quality". In the present context the reference is to nature-modality. Hence this chapter is called "The Unitive Way of Transcending the Three Nature Modalities". All of us and everything in nature are evolutes of the three modalities of nature.

The fifteenth chapter is called Puruṣottama-Yoga. In the Sāṁkhyan philosophy there are two primary factors called *puruṣa* and *prakṛti*. *Puruṣa* is equivalent to the "Supreme Spirit", and *prakṛti* is primordial matter from which nature is supposed to have evolved. The duality of *puruṣa* and *prakṛti* (spirit and matter), is transcended by conceiving the "Supreme Spirit" as the highest reality. The Gītā names it *puruṣottama*. The title of this chapter is translated as "The Unitive Approach to the Paramount Person".

The sixteenth chapter is called Daivāsura-Sampad-Vibhāga-Yoga. The three *guṇa*s mentioned in the previous chapters are said to create all conditioning impressions which are responsible for building up one's character. Once they are formed, they persist even through several lives. In the present chapter, reference is made to two main tendencies which run vertically through one's life, giving a contiguous character to one's habitual choice. The higher nature is called *daivī sampatti*, and the lower nature is called *āsurī sampatti*. *Daiva* means "divine", and *āsura* means "demonic". *Daivī sampatti* therefore means tendencies which are spiritually rich. The opposite is *āsurī*. To assess the value-structure of your personality, you should discern these two tendencies clearly, and should see how far your thoughts, beliefs, and behaviour are influenced by each.

How does a man diagnose the influence of inherent tendencies?

The seventeenth chapter is called Śraddhātraya-Vibhāga-Yoga. It is very much diagnostic in character. *Śraddhā* literally means "deep interest". Interest is an indicator of one's innate disposition, nature, and character. By observing symptoms, a doctor can diagnose a disease. In this chapter we get a symptomatic diagnosis of one's basic character. The Gītā teaches us how to analyze our individual self in terms of the three nature-modalities discussed earlier. It also teaches us how to take into account our higher and lower nature. It further discusses five types which are somewhat akin to the psychological types of Jung. These are the *saṁnyāsī* (renunciate), the brāhmin (scholarly priest), the kṣatriya, (warrior) the vaiśya (tradesman) and the śūdra (servant). We should be cautious not to treat these as social classes belonging to the stratified social system of India, indiscriminately termed as *varṇa* or *jāti*. The types discussed here are universal. This chapter is aptly called "The Unitive Recognition of the Three Patterns of Faith".

The last chapter, which is the eighteenth, is called Saṁnyāsa-Yoga. For one who seeks the highest Truth, there is no knowledge greater than *brahmavidyā*. Realization of the Absolute gives release from all bondage. It is preceded by renunciation resulting from proper discrimination. Correctly conceived renunciation is called *saṁnyāsa*. Hence this chapter is described as "The Unitive Way in Behaviour Patterns".

Does the Gītā teach Yoga, or the Science of the Absolute?

Each chapter of the Gītā ends with a reference to *brahma-vidyā*, *yoga-śāstra*, and *saṁvāda*. Each of these terms connotes a different meaning. There is no doubt the Gītā is a textbook of the Science of the Absolute, (*brahma-vidyā*). The Absolute is not a thing or an event. It gives rise to many relative notions. That means it can be approached from many angles of vision. The method of discussion employed in the Gītā is dialectical, not basically inferential. Hence it is called Yogaśāstra. The literary device employed by the author is in the form of a dialogue between Kṛṣṇa as teacher and Arjuna as disciple. That is why it is called a dialogue (a *saṁvāda*). The parables and dialogues in the Upaniṣads are given a more cogent and philosophically structured presentation in the Gītā. For all practical purposes, the Gītā can be considered the essence of the Upaniṣads.

Why is such a special device adopted?

In philosophical discussions there are bound to be anterior scepticisms, as well as finalized, conclusive teaching. Arjuna represents the anterior skeptic. He raises doubts, apprehensions, and uncritically believed dogmas. Kṛṣṇa examines the stand of Arjuna in each case, and gives Arjuna his conclusive teaching. In the Sanskrit tradition such an anterior critic is called *pūrvapakṣin*, and the person who gives conclusive or final teaching is called *siddhāntin*.

What troubles me is the description of the Gītā as Yogaśāstra. Each chapter is described as a different yoga. *Patañjali describes* yoga *as a state of the cessation of the modification of mind,* citta-vṛtti-nirodha. *Does the Gītā use the term in the same sense? If it does, why is the first chapter called Viṣāda-Yoga? Viṣāda is a state of mental distress. Naturally a disturbed state cannot be described as* yoga.

The Gītā does not exclude Patañjali's meaning of *yoga*. *Yoga* is conceived in a wider sense in the Gītā. The end and means are so interlaced in *yoga* that they cannot be dualistically separated. *Yoga* literally means "union". It is etymologically related to the English term "to yoke". Dialectical thinking implies synthesis of a thesis and its antithesis. The Bhagavadgītā employs a type of reasoning which is more dialectical than linear or inferential. Dialectical reasoning in Sanskrit is called *yoga-mīmāṁsā*. The *viṣāda* (mental perturbance), of Arjuna is highlighted in the first chapter as the stand of an anterior critic who is fit to become an accomplished dialectician. The chapters which follow reject Arjuna's contentions by cancelling them out with counter-theses before Kṛṣṇa's conclusive teaching is given. The specific sense in which *viṣāda-yoga* is used will be elaborated later.

When yoga is popularly understood as a state of perfection or spiritual absorption, why do you say that Vyāsa uses the term yoga *in this book only to indicate the type of methodology he has adopted?*

Most people think of ends and means dualistically. When taken separately, "means" can become a painful anticipation, and can lead one ultimately even to frustration. When ends and means are unitively conceived there is a continuous and progressive realization of the end in the application of the means. For instance, when a child runs after a ball, his game is a "means" to gain the "end" of happiness. Here, ends and means have no real dichotomy between them. Happiness is not an award given at the end of the game. Right from the beginning, when the child kicks as well as misses the ball, he is in a state of happiness which is the natural end of the game. In other words, the game provides to the child a *yoga* of ends and means. The Bhagavadgītā treats the whole of life as a game presided over by the Supreme Lord (*Īśvaraḥ*). The various positions within the game offer different roles and each person is expected to approach it from a stipulated angle in a certain manner. That is why each chapter of the Gītā focuses its attention on a different aspect.

Realization is not a static event; it is a continuous process. In all states and stages of life, the higher Self is to be realized in the lower self, and the lower self is to be seen as an expression of the higher Self. Arjuna is presented in the Gītā as the individual mind or personal psyche, and Kṛṣṇa, as the Guru, stands for the cosmic mind or universal psyche. Arjuna is confused because of a disparity or incompatibility in his notion of the personal and the universal. The Gītā attempts to avoid this implied duality by bringing Arjuna's mind in line with Kṛṣṇa's wisdom or, say, the oneness of the *jīva* (individual self), and *Īśvaraḥ* (Lord). Agreement in a certain approach need not necessarily imply agreement in all others. Hence, the Gītā takes into account the various possible approaches to the Absolute, and establishes an abiding rapport between Kṛṣṇa and Arjuna on different levels. This accounts for each chapter of the Gītā being termed an Upaniṣad. In that sense we have in the Gītā eighteen songs and eighteen Upaniṣads.

The Gītā was written in India by a ṛṣi, *who probably lived before Plato. From your description, it would look as if the* ṛṣi *learned dialectics from the Greeks to write the Gītā.*

We do not say so. Perhaps the Greeks might have learned dialectics from India. There is evidence that Alexandria and Crotona were frequented by

Indian thinkers even before the commencement of the Christian era. We use here the term dialectical not with any historical reference to Greek philosophy.

Suppose I say the word "wife". This will make sense to you only if you also think of the word "husband" and relate the meaning of the word "wife" to the meaning of the word "husband". Similarly, in the world of meaning many pairs of words occur with an internal togetherness: one forming the counterpart of the other. This is indicative of dialectical reasoning in the world of semantics.

Suppose a man offers a lady full protection and all the luxuries of life, on the condition that she leave her beloved husband and dear child. She will certainly refuse this with contempt, because her personal joy is tied up with the joy of her husband, as his wife, and the joy of the child, as its mother. This is an instance in which we see a dialectical interplay of counterparts that occurs very often in the field of sociology. Thus, in all walks of life, and in every phase of it, we come across a number of situations which cannot be understood or appreciated unless dialectical reasoning is properly applied.

Despite the fact that each chapter is a separate song, has the Gītā an inner consistency?

The Gītā certainly is a book of inner homogeneity and doctrinal consistency. We know that there were a few scholars who have failed to see this consistency. It is true that each chapter has its own frame of reference. Unless you understand the mind of Vyāsa, the author, and employ the same scheme of correlation which was in his mind when he was structuring these chapters, you will not see how one chapter leads to another. Certain philosophical stands accepted as bases for discussion in the earlier chapters are seen to be rejected later. This is very much in consistency with the method applied by all classical dialecticians. What is presented as a thesis should necessarily have its antithesis. Those who want to interpret the Gītā doctrines should be careful not to isolate any particular verse from the context within which each verse organically and functionally belongs. In a book like the Gītā, a verse lifted out of its context can give an absurd meaning. There is a purposive thread of correlation running not only through all chapters, but through all verses as well, even including the words. Even such an insignificant word as *ca*, meaning "and", has a great role to play in giving judgements of the utmost importance. It is significant, for instance, that at one place Kṛṣṇa describes himself as a *samāsa* (a compound). In short, the 700 verses of the Gītā are not to be treated as 700 separate maxims. It presents a dialectical structure in which eighteen units of correlatives are employed.

It will be interesting to know the structure as a whole, as well as by chapters.

I shall give you a table which will speak for itself. From it we can see how many questions Arjuna asks, how many times Sañjaya is brought in to keep the narrative unbroken, and how many verses in each chapter contain Kṛṣṇa's teaching.

Chapter	*Character*	*Verses*	*Total*
I	Dhṛtarāṣṭra	1	1
	Sañjaya	2-20, 24-27, 47	24
	Arjuna	21-23, 28-46	22
			47
II	Sañjaya	1, 9-10	3
	Arjuna	4-8, 54	6
	Kṛṣṇa	2-3, 11-53, 55-72	63
			72
III	Arjuna	1-2, 36	3
	Kṛṣṇa	3-35, 37-43	40
			43
IV	Arjuna	4	1
	Kṛṣṇa	1-3, 5-42	41
			42
V	Arjuna	1	1
	Kṛṣṇa	2-29	28
			29
VI	Arjuna	33, 37-39, 44	5
	Kṛṣṇa	1-32, 35-36, 40-47	42
			47
VII	Kṛṣṇa	1-30	30
VIII	Arjuna	1-2	2
	Kṛṣṇa	3-28	26
			28
IX	Kṛṣṇa	1-34	34
X	Arjuna	12-18	7
	Kṛṣṇa	1-11, 19-42	35
			42
XI	Sañjaya	9-14, 35, 50	8
	Arjuna	1-4, 15-31, 36-46, 51	33
	Kṛṣṇa	5-8, 32-34, 47-49, 52-55	14
			55

Chapter	*Character*	*Verses*	*Total*
XII	Arjuna	1	1
	Kṛṣṇa	2-20	19
			20
XIII	Kṛṣṇa	1-34	34
XIV	Arjuna	21	1
	Kṛṣṇa	1-20, 22-27	26
			27
XV	Kṛṣṇa	1-20	20
XVI	Kṛṣṇa	1-24	24
XVII	Arjuna	1	1
	Kṛṣṇa	2-28	27
			28
XVIII	Sañjaya	74-78	5
	Arjuna	1-73	2
	Kṛṣṇa	2-72	71
			78
TOTAL	Dhṛtarāṣṭra	1	
	Sañjaya	40	
	Arjuna	85	
	Kṛṣṇa	574	
	GRAND TOTAL	700	

Thank you for the table. It clearly shows the distribution of the verses. Are all the eighty-five verses attributed to Arjuna to be taken as the questions of an anterior critic?

All these eighty-five verses are not questions. Arjuna asks only thirty-eight questions, and they are given in thirty-three verses. The other fifty-two verses are used as literary devices to keep up the continuity of the dialogue. Some of the verses show Arjuna's appreciation of Kṛṣṇa's teaching, and some describe Arjuna's experience during the course of the revelation given, especially in the middle chapters. The relation between a question and its answer is analogous to the relation beween a disciple and his Guru. A silly question can evoke only a commonplace answer, while a serious question, in its turn, can open up rare secrets. Each man gets, as it were, a Guru according to his own merit. Śrī Kṛṣṇa represents a universal teacher. To merit such a Guru, the disciple also should be catholic in his vision and profound in his search. Arjuna is presented in the Gītā as an anterior critic, and Kṛṣṇa plays the role of the *siddhāntin*, the teacher who gives posterior conclusions.

Once upon a time, somewhere in India, a great Arjuna might have put unusual questions to a very wise Guru Kṛṣṇa, and he, in his turn, might have given Arjuna equally remarkable answers. Centuries have passed. Could it be of any importance to us, who live so far removed in time and place?

It is true that each man is unique, and that he differs even from his own brother. It is also true that in the course of time social problems do change, and value systems alter. In spite of such differences, man as a species has certain common characteristics. There are also values which do not change. Paradoxical situations of life which confronted the caveman are repeated time and again in the course of history. We see the same kind of enigmas confronting us more or less in the same way as experienced by our fathers and forefathers. The problems raised by Arjuna have a historical bias, but one can say that similar paradoxes come to all human beings irrespective of the time and place to which they belong. Kṛṣṇa's answers have a catholic ring and an apodictic authenticity which one cannot escape anytime or anywhere. Here, we are not examining a historical relic. In Arjuna's questions we can see our own enigmas and search for solutions. You will become convinced of this when you study the Gītā in more intimate detail. It is only natural that one becomes beset with doubts and hesitations when one enters the spiritual path. We intend to make this study fairly exhaustive.

To understand the Gītā is it imperative to study the Mahābhārata *also?*

The *Mahābhārata* is a rare classic. If one can afford the time to go through it even once, there is no doubt that it will be of great help. However, it is not imperative that we should know the whole of the *Mahābhārata* to know the purport of the Gītā. The *Mahābhārata* is used only as an epic-canvas upon which to paint the perennial philosophy of the Gītā. The texture of the canvas should be carefully discerned from the painting. The central teaching of the Gītā stands apart, complete in itself. To get the maximum benefit one should relate the teaching of the Gītā to one's own life.

Gītā Dhyānam

Meditation on the Gītā

1. *auṁ pārthāya pratibodhitāṁ bhagavatā nārāyaṇena svayaṁ* ।
vyāsena grathitāṁ purāṇa muninā madhye mahābhāratam ॥

advaitāmṛtavarṣiṇīṁ bhagavatīm aṣṭādaśādhyāyinīm ।
amba tvām anusaṁdadhāmi bhagavadgīte bhavadveṣiṇīm ॥

Auṁ: auṁ; *anusaṁdadhāmi*: I meditate; *tvām*: on Thee; *amba*: Oh Mother; *bhagavadgīte*: Bhagavadgītā; *bhagavatīm aṣṭādaśa adhyāyinīm*: made up of eighteen chapters; *advaita amṛta varṣiṇīṁ*: showering the nectar of *advaita* (non-dualism); *bhavadveṣiṇīm*: that can banish all (phenomenal) becoming; *grathitāṁ madhye mahābhāratam*: inserted into the middle of the *Mahābhārata*; *vyāsena*: by Vyāsa; *purāṇa muninā*: that antique Sage; *pārthāya pratibodhitāṁ*: as it was taught to Arjuna; *nārāyaṇena*: by Nārāyaṇa; *svayaṁ*: Himself; *bhagavatā*: the Blessed one

Auṁ — I meditate on Thee, Oh Mother Bhagavadgītā, made up of eighteen chapters, showering the nectar of Advaita that can banish all (phenomenal) becoming, (which is) inserted into the middle of the *Mahābhārata* by Vyāsa, that antique Sage (exactly), as it was taught to Arjuna by Nārāyaṇa Himself, the Blessed One.

2. *namo 'stu te vyāsa viśāla buddhe phullāravindāyata patra netra* ।
yena tvayā bhārata tailapūrṇaḥ prajvālito jñānamayaḥ pradīpaḥ ॥

namaḥ: salutations; *astu te*: to thee; *vyāsa*: Oh Vyāsa; *viśāla buddhe*: of expansive intellect; *phulla-aravinda-āyata-patra-netra*: having eyes like the petals of an open lotus; *yena tvayā*: who; *prajvālitaḥ*: has lit; *jñānamayaḥ pradīpaḥ*: the Wisdom-Lamp; *bhārata taila pūrṇaḥ*: filled with the oil which is the Bhārata epic

Salutations to thee, Oh Vyāsa of expansive intellect! having eyes like the petals of an open lotus, who has lit the Wisdom-Lamp filled with the oil which is the Bhārata epic.

3. *prapanna pārijātāya totravetraika pāṇaye* ।
jñāna mudrāya kṛṣṇāya gītāmṛta duhe namaḥ ॥

namaḥ: adoration; *kṛṣṇāya*: to Kṛṣṇa; *prapanna parijātāya*: representing in Himself that wish-fulfilling heavenly tree (the *summum bonum* of an eternal cosmology), brought within the reach of those who take refuge in Him; *totra vetra eka pāṇaye*: as He, wielding the whip of the charioteer in one hand; *jñāna mudrāya*: and the wisdom-Teacher's gesture (in the other hand); *gītā amṛta duhe*: milks the nectar of the *Gītā*

Adoration to Kṛṣṇa, representing in Himself that wish-fulfilling heavenly tree, brought within the reach of those who take refuge in Him as He, wielding the whip of the charioteer in one hand, and the wisdom-Teacher's gesture (in the other hand), milks the nectar of the *Gītā*.

4. *sarvopaniṣado gāvo dogdhā gopāla nandanaḥ* ।
pārtho vatsaḥ sudhīr bhoktā dugdhaṁ gītāmṛtaṁ mahat ॥

sarva upaniṣadaḥ: all the Upaniṣads; *gāvaḥ*: are cows; *dogdhā*: their milker; *gopāla nandanaḥ*: is the darling of the cowherds; *vatsaḥ*: the calf (inducing secretion); *pārthaḥ*: is Pārtha (Arjuna); *bhoktā*: and the drinkers thereof; *sudhīḥ*: are all men of good sense; *dugdhaṁ*: and what is milked is nothing but; *gītā*: the Gītā; *mahat*: the great; *amṛtaṁ*: nectar

All Upaniṣads are cows, their milker is the darling of the cowherds, the calf (inducing secretion) is Pārtha, the drinkers thereof are all men of good sense, and what is milked is nothing but the *Gītā*, the great nectar.

5. *vasudeva sutaṁ devaṁ kaṁsa cāṇūra mardanam* ।
devakī paramānandaṁ kṛṣṇaṁ vande jagad gurum ।

vande: I adore; *jagat gurum*: (that) World Teacher; *kṛṣṇaṁ*: Kṛṣṇa; *vasudeva sutaṁ*: son of Vasudeva; *devaṁ*: the Divine One; *kaṁsa cāṇūra mardanam*: who overcame Kaṁsa and Cāṇūra; *devakī parama ānandaṁ*: who was Devakī's bliss supreme

I adore that World Teacher Kṛṣṇa, son of Vasudeva, the Divine One, who overcame Kaṁsa and Cāṇūra, who was Devaki's bliss supreme!

6. *bhīṣma droṇa taṭā jayadratha jalā gāndhāra nīlopalā* ।
śalya grāhavatī kṛpeṇa vahanī karṇena velākulā ॥

aśvatthāma vikarṇa ghora makarā duryodhanāvartinī ।
sottīrṇā khalu pāṇḍavai raṇa nadī kaivartakaḥ keśavaḥ ॥

keśavaḥ: (with) Kṛṣṇa; *kaivartakaḥ*: at the helm; *uttīrṇā khalu*: was crossed over; *pāṇḍavaiḥ*: by the Pāṇḍavas (of yore); *saḥ*: that; *raṇa nadī*: battle-river; *bhīṣma droṇa taṭā*: (for which) the banks were Bhīṣma and Droṇa; *jayadratha jalā*: (whose) waters were Jayadratha; *gāndhāra nīlopalā*: (whose) black rocks were the Gāndhāras; *śalya grāhavatī*: the crocodile wherein was Śalya; *kṛpeṇa vahanī*: with Kṛpa as its current; *karṇena velākulā*: and Karṇa as its wave; *aśvatthāma vikarṇa ghora makarā*: the sharks Aśvatthāmā and Vikarṇa; *duryodhana āvartinī*: (and) the whirlpool Duryodhana

With Keśava at the helm, the Pāṇḍavas (of yore) crossed over that battle-river, for which the banks were Bhīṣma and Droṇa, and the waters were

Jayadratha, whose black rocks were the Gāndhāras, with Kṛpa as its current, and Karṇa as its wave, the crocodile wherein was Śalya, the sharks Aśvatthāmā and Vikarṇa, and the whirlpool Duryodhana.

7. *pārāśarya vacaḥ sarojam amalaṁ gītārtha gandhotkaṭaṁ* ।
nānākhyānaka kesaraṁ hari kathā saṁbodhanābodhitam ॥
loke sajjana ṣaṭpadair aharahaḥ pepīyamānaṁ mudā ।
bhūyād bhārata paṅkajaṁ kalimala pradhvaṁsinaḥ śreyase ॥

pārāśarya vacaḥ sarojam amalaṁ: born out of the limpid lake of the words of the son of Parāśara; *bhūyāt*: may; *bhārata paṇkajaṁ*: (such) a lotus, (which is even) the *Mahābhārata* epic; *gītā artha gandha utkaṭaṁ*: spreading the fragrance of Gītā-meaning; *nānā akhyānaka kesaraṁ*: containing numerous secondary anecdotes which are its pollen-bearing anthers; *harikathā saṁbodhana ābodhitam*: opening to wisdom-light because of having the story of Hari (Viṣṇu or Kṛṣṇa) as its content of good teaching; *śreyase*: be for our (everlasting) good; *kalimala pradhvaṁsinaḥ*: as it cleans away the dross incidental to the age of Kali (the evil cosmic period of thousands of years); *pepīyamānaṁ mudā*: as it is sucked; *ahaḥ ahaḥ*: day after day; *sat jana ṣaṭpadaiḥ*: by the bees who are none other than the good men; *loke*: on earth

Born out of the limpid lake of the words of the son of Parāśara, may such a lotus, which is even the *Mahābhārata* epic, spreading the fragrance of Gītā-meaning, containing numerous secondary anecdotes which are its pollen-bearing anthers, opening to wisdom-light because of having the story of Hari as its content of good teaching, be for our (everlasting) good, as it cleans away the dross incidental to the Age of Kali, as it is sucked day after day by the bees who are none other than the good men on earth.

8. *mūkaṁ karoti vācālaṁ paṅguṁ laṅghayate girim* ।
yatkṛpā tam ahaṁ vande paramānanda mādhavam ॥

ahaṁ vande tam: I adore that; *parama ānanda mādhavam*: Kṛṣṇa, source supreme of bliss; *yatkṛpa*: whose grace; *karoti*: can make; *vācālaṁ*: an orator; *mūkaṁ*: of a dumb man; *paṅguṁ*: (and enable) the lame; *laṅghayate*: to cross; *girim*: mountains

I adore that Mādhava, source supreme of bliss, whose grace can make an orator of a dumb man and enable the lame to cross mountains.

9. *yaṁ brahmā varuṇendra rudra marutaḥ stunvanti divyaiḥ stavaiḥ* ।
vedaiḥ sāṅga pada kramopaniṣadair gāyanti yaṁ sāmagāḥ ॥
dhyānāvasthita tadgatena manasā paśyanti yaṁ yogino ।
yasyāntaṁ na viduḥ surāsuragaṇā devāya tasmai namaḥ ॥

yaṁ: He whom; *brahmā*: Brahmā; *varuṇaḥ*: Varuṇa; *indraḥ*: Indra; *rudraḥ*: Rudra; *marutaḥ*: and Marut; *stunvanti*: ever praise; *divyaiḥ*: with celestial; *stavaiḥ*: hymns; *yaṁ*: whom; *sāmagāḥ*: the chanters of the *Sāma*(*Veda*); *gāyanti*: do extol with songs; *vedaiḥ*: comprising the Vedas; *sa aṅga padakrama upaniṣadaiḥ*: together with their sub-divisions respecting word and order, not omitting the Upaniṣads too; *yaṁ*: He whom; *yoginaḥ*: the contemplatives; *manasā dhyāna avasthita tadgatena*: with minds merged thereinto and established firm in meditation; *paśyanti*: can see; *yasya*: whose; *antaṁ*: end; *na viduḥ*: is beyond the ken; *sura asura gaṇāḥ*: equally of gods and their rival spirits; *tasmai*: to such; *devāya*: a Divinity; *namaḥ*: do I offer adoration

He whom Brahmā, Varuṇa, Indra, Rudra, and Marut ever praise. with celestial hymns, whom the chanters of the *Sāma* (*Veda*) do extol with songs comprising the Vedas together with their sub-divisions, respecting word and order, not omitting the Upaniṣads too, He whom the contemplatives with minds merged thereinto and established firm in meditation can see, whose end is beyond the ken equally of gods and their rival spirits — to such a Divinity do I offer adoration!

Meditation on the Gītā

AUṀ

I meditate on Thee, Oh Mother Bhagavadgītā! made up of eighteen chapters, showering the nectar of Advaita that can banish all (phenomenal) becoming, (which is) inserted into the middle of the *Mahābhārata* by Vyāsa, that antique Sage, (exactly) as it was taught to Arjuna by Nārāyaṇa Himself, the Blessed One.

Salutations to thee, Oh Vyāsa of expansive intellect! having eyes like the petals of an open lotus, who has lit the Wisdom-Lamp filled with the oil which is the Bhārata epic.

Adoration to Kṛṣṇa, representing in Himself that wish-fulfilling heavenly tree, brought within the reach of those who take refuge in Him as He, wielding the whip of the charioteer in one hand, and the wisdom-Teacher's gesture in the other hand, milks the nectar of the Gītā.

All the Upaniṣads are cows, their milker is the darling of the cowherds, the calf (inducing secretion) is Pārtha, the drinkers thereof are all men of good sense, and what is milked is nothing but the Gītā, the great nectar.

I adore that World Teacher Kṛṣṇa, son of Vasudeva, the Divine One, who overcame Kaṁsa and Cāṇūra, who was Devakī's bliss supreme!

With Keśava at the helm, the Pāṇḍavas (of yore) crossed over that battle-river, for which the banks were Bhīṣma and Droṇa, and the waters were Jayadratha, whose black rocks were the Gāndhāras, with Kṛpa as its current, and Karṇa as its wave, the crocodile wherein was Śalya, the sharks Aśvatthāmā and Vikarṇa, and the whirlpool Duryodhana.

Born out of the limpid lake of the words of the son of Parāśara, may such a lotus, which is even the *Mahābhārata* epic, spreading the fragrance of Gītā-meaning, containing numerous secondary anecdotes which are its pollen-bearing anthers, opening to wisdom-light because of having the story of Hari as its content of good teaching, be for our (everlasting) good, as it cleans away the dross incidental to the Age of Kali, as it is sucked day after day by the bees who are none other than the good men on earth.

I adore that Mādhava, source supreme of bliss, whose grace can make an orator of a dumb man and enable the lame to cross mountains.

He whom Brahmā, Varuṇa, Indra, Rudra, and Marut ever praise with celestial hymns, whom the chanters of the *Sāma* (*Veda*) do extol with songs comprising the Vedas together with their subdivisions, respecting word and order, not omitting the Upaniṣads too, He whom the contemplatives with minds merged thereinto and established firm in meditation can see, whose end is beyond the ken equally of gods and their rival spirits — to such a Divinity do I offer adoration!

I

Arjuna-Viṣāda-Yoga

The Yoga of Arjuna's Conflict

INTRODUCTION

THE word *yoga* in this Chapter does not refer to a state of happiness, as should be expected from the definition of *yoga* in the Gītā itself: "disaffiliation from the context of suffering" (VI. 23), but here, even referring to agony or unhappiness, it is still called a *yoga*. The agony of Arjuna is not the plight of a coward in the face of imminent danger. Note the phases of his despondency, beginning with pity and proceeding to philosophical, religious, and humanitarian considerations, all of a very respectable order. Although Kṛṣṇa smiles at Arjuna in disapproval, in the remaining chapters of the Gītā we find no contradiction of Arjuna's opinions, but rather a revalued statement of Arjuna's position in absolutist terms.

The only possible fault of Arjuna's attitude lurks in the expression "my own people" (*svajana*), in verse 28 where he begins his arguments. Ancestor worship, considerations of caste or clan, the non-hurting principle, and the principle of renunciation are not against the spirit of the Gītā as a whole. But Arjuna thinks as a relativist in these matters, while Kṛṣṇa teaches an absolutist revision of them.

The first chapter is thus the only one which contains the problems of the Gītā stated correctly before the discussion by the Guru, Kṛṣṇa. This chapter therefore requires very close attention. And yet, oddly enough, commentators – even Śaṅkara – have almost ignored it, even treating it as superfluous. Śaṅkara's commentary begins only with verse 10 of Chapter II, and he dismisses that which precedes it in a summary fashion not at all in proportion with the rest of his labours. The remaining seventeen chapters of the Gītā make an attempt to dialectically revalue the same problems as seen by a *yogī*.

It is therefore very important not to leave unnoticed even those minor peculiarities of this chapter in which the author hides here and there certain indications for the guidance of the intelligent reader.

This chapter is meant to indicate the nature of Arjuna's spiritual agony which, by the end of the chapter, attains the status of a religious conflict based on sin. Arjuna's scruples are vague, but still have the strength and virility of a representative skeptic of his time. As the anterior prerequisite for the whole teaching to follow, Arjuna's conflict deserves to be treated as a *yoga*.

The very first word of the Gītā is *dharma*, meaning right life that is in keeping with wisdom, which is to be set-off against the merely historical actuality of the Kuru battlefield. The latter is to be revalued in terms of the former by the battle that is about to begin. Absolute necessity or urgency in the Actual has to be understood in the light of the highest absolute sense of intelligent and normal living by Arjuna. He is called upon to be a man of unitive life without conflict, which is the life of a *yogī*.

TRANSLATION

धृतराष्ट्र उवाच –

1. धर्मक्षेत्रे कुरुक्षेत्रे समवेता युयुत्सवः।
मामकाः पाण्डवाश्चैव किमकुर्वत सञ्जय ।।

dhr̥tarāṣṭra uvāca –

dharmakṣetre kurukṣetre samavetā yuyutsavaḥ ।
māmakāḥ pāṇḍavāś cai 'va kim akurvata sañjaya ॥

dhr̥tarāṣṭra uvāca: Dhr̥tarāṣṭra said; *dharma kṣetre*: in the field of righteousness; *kuru kṣetre*: in the field of the Kurus; *samavetāḥ*: gathered together; *yuyutsavaḥ*: intent on battle; *kim akurvata*: what did; *māmakā*: my people; *pāṇḍavāḥ ca eva*: and also the Sons of Pāṇḍu (do); *sañjaya*: Oh Sañjaya.

Dhr̥tarāṣṭra said:

In the field of righteousness, the field of the Kurus, gathered together, intent on battle, what did my people and also the Sons of Pāṇḍu (do), Oh Sañjaya?

सञ्जय उवाच –

2. दृष्ट्वा तु पाण्डवानीकं व्यूढं दुर्योधनस्तदा ।
आचार्यमुपसङ्गम्य राजा वचनमब्रवीत् ।।

sañjaya uvāca –

dr̥ṣṭvā tu pāṇḍavānīkaṁ vyūḍhaṁ duryodhanas tadā ।
ācāryam upasaṁgamya rājā vacanam abravīt ॥

sañjaya uvāca: Sañjaya said; *dṛṣṭvā tu*: on seeing; *pāṇḍavānīkaṁ vyūḍhaṁ*: the army of the Pāṇḍavas in battle array; *rājā duryodhanaḥ*: Prince Duryodhana; *upasaṁgamya ācāryam*: having approached his teacher; *tadā*: then; *abravīt vacanam*: gave utterance to the following speech.

Sañjaya said:

On seeing the army of the Pāṇḍavas in battle array, Prince Duryodhana, having approached his teacher, then gave utterance to the following speech:

3. पश्यैतां पाण्डुपुत्राणामाचार्य महतीं चमूम् ।
व्यूढां द्रुपदपुत्रेण तव शिष्येण धीमता ।।

paśyai 'tāṁ pāṇḍuputrāṇām ācārya mahatīṁ camūm ।
vyūḍhāṁ drupada putreṇa tava śiṣyeṇa dhīmatā ॥

ācārya: Oh Teacher; *paśya etāṁ*: look at this; *mahatīṁ camūm*: grand army; *pāṇḍuputrāṇām*: of the Sons of Pāṇḍu; *vyūḍhāṁ*: marshalled by; *tava*: your; *dhimatā śiṣyeṇa*: talented pupil; *drupada putreṇa*: the son of Drupada (Dhṛṣṭadyumna).

Oh Teacher! look at this grand army of the Sons of Pāṇḍu, marshalled by your talented pupil, the Son of Drupada.

4. अत्र शूरा महेष्वासा भीमार्जुनसमा युधि ।
युयुधानो विराटश्च द्रुपदश्च महारथः ।।

atra śūrā maheṣvāsā bhīmārjunasamā yudhi ।
yuyudhāno virāṭaś ca drupadaś ca mahārathaḥ ॥

atra: here (are); *śūrāḥ*: heroes; *maheṣvāsāḥ*: mighty archers; *bhīma arjuna samāḥ yudhi*: equal in battle to Bhīma and Arjuna; *yuyudhāno*: Yuyudhāna; *virāṭaś ca*: Virāṭa and; *drupadaś ca*: Drupada; *mahā rathaḥ*: of the great chariot.

Here are heroes, mighty archers, equal in battle to Bhīma and Arjuna, Yuyudhāna, Virāṭa, and Drupada, of the great chariot.

5. धृष्टकेतुश्चेकितानः काशिराजश्च वीर्यवान् ।
पुरुजित्कुन्तिभोजश्च शैब्यश्च नरपुङ्गवः ।।

dhṛṣṭaketuś cekitānaḥ kāśirajaś ca vīryavān ।
purujit kuntībhojaś ca śaibyaś ca narapuṁgavaḥ ॥

dhṛṣṭaketuḥ: Dhṛṣṭaketu; *cekitānaḥ*: Cekitāna; *ca vīryavān kāśīrājaḥ*: and the valiant King of Kāśī; *purujit kuntibhojaḥ ca*: Purujit and Kuntībhoja; *ca narapuṁgavaḥ śaibyaḥ*: and that bull among men, Śaibya.

Dhṛṣṭaketu, Cekitāna, and the valiant King of Kāśī, Purujit and Kuntībhoja, and that bull among men, Śaibya.

6. युधामन्युश्च विक्रान्त उत्तमौजाश्च वीर्यवान् ।
सौभद्रो द्रौपदेयाश्च सर्व एव महारथाः ।।

yudhāmanyuś ca vikrānta uttamaujāś ca vīryavān ।
saubhadro draupadeyāś ca sarva eva mahārathāḥ ॥

vikrāntaḥ yudhāmanyuḥ ca: the heroic Yudhāmanyu and; *vīryavān uttamaujāḥ ca*: the brave Uttamaujās; *saubhadraḥ*: son of Subhadra (Abhimanyu); *draupadeyāḥ ca*: and the Sons of Draupadī; *sarva eva mahā rathāḥ*: all of great chariots.

The heroic Yudhāmanyu, and the brave Uttamaujas, the Son of Subhadrā, and the Sons of Draupadī, all of great chariots.

7. अस्माकं तु विशिष्टा ये तान्निबोध द्विजोत्तम ।
नायका मम सैन्यस्य संज्ञार्थं तान्ब्रवीमि ते ।।

asmākaṁ tu viśiṣṭā ye tān nibodha dvijottama ।
nāyakā mama sainyasya saṁjñārthaṁ tān bravīmi te ॥

tu nibodha: but know; *tān ye viśiṣṭāḥ asmākam*: those who are the most distinguished among us; *dvijottama*: Oh best of the twice born (Droṇa); *nāyakāḥ mama sainyasya*: the leaders of my army; *tān bravīmi te*: these I tell you; *saṁjñārthaṁ*: for recognizing by name.

But know who are the most distinguished among us, Oh Best of the Twice-born! the leaders of my army; these I tell you, for you to recognize by name.

8. भवान्भीष्मश्च कर्णश्च कृपश्च समितिञ्जयः ।
अश्वत्थामा विकर्णश्च सौमदत्तिस्तथैव च ।।

bhavān bhīṣmaś ca karṇaś ca kṛpaś ca samitiṁjayaḥ ।
aśvatthāmā vikarṇaś ca saumadattis tathai 'va ca ॥

bhavān: you; *bhīṣmaḥ ca*: and Bhīṣma; *karṇaḥ ca*: and Karṇa; *kṛpaḥ ca samitiṁjayaḥ*: and also Kṛpa, the victor in war; *aśvatthāmā vikarṇaḥ ca*: Aśvatthāmā and Vikarṇa; *saumadattis tathā eva ca*: and also the son of Somadatta (Bhūriśravas).

You and Bhīṣma, and Karṇa, and also Kṛpa, the victor in war, Aśvatthāmā and Vikarṇa, and also the Son of Somadatta,

9. अन्ये च बहवः शूरा मदर्थे त्यक्तजीविताः ।
नानाशस्त्रप्रहरणाः सर्वे युद्धविशारदाः ।।

anye ca bahavaḥ śūrā madarthe tyaktajīvitāḥ ।
nānāśastrapraharaṇāḥ sarve yuddhaviśārdāḥ ॥

ca bahavaḥ anye: and many other; *śūrāḥ*: heroes; *tyakta jīvitāḥ*: who are willing to die; *madarthe*: for me; *nānā śastra praharaṇāḥ*: (who have) various missiles and weapons; *sarve yuddha viśāradāḥ*: all skilled in warfare.

and many other heroes who are willing to die for me, who have various missiles and weapons, all skilled in warfare.

10. अपर्याप्तं तदस्माकं बलं भीष्माभिरक्षितम् ।
पर्याप्तं त्विदमेतेषां बलं भीमाभिरक्षितम् ।।

aparyāptaṁ tad asmākaṁ balaṁ bhīṣmābhirakṣitam ।
paryāptaṁ tv idam eteṣāṁ balaṁ bhīmābhirakṣitam ॥

tad balaṁ asmākaṁ: that army of ours; *bhīṣma abhirakṣitam*: which is under the care of Bhīṣma; *aparyāptaṁ*: is insufficient; *tu*: but; *idam balaṁ eteṣāṁ*: this army of theirs; *bhīma abhirakṣitam*: which is under the care of Bhīma; *paryāptaṁ*: is adequate.

That army of ours which is under the care of Bhīṣma is insufficient, but this army of theirs which is under the care of Bhīma is adequate.

11. अयनेषु च सर्वेषु यथाभागमवस्थिताः ।
भीष्ममेवाभिरक्षन्तु भवन्तः सर्व एव हि ।।

ayaneṣu ca sarveṣu yathābhāgam avasthitāḥ ।
bhīṣmam evā 'bhirakṣantu bhavantaḥ sarva eva hi ॥

yathā bhāgam avasthitāḥ: standing in your respective positions; *ayaneṣu sarveṣu*: at the entrance to every formation; *ca eva hi sarva bhavantaḥ*: and so, all of you; *abhirakṣantu bhīṣmam eva*: keep guard even on Bhīṣma.

And so let all of you, standing in your respective positions at the entrance to every formation, keep guard on Bhīṣma.

12. तस्य सञ्जनयन्हर्षं कुरुवृद्धः पितामहः ।
सिंहनादं विनद्योच्चैः शङ्खं दध्मौ प्रतापवान् ।।

tasya sañjanayan harṣaṁ kuruvṛddhaḥ pitāmahaḥ ।
siṁhanādaṁ vinadyo 'ccaiḥ śaṅkhaṁ dadhmau pratāpavān ॥

tasya sañjanayan harṣaṁ: so as to cheer him; *pratāpavān vṛddhaḥ*: the mighty old; *kuru pitāmahaḥ*: Kuru patriarch (Bhīṣma); *vinadya uccaiḥ siṁha nādam*: roared loudly like a lion; *dadhmau śaṅkhaṁ*; and blew a conch.

So as to cheer him, the mighty old Kuru patriarch roared loudly like a lion and blew a conch.

13. ततः शङ्खाश्च भेर्यश्च पणवानकगोमुखाः ।
सहसैवाभ्यहन्यन्त स शब्दस्तुमुलोऽभवत् ॥

tataḥ śaṅkhāś ca bheryaś ca paṇavānakagomukhāḥ ।
sahasai 'vā 'bhyahanyanta sa śabdas tumulo 'bhavat ॥

tataḥ: then; *śaṅkhāḥ*: conches; *ca bheryaḥ ca*: and drums and; *paṇava ānaka gomukhāḥ*: gongs, other drums and horns; *abhyahanyanta*: were played; *sahasa eva*: together suddenly; *saḥ śabdaḥ*: that sound; *abhavat tumulaḥ*: made a confused clang.

Then conches and drums and gongs, (other) drums, and horns, were played together suddenly, and that sound made a confused clang.

14. ततः श्वेतैर्हयैर्युक्ते महति स्यन्दने स्थितौ ।
माधवः पाण्डवश्चैव दिव्यौ शङ्खौ प्रदध्मतुः ॥

tataḥ śvetair hayair yukte mahati syandane sthitau ।
mādhavaḥ pāṇḍavaś cai 'va divyau śaṅkhau pradadhmatuḥ ॥

tataḥ: then; *sthitau mahati syandane*: (both) standing in (their) great chariot; *śvetaiḥ hayaiḥ yukte*: to which white horses were yoked; *mādhavaḥ*: Śrī Kṛṣṇa; *ca pāṇḍavaḥ eva*: and Arjuna; *pradadhmatuḥ*: the two together blew; *divyau śaṅkhau*: (their) divine conches.

Then standing in their great chariot, to which white horses were yoked, Mādhava and the Son of Pāṇḍu together blew their divine conches.

15. पाञ्चजन्यं हृषीकेशो देवदत्तं धनञ्जयः ।
पौण्ड्रं दध्मौ महाशङ्खं भीमकर्मा वृकोदरः ॥

pāñcajanyaṁ hṛṣīkeśo devadattaṁ dhanañjayaḥ ।
pauṇḍraṁ dadhmau mahāśaṅkhaṁ bhīmakarmā vṛkodaraḥ ॥

hṛṣīkeśaḥ: Kṛṣṇa; (*dadhmau*): blew; *pāñcajanyaṁ*: Pāñcajanya; *devadattaṁ dhanañjayaḥ*: (and) Arjuna (blew) Devadatta; *bhīma karmā vṛkodaraḥ*: Bhīma; *dadhmau mahā śaṅkhaṁ*: blew (his) great conch; *pauṇḍraṁ*; Pauṇḍra.

Hṛṣikeśa blew Pāñcajanya, and Arjuna blew Devadatta. He of wolf-like appetite and deeds of enormity blew his great conch, Pauṇḍra.

16. अनन्तविजयं राजा कुन्तीपुत्रो युधिष्ठिरः ।
नकुलः सहदेवश्च सुघोषमणिपुष्पकौ ॥

anantavijayaṁ rājā kuntīputro yudhiṣṭhiraḥ ।
nakulaḥ sahadevaś ca sughoṣamaṇipuṣpakau ॥

yudhiṣṭhiraḥ: Yudhiṣṭhira; *rājā*: the prince; *kuntī putraḥ*: Son of Kuntī;

(*dadhmau*): blew; *anantavijayaṁ*: Anantavijaya; *nakulaḥ sahadevaḥ ca*: Nakula and Sahadeva; *sughoṣa maṇipuṣpakau*: (blew together) the Sughoṣa and Maṇipuṣpaka.

Prince Yudhiṣṭhira, Son of Kuntī, blew Anantavijaya, and Nakula and Sahadeva (blew together) the Sughoṣa and Maṇipuṣpaka.

17. काश्यश्च परमेष्वासः शिखण्डी च महारथः ।
धृष्टद्युम्नो विराटश्च सात्यकिश्चापराजितः ।।

kāśyaś ca parameṣvāsaḥ śikhaṇḍī ca mahārathaḥ ।
dhṛṣṭadyumno virāṭaś ca sātyakiś cā 'parājitaḥ ॥

kāśyaḥ parameṣvāsaḥ ca: and the King of Kāśī, excellent bowman; *śikhaṇḍī ca mahā rathaḥ*: and Śikhaṇḍin, great charioteer; *dhṛṣṭadyumnaḥ*: Dhṛṣṭadyumna; *virāṭaḥ ca*: and Virāṭa; *aparājitaḥ sātyakiḥ ca*: and the unconquered Sātyaki.

And the King of Kāśī, excellent bowman, Śikhaṇḍin, great charioteer, Dhṛṣṭadyumna and Virāṭa and the unconquered Sātyaki,

18. द्रुपदो द्रौपदेयाश्च सर्वशः पृथिवीपते ।
सौभद्रश्च महाबाहुः शङ्खान्दध्मुः पृथक्पृथक् ।।

drupado draupadeyāś ca sarvaśaḥ pṛthivīpate ।
saubhadraś ca mahābāhuḥ śaṅkhān dadhmuḥ pṛthak-pṛthak ॥

drupadaḥ: Drupada; *draupade yāḥ ca*: and the Sons of Draupadī; *pṛthivī pate*: Oh Lord of the Earth (Dhṛtarāṣṭra); *saubhadraḥ ca*: and son of Subhadra (Abhimanyu); *mahābāhuḥ*: of mighty arms; *sarvaśaḥ*: from all sides; *dadhmuḥ śaṅkhān pṛthak-pṛthak*: blew conches separately.

Drupada, and the sons of Draupadī, Oh Lord of the Earth! and the Son of Subhadrā, of mighty arms – from all sides each blew his conch separately.

19. स घोषो धार्तराष्ट्राणां हृदयानि व्यदारयत् ।
नभश्च पृथिवीं चैव तुमुलो व्यनुनादयन् ।।

sa ghoṣo dhārtarāṣṭrāṇāṁ hṛdayāni vyadārayat ।
nabhaś ca pṛthivīṁ cai 'va tumulo vyanunādayan ॥

ca eva saḥ ghoṣaḥ: and indeed that loud blast; *vyanunādayan tumulaḥ*: filling with sound; *pṛthivīṁ ca nabhaḥ*: earth and sky; *vyadārayat hṛdayāni*: pierced the hearts; *dhārtarāṣṭrāṇāṁ*; of Dhṛtarāṣṭra's Sons.

That loud blast, filling earth and sky with sound, pierced the hearts of Dhṛtarāṣṭra's Sons.

20. अथ व्यवस्थितान्दृष्ट्वा धार्तराष्ट्रान्कपिध्वजः ।
प्रवृत्ते शस्त्रसंपाते धनुरुद्यम्य पाण्डवः ॥

atha vyavasthitān dṛṣṭvā dhārtarāṣṭrān kapidhvajaḥ ।
pravṛtte śastrasaṁpāte dhanur udyamya pāṇḍavaḥ ॥

atha: then; *dṛṣṭvā*: beholding; *dhārtarāṣṭrān*: the Sons of Dhṛtarāṣṭra; *vyavasthitān*: standing marshalled in order; *pravṛtte śastrasaṁpāte*: while the flight of arrows (was) beginning; *pāṇḍavaḥ*: Arjuna; *kapidhvajaḥ*: of monkey ensign; *udyamya dhanuḥ*: took up his bow.

Then, beholding the Sons of Dhṛtarāṣṭra standing marshalled in order, while the flight of arrows was beginning, the Son of Pāṇḍu, of monkey ensign, took up his bow;

21. हृषीकेशं तदा वाक्यमिदमाह महीपते ।
अर्जुन उवाच –
सेनयोरुभयोर्मध्ये रथं स्थापय मेऽच्युत ॥

hṛṣīkeśaṁ tadā vākyam idam āha mahīpate ।
arjuna uvāca –
senayor ubhayor madhye rathaṁ sthāpaya me 'cyuta ॥

tadā: and then; *mahīpate*; Oh King (said Sañjaya); *vākyam āha idam hṛṣīkeśaṁ*: (Arjuna) spoke thus to Kṛṣṇa; *acyuta*: Oh Kṛṣṇa; *sthāpaya*: stop; *me*: my; *rathaṁ*: chariot; *madhye ubhayoḥ senayoḥ*: in the middle between the two armies.

and, Oh King! he spoke thus to Hṛṣikeśa; Oh Acyuta! Stop my chariot right in the middle between the two armies,

22. यावदेतान्निरीक्षेऽहं योद्धुकामानवस्थितान् ।
कैर्मया सह योद्धव्यमस्मिन्रणसमुद्यमे ॥

yāvad etān nirīkṣe 'haṁ yoddhukāmān avasthitān ।
kair mayā saha yoddhavyam asmin raṇasamudyame ॥

yāvad: so that; *ahaṁ nirīkṣe*: I may behold; *etān*: these; *avasthitān*: standing; *yoddhukāmān*: eager to fight; *kaiḥ mayā saha*: by my side; *yoddhavyam asmin raṇa samudyame*: who must fight in this battle-undertaking.

so that I may behold these standing eager to fight by my side in the present battle-undertaking,

23. योत्स्यमानानवेक्षेऽहं य एतेऽत्र समागताः ।
धार्तराष्ट्रस्य दुर्बुद्धेर्युद्धे प्रियचिकीर्षवः ॥

yotsyamānān avekṣe 'haṁ ya ete 'tra samāgatāḥ ।
dhārtarāṣṭrasya durbuddher yuddhe priyacikirsavaḥ ॥

ahaṁ avekṣe ye ete atra: and I might observe those here; *yotsyamānān samāgatāḥ*: gathered together to fight; *priyacikīrṣavaḥ yuddhe*: who desire to please in war; *durbuddheḥ dhārtarāṣṭrasya*: the evil-minded Duryodhana.

and might observe those here gathered together who desire to please in war the evil-minded Son of Dhr̥tarāṣṭra.

24. सञ्जय उवाच –
एवमुक्तो हृषीकेशो गुडाकेशेन भारत ।
सेनयोरुभयोर्मध्ये स्थापयित्वा रथोत्तमम् ।।

sañjaya uvāca –

evam ukto hr̥ṣīkeśo guḍākeśena bhārata ।
senayor ubhayor madhye sthāpayitvā rathottamam ॥

sañjaya uvāca: Sañjaya said; *evam uktaḥ*: thus addressed; *guḍākeśena*: by Arjuna; *hr̥ṣīkeśaḥ*: Śrī Kr̥ṣṇa; *bhārata*: Oh Dhr̥tarāṣṭra; *sthāpayitvā*: having stationed; *rathottamam*: that excellent chariot; *madhye*: (right) in the middle (between); *ubhayoḥ senayoḥ*: the two armies.

Sañjaya said:

Thus addressed by Guḍākeśa, Hr̥ṣikeśa, Oh Bhārata! having stationed that excellent chariot right in the middle between the two armies,

25. भीष्मद्रोणप्रमुखतः सर्वेषां च महीक्षिताम् ।
उवाच पार्थ पश्यैतान् समवेतान्कुरूनिति ।।

bhīṣmadroṇapramukhataḥ sarveṣāṁ ca mahīkṣitām ।
uvāca pārtha paśyai 'tān samavetān kurūn iti ॥

bhīṣma droṇa pramukhataḥ: facing Bhīṣma and Droṇa; *ca sarveṣāṁ mahīkṣtām*: and all the rulers of the earth; *uvāca*: (Kr̥ṣṇa) said; *pārtha*: Oh Arjuna; *paśya etān*: behold these; *samavetān kurūn iti*: Kurus gathered (here).

facing Bhīṣma and Droṇa and all the rulers of the earth, (Kr̥ṣṇa) said; Oh Pārtha! Behold these Kurus gathered here.

26. तत्रापश्यत्स्थितान् पार्थः पितृनथ पितामहान् ।
आचार्यान्मातुलान्भ्रातृन्पुत्रान्पौत्रान्सखींस्तथा ।।

tatrā 'paśyat sthitān pārthaḥ pitr̄n atha pitāmahān ।
ācāryān mātulān bhrātr̄n putrān pautrān sakhīṁs tathā ॥

tatra: there; *pārthaḥ*: Arjuna; *apaśyat*: saw; *sthitān*: standing; *pitṛn*: fathers; *atha*: as well as; *pitāmahān*: grandfathers; *ācāryan*: teachers; *mātulān*: maternal uncles; *bhrātṛn*: brothers; *putrān*: sons; *pautrān*: grandsons; *sakhīn tathā*: and companions too.

Then Pārtha saw standing fathers as well as grandfathers, teachers, maternal uncles, brothers, sons, grandsons, and companions too.

27. श्वशुरान् सुहृदश्चैव सेनयोरुभयोरपि ।
तान्समीक्ष्य स कौन्तेयः सर्वान् बन्धूनवस्थितान् ॥

śvaśurān suhṛdaś cai 'va senayor ubhayor api ।
tān samīkṣya sa kaunteyaḥ sarvān bandhūn avasthitān ॥

saḥ kaunteyaḥ: he, Arjuna; *api samīkṣya tān*: also seeing these; *bandhūn*: relatives; *śvaśurān*: fathers-in-law; *ca eva suhṛdaḥ*: and friends; *sarvān avasthitān*: all standing; *ubhayoḥ senayoḥ*: in both the armies.

And the Son of Kuntī, also seeing these relatives, fathers-in-law, and friends, all standing, in both the armies,

28. कृपया परयाविष्टो विषीदन्निदमब्रवीत् ।
अर्जुन उवाच –
दृष्ट्वेमं स्वजनं कृष्ण युयुत्सुं समुपस्थितम् ॥

kṛpayā parayā 'viṣṭo viṣīdann idam abravīt ।
arjun uvāca –
dṛṣṭve 'maṁ svajanaṁ kṛṣṇa yuyutsuṁ samupasthitam ॥

āviṣṭaḥ parayā kṛpayā: filled by a supreme pity; *viṣīdan*: in mental distresses; *abravīt idam*: (Arjuna) said this; *dṛṣṭva imaṁ svajanaṁ*: beholding this my own people; *kṛṣṇa*: Oh Kṛṣṇa; *samupasthitam*: standing together; *yuyutsuṁ*: wanting to fight.

filled by a supreme pity, in mental distress, said: Beholding my own people, Oh Kṛṣṇa, standing together, wanting to fight,

29. सीदन्ति मम गात्राणि मुखं च परिशुष्यति ।
वेपथुश्च शरीरे मे रोमहर्षश्च जायते ॥

sīdanti mama gātrāṇi mukhaṁ ca pariśuṣyati ।
vepathuś ca śarīre me romaharṣaś ca jāyate ॥

mama gātrāṇi sīdanti: my limbs fail; *ca mukhaṁ pariśuṣyati*: and my mouth dries up; *ca me śarīre vepathuḥ*: and my body trembles; *ca roma harṣaḥ jāyate*: and my hair stands on end.

my limbs fail and my mouth dries up, my body trembles and my hair stands on end,

30. गाण्डीवं स्रंसते हस्तात्त्वक्चैव परिदह्यते ।
न च शक्नोम्यवस्थातुं भ्रमतीव च मे मनः ॥

gāṇḍīvaṁ sraṁsate hastāt tvak cai 'va paridahyate ।
na ca śaknomy avasthātum bhramatī 'va ca me manaḥ ॥

gāṇḍīvam: (the bow) Gāṇḍīva; *sraṁsate*: slips; *hastāt*: from (my) hand; *ca eva tvak paridahyate*: and (my) skin (feels as if it) is burning (all over); *na ca śaknomi avasthātuṁ*: and I am unable to stand; *ca me manaḥ bhramati iva*: and my mind is whirling round as it were.

(the bow) Gāṇḍīva slips from my hand, my skin feels as if burning all over, I am unable to stand, and my mind is whirling round;

31. निमित्तानि च पश्यामि विपरीतानि केशव ।
न च श्रेयोऽनुपश्यामि हत्वा स्वजनमाहवे ॥

nimittāni ca paśyāmi viparītāni keśava ।
na ca śreyo 'nupaśyāmi hatvā svajanam āhave ॥

paśyāmi viparītāni nimittāni ca: and I see conflicting portents; *keśava*: Oh Kṛṣṇa; *na ca anupaśyāmi śreyaḥ*: nor do I foresee good; *hatvā*: from killing; *svajanam ahave*: one's own people in battle.

and I see conflicting portents, Oh Keśava, nor do I foresee good from killing one's own people in battle.

32. न कांक्षे विजयं कृष्ण न च राज्यं सुखानि च ।
किं नो राज्येन गोविन्द किं भोगैर्जीवितेन वा ॥

na kāṅkṣe vijayaṁ kṛṣṇa na ca rājyaṁ sukhāni ca ।
kiṁ no rājyena govinda kiṁ bhogair jīvitena vā ॥

na kāṇkṣe vijayaṁ: I do not wish for victory; *kṛṣṇa*: Oh Kṛṣṇa; *na ca rājyaṁ*: nor kingdom; *sukhāni ca*: nor pleasures; *kiṁ rājyena naḥ govinda*: what is kingdom to us, Oh Kṛṣṇa; *kiṁ bhogaiḥ*: what enjoyments; *jīvitena vā*: or (even) life.

I do not wish for victory, Oh Kṛṣṇa, nor kingdom, nor pleasures; what is kingdom to us, Oh Govinda, what enjoyment, or even life?

33. येषामर्थे काक्षितं नो राज्यं भोगाः सुखानि च ।
त इमेऽवस्थिता युद्धे प्राणांस्त्यक्त्वा धनानि च ॥

yeṣām arthe kāṇkṣitaṁ no rājyaṁ bhogāḥ sukhāni ca ।
to ime 'vasthitā yuddhe prāṇāṁs tyaktvā dhanāni ca ॥

yeṣām arthe: they for whose sake; *rājyaṁ*: kingdom; *bhogāḥ*: enjoyments; *sukhāni ca*: and pleasures; *kāṅkṣitaṁ naḥ*: are desired by us; *te ime avasthitā*: they are standing (here); *yuddhe*: in battle; *tyaktvā prāṇān*: having renounced their lives; *dhanāni ca*: and wealth.

They for whose sake kingdom, enjoyments, and pleasures are desired by us, are standing here in battle, having renounced their interests in life and in wealth –

34. आचार्याः पितरः पुत्रास्तथैव च पितामहाः ।
मातुलाः श्वसुराः पौत्राः श्यालाः सम्बन्धिनस्तथा ।।

ācāryāḥ pitaraḥ putrās tathai 'va ca pitāmahāḥ ।
mātulāḥ śvaśurāḥ pautrāḥ śyālāḥ saṁbandhinas tathā ॥

ācāryāḥ: teachers; *pitaraḥ*: fathers; *putrāḥ*: sons; *ca tathā eva*: and also; *pitāmahāḥ*: grandfathers; *mātulāḥ*: maternal uncles; *śvaśurāḥ*: fathers-in-law; *pautrāḥ*: grandsons; *śyālāḥ*: brothers-in-law; *tathā saṁbandhinaḥ*: as well as (other) kinsmen.

teachers, fathers, sons, and also grandfathers, maternal uncles, fathers-in-law, grandsons, brothers-in-law, as well as other kinsmen.

35. एतान्न हन्तुमिच्छामि घ्नतोऽपि मधुसूदन ।
अपि त्रैलोक्यराज्यस्य हेतोः किं नु महीकृते ।।

etān na hantum icchāmi ghnato 'pi madhusūdana ।
api trailokyarājyasya hetoḥ kiṁ nu mahīkṛte ॥

etān: these; *na icchāmi hantum*: I do not want to kill; *api ghnataḥ*: though they kill (me); *madhusūdana*: Oh Kṛṣṇa; *api hetoḥ trailokya rājyasyaḥ*: not even for the sake of dominion over the three worlds; *kiṁ nu mahīkṛte*: how then for the sake of the earth.

These I do not want to kill, though they kill me, Oh Kṛṣṇa, not even for the sake of dominion over the three worlds: how then for the sake of the earth?

36. निहत्य धार्तराष्ट्रान्नः का प्रीतिः स्याज्जनार्दन ।
पापमेवाश्रयेदस्मान्हत्वैतानाततायिनः ।।

nihatya dhārtarāṣṭrān naḥ kā prītiḥ syāj janārdana ।
pāpam evā 'śrayed asmān hatvai 'tān ātatāyinaḥ ॥

nihatya: having killed; *dhārtarāṣṭrān*: the Sons of Dhṛtarāṣṭra; *kā prītiḥ*: what delight; *syāt naḥ*: can there be for us; *janārdana*: Oh Kṛṣṇa; *eva pāpam*: only sin; *āśrayet asmān*: would come to us; *hatvā etān*: after killing this; *ātatāyinaḥ*: marauding rabble.

Having killed the Sons of Dhṛtarāṣṭra, what delight can there be for us, Oh Janārdana? Only sin would come to us after killing this marauding rabble.

37. तस्मान्नार्हा वयं हन्तुं धार्तराष्ट्रान् स्वबान्धवान् ।
स्वजनं हि कथं हत्वा सुखिनः स्याम माधव ॥

tasmān nā 'rhā vayaṁ hantuṁ dhārtarāṣṭrān svabāndhavān ।
svajanaṁ hi kathaṁ hatvā sukhinaḥ syāma mādhava ॥

tasmāt: and so; *vayaṁ na arhā hantuṁ*: we ought not to kill; *dhārtarāṣṭrān*: the Sons of Dhṛtarāṣṭra; *svabāndhavān*: our relations; *kathaṁ*: (for) how; *hi*: indeed; *syāma sukhinaḥ*: can we be happy; *hatvā svajanaṁ*: after killing our own people; *mādhava*: Oh Kṛṣṇa.

And so we ought not to kill the Sons of Dhṛtarāṣṭra, our relations; for how, indeed, can we be happy after killing our own people, Oh Mādhava?

38. यद्यप्येते न पश्यन्ति लोभोपहतचेतसः
कुलक्षयकृतं दोषं मित्रद्रोहे च पातकम् ॥

yady apy ete na paśyanti lobhopahatacetasaḥ ।
kulakṣayakṛtaṁ doṣaṁ mitradrohe ca pātakam ॥

yadi api: even if; *ete lobha upahata cetasaḥ*: they whose minds are overpowered by greed; *paśyanti*: see; *na doṣaṁ kula kṣaya kṛtaṁ*: no wrong in causing the destruction of family; *ca (na) pātakam mitra drohe*: and no crime in treachery to friends.

Even if they, whose minds are overpowered by greed, see no wrong in the destruction of family, and no crime in treachery to friends,

39. कथं न ज्ञेयमस्माभिः पापादस्मान्निवर्तितुम् ।
कुलक्षयकृतं दोषं प्रपश्यद्भिर्जनार्दन ॥

kathaṁ na jñeyam asmābhiḥ pāpād asmān nivartitum ।
kulakṣayakṛtaṁ doṣaṁ prapaśyadbhir janārdana ॥

kathaṁ asmābhiḥ na jñeyam: (yet) why should we not learn; *nivartitum*: to turn away; *asmān pāpāt*: from this sin; *prapaśyadbhiḥ*: we who do see; *doṣaṁ kula kṣaya kṛtaṁ*: wrong in causing the destruction of family; *janārdana*: Oh Kṛṣṇa.

yet why should we not learn to turn away from this sin – we who do see wrong in the destruction of family – Oh Janārdana?

40. कुलक्षये प्रणश्यन्ति कुलधर्माः सनातनाः ।
धर्मे नष्टे कुलं कृत्स्नमधर्मोऽभिभवत्युत ॥

kulakṣaye praṇaśyanti kuladharmāḥ sanātanāḥ ।
dharme naṣṭe kulaṁ kṛtsnam adharmo 'bhibhavaty uta ॥

kula kṣaye: in the destruction of family; *sanātanāḥ kula dharmāḥ*: the immemorial clan traditions; *praṇaśyanti*: perish; *uta dharme naṣṭe*: and on the loss of tradition; *kṛtsnam kulaṁ*: the whole clan; *abhibhavati adharmaḥ*: comes under the sway of lawlessness.

In the destruction of family, the immemorial clan traditions perish, and on the loss of tradition the whole clan comes under the sway of lawlessness.

41. अधर्माभिभवात्कृष्ण प्रदुष्यन्ति कुलस्त्रियः ।
स्त्रीषु दुष्टासु वार्ष्णेय जायते वर्णसङ्करः ।।

adharmābhibhavāt kṛṣṇa praduṣyanti kulastriyaḥ ।
strīṣu duṣṭāsu vārṣṇeya jāyate varṇasaṁkaraḥ ॥

adharma abhibhavāt: when wrong ways prevail; *kṛṣṇa*: Oh Kṛṣṇa; *kula striyaḥ*: the women of the family; *praduṣyanti*: become corrupt; *strīṣu duṣṭāsu*: (and) when women become corrupt; *vārṣṇeya*: Oh Kṛṣṇa; *varṇa saṁkaraḥ jāyate*: mixing of clans arises.

When wrong ways prevail, Oh Kṛṣṇa, the women of the family become corrupt, and when women become corrupt, Oh Vārṣṇeya, mixing of clans arises.

42. सङ्करो नरकायैव कुलघ्नानां कुलस्य च ।
पतन्ति पितरो ह्येषां लुप्तपिण्डोदकक्रियाः ।।

saṅkaro narakāyai 'va kulaghnānāṁ kulasya ca ।
patanti pitaro hy eṣām luptapiṇḍodakakriyāḥ ॥

saṅkaraḥ: mixing (of clans); *narakāya eva kulasya kulaghnānāṁ ca*: (leads) to hell (both the) family and the destroyers of the family; *hi eṣām pitaraḥ patanti*: for their ancestors fall; *lupta piṇḍa udaka kriyāḥ*: (when) deprived of (their offerings of) rice balls and water rites.

This mixing leads (both the) family and the destroyers of the family to hell, for their ancestors fall when deprived of their offerings of rice balls and water rites.

43. दोषैरेतैः कुलघ्नानां वर्णसङ्करकारकैः ।
उत्साद्यन्ते जातिधर्माः कुलधर्माश्च शाश्वताः ।।

doṣair etaiḥ kulaghnānāṁ varṇasaṅkarakārakaiḥ ।
utsādyante jātidharmāḥ kuladharmāś ca śāśvatāḥ ॥

etaiḥ doṣaiḥ: by these misdeeds; *kulaghnānāṁ*: of the destroyers of families; *varṇa saṅkara kārakaiḥ*: causing intermixture of clans; *śāśvatāḥ*: the immemorial; *kula dharmāḥ*: traditions of clan; *ca jāti dharmāḥ*: and traditions of family; *utsādyante*: are destroyed.

By these misdeeds of the destroyers of families, causing intermixture of clans, the immemorial traditions of clan and family are destroyed.

44. उत्सन्नकुलधर्माणां मनुष्याणां जनार्दन ।
नरकेऽनियतं वासो भवतीत्यनुशुश्रुम ।।

utsannakuladharmāṇāṁ manuṣyāṇāṁ janārdana ।
narake niyataṁ vāso bhavatī 'ty anuśuśruma ॥

manuṣyāṅāṁ utsanna kula dharmāṇāṁ: of men of families whose clan traditions are destroyed; *janārdana*: Oh Kṛṣṇa; *niyataṁ vāsaḥ bhavati*: the destined dwelling is; *narake*: in hell; *iti*: thus; *anuśuśruma*: we have heard

Men of families whose clan traditions are destroyed, Oh Janārdana, are destined to live in hell – thus we have heard.

45. अहो बत महत्पापं कर्तुं व्यवसिता वयम् ।
यद्राज्यसुखलोभेन हन्तुं स्वजनमुद्यताः ।।

aho bata mahat pāpaṁ kartuṁ vyavasitā vayam ।
yad rājyasukhalobhena hantuṁ svajanam udyatāḥ ॥

aho bata: alas!; *mahat pāpaṁ*: a great sin; *vayam vyavasitā kartuṁ*: we are engaged in committing; *yad udyatāḥ hantuṁ svajanam*: in endeavouring to kill our own people; *rājya sukha lobhena*: through greed for the pleasures of kingdom.

Alas! A great sin are we engaged in committing in endeavouring to kill our own people through greed for the pleasures of kingdom!

46. यदि मामप्रतीकारमशस्त्रं शस्त्रपाणयः ।
धार्तराष्ट्रा रणे हन्युस्तन्मे क्षेमतरं भवेत् ।।

yadi mām apratīkāram aśastraṁ śastrapāṇayaḥ ।
dhārtarāṣṭrā raṇe hanyus tan me kṣemataraṁ bhavet ॥

bhavet kṣemataram me: it would he better for me; *yadi dhārtarāṣṭrāḥ*: if the Sons of Dhṛtarāṣṭra; *śastrapāṇayaḥ*: arms in hand; *hanyuḥ mām*: should kill me; *aśastraṁ*: unarmed; *apratīkāram*: (and) unresisting; *raṇe*: in the battle.

It would be better for me if the Sons of Dhṛtarāṣṭra, arms in hand, should kill me, unarmed and unresisting, in the battle.

सञ्जय उवाच –
47. एवमुक्त्वार्जुनः सङ्ख्ये रथोपस्थ उपाविशत् ।
विसृज्य सशरं चापं शोकसंविग्नमानसः ।।

sañjaya uvāca –

evam uktvā 'rjunaḥ saṁkhye rathopastha upāviśat ।
visṛjya saśaraṁ cāpaṁ śokasaṁvignamānasaḥ ॥

sañjaya uvāca: Sañjaya said; *evam uktvā*: thus having spoken; *saṁkhye*: in the midst of the battle; *arjunaḥ*: Arjuna; *upāviśat*: sat down; *ratha upastha*: in (his) chariot seat; *visṛjya*: casting away; *cāpaṁ saśaraṁ*: (his) bow and arrow; *śoka saṁvigna mānasaḥ*: (his) mind overwhelmed with sorrow.

Sañjaya said:

Thus having spoken in the midst of the battle, Arjuna sat down in his chariot seat, casting away his bow and arrow, his mind overwhelmed with sorrow.

DIALOGUE

TEACHER: This chapter is entitled Arjuna-Viṣāda-Yoga: (The Dialectical Conflict of Arjuna).

STUDENT: *Is this preliminary chapter important?*

Yes, it is. It contains the key to a proper understanding of the teaching in the rest of the book. The problems posed in this chapter are of a perennial kind. Such questions haunt the conscience of mankind again and again.

The Gītā is written in an archaic style. Even a name or a special word used in it can mean a lot if carefully studied. Take, for instance, the opening of the Gītā, which begins with the utterance of Dhṛtarāṣṭra. The Sanskrit word *Dhṛtarāṣṭra* literally means "the supporter of a nation", such as a king or president or chairman. In the present case, the reference is to a chief who was blind. If the premier of a country, who is destined to shape the fate of a people, is morally blind and does not see justice and wisdom, the country may become a stagnant pool of chaos. Whenever such tragedies occur, there is the dire need to revalue and restate the moral canons of personal ethics and social life. It is almost a miracle in the history of a country when it gets the leadership of a "Philosopher King" who is deep in his erudition, broad in his views, far-sighted in his visions, accommodative in his policies, generous in his judgements, and graceful in his public as well as personal behaviour. The Gītā does not conclude its teaching with the ideal of a recluse, but with the model of a wise ruler of the people, who can bring prosperity, victory, progress, and well-established justice. The mention of the blind king is an indication that the book will be a revaluation and restatement of moral and spiritual enlightenment.

Does this also mean that the Gītā is a book of political philosophy or social anthropology?

No. It teaches a sincere aspirant how to become well established in the Self, and to fully unfold his perfection. There is no doubt that the Gītā is a perennial source of inspiration and guidance, no matter what your vocation or career is, or who you are.

How do you equate Arjuna's problems with ours?

There might have been in the pre-history of India some legendary prince called Arjuna. We need not bother to know what his problems were. If the Gītā is accepted as a book of wisdom, then the Arjuna it refers to should be taken as a representative for all time, who epitomizes all that is best in man, plus man's natural misgivings and weaknesses. In the Sanskrit language, *Arjuna* means the "ever wakeful". In all of us there is an *Arjuna*, an awareness of our own being. That awareness is always alert behind all the altering states of consciousness, the wakeful as well as dream states, and in the sleep as well as the transcendental states. The same consciousness in its universal and purest form is none other than the Divine. It pervades everything, sees all as the one Eye behind all eyes, and knows all as the Overmind behind all minds. Yet at an individual level it is conditioned and coloured by the time and place of its expression, and filled with changing phases of fear and disbelief, hatred and rejection, withdrawal and resistance, a sense of guilt, emotional crisis, and every shade of neurosis and psychosis. The Gītā also reveals the need for intelligent acceptance and trust of the Divine. It gives us an enlightened vision of the Self, and an intimate knowledge of our basic drives and inner moorings. Based on that understanding, the Gītā recommends a healthy adherence to our social roles, while never forgetting that the ultimate goal of life is Realization.

According to you, Dhṛtarāṣṭra symbolizes the decline of an age and the failure of its dynamics. Arjuna symbolizes an earnest, truth-loving, good person of action confronted by dark and evil forces, and caught between the horns of a paradoxical dilemma. What does the battle symbolize?

The symbolism of war and battle represent the great struggle in the psyche between the human and animal factors, the lower and the higher selves, the individual and the mass-man, and the revolutionary contention of the negative and positive forces to create the new. In the battle of Kurukṣetra, the fight is essentially between the morbid *form* and the inner *spirit*. The *form* is of degenerate traditions preserved by kings, dogmas, creeds, rituals, organizations, laws, conventions, and customs, which turn out in the course of time to be mummified tyrants – abstract, cold, and dead – and yet to have the negative potential to strangle the spirit of man. The army of the Kurus, marshalled by Bhīṣma and commanded by Duryodhana, represents this *form* aspect. The *spirit* is the ever-bright life-aspect, which draws its light and strength from experience, mystical contemplation and insight, instrumentality of and obedience to the spirit of the tradition, an altruistic spirit of law, and spontaneity of expression. This is what Arjuna and his army, marshalled by Bhīma and commanded by Yudhiṣṭhira, represent.

Apart from Kṛṣṇa and Arjuna, why does the Gītā introduce in this chapter three other characters, Duryodhana, Droṇa, and Bhīṣma?

All around us we see people who are successful in their worldly pursuits. Most of them are not mindful of any moral principle: they just elbow their way through life. They easily slight their consciences, and engage in various acts of criminal deprivation. It is not that they do not know what is right. They simply do not have the sensibility of a Buddha or a Christ to sense the sufferings of others. Duryodhana, Droṇa, and Bhīṣma are three legendary men of gross action. They are well known in the *Mahābhārata* epic for their political ferocity. In them we see the ruthless attitude of leaders committed to pressure tactics. They gamble with the lives of others. They are only mindful of their own ignoble ends. The ugly spectacle of such down-to-earth men of relativistic valour shows by contrast the rich refinement of Arjuna's mind. This chapter portrays vividly how sensitive he is to every value involved in the total war situation. The same sensibility can be seen in anyone who is spiritually vibrant.

Why should Arjuna be placed in a battlefield to highlight his refinement and sensibility?

It is well known that armchair philosophy does not bake any bread. Life is full of combats, conflicts, crises, and deadlocks. The clash of values is at its worst in a war situation. The strongest man of action can be reduced to the weakest if his morale is affected. You cannot hold out with fiery vengeance to one whom you dearly love, revere, or look upon with gratitude. Your inner strength of purpose, dedication, consistent adherence to basic principles, and identity with the Absolute are put to the acid test when you are called upon to play your role in a life and death contest. A conscientious examiner evaluating the answer-book of his own son which borders below the minimum grade required to pass may feel tempted to err. A judge passing the verdict of death to his own son, proved to be guilty, may have to spend many sleepless nights. Even a dog lover who must give a needle to his rabid pet will have a hard day. We can quote from everyday life hundreds of such instances in which we all share the conflict of Arjuna.

What exactly was Arjuna's conflict?

In ancient India there were two brothers. The elder was Dhṛtarāṣṭra, King of Hastināpura, and the younger was Pāṇḍu. Dhṛtarāṣṭra was blind – a symbol of the darkness of nescience. Pāṇḍu was white – a symbol of brightness and clear vision. Dhṛtarāṣṭra's wife, Gāndhārī, gave birth to a mass of flesh – a symbol of insensitivity and inertia. This mass was cut into bits and each became a child, one hundred sons and one daughter. The eldest son was named Duryodhana, meaning "difficult to be fought with". The next eldest was named Duḥśāsana, meaning "difficult to be disciplined". In short, this was a whole brood of heartless brutes. Pāṇḍu was forbidden by a curse to procreate children. His wife, Kuntī, had a boon to bring forth children, begotten by gods, by a mere wish. Before her marriage to Paṇḍu, she gave birth to Karṇa by parthenogenesis. Karṇa was the begotten son of Sūrya (sun god). After her marriage to Pāṇḍu, time at his behest, she gave birth to Yudhiṣṭhira (son of Dharmarāja, the god of time and cosmic law), Bhīma (son of Vāyu, the wind god), and Arjuna (son of Indra, the god of the shining ones). With a vicarious effect of the same magic power, Pāṇḍu's second wife, Mādrī, also conceived in the same manner, and gave birth to the twins Nakula and Sahadeva, begotten by the Aśvinīs, the Indian version of the Gemini. After the death of Pāṇḍu and Mādrī, his first wife Kuntī, and all the five children went to stay with Dhṛtarāṣṭra, Pāṇḍu's elder brother, and Bhīṣma, patriarch of the Kuru clan. Dhṛtarāṣṭra divided the kingdom, which belonged to him and his brother, Pāṇḍu, and gave one half to his own son, Duryodhana, and the other half to Yudhiṣṭhira.

Yudhiṣṭhira and his brothers were called the Pāṇḍavas, and Duryodhana and his brothers were called the Kauravas. The Pāṇḍavas built up a great capital, and their share of the country became very prosperous. This led to the political jealousy of Duryodhana and the Kauravas. They played a deceitful trick on the Pāṇḍavas and sent them into exile for fourteen years. According to the terms of the exile, the Pāṇḍavas could reclaim their kingdom after the fourteen years. But when they returned after fulfilling the term, Duryodhana refused to grant them re-entry. Instead of returning their country to them, he challenged them to wage war. Śrī Kṛṣṇa, as a peacemaker, tried his best to avoid war. His appeals did not succeed. This led to the great battle of Mahābhārata.

When Arjuna came to the battlefield, he asked Kṛṣṇa, his charioteer, to station his chariot between the two armies. On the one side stood Duryodhana with his army marshalled by the Patriarch Bhīṣma, and aided by his military adviser, Droṇa. On the other side was Arjuna's own army under the command of his brother Bhīma, marshalled by his wife's brother, Dhṛṣṭadyumna. Before seeing the actual persons holding arms against each other, Arjuna accepted the challenge and the warfare began. Thus he committed himself fully to the situation, but he regretted it as soon as he saw friends and relatives standing on either side waiting to kill each other. Seeing this, he shifted his position from an active participation to one of witnessing. There is a paradoxical incompatibility between the attitude of a participant and that of a neutral witness. While the former belongs to the field of action, the latter belongs to the realm of knowledge. When action moves in one direction and knowledge points towards another, there comes a deadlock. This is exactly what happened to Arjuna on the battlefield.

In Arjuna we see the enigmatic case of the dynamics of social mechanisms urging him to carry out the duty of a warrior, and, at the same time, a philosophic disposition that was essentially compassionate and altruistic, compelling him to give up war. Arjuna found the situation too hard to tackle. According to his station in life – a role that he deliberately opted for – the action that was most natural for him was to kill his enemies before they could retaliate. Killing an enemy by fair means in an all-out battle is an act of valour. But killing one's own teacher (Droṇa), one's own brother (Karṇa), and one's own grandfather (Bhīṣma), had no moral justification. In other words, the problem was choosing between two universes of values, both of which had merit and obligations.

Does this chapter contribute anything to the study of the Indian school of psychology?

In terms of the Indian schools of psychology, what happened to Arjuna on the battlefield was *vikalpa*, a process of misconception in which the whole mechanism of the mind is subjected to a series of hindrances. A major symptom of *vikalpa* is seeing a predicate relation that is not based on the true form presented to the person concerned. The interpersonal ensemble of a family or class or community is different from the interpersonal ensemble of an enemy camp in a battlefield. There, the nature of interpersonal relationship is one of rivalry and not of friendship. Arjuna's conflict actually originated from this misconception. Other forms of his misconceptions were:

- Non-differentiation of conceptual forms in terms of each one's relevant frame of reference.
- Trying to see an effect where it is not to be expected.
- Recall of memories irrelevant to the present context.
- A kind of infatuation caused by an exaggerated notion of interpersonal dependency.

Craving to identify only with the commendable or glorious.
Withdrawal tactics resulting in negativism.

Could you explain to me how Arjuna was affected by his misconceptions?

Arjuna's crisis had three phases:

- Psychosomatic affliction resulting in physical incapacitation and mental delusion.
- Developing a concealed sense of castration, to which Kṛṣṇa, alludes in verse 3 of Chapter II as *klaibyaṁ* (impotency).
- Rationalizing his inability and making a virtue out of it.

Arjuna himself describes the first phase:

> My limbs fail and my mouth dries up, my body trembles and my hair stands on end, the bow slips from my hand and my skin feels as if burning all over, I am unable to stand and my mind is whirling round as it were.

In the second phase he sees the war as a gaping mouth of *becoming* wanting to devour all forms of *being*. This frightens him. He wants to escape. He sees the blind and helpless march into the mouth of homicide (vv. 26-27); he sees sin and feels guilty for it (vv. 36-39); he laments the destruction of tradition, fears that widowed women may seek other men. He is even afraid that this will dislodge the departed souls from the heavens where they rest. In the third phase he sits down in his chariot seat, casting aside his bow and arrows, his mind overwhelmed with sorrow.

In the next chapter we shall see how Śrī Kṛṣṇa, as a Guru and healer of psychic and spiritual maladies, tackles the dialectical conflict of Arjuna.

What are the questions in Arjuna's mind in this chapter? To what extent are they relevant to a reader of the present-day society?

In this chapter Arjuna is presenting his case by describing his bodily state and state of mind. Then he makes a number of observations, which all imply questions. Arjuna is asking, as it were:

> Kṛṣṇa, I came to this battlefield fully resolved to fight. When I asked you to station my chariot between the two armies, I did so in order that I might have a good look at my friends and enemies. But see what has happened to me! And where I looked for enemies, I can see only people worthy of being worshipped.
>
> Should one fight, killing kith and kin, even though they are seen as perverted in their ambitions? Should I not be grateful to the people who have helped me sincerely and affectionately over a long period of time to become what I am now? If it is natural for me to fight, why is it that my body is so

> adversely affected? Why does my mouth go dry, my limbs quail, my body shake, my hair stand on end, and my bow slip from my hand? What has happened to my firm resolve? Why am I subjected to this terrible conflict? Should I fight and kill when I do not see any value in possessing a kingdom nor do I care for the pleasures of life? What prevents me from becoming a renunciate instead of becoming a killer? Is it not noble to dissuade these people from committing genocide by setting before them a good example of non-violence? Is not killing a sin? After committing this hideous sin, how can one escape its consequences? Are we not as much addicted to the evils of greed and the sense of revenge as our own adversaries? Should a wise man copy the example of dull-headed people?
>
> Should we exterminate a whole clan to correct the misdeeds of their rulers? Is not the law preserved by the integrity of a clan? By destroying a whole people, are we not also destroying their laws, their traditions, and their culture? Is not the caste system a well-regulated social institution? Is it good to create a situation which will lead to the promiscuous mixing of people? Is there a moral agency that decides the merit of our actions? Is not hell a horrid place to purge us of our sins? Should we opt for it? Do we have obligations to our departed ancestors? Should we engage in activities which will disturb their astral peace? What will become of me if I decide to become a conscientious objector?

Although these are not the exact words of Arjuna, all the questions enumerated here are implied in the verses 29 to 47. Some of Arjuna's questions are based on unexamined beliefs, and some are precipitated by his prejudices. However, most of his questions have a great moral relevancy. He asks more pointed questions in the subsequent chapters.

Does Kṛṣṇa answer all these questions?

When Kṛṣṇa employs a methodology by which he can systematically correct Arjuna step by step, he keeps in his mind all the psychological, moral, and intellectual problems of Arjuna. He does not ignore any of his questions. The student has to keep his mind sharp to know which question of Arjuna's Kṛṣṇa is taking up in the course of the development of his encounter and counselling.

II

Sāṁkhya-Yoga
Unitive Reasoning

INTRODUCTION

ARJUNA'S conflict is carried over from the previous chapter, where we should normally have expected it to terminate. The literary device of a Sañjaya talking to a Dhṛtarāṣṭra is again introduced. Kṛṣṇa himself tries to rouse Arjuna from his apparent inertia or lethargy by sharp stinging expressions. Arjuna, instead of being cowed by them, justifies himself further in a manner that reflects a certain state of abandonment.

In this chapter the structure of the verses attains a new dialectical perfection, reciprocal expressions being used with a striking symmetry, neutralizing factors or values into a vague sense of wonder of the numinous. Arjuna himself thus gains a new status as a representative contemplative disciple who properly belongs to the *guru–śiṣya* context. Arjuna's conflict, condition, and attitude are typical of a wisdom seeker. From the mere emotion of the first chapter, here in the second chapter Arjuna has come to a state of philosophical doubt which he is quite capable of stating consciously and precisely in conformity with other scriptures.

Kṛṣṇa now begins the role of a Guru (wisdom teacher). This is inaugurated with verse 11. The smile on his lips in verse 10 is characteristically in contrast with the pessimistic state of Arjuna, who is gloomy and pensive. Between this bright smile and the *tedium vitae* is to take place presently a normal dialectical revaluation of wisdom values.

It has been generally admitted on the part of scholars (e.g. Franklin Edgerton and Radhakrishnan) that the Sāṁkhya system described in the Gītā is not the same as the Sāṁkhya of Kapila, nor does the Yoga of this chapter conform to Patañjali's Yoga. Many scholars find it difficult to explain why two familiar terms of the classical *darśanas* (philosophical visions) are used here in an unfamiliar sense.

Though renunciates, *saṁnyāsins*, and *yogīs* are usually looked upon as the same, for all practical purposes they are to be treated separately. It is hard for those who are not familiar with the history of India's spiritual evolution to distinguish between these two groups of spiritual people.

Before the supremacy of Vedic Brāhmanism in India, there were two other spiritual patterns known to the people of pre-Vedic times. The spiritual model of one group was the contemplative Śiva model, and the other was what developed afterwards into the proto-Jaina model of renunciation. Both the Śaivite mystics and the proto-Jaina ascetics were austere people who emphasized the need to withdraw from all competitive aspects of life to merge in the oneness of the spirit through meditation. The Vedic people, on the other hand, were positive in their outlook, and their love and enjoyment of life sometimes even bordered on aggression. The main theme of their spirituality was the fire sacrifice (Agnihotra). Pre-Vedic people, who belonged either to the Śaivite or proto-Jaina spiritual grass-roots, and who came to live in the Aryan fold, found the Veda utilitarian in its stress and lacking in the climate of contemplation. As a result, the Vedas were soon complemented by contemplative adjuncts called the Upaniṣads. Though the Upaniṣads had their allegiance to the Vedas, they spoke disparagingly of them and held out the ideal of renunciation rather than ritualism. Those who dropped out of the early Vedic society were called *saṁnyāsins*. Their heterodox attitude and way of thinking are more similar to that of the Sāṁkhyans than of any other system in India. Though the *ṛṣis* of the Upaniṣads were endowed with great intuitive penetration, they very often used the language of dialectical criticism similar to that of the Sāṁkhyans. This explains why the first part of the second chapter (vv. 1-38) is qualified as Saṁkhyan in its mode of reasoning.

Those who adhered to the society and continued to participate in the ritualism also found it necessary to revise their stand by renouncing the benefit of their action. Like Patañjali, they had no objection to accepting the postulate of *Īśvaraḥ* as Supreme Being. This, however, is not merely a theistic afterthought, as some scholars, such as Dr. Radhakrishnan, think. The Science of the Absolute, *brahma-vidyā*, should not be confused with mere religious theism. The revaluation of the attitude of those who continued to participate in social life is seen in the second part of this chapter (vv. 39-72).

TRANSLATION

सञ्जय उवाच –

1. तं तथा कृपयाविष्टमश्रुपूर्णाकुलेक्षणम् ।
विषीदन्तमिदं वाक्यमुवाच मधुसूदनः ।।

sañjaya uvāca –

taṁ tathā kṛpayā 'viṣṭam aśrupūrṇākulekṣaṇam ।
viṣīdantaṁ idaṁ vākyam uvāca madhusūdanaḥ ॥

sañjaya uvāca: Sañjaya said; *taṁ tathā*: to him who was thus; *āviṣṭam kṛpayā*: filled with tenderness; *aśrupūrṇa ākula īkṣaṇam*: whose eyes were filled with tears, and agitated; *viṣīdantam*: who was in distress; *madhusūdanaḥ*: Kṛṣṇa; *uvāca idaṁ vākyam*: spoke this word.

Sañjaya said:

To him who was thus filled with tenderness, whose eyes were filled with tears, and agitated, and who was in distress, the Destroyer of Madhu spoke these words:

श्रीभगवानुवाच –

2. कुतस्त्वा कश्मलमिदं विषमे समुपस्थितम् ।
अनार्यजुष्टमस्वर्ग्यमकीर्तिकरमर्जुन ।।

śrībhagavān uvāca –

kutas tvā kaśmalam idaṁ viṣame samupasthitam ।
anāryajuṣṭam asvargyam akīrtikaram arjuna ॥

śrī bliagavān uvāca: the Lord said; *samupasthitaṁ viṣame*: in the midst of this difficulty (war); *kutaḥ*: whence comes; *tvā*: to you; *idaṁ kaśmalam*: this dejection; *anārya juṣṭam*: typical of non-Aryans; *asvargyam*: heaven-barring; *akīrti karam*: (and) disreputable; *arjuna*: Oh Arjuna.

The Lord said:

In the midst of this difficulty, whence comes to you this dejection typical of non-Aryans, heaven-barring and disreputable, Oh Arjuna?

3. क्लैब्यं मा स्म गमः पार्थ नैतत्त्वय्युपपद्यते ।
क्षुद्रं हृदयदौर्बल्यं त्यक्त्वोत्तिष्ठ परन्तप ।।

klaibyaṁ mā sma gamaḥ pārtha nai 'tat tvayy upapadyate ।
kṣudraṁ hṛdayadaurbalyaṁ tyaktvo 'ttiṣṭha paraṁtapa ॥

mā sma gamaḥ: give not yourself to; *klaibyaṁ*: impotence; *pārtha*: Oh Arjuna; *etat*: it; *na upapadyate*: is not fitting; *tvayi*: in you; *tyaktvā*: cast off; *kṣudraṁ hṛdaya daurbalyaṁ*: (this) base faint-heartedness; *uttiṣṭha*: arise; *paraṁtapa*: Oh Arjuna.

Give not yourself to impotence, Oh Arjuna! it does not befit you. Cast off this base faint-heartedness. Arise, Oh Terrror of Foes!

अर्जुन उवाच –

4. कथं भीष्ममहं सङ्ख्ये द्रोणं च मधुसूदन ।
इषुभिः प्रतियोत्स्यामि पूजार्हावरिसूदन ।।

arjuna uvāca –

kathaṁ bhīṣmam ahaṁ saṁkhye droṇaṁ ca madhusūdana ।
iṣubhiḥ pratiyotsyāmi pūjārhāv arisūdana ॥

arjuna uvāca: Arjuna said; *kathaṁ ahaṁ*: how could I; *madhusūdana*: Oh Kṛṣṇa; *pratiyotsyāmi iṣūbhiḥ saṁkhye*: encounter with arrows in battle; *bhīṣmam ca droṇaṁ*: Bhīṣma and Droṇa; *pūjā arhau*: who are worthy of worship; *arisūdana*: Oh Kṛṣṇa.

Arjuna said:

How could I, Oh Slayer of Madhu! encounter with arrows in battle Bhīṣma and Droṇa, who are worthy of worship, Oh Slayer of Foes?

5. गुरूनहत्वा हि महानुभावान् श्रेयो भोक्तुं भैक्ष्यमपीह लोके ।
हत्वार्थकामांस्तु गुरूनिहैव भुञ्जीय भोगान् रुधिरप्रदिग्धान् ।।

gurūn ahatvā hi mahānubhāvān śreyo bhoktum bhaikṣyam api 'ha loke ।
hatvā 'rthakāmāṁs tu gurūn ihai 'va bhuñjīya bhogān rudhirapradigdhān ॥

ahatvā hi: desisting from killing indeed; *gurūn*: the Gurus; *mahānubhāvān*: who are highly honourable; *śreyaḥ*: (it would be) more meritorious; *iha loke*: in this world; *api bhoktum bhaikṣyam*: even to have to eat of a beggar's pittance; *tu hatvā*: on the other hand, killing; *gurūn arthakāmān*: (these) Gurus as fortune-seekers; *bhuñjiya*: I should be feasting on; *eva iha*: even here; *rudhirapradigdhān bhogān*: blood-stained benefits of life.

Desisting from the killing of the Gurus, who are highly honourable, it would be more meritorious in this world even to have to eat of a beggar's pittance. Choosing, on the other hand, to kill these Gurus as fortune-seekers, I should be feasting even here on blood-stained benefits of life.

6. न चैतद्विद्मः कतरन्नो गरीयो यद्वा जयेम यदि वा नो जयेयुः ।
यानेव हत्वा न जिजीविषामस्तेऽवस्थिताः प्रमुखे धार्तराष्ट्राः ।।

na cai 'tad vidmaḥ kataran no gariyo yad vā jayema yadi vā no jayeyuḥ ।
yān eva hatvā na jijīviṣāmas te 'vasthitāḥ pramukhe dhārtarāṣṭrāḥ ॥

na ca etat vidmaḥ: neither is it clear; *katarat gariyaḥ naḥ*: which (would be) of greater advantage to us; *yad vā jayema*: that we win; *vā yadi jayeyuḥ naḥ*: or that they win over us; *te eva avasthitāḥ pramukhe*: those very persons are standing ranged before us; *dhārtarāṣṭrāḥ*: the Sons of Dhṛtarāṣṭra; *hatvā yān*: killing whom; *na jijīviṣāmaḥ*: (we would) no longer wish to live.

Neither is it clear which would be of greater advantage to us: that we win, or that they win over us. Those very persons are standing ranged before us, the Sons of Dhṛtarāṣṭra, killing whom we would no longer wish to live.

7. कार्पण्यदोषोपहतस्वभावः पृच्छामि त्वां धर्मसम्मूढचेताः ।
यच्छ्रेयः स्यान्निश्चितं ब्रूहि तन्मे शिष्यस्तेऽहं शाधि मां त्वां प्रपन्नम् ।।

kārpaṇyadoṣopahatasvabhāvaḥ pṛcchāmi tvāṁ dharmasammūḍhacetāḥ ।
yac chreyaḥ syān niścitaṁ brūhi tan me śiṣyas te 'haṁ śādhi māṁ tvāṁ prapannam ॥

kārpaṇya doṣa upahata svabhāvaḥ: struck down by the evil of a tender disposition; *dharma sammūḍha cetāḥ*: with a mind confounded in regard to what is right (to do); *pṛcchāmi tvāṁ*: I ask you; *yat syāt niścitaṁ śreyaḥ*: that which should be definitely more meritorious; *tat brūhi me*: that do indicate to me; *ahaṁ tvaṁ śiṣyaḥ*: I am your disciple; *śādhi māṁ*: do discipline me; *prapannam*: coming for refuge.

Struck down by the evil of a tender disposition, with a mind confounded in regard to what is right to do, I ask you: that which is definitely more meritorious do indicate to me. I am your disciple; do discipline me coming thus for refuge to you.

8. न हि प्रपश्यामि ममापनुद्याद् यच्छोकमुच्छोषणमिन्द्रियाणाम् ।
अवाप्य भूमावसपत्नमृद्धं राज्यं सुराणामपि चाधिपत्यम् ।।

na hi prapaśyāmi mamā 'panudyād yac chokam ucchoṣaṇam indriyāṇām ।
avāpya bhūmāv asapatnam ṛddhaṁ rājyaṁ surāṇām api cā 'dhipatyam ॥

hi na prapaśyāmi: indeed, I cannot visualize; *yat apanudyāt mama śokam*: what could remove my distress; *ucchoṣaṇam indriyāṇām*: which dries up the senses (in this way); *avāpya asapatnaṁ rājyaṁ bhūmau ṛddhaṁ*: (even) should (it transpire that) I obtain unrivalled dominion of the earth's plenty; *ca ādhipatyam surāṇām api*: or overlordship of the gods (in heaven) too.

I cannot visualize what could rid me of this distress which dries up the senses in this way – even should (it transpire that) I obtain unrivalled dominion of the earth's plenty or overlordship of the gods in heaven too.

सञ्जय उवाच –

9. एवमुक्त्वा हृषीकेशं गुडाकेशः परन्तप ।
न योत्स्य इति गोविन्दमुक्त्वा तूष्णीं बभूव ह ॥

sañjaya uvāca –

evam uktvā hṛṣīkeśaṁ guḍākeśaḥ paraṁtapaḥ ।
na yotsya iti govindam uktvā tūṣṇīṁ babhūva ha ॥

sañjaya uvāca: Sañjaya said; *uktvā evam*: having spoken thus; *hṛṣīkeśaṁ*: to Kṛṣṇa; *guḍākeśaḥ*: Arjuna; *paraṁtapaḥ*: the Terror of the Foe; *uktvā*: saying; *na yotsye iti*: I will not fight; *govindam*: to Kṛṣṇa; *babhūva ha tūṣṇīṁ*: lapsed finally into silence.

Sañjaya said:

Having spoken thus to Hṛṣikeśa, Guḍākeśa, the Terror of the Foe, saying "I will not fight" to Govinda, lapsed finally into silence.

10. तमुवाच हृषीकेशः प्रहसन्निव भारत ।
सेनयोरुभयोर्मध्ये विषीदन्तमिदं वचः ॥

taṁ uvāca hṛṣikeśaḥ prahasann iva bhārata ।
senayor ubhayor madhye viṣīdantam idam vacaḥ ॥

hrsīkeśaḥ: Kṛṣṇa; *prahasan iva*: with a semblance of smiling; *bhārata*: Oh Dhṛtarāṣṭra; *idaṁ vacaḥ*: (spoke) this word; *tam viṣīdantam*: to him who was in grief; *madhye ubhayoh senayoḥ*: between the two armies.

On this, Hṛṣikeśa, with a semblance of smiling, Oh Dhṛtarāṣṭra! spoke these words to him who was in grief between the two armies:

श्रीभगवानुवाच –

11. अशोच्यानन्वशोचस्त्वं प्रज्ञावादांश्च भाषसे ।
गतासूनगतासूंश्च नानुशोचन्ति पण्डिताः ॥

śrībhagavān uvāca –

aśocyān anvaśocas tvaṁ prajñāvādāṁś ca bhāṣase ।
gatāsūn agatāsūṁś ca nā 'nuśocanti paṇḍitāḥ ॥

śrī bhagavān uvāca: the Lord said; *tvaṁ anvaśocaḥ aśocyān*: you are sorry for those for whom sorrow is unreasonable; *bhāṣase prajñāvādāṁś ca*: you speak in terms of reason too; *paṇḍitāḥ na anuśocanti*: veritable philosophers (*paṇḍits*) are not affected; *gatāsūn ca agatāsūn*: (in regard to) those whose breath has gone and those whose breath has not gone.

The Lord said:

You are sorry for those for whom sorrow is unreasonable. You speak in terms of reason too. Veritable philosophers are not affected in regard to those whose breath has gone and those whose breath has not gone.

12. न त्वेवाहं जातु नासं न त्वं नेमे जनाधिपाः ।
न चैव न भविष्यामः सर्वे वयमतः परम् ।।

na tv evā 'haṁ jātu nā 'saṁ na tvaṁ ne 'me janādhipāḥ ।
na cai 'va na bhaviṣyāmaḥ sarve vayam ataḥ param ॥

tu eva na jātu ahaṁ na āsaṁ: further, never was I non-existent; *na tvaṁ*: nor you; *na ime janādhipāḥ*: nor these chiefs of men; *na vayam sarve*: neither (shall) we, all of us; *ca eva na bhaviṣyāmaḥ param*: ever cease becoming hereafter.

Further, never was I non-existent, nor you, nor these chiefs of men; neither shall we, all of us, ever cease becoming hereafter.

13. देहिनोऽस्मिन्यथा देहे कौमारं यौवनं जरा ।
तथा देहान्तरप्राप्तिर्धीरस्तत्र न मुह्यति ।।

dehino 'smin yathā dehe kaumāraṁ yauvanaṁ jarā ।
tathā dehāntaraprāptir dhīras tatra na muhyati ॥

yathā asmin: as there is here; *dehinaḥ dehe*: in the body, for the embodied; *kaumāraṁ*: childhood; *yauvanaṁ*: youth; *jarā*: and old age; *tathā deha antara prāptiḥ*: so also the passing on to another body in the same manner; *tatra dhīraḥ*: those firm in mind; *na muhyati*: are not thereby bewildered.

As there is here in the body, for the embodied, childhood, youth, and old age, so also the passing on to another body in the same manner; those firm in mind are not thereby bewildered.

14. मात्रास्पर्शास्तु कौन्तेय शीतोष्णसुखदुःखदाः ।
आगमापायिनोऽनित्यास्तांस्तितिक्षस्व भारत ।।

mātrāsparśās tu kaunteya śītoṣṇasukhaduḥkhadāḥ ।
āgamāpāyino 'nityās tāṁs titikṣasva bhārata ॥

mātrā sparśāḥ: momentary sense contacts; *tu*: on the other hand; *kaunteya*: Oh Arjuna; *śīta uṣṇa sukha duḥkhadāḥ*: yielding cold warmth, joy pain; *āgama apāyinaḥ*: alternatively coming and going; *anityāḥ*: are transitory; *titikṣasva tān*: do you endure them; *bhārata*: Oh Arjuna.

Momentary sense contacts, on the other hand, Oh Kaunteya!, yielding cold-warmth, joy-pain, alternately coming and going, are transitory. Do you endure them, Oh Bhārata.

15. यं हि न व्यथयन्त्येते पुरुषं पुरुषर्षभ ।
समदु:खसुखं धीरं सोऽमृतत्वाय कल्पते ।।

yaṁ hi na vyathayanty ete puruṣaṁ puruṣarṣabha ।
samaduḥkhasukhaṁ dhīraṁ so 'mr̥tatvāya kalpate ॥

yam hi puruṣam dhīraṁ: that man indeed of firm mind; *na vyathayanti ete*: who is unaffected by these; *puruṣarṣabha*: Oh Arjuna; *sama duḥkha sukham*: equal-minded in joy as well as pain; *saḥ amr̥ta tvāya kalpate*: he is destined for immortality.

That man indeed of firm mind who is unaffected by these, Oh Best of Men! equal-minded in joy as well as pain – he is destined for immortality.

16. नासतो विद्यते भावो नाभावो विद्यते सतः ।
उभयोरपि दृष्टोऽन्तस्त्वनयोस्तत्त्वदर्शिभिः ।।

na 'sato vidyate bhāvo nā 'bhāvo vidyate sataḥ ।
ubhayor api dr̥ṣṭo 'ntas tv anayos tattvadarśibhiḥ ॥

asataḥ na vidyate bhāvaḥ: what is unreal cannot have being; *tu abhāvaḥ na vidyate sataḥ*: and non-being cannot be real; *antaḥ api ubhayoḥ anayoḥ*: the conclusion in regard to both these; *dr̥ṣṭaḥ tattvadarśibhiḥ*: has been known to philosophers.

What is unreal cannot have being, and non-being cannot be real; the conclusion in regard to both these has been known to philosophers.

17. अविनाशि तु तद्विद्धि येन सर्वमिदं ततम् ।
विनाशमव्ययस्यास्य न कश्चित्कर्तुमर्हति ।।

avināśi tu tad viddhi yena sarvam idaṁ tatam ।
vināśam avyayasyā 'sya na kaścit kartum arhati ॥

tad viddhi: know That; *avināśi tu*: to be indestructible; *yena*: by which; *sarvam idaṁ tatam*: all this is pervaded; *na kaścit kartum arhati vināśam*: none can bring about the destruction; *asya avyayasya*: of This that knows no decrease.

Know That to be indestructible by which all this is pervaded. None can bring about the destruction of This that knows no decrease.

18. अन्तवन्त इमे देहा नित्यस्योक्ताः शरीरिणः ।
अनाशिनोऽप्रमेयस्य तस्माद्युध्यस्व भारत ।।

antavanta ime dehā nityasyo 'ktāḥ śaririṇaḥ ।
anāśino 'prameyasya tasmād yudhyasva bhārata ॥

ime dehā: these bodies; *nityasya*: (however) of the everlasting; *anāśinaḥ*:

indestructible; *aprameyasya*: and undefinable; *śarīriṇaḥ*: embodied One; *uktāḥ*: are spoken of; *antavantaḥ*: as having an end; *tasmād*: therefore; *yudhyasva*: go on with the battle; *bhārata*: Oh Arjuna.

These bodies (however) of the everlasting indestructible and undefinable embodied One are spoken of as having an end. Therefore go on with the battle, Oh Bhārata!

19. य एनं वेत्ति हन्तारं यश्चैनं मन्यते हतम् ।
उभौ तौ न विजानीतो नायं हन्ति न हन्यते ॥

ya enaṁ vetti hantāraṁ yaś cai 'naṁ manyate hatam ।
ubhau tau na vijānīto nā 'yaṁ hanti na hanyate ॥

ya vetti: he who thinks of; *enaṁ hantāraṁ*: This as the killer; *ca yaḥ manyate enaṁ hatam*: and he who thinks of This as killed; *ubhau tau na vijānītaḥ*: both these know not; *ayaṁ na hanti na hanyate*: This does not kill, is not killed.

He who thinks of This as the killer, and he who thinks of This as killed – both these know not. This does not kill, is not killed.

20. न जायते म्रियते वा कदाचिन्नायं भूत्वा भविता वा न भूयः ।
अजो नित्यः शाश्वतोऽयं पुराणो न हन्यते हन्यमाने शरीरे ॥

na jāyate mriyate vā kadācin nā 'yaṁ bhūtvā bhavitā vā na bhūyaḥ ।
ajo nityaḥ śāśvato 'yaṁ purāṇo na hanyate hanyamāne śarīre ॥

ayaṁ na jāyate mriyate vā kadācit: This is neither born nor does This die; *na bhūtvā bhavitā vā na bhūyaḥ*: nor having once come into being, cease to become any more; *ajaḥ*: unborn; *nityaḥ*: perpetual; *śāśvataḥ*: eternal; *ayaṁ purāṇaḥ*: is This Ancient One; *na hanyate*: It is not killed; *hanyamāne śarīre*: on the killing of the body.

This is neither born nor does This die, nor, having once come into being, cease to become any more: unborn, perpetual, eternal is This Ancient One. It is not killed on the killing of the body.

21. वेदाविनाशिनं नित्यं य एनमजमव्ययम् ।
कथं स पुरुषः पार्थ कं घातयति हन्ति कम् ॥

vedā 'vināśinaṁ nityaṁ ya enam ajam avyayam ।
kathaṁ sa puruṣaḥ pārtha kaṁ ghātayati hanti kam ॥

yaḥ vedā enam: about him who knows This; *avināśinaṁ*: as the indestructible; *nityaṁ*: the everlasting; *ajam*: the unborn; *avyayam*: never-decreasing one; *saḥ puruṣaḥ*: of such a person; *kathaṁ*: how could the question arise; *kaṁ ghātayati*: whose death he causes; *hanti kam*: whom he kills; *pārtha*: Oh Arjuna.

About him who knows This as the indestructible, the everlasting, the unborn, never-decreasing one – of such a person how could the questions arise "whose death he causes", "whom he kills", Oh Pārtha?

22. वासांसि जीर्णानि यथा विहाय नवानि गृह्णाति नरोऽपराणि ।
तथा शरीराणि विहाय जीर्णान्यन्यानि संयाति नवानि देही ।।

vāsāṁsi jīrṇāni yathā vihāya navāni gṛhṇāti naro 'parāṇi ।
tathā śarīrāṇi vihāya jīrṇāny anyāni saṁyāti navāni dehī ॥

yathā: as; *naraḥ*: a man; *vihāya*: casting off; *jīrṇāni vāsāṁsi*: his worn-out garments; *gṛhṇāti*: assumes; *aparāṇi*: others; *navāni*: that are new; *tathā*: likewise; *vihāya*: casting off; *śarīrāṇi*: bodies; *jīrṇāni*: that are worn-out; *dehī*: the embodied One; *saṁyāti anyāni*: takes to others; *navāni*: that are new.

As a man casting off his worn-out garments assumes others that are new, likewise casting off bodies that are worn-out, the embodied One takes to others that are new.

23. नैनं छिन्दन्ति शस्त्राणि नैनं दहति पावकः ।
न चैनं क्लेदयन्त्यापो न शोषयति मारुतः ।।

nai 'naṁ chindanti śastrāṇi nai 'naṁ dahati pāvakaḥ ।
na cai 'naṁ kledayanty āpo na śoṣayati mārutaḥ ॥

śastrāṇi: weapons; *na chindanti*: do not cut; *enaṁ*: This; *pāvakaḥ*: fire; *na dahati*: does not burn; *enaṁ*: This; *ca āpaḥ*: and waters; *na kledayanti*: do not wet; *enaṁ*: This; *mārutaḥ*: wind; *na śoṣayati*: does not dry (This).

Weapons do not cut This, fire does not burn This, and water does not wet This; wind does not dry This:

24. अच्छेद्योऽयमदाह्योऽयमक्लेद्योऽशोष्य एव च ।
नित्यः सर्वगतः स्थाणुरचलोऽयं सनातनः ।।

acchedyo 'yam adāhyo 'yam akledyo 'śoṣya eva ca ।
nityaḥ sarvagataḥ sthāṇur acalo 'yaṁ sanātanaḥ ॥

ayam acchedyaḥ: indeed It is uncleavable; *ayam adāhyaḥ*: It is non-inflammable; (*ayam*) *akledyaḥ*: It is unwettable; *aśoṣyaḥ eva ca*: and non-dryable also; *nityaḥ*: everlasting; *sarvagataḥ*: all-pervading; *sthāṇuḥ*: stable; *acalaḥ*: immobile; *ayaṁ sanātanaḥ*: It is eternal.

Indeed It is uncleavable; It is non-inflammable; It is unwettable and non-dryable also – everlasting, all-pervading, stable, immobile; It is eternal.

25. अव्यक्तोऽयमचिन्त्योऽयमविकार्योऽयमुच्यते ।
तस्मादेवं विदित्वैनं नानुशोचितुमर्हसि ।।

avyakto 'yam acintyo 'yam avikāryo 'yam ucyate ।
tasmād evaṁ viditvai 'naṁ nā 'nuśocitum arhasi ॥

ayam avyaktaḥ: It is undefined; *acintyaḥ ayam*: unthinkable is It; *avikāryaḥ ayam ucyate*: as non-subject to change is It spoken of; *tasmād*: therefore; *viditvā enaṁ evaṁ*: knowing It as such; *na arhasi anuśocitum*: there is no reason for you to feel sorry for It.

It is undefined, unthinkable is It, as non-subject to change is It spoken of: therefore, knowing It as such, there is no reason for you to feel sorry for It.

26. अथ चैनं नित्यजातं नित्यं वा मन्यसे मृतम् ।
तथापि त्वं महाबाहो नैवं शोचितुमर्हसि ।।

atha cai 'naṁ nityajātaṁ nityaṁ vā manyase mṛtaṁ ।
tathā 'pi tvaṁ mahābāho nai 'naṁ śocitum arhasi ॥

atha ca: or again; *manyase*: if you should hold; *enaṁ nityajātaṁ*: This to be constantly-ever-born; *vā*: or; *nityaṁ mṛtaṁ*: as constantly-ever-dying; *tathā api*: even then; *tvaṁ mahābāho*: Oh Arjuna, you; *na arhasi śocitum enaṁ*: have no reason to regret it.

Or again if you should hold This to be constantly-ever-born or as constantly-ever-dying, even then, Oh Mighty-Armed! you have no reason to regret it.

27. जातस्य हि ध्रुवो मृत्युर्ध्रुवं जन्म मृतस्य च ।
तस्मादपरिहार्येऽर्थे न त्वं शोचितुमर्हसि ।।

jātasya hi dhruvo mṛtyur dhruvam janma mṛtasya ca ।
tasmād aparihārye 'rthe na tvaṁ śocitum arhasi ॥

hi jātasya: in respect of anyone born; *mṛtyuḥ*: death; *dhruvaḥ*: is certain; *ca dhruvam janma mṛtasya*: and certain is birth likewise for anyone dead; *tasmāt*: therefore; *arthe aparihārye*: regarding something inevitable; *tvaṁ na arhasi śocitum*: you have no reason to feel any regret.

In respect of anyone born, death is certain, and certain is birth likewise for anyone dead; therefore, regarding something inevitable, you have no reason to feel any regret.

28. अव्यक्तादीनि भूतानि व्यक्तमध्यानि भारत ।
अव्यक्तनिधनान्येव तत्र का परिदेवना ।।

avyaktādīni bhūtāni vyaktamadhyāni bhārata ।
avyaktanidhanāny eva tatra kā paridevanā ॥

bhūtāni: beings; *avyaktādīni*: have an unmanifested origin; (*ca*): and; *vyakta madhyāni*: manifested middle states; *bhārata*: Oh Arjuna; *eva*: and again; *avyakta nidhanānī*: unmanifested terminations; *kā paridevanā*: where is room for plaint; *tatra*: herein.

Beings have an unmanifested origin and manifested middle states, Oh Bhārata, and again unmanifested terminations. Where is room for plaint herein?

29. आश्चर्यवत्पश्यति कश्चिदेनमाश्चर्यवद्वदति तथैव चान्यः ।
आश्चर्यवच्चैनमन्यः शृणोति श्रुत्वाप्येनं वेद न चैव कश्चित् ॥

āścaryavat paśyati kaścid enam āścaryavad vadati tathāi 'va cā 'nyaḥ ।
āścaryavac cai 'nam anyaḥ śṛṇoti śrutvā 'py enaṁ veda na cai 'va kaścit ।

kaścid: a certain person; *paśyati enam*: sees This; *āścaryavat*: as a wonder; *tathā eva ca*: likewise; *anyaḥ*: another; *vadati*: speaks about (This); *āścaryavat*: as a wonder; *anyaḥ*: another; *śṛṇoti*: hears; *āścaryavat ca enam*: of It even as a wonder; *śrutvā api*: but even hearing; *na kaścit*: no one; *veda enaṁ ca eva*: understands This at all.

A certain person sees This as a wonder, likewise another speaks about This as a wonder. Another hears of It even as a wonder, but even hearing no one understands This at all.

30. देही नित्यमवध्योऽयं देहे सर्वस्य भारत ।
तस्मात्सर्वाणि भूतानि न त्वं शोचितुमर्हसि ॥

dehī nityam avadhyo 'yaṁ dehe sarvasya bhārata ।
tasmāt sarvāṇī bhūtāni na tvaṁ śocitum arhasi ॥

ayaṁ dehi dehe sarvasya: this embodied One within the bodies of all; *nityam avadhyaḥ*: is ever immune to killing; *bhārata*: Oh Arjuna; *tasmāt*: therefore; *sarvāṇi bhūtāni*: in respect of any being; *tvaṁ na arhasi śocitum*: you have no reason for regretting.

This embodied One within the bodies of all is ever immune to killing, Oh Bhārata. Therefore in respect of any being you have no reason for regretting.

31. स्वधर्ममपि चावेक्ष्य न विकम्पितुमर्हसि ।
धर्म्याद्धि युद्धाच्छ्रेयोऽन्यत्क्षत्रियस्य न विद्यते ॥

svadharmam api cā 'vekṣya na vikampitum arhasi ।
dharmyād dhi yuddhāc chreyo 'nyat kṣatriyasya na vidyate ॥

api ca avekṣya: further, having regard also; *svadharmam*: (for) the pattern of behaviour natural to you; *na arhasi*: there is no reason; *vikampitum*: for vacillation; *na vidyate anyat śreyaḥ*: for there could be nothing more meritorious; *dharmyāt hi yuddhāt*: than a war that is right; *kṣatriyaṣya*: for a true fighter.

Further, having regard also for the pattern of behaviour natural to you there is no reason for vacillation, for there could be nothing more meritorious than a war that is right for a true fighter.

32. यदृच्छया चोपपन्नं स्वर्गद्वारमपावृतम् ।
सुखिनः क्षत्रियाः पार्थ लभन्ते युद्धमीदृशम् ।।

yadṛcchayā co 'papannaṁ svargadvāram apāvṛtam ।
sukhinaḥ kṣatriyāḥ pārtha labhante yuddham īdṛśam ॥

kṣatriyāḥ: true warriors; *sukhinaḥ*: have reason to be happy; *pārtha*: Oh Arjuna; *labhante*: to have the chance; *īdṛśam yuddham*: of such a war; *yadṛcchayā ca upapannaṁ*: presenting itself unsought before them; *apāvṛtaṁ svargadvāram*: as an open door to heaven.

True warriors have reason to be happy, Oh Pārtha, to have the chance of such a war presenting itself unsought before them as an open door to heaven.

33. अथ चेत्त्वमिमं धर्म्यं सङ्ग्रामं न करिष्यसि ।
ततः स्वधर्मं कीर्तिं च हित्वा पापमवाप्स्यसि ।।

atha cet tvam imaṁ dharmyaṁ saṁgrāmaṁ na kariṣyasi ।
tataḥ svadharmaṁ kīrtiṁ ca hitvā pāpam avāpsyasi ॥

atha cet: if on the other hand; *tvam*: you; *na kariṣyasi*: will not take to; *imaṁ saṁgrāmaṁ dharmyaṁ*: this battle which conforms to the requirements of righteousness; *tataḥ*: then; *hitvā svadharmaṁ ca kīrtiṁ*: thwarting what is consistent with your own nature and your good repute; *avāpsyasi pāpam*: you will become involved in evil.

If, on the other hand, you will not take to this battle which conforms to the requirements of righteousness, then thwarting what is consistent with your own nature and your good repute you will become involved in evil.

34. अकीर्तिं चापि भूतानि कथयिष्यन्तितेऽव्ययाम् ।
सम्भावितस्य चाकीर्तिर्मरणादतिरिच्यते ।।

akīrtiṁ cā 'pi bhūtāni kathayiṣyanti te 'vyayām ।
saṁbhāvitasya cā 'kīrtir maraṇād atiricyate ॥

bhūtāni: living beings; *ca api*: also; *kathayiṣyanti*: will pronounce; *avyayām*: a never-ending; *akīrtim*: verdict of calumny; *te*: on you; *ca*: and; *sambhāvitasya*: to one used to honour; *akīrtiḥ*: dishonour; *atiricyate*: is worse; *maraṇāt*: than death.

Living beings will also pronounce a never-ending verdict of calumny on you, and to one used to honour, dishonour is worse than death.

35. भयाद्रणादुपरतं मंस्यन्ते त्वां महारथाः ।
येषां च त्वं बहुमतो भूत्वा यास्यसि लाघवम् ॥

bhayād raṇād uparataṁ maṁsyante tvāṁ mahārathāḥ ।
yeṣāṁ ca tvaṁ bahumato bhūtvā yāsyasi lāghavam ॥

mahārathāḥ: the great car-generals; *maṁsyante tvāṁ*: will look upon you; *raṇāt uparatam bhayāt*: as quitting the battle from fear; *ca*: and; *bhūtvā*: having been; *bahumataḥ*: honourably looked upon; *yeṣāṁ*: by them; *tvaṁ*: you; *yāsyasi lāghavam*: will be held in derision.

The great car-generals will look upon you as quitting the battle from fear, and having been honourably looked upon by them you will be held in derision.

36. अवाच्यवादांश्च बहून्वदिष्यन्ति तवाहिताः ।
निन्दन्तस्तव सामर्थ्यं ततो दुःखतरं नु किम् ॥

avācyavādāṁś ca bahūn vadiṣyanti tavā 'hitāḥ ।
nindantas tava sāmarthyaṁ tato duḥkhataraṁ nu kim ॥

tava ahitāḥ: those against you; *vadiṣyanti*: will speak of you; *avācyavādān ca bahūn*: in unspeakable terms; *nindantaḥ*: scorning; *tava*: your; *sāmarthyaṁ*: ability; *kim to duḥkhataraṁ tataḥ*: what pain could there be keener than this?

Those against you will speak of you in unspeakable terms, scorning your ability; what pain could there be keener than this?

37. हतो वा प्राप्स्यसि स्वर्गं जित्वा वा भोक्ष्यसे महीम् ।
तस्मादुत्तिष्ठ कौन्तेय युद्धाय कृतनिश्चयः ॥

hato vā prāpsyasi svargaṁ jitvā vā bhokṣyase mahīm ।
tasmād uttiṣṭha kaunteya yuddhāya kṛtaniścayaḥ ॥

hataḥ: dying; *prāpsyasi*: you will attain; *svargaṁ*: heaven; *vā*: or; *jitvā*: winning; *bhokṣyase*: you will have the enjoyment of; *mahīm*: the earth; *tasmāt*: therefore; *uttiṣṭha*: arise; *kaunteya*: Oh Arjuna; *kṛtaniścayaḥ*: making up your mind; *yuddhāya*: to fight.

Dying you will attain heaven, or winning you will have the enjoyment of the earth. Therefore arise, Oh Kaunteya! making up your mind to fight.

38. सुखदुःखे समे कृत्वा लाभालाभौ जयाजयौ ।
ततो युद्धाय युज्यस्व नैवं पापमवाप्स्यसि ॥

sukhaduḥkhe same kṛtvā lābhālābhau jayājayau ।
tato yuddhāya yujyasva nai 'vaṁ pāpam avāpsyasi ॥

same kṛtvā: equalizing; *sukha duḥkhe*: both pleasure and pain; *lābha alābhau*: both gain and loss; *jaya ajayau*: both victory and defeat; *tataḥ yujyasva*: then enter wholly; *yuddhāya*: into battle; *evaṁ*: thus; *na avāpsyasi*: you will avoid; *pāpam*: sin.

Equalizing both pleasure and pain, both gain and loss, both victory and defeat, enter wholly into battle. Thus you will avoid sin.

39. एषा तेऽभिहिता साङ्ख्ये बुद्धिर्योगे त्विमां शृणु ।
बुद्ध्या युक्तो यया पार्थ कर्मबन्धं प्रहास्यसि ।।

eṣā te 'bhihitā sāṁkhye buddhir yoge tv imāṁ śṛṇu ।
buddhyā yukto yayā pārtha karmabandhaṁ prahāsyasi ॥

eṣā te abhihitā: what has just been taught; *buddhiḥ*: is reasoning; *sāṁkhye*: according to Sāṁkhya; *tu*: but; *śṛṇu*: hear now; *imāṁ*: of the same; *yoge*: according to Yoga; *yuktaḥ yayā buddhyā*: attaining to the unity of which reasoning; *pārtha*: you (Arjuna); *prahāsyasi*: will be able to throw off; *karma bandhaṁ*: the bondage of works.

What has just been taught is reasoning according to Sāṁkhya; but hear now of the same according to Yoga, attaining to the unity of which reasoning you will be able to throw off the bondage of works.

40. नेहाभिक्रमनाशोऽस्ति प्रत्यवायो न विद्यते ।
स्वल्पमप्यस्य धर्मस्य त्रायते महतो भयात् ।।

ne 'hā 'bhikramanāśo 'sti pratyavāyo na vidyate ।
svalpam apy asya dharmasya trāyate mahato bhayāt ॥

iha: in such (a path); *asti*: there is; *na*: no; *abhikrama nāśaḥ*: forfeiture of any merit; *na vidyate*: nor is there; *pratyavāyaḥ*: involved any demerit by transgression; *api*: even; *svalpam*: a little; *asya*: of such; *dharmasya*: a way of life; *trāyate*: saves one; *mahataḥ*: from great; *bhayāt*: apprehension.

In such (a path) there is no forfeiture of any merit, nor is there involved any demerit by transgression. Even a little of such a way of life saves one from great apprehension.

41. व्यवसायात्मिका बुद्धिरेकेह कुरुनन्दन ।
बहुशाखा ह्यनन्ताश्च बुद्धयोऽव्यवसायिनाम् ।।

vyavasāyātmikā buddhir eke 'ha kurunandana ।
bahuśākhā hy anantāś ca buddhayo 'vyavasāyinām ॥

iha: here; *kuru nandana*: Oh Arjuna; *vyavasāyātmikā*: the well-founded; *buddhiḥ*: reasoning; *ekā*: *is* unitive; *hi*: but; *bahuśākhāḥ*: many-branched; *ca*: and; *anantāḥ buddhayaḥ*: endless are the reasonings; *avyavasāyinām*: of those in whom reason is ill-founded.

Here, Oh Prize of the Kurus! the well-founded reasoning is unitive, but many-branched and endless are the reasonings of those in whom reason is ill-founded.

42. यामिमां पुष्पितां वाचं प्रवदन्त्यविपश्चितः ।
वेदवादरताः पार्थ नान्यदस्तीति वादिनः ॥

yām imāṁ puṣpitāṁ vācaṁ pravadanty avipaścitaḥ ।
vedavādaratāḥ pārtha na 'nyad astī 'ti vādinaḥ ॥

imāṁ: such; *puṣpitāṁ*: flowery; *vācaṁ*: speech; *yām*: as; *pravadanti*: uttered by; *avipaścitaḥ*: the foolish; *veda vāda ratāḥ* (*pārtha*): adhering to the doctrine of the Veda, Oh Arjuna; *na anyat asti iti vādinaḥ*: negating any other (transcendental) verity.

43. कामात्मानः स्वर्गपरा जन्मकर्मफलप्रदाम् ।
क्रियाविशेषबहुलां भोगैश्वर्यगतिं प्रति ॥

kāmātmānaḥ svargaparā janmakarmaphalapradām ।
kriyāviśeṣabahulāṁ bhogaiśvaryagatiṁ prati ॥

kāmātmānaḥ: the self of which is nothing but desire-made; *svargaparāḥ*: holding heaven to be the highest goal; *pradām janma karma phala*: offering only birth as the result of works; *bahulām viśeṣa kriyā*: abounding in many special observances; *bhoga aiśvarya gatiṁ*: which aim at enjoyment and domination; *prati*: in the case of those.

44. भोगैश्वर्यप्रसक्तानां तयापहृतचेतसाम् ।
व्यवसायात्मिका बुद्धिः समाधौ न विधीयते ॥

bhogaiśvaryaprasaktānāṁ tayā 'pahṛtacetasām ।
vyavasāyātmikā buddhiḥ samādhau na vidhīyate ॥

cetasām apahṛta: whose minds are under the sway of; *tayā*: such teachings; *prasaktānāṁ bhogaiśvarya*: who are attached to enjoyment and domination; *vyavasāyātmikā*: a well-founded; *buddhiḥ*: reason; *na vidhīyate*: does not come under the sway of; *samādhau*: the peace of contemplation (*samādhi*).

Such flowery speech as uttered by the foolish, adhering to the doctrine of the Veda, negating any other (transcendental) verity, the self of which is nothing but desire-made, holding heaven to be the highest goal, offering only birth as the result of works abounding in many special observances, which aim at enjoyment and domination: in the case of those whose minds are under the sway of such teachings, who are attached to enjoyment and domination, a well-founded reason does not come under the sway of the peace of contemplation.

45. त्रैगुण्यविषया वेदा निस्त्रैगुण्यो भवार्जुन ।
निर्द्वन्द्वो नित्यसत्त्वस्थो निर्योगक्षेम आत्मवान् ॥

traiguṇyaviṣayā vedā nistraiguṇyo bhavā 'rjuna ।
nirdvandvo nityasattvastho niryogakṣema ātmavān ॥

vedāḥ: the Vedas; *viṣayāḥ*: (treat of) matters related to; *traiguṇya*: the three *guṇa*s (modalities of nature); *bhava nistraiguṇyaḥ*: (you should) be free from these three modalities; *arjuna*: Oh Arjuna; *nirdvandvaḥ*: free from (relative) pairs of opposites; *nitya sattvasthaḥ*: established ever in pure being; *niryoga kṣemaḥ*: without any *yoga* (discipline) or well-being (as dual factors); *ātmavān*: (but remain one who is unitively) Self-possessed.

The Vedas treat of matters related to the three *guṇa*s you should be free from these three modalities, Oh Arjuna free from (relative) pairs of opposites, established ever in pure being, without any *yoga* or well-being (as dual factors), (unitively) Self-possessed.

46. यावानर्थ उदपाने सर्वतः सम्प्लुतोदके ।
तावान्सर्वेषु वेदेषु ब्राह्मणस्य विजानतः ॥

yāvān artha udapāne sarvataḥ saṁplutodake ।
tāvān sarveṣu vedeṣu brāhmaṇasya vijānataḥ ॥

yāvān: there would be as much; *arthaḥ*: use; *sarveṣu vedeṣu*: for all the Vedas; *brāhmaṇasya*: to a brāhmin; *vijānataḥ*: of wisdom; *tāvān*: as there could be; *udapāne*: for a pool of water; *saṁpluta udake*: when a full flood prevails; *sarvataḥ*: all over.

There would be as much use for all the Vedas to a brāhmin of wisdom as there could be for a pool of water when a full flood prevails all over.

47. कर्मण्येवाधिकारस्ते मा फलेषु कदाचन ।
मा कर्मफलहेतुर्भूर्मा ते सङ्गोऽस्त्वकर्मणि ॥

karmaṇy evā 'dhikāras te mā phaleṣu kadācana ।
mā karmaphalahetur bhūr mā te saṅgo 'stv akarmaṇi ॥

te: your; *adhikāraḥ*: concern (should be); *karmaṇi*: with action (as such); *eva*: alone; *mā*: not; *phaleṣu*: for any benefits; *kadācana*: ever; *mā*: do not; *bhūḥ karma phala hetuḥ*: become benefit-motivated; *astu te mā sangaḥ*: be you not attached to; *akarmaṇi*: inaction (either).

Your concern should be with action (as such) alone, not for any benefits ever. Do not become benefit-motivated; be not attached to inaction (either).

48. योगस्थः कुरु कर्माणि सङ्गं त्यक्त्वा धनञ्जय ।
सिद्ध्यसिद्ध्योः समो भूत्वा समत्वं योग उच्यते ।।

yogasthaḥ kuru karmāṇi saṅgaṁ tyaktvā dhanañjaya ।
siddhyasiddhyoḥ samo bhūtvā samatvaṁ yoga ucyate ॥

kuru karmāṇi: engage in activities; *dhanañjaya*: Oh Arjuna; *yogasthaḥ*: taking your stand on the unitive way (of *yoga*); *tyaktvā*: discarding; *saṅgaṁ*: attachments; *bhūtvā samaḥ*: and capable of regarding as the same; *siddhi asiddhyoḥ*: both attainment and non-attainment; *samatvaṁ*: in sameness; *ucyate*: is said to be; *yogaḥ*: the unitive way (*yoga*).

Engage in activity, Oh Dhanañjaya, taking your stand on the unitive way, discarding attachments, and capable of regarding both attainment and non-attainment as the same: in sameness consists the unitive way.

49. दूरेण ह्यवरं कर्म बुद्धियोगाद्धनञ्जय ।
बुद्धौ शरणमन्विच्छ कृपणाः फलहेतवः ।।

dūreṇa hy avaraṁ karma buddhiyogād dhanañjaya ।
buddhau śaraṇam anviccha kṛpanāḥ phalahetavaḥ ॥

dūreṇa: far; *avaraṁ*: inferior; *hi*: is; *karma*: (the way of) action; *buddhiyogāt*: to the unitive way of reason; *dhanañjaya*: Oh Arjuna; *anviccha buddhau śaraṇam*: resort to reason for final refuge; *kṛpaṇāḥ*: pitiful are they; *phalahetavaḥ*: who are benefit-motivated.

Far inferior is (the way of) action to the unitive way of reason, Oh Dhanañjaya; resort to reason for final refuge; pitiful are they who are benefit-motivated.

50. बुद्धियुक्तो जहातीह उभे सुकृतदुष्कृते ।
तस्माद्योगाय युज्यस्व योगः कर्मसु कौशलम् ।।

buddhiyukto jahāti 'ha ubhe sukṛtaduskṛte ।
tasmād yogāya yujyasva yogaḥ karmasu kauśalam ॥

buddhiyuktaḥ: affiliated to reason; *jahāti*: one leaves behind; *iha*: here; *ubhe*: both; *sukṛta duṣkṛte*: meritorious and unmeritorious deeds; *tasmāt*: therefore; *yujyasva*: affiliate yourself; *yogāya*: to the unitive way (of *yoga*); *yogaḥ*: *yoga* (is); *kauśalam*: reason; *karmasu*: in action.

Affiliated to reason one leaves behind here both meritorious and unmeritorious deeds. Therefore affiliate yourself to the unitive way; *yoga* is reason in action.

51. कर्मजं बुद्धियुक्ता हि फलं त्यक्त्वा मनीषिणः ।
जन्मबन्धविनिर्मुक्ताः पदं गच्छन्त्यनामयम् ।।

karmajaṁ buddhiyuktā hi phalaṁ tyaktvā manīṣiṇaḥ ।
janmabandhavinirmuktāḥ padaṁ gacchanty anāmayam ॥

karmajaṁ buddhiyuktā hi: by affiliation to unitive reason; *manīṣiṇaḥ*: wise men; *vinirmuktāḥ janma bandha*: transcending birth-bondage; *tyaktvā*: renouncing; *phalaṁ*: benefit-interest; *gacchanti*: go onward to; *padaṁ*: a state; *anāmayam*: beyond all pain.

By affiliation to unitive reason wise men, transcending birth-bondage, renouncing benefit-interest, go onward to a state beyond all pain.

52. यदा ते मोहकलिलं बुद्धिर्व्यतितरिष्यति ।
तदा गन्तासि निर्वेदं श्रोतव्यस्य श्रुतस्य च ।।

yadā te mohakalilaṁ buddhir vyatitariṣyati ।
tadā gantāsi nirvedaṁ śrotavyasya śrutasya ca ॥

yadā: when; *te*: your; *buddiḥ*: reason; *vyatitariṣyati*: has transcended; *moha kalilaṁ*: the dross of vagueness; *tadā*: then; *gantāsi*: you attain to; *nirvedaṁ*: that neutral attitude; *śrotavyasya śrutasya ca*: both in respect of what is to be learnt and what has already been heard.

When your reason has transcended the dross of vagueness, then you attain to that neutral attitude, both in respect of what is to be learnt and what has already been heard.

53. श्रुतिविप्रतिपन्ना ते यदा स्थास्यति निश्चला ।
समाधावचला बुद्धिस्तदा योगमवाप्स्यसि ।।

śutivipratipannā te yadā sthāsyati niścalā ।
samādhāv acalā buddhis tadā yogam avāpsyasi ॥

yadā: when; *śruti vipratipannā*: disillusioned respecting the (contradictory injunctions of the) scriptures (Vedas); *te*: your; *buddhiḥ*: reason; *sthāsyati niścala*: stands unshaken; *acalā*: steady; *samādhau*: in *samādhi* (supreme peace); *tadā*: then; *avāpsyasi*: you shall have reached; *yogam*: *yoga* (unitive contemplation).

When, disillusioned respecting the (contradictory injunctions of the) scriptures, your reason stands unshaken and steady in *samādhi* – then you shall have reached *yoga*.

अर्जुन उवाच –

54. स्थितप्रज्ञस्य का भाषा समाधिस्थस्य केशव ।
स्थितधीः किं प्रभाषेत किमासीत व्रजेत किम् ।।

arjuna uvāca –

sthitaprajñasya kā bhāṣā samādhisthasya keśava ।
sthitadhīḥ kiṁ prabhāṣeta kim āsīta vrajeta kim ॥

arjuna uvāca: Arjuna said; *kā*: what; *bhāṣā*: is the way; *sthitaprajñasya*: of one whose reason is well-founded; *samādhisthasya*: who is estalished in *samādhi* (supreme peace); *keśava*: Oh Kṛṣṇa; *kim sthitadhīḥ prabhāṣeta*: how does he (whose thoughts are well-founded) discourse; *kim āsita*: what is his state of being; *kim vrajeta*: how does he move about.

Arjuna said:

What is the way of one whose reason is well-founded, who is established in *samādhi*, Oh Keśava? How does he discourse, what is his state of being, how does he move about?

श्रीभगवानुवाच –

55. प्रजहाति यदा कामान्सर्वान्पार्थ मनोगतान् ।
आत्मन्येवात्मना तुष्टः स्थितप्रज्ञस्तदोच्यते ।।

śrībhagavān uvāca –

prajahāti yadā kāmān sarvān pārtha manogatān ।
āmany evā 'tmanā tuṣṭaḥ sthitaprajñas tado 'cyate ॥

śrī bhagavān uvāca: Kṛṣṇa said; *yadā*: when; *prajahāti*: one banishes; *sarvān*: all; *kāmān*: desires; *manogatān*: that enter the mind; *pārtha*: Oh Arjuna; *tuṣṭaḥ*: satisfied; *ātmani*: in the Self; *ātmanā*: by the Self; *eva*: alone; *tadā*: then; *ucyate*: he is said to be; *sthitaprajñaḥ*: one of well-founded reason.

Kṛṣṇa said:

When one banishes all desires that enter the mind, Oh Pārtha, satisfied in the Self by the Self alone, then he is said to be one of well-founded reason.

56. दुःखेष्वनुद्विग्नमनाः सुखेषु विगतस्पृहः ।
वीतरागभयक्रोधः स्थितधीर्मुनिरुच्यते ।।

duḥkheṣv anudvignamanāḥ sukheṣu vigataspṛhaḥ ।
vītarāgabhayakrodhaḥ sthitadhīr munir ucyate ॥

anudvigna manāḥ: he whose mind is unaffected; *duḥkheṣu*: by mishaps; *vigata spṛhaḥ*: who evinces no interest; *sukheṣu*: on happy occasions (too); *vīta rāga bhaya krodhaḥ*: rising above attachment, anxiety, or anger; *muniḥ*: (such) a sage-recluse; *ucyate*: is said to be; *sthitadhiḥ*: of well-founded reason.

He whose mind is unaffected by mishaps, who on happy occasions, too, evinces no interest, rising above attachment, anxiety, or anger – such a sage-recluse is said to be of well-founded reason.

57. यः सर्वत्रानभिस्नेहस्तत्तत्प्राप्य शुभाशुभम् ।
नाभिनन्दति न द्वेष्टि तस्य प्रज्ञा प्रतिष्ठिता ॥

yaḥ sarvatrā 'nabhisnehas tat-tat prāpya śubhāśubham ।
nā 'bhinandati na dveṣṭi tasya prajñā pratiṣṭhitā ॥

yaḥ: he who; *sarvatra anabhisnehas*: remains in all cases unattached; *prāpya*: on gaining; *tat-tat*: such or such; *śubha aśubham*: desirable–undesirable end; *na abhinandati*: who neither welcomes (anything); *na dveṣṭi*: nor rejects in anger; *tasya prajñā*: his wisdom; *pratiṣṭhitā*: is well-founded.

He who remains in all cases unattached on gaining such or such desirable–undesirable end, who neither welcomes (anything) nor rejects in anger – his reason is well-founded.

58. यदा संहरते चायं कूर्मोऽङ्गानीव सर्वशः ।
इन्द्रियाणीन्द्रियार्थेभ्यस्तस्य प्रज्ञा प्रतिष्ठिता ॥

yadā saṁharate ca 'yaṁ kūrmo 'ṅgānī 'va sarvaśaḥ ।
indriyāni 'ndriyārthebhyas tasya prajñā pratiṣṭhitā ॥

ca ayaṁ: again this; *yadā*: when; *iva*: as; *kūrmaḥ*: a tortoise; *saṁharate*: retracts; *aṅgāni*: its limbs; *sarvaśaḥ*: from all sides; *indriyāṇi*: the senses; *indriyārthebhyaḥ*: (are withdrawn) from objects of sense-interest; *tasya*: his; *prajñā*: reason; *pratiṣṭhitā*: is well-founded.

Again, when, as a tortoise retracts its limbs from all sides, the senses (are withdrawn) from objects of sense-interest – his reason is well-founded.

59. विषया विनिवर्तन्ते निराहारस्य देहिनः ।
रसवर्जं रसोऽप्यस्य परं दृष्ट्वा निवर्तते ॥

viṣayā vinivartante nirāhārasya dehinaḥ ।
rasavarjaṁ raso 'py asya paraṁ dṛṣṭvā nivartate ॥

viṣayāḥ: objective interests; *vinivartante*: revert; *rasavarjaṁ*: without the relish (for them); *nirāhārasya*: on starving; *dehinaḥ*: the embodied (of them); *api*: even; *rasaḥ asya*: that (residual) relish; *nivartate*: reverts; *paraṁ dṛṣṭvā*: on the One Beyond being sighted.

Objective interests revert without the relish for them on starving the embodied (of them). Even the (residual) relish reverts on the One Beyond being sighted.

60. यततो ह्यपि कौन्तेय पुरुषस्य विपश्चितः ।
इन्द्रियाणि प्रमाथीनि हरन्ति प्रसभं मनः ॥

yatato hy api kaunteya puruṣasya vipaścitaḥ ।
indriyāṇi pramāthīni haranti prasabhaṁ manaḥ ॥

hi api: even; *puruṣasya*: with a man; *vipaścitaḥ*: of wisdom; *kaunteya*: Oh Arjuna; *yatataḥ*: in spite of his effort; *pramāthīni*: excited; *indriyāṇi*: sense interests; *prasabhaṁ*: forcibly; *haranti*: can distract; *manaḥ*: the mind.

Even with a man of wisdom, Oh Son of Kuntī, in spite of his effort, excited sense-interests can forcibly distract the mind.

61. तानि सर्वाणि संयम्य युक्त आसीत मत्परः ।
वशे हि यस्येन्द्रियाणि तस्य प्रज्ञा प्रतिष्ठिता ॥

tāni sarvāṇi saṁyamya yukta āsīta matparaḥ ।
vaśe hi yasye 'ndriyāṇi tasya prajñā pratiṣṭhitā ॥

saṁyamya: restraining; *sarvāṇi tāni*: every one of them; *āsīta*: he should rest; *yuktaḥ*: unitively established; *matparaḥ*: having Me for his Supreme (ideal); *hi yasya*: he in whom; *indriyāṇi*: sense-interests; *vaśe*: are subdued; *tasya*: his; *prajñā*: reason; *pratiṣṭhitā*: is well-founded.

Restraining every one of them, he should rest unitively established, having Me for his Supreme (ideal). He in whom sense-interests are subdued – his reason is well-founded.

62. ध्यायतो विषयान्पुंसः सङ्गस्तेषूपजायते ।
सङ्गात्सञ्जायते कामः कामात्क्रोधोऽभिजायते ॥

dhyāyato viṣayān puṁsaḥ saṅgas teṣū 'pajāyate ।
saṅgāt sañjāyate kāmaḥ kāmāt krodho 'bhijāyate ॥

dhyāyataḥ: meditating; *viṣayān*: on objects of sense-interest; *upajāyate*: there is born; *puṁsaḥ*: in man; *saṅgaḥ*: an attachment; *teṣu*: for them; *saṅgāt*: from attachment; *sañjāyate*: rises; *kāmaḥ*: passion; *kāmāt*: from passion (frustrated); *abhijāyate*: arises; *krodhaḥ*: rage.

Meditating on objects of sense-interest there is born in man an attachment for them; from attachment rises passion; in the face of passion (frustrated) arises rage.

63. क्रोधाद्भवति सम्मोहः सम्मोहात्स्मृतिविभ्रमः ।
स्मृतिभ्रंशाद् बुद्धिनाशो बुद्धिनाशात्प्रणश्यति ॥

krodhād bhavati saṁmohaḥ saṁmohāt smṛtivibhramaḥ ।
smṛtibhraṁśād buddhināśo buddhināśāt praṇaśyati ॥

krodhāt: from rage; *bhavati*: is produced; *saṁmohaḥ*: distortion of values; *saṁmohāt*: from distortion of values; *smṛtivibhramaḥ*: memory-lapse; *smṛti bhraṁśāt*: from memory-lapse; *buddhi nāśaḥ*: (comes) loss of reason; *buddhināśāt*: (and) from loss of reason; *praṇaśyati*: he perishes.

From rage is produced distortion of values, from distortion of values memory-lapse, from memory-lapse comes loss of reason, and from loss of reason he perishes.

64. रागद्वेषवियुक्तैस्तु विषयानिन्द्रियैश्चरन् ।
आत्मवश्यैर्विधेयात्मा प्रसादमधिगच्छति ॥

rāgadveṣaviyuktais tu viṣayān indriyaiś caran ।
ātmavaśyair vidheyātmā prasādam adhigacchati ॥

tu: but; *rāga dveṣa viyuktaiḥ ātmavaśyaiḥ*: whose attachment and aversion are both within the sway of the Self; *indriyaiḥ*: although his senses; *caran*: still move; *viṣayān*: amidst sense-interests; *vidheyātmā*: (he) whose Self is thus subdued; *adhigacchati*: wends toward; *prasādam*: a state of spiritual clarity.

But he whose Self is subdued, whose attachment and aversion are both within the sway of the Self, although his senses still move amidst sense-interests – he wends toward a state of spiritual clarity.

65. प्रसादे सर्वदुःखानां हानिरस्योपजायते ।
प्रसन्नचेतसो ह्याशु बुद्धिः पर्यवतिष्ठते ॥

prasāde sarvaduḥkhānāṁ hānir asyo'pajāyate ।
prasannacetaso hy āśu buddhiḥ paryavatiṣṭhate ॥

prasāde: by spiritual clarity; *upajāyate*: there takes place; *hāniḥ*: the effacement; *asya*: for him; *sarva duḥkhānāṁ*: of all sufferings; *prasanna cetasaḥ hi*: and for one whose spirit has become lucid; *āśu*: very soon; *buddhiḥ*: reason; *paryavatiṣṭhate*: becomes properly founded.

By spiritual clarity there takes place the effacement for him of all suffering, and for one whose spirit has become lucid, very soon reason becomes properly founded.

66. नास्ति बुद्धिरयुक्तस्य न चायुक्तस्य भावना ।
न चाभावयतः शान्तिरशान्तस्य कुतः सुखम् ॥

nā 'sti buddhir ayuktasya na cā 'yuktasya bhāvanā ।
na cā 'bhāvayataḥ śāntir aśāntasya kutaḥ sukham ॥

ayuktasya: for one unbalanced; *asti na*: there can be no; *buddhiḥ*: reason; *na ca*: nor is there any; *bhāvanā*: creative intuition; *ayuktasya*: for the unbalanced; *ca abhāvayataḥ*: and for one incapable of creative intuition; *na śāntiḥ*: (there could be) no peace; *aśāntasya*: (and) for the unpeaceful; *kutaḥ sukham*: where could there be happiness.

For one unbalanced there can be no reason, nor is there any creative intuition for the unbalanced, and for one incapable of creative intuition there could be no peace, and for the unpeaceful where could there be happiness?

67. इन्द्रियाणां हि चरतां यन्मनोऽनुविधीयते ।
तदस्य हरति प्रज्ञां वायुर्नावमिवाम्भसि ॥

indriyāṇām hi caratāṁ yan mano 'nuvidhīyate ।
tad asya harati prajñāṁ vāyur nāvam ivā 'mbhasi ॥

hi caratāṁ: still moving amid; *indriyāṇāṁ*: sense-interests; *yat*: that (item) to which; *manaḥ*: the mind; *anuvidhīyate*: submits; *tat asya*: that very item; *harati*: draws away; *prajñām*: the reasoning; *iva*: as; *vāyuḥ*: the wind (does); *nāvam*: a ship; *ambhasi*: on the waters.

Still moving amid sense-interests, that (item) to which the mind submits draws away the reasoning as the wind does a ship on the waters.

68. तस्माद्यस्य महाबाहो निगृहीतानि सर्वशः ।
इन्द्रियाणीन्द्रियार्थेभ्यस्तस्य प्रज्ञा प्रतिष्ठिता ॥

tasmād yasya mahābāho nigṛhītāni sarvaśaḥ ।
indriyāṇī 'ndriyārthebhyas tasya prajñā pratiṣṭhitā ॥

tasmāt: therefore; *mahābāho*: Oh Arjuna; *yasya*: he whose; *indriyāṇī*: senses; *sarvaśaḥ*: in every way; *nigṛhītāni*: have been withdrawn; *indriyārthebhyaḥ*: from sense-interests; *tasya*: his; *prajñā*: reason; *pratiṣṭhitā*: is well-founded.

Therefore, Oh Mighty-Armed, he whose senses have been in every way withdrawn from sense-interests – his reason is well-founded.

69. या निशा सर्वभूतानां तस्यां जागर्ति संयमी ।
यस्यां जाग्रति भूतानि सा निशा पश्यतो मुनेः ॥

yā niśā sarvabhūtānāṁ tasyāṁ jāgarti saṁyamī ।
yasyāṁ jāgrati bhūtāni sā niśā paśyato muneḥ ॥

yā: what is; *niśā*: night; *sarvabhūtānāṁ*: for all creatures; *saṁyamī*: the one of self-control; *jāgarti*: keeps awake; *tasyāṁ*: therein; *yasyāṁ*: wherein; *bhūtāni*: (all) creatures; *jāgrati*: are wakeful; *sā*: that is; *niśā*: night; *muneḥ*: for the sage-recluse; *paśyataḥ*: who sees.

What is night for all creatures: the one of self-control keeps awake therein; wherein all creatures are wakeful – that is night for the sage-recluse who sees.

70. आपूर्यमाणमचलप्रतिष्ठं समुद्रमापः प्रविशन्ति यद्वत् ।
तद्वत्कामा यं प्रविशन्ति सर्वे स शान्तिमाप्नोति न कामकामी ॥

āpūryamāṇam acalapratiṣṭhaṁ samudram āpaḥ praviśanti yadvat ।
tadvat kāmā yaṁ praviśanti sarve sa śāntim āpnoti na kāmakāmī ॥

yadvat: while; *āpūryamāṇam*: getting filled; *āpaḥ*: (with) water; *samudram*: the ocean; *acalapratiṣṭhaṁ*: remains fixed firm in immobility; *tadvat*: so, too; *yaṁ*: he into whom; *sarve*: all; *kāmāḥ*: interests; *praviśanti*: enter; *saḥ*: he; *āpnoti*: attains to; *śāntim*: peace; *na*: not; *kāmakāmī*: the craver of desires.

Still getting filled, while fixed firm in immobility, the ocean remains; so, too, he into whom all interersts enter – he attains to peace, not the craver of desires.

71. विहाय कामान्यः सर्वान्पुमांश्चरति निःस्पृहः ।
निर्ममो निरहङ्कारः स शान्तिमधिगच्छति ॥

vihāya kāmān yaḥ sarvān pumāṁś carati niḥspṛhaḥ ।
nirmamo nirahaṁkāraḥ sa śāntim adhigacchati ॥

pumān yaḥ: that man who; *vihāya*: giving up; *sarvān*: all; *kāmān*: attachments; *carati*: moves about; *niḥspṛhaḥ*: desirelessly; *nirmamaḥ*: without owning anything; *nirahaṁkāraḥ*: (and) without egoism; *saḥ*: he; *adhigacchati*: goes; *śāntim*: to peace.

That man who, giving up all attachments, moves about desirelessly, without owning anything, and without egoism – he goes to peace.

72. एषा ब्राह्मी स्थितिः पार्थ नैनां प्राप्य विमुह्यति ।
स्थित्वास्यामन्तकालेऽपि ब्रह्मनिर्वाणमृच्छति ॥

eṣā brāhmī sthitiḥ pārtha nai 'nām prāppya vimuhyati ।
sthitvā 'syām antakāle 'pi brahmanirvāṇam ṛcchati ॥

eṣā: this; *brāhmī sthitiḥ*: is the state of being in the Absolute (*Brahman*); *pārtha*: Oh Arjuna; *prāpya*: on reaching; *enām*: which; *vimuhyati na*: one suffers from delusion no more; *sthitvā*: established; *asyām*: in this; *antakāle api*: at the (very) last moments of life; *ṛcchati brahma nirvāṇam*: one reaches that final state of pure being in the Absolute.

This is the state of being in the Absolute, Oh Pārtha! on reaching which one suffers from delusion no more. Established in this at the very last moments of life, one reaches that final state of pure being in the Absolute.

DIALOGUE

TEACHER: This chapter introduces us to the most complex of God–man relations. I refer to the relation between Śrī Kṛṣṇa and Arjuna. Śrī Kṛṣṇa in the Gītā represents God or the Absolute. Arjuna represents man. Perhaps this is the only religious literature which presents God as a servant of man. Śrī Kṛṣṇa comes to the battlefield as a mere driver of Arjuna's chariot. Kṛṣṇa is willing to obey the command of a man as a dutiful servant. Arjuna looks upon Kṛṣṇa as a friend and playmate. Kṛṣṇa is too familiar to him to be treated as the Divine. Now the zero hour has come for Arjuna to incline before Kṛṣṇa and accept him as his Guru. He sees in Kṛṣṇa his guide, a philosopher and teacher. In verse 7 of this chapter Arjuna recognizes him as his Guru, and appeals to him to accept him as a disciple.

According to the Upaniṣads, the Guru is beyond the creator Brahmā, beyond the preserver Viṣṇu, and behind the divine solvent of all creation, Maheśvara. He is none other than the Absolute. In a later chapter we will see Arjuna standing with worshipfully joined palms, trembling, bowing down with emotional stuttering in sustained fear and saying, "You are the Imperishable One, Existence and Non-Existence, and what is beyond even that!"

STUDENT: *Why do you say the Guru is beyond even the creator? Is that not deifying a man? Does that not lead to a puerile form of personality cult?*

The Guru is not a person. Sometimes when a mind is beset with doubts and fears, frustrations and agony, the purest of light may dawn upon it, bringing wisdom and certitude, confidence and joy, strength and courage, all-embracing vision and love: the source of that light is the Guru. A mirror is not the sun, but it can reflect the sun. The mirrored sun also radiates light and warmth, although to a lesser degree, and it cannot be the same as direct radiation from the sun itself. In a similar way, the Guru very often shines through the eternal Word, through Silence, and through the silent model of an enlightened person. Such a person is described by Śaṅkara in his *Vivekacūḍāmaṇi* as a wise preceptor who is well versed in scripture, sinless, unsmitten by desire, who is withdrawn into the Absolute, and who is calm and compassionate for no reason. A person through whom the Guru shines may be called a man of God, but the Guru is the Absolute Itself – *sat-cit-ānanda*. In effect the Absolute, shining through Kṛṣṇa, says in Chapter IX, "The foolish misunderstand Me because of My adopting the human form, ignorant as they are of My being that is beyond, as the Lord of all beings".

Is Arjuna's conflict neurotic, psychotic, or truly philosophic?

Some of the symptoms enumerated in the previous chapter could have made us feel that Arjuna's condition was rather psychopathological. Had this been so, one would have perhaps expected Kr̥ṣṇa to act as a psychiatrist of some sort. In the present chapter all such doubts are lifted from our minds. Arjuna is only numbed, or dazed, intellectually. In the first chapter what looked like a somatization reaction, an anxiety state, and a depressive reaction now prove to be only a transient situational personality disturbance. In the second chapter Arjuna comes to his own rescue and plainly states his case. It is a purely intellectual confrontation which involves both his moral obligations as well as his spiritual beliefs or convictions. Hence, what is appropriate in the present situation is the timely attention of a Guru-representative and not a psychiatrist.

When it is well known that Kapila's Sāṁkhya is atheistic, why in a religious book like the Gītā does Kr̥ṣṇa, who is identified as God (Īśvara), bring in the Sāṁkhya?

The Gītā is not a religious book. Religion in the Hindu terminology is *dharma*. In the 18th chapter of the Gītā, Kr̥ṣṇa advises Arjuna to give up all religions and to take his refuge in the Absolute. The Gītā does not teach any cult, nor does it ask affiliation with any special pattern of behaviour that binds people together to form a religious group. What Kr̥ṣṇa teaches is neither theism nor atheism. Arjuna's fears touch the fringes of irrational beliefs. As a counter card, Kr̥ṣṇa places before him the time-honoured Sāṁkhyan rationalism and revaluates it in terms of the finalized teaching of Vedānta, which is both philosophically and mystically monistic.

Why does Kr̥ṣṇa accuse Arjuna of impotency? In the previous chapter you have made reference to Arjuna's concealed threat of castration. In the present chapter you have qualified Arjuna's conflict as a transient situational disturbance. Can you elaborate?

Śrī Kr̥ṣṇa's reference to impotency is to be taken as a symbolic, not factual, castration. To take the example of a modern writer, Jean-Paul Sartre explains the fear of castration by alluding to the analogy of a hole that seeks plugging, or a voracious mouth that wants to devour. A situation which should normally delight a chivalrous warrior creates in Arjuna a feeling of disgust and repulsion. Here he has to woo a war and not a girl, and what he has to produce is victory and not a child. His potential to father victory has to come from his physical prowess as a warrior and from his skill in archery. He is afraid that he will be castrated of this potential, since he is caught in a situation similar to Kronos devouring his children. The very Bhīṣma to whom Arjuna is bound by filial piety, and from whom Arjuna's physical prowess comes, stands against him. No less is the threat that comes from the source of his skill in archery. Droṇa expects from Arjuna love and gratitude for teaching him archery. By a cruel irony of fate, Arjuna is now asked to aim his arrow at his own preceptor. This very unusual and tragic situation breeds in him fear and impotency.

If Arjuna is convinced of his love and reverence, that are due these venerable men, where is there any room for conflict? What makes it imperative for him to fight and kill them?

To him it does not look as simple as that. He describes Bhīṣma and Droṇa in one and the same verse as Gurus of *great sympathy* as well as *grabbers of wealth.* The Guru of sympathy deserves veneration, but not the greedy grabber of somebody's property.

What is Arjuna's philosophical conflict?

He finds that most people assembled on the battlefield have no personal enmity between them, and yet some strange quirk seems to drive them into a fateful homicide. This particular war is being waged to recover a country from Arjuna's own cousins. It is likely that most of these people, with whom he would very much love to live and enjoy the country, would not survive. Hence, to his mind it is most suicidal. When Arjuna puts on one side values such as riches and victory in war, and on the other side values such as reverence for the aged, love for friends and relatives, and a need for inner peace and contentment, he finds the course of action he has chosen dragging him into a wrong tangent. According to him, man's true pursuit should be wisdom and release from the bondage of all action. He does not see how war could lead him or anyone else to the soul's liberation.

Arjuna's quest has a parallel in the *Kaṭha Upaniṣad*. In it a young aspirant named Naciketas asks Death:

> As one passes from birth to birth and death to death, what is it that endures and continues as the substratum of conditioned experience, of the happy and unhappy results of acts? What is it in man that forms the basis of all this transmigratory drama? If there is something which survives such changes, it should yield the secret of restfulness, infinite peace, and lasting happiness. To attain this, should we not turn away from all that is conditional?

It is for this reason that Arjuna here places himself most devoutly at the feet of Śrī Kṛṣṇa and accepts him as his Guru.

What does Kṛṣṇa teach?

Kṛṣṇa gives Arjuna his teaching in the traditional way of the Upaniṣads. The Absolute is not an object to be perceived. It is not an experience of the past to be inferred. It has no parallel with which to compare it by analogy. It is not a residual factor to be known by a process of elimination. So the only way of presenting it is by the a priori method of revelation. The traditional way of learning this great wisdom is by listening to the Word of the Guru, pondering on it continuously, and experiencing it as an intimate vision of the Absolute. The classical expression of the Word is, "That you are", "This knowledge is the Absolute", "This Self is the Absolute", and "I am the Absolute". Of these, the first one is defined as teaching, the second and third are used as aids for contemplation, and the fourth is the final experience in meditation. Of course, Kṛṣṇa puts it in a manner which is most appropriate to the situation. He says:

> You are sorry for those with whom sorrow is unreasonable. ... Never was I non-existent, nor you nor these chiefs of men; neither shall we, all of us, ever cease becoming hereafter. ... This is neither born nor does This die, nor having once come into being, cease to become any more: unborn, perpetual, eternal is This Ancient One.

Why does Kṛṣṇa begin with the highest of all teachings, when Arjuna only wanted to know how he could get rid of his distress?

Even a child knows that a war is not fought on a bed of roses. Arjuna is serious in his search for salvation from the imperative bindings of action, which are fraught with dreadful consequences. What frightens him is the horizontal aspect of the world of actuality. A man of realization sees nothing but the all-pervading existence of One Supreme Knowledge as the most adorable value of all. But the man in whom the knowledge of Self has shrunk into the shell of his social and physical ego will see the world appearing to alternate between a dreadful place of demonic idiosyncrasies and one of dear values. Jesus said, "Seek ye first the Kingdom of God; then everything else shall be added unto you". Similarly, Kṛṣṇa tells Arjuna the position of a thorough-going absolutist, *jñānī*, for all it is worth, to be elaborated stage by stage afterwards.

Arjuna's immediate problem is his becoming a cause for the death of his dear ones on the battlefield. This fear is born of the misconceptions which we have referred to earlier. These misconceptions are:

> Arjuna identifies a person with his body;
> he thinks that with the death of the body a person perishes;
> he imagines that the other person's death depends on his action,
> and that he is responsible for the life of others.

To remove this misconception, Kṛṣṇa says that whatever exists now has been existing always, and will ever continue to exist. Vertically, there is conservation of the One which alone truly exists all the time. Horizontally there is endless transformation. Even in the same body there are changes like childhood, youth, old age, and decay. Nobody can stop these transformations. It is foolish to grieve over the inevitable transience of the physical world and the beings that inhabit it. Alternating sensations of heat and cold, and joy and pain, belong to the flux of life. Only that person who is firm of mind and who is unaffected by these dualities is destined for immortality. What is unreal cannot have being, and non-being cannot be real.

If you look at this world from the side of the spirit, it shines forth for all eternity, unexpended. If you look at it from the side of the body or matter, there are countless millions of finite forms surging up from the abyss of becoming. Each form is born, appearing in the perceptible world of the senses, and later dying to disappear back into the indistinct vortex of being. As a garment is to the body, so is the body to the spirit. Nobody regrets having changed a costume. Death is inevitable to the body; it cannot be averted.

All this is true. Why should Arjuna remain in the bewildering world of the physical order of eternal flux, when he could easily switch over to the world of the spirit and remain peacefully in a long-drawn meditation as a recluse, rather than shooting arrows?

This question actually brings us to a very difficult, yet most important, aspect of the whole problem. From a lump of porcelain or china clay one can make a flower vase, a soup bowl, a toilet commode, or a wash basin. Vertically viewed they are not different. Their existential reality belongs to one and the same lump of clay. Horizontally viewed, each object has a different form, meaning, purpose, and significance. You cannot serve soup in the wash basin, or put flowers in the commode. It is in bad taste to drink coffee from a flower vase. We are all one in spirit, however, your personal fulfilment is different from mine. The spirit in you and me has no form, no name, no clan, and no adherence to pain or pleasure, good or evil; but the individuated self becomes distinct in this body, and has to function in a certain way, and only in a certain way, to give purpose and meaning to that specific form. Our horizontal specificity is worked out by a number of factors, such as our physical features, physical strength, the functional ability of our nerves and glandular system, family and hereditary factors, socio-economic backgrounds, education, special talents, and the social contract we have knowingly or unknowingly entered into. A truthful expression of one's specific nature is termed in Indian philosophy as *svadharma.* Arjuna has to fulfil his *svadharma.*

What is svadharma?

As followers of Christ, Peter and Paul can both be classified as Christians. As individuals with differing tastes, reactions, temperaments, and spiritual calibre, Paul is very different from Peter. In other words, we may say that the intrinsic nature of Peter is different from the intrinsic nature of Paul. The intrinsic nature, or what basically constitutes the uniqueness of personality, is called *svadharma*. Your personality has its own action–reaction mechanism, value-sense, and dynamic drive. You cannot shun this hidden anatomy of your personality. This is what the Gītā refers to as *svadharma*.

According to scholars, *svadharma* is one of the major doctrinal contributions of the Gītā. People with vested interests misinterpreted and misapplied it over several centuries in India to keep the less fortunate multitudes from gaining socio-economic and religio-cultural advantages. Actually, *svadharma* has nothing to do with caste-oriented or career-oriented duties, upheld in books like *Manusmṛti* (the Laws of Manu). All the same, vocational compatibility depends on one's *svadharma*.

Svadharma as a general doctrine is to be distinguished from its particular application to Arjuna in the given situation. As a general theory it has many implications in common with the *Nichomachean Ethics* of Aristotle, according to which that quality which specifies a character and distinguishes one from another is the basis of virtue. If an apple tree bears apples and a peach tree bears peaches, each one is fulfilling its *svadharma*, or unfolding its own innate character. The virtue of a good cow may be said to be the quantity and quality of its milk. Man's humanity distinguishes humankind. Arjuna's *svadharma* is of a warrior. This has no refernce to his caste or birth. For instance, Droṇa, though recognized as a brāhmin by caste, stands on the battlefield as a warrior to fulfil his *svadharma*.

Ethnologically, neither Arjuna nor his four brothers can be traced to Aryan origin. Hence, the theory of *varṇa*, implied in the fourfold classification of the Aryans, is not applicable to Arjuna. Time and again one reads in the *Mahābhārata* that Arjuna, his four brothers, his mother Kuntī and wife Draupadī, are all dark-skinned. It is well known that the Aryan invaders of India were of pale skin and the proto-Dravidians were dark-skinned. From the Upaniṣads (e.g. *Bṛhadāraṇyaka*) we also know that kṣatriya was a name loosely used in those days to refer to kings and chiefs of native Indian origin. The pure fulfilment of Arjuna's *svadharma* lies in his determined stand to play the role of a warrior. Otherwise, he will lose both his *śreyas* as well as his *preyas*.

What are śreyas *and* preyas?

Perennial values belonging to humanity as a whole are called *śreyas*. *Preyas* is that which belongs to our here and now achievements of an earthly nature. Arjuna was looked upon by all as a great hero of matchless chivalry. If he now leaves the battlefield he will be looked upon as a coward. He will not gain any merit, nor achieve the goal of averting bloodshed and death among his relatives. *Preyas* for him is gaining victory, the kingdom, riches, fame, and the like. If he runs away, he will lose all these. *Śreyas* for him is wisdom, or higher knowledge that leads to realization. If he does not attend to the necessary requirements to actualize his immediate goals and natural obligations, he will also lose track of his higher wisdom, by which alone he can see all as his Self, and that he is all as the one Self without a second.

Why is this chapter split into two sections?

Such a division is suggested in verse 39. Actually, the second chapter could more correctly be called Sāṁkhya and Yoga, instead of just Sāṁkhya–Yoga. The second half of this chapter is the *yoga* corollary of the Sāṁkhyan philosophy of the first half. In verse 39 Kṛṣṇa says:

> What has just been taught is reason according to Sāṁkhya; but hear now the same according to *yoga*, attaining to the unity of which reasoning you will be able to throw off the bondage of works.

This changeover from the Sāṁkhya to the *yoga* implies a great secret of higher realization. The same secret occurs in all scriptures of the world, whether the Upaniṣads or the Bible, the Koran or the Tao Teh Ching. The *Īśa Upaniṣad* says:

> To darkness are they doomed who are engrossed in nescience (*avidyā*), and to greater darkness they go who are devoted only to knowledge (*vidyā*). The secret of nescience leads to one result, and the secret of knowledge to another. By knowing both, they transcend death with the secret of nescience and attain immortality with the secret of knowledge.

The secret of knowledge is Sāṁkhyan, while the secret of nescience belongs to *yoga*. Those who understand only the Sāṁkhyan view visualize the vertical and pure aspect of the Universal Self, but they miss how the horizontal world of actuality presents itself in myriad names and forms. Even when they see truth they will fail to uphold it. When they see goodness they will be helpless to preserve it, because their discipline is one-sided. On the other hand, those who act impulsively, guided by their selfish ends, run into frustration and misery, and bring woes to others also. If you want to become adept in classical music, you should know both the science of music as well as the art of singing correctly and effectively. This secret is taught in all scriptures. In the Gospel of St. Mark, Jesus gives the same teaching as he interprets the first commandment:

> ... And thou shalt love the Lord thy God with all thy heart, and with all thy soul, and with all thy mind, and with all thy strength: this is the first commandment. And the second is like, namely this: Thou shalt love thy neighbour as thyself.

Here Jesus puts these two commandments in brackets and makes the second one a corollary of the first, just as Kṛṣṇa makes the reasoning according to *yoga* a corollary of the reasoning according to Sāṁkhya. In the Christian frame of reference, loving the unseen Universal Father is the basic fundamental. It is man's vertical acceptance of the oneness of mankind. However, his love for the unseen God can be lived in the everyday actuality of life only by showering it on his neighbour. Thus, the fatherhood of God lends meaning to human fraternity, and conversely, by loving his brother man loves his Father. In other words, every specific item of life here and now has its assigned place in the universal expression of the manifested Absolute.

How is it possible for us to know that every detail of our life is related to the Absolute? The pros and cons of the train of events that unfold in our lives have such an infinite range that it is not possible to pick up each item and relate it to the Absolute, or, to put it in more familiar terms, to God's scheme of things. How do we achieve this seemingly impossible feat?

If you once learn how to walk, you need not thereafter consciously guide every step; they automatically come the right way. In the Upaniṣads it is said that to know the nature of water you need not drain all the seven seas and examine each drop of water; if you know the nature of a cup of water you know the nature of water wherever it is. The homogeneity of the Universal Self and the individual self is maintained by an inner participation. In the Upaniṣads it is termed *ṛta.* It belongs to the phenomenal, while its counterpart, called *satya*, belongs to the numinous, or the Absolute. If you know the secret of holding together the *satya* and the *ṛta*, you have learned the *dharma* of the Upaniṣads, which is different from the *dharma* of the Vedas and of other forms of religion. Even a little knowledge of the Upaniṣadic *dharma* can save you from great peril. Kṛṣṇa says in verse 40:

> In such a path there is no forfeiture of any merit nor is there involved any demerit by transgression. Even a little of this *dharma* saves one from great apprehension.

How do you distinguish Upaniṣadic dharma *from other kinds of religious dogmas or canons?*

The Upaniṣadic *dharma* is not a social norm or a mechanical scheme of production. In relativistic *dharma* a failure can result in a total destruction of whatever is accomplished. This is called *abhikrama nāśa.* For instance, if someone earns a good name in the society and is afterwards caught indulging in a vicious act, his whole reputation will be at stake. Similarly, when a man takes to cultivation, and after tending his crop for a couple of months he fails to manure and irrigate, it may perish, giving no return for his labour. Absolutist *dharma* taught by the Upaniṣads is the natural fulfilment of what is true for each person. Even if a Beethovan goes deaf and later becomes incapable of composing music, that which he has already accomplished as a creative genius will not lose its value in the least.

Another defect of the relativistic *dharma* is called *pratyavāya.* In a closed society a man found seriously guilty is disqualified from holding any prospective office. In some religious groups it is thought that the sins of the parents descend even to their children. According to the Absolutist *dharma,* nothing stops a man from reforming himself at any moment of his life. He is never victimized by the prejudice or fear of his fellow men. There is no admitting of any vicarious perpetrating of sin. Those who subscribe to closed faiths and belong to relativistic societies remain bound to obligatory customs or conventions. The Gītā promises freedom from this bondage, under which so much of humanity groans in one form or another.

What should we do to free ourselves from such a bondage?

Every interest in life, every thought that occurs to the mind, every word that is articulated, and every action that is initiated, should point toward the one ultimate end, the only goal in life – Realization. The reasoning that is well-founded, and regulated and directed to this sole purpose of Realization is called *yoga-buddhi.*

Should we not adopt some special discipline or practice to achieve this end?

Life is spontaneous. Look at the flowering lilies and the singing birds in the garden. They need no special lessons or rehearsals, they spontaneously bring out their best. The only trouble with man is that he has a will to choose. To plants and all animals other than man, nature itself has taken the responsibility of fixing their habitual choice. In the case of man, a wrong conditioning of his happiness can tend to make him choose the wrong way. If he is enlightened he will habitually choose the right path. That is why Socrates said Knowledge is Virtue. Personal education and self-correction is a lifelong business.

According to the Gītā there is no special panacea or short-cut to Realization. *Yoga* is the whole of life. The entire course of life and every value implied in it should bear the stamp of Realization. Kr̥ṣṇa says:

> There would be as much use for all the Vedas to a seer of the Absolute as there could be for a pool of water when a full flood prevails all over.

The revised attitude proper to a fully dedicated person is to have a course of life uninfluenced by the consideration of the pairs of opposites, such as pain or pleasure, fame or shame, or victory or failure, but to remain ever-established in the Timeless or the Pure Being. He should not be the least concerned or anxious about his yesterdays or tomorrows. Yet he should be alive and wakeful, to carve out of yesterday and today the most beautiful tomorrow his mind can conceive of. Jesus Christ puts it this way:

> And why take ye thought for raiment? Consider the lilies of the field, how they grow; they toil not, neither do they spin: And yet I say unto you that even Solomon in all his glory was not arrayed like one of these.

Śrī Kr̥ṣṇa imparts the same wisdom to Arjuna in the following words:

> Your concern should be with action (as such) alone, not for any benefit ever. Do not become benefit-motivated; be not attached to inaction (either).

Action is a performance. The quality of a performance depends on the sincerity of the agent's motivation. A mercenary soldier, for example, cannot fight with the enthusiasm of a dedicated patriot. Don't you think the indifference of a disinterested agent of action will vitiate the quality of his performance?

The Gītā uses the word action (*karma*) in a special sense. The reference here is not to the mechanical performance of an automation. Action is the actualization of the agent's will. The will is a wish which conscience gives the sanction to act upon. A wish is promoted from a universe of several desires. The choice is made on moral grounds. The normative notion of an enlightened person is the Absolute Good or Beauty or Truth. When someone chooses to act in the name of the Absolute, he identifies his will with the will of the Absolute. This only enhances the importance of the will in his mind. In such a case, the opportunity to act is itself looked upon as an occasion to relate oneself with the Absolute. In other words, the *yogī* acts with an Absolutist vision. That is why Kr̥ṣṇa defines *yoga* as "dexterity in action": *yogaḥ karmasu kauśalam.* When once you are established in the Absolute, life becomes spontaneously harmonized. It is the same as saying, "Seek ye first the kingdom of God, and his righteousness; and all these things shall be added unto you".

How do you establish yourself in the Absolute?

Arjuna puts the same question to Śrī Kṛṣṇa. He asks:

> What is the way of one whose reason is well-founded, who is established in *samādhi*, Oh Keśava? How does he discourse, what is his state of being, and how does he move about?

Śrī Kṛṣṇa then describes one of well-founded reason as follows:

> When one banishes all desires that enter the mind, Oh Pārtha, satisfied in the Self by the Self alone, then he is said to be one of well-founded reason.
>
> He whose mind is unaffected by mishaps, who on happy occasions too evinces no interest, rising above attachment, anxiety or anger – such a sage-recluse is said to be of well-founded reason.
>
> He who remains in all cases unattached on gaining such or such desirable–undesirable end, who neither welcomes (anything) nor rejects in anger – his reason is well-founded.
>
> Again, when, as a tortoise retracts its limbs from all sides, the senses (are withdrawn) from objects of sense-interest – his reason is well-founded.
>
> Objective interests revert without the relish for them on starving the embodied (of them). Even the (residual) relish reverts on the One Beyond being sighted.

After having attained Realization, will this well-founded reason remain steadfast forever?

Realization is not a sporadic or solitary event. The phenomenal world is a continuous flux. As in a kaleidoscope, every new situation has its own challenge to make. There has to be a continuous and contiguous chain of realization running through the whole of life. Hear what Kṛṣṇa says:

> Even with a man of wisdom, Oh Arjuna, in spite of his effort, excited sense-interests can forcibly distract the mind.
>
> Restraining every one of them, he should rest unitively established, having me for his Supreme (ideal). He in whom sense-interests are subdued – his reason is well-founded.

How is it that sometimes we are dragged away from a state of calm and tranquillity to indulge in vile and ignoble actions?

Śrī Kṛṣṇa elucidates that also to Arjuna:

> Meditating on objects of sense-interest there is born in man an attachment for them; from attachment rises passion; in the face of passion frustrated arises rage. From rage is produced distortion of values, from distortion of

> values memory-lapse, from memory-lapse comes loss of reason, and from loss of reason he perishes.
>
> But he whose Self is subdued, whose attachment and aversion are both within the sway of the Self, although his senses still move amidst sense-interests – he wends toward a state of spiritual clarity.
>
> By spiritual clarity there takes place the effacement for him of all sufferings, and for one whose spirit has become lucid, very soon reason becomes properly founded.

However illusory the phenomenal world is, we empirically accept it for our everyday transactions. Our senses and minds are all attuned to that. We are bound to be affected by its vicissitudes of infatuation and frustration. How do we escape from them?

Our escape lies in the verticalization of our entire life interest. Our senses operate between the objects outside and the mind within. The mind directs the senses according to the *vāsanā*s (conditioned impressions), which seek revival through fresh experiences. Each of these propensities has its own value-dynamics. When an object in which the same value is inherent comes in contact with the relevant sense organ, the corresponding mind becomes extroverted. The arrow of this interest, which points outward, should be reversed so that every value symbol outside will turn the mind to the Self, to appreciate all values as aspects of one's own Self. Because of this reversing technique used by *yogī*s, their attitudes and reactions look very different from those of others. Śrī Kṛṣṇa says:

> What is night for all creatures – the one of self-control keeps awake therein; wherein all creatures are wakeful – that is night for the sage-recluse who sees.

He further compares the mind of a person well-established in the Self to a sea which does not increase or decrease because of the several rivers flowing into it. Supreme peace comes to those who move about desirelessly, having given up all attachments and cured of the fever of egoism. The concluding verse assures final liberation to those who are free of passion, fear, and anger:

> This is the state of being in the Absolute, Oh Pārtha, on reaching which one suffers from delusion no more. Established in this at the very last moments of life, one reaches that final state of pure being in the Absolute.

III

Karma-Yoga

The Unitive Way of Action

INTRODUCTION

MAN'S need to act arises not only out of his biological and sociological reality but also out of his cosmic reality. We do not know how vast the mental horizon of non-human beings is. As far as we are concerned, the starry heavens above and the moral world below are all parts of a single homogeneous universe which has systems within systems. The sun, moon, and stars are all exerting their influences on our body and mind. Even the little violet in the brush and the humming bird in the garden are in intimacy with our inspired moments. Man's oneness with the rest of the world is the theme of cosmo-sociology and cosmo-psychology. Unfortunately these fields have only just entered into the domain of academic interest. Three studies that have paid close attention to cosmo-sociology and cosmo-psychology are astrology, the Chinese I-Ching (the Book of Changes), and the Ayurvedic school of Indian medicine. In the present chapter the Gītā introduces us to this very fascinating study of tracing the causal origin of action to our cosmic reality.

After listening to Kṛṣṇa's description of a man of steadfast wisdom (*sthitaprajña*), Arjuna's negative feelings about war intensify. Anger, greed, and fear are mentioned in Chapter II as the three gateways to hell. It is well known that attachment causes these evils, and that ultimately these prompting lead to action. Arjuna knows that there is no need for him to fight if he has no desire to retrieve his lost kingdom. Kṛṣṇa is prompting him to give up his attachment to Bhīṣma and Droṇa. He may overcome that sentiment, however, he cannot forget the fact that his obligation to fight arises out of his attachment to his brothers, mother, wife, and children. What he opts for is wisdom, and not either a kingdom or victory in warfare. On this ground he becomes more inimical to the idea of action, especially the act of killing which he is obliged to perform on the battlefield.

When Arjuna's scepticism is roused by Kṛṣṇa, by paradoxically glorifying the model of the contemplative man of wisdom, and at the same time asking Arjuna to adopt the contrary model of a warrior of action, he cannot contain his strong dissatisfaction with Kṛṣṇa's teaching. This chapter opens with Arjuna's sceptical outburst:

> If you are of the opinion, Oh Kṛṣṇa, that reason is superior to action, why then in an action that is ghastly do you enjoin me?
>
> By words that appear to be mixed up you seem to confound my reasoning. Tell me, after taking a decision, of that one (way) by which I may obtain spiritual merit.

In response to Arjuna's question and passionate appeal, Kṛṣṇa goes into a detailed examination of the unavoidable nature of action in the manifested world of becoming. He throws light on the cosmic implications of action, its social relevancy, and its biological imperativeness.

TRANSLATION

अर्जुन उवाच –

1. ज्यायसी चेत्कर्मणस्ते मता बुद्धिर्जनार्दन ।
तत्किं कर्मणि घोरे मां नियोजयसि केशव ।।

arjuna uvāca –

jyāyasī cet karmaṇas te matā buddhir janārdana ।
tat kiṁ karmaṇi ghore māṁ niyojayasi keśava ॥

arjuna uvāca: Arjuna said; *cet te matā*: if your opinion; *janārdana*: Oh Kṛṣṇa; *buddhiḥ*: (is that) reason; *jyāyasī karmaṇaḥ*: (is) superior to action; *kiṁ tat*: why then; *karmaṇi ghore*: in an action (that is) ghastly; *niyojayasi māṁ*: do you enjoin me; *keśava*: Oh Kṛṣṇa.

Arjuna said:

If you are of the opinion, Oh Janārdana, that reason is superior to action, why then in an action that is ghastly do you enjoin me, Oh Keśava?

2. व्यामिश्रेणेव वाक्येन बुद्धिं मोहयसीव मे ।
तदेकं वद निश्चित्य येन श्रेयोऽहमाप्नुयाम् ।।

vyāmiśreṇe 'va vākyena buddhiṁ mohayasī 'va me ।
tad ekaṁ vada niścitya yena śreyo 'ham āpnuyām ॥

vākyena: by words; *iva vyāmiśreṇa*: (which are) as if mixed up *mohayasi iva*: you seem to confound; *me buddhiṁ*: my reasoning; *vada*: tell (me); *niścitya*: after taking a decision; *tat ekaṁ*: that one (way); *yena*: by which; *aham āpnuyām*: I may obtain; *śreyaḥ*: merit.

By words that appear to be mixed up you seem to confound my reasoning. Tell me, after taking a decision, of that one (way) by which I may obtain merit.

श्रीभगवानुवाच –

3. लोकेऽस्मिन्द्विविधा निष्ठा पुरा प्रोक्ता मयानघ ।
ज्ञानयोगेन साङ्ख्यानां कर्मयोगेन योगिनाम् ।।

śrībhagavān uvāca –

loke 'smin dvividā niṣṭhā purā proktā mayā 'nagha ।
jñānayogena sāṁkhyānāṁ karmayogena yoginām ॥

śrī bhagavān uvāca: Kṛṣṇa said; *dvividhā niṣṭhā*: (there are) two kinds of discipline; *asmin loke*: in this world; *proktā purā*: (as) declared in ancient times; *mayā*: by Me; *anagha*: Oh Arjuna; *jñānayogena*: by the unitive way of wisdom; *sāṁkhyānāṁ*: of the Sāṁkhyas; *karmayogena*: by the unitive way of action; *yoginām*: of the *yogī*s.

Kṛṣṇa said:

There are two kinds of discipline in this world, as declared in ancient times by Me, Oh Sinless One – the unitive way of wisdom of the Sāṁkhyas and the unitive way of action of the *yogī*s.

4. न कर्मणामनारम्भान्नैष्कर्म्यं पुरुषोऽश्नुते ।
न च सन्न्यसनादेव सिद्धिं समधिगच्छति ।।

na karmaṅām anārambhān naiṣkarmyaṁ puruṣo 'śnute ।
na ca saṁnyasanād eva siddhiṁ samadhigacchati ॥

anārambhāt karmaṇām: by refraining from initiating activities; *puruṣaḥ*: a person; *na aśnute*: does not attain; *naiṣkarmyaṁ*: transcending action; *na ca saṁnyasanāt*: nor (can one) by renunciation; *eva*: alone; *samadhigacchati siddhiṁ*: come to perfection.

By refraining from initiating activities a person does not come to have the attainment of transcending action, nor can one by renunciation alone come to perfection.

5. न हि कश्चित्क्षणमपि जातु तिष्ठत्यकर्मकृत् ।
कार्यते ह्यवशः कर्म सर्वः प्रकृतिजैर्गुणैः ।।

na hi kaścit kṣaṇam api jātu tiṣṭhaty akarmakṛt ।
kāryate hy avaśaḥ karma sarvaḥ prakṛtijair guṇaiḥ ॥

na hi api: not even; *kṣaṇam*: (for) a single instant; *kaścit jātu tiṣṭhati*: (can) one ever remain; *akarmakṛt*: engaged in no action (at all); *guṇaiḥ*: by (virtue of) modalities (*guṇas*); *prakṛtijaiḥ*: born from nature; *sarvaḥ*: all; *kāryate*: are made to engage in; *karma*: action; *hi avaśaḥ*: helplessly.

Not even for a single instant can one ever remain engaged in no action at all. By virtue of modalities born from nature, all are made to engage in action helplessly.

6. कर्मेन्द्रियाणि संयम्य य आस्ते मनसा स्मरन् ।
इन्द्रियार्थान्विमूढात्मा मिथ्याचारः स उच्यते ।।

karmendriyāṇi saṁyamya ya āste manasā smaran ।
indriyārthān vitmūḍhātmā mithyācāraḥ sa ucyate ॥

yaḥ āste: he who sits; *saṁyamya*: controlling; *karma indriyāṇi*: the organs of activity; *manasā smaran*: (while) mentally ruminating over; *indriya arthān*: items of sensuous interest; *saḥ vimūḍha ātmā*: such a lost soul; *ucyate*: is said to be; *mithyācāraḥ*: one of spurious conduct.

He who sits controlling the organs of activity while ruminating mentally over items of sensuous interest – such a lost soul is said to be one of spurious conduct.

7. यस्त्विन्द्रियाणि मनसा नियम्यारभतेऽर्जुन ।
कर्मेन्द्रियैः कर्मयोगमसक्तः स विशिष्यते ।।

yas tv indriyāṇi manasā niyamyā 'rabhate 'rjuna ।
karmendriyaiḥ karmayogam asaktaḥ sa viśiṣyate ॥

yaḥ tu: (he) who, on the other hand; *niyamya indriyāṇi*: keeps under control the senses; *manasā*: by (means of) the mind; *arjuna*: Oh Arjuna; *ārabhate*: (and then) commences; *karma indriyaiḥ*: with the organs of activity; *karmayogam*: unitive activity; *asaktaḥ*: (while still) unattached; *saḥ viśiṣyate*: he excels.

He, on the other hand, who keeps the senses under control by means of the mind, and then commences unitive activity while still unattached – he excels.

8. नियतं कुरु कर्म त्वं कर्म ज्यायो ह्यकर्मणः ।
शरीरयात्रापि च ते न प्रसिद्ध्येदकर्मणः ।।

niyataṁ kuru karma tvaṁ karma jyāyo hy akarmaṇaḥ ।
śarīrayātrā 'pi ca te na prasiddhyed akarmaṇaḥ ॥

kuru tvaṁ: do engage yourself; *niyataṁ karma*: (in) necessary action; *karma hi jyāyaḥ*: activity (is) indeed better; *akarmaṇaḥ*: than non-activity; *ca api*: and even; *śarīra yātrā*: the bodily life; *te*: of yours; *na prasiddhyet*: would not progress satisfactorily; *akarmaṇaḥ*: through non-action.

Do engage yourself in action that is necessary; activity is indeed better than non-activity, and even the bodily life of yours would not progress satisfactorily through non-action.

9. यज्ञार्थात्कर्मणोऽन्यत्र लोकोऽयं कर्मबन्धनः ।
तदर्थं कर्म कौन्तेय मुक्तसङ्गः समाचर ।।

yajñārthāt karmaṇo 'nyatra loko 'yam karmabandhanaḥ ।
tadarthaṁ karma kaunteya muktasaṅgaḥ samācara ॥

anyatra: outside; *karmaṇaḥ*: of activity; *yajña arthāt*: with a sacrificial purpose; *ayam lokaḥ*: this world; *karma bandhanaḥ*: is bound by action; *tad arthaṁ*: (even with) such a purpose; *samācara karma*: do engage in work; *kaunteya*: Oh Arjuna; *mukta saṅgaḥ*: freed of (all) attachments.

Outside of activity with a sacrificial purpose, this world is bound by action. Even with such a purpose, do engage in work, Oh Kaunteya, freed of all attachments.

10. सहयज्ञाः प्रजाः सृष्ट्वा पुरोवाच प्रजापतिः ।
अनेन प्रसविष्यध्वमेष वोऽस्त्विष्टकामधुक् ।।

sahayajñāḥ prajāḥ sṛṣṭvā puro 'vāca prajāpatiḥ ।
anena prasaviṣyadhvam eṣa vo 'stv iṣṭakāmadhuk ॥

purā: in ancient times; *sṛṣṭvā prajāḥ*: having created the peoples; *sahayajñāh*: along with sacrifice; *prajāpatiḥ uvāca*: Prajāpati (the Lord of the Peoples) said; *anena*: by this; *prasaviṣyadhvam*: shall you grow and multiply; *astu eṣaḥ*: let this be; *vaḥ*: to you; *iṣṭakāmadhuk*: the milch-cow of all desires.

In ancient times, having created the peoples with sacrifice as pertaining to them (necessarily), Prajāpati said: "By this shall you grow and multiply; let this be to you the milch-cow of all desires.

11. देवान्भावयतानेन ते देवा भावयन्तु वः ।
परस्परं भावयन्तः श्रेयः परमवाप्स्यथ ।।

devān bhāvayatā 'nena te devā bhāvayantu vaḥ ।
parasparaṁ bhāvayantaḥ śreyaḥ param avāpsyatha ॥

anena: with this; *bhāvayata devān*: do you gratify the gods; *te devāḥ*: (and) they, the gods; *bhāvayantu vaḥ*: gratify you; *bhāvayantaḥ parasparaṁ*: (thus) gratifying reciprocally; *avāpsyatha*: you shall reach to; *param śreyaḥ*: supreme merit.

With this do you gratify the gods, and the gods gratify you; thus gratifying reciprocally you shall reach to supreme merit.

12. इष्टान्भोगान्हि वो देवा दास्यन्ते यज्ञभाविताः ।
तैर्दत्तानप्रदायैभ्यो यो भुङ्क्ते स्तेन एव सः ॥

iṣṭān bhogān hi vo devā dāsyante yajñabhāvitāḥ ।
tair dattān apradāyai 'bhyo yo bhuṅkte stena eva saḥ ॥

devāḥ hi: (those) gods indeed; *yajña bhāvitāḥ*: by sacrifice gratified; *dāsyante*: shall bestow; *vaḥ*: on you; *bhogān iṣṭān*: (all) gratifications desired; *yaḥ bhuṅkte*: one who eats; *dattān taiḥ*: what is given by them; *apradāya ebhyaḥ*: without giving (in turn) to them; *saḥ stenaḥ eva*: he (is) a thief indeed.

Those gods shall bestow on you all the gratifications you desire; one who eats what is given by them without giving in turn to them – he is a thief indeed."

13. यज्ञशिष्टाशिनः सन्तो मुच्यन्ते सर्वकिल्बिषैः ।
भुञ्जते ते त्वघं पापा ये पचन्त्यात्मकारणात् ॥

yajñaśiṣṭāśinaḥ santo mucyante sarvakilbiṣaiḥ ।
bhuñjāte te tv aghaṁ papā ye pacanty ātmakāraṇāt ॥

santaḥ: the good man; *yajñaśiṣṭa āśinaḥ*: who eats of the remnants of a sacrifice; *mucyante*: is absolved; *sarva kilbiṣaiḥ*: of all faults; *tu*: however; *te pāpāḥ*: those sinners; *bhuñjate aghaṁ*: eat (of) evil (itself); *ye pacanti*: who cook; *ātmakāraṇāt*: (with) themselves (alone) for motive.

The good man who eats of the remnants of a sacrifice is absolved of all faults; however, those sinners eat of evil (itself) who cook with themselves (alone) for motive.

14. अन्नाद्भवन्ति भूतानि पर्जन्यादन्नसम्भवः ।
यज्ञाद्भवति पर्जन्यो यज्ञः कर्मसमुद्भवः ॥

annād bhavanti bhūtāni parjanyād annasaṁbhavaḥ ।
yajñād bhavati parjanyo yajñaḥ karmasamudbhavaḥ ॥

annāt: from food; *bhūtāni bhuvanti*: beings come to be; *parjanyāt*: (and) from rain; *anna saṁbhavaḥ*: food is produced; *yajñāt bhavati*: sacrifice becomes; *parjanyaḥ*: rain; *yajñaḥ*: (and) sacrifice; *karma samudbhavaḥ*: has its origin in action.

Food is the cause of beings, and from rain food is produced; sacrifice has its effect in rain, and sacrifice has its origin in action.

15. कर्म ब्रह्मोद्भवं विद्धि ब्रह्माक्षरसमुद्भवम् ।
तस्मात्सर्वगतं ब्रह्म नित्यं यज्ञे प्रतिष्ठितम् ॥

karma brahmodbhavaṁ viddhi brahmā 'kṣarasamudbhavam ।
tasmāt sarvagataṁ brahma nityaṁ yajñe pratiṣṭhitam ॥

viddhi karma: know (that) action; *brahmā udbhavaṁ*: arises from Brahmā (god of creation); *brahmā*: (and that) Brahmā; *samudbhavam akṣara*: traces his being to the Imperishable; *tasmāt sarvagataṁ*: therefore the all-pervasive; *brahma*: the Absolute (the Imperishable); *nityaṁ pratiṣṭhitam*: eternally remains; *yajñe*: in sacrifice.

Know that action arises from Brahmā, and that Brahmā traces his being to the Imperishable. Therefore the all-pervasive Absolute is eternally bound up with sacrifice.

16. एवं प्रवर्तितं चक्रं नानुवर्तयतीह यः ।
अघायुरिन्द्रियारामो मोघं पार्थ स जीवति ।।

evaṁ pravartitaṁ cakraṁ nā 'nuvartayatī 'ha yaḥ ।
aghāyur indriyārāmo moghaṁ pārtha sa jīvati ॥

yaḥ: he who; *na anuvartayati iha*: does not cause to turn hereunder; *pravartitaṁ*: the rotation; *evaṁ cakraṁ*: (of) such a wheel; *aghāyuḥ indriyārāmaḥ*: vicious, delighted by the senses; *saḥ jīvati*: he lives; *pārtha*: Oh Arjuna; *moghaṁ*: in vain (indeed).

He who leads a life hereunder that does not conform to the rotation of such a wheel – such a man of vicious lifetime lives, Oh Pārtha! in vain (indeed).

17. यस्त्वात्मरतिरेव स्यादात्मतृप्तश्च मानवः ।
आत्मन्येव च सन्तुष्टस्तस्य कार्यं न विद्यते ।।

yas tv ātmaratir eva syād ātmatṛptaś ca mānavaḥ ।
ātmany eva ca saṁtuṣṭas tasya kāryaṁ na vidyate ॥

tu yaḥ: but he who; *syāt*: happens to be; *ātma ratiḥ eva*: attached to the Self alone; *ca ātma tṛptaḥ*: and (who finds) full satisfaction in the Self; *mānavaḥ saṁtuṣṭaḥ*: a man who is happy; *ātmani*: in the Self; *eva ca*: as such, too; *tasya*: for him; *vidyate na*: there is nothing; *kāryaṁ*: he should do.

But for him who happens to be attached to the Self alone, who finds full satisfaction in the Self – for such a man who is happy in the Self as such, too, there is nothing that he should do.

18. नैव तस्य कृतेनार्थो नाकृतेनेह कश्चन ।
न चास्य सर्वभूतेषु कश्चिदर्थव्यपाश्रयः ।।

nai 'va tasya kṛtenā 'rtho nā 'kṛtene 'ha kaścana ।
na cā 'sya sarvabhūteṣu kaścid arthavyapāśrayaḥ ॥

na eva: neither (is there) anything indeed; *tasya*: for him; *kṛtena arthaḥ*: resulting from work done; *na kaścana*: nor anything; *akṛtena*: from work omitted; *iha*: here; *na ca*: nor is there either; *asya*: for him; *kaścit*: any whatsoever; *artha vyapāśrayaḥ*: dependence on anything derivable; *sarvabhūteṣu*: from any being.

Neither is there anything indeed for him resulting from work done, nor anything from work omitted here, nor is there either for him any dependence in respect of anything derivable from any being whatsoever.

19. तस्मादसक्तः सततं कार्यं कर्म समाचर ।
असक्तो ह्याचरन्कर्म परमाप्नोति पूरुषः ।।

tasmād asaktaḥ satataṁ kāryaṁ karma samācara ।
asakto hy ācaran karma param āpnoti pūruṣaḥ ॥

tasmāt: therefore; *satataṁ asaktaḥ*: always remaining detached; *samācara*: engage (yourself) in; *karma kāryaṁ*: actions that are necessary; *hi*: indeed; *ācaran karma*: performing actions; *asaktaḥ*: with detachment; *pūruṣaḥ āpnoti*: man attains to; *param*: the Supreme.

Therefore always remain detached, engage yourself in actions that are necessary, indeed, performing actions with detachment man attains to the Supreme.

20. कर्मणैव हि संसिद्धिमास्थिता जनकादयः ।
लोकसङ्ग्रहमेवापि सम्पश्यन्कर्तुमर्हसि ।।

karmaṇai 'va hi saṁsiddhim āsthitā janakādayaḥ ।
lokasaṁgrahaṁ evā 'pi sampaśyan kartum arhasi ॥

janaka ādayaḥ: Janaka and such others; *āsthitāḥ saṁsiddhim*: reached perfection; *eva hi*: even; *karmaṇā*: performing acts; *eva*: again; *saṁpaśyan*: having due regard for; *loka saṁgraham api*: the integration of the world too; *arhasi kartum*: you have to act.

Janaka and such others reached perfection even performing acts. Again, having due regard for the integration of the world too, you have to act.

21. यद्यदाचरति श्रेष्ठस्तत्तदेवेतरो जनः ।
स यत्प्रमाणं कुरुते लोकस्तदनुवर्तते ।।

yad-yad ācarati śreṣṭhas tat-tad eve 'taro janaḥ ।
sa yat pramāṇaṁ kurute lokas tad anuvartate ॥

yat yat: whichever (may be); *śreṣṭhaḥ ācarati*: (the way of life that) a superior man adopts; *tat tat eva*: that very one; *itaraḥ janaḥ*: (is by) other people (followed); *yat saḥ*: what he; *kurute*: makes; *pramāṇaṁ*: his guiding principle; *lokaḥ*: the world (too); *anuvartate tat*: follows that.

Whichever may be the way of life that a superior man adopts – that very one is by other people (followed). What he makes his guiding principle, the world too behaves even according to the same.

22. न मे पार्थास्ति कर्तव्यं त्रिषु लोकेषु किञ्चन ।
नानवाप्तमवाप्तव्यं वर्त एव च कर्मणि ॥

na me pārthā 'sti kartavyaṁ triṣu lokeṣu kiñcana ।
nā 'navāptam avāptavyaṁ varta eva ca karmaṇi ॥

asti na: there is nothing; *triṣu lokeṣu*: in the three worlds; *kartavyaṁ*: to be done; *me*: by me; *pārtha*: Oh Arjuna; *na kiñcana*: nor anything; *anavāptam*: unaccomplished; *avāptavyaṁ*: to be accomplished; *eva ca*: while still; *varta karmaṇi*: I remain active (in principle).

There is nothing in the three worlds that I am obliged to do, Oh Pārtha, nor anything unaccomplished to be accomplished, while still I remain active (in principle).

23. यदि ह्यहं न वर्तेयं जातु कर्मण्यतन्द्रितः ।
मम वर्त्मानुवर्तन्ते मनुष्याः पार्थ सर्वशः ॥

yadi hy ahaṁ na varteyaṁ jātu karmaṇy atandritaḥ ।
mama vartmā 'nuvartante manuṣyāḥ pārtha sarvaśaḥ ॥

yadi hi: if indeed; *ahaṁ*: I; *na varteyaṁ karmaṇi*: should not remain active (in principle); *jātu atandritaḥ*: never relaxing; *manuṣyāḥ*: men; *sarvaśaḥ*: everywhere; *pārtha*: Oh Arjuna; *anuvartante*: would follow; *mama vartmā*: my way

If I should not remain active (in principle), never relaxing, men in every walk of life, Oh Pārtha, would take to my way.

24. उत्सीदेयुरिमे लोका न कुर्यां कर्म चेदहम् ।
सङ्करस्य च कर्ता स्यामुपहन्यामिमाः प्रजाः ॥

utsīdeyur ime lokā na kuryāṁ karma ced aham ।
saṅkarasya ca kartā syām upahanyām imāḥ prajāḥ ॥

ime: these (various); *lokāḥ*: worlds (value systems); *utsīdeyuḥ*: would fall into ruin; *cet aham*: should I; *na kuryāṁ karma*: refrain from activity; *ca syām kartā*: and I would become the agent; *saṅkarasya*: of (evolutive) confusion; *upahanyām*: killing (in effect); *imāḥ prajāḥ*: these people.

These (various) worlds would fall into ruin should I refrain from activity, and I would become the agent of evolutive confusion, killing in effect the peoples.

25. सक्ताः कर्मण्यविद्वांसो यथा कुर्वन्ति भारत ।
कुर्याद्विद्वांस्तथासक्तश्चिकीर्षुर्लोकसङ्ग्रहम् ॥

saktāḥ karmaṇy avidvāṁso yathā kurvanti bhārata ।
kuryād vidvāṁs tathā 'saktaś cikīrṣur lokasaṁgraham ॥

yathā: in the same manner as; *avidvāṁsaḥ*: the uninstructed; *kurvanti*: would take to activity; *saktāḥ karmaṇi*: with attachment to work; *bhārata*: Oh Arjuna; *vidvān tathā*: the instructed man likewise; *kuryāt asaktaḥ*: should act without attachment; *cikīrṣuḥ*: interested (merely); *loka saṁgraham*: in world order.

In the same manner as uninstructed people would take to activity with attachment to work, Oh Bhārata, the instructed man likewise should act without attachment, interested (merely) in world order.

26. न बुद्धिभेदं जनयेदज्ञानां कर्मसङ्गिनाम् ।
जोषयेत्सर्वकर्माणि विद्वान्युक्तः समाचरन् ॥

na buddhibhedaṁ janayed ajñānāṁ karmasaṅginām ।
joṣayet sarvakarmāṇi vidvān yuktaḥ samācaran ॥

vidvān: the person who is wise; *na janayet*: should not give rise to; *buddhi bhedam*: disruption in the way of thinking; *ajñānāṁ*: of those who have not attained to wisdom; *karma saṅginām*: (who are) attached to action; *samācaran yuktaḥ*: (but by) behaving unitively; *joṣayet*: he should render enjoyable; *sarva karmāṇi*: every (kind of) action.

The person who is wise should not give room for disruption in the way of thinking of those who have not attained to wisdom, but by behaving unitively should render every kind of action enjoyable.

27. प्रकृतेः क्रियमाणानि गुणैः कर्माणि सर्वशः ।
अहङ्कारविमूढात्मा कर्ताहमिति मन्यते ॥

prakṛteḥ kriyamāṇāni guṇaiḥ karmāṇi sarvaśaḥ ।
ahaṁkāravimūḍhātmā kartā 'ham iti manyate ॥

sarvaśaḥ: on every occasion; *guṇaiḥ*: through the *guṇas* (three modalities); *prakṛteḥ*: of nature; *karmāṇi kriyamāṇāni*: every act is accomplished; *ahaṁkāra vimūḍhātmā*: one possessed of egoism; *iti*: however; *manyate*: thinks; *aham kartā*: I am the actor.

Irrespective of the occasion, it is nature that through the *guṇas* accomplishes every act. One possessed of egoism, however, thinks of himself as the actor.

28. तत्त्ववित्तु महाबाहो गुणकर्मविभागयोः ।
गुणा गुणेषु वर्तन्त इति मत्वा न सज्जते ॥

tattvavit tu mahābāho guṇakarmavibhāgayoḥ ।
guṇā guṇeṣu vartanta iti matvā na sajjate ॥

tu: on the other hand; *mahābāho*: Oh Arjuna; *tattvavit*: the one who knows the principle (underlying); *guṇa karma vibhāgayoḥ*: *guṇa* (nature mode) as distinct from *karma* (its functional counterpart); *iti matvā*: holding the view (that); *guṇāḥ*: (subjective) modes; *vartante*: inhere; *guṇeṣu*: in (their corresponding objective) modes; *na sajjate*: is not affected.

On the other hand, Oh Mighty-Armed, the one who knows the principle underlying *guṇa* as distinct from *karma*, holding the view that (subjective) modes inhere in (their corresponding objective) modes, is not affected.

29. प्रकृतेर्गुणसम्मूढाः सज्जन्ते गुणकर्मसु ।
तानकृत्स्नविदो मन्दान्कृत्स्नविन्न विचालयेत् ॥

prakṛter guṇasaṁmūḍhāḥ sajjante guṇakarmasu ।
tān akṛtsnavido mandān kṛtsnavin na vicālayet ॥

guṇa saṁmūḍhāḥ: those confounded by the modalities; *prakṛteḥ*: of nature; *sajjante*: become attached to; *guṇa karmasu*: (objective) modalities (existing) in works; *tān*: such men; *akṛtsnavidaḥ mandān*: (who are) not all wise, (and are) dull; *kṛtsnavit*: those who are all-wise; *na vicālayet*: should not unsettle.

Those confounded by the modalities of nature become attached to objective modalities existing in works. Such men who are not all-wise, and are dull, should not be unsettled by those who are all-wise.

30. मयि सर्वाणि कर्माणि संन्यस्याध्यात्मचेतसा ।
निराशीर्निर्ममो भूत्वा युध्यस्व विगतज्वरः ॥

mayi sarvāṇi karmāṇi saṁnyasyā 'dhyātmacetasā ।
nirāśir nirmamo bhūtvā yudhyasva vigatajvaraḥ ॥

saṁnyasya: renouncing; *mayi*: in Me (the Absolute); *sarvāṇi karmāṇi*: all works; *bhūtvā*: coming to be; *nirāśīḥ*: without expectations; *nirmamaḥ*: without possessiveness; *adhyātma cetasā*: with a full awareness about the Self; *yudhyasva*: do fight; *vigata jvaraḥ*: with fever gone.

Renouncing in Me all works, coming to be without expectations or possessiveness, with a full awareness about the Self, do fight with fever gone.

31. ये मे मतमिदं नित्यमनुतिष्ठन्ति मानवाः ।
श्रद्धावन्तोऽनसूयन्तो मुच्यन्ते तेऽपि कर्मभिः ॥

ye me matam idaṁ nityam anutiṣṭhanti mānavāḥ ।
śraddhāvanto 'nasūyanto mucyante te 'pi karmabhiḥ ॥

ye api: they who, too; *nityam anutiṣṭhanti*: ever adhere to; *idaṁ matam me*: this doctrine of mine; *mānavāḥ*: men; *śraddhāvantaḥ anasūyantaḥ*: full of faith and free from any mistrust (in respect of it); *te mucyante*: they gain release; *karmabhiḥ*: from works.

They, too, who ever adhere to this doctrine of mine, men full of faith and free from any mistrust in respect of it – they gain release from works.

32. ये त्वेतदभ्यसूयन्तो नानुतिष्ठन्ति मे मतम् ।
सर्वज्ञानविमूढांस्तान्विद्धि नष्टानचेतसः ॥

ye tv etad abhyasūyanto nā 'nutiṣṭhanti me matam ।
sarvajñānavimūḍhāṁs tān viddhi naṣṭān acetasaḥ ॥

tu: on the other hand; *ye abhyasūyantaḥ*: those who look with mistrust (upon); *etat me matam*: this my doctrine; *na anutiṣṭhanti*: (and) adhere not (to it); *sarva jñāna vimūḍhān*: who are deluded regarding all wisdom; *viddhi tān*: know them; *acetasaḥ*: (as) shut away from all knowledge; *naṣṭān*: (and as) lost.

On the other hand, those soulless ones who look upon my doctrine with mistrust and adhere not to it – know them as shut away from all knowledge and as lost.

33. सदृशं चेष्टते स्वस्याः प्रकृतेर्ज्ञानवानपि ।
प्रकृतिं यान्ति भूतानि निग्रहः किं करिष्यति ॥

sadṛśaṁ ceṣṭate svasyāḥ prakṛter jñānavān api ।
prakṛtiṁ yānti bhūtāni nigrahaḥ kiṁ kariṣyati ॥

api jñānavān: even a man of wisdom; *ceṣṭate sadṛśaṁ*: behaves in conformity with; *svasyāḥ prakṛteḥ*: his own nature; *bhūtāni yānti*: all creation goes on (subject to); *prakṛtiṁ*: nature; *kiṁ kariṣyati*: (of) what avail is; *nigrahaḥ*: control.

Even a man of wisdom behaves in conformity with his own nature. All creation goes on subject to nature. Of what avail is control?

34. इन्द्रियस्येन्द्रियस्यार्थे रागद्वेषौ व्यवस्थितौ ।
तयोर्न वशमागच्छेत्तौ ह्यस्य परिपन्थिनौ ॥

indriyasye 'ndriyasyā 'rthe rāgadveṣau vyavasthitau ।
tayor na vaśam āgacchet tau hy asya paripanthinau ॥

rāga dveṣau: attraction-repulsion; *vyavasthitau*: abide (mutually); *indriyasya indriyasya arthe*: between the senses and their sense-objects; *na āgacchet*: never should one come under; *tayoḥ vaśam*: their double sway; *tau hi*: they are indeed; *asya paripanthinau*: one's twin path-hindering factors.

Attraction-repulsion abide mutually, between the senses and their sense-objects. One should never come under their double sway. They indeed are one's twin path-hindering factors.

35. श्रेयान्स्वधर्मो विगुणः परधर्मात्स्वनुष्ठितात् ।
स्वधर्मे निधनं श्रेयः परधर्मो भयावहः ।।

śreyān svadharmo viguṇaḥ paradharmāt svanuṣṭhitāt ।
svadharme nidhanaṁ śreyaḥ paradharmo bhayāvahaḥ ॥

śreyān: better (is); *svadharmaḥ*: activity rightly conforming to one's own nature; *viguṇaḥ*: (though) lacking in superior quality; *paradharmāt*: than activity foreign to one's own nature; *svanuṣṭhitāt*: although (it may be) well done (otherwise); *nidhanaṁ*: (even) death; *svadharme*: by the performance of what fits one properly; *śreyaḥ*: has merit; *paradharmaḥ*: activity foreign to oneself; *bhaya āvahaḥ*: is fraught with danger.

Better is activity rightly conforming to one's own nature, though lacking in superior quality, than activity foreign to one's own nature, although it may be well done (otherwise). (Even) death by the performance of what fits one properly has merit. Activity foreign to oneself is fraught with danger.

अर्जुन उवाच –

36. अथ केन प्रयुक्तोऽयं पापं चरति पूरुषः ।
अनिच्छन्नपि वार्ष्णेय बलादिव नियोजितः ।।

arjuna uvāca –

atha kena prayukto 'yaṁ pāpaṁ carati pūruṣaḥ ।
anicchann api vārṣṇeya balād iva niyojitaḥ ॥

arjuna uvāca: Arjuna said; *atha*: then; *prayuktaḥ kena*: impelled by what; *pūruṣaḥ carati ayaṁ pāpaṁ*: man does this sin; *api anicchan*: even against his will; *vārṣṇeya*: Oh Kṛṣṇa; *iva*: as if; *balāt niyojitaḥ*: forcibly enjoined.

Arjuna said:

Then impelled by what does man lead such a life of sin even against his will, Oh Vārṣṇeya, as if forcibly enjoined?

श्रीभगवानुवाच –

37. काम एष क्रोध एष रजोगुणसमुद्भवः ।
महाशनो महापाप्मा विद्ध्येनमिह वैरिणम् ।।

śrībhagavān uvāca –

kāma eṣa krodha eṣa rajoguṇasamudbhavaḥ ।
mahāśano mahāpāpmā viddhy enam iha vairiṇam ॥

śrī bhagavām uvāca: Kṛṣṇa said; *eṣah kāmaḥ*: such (is) desire; *eṣaḥ krodhaḥ*: such (is) anger; *rajoguṇa samudbhavaḥ*: born out of the modality (*guṇa*) (called) *rajas* (the active-affective); *mahā aśanaḥ*: all devouring; *mahā pāpmāḥ*: all-vitiating; *viddhi enam*: know this (to be); *vairiṇam iha*: the enemy here.

Kṛṣṇa said:

Such is desire, such is anger, born out of the modality called *rajas*, all-devouring, all-vitiating; know this to be the enemy here.

38. धूमेनाव्रियते वह्निर्यथादर्शो मलेन च ।
यथोल्बेनावृतो गर्भस्तथा तेनेदमावृतम् ।।

dhūmenā 'vriyate vahnir yathā 'darśo malena ca ।
yatho 'lbenā 'vṛto garbhas tathā tene 'dam āvṛtam ॥

yathā vahniḥ: as fire; *āvriyate dhūmena*: is shrouded by smoke; *ca ādarśaḥ*: and a mirror (is beclouded); *malena*: by dirt; *yathā garbhaḥ*: as the foetus; *āvṛtaḥ ulbena*: is enclosed in the amnion; *tathā tena*: likewise by such; *idam āvṛtam*: (is) This surrounded.

As smoke shrouds fire, as a mirror (is beclouded) by dirt, as the foetus is enclosed in the amnion, likewise by such is This surrounded.

39. आवृतं ज्ञानमेतेन ज्ञानिनो नित्यवैरिणा ।
कामरूपेण कौन्तेय दुष्पूरेणानलेन च ।।

āvṛtaṁ jñānam etena jñānino nityavairiṇā ।
kāmarūpeṇa kaunteya duṣpūreṇā 'nalena ca ॥

jñānam āvṛtaṁ: wisdom is enveloped; *etena*: by this; *nityavairiṇā*: (which is) the eternal enemy; *jñāninaḥ*: (of) the wise; *kāma rūpeṇa*: with the form of desire; *kaunteya*: Oh Arjuna; *analena ca duṣpūreṇa*: by a fire, too, that is difficult to satiate.

Wisdom is enveloped by this which is the eternal enemy of the wise, remaining in the form of desire, Oh Kaunteya! which is a fire that is difficult to satiate.

40. इन्द्रियाणि मनो बुद्धिरस्याधिष्ठानमुच्यते ।
एतैर्विमोहयत्येष ज्ञानमावृत्य देहिनम् ।।

indriyāṇi mano buddhir asyā 'dhiṣṭhānam ucyate ।
etair vimohayaty eṣa jñānam āvṛtya dehinam ॥

indriyāṇi: the senses; *manaḥ buddhiḥ*: mind (and) reason; *ucyate*: are said to be; *adhiṣṭhānam asya*: the abode of this; *etaiḥ*: by means of these;

eṣaḥ vimohayati: this (desire) bewilders; *dehinam*: the embodied One; *āvṛtya jñānam*: (by) veiling (his) wisdom.

This is said to be lodged in the senses, mind, and reason. By means of these, this (desire) bewilders the embodied One by veiling his wisdom.

41. तस्मात्त्वमिन्द्रियाण्यादौ नियम्य भरतर्षभ ।
पाप्मानं प्रजहि ह्येनं ज्ञानविज्ञाननाशनम् ॥

tasmāt tvam indriyāṇy ādau niyamya bharatarṣabha ।
pāpmānaṁ prajahi hy enaṁ jñānavijñānanāśanam ॥

tasmāt: therefore; *bharatarṣabha*: Oh Arjuna; *ādau*: first; *niyamya indriyāṇi*: mastering the senses; *tvaṁ prajahi hi*: you slay indeed; *enaṁ pāpmānaṁ*: this which is of sin; *jñāna vijñāna nāśanam*: destroying (both) pure and practical wisdom.

Therefore, Oh Best of Bhāratas, mastering first the senses, slay this which is of sin, which can destroy both pure and practical wisdom.

42. इन्द्रियाणि पराण्याहुरिन्द्रियेभ्यः परं मनः ।
मनसस्तु परा बुद्धिर्यो बुद्धेः परतस्तु सः ॥

indriyāṇi parāṇy āhur indriyebhyaḥ paraṁ manaḥ ।
manasas tu parā buddhir yo buddheḥ paratas tu saḥ ॥

āhuḥ: it is taught (in ancient tradition) that; *indriyāṇi*: the senses; *parāṇi*: (are) beyond (transcendental); *paraṁ indriyebhyaḥ*: beyond the senses; *manaḥ*: (is) the mind; *tu parā manasaḥ*: and beyond the mind; *buddhiḥ*: (is) reason; *yaḥ parataḥ buddheḥ*: what is beyond reason; *tu saḥ*: (is) indeed He (the Absolute).

It is taught that the senses are beyond; beyond the senses is the mind, beyond the mind is reason, and beyond reason is He.

43. एवं बुद्धेः परं बुद्ध्वा संस्तभ्यात्मानमात्मना ।
जहि शत्रुं महाबाहो कामरूपं दुरासदम् ॥

evaṁ buddheḥ paraṁ buddhvā saṁstabhyā 'tmānam ātmanā ।
jahi śatruṁ mahābāho kāmarūpaṁ durāsadam ॥

evaṁ: thus; *buddhvā*: knowing (Him to be); *paraṁ buddheḥ*: beyond reason; *saṁstabhya ātmānam*: immobilizing the Self; *ātmanā*: by the Self; *mahābāho*: Oh Arjuna; *jahi śatruṁ*: kill (that) enemy; *kāma rūpaṁ*: in the form of desire; *durāsadam*: (so) difficult to encounter.

Thus knowing Him to be beyond reason, immobilizing the Self by the Self, Oh Mighty-Armed! kill that enemy in the form of desire, (so) difficult to encounter.

DIALOGUE

TEACHER: This chapter is on Karma-Yoga. *Karma* means action. In the previous chapter, you will remember, Kṛṣṇa referred to four fundamental concepts of Vedānta:

- The Spirit that animates all beings is One.
- This One is the Supreme Self, without a second, which has no beginning or end. Except for the Self, everything has only a dependent existence.
- Freedom from the conditionings that cause bondage is the chief aim of life. That is possible only through the realization of the Self. One realizes by unitive reasoning.
- The world that we experience as actual is only phenomenal. But it has a status of its own as an empirical fact of everyday life. As such, one has to respect the role that is assigned by nature or social circumstances, and has to carry out one's duties in conformity with one's intrinsic nature or innate disposition. Even after being established in the knowledge of the Self, so long as there persists the sense of personal ego one should regulate his appreciations and reactions with a unitive vision that transcends all sense of duality.

STUDENT: *After discussing karma in the second chapter, why does Kṛṣṇa bring it up again here?*

Although *karma* is generally translated as "action", in the social, cultural, religious, and spiritual contexts in India this word has many other operational meanings, each distinct from the others. I shall recall here some of these specific connotations.

According to Pūrva-Mīmāṁsā, one of the six systems of the Hindu philosophy, *karma* is action regulated by *vidhi*, a command, precept, or injunction. There are three kinds of *vidhis*:

- *Utpatti vidhi*, which lays down a command with a certain object, thereby creating a desire.
- *Viniyoga vidhi*, which lays the details of a sacrifice. There are two kinds of actions enjoyed by *viniyoga vidhi*:
  a. *Principle* – that which produces the transcendental effect called *apūrva*, which is an invisible result maturing in another life, and
  b. *Subordinate* – that which leads up to the completion of the principle action. These are called *aṅga* and are also of two types, *siddharūpa* and *kriyārūpa*. Of these, *siddharūpa* is the effect that is accomplished

by an action. It is visible. The action by which one effects this is called *kriyārūpa*. Among the actions that bring results, the primary is *pradhāna-karma*, and the secondary is called *guṇa-karma*.

- *Prayoga vidhi*, which is the injunction that lays down the order of performance of the subsidiary or minor parts of the ritual.

Thus, the *karma* of Mīmāṁsā falls under a special category of rituals, and it is not applied to any other kind of action.

According to the Vedānta philosophy, *karma* is equated with nescience or ignorance. Even good actions are not capable of bringing about realization. In the *Vivekacūḍāmaṇi* Śaṅkara says:

> Actions lead to purification of the mind, not to perception of Reality. The realization of Truth is brought about by philosophical discrimination and not in the least even by ten million actions.

According to Śaṅkara's *Brahmasūtra-Bhāṣya*, *karma* is that primordial cause of nescience from which follows the endless chain of cause and effect. Other connotations of *karma* in which they are commonly used include:

- Any action which implies an end and a means.
- The daily routines of life, such as waking up, ablutions, taking food, resting, sleeping, etc. called *nitya-karma*.
- The performance of one's duties enjoined by one's career or vocation. Any action that one is impelled to do by force of circumstance (like saving a man from drowning), called *naimittika-karma*.
- Accumulation of the causal potentials of action, which can cause good or bad experience in this life or the next if not erased by counter-acts of opposite potential. These are called *sañcita-karma*.
- The essence of the various actions that remain as part of the individuated life and cause a determined course of life, called *prārabdha-karma*.

As *karma* is used in such a vast range of various and variegated senses, it is taken up in this chapter and some of the subsequent ones for revaluation.

How does this help Arjuna?

In the second chapter Śrī Kṛṣṇa teaches Arjuna the merit of unitive reasoning and also points out to him the categorical imperativeness of action on the part of those who have in them the vestige of personal ego. He is asked to perform his duty. This appears to Arjuna like showing him both the superior and inferior paths of action, and then asking him to resort to the inferior one, which makes him both confused and annoyed.

Does Kṛṣṇa really contradict himself?

No, Kṛṣṇa knows Arjuna through and through. He wants him to conform to a pattern that is basically true to his own outgoing mind and active temperament. Kṛṣṇa replies:

- There are two kinds of discipline in this world, as declared in ancient times by Me, Oh Sinless One – the unitive way of wisdom (*jñāna-yoga*) of the Sāṁkhyas, and the unitive way of action (*karma-yoga*) of the *yogīs*.
- By refraining from initiating activities a person does not come to have the attainment of transcending action, nor can one by renunciation alone come to perfection.

That is a tricky way of answering. Do you notice that Kṛṣṇa avoids a straight answer and compares the merit of action to inaction when he was asked to compare action to meditative reasoning.

Kṛṣṇa plays no tricks here. He takes into account Arjuna's negativism and his attempt to take shelter in the passivity of renunciation. As a Guru, Kṛṣṇa speaks to Arjuna's immediate need, rather than engaging him in formal conversation. Realization comes as a result of removing the blemish of ignorance that shrouds the clear light of one's own Self (*ātman*). Action is generated by nature. The body, senses, and mind belong to nature. Arjuna does not seem to have recognized this distinction between nature and the spirit. Hence, Kṛṣṇa says:

> Not even for a single instant can one ever remain engaged in no action at all. By virtue of modalities (*guṇas*) born from nature, all are made to engage in action helplessly.

Our lower nature may prompt us to engage in many vicious actions. Should we allow them to have their natural course on the plea that the lower nature is different from our pure self?

Our body is like an instrument aided by the senses. These are operated by the mind. Mind is a general term used to indicate the interrogative or enquiring aspect, remembrance and recall, judgement, and evaluation in terms of values related to the ego factor. These fourfold functions of the mind are likely to be coloured by previous impressions left on the animating self. These impressions are the essence of whatever we experience, good or bad, painful or pleasure-giving. When any such essence of a previous experience influences the mind, it judges or wills according to the colouration of that impression. This essence of an impression is called *vāsanā*. If one knows that *vāsanā* causes a certain motivation, the very knowledge of the motivational cause will correct it. Mere brute suppression is not only unhelpful, it can be disastrous also. Kṛṣṇa says:

> He who sits controlling the organs of activity while ruminating mentally over items of sensuous interest – such a lost soul is said to be one of spurious conduct.
>
> He, on the other hand, who keeps the senses under control by means of the mind, and then commences unitive activity (*karma-yoga*) while still unattached – he excels.

True restraint or control comes from understanding the Self and the non-Self, and the possible errors of seeing the non-Self as Self. In the stimulus–response process, both the afferent and efferent mechanisms are activated or inhibited by a more deep-seated aspect of the mind where all latent impressions remain hidden. Control or restraint is to be first applied at the level of the latent impressions and not at the level of the organs of action or sense organs. When the Self knows itself, it is no longer difficult to see the real from the superimposed.

Does Kr̥ṣṇa speak here of action in its general sense, or does he include obligatory religious rituals also when he recommends action?

Although the word *karma* covers all activity, the attention is focused in verses 9 through 17 on sacrificial ritualism. However, action is taken in its most comprehensive sense in this chapter. Necessary action binds the whole of humanity. Free and contingent action should be distinguished from this general mass of human action taken as a whole. This is attempted in verse 9:

> Outside of activity with a sacrificial purpose, this world is bound by action. Even with such a purpose, do engage in work, Oh Arjuna! freed of all attachments.

All creative processes can be likened to a sacrifice. Something of worth is to be sacrificed to create something of greater value. The seed has to perish to give life to its sprout. The egg has to break to bring out its chicken. From the mighty stars to a biologic molecule, all are born at the cost and labour of something else. The cosmic world order is a grand scheme which provides for the spiral currents of the cosmic nebula cloud as well as the complex structuring of chromosomes and ribosomes. When we see how integrally we belong to that never-ending flux of creation and transformation, our own action falls in line with the rhythm of the cosmic becoming. A person with such conscious identity with the Absolute cannot any longer have selfish motivations. His action becomes a pure act like the radiation of a star, the wafting of a breeze, the showering of rain, or the blooming of a flower. Here the man of realization, as in a sacrifice, gives up everything of his own to the singular purpose of the fulfilment of the cosmic plan. It is this sacrifice that the Gītā recommends. Also, the Gītā develops the idea of action at three levels: the cosmologic, the psychologic, and the theologic.

What accounts for the inclusion of cosmology and theology when we are concerned here with something of psycho-physical import?

Three basic questions that have been haunting the mind of man from the dawn of reason are: From where did this world come? Who am I? and, How am I related to this world? Many have attempted to answer these questions either from the point of view of cosmology or of theology.

Those who tried to answer from the side of cosmology postulated a primordial substance evolving through a long process in such cosmic orders as the nebular, the stellar, and the solar systems. These systems, through sheer chance, gave rise to a planetary system in which, by some freak of nature, the planet Earth happened to have physical conditions that promoted on it the origin of life. After billions of years of evolution, life became more and more organized, finally becoming self-conscious, as is seen today in the *homo sapiens.* According to this postulation, man is an insignificant speck whose emergence or extinction is not going to affect the vast cosmos with its trillions of stars.

Theologians, on the other hand, tried to answer the above questions on the hypothesis of a benevolent creator. This is identified with the Supreme Being, who has a master plan of unfoldment in His mind. According to His own scheme, He creates or projects the world. This vast universe, according to theologians, is a living environment which God created out of his infinite mercy for man, whom He created in his own image. God gave man the facility of living a perfect life by his own choice and free will, or of defying His laws and perishing.

Cosmology and theology make sense to us only if we relate them to our own selves, by conceiving the same issues in terms of psychology. Therefore the disciplines of cosmology, theology, and psychology are related to each other. Kṛṣṇa, after having referred to the cosmologic binding of action, and to the individual action of the person as a pure act, now turns to the theologic concept:

> In anciet times, having created the peoples with sacrifice as pertaining to them (necessarily), Prajāpati said: "By this shall you grow and multiply; let this be you the milch-cow of all desires.
>
> With this do you gratify the gods, and the gods gratify you; thus gratifying reciprocally you shall reach to supreme merit.
>
> ṭhose gods shall bestow on you all the gratifications you desire; one who eats what is given by them without giving in turn to them – he is a theif indeed."
>
> The good man who eats of the remnants of a sacrifice is absolved of all

> faults; however, those sinners eat of evil (itself) who cook with themselves (alone) for motive.
>
> Food is the cause of beings, and from rain food is produced; sacrifice has its effect in rain, and sacrifice has its origin in action.
>
> Know that action arises from Brahmā and that Brahmā traces his being to the Imperishable. Therefore the all-pervasive Absolute is eternally bound up with sacrifice.
>
> He who leads a life hereunder that does not conform to the rotation of such a wheel – such a man of vicious lifetime lives, Oh Pārtha, in vain (indeed).

Does this mean that no man can escape these three types of action – natural, socio-religious, and personal?

Not so. One who has realized and is emancipated is not obliged to engage in any action. Kṛṣṇa says:

> But for him who happens to be attached to the Self alone, who finds full satisfaction in the Self – for such a man who is happy in the Self as such, too, there is nothing that he should do.
>
> Neither is there anything indeed for him resulting from work done, nor anything from work omitted here, nor is there either for him any dependence in respect of anything derivable from any being whatsoever.

In that case, why should Arjuna not remain as a passive witness rather than engaging in the tragic action of homicide?

Arjuna does not find his fulfilment in his own Self. He is still in the realm of duality. He sees himself and his relatives in terms of one who kills and one who is to be killed. Hence, what is said above is not applicable to him. Kṛṣṇa's advice to Arjuna is as follows:

> Therefore always remaining detached, engage yourself in actions that are necessary; indeed, performing actions with detachment man attains to the Supreme.
>
> Janaka and such others reached perfection even performing acts. Again, having due regard for the integration of the world too, you have to act.
>
> Whichever may be the way of life that a superior man adopts – that very one is by other people (followed). What he makes his guiding principle, the world too behaves even according to the same.

After making the categorical assertion that only through unitive reasoning can one reach perfection, how could Kṛṣṇa now say that Janaka reached perfection by performing acts? That sounds contradictory.

Kṛṣṇa does not say that Janaka attained perfection through action. All that he means is that action is not opposed to the pursuit of wisdom. Here action is regarded from a different angle; action that is not opposed to wisdom, and that clearly shows itself to be an expression of wisdom, sets a good example for others. The ideal of a wise man who has transcended the need for action may set a wrong example for an unwise man to become lazy, and in that way the wise man's example of non-action may cramp the dynamics of the society. The king-seer Janaka is cited as an instance of a wise man who continued to act as if bound to normal or necessary duties. It is optional for such a person to adhere to a programme of action. Such adherence is always to be permissively understood. Janaka's wisdom did not suffer even a bit because of his adherence to the duties of a king; that is why he is mentioned.

But wherein does karma-yoga *come here?*

Kṛṣṇa, representing the Absolute as the spiritual core of all beings, equates his will with the activating Self in all and shows how the whole world would come to a standstill and fall to pieces if the central Will that operates behind all suspended itself. Realization is the identity of the individual or relative self with the Absolute or Universal Self. Such being the case, every action provides for an opportunity to link oneself with the Absolute consciously and by habitual choice. That changes the status of individual action to the unitive way of action – *karma-yoga*.

Do you think we can change our basic nature?

We are a blend of two aspects of nature: one is categorical, which we share with all other living organisms as the *elan vital*, and the other is an acquisition built up in the form of character or second nature, very similar to "Pavlovian conditioning". The former exerts itself as a steady pressure of life against which we have little or no control, and the system becomes deranged if this natural function is mechanically stifled. The latter category is value oriented. Evil or negative tendencies generated by lower nature are motivated by false or irregularly conditioned value senses. When corrected with wisdom, its motive counterpart also undergoes correction automatically. This is the same as deconditioning a wrong stimulus.

Does this mean that everyone has to adhere to their true nature?

In our own age we seek educational, vocational, and marital guidance. This is based on the need to conform to our own individual basic nature. Here, Kṛṣṇa gives one of the most fundamental guidances in spiritual life:

> Better is activity rightly conforming to one's own nature, though lacking in superior quality, than activity foreign to one's own nature, although it may be well done (otherwise). (Even) death by the performance of what fits one properly has merit. Activity foreign to oneself is fraught with danger.

Could we equate svadharma *to one's suitable vocation?*

Svadharma here refers to the whole of life. It should not be just considered partially as preference for a certain vocation.

In spite of our not wanting to indulge in sin, what impels a person to lead a life against his own will?

To the same question asked by Arjuna, Kṛṣṇa replies:

> Such is desire, such is anger, born out of the modality (*guṇa*) called *rajas* (the active-affective), all-devouring, all-vitiating; know this to be the enemy here.
>
> As smoke shrouds fire, as a mirror (is beclouded) by dirt, as the foetus is enclosed in the amnion, likewise by such is This surrounded.
>
> Wisdom is enveloped by this which is the eternal enemy of the wise, remaining in the form of desire, Oh Kaunteya! which is a fire that is difficult to satiate.
>
> This is said to be lodged in the senses, mind, and reason. By means of these, this (desire) bewilders the embodied One by veiling his wisdom.
>
> Therefore, Oh best of Bhāratas! mastering first the senses, slay this which is of sin, which can destroy both pure and practical wisdom.
>
> It is taught that the senses are beyond; beyond the senses is the mind, beyond the mind is reason, and beyond reason is He.
>
> Thus knowing Him to be beyond reason, immobilizing the Self by the Self, Oh mighty-Armed! kill that enemy in the form of desire, (so) difficult to encounter.

IV

Jñāna-Yoga

Unitive Wisdom

INTRODUCTION

IN THIS chapter Kṛṣṇa openly declares that his one purpose is to restore the secret of *yoga*. But the initial claim he makes may sound strange to those who are not familiar with Indian mythology and symbolism and the archaic literary style of the Gītā. Kṛṣṇa says:

> This perennial unitive wisdom (*yoga*) did I declare to Vivasvān, Vivasvān taught it to Manu, and Manu told it to Ikṣvāku. Thus handed down the line in succession, this (wisdom) the king-sages (*rāja-ṛsis*) understood; by great lapse of time here (however) this unitive wisdom (*yoga*) came to be lost, Oh Paraṁtapa. That very same ancient secret is being today declared to you by me, seeing that you are both my devotee and friend.

A number of questions arise from this. Arjuna himself raises those doubts, so we need not discuss them here. In this statement mythology intertwines with reason, and the serialization of Vivasvata, Manu, Ikṣvāku, and the *rāja-ṛṣis* is not clear. It will be helpful to know the mythological and symbolic relevancy of these names. According to the Hindu mythology, Vivasvata (Vivasvān), is Āditya (sun). The word *vivasvat* means "fire", "shining forth", "diffusing light", and the "brilliant one". His wife was Saṁjñā, daughter of the Divine Architect Viśvakarmā, and by her he had three children, Manu Vaivasvata, Yama, and the Goddess Yamī. From Manu begins the human race. Manu's son was Ikṣvāku, the founder of the Solar dynasty. Vivasvata has several names, such as Savitṛ (nourisher), Vivasvat (brilliant), Bhāskara (giver of light), Dinakara (maker of the day), Sarvasākṣin (all-witnessing eye), Lokacakṣu (eye of the world), Karmasākṣin (witness of the deeds), Sahasrakiraṇa (having a thousand rays), Sūrya (sun) and more.

Physically the life on earth is causally related to solar energy. Imparting *yoga* to the sun only means that the harmony of life and its bipolar participation with the Absolute was engendered in the very first cause of life on earth. The cosmos itself is shown here as the primal ground of *yoga*. The second stage marks the link between the divine and the human. Manu is of divine origin, becoming the progenitor of the human race and imparting to his human successor the eternal law of the cosmic, social, and psychological order. At this level the natural law of the universe and its innate harmony are consciously felt, visualized, and lived by free choice. At the third stage it becomes an incorporated way of life and discipline taught and implemented by royal sages or philosopher kings. This divinely instituted course of harmonious living, or *yoga*, lost its way in the dreary desert of degeneration in the course of time. Kṛṣṇa wants to revalue and restate the same *yoga* which has its origin in him as the Absolute.

TRANSLATION

श्रीभगवानुवाच –

1. इमं विवस्वते योगं प्रोक्तवानहमव्ययम् ।
विवस्वान्मनवे प्राह मनुरिक्ष्वाकवेऽब्रवीत् ॥

śrībhagavān uvāca –

imaṁ vivasvate yogaṁ proktavān aham avyayam ।
vivasvān manave prāha manur ikṣvākave 'bravīt ॥

śrībhagavān uvāca: Kṛṣṇa said; *imaṁ avyayam*: this perennial; *yogaṁ*: unitive wisdom; *aham proktavān*: I declared; *vivasvate*: to Vivasvān (sun); *vivasvān prāha*: Vivasvān taught (it); *manave*: to Manu (law-giver); *manuḥ abravīt*: Manu told (it); *ikṣvākave*: to Ikṣvāku (first king of the Solar race).

Kṛṣṇa said:

This perennial unitive wisdom did I declare to Vivasvān, Vivasvān taught it to Manu, and Manu told it to Ikṣvāku.

2. एवं परम्पराप्राप्तमिमं राजर्षयो विदुः ।
स कालेनेह महता योगो नष्टः परन्तप ॥

evaṁ paraṁparāprāptam imaṁ rājarṣayo viduḥ ।
sa kālene 'ha mahatā yogo naṣṭaḥ paraṁtapa ॥

evaṁ: thus; *prātam paraṁparā*: handed down the line in succession; *imaṁ*: this (wisdom); *rāja ṛṣayaḥ*: the king-sages; *viduḥ*: understood; *mahatā kālena iha*: by great lapse of time here (however); *saḥ yogaḥ*: this unitive wisdom; *naṣṭaḥ*: came to be lost; *paraṁtapa*: Oh Arjuna.

Thus handed down the line in succession, this (wisdom) the king-sages understood; by great lapse of time here (however) this unitive wisdom came to be lost, Oh Paraṁtapa!

3. स एवायं मया तेऽद्य योगः प्रोक्तः पुरातनः ।
भक्तोऽसि मे सखा चेति रहस्यं ह्येतदुत्तमम् ॥

sa evā 'yaṁ mayā te 'dya yogaḥ proktaḥ purātanaḥ ।
bhakto 'si me sakhā ce 'ti rahasyaṁ hy etad uttamam ॥

saḥ eva ayaṁ: that very same; *purātanaḥ*: ancient; *uttamam*: supreme; *rahasyaṁ*: secret; *yogaḥ*: yoga; *adya proktaḥ*: today is being declared; *te*: to you; *mayā*: by me; *iti hi*: since; *asi*: you are; *me bhaktaḥ ca sakhā*: (both) my devotee and friend.

That very same ancient secret is being today declared to you by me, seeing that you are both my devotee and friend.

अर्जुन उवाच –

4. अपरं भवतो जन्म परं जन्म विवस्वतः ।
कथमेतद्विजानीयां त्वमादौ प्रोक्तवानिति ॥

arjuna uvāca –

aparaṁ bhavato janma paraṁ janma vivasvataḥ ।
katham etad vijānīyāṁ tvam ādau proktavān iti ॥

arjuna uvāca: Arjuna said; *bhavataḥ janma*: your birth; *aparaṁ*: (was) posterior; *janma*: (and) the birth; *vivasvataḥ*: of Vivasvān; *paraṁ*: (was) anterior; *katham iti*: how then; *vijānīyāṁ*: have I to understand (it); *tvam*: (that) you; *proktavān etat*: declared it; *ādau*: in the beginning.

Arjuna said:

Your birth was posterior and the birth of Vivasvān was anterior; how then have I to understand it that you declared it in the beginning?

श्रीभगवानुवाच –

5. बहूनि मे व्यतीतानि जन्मानि तव चार्जुन ।
तान्यहं वेद सर्वाणि न त्वं वेत्थ परन्तप ॥

śrībhagavān uvāca –

bahūni me vyatītāni janmāni tava cā 'rjuna ।
tāny ahaṁ veda sarvāṇi na tvaṁ vettha paraṁtapa ॥

śrī bhagavān uvāca: Kṛṣṇa said; *bahūni janmāni*: many (are) the lives; *vyatītāni*: that have gone past; *me*: for me; *ca tava*: as also for you; *arjuna*: Oh Arjuna; *ahaṁ veda*: I am conscious; *tāni sarvāṇi*: of them all; *tvaṁ paraṁtapa*: you, Oh Arjuna; *na vettha*: are not conscious (of them).

Kṛṣṇa said:

Many are the lives that have gone past for me, as also for you, Oh Arjuna; I am conscious of them all; you, Oh Paraṁtapa! are not conscious of them.

6. अजोऽपि सन्नव्ययात्मा भूतानामीश्वरोऽपि सन् ।
प्रकृतिं स्वामधिष्ठाय सम्भवाम्यात्ममायया ॥

ajo 'pi sann avyayātmā bhūtānām īśvaro 'pi san ।
prakṛtiṁ svām adhiṣṭhāya saṁbhavāmy ātmamāyayā ॥

api san ajaḥ: although being (ever) unborn; *avyaya ātmā*: (as) the never-diminishing Self; *san api*: (while) I am also; *īśvaraḥ bhūtānām*: the Lord of creation; *adhiṣṭhāya*: grounded on; *svām prakṛtiṁ*: my own nature; *saṁbhavāmi*: I assume being; *ātmamāyayā*: through the negative principle (*māyā*) of my own Self.

Although I remain ever unborn as the never-diminishing Self, while I am the Lord of creation too, grounded on my own nature I assume being through the negative principle of my own Self.

7. यदा यदा हि धर्मस्य ग्लानिर्भवति भारत ।
अभ्युत्थानमधर्मस्य तदात्मानं सृजाम्यहम् ॥

yadā-yadā hi dharmasya glānir bhavati bhārata ।
abhyutthānam adharmasya tadā 'tmānaṁ sṛjāmy aham ॥

yadā yadā hi: whenever; *bhavati*: there comes to be; *glāniḥ*: laxity; *dharmasya*: in regard to right life; *bhārata*: Oh Arjuna; *adharmasya*: (and) wrong; *abhyutthānam*: coming to assert (itself); *tadā aham*: then I; *sṛjāmi*: bring about the creation; *ātmānaṁ*: of myself.

Whenever there comes to be laxity in regard to right life, Oh Bhārata! and wrong coming to assert itself, then I bring about the creation of myself.

8. परित्राणाय साधूनां विनाशाय च दुष्कृताम् ।
धर्मसंस्थापनार्थाय सम्भवामि युगे युगे ॥

paritrāṇāya sādhūnāṁ vināśāya ca duṣkṛtām ।
dharmasaṁsthāpanārthāya saṁbhavāmi yuge-yuge ॥

paritrāṇāya: to protect; *sādhūnāṁ*: those who are good; *ca vināśāya*: and to destroy; *duṣkṛtām*: evil-doers; *dharma saṁsthāpana arthāya*: for establishing righteousness; *saṁbhavāmi*: I assume being; *yuge yuge*: age by age.

To protect those who are good and to destroy evil-doers, for establishing righteousness, I assume being, age by age.

9. जन्म कर्म च मे दिव्यमेवं यो वेत्ति तत्त्वतः ।
त्यक्त्वा देहं पुनर्जन्म नैति मामेति सोऽर्जुन ।।

janma karma ca me divyam evaṁ yo vetti tattvataḥ ।
tyaktvā dehaṁ punarjanma nai 'ti mān eti so 'rjuna ॥

saḥ yaḥ evaṁ: he who thus; *vetti*: understands; *divyam*: (this) divine (nature); *me janma*: of my birth; *ca karma*: and work; *tattvataḥ*: (consistently) with basic principles; *tyaktvā*: on leaving; *dehaṁ*: (this) body; *na eti*: does not attain to; *punaḥ janma*: repeated birth; *eti*: (but only) comes; *mām*: to Me; *arjuna*: Oh Arjuna.

He who understands this divine nature of my birth and work consistently with basic principles, on leaving this body does not attain to repeated birth, but (only) comes to Me, Oh Arjuna!

10. वीतरागभयक्रोधा मन्मया मामुपाश्रिताः ।
बहवो ज्ञानतपसा पूता मद्भावमागताः ।।

vītarāgabhayakrodhā manmayā mām upāśritāḥ ।
bahavo jñānatapasā pūtā madbhāvam āgatāḥ ॥

vīta rāga bhaya krodhāḥ: rid of attachment, fear, (and) anger; *manmayā*: wholly filled by Me (alone); *upāśritāḥ mām*: (and) surrendering to Me; *bahavaḥ*: many; *pūtāḥ*: (who have been) purified; *jñāna tapasā*: by the discipline of wisdom; *āgatāḥ*: have entered into; *mad bhāvam*: My (very) being.

Rid of attachment, fear, and anger, wholly filled by Me alone, and surrendering to Me many who have been purified by the discipline of wisdom have entered into My (very) being.

11. ये यथा मां प्रपद्यन्ते तांस्तथैव भजाम्यहम् ।
मम वर्त्मानुवर्तन्ते मनुष्याः पार्थ सर्वशः ।।

ye yathā māṁ prapadyante tāṁs tathai 'va bhajāmy aham ।
mama vartmā 'nuvartante manuṣyāḥ pārtha sarvaśaḥ ॥

yathā ye: as each; *prapadyante māṁ*: chooses to approach Me; *eva tathā*: even accordingly; *aham bhajāmi*: I have regard; *tān*: for him; *mama*: My; *vartma*: (very) path (it is); *pārtha*: Oh Arjuna; *manuṣyāḥ*: (that) all men; *anuvartante*: do tread; *sarvaśaḥ*: from every (possible) approach.

As each chooses to approach Me, even accordingly do I have regard for him. My very path it is, Oh Pārtha, that all men do tread from every (possible) approach.

12. काङ्क्षन्तः कर्मणां सिद्धिं यजन्त इह देवताः ।
क्षिप्रं हि मानुषे लोके सिद्धिर्भवति कर्मजा ।।

kāṅkṣantaḥ karmaṇāṁ siddhiṁ yajanta iha devatāḥ ।
kṣipraṁ hi mānuṣe loke siddhir bhavati karmajā ॥

kāṅkṣantaḥ: desiring; *siddhiṁ*: the benefits; *karmaṇāṁ*: coming from actions; *iha yajante*: and thus sacrificing; *devatāḥ*: to the gods; *kṣipraṁ hi*: quick indeed; *bhavati siddhiḥ*: are the results; *karmajā*: born of works; *loke*: in this world; *mānuṣe*: of men.

Desiring the benefits coming from actions and thus sacrificing to the gods, quick indeed are the results born of works in this world of men.

13. चातुर्वर्ण्यं मया सृष्टं गुणकर्मविभागशः ।
तस्य कर्तारमपि मां विद्ध्यकर्तारमव्ययम् ।।

cāturvarṇyaṁ mayā sṛṣṭaṁ guṇakarmavibhāgaśaḥ ।
tasya kartāram api māṁ viddhy akartāram avyayam ॥

cāturvarṇyaṁ: the fourfold colour-grades (*varṇas*); *sṛṣṭaṁ mayā*: were created by myself; *guṇa karma vibhāgaśaḥ*: (on the basis of) innate disposition (*guṇa*) and vocation (*karma*) that accorded with each; *viddhi māṁ*: know Me (to be); *kartāram*: the maker; *tasya*: of such; *api*: as also (to be); *akartāram*: its undoer; *avyayam*: unexpended.

The fourfold colour-grades were created by myself on the basis of innate disposition and vocation that accorded with each; know Me to be the maker of such as also to be its undoer, unexpended.

14. न मां कर्माणि लिम्पन्ति न मे कर्मफले स्पृहा ।
इति मां योऽभिजानाति कर्मभिर्न स बध्यते ।।

na māṁ karmāṇi limpanti na me karmaphale spṛhā ।
iti māṁ yo 'bhijānāti karmabhir na sa badhyate ॥

karmāṇi: works; *na limpanti māṁ*: do not affect Me; *na me spṛhā*: nor (is there) for me (any) interest; *karmaphale*: in the benefit of works; *saḥ yaḥ*: he who; *abhijānāti māṁ*: understands Me; *iti*: in this manner; *na badhyate*: comes no more under the bondage; *karmabhiḥ*: of works.

I am not affected by works, nor have I any interest in the benefit of works; he who understands Me in this manner comes no more under the bondage of works.

15. एवं ज्ञात्वा कृतं कर्म पूर्वैरपि मुमुक्षुभिः ।
कुरु कर्मैव तस्मात्त्वं पूर्वैः पूर्वतरं कृतम् ।।

evaṁ jñātvā kṛtaṁ karma pūrvair api mumukṣubhiḥ ।
kuru karmai 'va tasmāt tvaṁ pūrvaiḥ pūrvataraṁ kṛtam ॥

karma kṛtaṁ pūrvaiḥ: work was performed by the ancients; *jñātvā evaṁ*: after knowing in this manner; *tasmāt*: therefore; *evā karma*: such work; *kuru tvaṁ api*: do you also; *kr̥tam pūrvaiḥ*: as was performed by the ancients; *mumukṣubhiḥ*: desiring emancipation; *pūrvataraṁ*: in times more ancient.

The ancients performed work after knowing in this manner, therefore, do that kind of work also, as was performed by the ancients, desiring emancipation, in times more ancient.

16. किं कर्म किमकर्मेति कवयोऽप्यत्र मोहिताः ।
तत्ते कर्म प्रवक्ष्यामि यज्ज्ञात्वा मोक्ष्यसेऽशुभात् ।।

kiṁ karma kim akarme 'ti kavayo 'py atra mohitāḥ ।
tat te karma pravakṣyāmi yaj jñātvā mokṣyase 'śubhāt ॥

kiṁ karma: what is action; *kim akarma*: what is inaction; *iti api kavayaḥ*: thus, even intelligent men; *atra mohitāḥ*: here are confused; *pravakṣyāmi te*: I shall indicate to you; *tat karma*: that action; *jñātvā yat*: on knowing which; *mokṣyase*: you will be emancipated; *aśubhāt*: from evil.

On what is action and what is inaction even intelligent men here are confused. I shall indicate to you that action on knowing which you will be emancipated from evil.

17. कर्मणो ह्यपि बोद्धव्यं बोद्धव्यं च विकर्मणः ।
अकर्मणश्च बोद्धव्यं गहना कर्मणो गतिः ।।

karmaṇo hy api boddhavyaṁ boddhavyaṁ ca vikarmaṇaḥ ।
akarmaṇaś ca boddhavyaṁ gahanā karmaṇo gatiḥ ॥

boddhavyaṁ karmaṇaḥ hi: one has to understand about action, indeed; *ca boddhavyaṁ api*: and understand also; *vikarmaṇaḥ*: about wrong action; *ca*: again; *boddhavyaṁ*: one has to have a proper notion; *akarmaṇaḥ*: of non-action; *gatiḥ karmaṇaḥ*: the way of action; *gahanā*: (is) elusively subtle (indeed).

One has to understand about action and understand also what is wrong action; again, one has to have a proper notion of non-action; the way of action is elusively subtle (indeed).

18. कर्मण्यकर्म यः पश्येदकर्मणि च कर्म यः ।
स बुद्धिमान्मनुष्येषु स युक्तः कृत्स्नकर्मकृत् ।।

karmaṇy akarma yah paśyed akarmaṇi ca karma yaḥ ।
sa buddhimān manuṣyeṣu sa yuktaḥ kr̥tsnakarmakr̥t ॥

yaḥ paśyet: one who is able to see; *karma*: action; *akarmaṇi*: in inaction; *ca yaḥ*: and one who (sees); *akarma karmaṇi*: inaction in action; *ṣaḥ manuṣyeṣu*: he among men; *buddhimān*: (is) intelligent; *saḥ yuktaḥ*: he (is) one of unitive attitude (a *yogī*); *kṛtsna karmakṛt*: (while still) engaged in every (possible) kind of work.

One who is able to see action in inaction and inaction in action – he among men is intelligent; he is one of unitive attitude, while still engaged in every (possible) kind of work.

19. यस्य सर्वे समारम्भाः कामसङ्कल्पवर्जिताः ।
ज्ञानाग्निदग्धकर्माणं तमाहुः पण्डितं बुधाः ॥

yasya sarve samārambhāḥ kāmasaṅkalpavarjitāḥ ।
jñānāgnidagdhakarmāṇaṁ tam āhuḥ paṇḍitaṁ budhāḥ ॥

yasya: (that man) whose; *samārambhāḥ*: works; *sarve*: (are) all; *varjitāḥ kāma saṅkalpa*: devoid of desire and wilful motive; *jñāna agni dagdha karmāṇaṁ*: whose (impulse of) action has been reduced to nothing in the fire of wisdom; *tam āhuḥ*: he is recognized as; *paṇḍitaṁ*: a knowing person (*paṇḍit*); *budhāḥ*: by the wise.

That man whose works are all devoid of desire and wilful motive, whose (impulse of) action has been reduced to nothing in the fire of wisdom – he is recognized as a knowing person by the wise.

20. त्यक्त्वा कर्मफलासङ्गं नित्यतृप्तो निराश्रयः ।
कर्मण्यभिप्रवृत्तोऽपि नैव किञ्चित्करोति सः ॥

tyaktvā karmaphalāsaṅgaṁ nityatṛpto nirāśrayaḥ ।
karmaṇy abhipravṛtto 'pi nai 'va kiñcit karoti saḥ ॥

tyaktvā: relinquishing; *karma phala āsaṅgaṁ*: attachment for the benefit of works; *nitya tṛptaḥ*: ever happy; *nirāśrayaḥ*: (and) independent; *api abhipravṛttaḥ*: though engaged; *karmaṇi*: in work; *saḥ karoti*: he (in principle) does; *na kiñcit*: nothing; *eva*: at all.

Relinquishing attachment for the benefit of works, ever happy and independent, though such a man be engaged in work, he (in principle) does nothing at all.

21. निराशीर्यतचित्तात्मा त्यक्तसर्वपरिग्रहः ।
शारीरं केवलं कर्म कुर्वन्नाप्नोति किल्बिषम् ॥

nirāśīr yatacittātmā tyaktasarvaparigrahaḥ ।
śārīraṁ kevalaṁ karma kurvan nā 'pnoti kilbiṣam ॥

nirāśīḥ: (one) free of all expectancy; *yata citta ātmā*: (and) of subjugated (relational) self-consciousness; *tyakta sarva parigrahaḥ*: (who has) given up all possessiveness; *kurvan*: (and) is engaged; *kevalaṁ śārīraṁ*:

merely bodily (automatically); *karma*: (in) actions; *na āpnoti*: (he) does not acquire; *kilbiṣam*: evil.

One free of all expectancy and of subjugated relational self-consciousness, who has given up all possessiveness, and is engaged merely bodily in actions – he does not acquire evil.

22. यदृच्छालाभसंतुष्टो द्वन्द्वातीतो विमत्सरः ।
समः सिद्धावसिद्धौ च कृत्वापि न निबध्यते ।।

yadṛcchālābhasaṁtuṣṭo dvandvātīto vimatsaraḥ ।
samaḥ siddhāv asiddhau ca kṛtvā 'pi na nibadhyate ॥

yadṛcchā lābha saṁtuṣṭaḥ: satisfied (with) chance gain; *dvandva atītaḥ*: (by) conflicting pairs (of interests) unaffected; *vimatsaraḥ*: non-competitive; *samaḥ*: remaining the same; *siddhāu asiddhau*: in gain or no gain; *na nibadhyate*: (he) is not bound; *api ca*: in spite of; *kṛtvā*: having been active.

Satisfied with chance gains, unaffected by conflicting pairs (of interests), non-competitive, remaining the same in gain or no gain, he remains unbound in spite of having been active.

23. गतसङ्गस्य मुक्तस्य ज्ञानावस्थितचेतसः ।
यज्ञायाचरतः कर्म समग्रं प्रविलीयते ।।

gatasaṅgasya muktasya jñānāvasthitacetasaḥ ।
yajñāyā 'carataḥ karma samagraṁ pravilīyate ॥

gata saṅgasya: (in the case) of one whose attachments are gone; *muktasya*: who has gained freedom; *jñāna avasthita cetasaḥ*: whose spiritual being has been founded on wisdom; *karma yajñāya ācarataḥ*: (his) works, having a sacrificial character (only); *samagraṁ pravilīyate*: became wholly dissolved.

In the case of one whose attachments are gone, who has gained freedom, whose spiritual being has been founded on wisdom, his works, having a sacrificial character only, become wholly dissolved.

24. ब्रह्मार्पणं ब्रह्म हविर्ब्रह्माग्नौ ब्रह्मणा हुतम् ।
ब्रह्मैव तेन गन्तव्यं ब्रह्मकर्मसमाधिना ।।

brahmā 'rpaṇaṁ brahma havir brahmāgnau brahmaṇā hutam ।
brahmai 'va tena gantavyaṁ brahmakarmasamādhinā ॥

brahma: (for him) the Absolute; *arpaṇaṁ*: (is) the act of offering; *brahma haviḥ*: the Absolute (is) the substance offered; *brahma agnau*: into the fire of the Absolute; *hutam brahmaṇā*: offered by (him), the Absolute;

gantavyaṁ tena: the end to be reached by him; *eva brahma*: (being) even the Absolute; *brahma karma samādhinā*: by the supreme peace of absolutist action.

(For him) the Absolute is the act of offering, the Absolute is the substance offered into the Absolute which is the fire, offered by (him), the Absolute, the end to be reached by him being even the Absolute, by means of his peace supreme of absolutist action.

25. दैवमेवापरे यज्ञं योगिनः पर्युपासते ।
ब्रह्माग्नावपरे यज्ञं यज्ञेनैवोपजुह्वति ।।

daivam evā 'pare yajñaṁ yoginaḥ paryupāsate ।
brahmāgnāv apare yajñaṁ yajñenai 'vo 'pajuhvati ॥

daivam: (as referring) to the gods (of the Vedas); *apare yoginaḥ*: some *yogīs* (men of unitive discipline); *eva paryupāsate yajñaṁ*: indeed practise sacrifice; *apare*: others; *upajuhvati yajñaṁ*: offer sacrifice; *brahma agnau*: into the fire of the Absolute; *yajñena eva*: by sacrifice itself.

As referring to the gods (of the Vedas) is (the nature of) the sacrifice of some *yogīs*; others offer sacrifice into the fire of the Absolute by sacrifice itself.

26. श्रोत्रादीनीन्द्रियाण्यन्ये संयमाग्निषु जुह्वति ।
शब्दादीन्विषयानन्य इन्द्रियाग्निषु जुह्वति ।।

śrotrādīnī 'ndriyāṇy anye saṁyamāgniṣu juhvati ।
śabdādīn viṣayān anya indriyāgniṣu juhvati ॥

anye juhvati: others offer (as sacrifice); *śrotra ādīni indriyāṇi*: the ear and other such sense organs; *saṁyama agniṣu*: into the fire of restraint; *anye juhvati*: others offer (the sacrifice); *śabda ādīn viṣayān*: of sound and other sense interests; *indriya agniṣu*: into the fire of the senses.

Some offer as sacrifice the ear and other such sense organs into the fire of restraint; others offer the sacrifice of sound and other sense interests into the fire of the senses.

27. सर्वाणीन्द्रियकर्माणि प्राणकर्माणि चापरे ।
आत्मसंयमयोगाग्नौ जुह्वति ज्ञानदीपिते ।।

sarvāṇī 'ndriyakarmāṇi prāṇakarmāṇi cā 'pare ।
ātmasaṁyamayogāgnau juhvati jñānadīpite ॥

sarvāṇī: all; *indriya karmāṇi*: the functions of the senses; *ca prāṇa karmāṇi*: as also the vital functions; *apare juhvati*: others offer; *ātmasaṁyama yogāgnau*: into the fire of unitive discipline (*yoga*), consisting of self-restraint; *jñāna dīpite*: kindled by knowledge.

All the functions of the senses as also the vital functions, others make as an offering into the fire of unitive discipline, consisting of self-restraint.

28. द्रव्ययज्ञास्तपोयज्ञा योगयज्ञास्तथापरे ।
स्वाध्यायज्ञानयज्ञाश्च यतयः संशितव्रताः ।।

dravyayajñās tapoyajñā yogayajñās tathā 'pare ।
svādhyāyajñānayajñāś ca yatayaḥ saṁśitavratāḥ ॥

tathā apare: likewise, (there are) others; *dravya yajñāḥ*: of object-sacrifice; *tapaḥ yajñāḥ*: those of austerity-sacrifice; *yoga yajñāḥ*: those who sacrifice unitive discipline; *ca*: and; *svādhyāya jñāna yajñaḥ*: those of self-study and wisdom-sacrifice; *yatayaḥ*: (who are all) men of self-control; *saṁśita vratāḥ*: (and) fully accomplished vows.

Likewise there are others of object-sacrifice, those of austerity-sacrifice, those who sacrifice unitive discipline, and those of self-study and wisdom-sacrifice, who are (all) men of self-control and fully accomplished vows.

29. अपाने जुह्वति प्राणं प्राणेऽपानं तथापरे ।
प्राणापानगती रुद्ध्वा प्राणायामपरायणाः ।।

apāne juhvati prāṇaṁ prāṇe 'pānaṁ tathā 'pare ।
prāṇāpānagatī ruddhvā prāṇāyāmaparāyaṇāḥ ॥

apāne: into the downward (inward) vital tendency; *apare juhvati*: others sacrifice; *prāṇaṁ*: the upward (outward) one; *prāṇe*: (and) in the outward one; *apānaṁ*: the inward (likewise); *tathā*: thus; *ruddhvā prāṇa apāna gati*: countering the outward and inward tendencies; *prāṇāyāma parāyaṇāḥ*: (they remain) intent upon vital breath control.

Into the downward (inward) vital tendency others sacrifice the upward (outward) one and in the outward one the inward likewise; thus countering the tendencies, they remain ever as those (who resort to the way) of vital breath control.

30. अपरे नियताहाराः प्राणान्प्राणेषु जुह्वति ।
सर्वेऽप्येते यज्ञविदो यज्ञक्षपितकल्मषाः ।।

apare niyatāhārāḥ prāṇān prāṇeṣu juhvati ।
sarve 'py ete yajñavido yajñakṣapitakalmaṣāḥ ॥

apare: others; *niyatāhārāḥ*: abstemious in food; *juhvati*: make an offering of; *prāṇān*: vital breaths; *prāṇeṣu*: into vital breaths; *sarve ete api*: all these also (are); *yajñavidaḥ*: connoisseurs of sacrifice; *yajña kṣapita kalmaṣāḥ*: who have got rid of evil through sacrifice.

Others, abstemious in food, make an offering of vital breaths into vital breaths. All these are connoisseurs of sacrifice who have gotten rid of evil through sacrifice.

31. यज्ञशिष्टामृतभुजो यान्ति ब्रह्म सनातनम् ।
नायं लोकोऽस्त्ययज्ञस्य कुतोऽन्यः कुरुसत्तम ।।

yajñaśiṣṭāmṛtabhujo yānti brahma sanātanam ।
nā 'yaṁ loko 'sty ayajñasya kuto 'nyaḥ kurusattama ॥

yajñaśiṣṭa amṛta bhujaḥ: those who partake of the immortal nectar of sacrificial remains; *yānti*: go to; *sanātanam brahma*: the eternal Absolute; *ayaṁ lokaḥ*: this world; *asti na*: is not; *ayajñasya*: for one of no sacrifice; *kutaḥ*: how (can he have); *anyaḥ*: the next; *kuru sattama*: Oh Arjuna.

Those who partake of the immortal nectar of sacrificial remains go to the eternal Absolute. This world is not for one of no sacrifice. How can he have the next, Oh Best of Kurus?

32. एवं बहुविधा यज्ञा वितता ब्रह्मणो मुखे ।
कर्मजान्विद्धि तान्सर्वानेवं ज्ञात्वा विमोक्ष्यसे ।।

evaṁ bahuvidhā yajñā vitatā brahmaṇo mukhe ।
karmajān viddhi tān sarvān evaṁ jñātvā vimokṣyase ॥

evaṁ bahuvidhāḥ: thus, many and varied; *yajñāḥ*: (are) the sacrifices; *vitatāḥ mukhe*: spread in front; *brahmaṇaḥ*: of the Absolute; *viddhi tān sarvān*: know them all; *karmajān*: (as) originating in action; *evaṁ jñātvā*: thus understanding (them); *vimokṣyase*: you shall gain release.

Thus, many and varied are the sacrifices spread in front of the Absolute. Know them all as originating in action. Thus understanding them, you shall gain release.

33. श्रेयान्द्रव्यमयाद्यज्ञाज्ज्ञानयज्ञः परन्तप ।
सर्वं कर्माखिलं पार्थ ज्ञाने परिसमाप्यते ।।

śreyān dravyamayād yajñāj jñānayajñaḥ paraṁtapa ।
sarvaṁ karmā 'khilaṁ pārtha jñāne parisamāpyate ॥

śreyān yajñāt: superior to (any) sacrifice; *dravyamayāt*: with (valuable) objects; *jñāna yajñaḥ*: (is) the wisdom sacrifice; *paraṁtapa*: Oh Arjuna; *sarvaṁ karma akhilaṁ*: all actions without exception; *pārtha*: Oh Arjuna; *parisamāpyate*: have their culmination; *jñāne*: in wisdom.

Superior to any sacrifice with (valuable) objects is the wisdom-sacrifice, Oh Paraṁtapa; all actions, Oh Pārtha, have their culmination in wisdom.

34. तद्विद्धि प्रणिपातेन परिप्रश्नेन सेवया ।
उपदेक्ष्यन्ति ते ज्ञानं ज्ञानिनस्तत्त्वदर्शिनः ॥

tad viddhi praṇipātena paripraśnena sevayā ।
upadekṣyanti te jñānaṁ jñāninas tattvadarśinaḥ ॥

viddhi tat: learn this; *praṇipātena*: by prostration; *paripraśnena*: by searching questioning; *sevayā*: (and) by service; *upadekṣyanti te*: they will instruct you (duly); *jñānaṁ*: (in) wisdom; *jñāninaḥ*: those wise men; *tattva darśinaḥ*: who can see the basic principles.

Learn this by prostration, by searching questioning, and by service; they will instruct you (duly) in wisdom – those wise men who can see the basic principles.

35. यज्ज्ञात्वा न पुनर्मोहमेवं यास्यसि पाण्डव ।
येन भूतान्यशेषेण द्रक्ष्यस्यात्मन्यथो मयि ॥

yaj jñātvā na punar moham evaṁ yāsyasi pāṇḍava ।
yena bhūtāny aśeṣeṇa drakṣyasy ātmany atho mayi ॥

yat jñātvā: which having known; *pāṇḍava*: Oh Arjuna; *na yāsyasi*: you will not give way to; *moham*: delusion; *evaṁ punaḥ*: thus any more; *yena*: by this; *bhūtāny aśeṣeṇa*: (all) beings without exception; *drakṣyasi*: will be seen by you; *ātmani*: in the Self; *atho mayi*: and thus in Me.

Having known this, Oh Pāṇḍava, you will not give way to delusion thus any more; by this all beings without exception will be seen by you in the Self and thus in Me.

36. अपि चेदसि पापेभ्यः सर्वेभ्यः पापकृत्तमः ।
सर्वं ज्ञानप्लवेनैव वृजिनं सन्तरिष्यसि ॥

api ced asi pāpebhyaḥ sarvebhyaḥ pāpakṛttamaḥ ।
sarvaṁ jñānaplavenai 'va vṛjinaṁ saṁtariṣyasi ॥

api cet asi: even if you are; *sarvebhyaḥ pāpebhyaḥ*: among all evil-doers; *pāpakṛttamaḥ*: the most evil-doing (man); *jñāna plavena eva*: by the very raft of wisdom; *saṁtariṣyasi*: you will be able to cross over; *sarvaṁ vṛjinaṁ*: all sin.

Even if you should happen to be among evil-doers the most evil-doing man, by the very raft of wisdom you will be able to cross over all sin.

37. यथैधांसि समिद्धोऽग्निर्भस्मसात्कुरुतेऽर्जुन ।
ज्ञानाग्निः सर्वकर्माणि भस्मसात्कुरुते तथा ॥

yathai 'dhāṁsi samiddho 'gnir bhasmasāt kurute 'rjuna ।
jñānāgniḥ sarvakarmāṇi bhasmasāt kurute tathā ॥

yathā agniḥ: just as fire; *samiddhaḥ*: when kindled; *kurute bhasmasāt*: reduces to ashes; *edhāṁsi*: the fuel; *arjuna*: Oh Arjuna; *tathā jñāna agniḥ*: so the fire of wisdom; *kurute bhasmasāt*: reduces to ashes; *sarvakarmāṇi*: all works.

Just as fire when kindled reduces to ashes the fuel, Oh Arjuna! likewise the fire of wisdom reduces all works to ashes.

38. न हि ज्ञानेन सदृशं पवित्रमिह विद्यते ।
तत्स्वयं योगसंसिद्धः कालेनात्मनि विन्दति ।।

na hi jñānena sadṛśaṁ pavitram iha vidyate ।
tat svayaṁ yogasaṁsiddhaḥ kālenā 'tmani vindati ॥

na hi: there is nothing indeed; *iha vidyate*: here exists; *sadṛśaṁ pavitram*: equal in purity; *jñānena*: to wisdom; *tat*: that; *yoga saṁsiddhaḥ*: the man of perfection through unitive discipline; *svayaṁ vindati*: himself discovers; *ātmani*: in himself; *kālena*: in time.

There is nothing indeed here so purificatory as wisdom, which same the man of perfection through unitive discipline discovers in himself in due course.

39. श्रद्धावाँल्लभते ज्ञानं तत्परः संयतेन्द्रियः ।
ज्ञानं लब्ध्वा परां शान्तिमचिरेणाधिगच्छति ।।

śraddāvāṁl labhate jñānaṁ tatparaḥ saṁyatendriyaḥ ।
jñānaṁ labdhvā parāṁ śāntim acireṇā 'dhigacchati ॥

śraddhāvān: a man of faith; *labhate jñānaṁ*: comes to wisdom; *tat paraḥ*: (having) That (the Absolute) as highest; *saṁyata indriyaḥ*: (with) the senses subjugated; *labdhvā jñānaṁ*: on obtaining wisdom; *adhigacchati acireṇa*: he reaches without delay; *parāṁ śāntim*: (the state of) supreme peace.

A man of faith comes to wisdom being intent on That, with the senses subjugated. On obtaining wisdom he reaches without delay (the state of) supreme peace.

40. अज्ञश्चाश्रद्दधानश्च संशयात्मा विनश्यति ।
नायं लोकोऽस्ति न परो न सुखं संशयात्मनः ।।

ajñaś cā 'śraddadhānaś ca saṁśayātmā vinaśyati ।
nā 'yaṁ loko 'sti na paro na sukhaṁ saṁśayātmanaḥ ॥

ajñaḥ: he who is unwise; *aśraddadhānaḥ ca*: and the man without faith; *ca saṁśayātmā*: and with the Self held in (the conflict of) doubt; *vinaśyati*: is destroyed; *na asti*: neither is there; *ayaṁ lokaḥ*: this world; *na paraḥ*: nor (the world) beyond; *na*: nor (can there be); *sukhaṁ*: (any) happiness; *saṁśayātmanaḥ*: for a man (caught) in doubt.

The man who is unwise and without faith, with the Self held in (the conflict of) doubt, is destroyed; neither is there this world, nor the world beyond, nor can there be any happiness for a man (caught) in doubt.

41. योगसन्न्यस्तकर्माणं ज्ञानसञ्छिन्नसंशयम् ।
आत्मवन्तं न कर्माणि निबध्नन्ति धनञ्जय ।।

yogasaṁnyastakarmāṇaṁ jñānasañchinnasaṁśayam ।
ātmavantaṁ na karmāṇi nibadhnanti dhanañjaya ॥

yoga saṁnyasta karmāṇaṁ: one of unitively-renounced action; *jñāna sañchinna saṁśayam*: who by wisdom has sundered doubt; *ātmavantaṁ*: who is fully self-possessed; *karmāṇi*: works; *na nibadhnanti*: cannot bind; *dhanañjaya*: Oh Arjuna.

One of unitively-renounced action, who by wisdom has sundered doubt and come to full self-possession, cannot be bound by works, Oh Dhanañjaya!

42. तस्मादज्ञानसम्भूतं हृत्स्थं ज्ञानासिनात्मनः ।
छित्त्वैनं संशयं योगमातिष्ठोत्तिष्ठ भारत ।।

tasmād ajñānasaṁbhūtaṁ hr̥tsthaṁ jñānāsinā 'tmanaḥ ।
chittvai 'naṁ saṁśayaṁ yogam ātiṣṭho 'ttiṣṭha bhārata ॥

tasmāt chittvā: therefore, sundering; *jñāna asinā ātmanaḥ*: with the sword of Self-knowledge; *enaṁ*: this; *ajñāna saṁbhūtaṁ saṁśayaṁ*: ignorance-born doubt; *hr̥tsthaṁ*: residing in the heart; *ātiṣṭha yogam*: stand firm in the unitive way; *uttiṣṭha*: (and) stand up; *bhārata*: Oh Arjuna.

Therefore, sundering with the sword of Self-knowledge this ignorance-born doubt residing in the heart, stand firm in the unitive way, and stand up, Oh Bhārata!

DIALOGUE

Teacher: This chapter is titled differently in several editions of the Gītā. A few are:

- Jñāna-Yoga (Unitive Wisdom)
- Jñāna-Vibhāga-Yoga (Yoga of Wisdom Section)
- Jñāna-Karma-Saṁnyāsa-Yoga (Yoga of Knowledge, Action, and Renunciation).

From these titles we can easily see that this chapter pertains to a subject that is too elusive and difficult to pinpoint or describe in clear-cut terms. This discourse refers first to the timelessness or perennial nature of absolute Wisdom, taking it completely out of historical or even geographical limitations. Divine intervention in the affairs of this world is introduced before we are led to the typological concept of human nature. It is followed by a closer scrutiny of the true nature of action. From this, the discussion passes on to the examination of the various kinds of spiritual practice extant in the India of the time of the writing of the Gītā, such as burnt-sacrifice, restraints, and harmonization of breath. These are disposed of in a graded fashion, culminating in a crowning discipline which comprises them all under *brahma-vidyā* (Science of the Absolute), or Self-realization. It aptly closes with unqualified praise for wisdom which, like fire, should burn away all the dross of action, or practices of any kind. The sword of wisdom has to cleave asunder all doubts. Such is the nature of the triumph of wisdom as depicted in the closing verses of this chapter.

Action, as usually understood, is completely discredited here, although the eternally necessary urge for positive living is still retained. The word *saṁnyāsa*, which occurs in verse 41 rounds off the nature of the discipline in relation to renunciation which, however, is not just vacuous abandonment, leaving emptiness, but is to be understood as life lived in the fresh breezes of *yoga*, where all conflicting factors referred to in this chapter are brought into a unity of understanding. The unity of *yoga* of this chapter therefore lies in its treatment of wisdom as a perennial way of life in keeping with the Science of the Absolute.

STUDENT: *Who expounded this wisdom first?*

This wisdom is timeless. It originates from the Absolute. Kṛṣṇa says:

> This perennial unitive wisdom (*yoga*) did I declare to Vivasvān (Sun); Vivasvān taught it to Manu (law-giver) and Manu told it to Ikṣvāku (first king of the Solar race). Thus handed down the line in succession, this (wisdom) the king-sages (*rāja-ṛṣis*) understood; by great lapse of time here (however) this unitive wisdom (*yoga*) came to be lost, Oh Paraṁtapa.

This sounds like a fable. How could Kṛṣṇa, a contemporary of Arjuna, teach wisdom to the very sun itself even before the earth came into being? After all, the sun is a star and not an intelligent being. How could it ever be taught wisdom?

I told you earlier that the Gītā is written in an archaic language of myths and symbols. Its mystical or mythical language should first be deciphered in modern thought if we want to appreciate its great teaching.

Life on Earth originated from solar energy. Our vegetative existence is sustained by the sun. In short, the sun is the primary cause of our origination. To say that this wisdom existed even before the beginning of time, the Gītā says that the Absolute passed on its perennial truth first to the Sun. The Sun, according to Indian mythology, is the progenitor of time. We base our time-sense on the movement of the Earth in relation to the Sun. All that is to be inferred from this is that the Science of the Absolute is timeless.

First of all, Truth exists on its own, irrespective of the mind that grasps it. It becomes operative in the life of people when they comprehend it and can see the structural function of Truth in terms of laws – physical, mathematical, moral and aesthetic. That is why the law-giver, Manu, is mentioned next. In the Semitic world, God, or Jehovah, Himself first revealed the commandments to Moses, and from him they came down the hierarchy of kings, like David and Solomon. What Moses is to Semitic religions, Manu is to the Hindus.

Truth first exists on its own. Then it is known. After knowing it, what is known is lived. Implementation of the law belongs to the king, the ruler. Hence Ikṣvāku, the first king of the Solar race of India, is mentioned here as one who received the law from the law-giver. Thus the arrow of the pointer of wisdom shows the course from the timeless into the cycle of time, and then it moves down into the affairs of man on Earth. This unbroken flow of wisdom, preserved by long lines of the hierarchy of royal seers, lost its vigour in the course of time and disappeared in the dreary sand of decadence. Kṛṣṇa now revives, revalues, and restates the same age-old wisdom for Arjuna to pass on to posterity.

Does this not resemble the coming of Jesus Christ at a time of similar decadence, for the restatement of the spiritual norms of higher life and revision of the moral code revealed through Moses and other prophets?

Yes indeed. We can see many other parallels of such revaluation in history. In the Gospel of St. Matthew (5: 17, 18), Jesus says:

> Think not that I am come to destroy the law, or the prophets: I am come not to destroy but to fulfil. For verily I say unto you, till heaven and earth pass, one jot or one tittle shall in no wise pass from the law, till all be fulfilled.

In these words we get the same concept of perennial wisdom. Arjuna was as much a sceptic as any of modern days. He asks Kṛṣṇa:

> Your birth was posterior and the birth of Vivasvān was anterior; how then have I to understand it that you declared it in the beginning?

To this does Kṛṣṇa give the key of symbolism you have explained to me?

Kṛṣṇa puts it this way:

> Many are the lives that have gone past for me, as also for you, Oh Arjuna; I am conscious of them all; you, Oh Paraṁtapa, are not conscious of them.

> Although (I remain) ever unborn as the never-diminishing Self, while I am the Lord of creation too, grounded on my own nature I assume being through the negative principle (*māyā*) of my own Self.

Does that mean that Arjuna and Kṛṣṇa had many incarnations? Does God also incarnate like other beings?

Here Kṛṣṇa's first reference is to the transparency of the eternal duration of the Absolute Consciousness. It is contrasted with the obliteration of infinite awareness by the segmentation of time in terms of the past, present, and the future in the case of the relative consciousness. Kṛṣṇa's second reference is to the Absolute that assumes its own personified individuation in its own negative power. In other words, there is provision in the creative present to project a medium that can mirror the law of the total Being with clarity unaffected by the blemishes of relativism.

I do not understand either of these references.

There is a difference between the consciousness of Kṛṣṇa and that of Arjuna. The former is Absolute Consciousness and the latter is relative and conditioned. Arjuna's consciousness is of the phenomenal, in which duration is conceived in sequence in a homogeneous extension of time, using space as a model for time also. The time that Arjuna perceives, and which is just as you or I perceive it, is a symbolical duration and not a concrete duration. Bergson, in his *Duration and Simultaneity*, says:

> Time is first identical with the continuity of our inner life. (It is) a self-sufficient flow or passage, the flow not implying a thing that flows, and the passing not presupposing states through which we pass. The *thing* and the *state* are only artificially taken snap-shots of the transition; in this transition, all that is naturally experienced is duration itself. It is *memory*, but not personal memory.

In the above passage, what is interpreted as "memory" has identity with Kṛṣṇa's view: Arjuna's can be called "personal memory". As a counterpart of the spiritual symbiosis of the personal and universal self given here, Piaget speaks of "protoplasmic consciousness" as a continuation of the biological symbiosis of the foetus in the womb. He describes protoplasmic consciousness as the focusing of the universe on the self and the self on the universe. In *Civilization and Its Discontents*, Freud also puts it similarly. He says:

> Originally the ego includes everything, later it detaches from itself the external world. The ego-feeling we are aware of now is thus only a shrunken vestige of a far more extensive feeling – a feeling which embraced the universe and expressed an inseparable connection of the ego with the

> external world. If we may suppose that this primary ego-feeling has been preserved in the minds of many people, to a greater or lesser extent, it would coexist like a sort of counterpart with the narrower and more sharply outlined ego-feeling of maturity, and the ideational content belonging to it would be precisely the notion of limitless extension and oneness with the universe.

How does the Absolute assume individuality in its own negative principle?

Let us take the analogy of the sun shining on the saline crystals of a desert. When the sun is hot and there is not the slightest trace of water or water vapour in the desert, we see an expanse of clear blue water reflecting on its surface the blue sky above and its bright sun. Even though this reflected sun has no existence of its own, other than that of the original, it shines with the same brightness and radiates both light and heat. Where does it reflect when there is really no water below? It reflects on its own light. The principle of the individuation of the Absolute is the same.

What necessitates the personal intervention of the Absolute in the affairs of man in the form of a saviour?

Kṛṣṇa puts it this way:

> Whenever there comes to be laxity in regard to right life (*dharma*) Oh Bhārata! and wrong coming to assert itself, then I bring about the creation of myself.
>
> To protect those who are good and to destroy evil-doers, for establishing righteousness, I assume being, age by age.

When the natural sense of right and absolutist norms are abandoned in despair by humanity as a whole, and when the old order is ready to change, yielding its place to the new, the Absolute intervenes. When humanity is regimented or conscripted into forced labour or warfare, stifling its natural expression (cutting across the precious values which the individual needs to work out or express in a natural way, in keeping with a life of freedom in the Absolute), then the time is right for the absolutist pattern of life to assert itself by sheer necessity combined with the chance element which makes humanity balance itself again. It is then that persons who represent absolutist universal values in themselves gain a status as saviours of humanity. This phenomenon is familiar to us in the spiritual history of the world, when a Buddha or a Christ lives and moves among men.

The Gītā is a Hindu scripture and Kṛṣṇa a Hindu deity. So how do we relate his assurance to the advent of saviours like Christ and prophets like Muhammad?

It is only incidental that the Gītā was written in India. Its subject matter has no geographic or ethnic limitations. Kr̥ṣṇa says:

> As each chooses to approach Me, even accordingly do I have regard for him. My very path it is, Oh Arjuna, that all men do tread from every possible approach.

In a sense, all men belong to one religion and, in another sense, when they are not affiliated at all to absolutism, humanity stands in danger of being subjected to a process of disruption. As a corollary to this verse, it could be stated that there is but one religion for all men. That religion becomes one and the same, irrespective of the diverse forms or trappings with which it might outwardly be expressed. These expressions then are affiliated to be Most High or the Absolute, and finally are the same in effect. A Christian who worships Christ as a representative of the Most High belongs to the same religion to which a Muslim, who follows Muhammad as the Prophet of Allah, the Most High Absolute of Islam, affiliates himself. Even ideologies which seem atheistic or irreligious can imply a certain affiliation to absolute values, and to that extent these paths become in effect the same also.

How do we keep ourselves true to our dharma?

Psychologically viewed, one's own personality is moulded by his innate qualities (*guṇa*s). The total structure of a person's innate qualities constitutes his *dharma*. Every *dharma* demands its proper expression in a relevant context, or rather, its unfoldment through action. When such an action is unitively understood, and carried out with the same attitude of a sacrifice in which ends and means meet, one's own *dharma* leads to *karma-yoga*. In the performance of *karma* as *yoga* there is no postponement of the reward of the action to the future. Work itself becomes its enjoyment. One can decide the requirements of his or her personality by finding an identity with the type (*varṇa*) to which they naturally belong.

The world is already torn into shreds of contending factions based on colour and creed and all sorts of ideologies and "isms". Instead of finding ways and means to eradicate such separatistic tendencies, is it wise to identify oneself with this or that type? In the first chapter we see Arjuna expressing his fear of the mixing of varṇa *by intermarriage. From that I presume that the Gītā puts forward its theory of* varṇa *to form a narrow-minded community based on the puerile notion of a caste system.*

I admit that even some Indian scholars have unfortunately succumbed to such a false notion in their interpretation of the word *varṇa*. But you should carefully examine Kr̥ṣṇa's own words:

> The fourfold colour-grades (*varṇas*) were created by myself on the basis of innate disposition (*guṇa*) and vocation (*karma*) that accorded with each; know Me to be the maker of such as also to be its undoer, unexpended.

To understand Kṛṣṇa as both the creator as well as remover of these types or grades of colouration of the psyche, let us take the example of light productng varying shades or intensities. That same light can also remove the shades. When a man fully renounces his self in the bounty of the Absolute, he becomes a *saṁnyāsin*. When a man enters into a bipolarity with the Absolute and participates in the wisdom-dictates of the Science of the Absolute, he becomes a brāhmaṇa. When one comprehends the value of the Absolute in the relativistic plane with a coloured mind, and is swayed by his passions to stand by those values, he becomes a kṣatriya. When a person confines himself to the actualities of the work-a-day world, always getting and spending, and having only a feeble undercurrent of the vertical pull of the Absolute, he becomes a vaiśya. A person tied down to the harsh actualities of the mundane world and passing his days in a protracted agony for which he sees no alternative, becomes a śūdra. The first is atypical, and the remaining four are termed *catur-varṇya* (fourfold colouration of the psyche). The illumination of an object becomes bright or dark according to its proximity to, or distance from, the source of illumination. In this manner these colours are determined by one's intensity of affiliation with the Absolute. All these shades can be annulled by the same Absolute. One can obliterate his *varṇa* by a correction of his vision of the Absolute.

Karma *being the overt expression of a person's latent* dharma, *it must be as important to know the true nature of* karma … .

A proper understanding of *karma* is difficult even for the wise. Kṛṣṇa says:

> On what is action and what is inaction even intelligent men here are confused. I shall indicate to you that action on knowing which you will be emancipated from evil.
>
> One has to understand about action and understand also what is wrong action; again, one has to have a proper notion of non-action; the way of action is elusively subtle (indeed).
>
> One who is able to see action in inaction and inaction in action – he among men is intelligent; he is one of unitive attitude (a *yogī*), while still engaged in every (possible) kind of work.

How do we see action in inaction and inaction in action?

In our life there are ambivalent, dichotomous, or bipolar aspects of the soul of man which are interrelated, such as instinct with intelligence.

What instinct is convinced of, intelligence cannot appreciate, and what intelligence sees, instinct cannot. The soul of man as understood in its absolute sense is the meeting place of opposites. The neutral ground of wisdom is none other than the same. When our hands are inactive the mind is active, and when the mind is inactive the hands come into action. The man who sits still might be steeped in overpowering mental activity, as in the case of a bound Prometheus. To reduce both these opposing tendencies into a neutral whole is the *yoga* of wisdom spoken of here. Kṛṣṇa equates action carried out with such a unitive understanding to a sacrifice:

> In the case of one whose attachments are gone, who has gained freedom, whose spiritual being has been founded on wisdom, his works, having a sacrificial character only, become wholly dissolved.
>
> (For him) the Absolute is the act of offering, the Absolute is the substance offered into the Absolute which is the fire, offered by (him), the Absolute, the end to be reached by him being even the Absolute, by means of his peace supreme of absolutist action.

Could any action be conceived in terms of a sacrifice?

Kṛṣṇa gives a number of examples for treating different kinds of actions as sacrifices in verses 25 to 32. Of all these he considers the wisdom sacrifice as the highest. He says:

> Superior to any sacrifice with (valuable) objects is the wisdom-sacrifice, Oh Paraṁtapa; all actions, Oh Pārtha, have their culmination in wisdom.
>
> Learn this by prostration, by searching questioning, and by service; they will instruct you (duly) in wisdom – those wise men who can see the basic principles.

Will such actions bring cumulative impressions that may prolong the series of birth and death?

Kṛṣṇa says:

> One of unitively-renounced action, who by wisdom has sundered doubt and come to full self-possession, cannot be bound by works, Oh Dhanañjaya!
>
> Therefore, sundering with the sword of Self-knowledge this ignorance-born doubt residing in the heart, stand firm in the unitive way (*yoga*), and stand up, Oh Bhārata!

V

Karma-Saṁnyāsa-Yoga

Unitive Action and Renunciation

INTRODUCTION

WE HAVE stated earlier that the Gītā is a dialectical revaluation of spiritual or philosophical doctrines as they prevailed in India at the time it was written. The character of this revaluation consists of reconciling divergent traditions in the unitive terms of an absolutist way of life.

If we examine the history and nature of the six systems of Indian philosophy, we find that they fall into three pairs: Nyāya–Vaiśeṣika, Sāṁkhya–Yoga, and Pūrva-Mīmāṁsā–Uttara-Mīmāṁsā. Each pair taken separately reveals a rationalist side and another side in which matters of practice or discipline are introduced. Following up the development of Indian thought further, we notice that Vedic orthodoxy and heterodoxy also alternately change positions or take over primacy, as between the successive pairs, as the thought matures, to culminate in the final Vedāntic teaching of Bādarāyaṇa. This teaching contains, in revalued terms, all that is implied in the other anterior schools of a logical, methodological, or epistemological order. The final doctrinal aspects, however, belong to Vedānta as revalued and restated by masterminds like Vyāsa.

The critical student must therefore look out for the opposing tendencies and the alternating movement from orthodoxy to heterodoxy, or form reason to faith, that we find in the growth of the spiritual and philosophical thought of India, before he can be clear in his own mind about the exact nature of the revaluation accomplished chapter by chapter in the Gītā.

Yoga as a practical discipline is all that is alluded to as action here. Supreme peace is the note on which this chapter ends. To obey Kṛṣṇa, it is hardly necessary for Arjuna to stir from his posture of sitting.

TRANSLATION

अर्जुन उवाच –

1. संन्यासं कर्मणां कृष्ण पुनर्योगं च शंससि ।
यच्छ्रेय एतयोरेकं तन्मे ब्रूहि सुनिश्चितम् ।।

arjuna uvāca –

saṁnyāsaṁ karmaṇāṁ kṛṣṇa punar yogaṁ ca śaṁsasi ।
yac chreya etayor ekaṁ tan me brūhi suniścitam ॥

arjuna uvāca: Arjuna said; *śaṁsasi*: you recommend; *saṁnyāsaṁ karmaṇāṁ*: the (effective) transcending of action; *kṛṣṇa*: Oh Kṛṣṇa; *ca punaḥ*: and again; *yogaṁ*: *yoga*; *brūhi me tat*: tell me that; *suniścitam*: duly determined; *yat ekaṁ etayoḥ*: which one of these two; *śreyaḥ*: (is) spiritually better.

Arjuna said:

You recommend the effective transcending of action, Oh Kṛṣṇa, and again *yoga* also; tell me, duly determined, which one of these two is spiritually better.

श्रीभगवानुवाच –

2. संन्यासः कर्मयोगश्च निःश्रेयसकरावुभौ ।
तयोस्तु कर्मसंन्यासात्कर्मयोगो विशिष्यते ।।

śrībhagavān uvāca –

saṁnyāsaḥ karmayogaś ca niḥśreyasakarāv ubhau ।
tayos tu karmasaṁnyāsāt karmayogo viśiṣyate ॥

śrībhagavān uvāca: Kṛṣṇa said; *ubhau saṁnyāsaḥ*: both renunciation; *ca karma yogaḥ*: and unitive action; *niḥśreyasa karau*: have as their common effect emancipation; *tayoḥ tu*: of the two, however; *karma yogaḥ*: unitive action; *viśiṣyate*: is superior; *karma saṁnyāsāt*: to (mere) renunciation of action.

Kṛṣṇa said:

Both renunciation and unitive action have emancipation as their common effect; of the two, however, unitive action is superior to (mere) renunciation of action.

3. ज्ञेयः स नित्यसंन्यासी यो न द्वेष्टि न काङ्क्षति ।
निर्द्वन्द्वो हि महाबाहो सुखं बन्धात्प्रमुच्यते ।।

jñeyaḥ sa nityasaṁnyāsī yo na dveṣṭi na kāṅkṣati ।
nirdvandvo hi mahābāho sukhaṁ bandhāt pramucyate ॥

saḥ jñeyaḥ: he should be recognized as; *nitya saṁnyāsī*: a perennial renouncer; *yaḥ na dveṣṭi*: who neither hates; *na kāṅkṣati*: nor desires; *nirdvandvaḥ hi*: free from conflicting pairs (of interests) indeed; *mahābāho*: Oh Arjuna; *sukhaṁ pramucyate*: (he is) happily released; *bandhāt*: from the bondage (of necessity).

That man should be recognized as a perennial renouncer who neither hates nor desires; free indeed from conflicting pairs (of interests), Oh Mighty-Armed, he is happily released from the bondage (of necessity).

4. साङ्ख्ययोगौ पृथग्बालाः प्रवदन्ति न पण्डिताः ।
एकमप्यास्थितः सम्यगुभयोर्विन्दते फलम् ।।

sāṁkhyayogau pṛthag bālāḥ pravadanti na paṇḍitāḥ ।
ekam apy āsthitaḥ samyag ubhayor vindate phalam ॥

sāṁkhyayogau: (that) rationalism (*sāṁkhya*) and self-discipline (*yoga*); *pṛthak*: (are) distinct; *bālāḥ pravadanti*: (only) children say; *na paṇḍitāḥ*: not the well-informed; *samyak āsthitaḥ api ekam*: well-established even in one (of them); *vindate phalam*: one obtains the result; *ubhayoḥ*: of both.

That rationalism and self-discipline are distinct, only children say, not the well-informed; one well-established in either one of them obtains the result of both.

5. यत्साङ्ख्यैः प्राप्यते स्थानं तद्योगैरपि गम्यते ।
एकं साङ्ख्यं च योगं च यः पश्यति स पश्यति ।।

yat sāṁkhyaiḥ prāpyate sthānaṁ tad yogair api gamyate ।
ekaṁ sāṁkhyaṁ ca yogaṁ ca yaḥ paśyati sa paśyati ॥

yat sthānaṁ: what status; *prāpyate*: is attained; *sāṁkhyaiḥ*: by men of rationalist persuasion; *tad gamyate api*: that is reached also; *yogaiḥ*: by those of unitive discipline; *yaḥ paśyati*: he who (thus) sees; *sāṁkhyaṁ ca yogaṁ*: Sāṁkhya and Yoga; *ekaṁ*: as one; *saḥ paśyati*: he (alone) sees.

That status attained by men of Sāṁkhya is reached also by those of *yoga*; he who thus sees Sāṁkhya and Yoga as one – he (alone) sees.

6. संन्यासस्तु महाबाहो दुःखमाप्तुमयोगतः ।
योगयुक्तो मुनिर्ब्रह्म नचिरेणाधिगच्छति ।।

saṁnyāsas tu mahābāho duḥkham āptum ayogataḥ ।
yogayukto munir brahma nacireṇā 'dhigacchati ॥

tu saṁnyāsaḥ: but renunciation; *mahābāho*: Oh Arjuna; *ayogataḥ*: non-unitively (without *yoga*); *duḥkham āptum*: (is) full of pain to achieve;

yoga yuktaḥ muniḥ: one unitively harmonized, of subdued ways; *nacireṇa*: without any delay; *adhigacchati brahma*: attains the Absolute.

But non-unitive renunciation, Oh Mighty-Armed, is full of pain to achieve; one unitively harmonized, of subdued ways, without any delay attains the Absolute.

7. योगयुक्तो विशुद्धात्मा विजितात्मा जितेन्द्रियः ।
सर्वभूतात्मभूतात्मा कुर्वन्नपि न लिप्यते ।।

yogayukto viśuddhātmā vijitātmā jitendriyaḥ ।
sarvabhūtātmabhūtātmā kurvann api na lipyate ॥

yogayuktaḥ: one affiliated to the unitive way of life; *viśuddha ātmā*: who has attained to lucidity of Self; *vijita ātmā*: one of Self-conquest; *jita indriyaḥ*: one who has gained a victory over the senses; *sarva bhūtātma bhūtātmā*: whose Self-existence has become the same as the Self-existence of all; *api kurvan*: though active; *na lipyate*: is unaffected (thereby).

One affiliated to the unitive way of life, attained to lucidity of Self, of Self-conquest, who has gained a victory over the senses, whose Self-existence has become the same as the Self-existence of all, though active, is unaffected (thereby).

8. नैव किञ्चित्करोमीति युक्तो मन्येत तत्त्ववित् ।
पश्यञ्शृण्वन्स्पृशञ्जिघ्रन्नश्नन्गच्छन्स्वपञ्श्वसन् ।।

nai 'va kiñcit karomī 'ti yukto manyeta tattvavit ।
paśyañ śṛṇvan spṛśañ jighrann aśnan gacchan svapañ śvasan ॥

karomi: I do; *na kiñcit eva*: nothing at all; *iti*: (saying) thus; *yuktaḥ*: (one) of unitive ways; *tattvavit*: (who is) a philosopher; *manyeta*: he thinks; *paśyañ śṛṇvan*: (while) seeing, hearing; *spṛśañ jighran*: touching, smelling; *aśnan gacchan*: eating, going; *svapañ śvasan*: sleeping, breathing

9. प्रलपन्विसृजन्गृह्णन्नुन्मिषन्निमिषन्नपि ।
इन्द्रियाणीन्द्रियार्थेषु वर्तन्त इति धारयन् ।।

pralapan visṛjan gṛhṇann unmiṣan nimiṣann api ।
indriyāṇī 'ndriyārtheṣu vartanta iti dhārayan ॥

pralapan visṛjan: speaking, excreting; *gṛhṇan*: grasping; *unmiṣan nimiṣan api*: opening and closing the eyes; *dhārayan indriyāṇi*: treating the senses; *vartante iti*: as (merely) related to; *indriyārtheṣu*: (their corresponding) sense-objects.

"I do nothing at all" – saying thus, he of unitive ways, who is a philosopher, should think, (while) seeing, hearing, touching, smelling, eating, going, sleeping, breathing, speaking, excreting, grasping, opening and closing the eyes – treating the senses as (merely) related to their (corresponding) sense-objects.

10. ब्रह्मण्याधाय कर्माणि सङ्गं त्यक्त्वा करोति यः ।
लिप्यते न स पापेन पद्मपत्रमिवाम्भसा ॥

brahmaṇy ādhāya karmāṇi saṅgaṁ tyaktvā karoti yaḥ ।
lipyate na sa pāpena padmapatram ivā 'mbhasā ॥

saḥ yaḥ karoti: he who acts; *ādhāya karmāṇi*: placing (all) actions; *brahmaṇi*: in the Absolute; *tyaktvā saṅgaṁ*: having given up attachment; *na lipyate pāpena*: is not affected by sin; *iva padma patram*: like a lotus leaf; *ambhasā*: by water.

He who acts, placing all actions in the Absolute, having given up attachment, is not affected by sin, like a lotus leaf by water.

11. कायेन मनसा बुद्ध्या केवलैरिन्द्रियैरपि ।
योगिनः कर्म कुर्वन्ति सङ्गं त्यक्त्वात्मशुद्धये ॥

kāyena manasā buddhyā kevalair indriyair api ।
yoginaḥ karma kurvanti saṅgaṁ tyaktvā 'tmaśuddhaye ॥

kāyena manasā: by the body, by the mind; *buddhyā*: by intelligence; *api indriyaiḥ kevalaiḥ*: (and) even by the senses alone; *yoginaḥ kurvanti*: *yogī*s engage in; *karma*: action; *tyaktvā saṅgaṁ*: abandoning attachment; *ātma śuddhaye*: for (purposes of) purity of Self.

By the body, by the mind, by intelligence, and even by the senses alone, *yogī*s engage in action, abandoning attachment, for (purposes of) purity of Self.

12. युक्तः कर्मफलं त्यक्त्वा शान्तिमाप्नोति नैष्ठिकीम् ।
अयुक्तः कामकारेण फले सक्तो निबध्यते ॥

yuktaḥ karmaphalaṁ tyaktvā śāntim āpnoti naiṣṭhikīm ।
ayuktaḥ kāmakāreṇa phale sakto nibadhyate ॥

yuktaḥ: the one of unitive discipline; *tyaktvā karma phalaṁ*: discarding benefit-motive; *āpnoti*: attains to; *naiṣṭhikīm śāntim*: ultimate peace; *ayuktaḥ*: the one of non-unitive discipline; *kāmakāreṇa*: being desire-motivated; *saktaḥ phale*: attached to results; *nibadhyate*: is bound.

The one of unitive discipline, discarding benefit-motive, attains to ultimate peace; the one of non-unitive discipline, being desire-motivated, attached to results, is bound.

13. सर्वकर्माणि मनसा संन्यस्यास्ते सुखं वशी ।
नवद्वारे पुरे देही नैव कुर्वन्न कारयन् ।।

sarvakarmāṇi manasā saṁnyasyā 'ste sukhaṁ vaśī ।
navadvāre pure dehī nai 'va kurvan na kārayan ॥

saṁnyasya: relinquishing; *manasā*: by means of the mind; *sarva karmāṇi*: all activities; *dehī āste sukhaṁ*: the embodied One sits happily; *vaśī*: a victor; *nava dvāre pure*: in the nine-gated city; *na eva kurvan*: neither acting; *na kārayan*: nor causing to act.

Relinquishing by means of the mind all activities, the embodied One sits happily, a victor, in the nine-gated city, neither acting nor causing to act.

14. न कर्तृत्वं न कर्माणि लोकस्य सृजति प्रभुः ।
न कर्मफलसंयोगं स्वभावस्तु प्रवर्तते ।।

na kartṛtvaṁ na karmāṇi lokasya sṛjati prabhuḥ ।
na karmaphalasaṁyogaṁ svabhāvas tu pravartate ॥

prabhuḥ: the Supreme; *na sṛjati*: does not generate; *kartṛtvaṁ na karmāṇi*: either (the idea of) agency or activity; *lokasya*: in regard to the world; *na karmaphala saṁyogaṁ*: nor the union of action and benefit; *svabhāvaḥ*: the innate urge in beings; *tu*: however; *pravartate*: exerts itself.

The Supreme does not generate either the idea of agency or activity in regard to the world, nor the union of action and benefit; the innate urge in beings, however, exerts itself.

15. नादत्ते कस्यचित्पापं न चैव सुकृतं विभुः ।
अज्ञानेनावृतं ज्ञानं तेन मुह्यन्ति जन्तवः ।।

nā 'datte kasyacit pāpaṁ na cai 'va sukṛtaṁ vibhuḥ ।
ajñānenā 'vṛtaṁ jñānaṁ tena muhyanti jantavaḥ ॥

vibhuḥ: the all-pervading One; *ādatte*: takes cognizance of; *na pāpaṁ*: neither the sinful; *ca eva sukṛtaṁ*: nor the meritorious actions; *kasyacit*: of anyone; *jñānaṁ āvṛtaṁ*: wisdom is veiled; *ajñānena*: by unwisdom; *jantavaḥ muhyanti tena*: beings are deluded thereby.

The All-pervading One takes cognizance neither of the sinful nor of the meritorious actions of anyone; wisdom is veiled by unwisdom; beings are deluded thereby.

16. ज्ञानेन तु तदज्ञानं येषां नाशितमात्मनः ।
तेषामादित्यवज्ज्ञानं प्रकाशयति तत्परम् ।।

jñānena tu tad ajñānaṁ yeṣāṁ nāśitam ātmanaḥ ।
teṣām ādityavaj jñānaṁ prakāśayati tat param ॥

yeṣāṁ tu: to whom, however; *tat ajñānaṁ*: that unwisdom; *ātmanaḥ*: in the Self; *nāśitam*: has been destroyed; *teṣām*: to those; *jñānaṁ prakāśayati*: wisdom shines; *ādityavat*: sunlike; *tat param*: (as) that Ultimate (the Absolute).

To those, however, in whom that unwisdom in the Self has been destroyed, wisdom shines sunlike as the Ultimate.

17. तद्बुद्धयस्तदात्मानस्तन्निष्ठास्तत्परायणाः ।
गच्छन्त्यपुनरावृत्तिं ज्ञाननिर्धूतकल्मषाः ॥

tadbuddhayas tadātmānas tanniṣṭhās tatparāyaṇāḥ ।
gacchanty apunarāvṛttiṁ jñānanirdhūtakalmaṣāḥ ॥

tat buddhayaḥ: those having That (the Absolute) for reasoning; *tat ātmānaḥ*: who have That for the Self; *tat niṣṭhāḥ*: who have That for finalized discipline; *tat parāyaṇāḥ*: who have That for supreme goal; *gacchanti*: they go; *apunar āvṛttiṁ*: to a state of (final) non-return; *jñāna nirdhūta kalmaṣāḥ*: (all) their (relativistic) dross being cancelled out by wisdom.

Thus having That for reasoning, That for the Self, That for finalized discipline, That for supreme goal, they go to a state of final non-return, all their (relativistic) dross being cancelled out by wisdom.

18. विद्याविनयसंपन्ने ब्राह्मणे गवि हस्तिनि ।
शुनि चैव श्वपाके च पण्डिताः समदर्शिनः ॥

vidyāvinayasaṁpanne brāhmaṇe gavi hastini ।
śuni cai 'va śvapāke ca paṇḍitāḥ samadarśinaḥ ॥

brāhmaṇe: in regard to a brāhmin; *vidyā vinaya saṁpanne*: endowed with learning or humility; *gavi hastini*: in a cow, in an elephant; *ca eva śuni*: and even in a dog; *ca śvapāke*: (as) also in one who cooks the dog (for food); *paṇḍitāḥ*: the well-informed ones; *sama darśinaḥ*: see the same (differenceless reality).

In regard to a brāhmin endowed with learning or humility, a cow, an elephant, and even a dog, as also one who cooks the dog (for food), the well-informed ones see the same (differenceless reality).

19. इहैव तैर्जितः सर्गो येषां साम्ये स्थितं मनः ।
निर्दोषं हि समं ब्रह्म तस्माद् ब्रह्मणि ते स्थिताः ॥

ihai 'va tair jitaḥ sargo yeṣāṁ sāmye sthitaṁ manaḥ ।
nirdoṣaṁ hi samaṁ brahma tasmād brahmaṇi te sthitāḥ ॥

eva iha: even here; *sargaḥ jitaḥ*: creative urge(s) (are) conquered; *taiḥ yeṣāṁ manaḥ*: by those whose minds; *sthitaṁ sāmye*: (are) balanced in sameness; *nirdoṣaṁ*: free from blemish; *samaṁ*: and unitively balanced; *hi brahma*: (is) indeed the Absolute; *tasmāt*: therefore; *te sthitāḥ*: they become grounded; *brahmaṇi*: in the Absolute.

Even here creative urges are conquered by those whose minds are balanced in sameness; free from blemish and unitively balanced is indeed the Absolute; therefore such persons become grounded in the Absolute.

20. न प्रहृष्येत्प्रियं प्राप्य नोद्विजेत्प्राप्य चाप्रियम् ।
स्थिरबुद्धिरसम्मूढो ब्रह्मविद् ब्रह्मणि स्थितः ॥

na prahṛṣyet priyaṁ prāpya no 'dvijet prāpya cā 'priyam ।
sthirabuddhir asaṁmūḍho brahmavid brahmaṇi sthitaḥ ॥

na prahṛṣyet: he should not rejoice; *priyam prāpya*: on good befalling him; *ca na udvijet*: nor should be disturbed; *apriyam prāpya*: on a mishap befalling (him); *sthira buddhiḥ*: stabilized in reason; *asaṁmūḍhaḥ*: delusion-free; *brahmavit*: a knower of the Absolute; *sthitaḥ*: (is) firmly established; *brahmaṇi*: in the Absolute.

He should not rejoice on good befalling him nor be disturbed by a mishap; stabilized in reason, delusion-free, as knower of the Absolute, firmly established is he in the Absolute.

21. बाह्यस्पर्शेष्वसक्तात्मा विन्दत्यात्मनि यत्सुखम् ।
स ब्रह्मयोगयुक्तात्मा सुखमक्षयमश्नुते ॥

bāhyasparśeṣv askatātmā vindaty ātmani yat sukham ।
sa brahmayogayuktātmā sukham akṣayam aśnute ॥

yat sukham: that joy which; *vindati*: one feels; *ātmani*: in his own Self; *asakta ātmā*: whose Self is unattached; *bāhya sparśeṣu*: to outer contacts (such as touch); *saḥ*: he; *brahma yoga yuktātmā*: whose Self has established unity with the Absolute; *aśnute*: experiences; *akṣayam sukham*: never-decreasing joy.

That (same) joy which is felt by one in his own Self when he is unattached to outer contacts (such as touch), he whose Self has established unity with the Absolute experiences never-decreasingly.

22. ये हि संस्पर्शजा भोगा दुःखयोनय एव ते ।
आद्यन्तवन्तः कौन्तेय न तेषु रमते बुधः ॥

ye hi saṁsparśajā bhogā duḥkhayonaya eva te ।
ādyantavantaḥ kaunteya na teṣu ramate budhaḥ ॥

ye: those; *saṁsparśajāḥ bhogāḥ*: contact-born pleasures; *hi te eva*: indeed they (are) alone; *duḥkha yonayaḥ*: the sources (wombs) of pain; *ādyantavantaḥ*: having a beginning and an end; *kaunteya*: Oh Arjuna; *budhaḥ*: the wise man; *na ramate teṣu*: does not take pleasure in them.

Those contact-born pleasures indeed are the sources of pain, having a beginning and an end, Oh Son of Kuntī! the wise man does not take pleasure in them.

23. शक्नोतीहैव यः सोढुं प्राक्शरीरविमोक्षणात् ।
कामक्रोधोद्भवं वेगं स युक्तः स सुखी नरः ।।

śaknotī 'hai 'va yaḥ soḍhuṁ prāk śariravimokṣaṇāt ।
kāmakrodhodbhavaṁ vegaṁ sa yuktaḥ sa sukhī naraḥ ॥

yaḥ śaknoti: he who is able; *soḍhuṁ*: to experience undisturbed; *iha eva*: here itself; *prāk śarīra vimokṣaṇāt*: before liberation from the body; *vegaṁ*: (that) impulse; *kāma krodha udbhavaṁ*: arising out of desire and hatred; *saḥ yuktaḥ*: he is the unified; *saḥ sukhī naraḥ*: he is the happy man.

He who is able to experience undisturbed here itself, before liberation from the body, that impulse arising out of desire and hatred – he is the unified and happy man.

24. योऽन्तःसुखोऽन्तरारामस्तथान्तर्ज्योतिरेव यः ।
स योगी ब्रह्मनिर्वाणं ब्रह्मभूतोऽधिगच्छति ।।

yo 'ntaḥsukho 'ntarārāmas tathā 'ntarjyotir eva yaḥ ।
sa yogī brahmanirvāṇaṁ brahmabhūto 'dhigacchati ॥

yaḥ antaḥ sukhaḥ: he of inward happiness; *antarārāmaḥ*: whose inner life is free and easy; *tathā eva*: and likewise; *yaḥ antaḥ jyotiḥ*: who is of inward brilliance; *saḥ yogī*: he of unitive understanding; *brahma bhūtaḥ*: having become the Absolute; *adhigacchati*: (he) enters; *brahma nirvāṇaṁ*: the self-effacement of the Absolute.

He of inward happiness, whose inner life is free and easy, and likewise of inward brilliance – he of unitive understanding, having become the Absolute, enters the self-effacement of the Absolute.

25. लभन्ते ब्रह्मनिर्वाणमृषयः क्षीणकल्मषाः ।
छिन्नद्वैधा यतात्मानः सर्वभूतहिते रताः ।।

labhante brahmanirvāṇam ṛṣayaḥ kṣīṇakalmaṣāḥ ।
chinnadvaidhā yatātmānaḥ sarvabhūtahite ratāḥ ॥

ṛṣayaḥ: seers; *kṣīṇa kalmaṣāḥ*: (their) evils weakened; *chinna dvaidhāḥ*:

cut away (from) conflicting pairs (of interests); *yata ātmānaḥ*: who are self-controlled; *sarva bhūta hite ratāḥ*: who are (ever) kindly disposed to all beings; *labhante*: attain to; *brahma nirvāṇam*: self-effacement in the Absolute.

Seers, their evils weakened, cutting themselves away from conflicting pairs of interests, who are self-controlled, who are ever kindly disposed to all beings, attain to self-effacement in the Absolute.

26. कामक्रोधवियुक्तानां यतीनां यतचेतसाम् ।
अभितो ब्रह्मनिर्वाणं वर्तते विदितात्मनाम् ॥

kāmakrodhaviyuktānāṁ yatīnāṁ yatacetasām ।
abhito brahmanirvāṇaṁ vartate viditātmanām ॥

kāma krodha viyuktānāṁ: to those disjoined from desire and anger; *yatīnāṁ*: those self-controlled ones; *yata cetasām*: whose vital consciousness is subdued; *vidita ātmanām*: (who are also) knowers of the Self; *brahma nirvāṇaṁ*: self-effacement in the Absolute; *vartate abhitaḥ*: lies near at hand.

To those disjoined from desire and anger, those self-controlled ones whose vital consciousness is subdued, (who are also) knowers of the Self, self-effacement in the Absolute lies near at hand.

27. स्पर्शान्कृत्वा बहिर्बाह्यांश्चक्षुश्चैवान्तरे भ्रुवोः ।
प्राणापानौ समौ कृत्वा नासाभ्यन्तरचारिणौ ॥

sparśān kṛtvā bahir bāhyāṁś cakṣuś cai 'vā 'ntare bhruvoḥ ।
prāṇāpānau samau kṛtvā nāsābhyantaracārinau ॥

kṛtvā bāhyān: having (peripherally) discarded; *bahiḥ sparśān*: outward contacts (such as touch); *ca eva*: and also; *cakṣuḥ antare*: (with) eyes (fixed) between; *bhruvoḥ*: the eyebrows; *samau*: equalizing; *prāṇa apānau*: the positive (outward *prāna*) and negative (inward *apāna* – vital tendencies; *kṛtvā nāsā abhyantara cārinau*: moving within the nasal orifice.

28. यतेन्द्रियमनोबुद्धिर्मुनिर्मोक्षपरायणः ।
विगतेच्छाभयक्रोधो यः सदा मुक्त एव सः ॥

yatendriyamanobuddhir munir mokṣaparāyaṇaḥ ।
vigatecchābhayakrodho yaḥ sadā mukta eva saḥ ॥

yata indriya manaḥ buddhiḥ: with the senses, mind, and reason controlled; *muniḥ*: the silent recluse; *mokṣa parāyaṇaḥ*: wholly intent on liberation; *vigata icchā bhaya krodhaḥ*: with desire, fear, and anger gone; *eva yaḥ*: (is) even who; *sadā saḥ*: (is) ever himself; *muktaḥ*: the liberated one.

Having peripherally discarded outward factors (such as touch), and also with eyes fixed between the eyebrows, equalizing the positive and negative vital tendencies moving within the nasal orifice, with the senses, mind, and reason controlled, the silent recluse, wholly intent on liberation, with desire, fear, and anger gone, is ever himself, the liberated one.

29. भोक्तारं यज्ञतपसां सर्वलोकमहेश्वरम् ।
सुहृदं सर्वभूतानां ज्ञात्वा मां शान्तिमृच्छति ।।

bhoktāraṁ yajñatapasāṁ sarvalokamaheśvaram ।
suhṛdaṁ sarvabhūtānāṁ jñātvā māṁ śāntim ṛcchati ॥

jñātvā māṁ: having known Me; *bhoktāraṁ*: as the Enjoyer, the Acceptor; *yajña tapasāṁ*: of ritual sacrifices and austerities; *sarva loka maheśvaram*: the great Lord of all worlds; *suhṛdaṁ sarva bhūtānāṁ*: (and) the Friend of all beings; *ṛcchati śāntim*: one reaches peace.

Having known Me as the Enjoyer of ritual sacrifices, the Acceptor of austerities, the great Lord of all worlds, and the Friend of all beings, one reaches peace.

DIALOGUE

TEACHER: There is a complementarity between renunciation resulting from unitive reasoning (*saṁnyāsa*), and the performance of action with an identity of the personal self with the Universal Self (*karma-yoga*).

STUDENT: *Could you give me a typical example of each of these?*

On seeing that everything is an aggregate of dependent origination, born of desire, Gautama, the Prince of Kapilavastu, became the Awakened One, the Buddha. Having found nothing greater than *nibbāna*, the Great Liberation, he lived the life of a renunciate. He typifies *saṁnyāsa*. Jesus of Nazareth found his self-identity with God and guided all his actions on that sense of identity expressed in the dictum: "Thy will be done and not mine". He typifies the highest form of the unitive way of action. In both these cases everything personal, private, narrow, closed, limited, or relativistic is transcended. Instead of seeing the complementarity of these two approaches, many see only the apparent contradiction between rejection and acceptance, and place these two visions of life as opposed to each other. Arjuna also is not free from such a fallacy of judgement. He asks:

> You recommend the effective transcending of action, Oh Kṛṣṇa, and again *yoga* also; tell me, duly determined, which one of these two is spiritually better.

Earlier, in Chapters II, III, and IV, unitive reasoning was referred to as superior to the performance of action. It was never made clear that they are complementary as in the two cases you have cited above. Hence Arjuna's confusion is legitimate.

Kṛṣṇa makes it very clear in the following verse:

> Both renunciation and unitive action have emancipation as their common effect; of the two, however, unitive action is superior to (mere) renunciation of action.

I think even in this verse there remains a vestige of the same semantic confusion that led Arjuna to think of unitive reasoning and the unitive way of action as mutually contradictory, or at least contrary, with the latter having a special stress of superiority over the former. When Kṛṣṇa is asked to compare and evaluate renunciation (saṁnyāsa) *and the unitive way of action* (karma-yoga), *he compares the unitive way of action (karma-yoga) with inaction* (karma-saṁnyāsa). *It is hard to see what distinction Kṛṣṇa makes between saṁnyāsa, in the sense of renunciation of one's sense of agency in action, or of the enjoyment or suffering as the result of action, and* karma-saṁnyāsa, *in the sense of the mere rejection of action and resorting to inaction.*

Yes, you are right. There is a possible confusion in the different senses in which the word renunciation (*saṁnyāsa*) is used here. In the above verse, Kṛṣṇa speaks of *saṁnyāsa* as being equal to *karma-yoga* when judged by their common effect of spiritual emancipation. When judged merely on the basis of effect or end, rather than by the method or means employed, they are equal. When we take into consideration the means, there is a difference. The Gītā decides in favour of *karma-yoga*, unitive action, as against mere omission of action, given in the above verse as *karma-saṁnyāsa*. The revaluation of *saṁnyāsa* in the light of *yoga* may be said to be one of the important contributions of the Gītā.

What is Kṛṣṇa's definition of saṁnyāsa?

Kṛṣṇa defines *saṁnyāsa* in verse 3:

> That man should be recognized as a perennial renouncer (*nitya saṁnyāsī*) who neither hates nor desires; free indeed from conflicting pairs (of interests), Oh Mighty-Armed, he is happily released from the bondage (of necessity).

Further, in verses 4 and 5, Kṛṣṇa points out the complementarity and axiological identity of the two disciplines:

> That rationalism (Sāṁkhya) and self-discipline (Yoga) are distinct, only children say, not the well-informed; one well-established in either one of them obtains the result of both.

> That status attained by men of Sāṁkhya (rationalist persuasion) is reached also by those of Yoga (unitive discipline); he who thus sees Sāṁkhya and Yoga as one – he (alone) sees.

In that case why is so much fuss made in the name of unitive action? Why cannot Arjuna be left to himself to make his own decisions?

Nobody asks Arjuna to defer from making his decision. On his own accord he came to the battlefield. It was his own choice to take up the challenge and declare war on behalf of his brothers when it was not warranted in the least for him to blow his conch in response to the war challenge. He was overriding the privileges of both Yudhiṣṭhira, who was the king and his elder brother, and Bhīma, who was the commander-in-chief. After having initiated the warfare he himself stood up, raised his bow, and decided to fight. Nobody prompted him to make any of these decisions. The decisions to blow his conch before the king, and to station his chariot in between the two armies, were his own unilateral decisions. Kr̥ṣṇa would not have said a word to him, except in obedience, had he not placed himself at his feet as a disciple and asked for his advice. The least to be expected from a Guru is telling his disciple what he can and cannot do when the latter by himself cannot decide upon his own course. The type of renunciation Arjuna had in mind was the antique form of *saṁnyāsa* which was full of taboos, denials, harsh obligations, bans, and painful austerities. Hence Kr̥ṣṇa offers him the alternative of the Yoga of Action:

> One affiliated to the unitive way of life, attained to lucidity of Self, of Self-conquest, who has gained a victory over the senses, whose Self-existence has become the same as the Self-existence of all, though active, is unaffected (thereby).
>
> "I do nothing at all" – saying thus, he of unitive ways, who is a philosopher, should think, (while) seeing, hearing, touching, smelling, eating, going, sleeping, breathing, speaking, excreting, grasping, opening and closing the eyes – treating the senses as (merely) related to their (corresponding) sense-objects.
>
> He who acts, placing all actions in the Absolute, having given up attachment, is not affected by sin, like a lotus leaf by water.

In unitive action also it is the continuous remembrance of the yogī's *identity with the Absolute that makes his action an occasion of union. There also, the emphasis is on knowledge. What special role does action play in the search for realization?*

Performance of action with the right attitude is for the purpose of the purity of the Self. Kr̥ṣṇa says:

> By the body, by the mind, by intelligence, and even by the senses alone, *yogīs* engage in action, abandoning attachment, for purposes of purity of Self.

Here the term "purity of Self" calls for an explanation, since it has just now been stated that actions do not affect the actor if he is a *yogī*. To avoid the stagnation produced by willful inaction and its consequent morbid psychic states, and to permit the free interplay of natural tendencies and impulses, some sort of non-obstructive working out of these tendencies is required. Repressions benumb the spirit, and cathartic easing is a remedy known to modern psychology. It is in this sense that the purification is to be understood here.

Haven't we discussed karma-yoga *threadbare in Chapters II, III, and IV?*

This chapter is intended to give an integral vision of both *karma-yoga* and *saṁnyāsa*. After having shown how a *yogī* resorts to action without being bogged down by its binding consequences, Kṛṣṇa complements the same discipline with the life pattern of a renunciate:

> The one of unitive discipline, discarding benefit-motive, attains to ultimate peace; the one of non-unitive discipline being desire-motivated, attached to results, is bound.
>
> Relinquishing by means of the mind all activities, the embodied One sits happily, a victor, in the nine-gated city, neither acting nor causing to act.

But the renunciate also does not seem absolutely inactive. What impels him to act?

Kṛṣṇa explains it in verses 14 and 15:

> The Supreme does not generate either the idea of agency or activity in regard to the world, nor the union of action and benefit; the innate urge in beings, however, exerts itself.
>
> The All-pervading One takes cognizance neither of the sinful nor of the meritorious actions of anyone; wisdom is veiled by unwisdom; beings are deluded thereby.

In the two verses above, the "Supreme" and "the Pervading One", given in the Sanskrit respectively as *prabhu* and the *vibhu*, need special attention. These expressions are often taken as a reference to God in a theistic sense, but the context here does not demand such an interpretation. The perfected man who has been referred to as a *yogī* untouched by peripheral aspects of ordinary existence is automatically raised in his spiritual status, which can even amount to that of a lordship, described by Patañjali as *īśatva*. It is not uncommon to refer to the soul as *vibhu*, meaning "that which persists as the primeval cause" and also as "the all-pervading One", in and through all the manifested forms and effects.

From the standpoint of pure contemplation there is no plurality of selves, and there is no Truth other than the Self. What is given in verse 14 above as "innate urge" should be taken in its most general term as an equally all-pervading negative principle or vital impulse to which is attributed all the creative functions known in nature.

From this, I understand Kṛṣṇa does not favour any special religious creed or discipline of piety. It seems such a yogī should treat the whole universe as his own negative counterpart, just as an ordinary man considers his body as a perishable counterpart of his soul. Am I right?

Kṛṣṇa puts it this way:

> In regard to a brāhmin endowed with learning or humility, a cow, an elephant, and even a dog, as also one who cooks the dog (for food), the well-informed ones see the same difference-less reality.

This clearly shows that the doctrine of the Gītā rises above all forms of holiness or relativistic spirituality. This is different from any religious or theologic contexts, in which we see all sorts of grades distinguishing man from man on the basis of considerations of virtue or vice, of the sacred or the profane. The reference to the dog and the brāhmin is to demolish all sense of sacredness and profanity that was prevalent in the Indian mind through many centuries. All are equals in the Light of the Absolute. In the second chapter we had the description of one established in unitive wisdom. Here again Kṛṣṇa gives the characteristics of the wise established in the Absolute. Such a state is called *brāhmī sthiti.*

Is there any difference between the state of being well-founded in unitive reason, sthitaprajñatā, *and grounded in the Absolute,* brāhmī sthiti?

In the course of the Gītā you will find different descriptions of the same state of the highest realization. If there is any subtle difference at all, it only belongs to the kind of discipline or the gestalt of the vision by which one arrives at such a state. One in *brāhmī sthiti*, meaning "grounded in the Absolute", is one whose mind is balanced in unity, who is no longer disturbed by turbulent vital urges. He will not rejoice on good befalling him nor be disturbed by a mishap. As he verticalizes all his external happenings in terms of his inner life, he knows no joy but the oneness of his Self with the Absolute. He does not need to wait for the fall of his body to live the life of the eternally free. His inward happiness shines like a bright light that fills his inner and outer life with the same brilliance and joy. As he sees none but his own Self in all, he becomes a veritable refuge for all who seek love and compassion. Being one with all, such a person has nothing to desire. As there is none other than him, there is no one to rob him of his joy and provoke him to be hateful. He basks on the banks of the Absolute in Whom he can dissolve his identity any time and forever.

What happens to such a person when he leaves his body?

Most people think of death with dread. The time of death is the most difficult time to keep in perfect attunement with the Absolute. The discipline of a lifetime brings the reward of the most graceful exit from the body, and blesses the mind with an attitude which leads one to final liberation. Kṛṣṇa describes the state of such blessed ones in verses 27 and 28:

> Having peripherally discarded outward factors (such as touch), and also with eyes fixed between the eyebrows, equalizing the positive and negative vital tendencies moving within the nasal orifice, with the senses, mind, and reason controlled, the silent recluse, wholly intent on liberation, with desire, fear, and anger gone, is ever himself, the liberated one.

VI

Dhyāna-Yoga
Unitive Contemplation

INTRODUCTION

HOWEVER glorious action is, it does not bring realization or ultimate release. When action is performed with dedication in a sacrificial sense, it purifies the mind and indirectly helps to attain an attitude that is conducive to realization. This chapter begins with praise for the renunciation of the fruits of action. The previous chapter ended with the description of a contemplative. As such a contemplative has no desire to fulfil, and his action is in tune with the symphony of universal well-being; he is described here as a *yogī* and a *saṁnyāsī*. The Sāṁkhyan ideal of *saṁnyāsa* and the Yogic path of unitive action are here fused into an integrated model.

In this chapter the attitude and inner experience of a *yogī* are so clearly described that one can look upon the *yogī* as a model of perfection. The perfection conceived by the Bhagavadgītā is not confined to the present life alone. Just as Keats said "A thing of beauty is a joy forever", the perfection achieved by a *yogī* will leave its stamp of reminiscence as an eternal inspiration to mankind. A progression towards perfection is not cut-off by the termination of life in one body, but will continue in the next incarnation from where it left off.

TRANSLATION

श्रीभगवानुवाच –

1. अनाश्रितः कर्मफलं कार्यं कर्म करोति यः ।
स संन्यासी च योगी च न निरग्निर्न चाक्रियः ॥

śrībhagavān uvāca –

anāśritaḥ karmaphalaṁ kāryaṁ karma karoti yaḥ ।
sa saṁnyāsī ca yogī ca na niragnir na cā 'kriyaḥ ॥

śrībhagavān uvāca: Kṛṣṇa said; *anāśritaḥ*: without depending on; *karmaphalaṁ*: the results of action; *yaḥ karoti*: he who does; *kāryaṁ karma*: necessary action; *saḥ saṁnyāsī ca*: he is a renunciate and; *ca yogī*: also a contemplative; *na niragniḥ*: not he who has (merely) given up sacrificial fire; *na ca akriyaḥ*: nor he who (merely) abstains from ritualist (or other) action.

Kṛṣṇa said:

Without depending on the results of action, he who does necessary action is a renouncer and also a contemplative, not he who has (merely) given up sacrificial fire, or who (merely) abstains from ritualist (or other) action.

2. यं संन्यासमिति प्राहुर्योगं तं विद्धि पाण्डव ।
न ह्यसंन्यस्तसङ्कल्पो योगी भवति कश्चन ॥

yaṁ saṁnyāsam iti prāhur yogaṁ taṁ viddhi pāṇḍava ।
na hy asaṁnyastasaṅkalpo yogī bhavati kaścana ॥

yaṁ prāhuḥ: that which (people) call; *saṁnyāsam*: renunciation; *iti viddhi taṁ*: thus know that (to be); *yogaṁ*: *yoga*; *pāṇḍaya*: Oh Arjuna; *asaṁnyasta saṅkalpaḥ kaścana*: one who has not given up his wilful desires for particularized ends; *na hi bhavati yogī*: never indeed becomes a *yogī*.

That which people call renunciation: know that to be *yoga*, Oh Pāṇḍava; one who has not given up his willful desires for particularized ends never indeed becomes a *yogī*.

3. आरुरुक्षोर्मुनेर्योगं कर्म कारणमुच्यते ।
योगारूढस्य तस्यैव शमः कारणमुच्यते ॥

ārurukṣor muner yogaṁ karma kāraṇam ucyate ।
yogārūḍhasya tasyaī 'va śamaḥ kāraṇam ucyate ॥

yogaṁ muneḥ: the *yoga* of a man of self-control; *ārurukṣoḥ*: who is still an aspirant (for it); *ucyate*: is said to have; *karma kāraṇam*: action (as its) motive-principle; *tasya eva*: for him indeed; *yoga ārūḍhasya*: who has ascended to the unitive state; *śamaḥ ucyate*: tranquillity is said to be; *kāraṇam*: (its) motive-principle.

The *yoga* of a man of self-control, who is still an aspirant for it, is said to have action as its motive-principle; for the same person, when he has ascended to the unitive state, tranquillity is said to be its motive-principle.

4. यदा हि नेन्द्रियार्थेषु न कर्मस्वनुषज्जते ।
सर्वसङ्कल्पसंन्यासी योगारूढस्तदोच्यते ॥

yadā hi ne 'ndriyārtheṣu na karmasv anuṣajjate ।
sarvasaṅkalpasaṁnyāsī yogārūḍhas tado 'cyate ॥

yadā hi: when however; *na indriyārtheṣu*: neither in the objects of the senses; *na karmasu*: nor in actions; *anuṣajjate*: one is attached; *sarva saṅkalpa saṁnyāsī*: (such a man) who has renounced all wilful desires for particularized ends; *tadā ucyate*: then is said to be; *yogārūḍhaḥ*: one who has ascended to *yoga.*

When, however, neither in the objects of the senses nor in actions one finds attachment – such a man, who has renounced all wilful desires for particularized ends, is said to be one who has ascended to *yoga*.

5. उद्धरेदात्मनात्मानं नात्मानमवसादयेत् ।
आत्मैव ह्यात्मनो बन्धुरात्मैव रिपुरात्मनः ।।

uddhared ātmanā 'tmānaṁ nā 'tmānam avasādayet ।
ātmai 'va hy ātmano bandhur ātmai 'va ripur ātmanaḥ ॥

ātmanā: by the Self; *ātmānaṁ uddharet*: the Self must be upheld; *ātmānam na avasādayet*: the Self should not be let down; *ātmā eva hi*: the Self alone indeed; *ātmanaḥ bandhuḥ*: (is) its own dear relative; *ātmā eva*: the Self indeed; *ripuḥ ātmanaḥ*: (is) the enemy of the Self.

By the Self the Self must be upheld; the Self should not be let down; the Self indeed is its own dear relative; the Self indeed is the enemy of the Self.

6. बन्धुरात्मात्मनस्तस्य येनात्मैवात्मना जितः।
अनात्मनस्तु शत्रुत्वे वर्तेतात्मैव शत्रुवत् ।।

bandhur ātmā 'tmanas tasya yenā 'tmai vā 'tmanā jitaḥ ।
anātmanas tu śatrutve vartetā 'tmai 'va śatruvat ॥

ātmā bandhuḥ: the Self is dear; *tasya ātmanaḥ*: to one (possessed) of Self; *yena eva ātmā*: by whom even the Self; *ātmanā*: by the Self; *jitaḥ*: has been won; *tu anātmanaḥ*: but for one not (possessed) of Self; *ātmā varteta*: the Self would be; *śatrutve eva*: in confllict indeed; *śatruvat*: as if an enemy

The Self is dear to one (possessed) of Self, by whom even the Self by the Self has been won; for one not (possessed) of Self, the Self would be in conflict with the very Self, as if an enemy.

7. जितात्मनः प्रशान्तस्य परमात्मा समाहितः ।
शीतोष्णसुखदुःखेषु तथा मानापमानयोः ।।

jitātmanaḥ praśāntasya paramātmā samāhitaḥ ।
śītoṣṇasukhaduḥkheṣu tathā mānāpamānayoḥ ॥

jitātmanaḥ: to one of conquered Self; *praśāntasya*: who rests in peace; *paramātmā*: the Supreme Self; *tathā samāhitaḥ*: (is) thus in (a state of) neutral balance; *śīta uṣṇa sukha duḥkheṣu*: in cold–heat, happiness–suffering; *māna apamānayoḥ*: in honour–disgrace.

To one of conquered Self, who rests in peace, the Supreme is in a state of neutral balance in heat–cold, happiness–suffering, honour–disgrace.

8. ज्ञानविज्ञानतृप्तात्मा कूटस्थो विजितेन्द्रियः ।
युक्त इत्युच्यते योगी समलोष्टाश्मकाञ्चनः ॥

jñānavijñānatṛptātmā kūṭastho vijitendriyaḥ ।
yukta ity ucyate yogī samaloṣṭāśmakāñcanaḥ ॥

iti yogī: that *yogī*; *jñāna vijñāna tṛpta ātmā*: whose Self is satisfied by (synthetic) wisdom and (analytic) knowledge; *kūṭasthaḥ*: established in unchanging immobility; *vijita indriyaḥ*: who has gained full control over sense-attachments; *ucyate yuktaḥ*: is said to be unified; *sama loṣṭa aśma kāñcanaḥ*: one to whom a lump of earth, a stone, and gold are the same.

That *yogī* whose Self is satisfied by (synthetic) wisdom and (analytic) knowledge, established in unchanging immobility, who has gained full control over sense-attachments, is said to be unified – one to whom a lump of earth, a stone, and gold are the same.

9. सुहृन्मित्रार्युदासीनमध्यस्थद्वेष्यबन्धुषु ।
साधुष्वपि च पापेषु समबुद्धिर्विशिष्यते ॥

suhṛnmitrāryudāsīna madhyasthadveṣyabandhuṣu ।
sādhuṣv api ca pāpeṣu samabuddhir viśiṣyate ॥

suhṛt mitra ari udāsīna madhyastha dveṣya bandhuṣu: as between dear well-wishers, friends, enemies, those indifferent, those in-between, haters, relations; *api sādhuṣu ca pāpeṣu*: also as between good people and sinners; *sama buddhiḥ*: he who can maintain an equal attitude; *viśiṣyate*: excels.

As between dear well-wishers, friends, enemies, those indifferent, those in-between, haters, relations, and also as between good people and sinners, he who can maintain an equal attitude, excels.

10. योगी युञ्जीत सततमात्मानं रहसि स्थितः ।
एकाकी यतचित्तात्मा निराशीरपरिग्रहः ॥

yogī yuñjīta satatam ātmānaṁ rahasi sthitaḥ ।
ekākī yatacittātmā nirāśīr aparigrahaḥ ॥

yogī satatam: the *yogī* constantly; *yuñjita ātmānaṁ*: should gather unitively his own Self; *sthitaḥ rahasi*: established (in a place) by himself; *ekākī*: alone; *yata citta ātmā*: with relational mind and Self under control; *nirāśīḥ*: without expectations; *aparigrahaḥ*: (and) without possessive intentions.

The *yogī* should constantly gather his own Self unitively, established in a place where he can be by himself, alone, with relational mind and Self control, without expectations and without possessive intentions.

11. शुचौ देशे प्रतिष्ठाप्य स्थिरमासनमात्मनः ।
नात्युच्छ्रितं नातिनीचं चैलाजिनकुशोत्तरम् ।।

śucau deśe pratiṣṭhāpya sthiram āsanam ātmanaḥ ।
nā 'tyucchritaṁ nā 'tinīcaṁ cailājinakuśottaram ॥

pratiṣṭhāpya sthiram: having established firmly; *śucau deśe*: in a clean place; *āsanam ātmanaḥ*: a seat for himself; *na ati ucchritam*: neither too high; *na ati nīcaṁ*: nor no low; *caila ajina kuśa uttaram*: (and) covered (respectively) with cloth, skin, and grass.

12. तत्रैकाग्रं मनः कृत्वा यतचित्तेन्द्रियक्रियः ।
उपविश्यासने युञ्ज्याद्योगमात्मविशुद्धये ।।

tatrai 'kāgraṁ manaḥ kṛtvā yatacittendriyakriyaḥ ।
upaviśyā 'sane yuñjyād yogam ātmaviśuddhaye ॥

tatra kṛtvā manaḥ ekāgraṁ: there having made the mind one-pointed; *yata citta indriyakriyaḥ*: and with relational mind and sense-functions subdued; *upaviśya āsane*: (duly) taking his place on his seat; *yuñjyāt yogam*: let him unitively engage in *yoga*; *ātma viśuddhaye*: for transparent Self-consciousness.

Having established firmly in a clean place a seat for himself, one neither too high nor too low, and covered respectively with cloth, skin, and grass,

there having made the mind one-pointed, and with relational mind and sense-functions subdued, (duly) taking his place on his seat, let him unitively engage in *yoga* for transparent Self-consciousness.

13. समं कायशिरोग्रीवं धारयन्नचलं स्थिरः ।
सम्प्रेक्ष्य नासिकाग्रं स्वं दिशश्चानवलोकयन् ।।

samaṁ kāyaśirogrīvaṁ dhārayann acalaṁ sthiraḥ ।
saṁprekṣya nāsikāgraṁ svaṁ diśaś cā 'navalokayan ॥

kāya śiraḥ grīvaṁ: (with) body, head, and neck; *dhārayan samaṁ*: held evenly; *acalaṁ sthiraḥ*: (in) immobile poise; *saṁprekṣya svaṁ nāsikā agraṁ*: looking at one's nose-tip; *ca anavalokayan*: and not perceiving; *diśaḥ*: the (actual) directions (of space).

14. प्रशान्तात्मा विगतभीर्ब्रह्मचारिव्रते स्थितः ।
मनः संयम्य मच्चित्तो युक्त आसीत मत्परः ।।

praśantātmā vigatabhīr brahmacārivrate sthitaḥ ।
manaḥ saṁyamya maccitto yukta āsita matparaḥ ॥

praśānta ātmā: (with) tranquil Self; *vigata bhīḥ*: (with) fear gone; *sthitaḥ vrate brahmacārī*: established in the vow of a *brahmacārī* (aspirant walking in the Way of the Absolute); *manaḥ saṁyamya*: having mind subdued; *maccitaḥ*: contemplating Me; *āsīta yuktaḥ*: he may sit united; *matparaḥ*: having Me for (his) supreme goal.

With body, head, and neck held evenly and in immobile poise, looking at one's nose-tip and not perceiving the (actual) directions (of space), with tranquil Self, with fear gone, established in the vow of a *brahmacārī*, having mind subdued, related to Me through contemplative thought, he may sit, united, having Me for his supreme goal.

15. युञ्जन्नेवं सदात्मानं योगी नियतमानसः ।
शान्तिं निर्वाणपरमां मत्संस्थामधिगच्छति ।।

yuñjann evaṁ sadā 'tmānaṁ yogī niyatamānasaḥ ।
sāntiṁ nirvāṇaparamāṁ matsaṁsthām adhigacchati ॥

evaṁ sadā: thus, ever; *yuñjan ātmānaṁ*: unitively joining the Self; *yogī niyata mānasaḥ*: the *yogī* whose mind is subdued; *adhigacchati śāntiṁ*: enters into the peace; *matsaṁsthām*: which abides in Me; *nirvāṇa paramāṁ*: (having as its) ultimate phase total effacement.

Thus, ever unitively joining the Self, the *yogī* whose mind is subdued enters into that peace which abides in Me, which has as its ultimate phase total effacement.

16. नात्यश्नतस्तु योगोऽस्ति न चैकान्तमनश्नतः ।
न चातिस्वप्नशीलस्य जाग्रतो नैव चार्जुन ।।

nā 'tyaśnatas tu yogo 'sti na cai 'kāntam anaśnataḥ ।
na cā 'tisvapnaśīlasya jāgrato nai 'va cā 'rjūna ॥

tu: but; *asti na yogaḥ*: there is no *yoga*; *atyaśnataḥ*: (for) a glutton; *na ca*: nor; *ekāntam anaśnataḥ*: (for) one who eats nothing at all; *na ca*: nor; *arjuna*: Oh Arjuna; *ati svapna śīlasya*: for one who over-sleeps; *na ca eva jāgrataḥ*: nor even for the (over) wakeful.

To be sure, there is no *yoga* for a glutton, nor for one who fasts, nor, Oh Arjuna, is it either for one who over-sleeps or is (over) wakeful.

17. युक्ताहारविहारस्य युक्तचेष्टस्य कर्मसु ।
युक्तस्वप्नावबोधस्य योगो भवति दुःखहा ॥

yuktāhāravihārasya yuktaceṣṭasya karmasu ।
yuktasvapnāvabodhasya yogo bhavati duḥkhahā ॥

yukta āhāra vihārasya: to one of proper food (habits) and recreation; *yukta ceṣṭasya karmasu*: who engages in activities in (proper) moderation; *yukta svapna avabodhasya*: who sleeps and wakes in a well-regulated way; *yogaḥ bhavati*: *yoga* takes its course; *duḥkhahā*: painlessly.

To one of proper food (habits) and recreation, who engages in activities in proper moderation, who sleeps and wakes in a well-regulated way, *yoga* takes its course painlessly.

18. यदा विनियतं चित्तमात्मन्येवावतिष्ठते ।
निःस्पृहः सर्वकामेभ्यो युक्त इत्युच्यते तदा ॥

yadā viniyataṁ cittam ātmany evā 'vatiṣṭhate ।
niḥspṛhaḥ sarvakāmebhyo yukta ity ucyate tadā ॥

yadā viniyataṁ cittam: when the subdued relational mind; *avatiṣṭhate ātmani eva*: stays in the Self itself; *niḥspṛhaḥ sarva kāmebhyaḥ*: desireless of all desires; *tadā*: then; *iti ucyate yuktaḥ*: indeed (it) is said to be united.

When the subduced relational mind stays in the Self itself, desireless of all desires, then it is said to be united.

19. यथा दीपो निवातस्थो नेङ्गते सोपमा स्मृता ।
योगिनो यतचित्तस्य युञ्जतो योगमात्मनः ॥

yathā dīpo nivātastho ne 'ṅgate so 'pamā smṛtā ।
yogīno yatacittasya yuñjato yogam ātmanaḥ ॥

yathā dīpaḥ: as a lamp; *nivātasthaḥ*: set in a windless place; *na iṅgate*: does not flicker; *saḥ upamā smṛtā*: such a simile is thought of; *yoginaḥ*: in regard to a *yogī*; *yata cittasya*: who has brought under restraint his (relational) mind; *yuñjataḥ*: (ever) uniting (thus); *yogam ātmanaḥ*: in the union of the Self.

As a lamp set in a windless place does not flicker – such a simile is thought of in regard to a *yogī* who has brought under restraint his (relational) mind, (ever) uniting thus in the union of the Self.

20. यत्रोपरमते चित्तं निरुद्धं योगसेवया ।
यत्र चैवात्मनात्मानं पश्यन्नात्मनि तुष्यति ॥

yatro 'paramate cittaṁ niruddhaṁ yogasevayā ।
yatra cai 'vā 'tmanā 'tmānaṁ paśyann ātmani tuṣyati ॥

yatra cittaṁ: (that state) where the (relational) mind; *uparamate*: attains tranquillity; *niruddhaṁ*: restrained; *yoga sevayā*: through (continued) cultivation of a Yogic attitude; *ca yatra eva*: and where also; *paśyan ātmānaṁ*: seeing the Self; *ātmanā ātmani*: by the Self in the Self; *tuṣyati*: (he) enjoys happiness.

(That state) where the (relational) mind attains tranquillity, restrained through continued cultivation of a Yogic attitude, and where also the Self by the Self in the Self enjoys happiness,

21. सुखमात्यन्तिकं यत्तद्बुद्धिग्राह्यमतीन्द्रियम् ।
वेत्ति यत्र न चैवायं स्थितश्चलति तत्त्वतः ॥

sukham ātyantikaṁ yat tad buddhigrāhyam atīndriyam ।
vetti yatra na cai 'vā 'yaṁ sthitaś calati tattvataḥ ॥

tat yat: that (in) which; *vetti ātyantikaṁ sukham*: one cognizes the ultimate limit of happiness; *buddhi grāhyam*: (which can be) grasped by reason; *atīndriyam*: (and goes) beyond the senses; *ca sthitaḥ yatra*: and established wherein; *na eva calati*: there is no more moving; *ayaṁ tattvataḥ*: from this true principle.

that in which one cognizes the ultimate limit of happiness which can be grasped by reason and goes beyond the senses, and established wherein there is no more swerving from the true principle,

22. यं लब्ध्वा चापरं लाभं मन्यते नाधिकं ततः ।
यस्मिन्स्थितो न दुःखेन गुरुणापि विचाल्यते ॥

yaṁ labdhvā cā 'paraṁ lābhaṁ manyate nā 'dhikaṁ tataḥ ।
yasmin sthito na duḥkhena guruṇā 'pi vicālyate ॥

ca yaṁ labdhvā: and which having obtained; *tataḥ na aparaṁ lābhaṁ*: from there no other gain; *manyate*: is thought of; *adhikaṁ*: (which could be) greater (in value); *yasmin sthitaḥ*: in which, (when) established; *na vicālyate*: there is no swerving; *api guruṇā duḥkhena*: even by heavy suffering.

and which, having obtained, there is no other gain thought of which could be greater (in value), in which, when established, there is no swerving even by heavy suffering

23. तं विद्याद् दुःखसंयोगवियोगं योगसञ्ज्ञितम् ।
स निश्चयेन योक्तव्यो योगोऽनिर्विण्णचेतसा ॥

taṁ vidyād duḥkhasaṁyoga viyogaṁ yogasaṁjñitam ।
sa niścayena yoktavyo yogo'nirviṇṇacetasā ॥

taṁ vidyāt: that should be known; *yoga saṁjñitam*: by the name of *yoga*; *duḥkha saṁyoga viyogaṁ*: disaffiliation from the context of suffering; *saḥ yogaḥ*: such a *yoga*; *yoktavyaḥ*: should be adhered to; *niścayena*: with determination; *anirviṇṇa cetasā*: free from spiritual regret.

– that should be known by the name of *yoga*: disaffiliation from the context of suffering. Such a *yoga* should be adhered to with determination, free from spiritual regret.

24. सङ्कल्पप्रभवान्कामांस्त्यक्त्वा सर्वानशेषतः ।
मनसैवेन्द्रियग्रामं विनियम्य समन्ततः ।।

saṅkalpaprabhavān kāmāṁs tyaktvā sarvān aśeṣataḥ ।
manasai 've 'ndriyagrāmaṁ viniyamya samantataḥ ॥

tyaktvā aśeṣataḥ: abandoning completely; *sarvān kāmān*: all desires; *saṅkalpa prabhavān*: originating in the will for particularized ends; *viniyamya eva manasā*: curbing indeed with the mind; *indriya grāmaṁ*: the collection of sense-functionings; *samantataḥ*: on every side.

Abandoning completely all desires originating in the will for particularized ends, curbing the collection of sense-functionings on every side

25. शनैः शनैरुपरमेद्बुद्ध्या धृतिगृहीतया ।
आत्मसंस्थं मनः कृत्वा न किञ्चिदपि चिन्तयेत् ।।

śanaiḥ-śanair uparamed buddhyā dhṛtigṛhītayā ।
ātmasaṁsthaṁ manaḥ kṛtvā na kiñcid api cintayet ॥

śanaiḥ śanaiḥ: slowly, slowly; *uparamet*: activities should be brought to a standstill; *buddhyā dhṛti gṛhītayā*: by reason steadily applied; *kṛtvā manaḥ*: establishing the mind; *ātma saṁsthaṁ*: reflexively in the Self; *cintayet*: one should think of; *na kiñcit api*: nothing at all.

– slowly, slowly, activities should be brought to a standstill by reason steadily applied, establishing the mind reflexively in the Self, without thinking of anything whatever.

26. यतो यतो निश्चरति मनश्चञ्चलमस्थिरम् ।
ततस्ततो नियम्यैतदात्मन्येव वशं नयेत् ।।

yato-yato niścarati manaś cañcalam asthiram ।
tatas-tato niyamyai 'tad ātmany eva vaśaṁ nayet ॥

yataḥ yataḥ: from whatever (again and again); *cañcalam asthiram manaḥ*: the changeful, unsteady mind; *niścarati*: goes out to; *tataḥ tataḥ*: from that (again and again); *niyamya*: restraining (it); *etat nayet*: it should (ever) be led; *vaśaṁ ātmani eva*: to the control of the Self indeed.

Whatever causes the changeful, unsteady mind to go out (again and again), from each such, restraining it (again and again), it should ever be led to the side of the Self.

27. प्रशान्तमनसं ह्येनं योगिनं सुखमुत्तमम् ।
उपैति शान्तरजसं ब्रह्मभूतमकल्मषम् ।।

praśāntamanasaṁ hy enaṁ yoginaṁ sukham uttamam ।
upaiti śāntarajasaṁ brahmabhūtam akalmaṣam ॥

enaṁ yoginaṁ hi: such a *yogī*, verily; *praśānta manasaṁ*: of calmed mind; *śānta rajasaṁ*: of pacified passion; *brahma bhūtam*: who has become the Absolute; *akalmaṣaṁ*: free from (all) dross; *upaiti uttamam sukham*: comes to supreme happiness.

Such a *yogī*, verily, of calmed mind, of pacified passion, who has become the Absolute, free from all dross, comes to supreme happiness.

28. युञ्जन्नेवं सदात्मानं योगी विगतकल्मषः ।
सुखेन ब्रह्मसंस्पर्शमत्यन्तं सुखमश्नुते ।।

yuñjann evaṁ sadā 'tmānaṁ yogī vigatakalmaṣaḥ ।
sukhena brahmasaṁsparśam atyantaṁ sukham aśnute ॥

sadā yuñjan evaṁ ātmānaṁ: ever uniting thus the Self; *yogī vigata kalmaṣaḥ*: (that) *yogī*, rid of dross; *brahma saṁsparśam*: having contact with the Absolute; *aśnute sukhena*: experiences easily; *atyantaṁ sukham*: ultimate happiness.

Ever uniting thus the Self, that *yogī*, rid of dross, having contact with the Absolute, enjoys easily happiness that is ultimate.

29. सर्वभूतस्थमात्मानं सर्वभूतानि चात्मनि ।
ईक्षते योगयुक्तात्मा सर्वत्र समदर्शनः ।।

sarvabhūtastham ātmānaṁ sarvabhūtāni cā 'tmani ।
īkṣate yogayuktātmā sarvatra samadarśanaḥ ॥

yoga yuktātmā: one whose Self is united by *yoga*; *īkṣate ātmānaṁ*: sees the Self; *sarva bhūta stham*: (as) abiding in all beings; *ca sarva bhūtāni*: and all beings; *ātmani*: (as abiding) in the Self; *sarvatra sama darśanaḥ*: everywhere seeing the same.

One whose Self is united by *yoga* sees the Self as abiding in all beings and all beings as abiding in the Self, everywhere seeing the same.

30. यो मां पश्यति सर्वत्र सर्वं च मयि पश्यति ।
तस्याहं न प्रणश्यामि स च मे न प्रणश्यति ।।

yo māṁ paśyati sarvatra sarvaṁ ca mayi paśyati ।
tasyā 'haṁ na praṇaśyāmi sa ca me na praṇaśyati ॥

yaḥ paśyati māṁ sarvatra: he who sees Me everywhere; *ca paśyati*: and sees; *sarvaṁ mayi*: everything in Me; *tasya*: to him; *ahaṁ na praṇaśyāmi*: I am not lost; *ca saḥ na praṇaśyāti me*: and he is not lost to me.

He who sees me everywhere, and sees everything in Me – to him I am not lost and he is not lost to Me.

31. सर्वभूतस्थितं यो मां भजत्येकत्वमास्थितः ।
सर्वथा वर्तमानोऽपि स योगी मयि वर्तते ।।

sarvabhūtasthitaṁ yo māṁ bhajaty ekatvam āsthitaḥ ।
sarvathā vartamāno 'pi sa yogī mayi vartate ॥

saḥ yogī: that *yogī*; *yaḥ bhajati māṁ*: who honours Me; *sarva bhūta sthitaṁ*: (as) abiding in all beings; *āsthitaḥ ekatvam*: established in unity; *api vartamānaḥ*: though remaining; *sarvathā*: in whatever way; *vartate mayi*: he abides in Me.

That *yogī* who honours Me as abiding in all beings, established in unity, remaining as he may in every (possible) way – he abides in Me.

32. आत्मौपम्येन सर्वत्र समं पश्यति योऽर्जुन ।
सुखं वा यदि वा दुःखं स योगी परमो मतः ।।

ātmaupamyena sarvatra samaṁ paśyati yo 'rjuna ।
sukhaṁ vā yadi vā duḥkhaṁ sa yogī paramo mataḥ ॥

ātma aupamyena: by (establishing an) analogy with the Self; *yaḥ paśyati samaṁ sarvatra*: who sees equality everywhere; *arjuna*: Oh Arjuna; *vā yadi sukhaṁ*: whether (in) pleasant; *vā duḥkhaṁ*: or painful (situations); *saḥ mataḥ*: he is considered; *yogī paramaḥ*: a perfect *yogī*.

By establishing an analogy with the Self, he who sees equality everywhere, Oh Arjuna, whether (in) pleasant or painful (situations) – he is considered a perfect *yogī*.

अर्जुन उवाच –
33. योऽयं योगस्त्वया प्रोक्तः साम्येन मधुसूदन ।
एतस्याहं न पश्यामि चञ्चलत्वात्स्थितिं स्थिराम् ।।

arjuna uvāca –

yo 'yaṁ yogas tvayā proktaḥ sāmyena madhusūdana ।
etasyā 'haṁ na paśyāmi cañcalatvāt sthitiṁ sthirām ॥

arjuna uvāca: Arjuna said; *ayaṁ yogaḥ yaḥ*: this *yoga* which; *proktaḥ tvayā*: outlined by you; *sāmyena*: as (consisting of) sameness; *madhusūdana*: Oh Kr̥ṣṇa; *ahaṁ na paśyāmi*: I do not see; *etasya*: for this; *sthitiṁ sthirām*: a stable foundation; *cañcalatvāt*: owing to changefulness.

Arjuna said:

That *yoga* you have outlined as consisting of sameness, Oh Madhusūdana – I do not see for this any stable foundation, owing to changefulness.

34. चञ्चलं हि मनः कृष्ण प्रमाथि बलवद्दृढम् ।
तस्याहं निग्रहं मन्ये वायोरिव सुदुष्करम् ॥

cañcalaṁ hi manaḥ kr̥ṣṇa pramāthi balavad dr̥ḍham ।
tasyā 'haṁ nigrahaṁ manye vāyor iva suduṣkaram ॥

manaḥ cañcalaṁ hi: the mind is changeful indeed; *kr̥ṣṇa*: Oh Kr̥ṣṇa; *pramāthi balavat*: it is agitated, forceful; *dr̥ḍham*: (and) imperative (in character); *ivā vāyoḥ*: like the wind; *ahaṁ manye*: I consider; *tasya nigrahaṁ*: its control; *suduṣkaram*: difficult to do.

The mind is changeful indeed, Oh Kr̥ṣṇa; it is agitated, forceful, and imperative (in character); like the wind, I consider its control difficult.

श्रीभगवानुवाच –
35. असंशयं महाबाहो मनो दुर्निग्रहं चलम् ।
अभ्यासेन तु कौन्तेय वैराग्येण च गृह्यते ॥

śrībhagavān uvāca –

asaṁśayaṁ mahābāho mano durnigrahaṁ calam ।
abhyāsena tu kaunteya vairāgyeṇa ca gr̥hyate ॥

śrībhagavān uvāca: Kr̥ṣṇa said; *asaṁśayaṁ*: doubtless; *mahābāho*: Oh Arjuna; *manaḥ durnigrahaṁ*: the mind is difficult to control; *calam*: (and) changeful; *tu abhyāsena*: but by practice; *kaunteya*: Oh Arjuna; *ca vairāgyeṇa*: and by dispassion; *gr̥hyate*: (it) is held (together).

Kr̥ṣṇa said:

Doubtless, Oh Mighty-Armed, the mind is difficult to control and changeful. By practice, indeed, Oh Son of Kuntī, and by dispassion (it) is held together.

36. असंयतात्मना योगो दुष्प्राप इति मे मतिः ।
वश्यात्मना तु यतता शक्योऽवाप्तुमुपायतः ॥

asaṁyatātmanā yogo duṣprāpa iti me matiḥ ।
vaśyātmanā tu yatatā śakyo 'vāptum upāyataḥ ॥

asaṁyata ātmanā: by a self uncontrolled; *yogaḥ duṣprāpaḥ*: *yoga* is hard to attain; *iti me matiḥ*: such is my opinion; *tu vaśya ātmanā*: but by a Self controlled; *yatatā*: endeavouring; *śakyaḥ avāptum*: (it is) possible to reach; *upāyataḥ*: through the means (indicated).

By a self uncontrolled, *yoga* is hard to attain; such is my opinion; but by a Self which is its own support, endeavouring, it is possible to reach through the means (indicated).

अर्जुन उवाच –

37. अयतिः श्रद्धयोपेतो योगाच्चलितमानसः ।
अप्राप्य योगसंसिद्धिं कां गतिं कृष्ण गच्छति ।।

arjuna uvāca –

ayatiḥ śraddhayo 'peto yogāc calitamānasaḥ ।
aprāpya yogasaṁsiddhiṁ kāṁ gatiṁ kṛṣṇa gacchati ॥

arjuna uvāca: Arjuna said; *ayatiḥ*: he who is unsubdued; *śraddhayā upetaḥ*: (but) endowed with faith; *yogāt calita mānasaḥ*: whose mind has deviated from *yoga*; *aprāpya yogasaṁsiddhiṁ*: not reaching to Yogic attainments; *kāṁ gatiṁ*: what path; *gacchati*: he goes; *kṛṣṇa*: Oh Kṛṣṇa.

38. कच्चिन्नोभयविभ्रष्टश्छिन्नाभ्रमिव नश्यति ।
अप्रतिष्ठो महाबाहो विमूढो ब्रह्मणः पथि ।।

kaccin no 'bhayavibhraṣṭaś chinnābhram iva naśyati ।
apratiṣṭho mahābāho vimūḍho brahmaṇaḥ pathi ॥

kaccit na: is it not that; *vibhraṣṭaḥ ubhaya*: fallen (from) both; *iva chinna abhram*: like a riven cloud; *naśyati*: he is destroyed; *apratiṣṭhaḥ*: without a mainstay; *mahābāho*: Oh Kṛṣṇa; *vimūḍhāḥ pathi*: confounded on the path; *brahmaṇaḥ*: of the Absolute.

Arjuna said:

He who is unsubdued (but) endowed with faith, whose mind has deviated from *yoga*, not reaching to Yogic attainments – what path does he take, Oh Kṛṣṇa?

Is he not fallen from both like a riven cloud, destroyed without a mainstay, Oh Mighty-Armed, confounded regarding the path of the Absolute?

39. एतन्मे संशयं कृष्ण छेत्तुमर्हस्यशेषतः ।
त्वदन्यः संशयस्यास्य छेत्ता न ह्युपपद्यते ।।

etan me saṁśayaṁ kṛṣṇa chettum arhasy aśeṣataḥ ।
tvadanyaḥ saṁśayasyā 'sya chettā na hy upapadyate ॥

etat me saṁśayaṁ: this, my doubt; *kṛṣṇa*: Oh Kṛṣṇa; *arhasi*: you can; *chettum aśeṣataḥ*: dispel completely; *anyaḥ tvat*: other than you; *na upapadyate hi*: no one exists indeed; *chettā*: to dispel; *asya saṁśayasya*: of this doubt.

My doubt, Oh Kṛṣṇa, you should dispel completely. Other than you there is none to be found to dispel this doubt.

श्रीभगवानुवाच –

40. पार्थ नैवेह नामुत्र विनाशस्तस्य विद्यते ।
न हि कल्याणकृत्कश्चिद्दुर्गतिं तात गच्छति ।।

śrībhagavān uvāca –

pārtha nai 've 'ha nā 'mutra vināśas tasya vidyate ।
na hi kalyāṇakṛt kaścid durgatiṁ tāta gacchati ॥

śrībhagavān uvāca: Kṛṣṇa said; *pārtha*: Oh Arjuna; *na eva iha*: neither here; *na amutra*: nor hereafter; *vidyate vināśaḥ tasya*: is there destruction for him; *hi na kaścit kalyāṇakṛt*: indeed, no one of good deeds; *tāta*: Oh Son; *gacchati durgatim*: goes to perdition.

Kṛṣṇa said:

Oh Pārtha, neither here nor hereafter is there destruction for him, for none of good deeds, Oh Son, ever goes to perdition.

41. प्राप्य पुण्यकृतां लोकानुषित्वा शाश्वतीः समाः ।
शुचीनां श्रीमतां गेहे योगभ्रष्टोऽभिजायते ।।

prāpya puṇyakṛtāṁ lokān uṣitvā śāśvatīḥ samāḥ ।
śucīnāṁ śrīmatāṁ gehe yogabhraṣṭo 'bhijāyate ॥

prāpya lokān: having attained to the worlds; *puṇyakṛtāṁ*: of the righteous; *uṣitvā*: (and) having dwelt (there); *śāśvatīḥ samāḥ*: (for) eternal years; *yoga bhraṣṭah*: he who deviated from the path of *yoga*; *abhijāyate*: is reborn; *gehe śucīnāṁ śrīmatāṁ*: in a house of the pure and well-to-do.

Having attained to the worlds of the righteous, and having dwelt there for eternal years, he who deviated from the path of *yoga* is reborn in a house of the pure and well-to-do.

42. अथवा योगिनामेव कुले भवति धीमताम् ।
एतद्धि दुर्लभतरं लोके जन्म यदीदृशम् ।।

athavā yogināṁ eva kule bhavati dhīmatām ।
etad dhi durlabhataraṁ loke janma yad īdṛśam ॥

athavā bhavati: else he is born; *kule dhīmatām yogināṁ eva*: in a family of wise *yogīs* only; *janma yat īdṛśam*: a birth like this; *etat hi durlabhataraṁ*: this is very rate to obtain; *loke*: in this world.

Else he is born in a family of wise *yogīs* only. A birth like this is very rare to obtain in this world.

43. तत्र तं बुद्धिसंयोगं लभते पौर्वदेहिकम् ।
यतते च ततो भूयः संसिद्धौ कुरुनन्दन ।।

tatra taṁ buddisaṁyogaṁ labhate paurvadehikam ।
yatate ca tato bhūyaḥ saṁsiddhau kurunandana ॥

tatra labhate: there he obtains; *taṁ buddhi saṁyogaṁ*: that union with reason; *paurva dehikam*: pertaining to a previous body; *ca yatate*: and strives; *tataḥ bhūyaḥ*: thence again; *saṁsiddhau*: for perfection; *kuru nandana*: Oh Arjuna.

There he obtains that union with reason, pertaining to a previous body, and strives thence again for perfection, Oh Prize of the Kurus!

44. पूर्वाभ्यासेन तेनैव ह्रियते ह्यवशोऽपि सः ।
जिज्ञासुरपि योगस्य शब्दब्रह्मातिवर्तते ।।

pūrvābhyāsena tenai 'va hriyate hy avaśo 'pi saḥ ।
jijñāsur api yogasya śabdabrahmā 'tivartate ॥

tena pūrva abhyāsena eva: by this former practice itself; *saḥ hriyate hi*: he is drawn on indeed; *api avaśah*: though disabled; *api jijñāsuḥ yogasya*: (as) one merely desiring to know of *yoga*; *ativartate śabda brahma*: he transcends the Absolute of sound.

By the former practice itself he is drawn on, though disabled; as one merely desiring to know of *yoga*, he transcends the Absolute of sound.

45. प्रयत्नाद्यतमानस्तु योगी संशुद्धकिल्बिषः ।
अनेकजन्मसंसिद्धस्ततो याति परां गतिम् ।।

prayatnād yatamānas tu yogī saṁśuddhakilbiṣaḥ ।
anekajanmasaṁsiddhas tato yāti parāṁ gatim ॥

tu yogī: but the *yogī*; *yatamānaḥ*: who strives; *prayatnāt*: with perseverance; *saṁśuddha kilbiṣaḥ*: purified from evils; *aneka janma saṁsiddhaḥ*: (and) perfected by many births; *tataḥ yāti*: then goes; *parāṁ gatim*: to the supreme path.

But the *yogī* who strives with perseverance, purified from evils, and perfected by many births, then reaches the supreme path.

46. तपस्विभ्योऽधिको योगी ज्ञानिभ्योऽपि मतोऽधिकः ।
कर्मिभ्यश्चाधिको योगी तस्माद्योगी भवार्जुन ।।

tapasvibhyo 'dhiko yogī jñānibhyo 'pi mato 'dhikaḥ ।
karmibhyaś cā'dhiko yogī tasmād yogī bhavā 'rjuna ॥

yogī adhikaḥ: the *yogī* is greater; *tapasvibhyaḥ*: than men of austerity; *api mataḥ*: (and he is) even thought to be; *adhikaḥ jñānibhyaḥ*: greater than men of wisdom; *ca yogī adhikaḥ*: and the *yogī* is greater; *karmibhyaḥ*: than men of works; *tasmāt bhava yogī*: therefore become a *yogī*; *arjuna*: Oh Arjuna.

The *yogī* is greater than men of austerity, and he is thought to be greater than men of wisdom, and greater than men of works; therefore become a *yogī*, Oh Arjuna!

47. योगिनामपि सर्वेषां मद्गतेनान्तरात्मना ।
श्रद्धावान्भजते यो मां स मे युक्ततमो मतः ।।

yoginām api sarveṣāṁ madgatenā 'ntarātmanā ।
śraddhāvān bhajate yo māṁ sa me yuktatamo mataḥ ॥

api sarveṣāṁ yoginām: of all *yogīs*; *antarātmanā*: (he who) with inner Self; *madgatena*: merged in Me; *śraddhāvān*: full of faith; *yaḥ bhajate māṁ*: who is devoted to me; *saḥ mataḥ me*: he is considered by Me; *yuktatamaḥ*: the most unitive.

Of all *yogīs*, he who with inner Self is merged in Me, full of faith, devoted to Me, is considered by Me the most unitive.

DIALOGUE

STUDENT: *Does* dhyāna *mean "meditation" or "contemplation"?*

TEACHER: Neither of these terms are apt to bring out the proper meaning of the Sanskrit term *dhyāna.* It is actually a state in which the tranquillity of consciousness is not disturbed by any specific modulation. In the present context the reference is to unitive contemplation. The two ancient models of spiritual life, *saṁnyāsī* (renunciate) and *yogī* (one of unitive action), are taken again in this chapter for further integration. You should know a little more in detail about these two models as they existed at the time of the composition of the Gītā.

Pre-Vedic Indians were a very peace-loving, passive type of people who had developed a highly contemplative heritage. They differed from the Aryans in three respects:

> They did not offer any worship to *devas* (or "Shining Ones"), like Indra, Varuṇa, Mitra, Sūrya, and others.
>
> They did not perform any burnt sacrifice.
>
> They did not observe any caste distinction, nor did they exhibit such differences in their mode of dress. There was no painting of marks on the forehead, or keeping a tuft of hair, or wearing a sacred thread, whereas Aryans considered conformity to this mode essential to anyone who wanted to perform burnt sacrifices.

The Vedic adherents who desired heaven after death, and pleasures of the senses and the mind while they lived on earth, performed various rites and rituals with benefit-motive, and they even sacrificed animals. The give and take between the Aryans and the pre-Aryan natives of India brought out a new synthesis of the two cultures incorporating the best of both. This Aryan assimilation of pre-Aryan contemplative visions, and the pre-Aryan's acceptance of positive Vedic concepts and ideology, can be seen in a large part of the Brāhmaṇas and the Upaniṣads, especially in the *Bṛhadāraṇyaka*. In spite of such an admirable synthesis brought about by the *ṛṣi*s of the Upaniṣads, two definite trends continued in the spiritual field of India: one of orthodoxy, sticking to rites and rituals, and the other of heterodoxy, where aloneness and freedom from obligation were preferred. This heterodox group refused to conform to social obligations and the precepts of rites and rituals. They became the forerunners of the renunciates, *saṁnyāsī*s. The main features of the *saṁnyāsī* are:

> Undergoing civic death, and no longer living as a member of a closed family of relatives.
>
> Not paying any heed to differences in caste, creed, colour, religion, or nationality.
>
> Looking upon the world as his home and mankind as his brothers.
>
> Not performing any religious ritual or participating in obligatory rites.
>
> As a symbol of the acceptance of poverty and wholehearted dedication to the path of the Absolute, wearing rags, usually dipped in ochre-coloured mud.

Those who stood by orthodoxy also revised the old model and accepted a new contemplative pattern which was consistent with the final teaching of the Upaniṣads. They became *yogī*s. It was like the great river of Indian culture splitting into two rivers, one of the *saṁnyāsī*s and the other of the *yogīs*. In the present chapter of the Gītā we find a confluence of these two streams of culture once again continuing on as one unified river, with the integrated ideal of the renunciation of everything relativistic, personal, parochial, and private with the one goal of identity with the Absolute. Now listen to what Kṛṣṇa says:

> Without depending on the results of action, he who does necessary action is a renouncer (*saṁnyāsī*) and also a contemplative (*yogī*), not he who has (merely) given up sacrificial fire, or who (merely) abstains from ritualist or other) action.
>
> That which people call renunciation (*saṁnyāsa*) – know that to be *yoga* Oh Pāṇḍava! one who has not given up his willful desires for particularized ends never indeed becomes a *yogī*.

At the very outset of this chapter, mere negation is discredited. Out of the positive attitudes remaining when negative values are discarded, there remain two major alternatives before the spiritual aspirant: that of the non-ritualist who still has hopes or aspirations of a positive order, and that of the *yogī* who is not opposed to ritual, but treats it as merely incidental to his own necessary life. The latter should not consider ritual as a means for ends lying outside the scheme of spirituality. According to this chapter, the *yogī* has aspirations which are at least as noble and idealistic as those of the renouncer in the revised sense. The ends on which his mind is fixed approximate the "highest good" of Plato. The *yogī* is more of a realist, making allowances for an organically conceived process of spiritual development.

When we have only one mind, how can there be contradictory dispositions in it? Has the Self (ātman), *a superior as well as an inferior counterpart?*

Like polarized light and shadow, the pure and coloured aspects can make dichotomous counterparts of the same Self. Of these, one part can feel and react to environments in terms of pain or pleasure, virtue or vice, and confidence or diffidence, and that largely goes to make up the personality of an individual. The other half always remains passive as an eternal witness, unaffected and pure; it even remains hidden or unnoticed in the case of most people, who are lost in the feverishness of their everyday activities. The high tides of vital urges or the low tides of disinterestedness make many people either violent or depressed. Hence, it is necessary for the active part of the Self, affected by phenomenal distractions, to be salvaged by the pure and passive counterpart. Kṛṣṇa says:

> By the Self the Self must be upheld; the Self should not be let down; the Self indeed is its own dear relative; the Self indeed is the enemy of the Self.

The Self is dear to one (possessed) of Self, by whom even the Self by the Self has been won; for one not (possessed) of Self, the Self would be in conflict with the very Self, as if an enemy.

To one of conquered Self, who rests in peace, the Supreme (*paramātmā*) is in a state of neutral balance in heat–cold, happiness–suffering, honour–disgrace.

I see in these verses a series very similar to that for one established in unitive reasoning (sthitaprajña) *given in Chapter II, and for one grounded in the Absolute* (brāhmī sthiti) *given in Chapter V. When once you realize, don't you always remain established in wisdom and the Absolute* ?

We have already explained earlier that realization is not a singled out event. It has to be consistent, continuous, and contiguous:

That *yogī* whose Self is satisfied by (synthetic) wisdom and (analytic) knowledge, established in unchanging immobility, who has gained full control over sense-attachments, is said to be unified – one to whom a lump of earth, a stone, and gold are the same.

As between dear well-wishers, friends, enemies, those indifferent, those in-between, haters, relations, and also as between good people and sinners, he who can maintain an equal attitude, excels.

The *yogī* should constantly gather his own Self unitively, established in a place where he can be by himself, alone, with relational mind and Self under control, without expectations and without possessive intentions.

Apart from the performance of one's duties in the light of higher wisdom, should we have to make any psycho-physical attunement or adjustment of the body, mind, and inner self to keep up the above-mentioned vision of the realized in a contiguous state?

Even the bright light becomes brighter by increasing its voltage. That means even the brightest mind has in it shades of its own negative operations. One can reduce or abolish such stains by accelerating the inner vigil and neutralizing the positive and negative urges or tendencies of the mind. Kṛṣṇa says:

Having established firmly in a clean place a seat for himself, one neither too high nor too low, and covered respectively with cloth, skin, and grass, there having made the mind one-pointed, and with relational mind and sense-functions subdued, (duly) taking his place on his seat, let him unitively engage in *yoga* for transparent Self-consciousness.

With body, head, and neck held evenly and in immobile poise, looking at one's nose-tip and not perceiving the (actual) directions (of space), with tranquil Self, with fear gone, established in the vow of a *brahmacārī*, having mind subdued, related to Me through contemplative thought, he may sit, united, having Me for his supreme goal.

Is this path open to all, or is it only for the chosen few?

Nobody is prohibited from spiritual pursuit or from living a wholesome life. But, unfortunately, moved by the dark forces of *tamas*, a person may become gluttonous, sleepy, and idiotic, and he may have to go the hard way until his tendencies are polished and rounded off and his mind is cultivated for a better and brighter pursuit in life. Again, there are those affected by unbridled passions. Their minds smoulder with the flames of *rajas*. They overdo things, and can never get the poise and tranquillity that are needed for the dispassionate, contemplative attitude of the renunciate (*yogī*).

A *yogī* is not a man of extremes. He neither gives up sleep, nor does he indulge in too much sleep. He observes such moderation with regard to food as well as amusements. He need not be cold, serious, and reserved all the time. He should also have his lighter moments. When he is well-established, his relational mind stays within the limits of the Self. Kṛṣṇa says:

> As a lamp set in a windless place does not flicker – such a simile is thought of in regard to a *yogī* who has brought under restraint his (relational) mind, (ever) uniting thus in the union of the Self.
>
> (That state) where the (relational) mind attains tranquillity, restrained through continued cultivation of a Yogic attitude, and where also the Self by the Self in the Self enjoys happiness,

Has this simile of a lamp any special significance?

The simile here is not just one among many others. The idea of *yoga* is here pushed to its purest and furthermost meaning, where duality is completely effaced. The word *yoga* itself implies a duality, but the comparison consciously employed and referred to here as a simile is meant to finally abolish any duality between the object and subject of union as may be implied in the word *yoga*. The unflickering flame just keeps burning on steadily. A flame that flickers has on one hand the flame itself, and on the other hand the wind which makes it flicker, as something extraneous. In a windless place, however, where the extraneous factors causing the flickering are absent, the flame just burns on. Establishment of unity is a similar state. It requires only the removal of what is extraneous to the situation. Perfect *yoga* is unitiveness in the Self, of the Self, and by the Self. The subtle distinction brought out by this example has a more than casual interest.

Wind is an extraneous factor. Only in its absence does the flame become steady. What happens when a physical disease or a social tragedy befalls the yogī?

The *yoga* spoken of here is not merely a neutral state of sheer withdrawal, as in the case of Patañjali's Yoga. The Gītā gives *yoga* a positive content. Kṛṣṇa describes it adequately:

> that in which one cognizes the ultimate limit of happiness which can be grasped by reason and goes beyond the senses, and established wherein there is no more swerving from the true principle,
>
> and which, having obtained, there is no other gain thought of which could be greater (in value), in which, when established, there is no swerving even by heavy suffering
>
> – that should be known by the name of *yoga*: disaffiliation from the context of suffering. Such a *yoga* should be adhered to with determination free from spiritual regret.

But the mind is like quicksilver. As soon as our attention is directed toward it, it throws a hundred tantrums and may defeat the very purpose of meditation. ...

That is so when we approach the mind mechanistically with rude abruptness. One has to tame the mind gradually with insight and a sympathetic understanding of the several urges that lie dormant within it. Kṛṣṇa describes the whole procedure in verses 24-26, and 28. Please refer back to this important section.

Does Vedānta incorporate yoga in it?

The final realization of *yoga* as revalued in the Gītā has no difference whatsoever from that of Vedānta. The state of *yoga* described in verses 28 and 29 is the same as taught in the *Īśa Upaniṣad*:

> He who sees all beings in the Self, and the Self in all beings, hates none. To the illumined soul, the Self is all. For him who sees everywhere oneness, how can there be delusion or grief?

Suppose a yogī *fails to complete his discipline and to attain realization. If before that he meets with some tragic calamity by which he dies or is unable to continue his discipline, what will happen to him?*

Whatever he has attained by way of self-discipline and understanding will not perish. In his next birth he will find a good environment to continue from where he left off. There he obtains his union with reason that was pertaining to his previous body, and from there on he can strive again for perfection. That way, the *yogī* who strives with perseverance, purified from evils, and perfected by many births, then reaches the supreme path.

Is yoga the highest model of the Gītā?

Here are the concluding verses of this chapter:

> The *yogī* is greater than men of austerity, and he is thought to be greater than men of wisdom, and greater than men of works; therefore become a *yogī*, Oh Arjuna!
>
> Of all *yogīs*, he who with inner Self is merged in Me, full of faith, devoted to Me, is considered by Me the most unitive (*yuktatamaḥ*).

VII

Jñāna-Vijñāna-Yoga

The Unitive Way of Wisdom Synthesis

INTRODUCTION

THERE is an enigmatic movement of life between Being and Nothingness. No problem is encountered in Nothingness, that is self-evident. Also, in the pure or Absolute Being there is no duality, hence there is no one to know, feel, or will. So there is no problem in Being, either. However, countless are the possibilities within Being. Between the divine comedy of Absolute Being and the tragedy of total Nothingness there is staged an interlude called the world, or the flux of the phenomenal. The main character occupying the centre of that stage is Man, an embodied "being" animated by the spirit and enveloped by the unknown, somewhere culminating in Nothingness. In the present chapter, the interlude in which Man lives and strives to find his true bearing is highlighted.

One can either look from the core of Being into the void of Nothingness, or from the void of Nothingness into the enormity of Being. These two possibilities are personified in the Bhagavadgītā by Śrī Kr̥ṣṇa and Arjuna. In the present chapter we hear the voice of Kr̥ṣṇa identified with the Word of the Absolute. His counterpart is Arjuna. For Arjuna, everything stable under his feet, such as his country, clan, and family ties, his honour and sacred strongholds like love, compassion, justice, and gratitude, gave way to Nothingness like melting snowflakes. He turned to Kr̥ṣṇa for refuge and guidance only when he touched the zero point. The reunion of what is born of Being and what is destined to be blown in the winds of phenomenal Becoming is exemplified in the previous chapter by the model of the *yogī*. The penultimate verse in Chapter VI ends with the exhortation from Śrī Kr̥ṣṇa calling Arjuna to become a *yogī*.

If *yoga* is union with the Absolute, Arjuna should be told what the

Absolute is. At the very outset of the chapter Kṛṣṇa promises him full knowledge, both in its pure aspect and its application. In verse 4 Kṛṣṇa brackets the phenomena to be known. As Edmund Husserl would put it, through the *epoche* the aspirant's phenomenal experience is reduced to the eight categories of earth, water, fire, air, space, mind, intellect, and ego. Immediately in the next verse, a further reduction is employed, through which Arjuna is left with only one reality to relate to: the Transcendent Being. As in the phenomenology of Karl Jaspers, the Transcendent is given here as the ground or basis of phenomenological *existenz.*

In verse 6 a method of cancellation is employed in presenting the Absolute as both the origin of everything and the dissolution of everything. Thus the whole process of the return of the phenomenal man to Absolute Being is summarized in six verses. In the next six verses, Kṛṣṇa invites Arjuna to a brief exercise in eidetic reduction, a process by which he is to stand aside from all his own mental images in order to see the essential structural elements. From the sapidity of water to the zest for sexual union, all items of interest that can be coloured with the triple modalities of nature – ideation, activity, and inertia – are reviewed in a single sweep. Kṛṣṇa thus fulfils his promise of presenting both the pure and applied aspects of knowledge.

In the rest of the chapter Kṛṣṇa gives an appraisal of the benefits derived by different people employing different methods. He makes use of the occasion to state the correct attitude that should be adopted by a sincere seeker in establishing a total bipolarity with the Absolute. It is in conformity with the non-dual, transcendental reduction employed here that the whole chapter is dominated by the voice of Kṛṣṇa, and Arjuna is expected only "to listen, to reflect, and to meditate upon", as was required of Maitreyī in the *Bṛhadāraṇyaka Upaniṣad* when Yājñavalkya imparted to her the secret of *brahma-vidyā* (Science of the Absolute).

TRANSLATION

श्रीभगवानुवाच –

1. मय्यासक्तमनाः पार्थ योगं युञ्जन्मदाश्रयः ।
असंशयं समग्रं मां यथा ज्ञास्यसि तच्छृणु ॥

śrībhagavān uvāca –

mayy āsaktamanāḥ pārtha yogaṁ yuñjan madāśrayaḥ ।
asaṁśayaṁ samagraṁ māṁ yathā jñāsyasi tac chṛṇu ॥

śrībhagavān uvāca: Kṛṣṇa said; *āsakta manāḥ mayi*: having a mind attached in Me; *pārtha*: Oh Arjuna; *yogaṁ yuñjan*: joining unitively through *yoga*; *mat āśrayaḥ*: (and) having Me as refuge; *yathā jñāsyasi māṁ*: how you will know Me; *asaṁśayaṁ*: without any doubt; *samagraṁ*: comprehensively; *tat śṛṇu*: that do hear.

Kṛṣṇa said:

Having a mind attached to Me, Oh Pārtha, joining unitively through *yoga*, and having Me as refuge, how you will know Me without any doubt, comprehensively, that do hear.

2. ज्ञानं तेऽहं सविज्ञानमिदं वक्ष्याम्यशेषतः ।
यज्ज्ञात्वा नेह भूयोऽन्यज्ज्ञातव्यमवशिष्यते ।।

jñānaṁ te 'haṁ savijñānam idaṁ vakṣyāmy aśeṣataḥ ।
yaj jñātvā ne 'ha bhūyo 'nyaj jñātavyam avaśiṣyate ॥

ahaṁ vakṣyāmi te: I shall teach to you; *idaṁ jñānaṁ*: this (pure) wisdom; *savijñānam*: together with (applied) knowledge; *aśeṣataḥ*: without any omission; *jñātvā yat*: knowing which; *na anyat bhūyaḥ*: nothing other more; *iha avaśiṣyate*: here is left; *jñātavyam*: to be known.

I shall teach you this (pure) wisdom together with this (applied) knowledge, without any omission, knowing which, there will be nothing more here left over that should be known.

3. मनुष्याणां सहस्रेषु कश्चिद्यतति सिद्धये ।
यततामपि सिद्धानां कश्चिन्मां वेत्ति तत्त्वतः ।।

manuṣyāṇāṁ sahasreṣu kaścid yatati siddhaye ।
yatatām api siddhānāṁ kaścin māṁ vetti tattvataḥ ॥

sahasreṣu manuṣyāṇāṁ: among thousands of men; *kaścit*: (hardly) anyone; *yatati siddhaye*: strives for perfection; *api yatatām*: even among the striving; *siddhānāṁ*: who have attained; *kaścit*: one perchance; *vetti māṁ*: knows Me; *tattvataḥ*: acccording to proper principles.

Among thousands of men, one perchance strives for perfection. Even among the striving who have attained, one perchance knows Me according to proper principles.

4. भूमिरापोऽनलो वायुः खं मनो बुद्धिरेव च ।
अहङ्कार इतीयं मे भिन्ना प्रकृतिरष्टधा ।।

bhūmir āpo 'nalo vāyuḥ khaṁ mano buddhir eva ca ।
ahaṁkāra iti 'yaṁ me bhinnā prakṛtir aṣṭadhā ॥

bhūmiḥ āpaḥ: earth, water; *analaḥ vāyuḥ*: fire, air; *khaṁ manaḥ*: sky, mind; *buddhiḥ ca eva*: reason, and also; *ahaṁkāraḥ*: consciousness of individuality; *iti iyaṁ*: thus, this; *bhinnā*: is divided; *me aṣṭadhā prakṛtiḥ*: my eightfold nature.

Earth, water, fire, air, sky, mind, reason, and also consciousness of individuality – thus, here is divided My eightfold nature.

5. अपरेयमितस्त्वन्यां प्रकृतिं विद्धि मे पराम् ।
जीवभूतां महाबाहो ययेदं धार्यते जगत् ।।

apare 'yam itas tv anyāṁ prakṛtiṁ viddhi me parām ।
jivabhūtāṁ mahābāho yaye 'daṁ dhāryate jagat ॥

iyam aparā: this (is) the non-transcendental (immanent); *tu itas anyāṁ*: but this other; *viddhi me prakṛtiṁ*: know to be My nature; *parām*: (which is) transcendental; *jīvabhūtāṁ*: constituting life; *mahābāho*: Oh Arjuna; *yayā idaṁ jagat*: by which this phenomenal world; *dhāryate*: is sustained.

This is the non-transcendental. Know the other to be My nature, which is transcendental, constituting life, Oh Mighty-Armed, by which the phenomenal world is sustained.

6. एतद्योनीनि भूतानि सर्वाणीत्युपधारय ।
अहं कृत्स्नस्य जगतः प्रभवः प्रलयस्तथा ।।

etadyonini bhūtāni sarvāṇī 'ty upadhāraya ।
ahaṁ kṛtsnasya jagataḥ prabhavaḥ pralayas tathā ॥

iti upadhāraya: thus know; *sarvāṇi bhūtāni*: all beings (have); *etat yonini*: this (as their) common source (womb); *ahaṁ prabhavaḥ*: I am the becoming; *tathā pralayaḥ*: (as) also the dissolution; *kṛtsnasya jagataḥ*: of the whole (phenomenal) world.

Know that all beings have this as their common source. I am the becoming as also the dissolution of all this (phenomenal) world.

7. मत्तः परतरं नान्यत्किञ्चिदस्ति धनञ्जय ।
मयि सर्वमिदं प्रोतं सूत्रे मणिगणा इव ।।

mattaḥ parataraṁ nā 'nyat kiñcid asti dhanañjaya ।
mayi sarvam idaṁ protaṁ sūtre maṇigaṇā iva ॥

na anyat kiñcit: nothing else; *asti parataraṁ mattaḥ*: is higher than Me; *dhanañjaya*: Oh Arjuna; *mayi sarvam idaṁ*: in Me all this; *protaṁ*: is strung; *iva gaṇāḥ*: as a classified series; *maṇi*: (of) precious beads; *sūtre*: one a string.

Nothing else is higher than Me, Oh Winner of Wealth. In Me all this is strung as a classified series of precious beads on a string.

8. रसोऽहमप्सु कौन्तेय प्रभास्मि शशिसूर्ययोः ।
प्रणवः सर्ववेदेषु शब्दः खे पौरुषं नृषु ।।

raso 'ham apsu kaunteya prabhā 'smi śaśisūryayoḥ ।
praṇavaḥ sarvavedeṣu śabdaḥ khe pauruṣaṁ nṛṣu ॥

aham rasaḥ apsu: I (am) the taste in waters; *kaunteya*: Oh Arjuna; *asmi prabhā*: (I) am the light; *śaśi sūryayoḥ*: of the moon and the sun; *praṇavaḥ*: (I am) *AUṀ* (numinous exclamation); *sarva vedeṣu*: in all the Vedas; *śabdaḥ khe*: sound in the sky; *pauruṣaṁ nṛṣu*: (and) the human quality in men.

I am the taste in waters, Oh Son of Kuntī! I am the light in the moon and the sun, I am *AUṀ* in all the Vedas, sound in the sky, and the human quality in men.

9. पुण्यो गन्धः पृथिव्यां च तेजश्चास्मि विभावसौ ।
जीवनं सर्वभूतेषु तपश्चास्मि तपस्विषु ।।

puṇyo gandhaḥ pṛthivyāṁ ca tejaś cā 'smi vibhāvasau ।
jīvanaṁ sarvabhūteṣu tapaś cā 'smi tapasviṣu ॥

asmi puṇyaḥ gandhaḥ: (I) am the holy fragrance; *pṛthivyāṁ ca*: of the earth (divinity) and; *ca tejaḥ*: also the brilliance; *vibhāvasau*: of the luminary (presence); *jīvanaṁ*: the vital principle; *sarva bhūteṣu*: in all beings; *ca asmi*: and (I) am; *tapaḥ tapasviṣu*: the (essence of) austerity in (all) ascetics.

I am the holy fragrance of the earth (divinity), and also the brilliance of the luminary (presence), the vital principle in all beings, and the (essence of) austerity in all ascetics.

10. बीजं मां सर्वभूतानां विद्धि पार्थ सनातनम् ।
बुद्धिर्बुद्धिमतामस्मि तेजस्तेजस्विनामहम् ।।

bījaṁ māṁ sarvabhūtānāṁ viddhi pārtha sanātanam ।
buddhir buddhimatām asmi tejas tejasvinām aham ॥

viddhi māṁ: know me (to be); *pārtha*: Oh Arjuna; *sanātanam bījaṁ*: the perennial seed; *sarva bhūtānāṁ*: of all beings; *asmi buddhiḥ*: (I) am the reason; *buddhimatām*: of the intelligent; *aham tejaḥ*: (and) I the brightness; *tejasvinām*: of (those who are) the brilliant.

Know Me, Oh Pārtha! to be the perennial seed of all beings; I am the reason of the intelligent, and I the brightness of (those who are) the brilliant.

11. बलं बलवतां चाहं कामरागविवर्जितम् ।
धर्माविरुद्धो भूतेषु कामोऽस्मि भरतर्षभ ।।

balaṁ balavatāṁ cā 'haṁ kāmarāgavivarjitam ।
dharmāviruddho bhūteṣu kāmo 'smi bharatarṣabha ॥

ca ahaṁ: and I (am); *balaṁ balavatāṁ*: the strength of the strong; *vivarjitam kāma rāga*: deviod of desire and passion; *bhūteṣu*: in beings; *asmi kāmaḥ*: (I) am desire; *dharma aviruddaḥ*: which is not contray to righteousness; *bharatarṣabha*: Oh Arjuna.

I am the strength of the strong, devoid of desire and passion. In beings I am desire which is not contrary to righteousness, Oh Leader of the Bhāratas!

12. ये चैव सात्त्विका भावा राजसास्तामसाश्च ये ।
मत्त एवेति तान्विद्धि न त्वहं तेषु ते मयि ।।

ye cai 'va sāttvikā bhāvā rājasās tāmasāś ca ye ।
matta eve 'ti tān viddhi na tv ahaṁ teṣu te mayi ॥

ca eva ye bhāvāḥ: and even those manifestations; *sāttvikāḥ*: (recognized as) according with existence (sāttvic); *ca ye rājasāḥ*: and those which are active or dominant (rājasic); *tāmasāḥ*: (or) dark or inert (tāmasic); *viddhi tān*: know them; *eva iti*: even as; *mattaḥ*: from Me; *aham na teṣu*: I (am) not in them; *tu te mayi*: but they (are) in Me.

Even those manifestations recognized as according with existence, and active or dominant, and dark or inert – know them even to be My own. I am not in them, but they are in Me.

13. त्रिभिर्गुणमयैर्भावैरेभिः सर्वमिदं जगत् ।
मोहितं नाभिजानाति मामेभ्यः परमव्ययम् ।।

tribhir guṇamayair bhāvair ebhiḥ sarvam idaṁ jagat ।
mohitaṁ nā 'bhijānāti mām ebhyaḥ param avyayam ॥

mohitaṁ: deluded; *ebhiḥ tribhiḥ*: by these three; *bhāvaiḥ guṇamayaiḥ*: by manifestations of value; *idaṁ sarvam jagat*: this whole world; *na abbijānāti mām*: is unable to know Me; *param ebhyaḥ*: (who am) beyond them; *avyayam*: (and) unexpended.

Deluded by these three manifestations of value this whole world is unable to know Me, who am beyond them and unexpended.

14. दैवी ह्येषा गुणमयी मम माया दुरत्यया ।
मामेव ये प्रपद्यन्ते मायामेतां तरन्ति ते ।।

daivī hy eṣā guṇamayī mama māyā duratyayā ।
mām eva ye prapadyante māyām etāṁ taranti te ॥

hi eṣā: verily this; *daivī māyā mama*: divine illusion of Mine; *guṇamayī*: made up of the manifestations of value; *duratyayā*: (is) hard to surmount; *te ye prapadyante*: those who seek; *mām eva*: Me alone; *taranti*: pass over; *etāṁ māyām*: this illusion.

Verily this divine illusion of Mine, made up of the manifestations of value, is hard to surmount. Those who seek Me alone pass over this illusion.

15. न मां दुष्कृतिनो मूढाः प्रपद्यन्ते नराधमाः ।
माययापहृतज्ञाना आसुरं भावमाश्रिताः ।।

na māṁ duṣkṛtino mūḍhāḥ prapadyante narādhamāḥ ।
māyayā 'pahṛtajñānā āsuraṁ bhāvam āśritāḥ ॥

mūḍhāḥ duṣkṛtinaḥ: foolish evil-doers; *adhamāḥ narā*: lowest among men; *na prapadyante māṁ*: do not attain Me; *apahṛtajñānāḥ*: their wisdom being distracted; *māyayā*: by illusion; *āśritāḥ*: affiliated (as they are) to; *āsuraṁ*: the demonic (or non-intelligent) aspect; *bhāvam*: (of) nature.

Foolish evil-doers, lowest among men, do not attain Me, their wisdom being distracted by illusion, affiliated as they are to the demonic (or non-intelligent) aspect of nature.

16. चतुर्विधा भजन्ते मां जनाः सुकृतिनोऽर्जुन ।
आर्तो जिज्ञासुरर्थार्थी ज्ञानी च भरतर्षभ ।।

caturvidhā bhajante māṁ janāḥ sukṛtino 'rjuna ।
ārto jijñāsur arthārthī jñānī ca bharatarṣabha ॥

caturvidhāḥ: four kinds; *sukṛtināḥ janāḥ*: (of) good-doing men; *bhajante mām*: are intent on Me; *arjuna*: Oh Arjuna; *ārtaḥ*: the distressed; *jijñāsuḥ*: the seeker of knowledge; *arthārthī*: the seeker of the goods of life; *ca jñānī*: and the wise; *bharatarṣabha*: Oh Arjuna.

Among doers of the good, four kinds are intent on Me, Arjuna: the distressed, the seeker of knowledge, the seeker of the goods of life, and the wise, Oh Leader of the Bhāratas!

17. तेषां ज्ञानी नित्ययुक्त एकभक्तिर्विशिष्यते ।
प्रियो हि ज्ञानिनोऽत्यर्थमहं स च मम प्रियः ।।

teṣāṁ jñānī nityayukta ekabhaktir viṣiśyate ।
priyo hi jñānino 'tyartham ahaṁ sa ca mama priyaḥ ॥

teṣāṁ jnānī: of these, the wise man; *nitya yuktaḥ*: forever united; *eka bhaktiḥ*: (and) unitively affiliated to the One; *viśiṣyate*: excels; *hi priyaḥ*: for dear; *atyartham*: to the utmost limit; *aham*: (am) I; *jñāninaḥ*: to the wise one; *ca saḥ priyaḥ mama*: and he (is) dear to me.

Of these, the wise man, forever united and unitively affiliated with the Absolute, excels, for dear to the utmost limit am I to the wise one, and he is dear to Me.

18. उदाराः सर्व एवैते ज्ञानी त्वात्मैव मे मतम् ।
आस्थितः स हि युक्तात्मा मामेवानुत्तमां गतिम् ॥

udārāḥ sarva evai 'te jñānī tv ātmai 'va me matam ।
āsthitaḥ sa hi yuktātmā mām evā 'nuttamāṁ gatim ॥

sarva ete eva udārāḥ: all these (are) indeed honourable; *tu me matam*: but My firm opinion (is that); *jñānī*: the wise one; *ātmā eva*: (is) the Self itself; *saḥ yuktātmā*: he of unitively established Self; *hi āsthitaḥ*: indeed remains; *mām gatim*: in My path; *eva anuttamāṁ*: (which) indeed (has) nothing higher.

Honourable are all these, but My firm opinion is that the wise one is the Self itself. He of unitively established Self indeed remains in My path, which has nothing higher.

19. बहूनां जन्मनामन्ते ज्ञानवान्मां प्रपद्यते ।
वासुदेवः सर्वमिति स महात्मा सुदुर्लभः ॥

bahūnāṁ janmanām ante jñānavān māṁ prapadyate ।
vāsudevaḥ sarvam iti sa mahātmā sudurlabhaḥ ॥

ante bahūnāṁ janmanām: after many births; *jñānavān prapadyate māṁ*: the wise man attains Me; *saḥ mahātmā*: such a Great Self; *vāsudevaḥ sarvam*: (thinking) Vāsudeva is all; *iti sudurlabhaḥ*: thus (is) rare (indeed) to find.

After many births the wise man attains Me. Such a Great Self, thinking Vāsudeva to be all is rare indeed to find.

20. कामैस्तैस्तैर्हृतज्ञानाः प्रपद्यन्तेऽन्यदेवताः ।
तं तं नियममास्थाय प्रकृत्या नियताः स्वया ॥

kāmais tais-tair hṛtajñānāḥ prapadyante 'nyadevatāḥ ।
taṁ-taṁ niyamam āsthāya prakṛtyā niyatāḥ svayā ॥

hṛtajñānāḥ: those whose wisdom is distracted; *taiḥ taiḥ kāmaiḥ*: by such (or) such (other) desire (counterparts); *prapadyante anya devatāḥ*: (they) attain to other divinities; *āsthāya*: committed to; *taṁ taṁ niyamam*: this or that obligation (belonging to each); *niyatāḥ*: controlled; *svayā prakṛtyā*: by (their) own (particular) nature (in each case).

Their wisdom distracted by such (or) such (other) desire (counterparts), they attain to other divinities, committed to various obligations belonging to each, prompted by their own particular nature (in each case).

21. यो यो यां यां तनुं भक्तः श्रद्धयार्चितुमिच्छति ।
तस्य तस्याचलां श्रद्धां तामेव विदधाम्यहम् ॥

yo-yo yāṁ-yāṁ tanuṁ bhaktaḥ śraddhayā 'rcitum icchati ।
tasya-tasyā 'calāṁ śraddhāṁ tām eva vidadhāmy aham ॥

yāṁ yāṁ tanuṁ: (by) whichever (particular) form; *yaḥ yaḥ bhaktaḥ*: such and such a devotee; *śraddhayā*: with faith; *icchati arcitum*: wishes to worship; *tām eva*: this indeed; *tasya tasya*: of that (whatever it is); *acalāṁ śraddhāṁ*: unmoving faith; *aham vidadhāmi*: I confirm.

By whichever (particular) form such and such a devotee with faith wishes to worship, each to his own faith I confirm.

22. स तया श्रद्धया युक्तस्तस्याराधनमीहते ।
लभते च ततः कामान्मयैव विहितान्हि तान् ॥

sa tayā śraddhayā yuktas tasyā 'rādhanam īhate ।
labhate ca tataḥ kāmān mayai 'va vihitān hi tān ॥

saḥ: he; *yuktaḥ tayā śraddhayā*: endowed with that faith; *īhate ārādhanam*: seeks the worship; *tasya*: of such a one; *ca tataḥ*: and from him; *labhate kāmān*: obtains (his) desires; *tān hi vihitān*: those indeed decreed; *mayā eva*: by Me alone.

He, endowed with that faith, seeks the worship of such a one, and from him obtains his desires, the benefits being decreed by Me.

23. अन्तवत्तु फलं तेषां तद्भवत्यल्पमेधसाम् ।
देवान्देवयजो यान्ति मद्भक्ता यान्ति मामपि ॥

antavat tu phalaṁ teṣāṁ tad bhavaty alpamedhasām ।
devān devayajo yānti madbhaktā yānti mām api ॥

antavat: terminable; *tu bhavati tat*: indeed is that; *phalaṁ*: the benefit (accruing); *teṣāṁ*: to these; *alpa medhasām*: of small intelligence; *devayajaḥ*: sacrificers to the divinities; *yānti devān*: go to divinities; *mat bhaktaḥ*: (but) my devotees; *api yānti mām*: surely come to Me.

Terminable indeed is the benefit (accruing) to these of small intelligence; secrificers to the divinities go to the divinities, but My devotees come to Me.

24. अव्यक्तं व्यक्तिमापन्नं मन्यन्ते मामबुद्धयः ।
परं भावमजानन्तो ममाव्ययमनुत्तमम् ॥

avyaktaṁ vyaktim āpannaṁ manyante mām abuddhayaḥ ।
paraṁ bhāvam ajānanto mamā 'vyayam anuttamam ॥

abuddhayaḥ: unreasoning persons; *manyante mām*: consider Me; *avyaktaṁ*: (as) the unmanifest; *āpannaṁ vyaktim*: come to manifestation; *ajānantaḥ*: not knowing; *mama paraṁ bhāvam*: My supreme existence; *avyayam anuttamam*: unexpended, with no superior.

Unreasoning persons consider Me as the unmanifest come to manifestation, not knowing My supreme (value), unexpended, with no superior.

25. नाहं प्रकाशः सर्वस्य योगमायासमावृतः ।
मूढोऽयं नाभिजानाति लोको मामजमव्ययम् ॥

nā 'haṁ prakāśāḥ sarvasya yogamāyāsamāvṛtaḥ ।
mūḍho 'yaṁ nā 'bhijānāti loko mām ajam avyayam ॥

aham na: I (am) not; *prakāśaḥ*: revealed brightly; *sarvasya*: to all; *yoga māyā samāvṛtaḥ*: shrouded (as I am) by the illusive effect of negative reality; *ayaṁ mūḍhaḥ lokaḥ*: this deluded world; *na abhijānāti mām*: does not know Me; *ajaṁ avyayam*: unborn, unexpended.

I am not revealed brightly to all; shrouded as I am by the illusive effect of negative reality, this deluded world does not know Me, unborn, unexpended.

26. वेदाहं समतीतानि वर्तमानानि चार्जुन ।
भविष्याणि च भूतानि मां तु वेद न कश्चन ॥

vedā 'haṁ samatītāni vartamānāni cā 'rjuna ।
bhaviṣyāṇi ca bhūtāni māṁ tu veda na kaścana ॥

aham veda: I know; *bhūtāni samatītāni*: the beings that are past; *ca vartamānāni*: and present; *ca bhaviṣyāṇi*: and to come; *arjuna*: Oh Arjuna; *tu na kaścana*: but no one; *veda māṁ*: knows Me.

I know the beings that are past, present, and to come, Oh Arjuna! but no one knows Me.

27. इच्छाद्वेषसमुत्थेन द्वन्द्वमोहेन भारत ।
सर्वभूतानि सम्मोहं सर्गे यान्ति परन्तप ॥

icchādveṣasamutthena dvandvamohena bhārata ।
sarvabhūtāni saṁmohaṁ sarge yānti paraṁtapa ॥

dvandva mohena: from the delusion of the pairs of opposites; *icchā dveṣa samutthena*: arising from attraction and repulsion; *bhārata*: Oh Arjuna; *sarva bhūtāni*: all beings; *sarge*: on being created; *yānti*: (they) go; *saṁmohaṁ*: (to) confusion (of values); *paraṁtapa*: Oh Arjuna.

From the delusion of the pairs of opposites, arising from attraction and repulsion, Oh Bhārata! all beings, on being created, are subject to confusion (of values), Oh Burner of the Foe!

28. येषां त्वन्तगतं पापं जनानां पुण्यकर्मणाम् ।
ते द्वन्द्वमोहनिर्मुक्ता भजन्ते मां दृढव्रताः ॥

yeṣāṁ tv antagataṁ pāpaṁ janānāṁ puṇyakarmaṇām ।
te dvandvamohanirmuktā bhajante māṁ dṛḍhavratāḥ ॥

tu: but; *janānāṁ puṇya karmaṇām*: those persons of pure deeds; *yeṣāṁ pāpaṁ*: whose sin; *antagataṁ*: has come to an end; *dvandva moha nirmuktāḥ*: freed from the conflict of pairs of opposites; *te bhajante*: they adore; *māṁ*: Me; *dṛḍha vratāḥ*: with a firm resolve.

But those persons of pure deeds, whose sin has come to an end, freed from the conflict of pairs of opposites, adore Me with a firm resolve.

29. जरामरणमोक्षाय मामाश्रित्य यतन्ति ये ।
ते ब्रह्म तद्विदुः कृत्स्नमध्यात्मं कर्म चाखिलम् ।।

jarāmaraṇamokṣāya mām āśritya yatanti ye ।
te brahma tad viduḥ kṛtsnam adhyātmaṁ karma cā 'khilam ॥

ye: (those) who; *āśritya mām*: resorting to Me; *yatanti*: strive; *jarā maraṇa mokṣāya*: for liberation from decay and death; *te viduḥ tat*: they know That; *brahma*: the Absolute; *kṛtsnam*: all that constitutes; *adhyātmaṁ*: self-knowledge; *ca akhilam*: and everything; *karma*: (pertaining to ritualistic) action.

Those who, resorting to Me, strive for liberation from decay and death – they know That, the Absolute, all that constitutes Self-knowledge, and everything pertaining to (ritualistic) action.

30. साधिभूताधिदैवं मां साधियज्ञं च ये विदुः ।
प्रयाणकालेऽपि च मां ते विदुर्युक्तचेतसः ।।

sādhibhūatādhidaivaṁ māṁ sādhiyajñaṁ ca ye viduḥ ।
prayāṇakāle 'pi ca māṁ te vidur yuktacetasaḥ ॥

ye viduḥ: (those) who know; *māṁ*: Me; *sa adhibhūta adhidaivaṁ*: taking together (what refers to) existential, hypostatic; *ca sa adhiyajñaṁ*: and sacrificial (aspects); *te viduḥ māṁ*: they know Me; *yukta cetasaḥ*: in a unitive spirit; *api prayāṇa kāle*: even at the time of (their) departure.

Those who know Me, taking together what refers to existential, hypostatic, and sacrificial aspects – they know Me in a unitive spirit, even at the time of their departure.

DIALOGUE

TEACHER: Like pure mathematics, and applied mathematics, and theoretical and applied physics, in wisdom also there is pure knowledge and applied wisdom. Pure knowledge is called *jñāna*, and applied wisdom is called *vijñāna*. This chapter continues the discussion of the previous chapter, and teaches how pure knowledge and applied wisdom can together be treated integrally.

STUDENT: *In the course of life, at every turn, there arises a new problem which calls for a fresh approach. The flow of life is not in conformity with any pre-established system, even though there might be, as Leibnitz says, a pre-established harmony in its inner law. When eventualities and their consequences are unpredictable, what benefit can we derive from pure knowledge?*

It is true that unexpected events crop up spontaneously. Although in ordinary situations we can profitably use common sense and inferential reasoning, when it comes to dealing with situations that are essentially enigmatic or paradoxical, mere ratiocination or linear reasoning cannot help us very much. In the ordinary kind of thinking we treat the subject and the object separately as two distinct or disjunct entities. In wisdom synthesis, we have to integrate the subject and the object to be experienced as a single indivisible identity. Knowing a thing from outside is different from *being* it from inside. Bergson says:

> When you raise your arm, you accomplish a movement of which you have, from within, a simple perception; but for me, watching it from the outside, your arm passes through one point, then through another, and between these two there will still be other points; so that, if I began to count, the operation would go on forever. Viewed from the inside, then, an absolute is a simple thing; but looked at from the outside, that is to say, relatively to other things, it becomes, in relation to these signs which express it, the gold coin for which we never seem able to finish giving small change.[1]

When the mind is tied up with the symbols of analysis and cluttered with discursive thoughts, it cannot have any streak of intuition. Ratiocination and analytical reasoning are therefore to be dimmed or even abandoned in contemplation. Only in this state can the subject intuitively identify himself with the object.

It sounds very simple, but I doubt whether we can so easily abandon the many natural functions of the mind, such as curiosity, enquiry, observation, cognition, conation, affection, reaction, postulation, interrogation, admission of relevancy, rejection of irrelevancy, and a host of other conscious and unconscious modulations of the thinking process. What should we do to dim or negate these natural functions of the mind so that it can easily attune itself to intuition?

When a person dedicates himself wholeheartedly to the Absolute, and lifts himself from the dull and insipid state of drudgery or disinterest, he

---

[1] Henri Bergson, 1965, *An Introduction to Metaphysics*, New York: The Library of Liberal Arts, p. 23.

goes beyond the pale of egoistic interests and relativistic memories. The mind gains a new dimension, as it were. Such a mind can certainly have the benefit of intuitive penetration.

Kṛṣṇa speaks of pure knowledge and applied wisdom. How do we differentiate these two?

The reference to "pure knowledge" means the envisaging of a philosophy of life, and "applied wisdom" is the actual living of that philosophy. Although the Gītā teaches a way of life, it does not place before its student any particular creed or closed pattern of behaviour. The Gītā is not a book of mandatory injunctions, nor does it prescribe any obligatory duty. It teaches that each man should choose his own way of life. Wisdom by itself will be incomplete if it cannot be lived from moment to moment, despite the changing vicissitudes and alternating moods of man. In this chapter the term "applied wisdom" refers to the existential aspects of reality. Our body, mind, and the various impulses of life belong to the lower nature. The Gītā calls the lower aspect of the Absolute *apara Brahman*`1 Kṛṣṇa identifies his own lower nature with the following eight categories:

> Earth, water, fire, air, sky, mind, reason, and also consciousness of individuality – thus, here is divided My eightfold nature.

Does this classification conform to the Sāṁkhyan categories?

The Sāṁkhyan classification of categories is based on a descending scheme, and the Patañjali school of Yoga follows it up in an ascending scheme. The Gītā is applying a scheme which implies alternating phases of both ascending and descending dialectics.

Suppose that a man says that a pot is made of clay. His reference is not to any particular pot or specific lump of clay that he directly perceives. To him the pot and the clay are only mental images. When the same man puts a lump of clay on a potter's wheel and makes a pot, he is not dealing with mental images but the *actual* clay and pot with which he is directly related. After making the pot, when the same man sits back and appreciates the quality of the clay and the satisfactory moulding of the pot, he returns to his mental images which are now more vivid and specific, and which now have a direct reference to something which exists in the world of brute facts. If we schematically look at these three phases of pre-creation, creation, and post-creation, we can see pure knowledge descending into actuality and the experiences of the actual once again ascending into pure notions. In Vedānta, or integral wisdom, it is essential that the student should clearly see the alternating movements of the entire psyche in an ascending and descending order. Ascending and descending dialectics of wisdom-synthesis imply the stringing together of theoretical and practical values on the invisible thread of the Absolute, which passes through everyone and everything. Kṛṣṇa says:

> This is the non-transcendental. Know the other to be My nature, which is transcendental, constituting life, Oh Mighty-Armed by which the phenomenal world is sustained.
>
> Know that all beings have this as their common source. I am the becoming as also the dissolution of all this (phenomenal) world.
>
> Nothing else is higher than Me, Oh Winner of Wealth! In Me all this is strung as a classified series of precious beads on a string.

Even though in a garland the string is the concealed link that holds the beads together, the individual worth of the bead is what makes the garland valuable. If the author's intention is to give the phenomenal world, which is compared here to the beads, only a lower status, then this analogy looks inappropriate.

One of the worst curses in philosophy, whether of the East or the West, is philosophers emphasizing one aspect alone at the expense of another. When Parmenides spoke of *Being*, Heraclitus spoke of *Becoming*. Even though Zeno recognized the relevancy of both Being and Becoming, he could not extricate himself from the *paradox* of accepting them together. In the philosophy of Śaṅkara, cause is given primacy over effect. Rāmānuja refuted Śaṅkara, giving effect an equal status with cause. The followers of Śaṅkara and Rāmānuja interpreted these masters in terms of unreconcilable polemics. The secret implied in the analogy given by Kṛṣṇa of the beads and string of a cosmic garland could have saved many from unnecessary squabbles in the name of Being or Becoming, Cause and Effect, or Existence and Essence. The garland presents the picture of a global or unitive vision which is contrary to vivisecting analysis.

When an artist appreciates or enjoys a beautiful sunset, he sees the landscape or the sunset as an ensemble or *gestalt*. He does not separate the sun from the clouds or the clouds from their changing colours. The vision of the garland stated above should also be taken as one total reality, and not as fragmentary pieces standing separately. The beauty of the beads is obvious, and they do not escape our attention. However, the true appreciation is of the unitiveness of the garland and not the beads. Thus each one of us has our own value, and we all belong to a greater value when understood as belonging to the Absolute. Throughout the Gītā the same secret is used as a method of correlation between the necessary and the contingent, the relative and the Absolute, and the personal and the Universal. In an ascending scale of values ranging from the most actual to the most theoretical or sublime, we can imagine the highest point to be the Absolute itself, considered as a brilliant pearl of great price. This presiding Value is what gives coherence and correlation to all the other values at the different levels of human consciousness.

If the phenomenal world and its invisible inner coherence are aspects of the Supreme, do we realize the Absolute by meditating on all that pops up before us in the phenomenal world as the lower aspect of the Absolute, with the unknown as the higher?

What we term here as the Absolute is not the quantitative sum total of all things. When any value is self-founded, complete in itself and global in its significance, it is an expression of the Absolute. Kṛṣṇa says:

> I am the taste in waters, Oh Son of Kuntī, I am the light in the moon and the sun, I am *AUṀ* in all the Vedas, sound in the sky, and the human quality in men.
>
> I am the holy fragrance of the earth (divinity), and also the brilliance of the luminary (presence), the vital principle in all beings, and the (essence of) austerity in all ascetics.
>
> Know Me, Oh Pārtha! to be the perennial seed of all beings; I am the reason of the intelligent, and I the brightness of (those who are) the brilliant.

The way of entering into the unitive principle implied in the various entities enumerated is indicated in these verses. It involves initiation and a certain pressure of contemplation. The examples cited in the above verses by no means exhaust all the values that can be referred to as expressions of the Absolute. These are, more or less, model lessons for the aspirant to direct his contemplation in abstracting the most essential value from a complex and involved matrix of the systems to which they belong.

The Absolute is often defined as "existence, knowledge, and bliss" (sat-cit-ānanda). *Whether higher or lower, it cannot have qualities opposed to these three aspects, but the phenomenal world very often shows the non-existent to be existent, false or fabricated notions to be right knowledge, and a great many of our experiences are far from being blissful, if they are not truly miserable. I do not see the relevancy in treating the phenomenal world as Absolute, even if it were qualified as lower.*

The noumenal and the phenomenal can be compared to pure light and the rainbow, respectively. Pure light by itself has no form and colour, whereas the rainbow is a colourful spectrum with an arc-like shape. To a person's uncritical mind the rainbow, being visible and objective, will appear as positive, whereas pure light is what they might know only by mere inferential abstraction. On the other hand, someone with a discerning mind sees the rainbow as a negative phenomenon which falsifies the true nature of light. The relation between light and the rainbow is of an independent factor and a dependent accident. Light can shine on its own, whereas the rainbow cannot exist without the light even for a second. On that account, one can treat light as real and the rainbow as unreal. In spite of this philosophical verity, the fact remains that the rainbow is part of our experience. There must be something in the very nature of pure light that accounts for the emergence of the rainbow. To that extent it cannot be unreal. In the same way, the phenomenal, while being entirely dependent on the noumenal, cannot be dismissed as unreal. That is why the Vedāntins call the phenomenal world *sadasat*, meaning "real–unreal".

It is true that there is room for false notions and misery in the phenomenal world. Our definition of the Absolute is "existence, subsistence, and value" and not "bliss". We have explained earlier that however unpalatable misery is, it cannot be denied as a value, because negative values and positive values are both values alike. Though the Absolute is all-inclusive, the relation of specific values born of the modalities of nature are governed by a subtle dialectics which should be carefully understood, and this we get in verses 11 and 12:

> I am the strength of the strong, devoid of desire and passion. In beings I am desire which is not contrary to righteousness (*dharma*), Oh Leader of the Bhāratas!
>
> Even those manifestations recognized as according with existence (sāttvic), and active or dominant (rājasic), and dark or inert (tāmasic) – know them even to be My own. I am not in them, but they are in Me.

Just as in deductive logic, that which is true of a universal proposition is not true of its converse: what is true of an individual item in the phenomenal manifestation is not true of the Absolute. The Absolute, while being inclusive of the relative, also transcends it. In other words, a person who is wholeheartedly devoted to the Absolutue or an absolute Value can be considered as belonging to a distinct or superior order. The Upaniṣads speak of Raikva the cartman, poor and clad in rags, who lived under the shade of his cart. However worthless he looked, he could not condescend to teach the king higher wisdom until he proved his absolute devotion to wisdom.

What makes the psyche positively purified, promoting it from a darker realm of manifestation to a brighter one, or to colour or condition the psyche, thereby pushing it down to an inferior realm?

A person bound by his ego-consciousness while being engaged in action is caught in the eddy of relativistic obligations, which in turn bring many desires and frustrations. In that way, there ensues a long chain of action. The motivation of each action purifies or conditions the psyche, as the case may be. Thus, each person by his own action promotes himself to a better form of life or deteriorates his own value system.

Is it natural for all people to seek liberation or God-realization?

All people do not turn to God for the same reason. Kṛṣṇa names four kinds of devotees turning to Him for different favours:

> Among doers of the good, four kinds are intent on Me, Arjuna: the distressed, the seeker of knowledge, the seeker of the goods of life, and the wise, Oh Leader of the Bhāratas!
>
> Of these, the wise man, forever united and unitively affiliated with the Absolute, excels, for dear to the utmost limit am I to the wise one, and he is dear to Me.

There are several religions and many forms of worship. In some religions, God is conceived as a deity or as a supreme person intimately tied up in the affairs of each man. In some others God has no form and is impersonal. There are even religions which have no belief in God at all. Do they all turn to the same Absolute in their search?

Kṛṣṇa says:

> Their wisdom distracted by such (or) such (other) desire (counterparts), they attain to other divinities, committed to various obligations belonging to each, prompted by their own particular nature (in each case).
>
> By whichever (particular) form such and such a devotee with faith wishes to worship, each to his own faith I confirm.
>
> He, endowed with that faith, seeks the worship of such a one, and from him obtainss his desires, the benefits being decreed by Me.

That does not mean irregular and unintelligent devotion will have the same benefit as the wise man's wholehearted devotion to the Absolute. Kṛṣṇa further says:

> Terminable indeed is the benefit (accruing) to these of small intelligence; sacrificers to the divinities go to the divinities, but My devotees come to Me.

Is it justifed to use the terms Absolute, God, and deity all in the same sense when they are predicated differenlty?

The imcomparable and unpredicable aspect of the Absolute is offered in verse 24, which gives the key to the whole secret:

> Unreasoning persons consider Me as the unmanifest come to manifestation, not knowing My supreme (value), unexpended, with no superior.

This verse enunciates the overall character of the Absolute in terms of manifestation and non-manifestation. It postulates four possible ways of ruling out predications about the Absolute.

First, it denies that the manifest is the Absolute, though derived from a prior unmanifest. Second, it rules out the theory (which is more philosophical) that the unmanifest is the Absolute, although it attains to manifestation as the visible world. Third, it rules out the position where a philosopher thinks that the manifest and unmanifast are dual aspects of the same Absolute, a position which Śaṅkara has taken so much trouble to refute. Fourth, as a final residue there is the possible predication which states that the Absolute is an entity to be included among entities abstract or concrete which the mind is capable of conceiving statically or existentially. Here the Absolute is not to be thought of as a thing at all. The Absolute belongs to the unique order of the Absolute itself which has nothing in common with things or entities, however subtle or perceptual they may be. The Absolute is the Supreme and therefore above all, though comprehending all. Nothing can therefore be predicated of it, but everything that is predicated derives its reality from it.

When the Absolute is so inconceivable and incomprehensible, how can it ever be attained?

In trying to cut oneself away from all the ills of relativism, one has to focus one's attention on a value which constitutes a second pole representing freedom in the Absolute in the fullest possible sense. The value which can form the legitimate counterpart of the suffering or bondage of man, conceived in the most general terms, must be that Absolute, which can be considered in its most all-inclusive manner. Kṛṣṇa says:

> Those who, resorting to Me, strive for liberation from decay and death – they know That, the Absolute, all that constitutes Self-knowledge, and everything pertaining to (ritualistic) action.
>
> Those who know Me, taking together what refers to existential (*adhibhūta*), hypostatic (*adhidaiva*), and sacrificial (*adhiyajña*) aspects – they know Me in a unitive spirit, even at the time of their departure.

The final focusing of the Self in relation to that supreme value called the Absolute generally takes place when a man is about to leave life here. It is referred to here as *prayāṇa-kāla* (time of departure). If a man is capable of retaining a global or intuitive vision of the Absolute in all its three aspects mentioned, at the time of his passing, he may be said to have at that time a proper and complete vision of the Absolute as intended in this chapter.

VIII

Akṣara-Brahma-Yoga

The Unitive Way in Spiritual Progress

INTRODUCTION

IN CHAPTER VII the only articulation was from the side of the Absolute. It came through Kṛṣṇa, the conceivable personification of the Transcendental Immanence. In the present chapter the attention is shifted from the Absolute Being to the problem of the sum total of phenomenality, personified in Arjuna. Here he is pushed to the wall of death, the gaping mouth of the void. He sees in himself both the cause and the effect of a possible suicidal fratricide. His only choice is to turn in the direction of the Transcendent Being. At this crucial moment he puts eight pointed questions to Kṛṣṇa:

- Who or what is the Absolute?
- What is the Transcendent Being?
- What is action?
- What is phenomenality?
- What is God?
- Who is the beneficiary of sacrifice?
- How is the transcendental principle immanent in the physical body?
- How does one return to the Absolute through remembrance, at a crucial hour when the phenomenal makes its most nihilistic assault (at the time of death)?

Thus, in this chapter a proper dialogue is re-established between the voices of transcendence and existence. To make the teaching more effective for the student, the author has adopted as a literary device a form of mystical rhapsody. The verses are composed with exquisite poetic charm. The link between the counterparts is highlighted as one of great intimacy.

Mystical vision is alluded to as a sure way to relate the individual with the Absolute. The first step is centring the total Beingness of the individual in the heart. After experiencing union with the Absolute in the heart, the emphasis is brought to a level of consciousness where the deep feelings of the total personality can surface to positive awareness. This is done by meditating on the centre of the stream of consciousness, located between the eyebrows. Finally the progression of the experience is converted into the *logos* or *verbum*, *AUṀ*. Thereafter, the continuous remembrance of *AUṀ* ensures the link between the Absolute and the aspirant.

After clearly enunciating the whole process of mystical discipline, Kr̥ṣṇa passes on to the discussion of several miscellaneous subjects of topical or historical interest. He begins with a reference to the traditional belief in two paths for the departed souls, the bright path and the smoky one. He explains to Arjuna the cosmic cycle of time and the need to transcend it. He makes a passing reference to the idea of reincarnation. The relativistic merit of the hedonistic, heaven-seeking formulae of the Vedas is treated as of secondary importance only. Kr̥ṣṇa then makes a review of ritualistic sacrifice, the sharing of gifts to obtain spiritual merit, and the resorting to practices of mortification.

The highest emphasis is laid on the need to establish the best rapport possible between the intentionality of Transcendental Being and the existential ego of the person belonging to the transactional field. The key-words of this chapter are, "Reflect on Me and also fight".

TRANSLATION

अर्जुन उवाच –

1. किं तद्ब्रह्म किमध्यात्मं किं कर्म पुरुषोत्तम ।
अधिभूतं च किं प्रोक्तमधिदैवं किमुच्यते ।।

arjuna uvāca –

kiṁ tad brahma kim adhyātmaṁ kiṁ karma puruṣottama ।
adhibhūtaṁ ca kiṁ proktam adhidaivaṁ kim ucyate ॥

arjuna uvāca: Arjuna said; *kiṁ tat brahma*: what (is) that Absolute; *kim adhyātmaṁ*: what (is) the principle of the Self; *kiṁ karma*: what (is) action; *puruṣottama*: Oh Kr̥ṣṇa; *kiṁ proktam*: what is said to be; *adhibhūtaṁ*: the principle of existence; *ca kim ucyate*: and what is spoken of as; *adhidaivaṁ*: the principle of divinity.

Arjuna said:

What is that Absolute? What is the principle of the Self? What is action, Oh

Highest Spirit? What is said to be the principle of existence, and what is spoken of as the principle of divinity?

2. अधियज्ञः कथं कोऽत्र देहेऽस्मिन्मधुसूदन ।
प्रयाणकाले च कथं ज्ञेयोऽसि नियतात्मभिः ।।

adhiyajñah katham ko 'tra dehe 'smin madhusūdna ।
prayāṇakāle ca katham jñeyo 'si niyatātmabhiḥ ॥

atra asmin dehe: here in this body; *kaḥ katham*: what (and) how (is to be understood); *adhiyajñaḥ*: the principle of sacrifice; *madhusūdana*: Oh Kṛṣṇa; *ca katham asi jñeyaḥ*: again, how are you to be known; *niyatātmabhiḥ*: by self-controlled persons; *prayāṇakāle*: at the time of going forth (from the body).

Here in this body, what and how is (to be understood) the principle of sacrifice, Oh Madhusūdana? Again, how are You to be known by self-controlled persons at the time of going forth from the body?

श्रीभगवानुवाच –
3. अक्षरं ब्रह्म परमं स्वभावोऽध्यात्ममुच्यते ।
भूतभावोद्भवकरो विसर्गः कर्मसञ्ज्ञितः ।।

śrībhagavān uvāca –
akṣaraṁ brahma paramaṁ svabhāvo 'dhyātmam ucyate ।
bhūtabhāvodbhavakaro visargaḥ karmasaṁjñitaḥ ॥

śrībhagavān uvāca: Kṛṣṇa said; *akṣaraṁ brahma paramaṁ*: Perennial, the Absolute, Supreme; *svabhāvaḥ*: (its) own nature; *adhyātmam*: the principle of the Self; *ucyate*: is called; *visargaḥ*: the creative urge; *bhūtabhāva udbhava karaḥ*: the cause of the origin of existent beings; *saṁjñitaḥ karma*: is designated action.

Kṛṣṇa said:

Perennial, the Absolute, Supreme -- (its) own nature, the principle of the Self is called. The creative urge, the cause of the origin of existent beings, is designated action.

4. अधिभूतं क्षरो भावः पुरुषश्चाधिदैवतम् ।
अधियज्ञोऽहमेवात्र देहे देहभृतां वर ।।

adhibhūtaṁ kṣaro bhāvaḥ purușaś cā 'dhidaivatam ।
adhiyajño 'ham evā 'tra dehe dehabhṛtāṁ vara ॥

adhibhūtaṁ: the principle of existence; *kṣaraḥ bhāvaḥ*: (is) the transient aspect; *ca puruṣaḥ*: and spirit; *adhidaivatam*: (is) the principle of divinity; *adhiyajñāḥ*: what pertains to sacrifice (is); *aham eva*: I alone; *atra dehe*: here in the body; *dehabhṛtāṁ vara*: Oh Arjuna.

The principle of existence is the transient aspect, and spirit is the principle of divinity; what pertains to sacrifice is Myself here in the body Oh Most Superior Bearer of the Body.

5. अन्तकाले च मामेव स्मरन्मुक्त्वा कलेवरम् ।
यः प्रयाति स मद्भावं याति नास्त्यत्र संशयः ॥

antakāle ca mām eva smaran muktvā kalevaram ।
yaḥ prayāti sa madbhāvaṁ yāti nā 'sty atra saṁśayaḥ ।

ca saḥ yaḥ: and he who; *antakāle*: at the time of death; *smaran mām eva*: thinking of Me alone; *muktvā kalevaram*: leaving the body; *prayāti*: goes forth; *yāti madbhāvaṁ*: reaches My being; *atra*: herein; *asti na saṁśayaḥ*: there is no doubt.

And he who, at the time of death, thinking of Me alone, leaves the body and goes forth, reaches My being; herein there is no room for doubt.

6. यं यं वापि स्मरन्भावं त्यजत्यन्ते कलेवरम् ।
तं तमेवैति कौन्तेय सदा तद्भावभावितः ॥

yaṁ-yaṁ vā 'pi smaran bhāvaṁ tyajaty ante kalevaram ।
taṁ-tam evai 'ti kaunteya sadā tadbhāvabhāvitaḥ ॥

vā api yaṁ yaṁ: or also, whatever; *bhāvaṁ*: manifested aspect; *smaran*: (a man) is thinking of; *ante*: in the end; *tyajati kalevaram*: (when) he leaves the body; *taṁ tam eva*: that indeed; *kaunteya*: Oh Arjuna; *eti*: (he) reaches; *sadā bhāvitaḥ tad bhāva*: always made to become that (particular) life-expression.

Whatever manifested aspect a man might think of at death, when he leaves the body – that, Oh Son of Kuntī, he reaches, whose thoughts always conform to that particular life-expression.

7. तस्मात्सर्वेषु कालेषु मामनुस्मर युध्य च ।
मय्यर्पितमनोबुद्धिर्मामेवैष्यस्यसंशयः ॥

tasmāt sarveṣu kāleṣu mām anusmara yudhya ca ।
mayy arpitamanobuddhir mām evai 'ṣyasy asaṁśayaḥ ॥

tasmāt: therefore; *sarveṣu kāleṣu*: at all times; *anusmara mām*: remember Me; *ca yudhya*: and fight; *arpita manaḥ buddhiḥ mayi*: having mind and intelligence surrendered in Me; *eṣyasi*: you shall come; *mām eva*: to Me alone; *asaṁśayaḥ*: (have) no doubt.

Therefore, at all times remember Me and fight; when your mind and intelligence are surrendered to Me, you shall come to Me; (have) no doubt.

8. अभ्यासयोगयुक्तेन चेतसा नान्यगामिना ।
परमं पुरुषं दिव्यं याति पार्थानुचिन्तयन् ॥

abhyāsayogayuktena cetasā nā 'nyagāminā ।
paramaṁ puruṣaṁ divyaṁ yāti pārthā 'nucintayan ॥

anucintayan: meditating; *cetasā*: with the mind; *abhyāsa yoga yuktena*: engaged in the *yoga* of positive effort; *na anya gāminā*: undistracted by anything else; *yāti*: he goes; *paramaṁ divyaṁ puruṣaṁ*: (to) the supreme divine Person; *pārtha*: Oh Arjuna.

Meditating, with the mind engaged in the *yoga* involving positive effort, undistracted by anything else, he goes to the supreme divine Person, Oh Pārtha!

9. कविं पुराणमनुशासितारमणोरणीयांसमनुस्मरेद्यः ।
सर्वस्य धातारमचिन्त्यरूपमादित्यवर्णं तमसः परस्तात् ॥

kaviṁ purāṇam anuśāsitāram aṇor aṇiyāṁsam anusmared yaḥ ।
sarvasya dhātāram acintyarūpam ādityavarṇaṁ tamasaḥ parastāt ॥

yaḥ anusmaret: (he) who meditates on; *kaviṁ purāṇam*: the Poet-seer, the Ancient; *anuśāsitāram*: the Ordainer; *aṇīyāṁsam aṇoḥ*: minuter than the atom; *dhātāram sarvasya*: the Dispenser of all; *acintya rūpam*: of unthinkable nature; *āditya varṇaṁ*: sun-coloured; *parastāt tamasaḥ*: beyond the darkness.

10. प्रयाणकाले मनसाचलेन भक्त्या युक्तो योगबलेन चैव ।
भ्रुवोर्मध्ये प्राणमावेश्य सम्यक् स तं परं पुरुषमुपैति दिव्यम् ॥

prayāṇakāle manasā 'calena bhaktyā yukto yogabalena cai 'va ।
bhruvor madhye prāṇam āveśya samyak sa taṁ paraṁ puruṣam upaiti divyam ॥

prayāṇakāle: (who meditates) at the time of departure; *acalena manasā*: with a steady mind; *yuktaḥ bhaktyā*: possessed of devotion; *ca eva*: as also; *yoga balena*: of the strength that comes from *yoga*; *samyak āveśya*: well-fixing; *prāṇam*: the life-breath; *madhye bhruvoḥ*: betwixt the eyebrows; *saḥ upaiti taṁ*: he reaches that; *paraṁ divyam puruṣam*: supreme divine Person.

He who meditates on the Poet-seer, the Ancient, the Ordainer, minuter than the atom, the Dispenser of all, of unthinkable nature, sun-coloured beyond the darkness, who meditates at the time of departure with a steady mind possessed of devotion, as also of the strength that comes from *yoga*, well-fixing the life-breath betwixt the eyebrows – he reaches that supreme divine Person.

11. यदक्षरं वेदविदो वदन्ति विशन्ति यद्यतयो वीतरागाः ।
यदिच्छन्तो ब्रह्मचर्यं चरन्ति तत्ते पदं सङ्ग्रहेण प्रवक्ष्ये ॥

yad akṣaraṁ vedavido vadanti viśanti yad yatayo vītarāgāḥ ।
yad icchanto brahmacaryaṁ caranti tat te padaṁ saṁgraheṇa pravakṣye ॥

akṣaraṁ yat: (that) imperishable (value) which; *vedavidaḥ*: the knowers of the Vedas; *vadanti*: speak of; *yat yatayaḥ*: which the self-controlled; *vītarāgāḥ viśanti*: (and) passion-free enter; *icchantaḥ yat*: desiring which; *caranti*: (they) lead; *brahmacaryaṁ*: the life of the disciplined (Vedic) student; *tat padaṁ*: that state; *saṁgraheṇa pravakṣye*: succinctly I shall describe.

That imperishable (value) which the knowers of the Vedas speak of, which the self-controlled and passion-free enter, desiring which they lead the life of the disciplined (Vedic) student – that state I shall succinctly describe.

12. सर्वद्वाराणि संयम्य मनो हृदि निरुध्य च ।
मूर्ध्न्याधायात्मनः प्राणमास्थितो योगधारणाम् ॥

sarvadvārāṇi saṁyamya mano hṛdi nirudhya ca ।
mūrdhny ādhāyā 'tmanaḥ prāṇam āsthito yogadhāraṇām ॥

saṁyamya sarva dvārāṇi: inhibiting all exists; *ca nirudhya*: and holding; *manaḥ*: the mind-factors; *hṛdi*: (convergent) in the heart; *ātmanaḥ prāṇam*: one's vitality-functionings; *ādhāya mūrdhni*: placed in the head; *āsthitaḥ*: well-established in; *yoga dhāraṇām*: sustained unitive contemplation.

13. ओमित्येकाक्षरं ब्रह्म व्याहरन्मामनुस्मरन् ।
यः प्रयाति त्यजन्देहं स याति परमां गतिम् ॥

aum ity ekākṣaraṁ brahma vyāharan mām anusmaran ।
yaḥ prayāti tyajan dehaṁ sa yāti paramāṁ gatim ॥

vyāharan: uttering; *ekākṣaraṁ*: the one-syllabled word; *aum*: *AUṀ* (Vedic symbol of the Supreme); *iti brahma*: which is the Absolute; *anusmaran mām*: remembering Me; *saḥ yaḥ prayāti*: he who departs; *tyajan dehaṁ*: abandoning the body; *yāti paramāṁ gatim*: treads the highest path.

Inhibiting all exits, holding the mind-factors convergent in the heart, vitality-functionings operating centred between the eyebrows, well-established in sustained unitive contemplation,

uttering the one-syllabled word *AUṀ*, which is the Absolute, while constantly remembering Me, he who departs, abandoning the body, treads the highest path.

14. अनन्यचेताः सततं यो मां स्मरति नित्यशः ।
तस्याहं सुलभः पार्थ नित्ययुक्तस्य योगिनः ॥

ananyacetāḥ satataṁ yo māṁ smarati nityaśaḥ ।
tasyā 'haṁ sulabhaḥ pārtha nityayuktasya yoginaḥ ॥

yaḥ: one; *ananya cetāḥ*: without extraneous relational mental interests; *satataṁ smarati māṁ*: ever remembering Me; *nityaśaḥ*: day in and day out; *tasya*: to such; *nitya yuktasya yoginaḥ*: an ever unitively affiliated man of contemplation; *aham sulabhaḥ*: I (am) easy of attainment; *pārtha*: Oh Arjuna.

One without extraneous relational mental interests, remembering Me day in and day out – to such an ever unitively affiliated man of contemplation I am easy of attainment, Oh Pārtha!

15. मामुपेत्य पुनर्जन्म दुःखालयमशाश्वतम् ।
नाप्नुवन्ति महात्मानः संसिद्धिं परमां गताः ॥

mām upetya punarjanma duḥkhālayam aśāśvatam ।
nāpnuvanti mahātmānaḥ saṁsiddhiṁ paramāṁ gatāḥ ॥

upetya mām: having attained to Me; *mahātmānaḥ*: the great ones; *na apnuvanti punaḥ janma*: do not get again birth; *aśāśvatam*: (in this) transitory; *duḥkha alayam*: abode of suffering; *gatāḥ paramāṁ saṁsiddhiṁ*: gone to the highest attainment.

Having attained to Me, they do not return to this transitory abode of suffering, having reached the highest attainment.

16. आब्रह्मभुवनाल्लोकाः पुनरावर्तिनोऽर्जुन ।
मामुपेत्य तु कौन्तेय पुनर्जन्म न विद्यते ॥

ā brahmabhuvanāl lokāḥ punarāvartino 'rjuna ।
mām upetya tu kaunteya punarjanma na vidyate ॥

lokāḥ: (all) worlds; *ā brahma bhuvanāt*: (beginning from here) to the world of Brahmā; *punarāvartinaḥ*: (are subject to) return to rebirth; *arjuna*: Arjuna; *tu upetya mām*: but on reaching Me; *kaunteya*: Oh Arjuna; *vidyate*: there is; *na punaḥ janma*: not another birth.

All worlds, beginning from here to the world of Brahmā, are subject to phenomenal repetition, Arjuna; but on reaching Me, Oh Son of Kuntī, there is not another birth.

17. सहस्रयुगपर्यन्तमहर्यद्ब्रह्मणो विदुः ।
रात्रिं युगसहस्रान्तां तेऽहोरात्रविदो जनाः ।।

sahasrayugaparyantam ahar yad brahmaṇo viduḥ ।
rātriṁ yugasahasrāntāṁ te 'horātravido janāḥ ॥

yat viduḥ: (those) who know; *ahaḥ brahmaṇaḥ*: the day of Brahmā; *paryantam sahasra*: extends to a thousand; *yuga*: unit periods in the cosmic cycle (of 4,320,000 years duration); *rātriṁ*: (and) the night; *sahasrāntāṁ yuga*: (of) a thousand (such) units; *te janāḥ*: they (are) men (who); *aho rātra vidaḥ*: know the day and night (principle).

Those who know that the day of Brahmā is a thousand unit periods in the cosmic cycle, and the night of a thousand (such) units – they are knowers of the day and night (principle).

18. अव्यक्ताद्व्यक्तयः सर्वाः प्रभवन्त्यहरागमे ।
रात्र्यागमे प्रलीयन्ते तत्रैवाव्यक्तसञ्ज्ञके ।।

avyaktād vyaktayaḥ sarvāḥ prabhavanty aharāgame ।
rātryāgame pralīyante tatrai 'vā 'vyaktasaṁjñake ॥

avyaktāt: from the unmanifested; *sarvāḥ vyaktayaḥ*: all the manifested; *prabhavanti*: proceed; *ahaḥ āgame*: at the coming of day; *rātri āgame*: at the coming of night; *pralīyante tatra eva*: (they) merge there indeed; *avyakta saṁjñake*: named the unmanifested.

From the unmanifested all the manifested proceed at the coming of day; at the coming of night they merge in that same, named the unmanifested.

19. भूतग्रामः स एवायं भूत्वा भूत्वा प्रलीयते ।
रात्र्यागमेऽवशः पार्थ प्रभवत्यहरागमे ।।

bhūtagrāmaḥ sa evā 'yaṁ bhūtvā-bhūtvā pralīyate ।
rātryāgame 'vaśaḥ pārtha prabhavaty aharāgame ॥

saḥ eva ayam: this very same; *bhūta grāmaḥ*: aggregate of beings; *bhūtvā bhūtvā*: coming into existence again and again; *pralīyate*: merges; *avaśaḥ*: subject to necessity; *rātri āgame*: at the onset of night; *pārtha*: Oh Arjuna; *prabhavati*: (and) comes into being; *ahaḥ āgame*: at the coming of day.

This very same aggregate of beings, coming into existence again and again, merges, subject to necessity, at the onset of night, Oh Pārtha, and comes into being at the coming of day.

20. परस्तस्मात्तु भावोऽन्योऽव्यक्तोऽव्यक्तात्सनातनः ।
यः स सर्वेषु भूतेषु नश्यत्सु न विनश्यति ।।

paras tasmāt tu bhāvo 'nyo 'vyakto 'vyaktāt sanātanaḥ ।
yaḥ sa sarveṣu bhūteṣu naśyatsu na vinaśyati ॥

tu paraḥ tasmāt: but beyond this; *avyaktaḥ*: unmanifested; *anyaḥ*: (there is yet) another; *avyaktāt sanātanaḥ*: unmanifested, perennial; *bhāvaḥ*: existence; *yaḥ*: which; *sarveṣu bhūteṣu naśyatsu*: among all perishable beings; *saḥ*: itself; *na vinaśyati*: does not perish.

But beyond this unmanifested there is yet another unmanifested perennial existence, which among perishables itself does not perish.

21. अव्यक्तोऽक्षर इयुक्तस्तमाहुः परमां गतिम् ।
यं प्राप्य न निवर्तन्ते तद्धाम परमं मम ।।

avyakto 'kṣara ity uktas tam āhuḥ paramāṁ gatim ।
yaṁ prāpya na nivartante tad dhāma paramaṁ mama ॥

avyaktaḥ: (that) unmanifested; *uktaḥ iti*: is called thus; *akṣaraḥ*: the imperishable; *āhuḥ tam*: (they) speak of that; *paramāṁ gatiṁ*: (as) the highest (spiritual) path; *prāpya yam*: attaining which; *nivartante na*: they return not; *tat mama*: that (is) My; *paramaṁ dhāma*: supreme abode.

That unmanifested is called the imperishable. That they speak of as the highest (spiritual) path, attaining which they return not. Such is My supreme abode.

22. पुरुषः स परः पार्थ भक्त्या लभ्यस्त्वनन्यया ।
यस्यान्तःस्थानि भूतानि येन सर्वमिदं ततम् ।।

puruṣaḥ sa paraḥ pārtha bhaktyā labhyas tv ananyayā ।
yasyā 'ntaḥsthāni bhūtāni yena sarvam idaṁ tatam ॥

saḥ paraḥ puruṣaḥ: this (is) the supreme Spirit; *pārtha*: Oh Arjuna; *yasya antaḥ sthāni*: within whom abide; *bhūtāni*: (all) existences; *yena*: (and) by whom; *sarvam idam*: all this; *tatam*: is pervaded; *labhyaḥ tu*: (who is) attainable, however; *bhaktyā*: by devotion; *ananyayā*: exclusive of (all) extraneous factors.

This is the supreme Spirit, Oh Pārtha! within whom all existences abide and by whom all this is pervaded, who is attainable, however, by devotion exclusive of all extraneous factors.

23. यत्र काले त्वनावृत्तिमावृत्तिं चैव योगिनः ।
प्रयाता यान्ति तं कालं वक्ष्यामि भरतर्षभ ।।

yatra kāle tv anāvr̥ttim āvr̥ttiṁ cai 'va yoginaḥ ।
prayātā yānti taṁ kālaṁ vakṣyāmi bharatarṣabha ॥

yatra kāle: that time at which; *yoginaḥ*: *yogīs*; *tu prayātāḥ yānti*: indeed go forth; *āvr̥ttiṁ anāvr̥ttim ca eva*: (cause them) to return or not to return (as the case may be); *taṁ*: that; *kālaṁ*: temporal circumstance; *vakṣyāmi*: I am going to tell you; *bharatarṣabha*: Oh Arjuna.

That (cosmological) occasion in which *yogīs* go forth (causes them) to return or not to return (as the case may be) – that temporal circumstance I am going to tell you, Oh Chief of Bhāratas!

24. अग्निर्ज्योतिरहः शुक्लः षण्मासा उत्तरायणम् ।
तत्र प्रयाता गच्छन्ति ब्रह्म ब्रह्मविदो जनाः ।।

agnir jyotir ahaḥ śuklaḥ ṣaṇmāsā uttarāyaṇam ।
tatra prayātā gacchanti brahma brahmavido janāḥ ॥

agniḥ jyotiḥ: fire, light; *ahaḥ*: day-time; *śuklaḥ*: the bright lunar fortnight; *ṣaṇmāsāḥ*: the six months; *uttarāyaṇam*: of the (summer) northern solstice; *prayātāḥ tatra*: going forth there; *janāḥ brahmavidaḥ*: people who can understand the Absolute; *gacchanti brahma*: reach the Absolute.

25. धूमो रात्रिस्तथा कृष्णः षण्मासा दक्षिणायनम् ।
तत्र चान्द्रमसं ज्योतिर्योगी प्राप्य निवर्तते ।।

dhūmo rātris tathā kr̥ṣṇaḥ ṣaṇmāsā dakṣiṇāyanam ।
tatra cāndramasaṁ jyotir yogī prāpya nivartate ॥

dhūmah rātriḥ: smoke, night; *tathā kr̥ṣṇaḥ*: thus the dark and lunar fortnight; *ṣaṇmāsāḥ*: the six months; *dakṣiṇāyanam*: of the (winter) southern solstice; *tatra yogī*: there the *yogī*; *prāpya*: attaining; *cāndramsaṁ jyotiḥ*: the lunar (relativist) light; *nivartate*: returns.

Fire, light, day-time, the bright fortnight, the six months of the (summer) northen solstice – going forth on that (cosmological) occasion, those people who can understand the Absolute reach the Absolute.

Smoke, night, the dark fortnight, the six months of the (winter) southern solstice – on that (cosmological) occasion, the *yogī*, attaning the lunar (relativist) light, returns.

26. शुक्लकृष्णे गती ह्येते जगतः शाश्वते मते ।
एकया यात्यनावृत्तिमन्ययावर्तते पुनः ।।

śuklakr̥ṣṇe gatī hy ete jagataḥ śāśvate mate ।
ekayā yāty anāvr̥ttim anyayā 'vartate punaḥ ॥

ete: these two; *śukla kṛṣṇe*: the white and the black; *mate*: are known to be; *jagataḥ*: in the world; *gatī śāśvate hi*: the twin perennial paths indeed; *ekayā*: by one (of them); *yāti anāvṛttim*: (one) attains to non-return; *anyayā*: (while) by the other; *āvartate punaḥ*: (one) comes back again.

These, the white and the black, are known to be in this world the twin perennial paths; by one of them one attains to non-return, while by the other one comes back.

27. नैते सृती पार्थ जानन्योगी मुह्यति कश्चन ।
तस्मात्सर्वेषु कालेषु योगयुक्तो भवार्जुन ॥

nai 'te sṛtī pārtha jānan yogī muhyati kaścana ।
tasmāt sarveṣu kāleṣu yogayukto bhavā 'rjuna ॥

jānan: understanding (the basic nature of); *ete sṛtī*: these two paths; *pārtha*: Oh Arjuna; *yogī*: one of contemplation; *na muhyati kaścana*: is not confounded at all; *tasmāt*: therefore; *sarveṣu kāleṣu*: at all times; *arjuna*: Oh Arjuna; *bhava*: be; *yoga yuktaḥ*: unitively established in *yoga*.

Understanding (the basic nature of) these two paths, Oh Pārtha, one of contemplation is not confounded at all; therefore, at all times, Oh Arjuna! be unitively established in *yoga*.

28. वेदेषु यज्ञेषु तपःसु चैव दानेषु यत्पुण्यफलं प्रदिष्टम् ।
अत्येति तत्सर्वमिदं विदित्वा योगी परं स्थानमुपैति चाद्यम् ॥

vedeṣu yajñeṣu tapaḥsu cai 'va dāneṣu yat puṇyaphalaṁ pradiṣṭam ।
atyeti tat sarvam idaṁ viditvā yogī paraṁ sthānaṁ upaiti cā 'dyam ॥

yat: whatever; *puṇya phalaṁ*: meritorious result; *pradiṣṭam*: is (found) implied; *vedeṣu yajñeṣu*: in the Vedas, in sacrifices; *tapaḥsu ca eva dāneṣu*: in austerities and indeed in gifts; *yogī*: the contemplative who is unitively established; *viditvā idaṁ*: having understood this (teaching); *atyeti sarvam tat*: transcends all this; *ca upaiti*: and attains to; *paraṁ ādyam sthānam* – the supreme primal state.

Whatever meritorious result is found implied in the Vedas, in sacrifices, austerities, and in gifts, the contemplative who is unitively established, having understood this (teaching), transcends all these and attains to the supreme primal state.

DIALOGUE

TEACHER: This chapter is also called Tāraka-Brahma-Yoga. *Akṣara* means that which is the perennial or imperishable. *Tāraka* means that which is luminous like a guiding star. Hence this chapter is to be treated as one of supreme guidance to the Absolute given by the Lord Himself. The most fundamental questions in spirituality are here raised by Arjuna for Kṛṣṇa's divine guidance. He asks Kṛṣṇa:

> What is that Absolute? What is the principle of the Self? What is action.
>
> Oh Highest Spirit? What is said to be the principle of existence, and what is spoken of as the principle of divinity?
>
> Here in this body, what and how is (to be understood) the principle of sacrifice, Oh Madhusūdana? Again, how are You to be known by self-controlled persons at the time of going forth from the body?

STUDENT: *Why does Arjuna put a volley of questions instead of putting them singly?*

The reason is that the author wants to fuse together and revalue the spiritual content of many anterior traditional trends. In the previous chapters there were several references to the Absolute (*Brahman*), the Self (*ātman*), action (*karma*), the phenomenal world, the world of the Shining Ones, sacrifice, and union with the Absolute. All these are lying in Arjuna's mind as loose ends. Here they are all to be picked up and correlated meaningfully.

At the time of death man is filled with remorse and many regrets, and he looks for redemption. In such a mood he looks for solace within himself and also to God, and all currents of spirituality tend to come together in one single masterdrive. In such a state the urge for fulfilment can only be satisfied by gaining an integrated vision of the many factors which Arjuna brings in here for discussion. Kṛṣṇa answers Arjuna in the same style in which Arjuna put his questions:

> Perennial, the Absolute, Supreme – (its) own nature, the principle of the Self is called. The creative urge, the cause of the origin of existent beings, is designated action.
>
> The principle of existence is the transient aspect, and spirit is the principle of divinity; what pertains to sacrifice is Myself here in the body, Oh Most Superior Bearer of the Body!
>
> And he who, at the time of death, thinking of Me alone, leaves the body and goes forth, reaches My being; herein there is no room for doubt.

The above definition of the Absolute is, in the original Sanskrit, *akṣaram brahma paramaṁ*. This can be translated in three ways: the Imperishable is the Absolute Supreme; the Supreme is the Imperishable Absolute; or the Absolute is the Supreme Imperishable.

These definitions are very cryptic. Please elaborate.

Brahman, which is translated here as "the Absolute", has no parts. It is self-founded and is beyond the concept of time and space and all other relative notions. If the transformation of matter and the conservation of energy are brought under one common universal reference, and correlated to all that is experienced in the alternating states of consciousness as well as that which transcends consciousness – that universal reference of a single immutable and unchanging homogeneous Reality can be accepted as the general ground of all, and it can be called the Absolute.

Is the Absolute different from God?

God is the theological concept of the Absolute. In Vedānta, God is called *Īśvara* and is treated differently from *Brahman*, which is the Sanskrit equivalent for the Absolute. When the pure and transcendent aspect of the Absolute is conjoined with its own negative principle of nescience, the Absolute appears, as it were, in a state of immanence. As a result of this, there emerges the phenomenal world of manifestation. Vedānta recognizes only this immanent aspect of the Absolute as *Īśvara* or God. Such a theological concept is not absolutely free of anthropomorphic personification. The Absolute, on the other hand, should be understood as a pure notion of the All, or Totality.

When we think of the soul, what comes to our mind is some sort of subtle substance which animates our body. Our notion of it is very vague. To comprehend it as an indivisible, all-embracing Absolute seems even theoretically impossible. How can this seemingly unattainable identity ever be accomplished?

What is commonly understood as knowledge is a conditioning or colouration that circumlimits consciousness. This process of psychosis makes the infinite consciousness appear finite and its own modifications seem to be objects other than itself. Thus it implies at once a veiling and a projecting feature. These self-propelled operations which cause the dichotomy of a subject and its many objects are called nescience. From this it follows that knowledge of the world means ignorance of the Self. Because of this ever-persisting ignorance the Self is obscured by the non-Self, and the attributes of the non-Self are superimposed upon the Self.

The Self is defined as "Existence, Subsistence, and Self-founded Value" (*sat-cit-ānanda*). Such a definition may look odd to the empiricist and the existentialist, who may easily brush aside such a definition as a mere verbal abstraction. In the present case we should not forget that the Vedāntin is as much aware of the need to recognize ontologic existence, and so primacy is given to Existence in the definition. Recognition is also given to the apodictic verity of empirical facts. There is a third factor of equal importance: the value involvement in all that exists and is known. The core of our value structure is mankind's happiness.

The veracity of a value is judged on the grounds of its necessary existence and the apodictic quality of the awareness in which it is presented to the mind. Though all experiences are specific cases of existence, subsistence, and value, we relate ourselves to them as items that belong to a continuous and homogeneous whole. Nobody thinks of himself as so many disjunct and fragmentary bits of "I". The self identifies itself with an unbroken continuum. If the all-embracing Existence-Subsistence-Value is an abstraction, we are all abstractions. Whether abstract or not, the notion of "I" as well as the notion of the "Supreme", whether called God or the Absolute, have the dynamics to affect our lives physically, mentally, morally, and spiritually.

The very first fact that Vedānta admits is existence. The ontological verity of truth is intimately related to its own teleological possibilities. All possibilities are actualized here and now, and not in a shadowy world of speculation.

Arjuna is a young man. Why should he hurry to know with such urgency what the state of mind will be at the time of death?

You must remember that Arjuna is standing in the middle of a battlefield, where deadly arrows are flying past him. In such a context, with death staring him in the face, all life values come into focus toward a unified stream of interest. The minor or trivial interests of everyday life tend to recede into the background, and a master interest is bound to prevail. If the object of such an interest is no less than the Absolute, one will be drawn into the Being of the Absolute, like a stream that is drawn to the sea.

All thoughts and attitudes have the potential to cause another thought or attitude immediately or in the future. Hence, there is nothing wrong with presuming that the last thought of a person at the time of death can causally relate itself to the mode of a subsequent reincarnation. The idea of a single unitary soul wandering in time, assuming different bodily forms in successive phases of time is a far too simplified picture, which many people seem to hold. Such a view is not philosophically tenable. Even in this life there are many cross-currents of personal and group interests entering into each person's life in the form of sensations, feelings, ideations, and volitional reactions, causing an ever-changing and transforming persona that will become very bare in its existence if it is separated from the social matrix to which it belongs. However, in and through the flux of becoming there persists a nucleus bearing the personal identity of "I". Its continuity in this very life as well as in life after life depends on the same principle of participation in the never-expending existence of the Absolute. Arjuna wants to know clearly how a dying man can best relate himself to the source of his life – the Absolute.

Does the Gītā share the theory of the Rāmāyaṇa *and the* Yoga-Vāsiṣṭha, *that the last thoughts of a man propel his departed soul to its next birth?*

Kṛṣṇa states the general law without any reference to the Absolute:

> Whatever manifested aspect a man might think of at death, when he leaves the body – that, Oh Son of Kuntī, he reaches, whose thoughts always conform to that particular life-expression.

As a man thinks, so he becomes. This is a popular saying, recognized by the Buddhist *Dhammapada* when it says in the beginning, "All that we are is the result of what we have thought". In the light of the above teaching Kṛṣṇa gives his advice to Arjuna:

> Therefore, at all times remember Me and fight; when your mind and intelligence are surrendered to Me, you shall come to Me; (have) no doubt.

Does Kṛṣṇa suggest any special method or way of meditation to attune one's mind to the Absolute?

Kṛṣṇa's words that follow have the quality of a rhapsody, and are presented almost like a psalm:

> He who meditates on the Poet-Seer, the Ancient, the Ordainer, minuter than the atom, the Dispenser of all, of unthinkable nature, sun-coloured, beyond the darkness,
>
> who meditates at the time of departure with a steady mind possessed of devotion, as also the strength that comes from *yoga*, well-fixing the life-breath betwixt the eyebrows – he reaches that supreme divine Person.
>
> That imperishable (value) which the knowers of the Vedas speak of, which the Self-controlled and passion-free enter, desiring which they lead the life of the disciplined (Vedic) student – that state I shall succinctly describe.
>
> Inhibiting all exits, holding the mind-factors convergent in the heart, vitality-functionings operating centred between the eyebrows, well-established in sustained unitive contemplation,
>
> uttering the one-syllabled word *AUṀ*, which is the Absolute, while constanly remembering Me, he who departs, abandoning the body, treads the highest path.

Is the perennial continuity of the cosmos preferable to the transient world of the psyche?

The bursting of a bubble and the burning out of a star are different only in a quantitative sense. In principle their impermanence is the same. According to Indian cosmogony there are several world-systems and time-structures. Kṛṣṇa alludes to this in verses 16 through 19:

> All worlds, beginning from here to the world of Brahmā, are subject to phenomenal repetition, Arjuna; but on reaching Me, Oh Son of Kuntī! there is not another birth.
>
> Those who know that the day of Brahmā is a thousand unit periods in the cosmic cycle, and the night of a thousand (such) units – they are knowers of the day and night (principle).
>
> From the unmanifested all the manifested proceed at the coming of day; at the coming of night they merge in that same, named the unmanifested.
>
> This very same aggregate of beings, coming into existence again and again, merges, subject to necessity, at the onset of night, Oh Pārtha! and comes into being at the coming of day.

Does the Absolute itself belong to such a world-system and time-structure?

All these relativistic systems referred to in the above verses are only of a different phenomenological content within the negative principle of the Absolute, which is known as manifestation. The unmanifested aspect remains beyond all time–space concepts and the norms of relative understanding. This unmanifested aspect is called the *akṣara*. This chapter is especially dedicated to the unmanifested and imperishable aspect of the Absolute.

Though the Absolute is said to have its major portion unmanifest and only a fragment manifest as the phenomenal world of several cosmological and psychological systems with varying time-structures, it is difficult to think of the Absolute as entirely unaffected by the manifested aspect.

This doubt arises from a very typical error of the mind: that of trying to understand the Absolute itself as an *object*, as well as in quantitative terms. The temporal and spatial understanding of manifest phenomena, being of the negative principle of the Absolute, along with the ratiocinating mind, should be given up in order to arrive at a proper understanding. In other words, the mind itself should cease to function before there is a merging in the total vision of the Absolute. This higher understanding comes only to a very few people, hence the courses of people with higher and lower understanding are both described in verses 24 and 25:

> Fire, light, day-time, the bright fortnight, the six months of the (summer) northern solstice – going forth on that (cosmological) occasion, those people who can understand the Absolute reach the Absolute.
>
> Smoke, night, the dark fortnight, the six months of the (winter) southern solstice – on that (cosmological) occasion, the *yogī*, attaining the lunar (relativist) light, returns.

I do not understand the significance of the reference to light and darkness in the above passage.

Some people are active by temperament, and are prone to be led by their immediate interests, which are usually tainted by sensual or materialistic considerations. Their path is described here as the dark. The bright path is of those who are contemplatives and have turned away from the relativistic world with wholehearted devotion to the Absolute. The theory of reincarnation uses these symbols to describe the return of the relativist again and again to the world of the phenomenal, and the deliverance of wise seers who have become one with the Absolute. The former are like those who are caught in the varying intensity and duration of darkness, such as the smoke, night, etc. going from one experience of dream to another. Dreams can be pleasant or they can be nightmares, but their status is only that of the apparent and recurring. Until one completely wakes up, the dreams continue. In the wakeful state also, there are degrees of clarity. That is why in an earlier chapter it was said that the wise, by many births, finally reach the Absolute.

Which of these paths does Arjuna resort to by accepting his role as a man of action?

Kṛṣṇa does not want Arjuna to have any confused idea that action can lead him to liberation. He should be clear that only contemplative wisdom can do this. Kṛṣṇa says:

> These, the white and the black, are known to be in this world the twin perennial paths; by one of them one attains to non-return, while by the other one comes back.
>
> Understanding (the basic nature of) these two paths! Oh Pārtha! one of contemplation is not confounded at all; therefore, at all times, Oh Arjuna, be unitively established in *yoga*.
>
> Whatever meritorious result is found implied in the Vedas, in sacrifices, austerities, and in gifts, the contemplative who is unitively established, having understood this (teaching), transcends all these and attains to the supreme primal state.

These paths, though everlastingly different, can be brought under a unitive vision by the *yogī*. When thus brought to union, all confusion and perplexity is abolished through the understanding of one's true nature. Though different, they belong to the same principle of light, the dark side being merely less bright. Relativism, while opposed to absolutism in a certain sense, is capable of being absorbed into the Absolute by the ascending dialectical method of *yoga*. Such a *yoga* is here recommended as being worthy of cultivation at all times.

IX

Raja-vidyā–Rāja-guhya-Yoga
Unitive Contemplation as a Royal Science and Crowning Secret

INTRODUCTION

THE title of this chapter is derived from verse 2:

> Royal science, crowning secret, purificatory is this, superior, objectively verifiable, conforming to right living, very easy to live, and subject to no decrease.

Those who are familiar with the rapport that is established between a Guru and disciple know how the disciple goes into total silence and gives his entire attention to the often subtle meaning of every word coming from the Guru. The natural language of a Guru is silence, and the spoken word is a great concession which he shows to the disciple. In the interpersonal rapport of Guru and disciple there come moments of great importance which the disciple intuitively understands, and he responds with full attention. He does not spoil the grandeur and beauty of such occasions by kicking up any dust of scepticism. Thus, in this chapter we see Arjuna giving his silent attention to Kṛṣṇa's teaching. Kṛṣṇa himself is encouraged to give his dear disciple what he considers his most secret and royal teaching.

A Western scholar who reads verse 4 may hastily conclude that the Gītā is teaching pantheism. Western critics have already dubbed Spinoza as a pantheist, which is not fair. Karl Jaspers quotes Spinoza to make this point clear:

> His (God's) essence would have to differ entirely from our intellect and will and could resemble ours in nothing except name. There could be no further likeness than between the celestial constellation of Dog and the animal which barks.

In the case of the Gītā, Kr̥ṣṇa does not leave the student with any doubt as to the fallacy of identifying God with the world. In verse 5 he unequivocally states:

> And further, beings do not exist in Me; behold My status as a divine mystery; further, Myself remaining that urge behind beings, I bear them but do not exist in them either.

The concept of the Absolute is further elucidated in verses 6-11, and the anthropomorphic view of looking upon the Absolute as of human form is condemned in verse 12 as totally irrelevant and foolish. However, the Gītā takes care to assure the lovers of God that the transcendence of the Absolute does not make it a mere metaphysical abstraction. In verses 17 and 18, Kr̥ṣṇa describes Himself as values adorable to Man.

Universal acceptance of the principle of bipolarity, even when it is not of a conformist kind, is recognized as valid. The only condition laid for all paths is the understanding of the Absolute according to first principles.

It is unusual to find in a religious or spiritual book the adoption of an attitude of neutrality between good and evil. In verse 28, as in II.57 and XII.17, we see an allusion to transcending good and evil alike.

The Gītā discredits the idea of people slowly evolving to perfection. In verses 30 and 31, Kr̥ṣṇa says that even if a person who has indulged in very evil action properly determines to dedicate himself to the Absolute with exclusive devotion, he will become instantly established in his own right nature and will enter into eternal peace.

The central teaching of the Gītā is *ekāntika bhakti*, devotion to the Absolute to the exclusion of everything else. It is given in the concluding verse of this chapter. The same teaching is repeated with a slight modification in Chapter XVIII, verse 65.

TRANSLATION

श्रीभगवानुवाच –

1. इदं तु ते गुह्यतमं प्रवक्ष्याम्यनसूयवे ।
ज्ञानं विज्ञानसहितं यज्ज्ञात्वा मोक्ष्यसेऽशुभात् ॥

śrībhagavān uvāca –

idaṁ tu te guhyatamaṁ pravakṣyāmy anasūyave ।
jñānaṁ vijñānasahitaṁ yaj jñātvā mokṣyase 'śubhāt ॥

śrībhagavān uvāca: Kr̥ṣṇa said; *te tu*: to you indeed; *anasūyave*: who do not mistrust; *pravakṣyāmi*: (I) shall declare; *idaṁ guhyatamaṁ*: this profound secret; *jñānaṁ*: wisdom; *sahitaṁ vijñāna*: together with its applied aspects; *jñātvā yat*: knowing which; *mokṣyase*: you shall be freed; *aśubhāt*: from (what savours of) evil.

Kṛṣṇa said:

To you indeed who do not mistrust I shall declare this profound secret of wisdom together with its applied aspects, by knowing which you shall be freed from what savours of evil.

2. राजविद्या राजगुह्यं पवित्रमिदमुत्तमम् ।
प्रत्यक्षावगमं धर्म्यं सुसुखं कर्तुमव्ययम् ।।

rājavidyā rājaguhyaṁ pavitram idam uttamam ।
pratyakṣāvagamaṁ dharmyaṁ susukhaṁ kartum avyayam ॥

rājavidyā: royal science; *rājaguhyaṁ*: crowning secret; *pavitram idam*: purificatory (is) this; *uttamam*: superior; *pratyakṣa avagamaṁ*: objectively verifiable; *dharmyaṁ*: conforming to right living; *susukhaṁ kartum*: very easy to live; *avyayam*: (and) subject to no decrease.

Royal science, crowning secret, purificatory is this, superior, objectively verifiable, conforming to right living, very easy to live, and subject to no decrease.

3. अश्रद्दधानाः पुरुषा धर्मस्यास्य परन्तप ।
अप्राप्य मां निवर्तन्ते मृत्युसंसारवर्त्मनि ।।

aśraddadhānāḥ puruṣā dharmasyā 'sya paraṁtapa ।
aprāpya māṁ nivartante mṛtyusaṁsāravartmani ॥

puruṣāḥ: men; *aśraddadhānāḥ*: without (wholehearted) faith-affiliation; *asya dharmasya*: to this way of right living; *paraṁtapa*: Oh Arjuna; *aprāpya mām*: not attaining to Me; *nivartante*: return; *vartmani mṛtyu saṁsāra*: in the path of mortality and cyclic repetition of existence.

Men without wholehearted faith-affiliation to this way of right living, Oh Burner of Foes! not attaining to Me, return to the paths of mortality and cyclic repetition of existence.

4. मया ततमिदं सर्वं जगदव्यक्तमूर्तिना ।
मत्स्थानि सर्वभूतानि न चाहं तेष्ववस्थितः ।।

mayā tatam idaṁ sarvaṁ jagad avyaktamūrtinā ।
matsthāni sarvabhūtāni na cā 'haṁ teṣv avasthitaḥ ॥

mayā: by me; *sarvaṁ idaṁ jagat*: all this world; *tatam*: is prevaded; *avyakta mūrtinā*: My form unmanifested; *sarva bhūtāni*: all beings; *mat sthāni*: have existence in Me; *ca aham*: and I; *na avasthitaḥ*: do not have existence; *teṣu*: in them.

By Me all this world is pervaded, My form unmanifested; all beings have existence in Me and I do not have existence in them.

5. न च मत्स्थानि भूतानि पश्य मे योगमैश्वरम् ।
भूतभृन्न च भूतस्थो ममात्मा भूतभावनः ।।

na ca matsthāni bhūtāni paśya me yogam aiśvaram ।
bhūtabhṛn na ca bhūtastho mamā 'tmā bhūtabhāvanaḥ ॥

ca: and (further); *bhūtāni na matsthāni*: beings do not exist in Me; *paśya*: behold; *me aiśvaram yogam*: My divine *yoga*; *ca*: further; *mama ātmā*: Myself; *bhūta bhāvanaḥ*: causing beings to exist; *bhūtabhṛt*: bearing beings; *na bhūtasthaḥ*: but not existing in beings.

And further, beings do not exist in Me; behold My status as a divine mystery; further, Myself remaining that urge behind beings, I bear them but do not exist in them either.

6. यथाकाशस्थितो नित्यं वायुः सर्वत्रगो महान् ।
तथा सर्वाणि भूतानि मत्स्थानीत्युपधारय ।।

yathā 'kāśasthito nityaṁ vāyuḥ sarvatrago mahān ।
tathā sarvāṇi bhūtāni matsthānī 'ty upadhāraya ॥

Yathā: as; *mahān*: the great (expanse of); *vāyuḥ*: air; *nityaṁ akāśasthitaḥ*: ever abides in space; *sarvatragaḥ*: going everywhere; *tathā upadhāraya*: thus, understand; *sarvāṇi bhūtāni*: all existences; *iti matsthāni*: as (having their) basis in Me.

As the great (expanse of) air filling all space has its basis in pure extension, thus you should understand all existences as having their basis in Me.

7. सर्वभूतानि कौन्तेय प्रकृतिं यान्ति मामिकाम् ।
कल्पक्षये पुनस्तानि कल्पादौ विसृजाम्यहम् ।।

sarvabhūtāni kaunteya prakṛtiṁ yānti māmikām ।
kalpakṣaye punas tāni kalpādau visṛjāmy aham ॥

sarva bhūtāni: all beings; *kaunteya*: Oh Arjuna; *yānti māmikām prakṛtiṁ*: go into My nature; *kalpakṣaye*: at the end of a unit of cosmic duration (a *kalpa* is equivalent to 1,000 *yuga*s, or 4,320,000,000 years); *punaḥ*: and; *kalpādau*: at the beginning of the same unit; *aham visṛjāmi tāni*: I emanate them.

8. प्रकृतिं स्वामवष्टभ्य विसृजामि पुनः पुनः ।
भूतग्राममिमं कृत्स्नमवशं प्रकृतेर्वशात् ।।

prakṛtiṁ svām avaṣṭabhya visṛjāmi punaḥ-punaḥ ।
bhūtagrāmam imaṁ kṛtsnam avaśaṁ prakṛter vaśāt ॥

avaṣṭabhya svām prakṛtiṁ: supported by (My) own nature; *visṛjāmi*: (I) emanate; *punaḥ punaḥ*: again and again; *imaṁ kṛtsnaṁ bhūta grāmam*: this whole aggregate of beings; *avaśaṁ*: powerless (as they are); *vaśāt*: by the (necessary) compulsion; *prakṛteḥ*: of nature.

All beings, Oh Son of Kuntī! pass into My nature at the end of a unit of cosmic duration, and at the beginning of the same unit I emanate them. By virtue of My nature, I emanate again and again the whole aggregate of beings, subject as they are to the necessary compulsion of nature.

9. न च मां तानि कर्माणि निबध्नन्ति धनञ्जय ।
उदासीनवदासीनमसक्तं तेषु कर्मसु ।।

na ca māṁ tāni karmāṇi nibadhnanti dhanañjaya ।
udāsīnavad āsīnam asaktaṁ teṣu karmasu ॥

ca tāni karmāṇi: and these works; *na nibadhnanti māṁ*: do not bind Me; *dhanañjaya*: Oh Arjuna; *āsīnam*: (for I am) seated; *udāsīnavat*: seemingly indifferent; *asaktaṁ*: unattached; *teṣu karmasu*: in these actions.

10. मयाध्यक्षेण प्रकृतिः सूयते सचराचरम् ।
हेतुनानेन कौन्तेय जगद्विपरिवर्तते ।।

mayā 'dhyakṣeṇa prakṛtiḥ sūyate sacarācaram ।
hetunā 'nena kaunteya jagad viparivartate ॥

mayā adhyakṣena: with Me presiding; *prakṛtiḥ sūyate*: nature gives birth; *sa cara acaram*: to both the movable and the immovable (entities); *hetunā anena*: because of this; *kaunteya*: Oh Arjuna; *jagat*: (this moving) world; *viparivartate*: revolves.

Further, these works do not bind Me, Oh Winner of Wealth! for I am seated, seemingly indifferent, unattached to those actions.

With Me presiding, nature gives birth to both the movable and the immovable entities; because of this, Oh Son of Kuntī! this (moving) world revolves.

11. अवजानन्ति मां मूढा मानुषीं तनुमाश्रितम् ।
परं भावमजानन्तो मम भूतमहेश्वरम् ।।

avajānanti māṁ mūḍhā mānuṣīṁ tanum āśritam ।
paraṁ bhāvam ajānanto mama bhūtamaheśvaram ॥

mūḍhāḥ: the foolish; *avajānanti māṁ*: misunderstand Me; *āśritam*: (because of My) adopting; *mānuṣīṁ tanum*: the human form; *ajānantaḥ*: ignorant (as they are) of; *mama bhāvam*: My being; *paraṁ*: (that is) beyond; *maheśvaram bhūta*: (as) the great Lord of (all) beings.

12. मोघाशा मोघकर्माणो मोघज्ञाना विचेतसः ।
राक्षसीमासुरीं चैव प्रकृतिं मोहिनीं श्रिताः ।।

moghāśā moghakarmāṇo moghajñānā vicetasaḥ ।
rākṣasīm āsuriṁ cai 'va prakṛtiṁ mohinīṁ śritāḥ ॥

moghāśāḥ: of frustrated hope; *mogha karmāṇaḥ*: of frustrated deeds; *moghajñānā*: empty of wisdom; *vicetasaḥ*: non-discriminating; *rākṣasīm*: like malignant titans; *ca eva āsurīṁ*: and indeed like demons; *śritāḥ*: submitting to; *prakṛtiṁ mohinīṁ*: a nature (of) confounding (values).

The foolish misunderstand Me because of My adopting the human form, ignorant as they are of My being that is beyond, as the Lord of all beings,

of frustrated hope, of frustrated deeds, empty of wisdom, non-discriminating, like malignant titans and demons, submitting themselves to a nature (of) confounding (values).

13. महात्मानस्तु मां पार्थ दैवीं प्रकृतिमाश्रिताः ।
भजन्त्यनन्यमनसो ज्ञात्वा भूतादिमव्ययम् ।।

matātmānas tu māṁ pārtha daivīṁ prakṛtim āśritāḥ ।
bhajanty ananyamanaso jñātvā bhūtādim avyayam ॥

tu mahātmānaḥ: but those of Great Self; *parthu*: Oh Arjuna; *āśritāḥ*: affiliated to; *māṁ daivīṁ prakṛtim*: My divine nature; *bhajanti*: adore (Me); *ananya manasaḥ*: with mind exclusive of (all) otherness; *jñātvā*: having known (Me); *avyayam*: (as) the unexpended; *bhūtādim*: primal Source of (all) beings.

But those of Great Self, Oh Pārtha! affiliated to My divine nature, adore Me with mind exclusive of all extraneous interests, having known Me as the unexpended primal Source of all beings.

14. सततं कीर्तयन्तो मां यतन्तश्च दृढव्रताः ।
नमस्यन्तश्च मां भक्त्या नित्ययुक्ता उपासते ।।

satataṁ kīrtayanto māṁ yatantaś ca dṛdhavratāḥ ।
namasyantaś ca māṁ bhaktyā nityayuktā upāsate ॥

satataṁ: always; *kīrtayantaḥ māṁ*: singing praises of Me; *yatantaḥ*: (ever) striving; *dṛdha vratāḥ*: firm in vows; *ca namasyantaḥ māṁ*: and saluting Me; *bhaktyā*: devotedly; *nitya yuktāḥ*: ever-united; *upāsate*: they are in worshipful attendance.

15. ज्ञानयज्ञेन चाप्यन्ये यजन्तो मामुपासते ।
एकत्वेन पृथक्त्वेन बहुधा विश्वतोमुखम् ।।

jñānayajñena cā 'py anye yajanto mām upāsate ।
ekatvena pṛthaktvena bahudhā viśvatomukham ॥

ca anye api: and others also; *yajantaḥ*: sacrificing; *jñāna yajñena*: with the wisdom-sacrifice; *ekatvena*: unitively; *pṛthaktvena*: dualistically; *bahudhā*: (as also) in many ways; *viśvato mukham*: facing universally everywhere; *upāsate mām*: worshipfully attend (on) Me.

Always singing praises of Me, ever striving, firm in vows, and saluting Me devotedly, they are ever-united in worshipful attendance;

Others also, sacrificing with the wisdom-sacrifice, unitively, dualistically, as also in many ways facing universally everywhere, worshipfully attend on Me.

16. अहं क्रतुरहं यज्ञः स्वधाहमहमौषधम् ।
मन्त्रोऽहमहमेवाज्यमहमग्निरहं हुतम् ।।

ahaṁ kratur ahaṁ yajñaḥ svadhā 'ham aham auṣadham ।
mantro 'ham aham evā 'jyam aham agnir ahaṁ hutam ॥

ahaṁ kratuḥ: I the ritual action; *ahaṁ yajñaḥ*: I the sacrifice; *aham svadhā*: I the ancestral oblation; *aham auṣadham*: I the potent medicinal herb; *aham mantraḥ*: I the holy formula; *aham eva ājyam*: I also the melted butter; *aham agniḥ*: I the fire; *ahaṁ hutaṁ*: I the offering.

I the ritual action, I the sacrifice, I the ancestral oblation, I the potent medicinal herb, I the holy formula, I also the melted butter, I the fire, I the offering.

17. पिताहमस्य जगतो माता धाता पितामहः ।
वेद्यं पवित्रमोङ्कार ऋक्साम यजुरेव च ।।

pitā 'ham asya jagato mātā dhātā pitāmahaḥ ।
vedyaṁ pavitram auṁkāra ṛk sāma yajur eva ca ॥

aham pitā: I the Father; *asya jagataḥ*: of this world; *mātā dhātā*: the Mother, Supporter; *pitāmahaḥ*: (and) the Grandsire (ancestor); *vedyaṁ*: (the Holy One) who is to be known; *pavitram*: the Purifier; *auṁkāra*: the syllable *AUṀ*; *eva ṛk*: (as) also the (Vedas called) *Ṛk*; *sāma ca yajuḥ*: *Sāma* and *Yajus*.

I the Father of this world, the Mother, the Supporter, and the Grandsire, the Holy One who is to be known, the Purifier, the syllable *AUṀ*, as also the Vedas called *Ṛk*, *Sāma* and *Yajus*,

18. गतिर्भर्ता प्रभुः साक्षी निवासः शरणं सुहृत् ।
प्रभवः प्रलयः स्थानं निधानं बीजमव्ययम् ।।

gatir bhartā prabhuḥ sākṣī nivāsaḥ śaraṇaṁ suhṛt ।
prabhavaḥ pralayaḥ sthānaṁ nidhānaṁ bījam avyayam ॥

gatiḥ: (I am) the Goal; *bhartā prabhuḥ*: the Supporter, the Lord; *sākṣī nivāsaḥ*: the Witness, the Abode; *śaraṇaṁ suhṛt*: the Refuge, the Friend; *prabhavaḥ pralayaḥ*: the Becoming, the Dissolution; *sthānaṁ nidhānaṁ*: the Ground of Being, ontological Basis; *avyayam bījam*: (and) never-expended Seed.

(I am) the Goal, the Supporter, the Lord, the Witness, the Abode, the Refuge, the Friend, the Becoming, the Dissolution, and Ground of Being, ontological Basis, and never-expended Seed.

19. तपाम्यहमहं वर्षं निगृह्णाम्युत्सृजामि च ।
अमृतं चैव मृत्युश्च सदसच्चाहमर्जुन ।।

tapāmy aham ahaṁ varṣaṁ nigṛhṇāmy utsṛjāmi ca ।
amṛtaṁ cai 'va mṛtyuś cā sad asac cā 'ham arjuna ॥

aham tapāmi: I radiate heat; *ahaṁ varṣaṁ*: (and) I rain; *nigṛhṇāmi*: (I) withhold; *ca utsṛjāmi*: and (I) send forth; *aham amṛtaṁ*: I (am) immortality; *ca mṛtyuḥ*: and death; *ca eva*: as also; *sat ca asat*: being and non-being; *arjuna*: Oh Arjuna.

I radiate heat and I rain, I withhold and I send forth, I am immortality and death, as also being and non-being, Oh Arjuna!

20. त्रैविद्या मां सोमपाः पूतपापा यज्ञैरिष्ट्वा स्वर्गतिं प्रार्थयन्ते ।
ते पुण्यमासाद्य सुरेन्द्रलोकमश्नन्ति दिव्यान्दिवि देवभोगान् ।।

traividyā māṁ somapāḥ pūtapāpā yajñair iṣṭvā svargatiṁ prārthayante ।
te puṇyam āsādya surendralokam aśnanti divyān divi devabhogān ॥

trai vidyāḥ: knowers of the three (Vedas); *somapāḥ*: *soma* drinkers; *pūta pāpāḥ*: purified from sin; *iṣṭvā yajñaiḥ*: worshipping by sacrifices; *prārthayante māṁ*: pray of Me; *svargatim*: the way to heaven; *te āsādya*: they attaining; *puṇyam lokam surendra*: the holy world of Indra (Lord of gods); *aśnanti divyān*: enjoy divine; *deva bhogān*: pleasures of the gods; *divi*: in heaven.

21. ते तं भुक्त्वा स्वर्गलोकं विशालं क्षीणे पुण्ये मर्त्यलोकं विशन्ति ।
एवं त्रयीधर्ममनुप्रपन्ना गतागतं कामकामा लभन्ते ।।

te taṁ bhuktvā svargalokaṁ viśalaṁ kṣīṇe puṇye martyalokaṁ viśanti ।
evaṁ trayīdharmam anuprapanṇā gatāgataṁ kāmakāmā labhante ॥

te bhuktvā: they having enjoyed; *taṁ vaśālaṁ*: that expansive; *svarga lokaṁ*: heaven-world; *puṇye kṣīṇe*: (their) merit exhausted; *viśanti*: (they) enter; *martya lokaṁ*: the world of mortality; *evaṁ anuprapannāḥ*:

thus conforming to; *trayī dharmam*: the righteous (notions implied) in the three (Vedas); *kāma kāmāḥ*: desiring desirable objects; *labhante*: (they) obtain; *gata āgataṁ*: (that which) comes and goes.

Knowers of the three Vedas, *soma* drinkers, purified from sin, worshipping by sacrifices, pray of Me the way to heaven; they, attaining the holy world of Indra, enjoy divine feasts in heaven.

They, having enjoyed that expansive heaven-world, their merit exhausted, enter the world of mortality, thus conforming to the righteous notions implied in the three Vedas, desiring desirable objects they obtain values which come and go.

22. अनन्याश्चिन्तयन्तो मां ये जनाः पर्युपासते ।
तेषां नित्याभियुक्तानां योगक्षेमं वहाम्यहम् ।।

ananyāś cintayanto māṁ ye janāḥ paryupāsate ।
teṣāṁ nityābhiyuktānāṁ yogakṣemaṁ vahāmy aham ॥

teṣāṁ janāḥ ye: to those persons who; *cintayantaḥ māṁ*: meditating on Me; *ananyāḥ*: to the exclusion of all else; *paryupāsate*: worship (Me); *nitya abhiyuktānāṁ*: ever established unitively; *aham vahāmi*: I bring; *yogakṣemaṁ*: the solace of the unitive way of *yoga.*

To those persons who, meditating on Me to the exclusion of all else, worship Me, ever established unitively, I bring that solace of the unitive way of *yoga*.

23. येऽप्यन्यदेवता भक्ता यजन्ते श्रद्धयान्विताः ।
तेऽपि मामेव कौन्तेय यजन्त्यविधिपूर्वकम् ।।

ye 'py anyadevatābhaktā yajante śraddhayā 'nvitāḥ ।
te 'pi mām eva kaunteya yajanty avidhipūrvakam ॥

api ye: even (those) who; *bhaktāḥ*: devoted to; *anya devatāḥ*: other gods; *yajante*: worship (them); *śraddhayā anvitāḥ*: with faith; *te api*: they also; *yajanti mām eva*: worship Me alone; *kaunteya*: Oh Arjuna; *avidhi pūrvakam*: (though) not conforming to (orthodox) rules.

Even those who, devoted to other gods, worship them with faith, they in fact worship Myself, Oh Son of Kuntī! though not conforming to orthodox rules.

24. अहं हि सर्वयज्ञानां भोक्ता च प्रभुरेव च ।
न तु मामभिजानन्ति तत्त्वेनातश्च्यवन्ति ते ।।

ahaṁ hi sarvayajñānāṁ bhoktā ca prabhur eva ca ।
na tu mām abhijānanti tattvenā 'taś cyavanti te ॥

ahaṁ hi: I (am) indeed; *bhoktā ca*: the Enjoyer and; *ca eva*: also indeed; *prabhuḥ sarva yajñānāṁ*: the Lord of all sacrifices; *tu te cyavanti ataḥ*:

but they fall indeed; *na abhijānanti mām*: who do not understand Me; *tattvena*: according to first principles.

I am indeed the Enjoyer, as also the Lord of all sacrifices; but they fall indeed who do not understand Me according to first principles.

25. यान्ति देवव्रता देवान्पितृन्यान्ति पितृव्रताः ।
भूतानि यान्ति भूतेज्या यान्ति मद्याजिनोऽपि माम् ।।

yānti devavratā devān pitṝn yānti pitṛvratāḥ ।
bhūtāni yānti bhūtejyā yānti madyājino 'pi mām ॥

deva vratāḥ: votaries of the divinities; *yānti devān*: go to the divinities; *pitṛ vratāḥ yānti pitṛn*: votaries of the ancestors go to the ancestors; *bhūtejyāḥ*: sacrificers to elemental existences; *yānti bhutāni*: go to elemental existences; *api*: so (too); *madyājinaḥ*: My worshippers; *yānti mām*: attain to Me.

Votaries of the divinities go to the divinities, votaries of the ancestors go to the ancestors, sacrificers to elemental existences go to elemental existences, and so too My worshippers attain to Me.

26. पत्रं पुष्पं फलं तोयं यो मे भक्त्या प्रयच्छति ।
तदहं भक्त्युपहृतमश्नामि प्रयतात्मनः ।।

pattraṁ puṣpaṁ phalaṁ toyaṁ yo me bhaktyā prayacchati ।
tad ahaṁ bhaktyupahṛtam aśnāmi prayatātmanaḥ ॥

yaḥ prayacchati me: (he) who offers to Me; *bhaktyā*: with devotion; *pattraṁ puṣpam*: a leaf, a flower; *phalaṁ toyaṁ*: a fruit, (or) water; *tat ahaṁ aśnāmi*: that (do) I accept; *upahṛtam bhakti*: (as being) offered with devotion; *prayata ātmanaḥ*: by one who makes the (right) effort.

He who offers to Me with devotion a leaf, a flower, a fruit, or water, that do I accept as being offered with devotion by one who makes the right effort.

27. यत्करोषि यदश्नासि यज्जुहोषि ददासि यत् ।
यत्तपस्यसि कौन्तेय तत्कुरुष्व मदर्पणम् ।।

yat karoṣi yad aśnāsi yaj juhoṣi dadāsi yat ।
yat tapasyasi kaunteya tat kuruṣva madarpaṇam ॥

yat karoṣi: what you do; *yat aśnāsi*: what you eat; *yat juhoṣi*: what you offer; *yat dadāsi*: what you give; *yat tapasyasi*: what austerity you practise; *kaunteya*: Oh Arjuna; *kuruṣva tat*: do that; *mad arpaṇam*: as an offering to Me

What you do, what you eat, what you offer, what you give, what austerity you practise, Oh Son of Kuntī! – let that be done as an offering to Me.

28. शुभाशुभफलैरेवं मोक्ष्यसे कर्मबन्धनैः ।
संन्यासयोगयुक्तात्मा विमुक्तो मामुपैष्यसि ।।

śubhāśubhaphalair evaṁ mokṣyase karmabandhanaiḥ ।
saṁnyāsayogayuktātmā vimukto mām upaiṣyasi ॥

evaṁ mokṣyase: thus (you) will be liberated; *karma bandhanaiḥ*: from the bonds of action; *śubha aśubha phalaiḥ*: from good or evil results; *saṁnyāsa yoga yuktātmā*: with Self affiliated to unitive Self-denial; *vimuktaḥ*: (as one thus) emancipated; *upaiṣyasi māṁ*: you will attain to me.

Thus you will be liberated from the bonds of action, whether its results are good or evil. With Self affiliated to unitive Self-denial, as one thus emancipated you will attain to Me.

29. समोऽहं सर्वभूतेषु न मे द्वेष्योऽस्ति न प्रियः ।
ये भजन्ति तु मां भक्त्या मयि ते तेषु चाप्यहम् ।।

samo 'haṁ sarvabhūteṣu na me dveṣyo 'sti na priyaḥ ।
ye bhajanti tu māṁ bhaktyā mayi te teṣu cā 'py aham ॥

ahaṁ: I (regard); *sarva bhūteṣu*: all beings; *samaḥ*: equally; *me asti na dveṣyaḥ na priyaḥ*: to me there is none hateful nor dear; *tu*: however; *ye bhajanti māṁ*: (they) who worship Me; *bhaktyā*: with devotion; *te mayi*: they (are) in Me; *ca aham api teṣu*: and I too (am) in them.

I regard all beings equally. To Me there is none hateful or dear. They, however, who worship with devotion – they are in Me and I too am in them.

30. अपि चेत्सुदुराचारो भजते मामनन्यभाक् ।
साधुरेव स मन्तव्यः सम्यग्व्यवसितो हि सः ।।

api cet sudurācāro bhajate mām ananyabhāk ।
sādhur eva sa mantavyaḥ samyag vyavasito hi saḥ ॥

api cet: even if; *sudurācāraḥ*: one of very evil actions; *bhajate mām*: worships Me; *ananyabhāk*: with a devotion exclusive of all else; *saḥ mantavyaḥ*: he should be accounted; *sādhuḥ hi*: (to be) good indeed; *eva*: merely (by the fact that); *saḥ*: he (has); *samyak vyavasitaḥ*: a properly settled determination.

Even if one of very evil actions should worship Me with a devotion exclusive of all else; he should be accounted to be good all the same, merely by the fact that he has a properly settled determination.

31. क्षिप्रं भवति धर्मात्मा शश्वच्छान्तिं निगच्छति ।
कौन्तेय प्रति जानीहि न मे भक्तः प्रणश्यति ।।

kṣipraṁ bhavati dharmātmā śaśvacchāntiṁ nigacchati ।
kaunteya pratijānīhi na me bhaktaḥ praṇaśyati ॥

kṣipraṁ: instantaneously; *bhavati*: he becomes (established); *dharmātmā*: in his own right nature; *nigacchati*: (and) enters into; *śaśvat śāntiṁ*: eternal peace; *pratijānīhi*: believe (Me in all confidence); *kaunteya*: Oh Arjuna; *bhaktaḥ me*: (that) one affiliated to Me with fidelity; *na praṇaśyati*: (knows) no destruction.

Instantaneously he becomes established in his own right nature and enters into eternal peace. Believe Me in all confidence, Oh Son of Kuntī! that one affiliated to Me with fidelity knows no destruction.

32. मां हि पार्थ व्यपाश्रित्य येऽपि स्युः पापयोनयः ।
स्त्रियो वैश्यास्तथा शूद्रास्तेऽपि यान्ति परां गतिम् ॥

māṁ hi pārtha vyapāśritya ye 'pi syuḥ pāpayonayaḥ ।
striyo vaiśyās tathā śūdrās te 'pi yānti parāṁ gatim ॥

māṁ hi vyapāśritya: (they too) who resort to Me indeed for refuge; *pārtha*: Oh Arjuna; *ye api*: whoever; *syuḥ*: they might be; *striyaḥ*: (whether) women; *śūdrāḥ*: workers (śūdras); *tathā*: as well as; *vaiśyaḥ*: farmer-merchants (vaiśyas); *pāpayonayaḥ*: (all) of sinful origin; *te api yānti*: they too attain to; *parāṁ gatim*: the supreme goal.

They too who resort to Me for refuge, Oh Pārtha! whoever they might be, (whether) women, workers, as well as farmer-merchants, (all) of sinful origin – they too attain to the supreme goal.

33. किं पुनर्ब्राह्मणाः पुण्या भक्ता राजर्षयस्तथा ।
अनित्यमसुखं लोकमिमं प्राप्य भजस्व माम् ॥

kiṁ punar brāhmaṇāḥ puṇyā bhaktā rājarṣayas tathā ।
anityam asukhaṁ lokam imaṁ prāpya bhajasva mām ॥

kiṁ punaḥ: how (much) more; *puṇyāḥ brāhmaṇāḥ*: (then) the pure brāhmaṇas; *tathā*: as also; *bhaktāḥ rājarṣayaḥ*: the devoted royal sages; *prāpya*: having reached; *imaṁ anityam*: this transient; *asukhaṁ lokam*: joyless world; *bhajasva mām*: (do you) worship Me.

How much more then the pure brāhmaṇas, as also the devoted royal sages! Having reached this transient joyless world do you worship Me.

34. मन्मना भव मद्भक्तो मद्याजी मां नमस्कुरु ।
मामेवैष्यसि युक्त्वैवमात्मानं मत्परायणः ॥

manmanā bhava madbhakto madyājī māṁ namaskuru ।
mām evai 'ṣyasi yuktvai 'yam ātmānaṁ matparāyaṇaḥ ॥

bhava manmanāḥ: become one with Me; *mat bhaktāḥ*: (be) devoted to Me; *madyājī*: sacrifice to Me; *namaskuru māṁ*: bow down to Me; *yuktvā evam ātmānaṁ*: unifying thus yourself; *eva eṣyasi*: you shall surely come; *mām*: to Me; *matparāyaṇaḥ*: your supreme Goal (none other than) Me.

Become one with Me; be devoted to Me; sacrifice to Me; bow down to Me; unifying thus yourself, you shall surely come to Me; your supreme Goal none other than Me.

DIALOGUE

TEACHER: In Chapter VII, entitled "The Unitive Contemplation of Wisdom-Synthesis", we have seen Arjuna observing silence. In the present chapter we see him resorting to a similar silence, leaving the entire initiative to Kṛṣṇa. Later, in Chapter XV, described as "The Unitive Approach to the Paramount Person" we will see him once more absorbed in his attentive silence, listening to Kṛṣṇa.

STUDENT: *After having conceived the Gītā to be a dialogue between Kṛṣṇa and Arjuna, why does the author resort to the literary device of a monologue here?*

In this and the other two chapters (VII and XV) the wisdom-synthesis reaches its height; both the exoteric and esoteric aspects, as well as pure and practical knowledge are taken together. In this finalized wisdom all shades of duality are abolished. The rapport between the teacher and the disciple becomes more complete and the mutual adoption implied in the situation becomes more patent. There is no complaint on the Guru's part of carping by the disciple, nor any complaint of the Guru confusing his mind on the part of the disciple. The Absolute represented by Kṛṣṇa is made to declare unequivocally that he is neither interested in the good or the bad people, but is indifferent to both alike. This aloofness and neutrality denotes the highest level of purity that can be attained in the teaching of the Gītā. Even the importance of his own personality tends to be minimized. The mythological or legendary aspects of Viṣṇu or Kṛṣṇa are effaced and merged into a comprehensive and pure notion of the Absolute. Further, the mystery and wonder of the Absolute is enhanced by cancelling out all mutual interdependence between the phenomenal and the noumenal. All theological scaffolding is removed, so that the notion of the Absolute emerges in all its purity and glory. The hope that the Gītā holds out is given to all without distinction, including those who may be termed as the worst sinners.

This chapter concludes with what we might call the central doctrine of the Gītā, if such a thing could be singled out at all. All forms of bipolar adoption that promote the final unity, whether of understanding or worship, surrender or *yoga*, are all brought together in the final verse, with which the first half of the Gītā closes its dialogue.

Kṛṣṇa begins with an open admission of Arjuna's perfect adoption:

> To you indeed who do not mistrust I shall declare this profound secret of wisdom together with its applied aspects, by knowing which you shall be freed from what savours of evil.

When the relation between a disciple and teacher implies the dichotomy of anterior scepticism and posterior certitude, why does Kṛṣṇa ask for implicit and absolute trust on the part of his disciple? Is it not right for Arjuna to doubt and question?

The power to listen is as important as the ability to teach, especially where such profound secrets are involved. The relation has to be strictly bipolar. Mistrust and rivalry between the two have to be implicitly eliminated. The reference here to the absence of a disadoption is therefore a necessary prerequisite before the proper teaching can begin.

What is the great secret which Kṛṣṇa wants to teach?

Kṛṣṇa says:

> Royal science, crowning secret, purificatory is this, superior, objectively verifiable, conforming to right living, very easy to live, and subject to no decrease.
>
> Men without wholehearted faith-affiliation to this way of right living, Oh Burner of Foes! not attaining to Me, return to the paths of mortality and cyclic repetition of existence.

The teaching becomes royal in the sense that it involves and affects the whole domain of one's life interest, and that it is open to all. It is called a crowning secret in the sense that it is most unique. It is called pure because it clears away the dross of evil, whether in the form of sin, action, or ignorance. It is objectively verifiable in the sense that its methods and results come within the purview of what could be observed in objective terms.

What is the way of right living referred to here?

Although the Gītā permits all forms of worship, including the most childish (such as offering fruit and flowers to God), it attaches no value to a discipline or form of worship which is lukewarm or half-hearted. The recognition of the Absolute should be implied in the attitude of one's affiliation and devotion. With the following remarks Kṛṣṇa begins the unravelling of the mystery of the Absolute:

By Me all this world is pervaded, My form unmanifested; all beings have existence in Me and I do not have existence in them.

And further, beings do not exist in Me; behold my status as a divine mystery; further, Myself remaining that urge behind beings, I bear them but do not exist in them either.

As the great (expanse of) air filling all space has its basis in pure extension, thus you should understand all existences as having their basis in Me.

All beings, Oh Son of Kuntī! pass into My nature at the end of a unit of cosmic duration (*kalpa*), and at the beginning of the same unit I emanate them.

By virtue of My nature, I emanate again and again the whole aggregate of beings, subject as they are to the necessary compulsion of nature.

These verses seem to be bristling with contradictions. If the Absolute has no existence in the relative, from where does the relative get its substratum to exist?

When Kr̥ṣṇa admits that he remains as the urge behind beings, how could he say that he does not exist in them?

It is true that this description implies a paradoxical wonder. Beings exist in the Absolute, but the converse is not true, and is here denied. Exactly what then the relation is between the Absolute and existence remains a wonder and a mystery. This mystery is further heightened by saying that manifested beings do not have existence in the Absolute either, although the relationship of ruler and ruled might yet be postulated between them. It is stated in the verse itself that this is His divine mystery. The wonder remains, unsolved by any logic. When the meaning is subjected to final scrutiny, it amounts to saying that Kr̥ṣṇa, as representing the Absolute, has no individual ego. The personal pronoun "I" is used only for the purpose of conforming to literary requirements.

It is not comfortable to stand bewildered holding on to an unresolved mystery. Could you throw more light on this?

The Absolute comes to be viewed as capable of having two aspects, one in which it is pure and another in which it is viewed as if conditioned or coloured by factors that come under nature. The relation between this nature and the pure Absolute itself is similar to the one between *māyā*, relativist appearance due to the principle of error, and *Brahman* (Absolute Reality). Nature is hidden in the Absolute at certain times, at other times it is evident. In other words, nature is virtually present in the Absolute at a cosmological moment, and cyclically it becomes actualized.

Nature may be said to be an instrument of the pure Absolute principle. Instead of creating the various aggregates of beings which we see in the universe, this nature principle has a status approximating to the Absolute itself, and to which all agency in the act of particularized creation is attributable. The unconditioned Absolute is to be left out of the picture; the relation between this nature instrument and its operator is only something like that of a controlling magnet in certain electrical instruments. By its mere presence, somewhat like a catalytic agent, the Absolute helps nature, as it were, from a distance, to fulfil its work with all the compulsive force of necessity belonging to it. While nature is fatalistic, the Absolute belongs to the side of providence, which is a witnessing presence with its own subtle influence, ever counteracting the fatality implied in nature. The subtle relationship here is as between sin and grace in Christian theology, or as between inexorable law and indeterminism in modern scientific theory.

When the Absolute is so mysterious, how can we justify the rites and rituals offered before idols? How could a person like Kṛṣṇa or Christ be deified as the Supreme, and all power and knowledge be relegated to them?

Kṛṣṇa does not condone this error, universally displayed by those of dull intelligence. He says:

> The foolish misunderstand Me because of My adopting the human form, ignorant as they are of My being that is beyond, as the Lord of all beings, of frustrated hope, of frustrated deeds, empty of wisdom, non-discriminating, like malignant titans and demons, submitting themselves to a nature (of) confounding (values).

From this outright condemnation of idolatry, personality cult, and relativistic creed, there hardly escapes any of the known religions and their popular forms of worship. Does this amount to heterodoxy?

Modern Hinduism, after the decadence of the philosophical schools of thought, has arrived at many forms of religious practice, some being but puerile forms of popular adoration, on a par perhaps with the kissing of the brass or plaster image of Jesus in Milan and elsewhere, violating even sanitary principles. The Gītā being a Yogaśāstra (textbook on unitive understanding) dealing with the Science of the Absolute, continues the rational philosophical tradition of India without giving any room for heterodoxy. Since this is its essential nature, it is but natural to expect that puerile or lazy forms of worship would not be upheld. The strong note here thus becomes levelled against people who would misunderstand the true nature of the Absolute. The protest is against giving importance to a particular object, as against its universal import as a principle. All static or fixed notions of the Absolute should be considered out of place in the strict light of Vedānta. A static view, even when it is glorified by myth and symbol, only becomes worse than the common sense reality of the Absolute when considered as a good, great, or lovable man in the ordinary sense. The misunderstanding referred to here covers all anthropomorphic forms and notions possible, from the most simple to the most elaborate.

This makes the Absolute so elusive that no man can turn to it and make it either the object of his devotion and love, or visualize it in any manner so that the presence might be felt, in order to draw consolation or inspiration. . . .

This is not so. Those who do not limit their Self to the body, and who have their one-pointed interest in the supreme Truth, are always spurred on by their very love for truth. In fact, there is no place, no object, no event outside the pale of the Absolute. How could it be missed? Kṛṣṇa says:

> I the ritual action, I the sacrifice, I the ancestral oblation, I the potent medicinal herb, I the holy formula, I also the melted butter, I the fire, I the offering.
>
> I the Father of this world, the Mother, the Supporter, and the Grandsire, the Holy One who is to be known, the Purifier, the syllable *AUṀ*, as also the Vedas called *Ṛk*, *Sāma*, and *Yajus*,
>
> I radiate heat and I rain, I withhold and I send forth, I am immortality and death, as also being and non-being, Oh Arjuna!

Thus every possible value in the contemplative context is so rich with the presence of the Absolute that it is not necessary to idealize or idolize any one of them particularly.

Is it necessary that one should have a clear understanding of all that is implied in one's worship? What about simple faith?

Kṛṣṇa gives due credence to faith. However, he insists on proper understanding also. Faith is to be directed in the right manner, with right affiliation. Blind faith can go off the mark, though in principle it need not necessarily do so.

Does this mean that the intention of the devotee is more important than the expression?

The soul of an action is its intention and the core of an understanding is its value.

Kṛṣṇa says:

> He who offers to Me with devotion a leaf, a flower, a fruit, or water, that do I accept as being offered with devotion by one who makes the right effort.

What you do, what you eat, what you offer, what you give, what austerity you practise, Oh Son of Kuntī! – let that be done as an offering to Me.

Thus you will be liberated from the bonds of action, whether its results are good or evil. With Self affiliated to unitive self-denial, as one thus emancipated you will attain to Me.

When the Absolute is understood as impersonal and without an individualized self, how could there be any bipolarity from the side of the Absolute in terms of reciprocation?

The neutrality and reciprocity of the Absolute are to be taken together as a unique feature of it. Kṛṣṇa says:

I regard all beings equally. To me there is none hateful or dear. They, however, who worship with devotion – they are in Me and I too am in them.

Even if one of very evil actions should worship Me with a devotion exclusive of all else, he should be accounted to be good all the same, merely by the fact he has a properly settled determination.

What is the central teaching of the Gītā?

This is stated in the exact middle of the text, in the last verse of the ninth chapter:

Become one with Me; be devoted to Me; sacrifice to Me; bow down to Me; unifying thus yourself, you shall surely come to Me, your supreme goal none other than Me.

When the mind attains identity with the Absolute it loses all its egoism and the sense of agency in actions. When union is thus established at the level of the mind, other attitudes follow in outward actions. Here, outward actions which belong to religious or spiritual disciplines are referred to one after the other. This teaching is repeated in the last chapter of the Gītā.

Why are these different attitudes referred to?

The expression "be devoted to Me" refers to a religious attitude, "sacrifice to Me" refers to the attitude of a ritualist. "Bow down to Me" refers to the most overt form of behaviour involving the body, again in the context of spirituality. Such wholesale affiliation at all levels representing different contexts brings together all possible attitudes into one total affiliation with the Absolute.

The Absolute is within oneself. Such is the pure position of the Upaniṣads as expressed in the *mahāvākyas* (great dictums), such as *tat tvam asi* (That thou art). The pure teaching intended in this chapter is thus naturally stated with the above difference. A certain balancing of two aspects of the same Self is what happens here when surrender to the Absolute has taken place.

The openness and catholicity implied in this chapter, and the high hope that it holds out to every human being, give this chapter a status of its own at the centre of the work. The technical and scientific details of establishing a bipolar relationship with the Absolute, which is perhaps the central teaching of the Gītā, find finalized expression. Being thus related to the Absolute is the way recommended for freedom from the ills of life, or salvation, as summed up in the antepenultimate verse. By treating good and bad on a par as items to be transcended by a unitive way of life, by speaking of the Absolute as both existent and non-existent, by stressing the need to transcend sin and even virtue, while yet extolling the numinous value-factor implied in the Absolute, and stressing the need for knowing the Absolute as it ought to be known, according to first principles – by all these features this chapter deserves to be considered as central in relation to the teaching of the Gītā taken as a whole.

X

Vibhūti-Yoga

The Unitive Recognition of Positive Values

INTRODUCTION

THREE main problems that confront all people are discerning true Being from what is only apparent, arriving at absolute certitude instead of entertaining hypothetical postulates, and actualizing the potentials of one's true being instead of running after phantom values. In Chapter II, when Kṛṣṇa assumed the role of a teacher, the very first mention he made of Arjuna's conflict was that he was sorry for those for whom sorrow was unreasonable. Thus, the dialogue of the Gītā was initiated to provide Arjuna with a normative notion of values.

Although the problem of values figured in Western philosophy from the time of Plato, it was always discussed piecemeal, such as the individual merit of values like truth, love, goodness, beauty, or justice. Even these inquiries became further delimited when Value was made the main concern of social sciences like Economics. Once again Value was given consideration on a broader basis by philosophers like Nietzsche, Brentano, Hartmann, and Husserl. In their studies we can see an attempt made to formulate a normative theory of values. Still, they also were dealing mostly with social virtues.

In the present chapter Kṛṣṇa draws a distinction between the One and the many. The One is the Absolute, in Itself, by Itself, and for Itself. The many covers the ontologic ground of the phenomenal, and items that belong to cosmology, theology, and psychology.

Hindu theology is not a systematically structured study of the existence of God and the meaning of His attributes. It mainly incorporates into metaphysical studies the mythological godheads as quasi-personal and allegoric allusions. For instance, in this chapter we find references to mythological figures like Bṛhaspati, the teacher of the gods, and Marīci, the son of Brahmā. The allegoric meaning of these names is evident from the names themselves. The psychological study of values covers human virtues that are attributable to the manifestation of the Divine in man.

Although Kṛṣṇa promises Arjuna to elucidate the values in a graded order, the scheme of grading employed is not explained. First of all, before giving the series, Kṛṣṇa speaks of himself as the absolute ground of all values, both human and cosmologic. After postulating himself as the supreme source of all values, he asks Arjuna to understand, in principle, the manifoldness of values arising out of the one source. Even the ground of manifestation is explicitly termed as his compassion (*anukampā*). This compassion prompts him to be seated in all beings as their soul, which dispels ignorance and fear by functioning as a lamp of knowledge (*jñānadīpam*).

Vyāsa highlights Arjuna's interest in knowing the manifested values of the Absolute by first making him recount the predicates of the Divine revealed by the seers of the past like Asita, Devala, and Vyāsa. Further, he requests the Lord to reveal in full all his unique values. Kṛṣṇa draws a vertical parameter and marks its beginning, middle, and end as aspects of his nature that bring about manifestation. He vouchsafes the illumination of every individuation by himself. This sounds like the monads of Leibnitz, except for the fact that these monads are not mirroring each other, but are imbibed with the one essence of all.

Kṛṣṇa enumerates the values in ensembles which do not immediately give away the principle of their interrelatedness. For example, in the first grouping are Viṣṇu (one of the twelve Ādityas), Ravi (sun), Marīci, and Śaśi (moon). By reflecting on their nature we can presume that the principle of luminosity is employed here for grading these values. Viṣṇu is the Self-effulgent personification of the Lord, hence he is given the primary place. Ravi (sun), comes second in line as the Grand Illuminator of the world. Marīci and Śaśī (moon) are, in principle, the reflection of the Creator's mind and of the sun, respectively.

In the second ensemble the principle used for grading is knowledge; under this group come *Sāmaveda*, Indra, mind, and intellect. As *Sāmaveda* is sung to glorify the Absolute, it is given the primary position. Indra is the lord of mind. Mind is a general category and intellect is its special faculty. In this way, with a close understanding of mythology, and the intuitive use of reflection, it is possible to discover the secret of the grading given in this chapter.

After giving several such graded ensembles, Kṛṣṇa asks Arjuna how he would be benefited by values of a transitory world which has for its ground only a spark of his brilliance. Evidently the advice of the Lord is to know the Absolute in full and to be it.

TRANSLATION

श्रीभगवानुवाच –

1. भूय एव महाबाहो शृणु मे परमं वचः ।
यत्तेऽहं प्रीयमाणाय वक्ष्यामि हितकाम्यया ।।

śrībhagavān uvāca –

bhūya eva mahābāho śṛṇu me paramaṁ vacaḥ ।
yat te 'haṁ prīyamāṇāya vakṣyāmi hitakāmyayā ॥

śrībhagavān uvāca: Śrī Kṛṣṇa said; *bhūyaḥ eva*: again indeed; *mahābāho*: Oh Arjuna; *śṛṇu me*: listen to My; *paramaṁ vacaḥ*: supreme word; *yat aham*: which I; *hitakāmyayā*: desiring (your) well-being; *vakṣyāmi te*: shall tell you; *prīyamāṇāya*: to the dear one (and favourably disposed).

Śrī Kṛṣṇa said:

Again, Oh Mighty-Armed! listen to My supreme word, which I, desiring your well-being, shall tell you, so dear (and favourably disposed).

2. न मे विदुः सुरगणाः प्रभवं न महर्षयः ।
अहमादिर्हि देवानां महर्षीणां च सर्वशः ।।

na me viduḥ suragaṇāḥ prabhavaṁ na maharṣayaḥ ।
aham ādir hi devānāṁ maharṣīṇāṁ ca sarvaśaḥ ॥

na suragaṇāḥ: neither the hosts of the gods; *na maharṣayaḥ*: nor the great sages; *viduḥ*: know; *me prabhavaṁ*: My origin; *aham hi sarvaśaḥ*: (for) I (am) indeed in every way; *ādiḥ devānāṁ*: the source of the gods; *ca maharṣīṇāṁ*: and of the great sages.

Neither the hosts of the gods, nor the great sages know My origin; for I am indeed in every way the source of the gods and the great sages.

3. यो मामजमनादिं च वेत्ति लोकमहेश्वरम् ।
असम्मूढः स मर्त्येषु सर्वपापैः प्रमुच्यते ।।

yo māṁ ajam anādiṁ ca vetti lokamaheśvaram ।
asaṁmūḍhaḥ sa martyeṣu sarvapāpaiḥ pramucyate ॥

yaḥ vetti māṁ: (he) who understands Me; *ajam*: (as) unborn; *ca anādiṁ*: and beginningless; *loka maheśvaram*: (as) the great Lord of the world; *saḥ asaṁmūḍhaḥ*: he (is) undeluded; *martyeṣu*: among mortals; *pramucyate*: (he is) absolved; *sarva pāpaiḥ*: from all sins.

He who understands Me as unborn and beginningless, as the great Lord of the world – that man, undeluded among mortals, is absolved from all sins.

4. बुद्धिर्ज्ञानमसम्मोहः क्षमा सत्यं दमः शमः ।
सुखं दुःखं भवोऽभावो भयं चाभयमेव च ॥

buddhir jñānam asaṁmohaḥ kṣamā satyaṁ damaḥ śamaḥ ।
sukhaṁ duḥkhaṁ bhāvo 'bhāvo bhayaṁ cā 'bhayam eva ca ॥

buddhiḥ jñānam: reason, wisdom; *asaṁmohaḥ*: non-delusion; *kṣamā satyaṁ*: patience, truth; *damaḥ śamaḥ*: self-restraint, calmness; *sukhaṁ duḥkhaṁ*: pleasure, pain; *bhavaḥ ca abhāvaḥ*: becoming and non-becoming; *bhayaṁ*: sense of danger; *ca eva abhayam*: and indeed security.

5. अहिंसा समता तुष्टिस्तपो दानं यशोऽयशः ।
भवन्ति भावा भूतानां मत्त एव पृथग्विधाः ॥

ahiṁsā samatā tuṣṭis tapo dānaṁ yaśo 'yaśaḥ ।
bhavanti bhāvā bhūtānāṁ matta eva pṛthagvidhāḥ ॥

ahiṁsā samatā: non-hurting, balance; *tuṣṭiḥ tapaḥ*: contentment, austerity; *dānaṁ*: benevolence; *yaśaḥ ayaśaḥ*: fame, shame; *pṛthagvidhāḥ*: are the various; *bhāvāḥ bhūtānāṁ*: distinct attitudes of beings; *bhavanti*: arising; *mattaḥ eva*: from Me alone.

Reason, wisdom, non-delusion, patience, truth, self-restraint, calmness, pleasure-pain, becoming and non-becoming, sense of danger and security, non-hurting, balance, contentment, austerity, benevolence, fame-shame, are the various distinct attitudes arising from Me alone.

6. महर्षयः सप्त पूर्वे चत्वारो मनवस्तथा ।
मद्भावा मानसा जाता येषां लोक इमाः प्रजाः ॥

maharṣayaḥ sapta pūrve catvāro manavas tathā ।
madbhāvā mānasā jātā yeṣāṁ loka imāḥ prajāḥ ॥

sapta maharṣayaḥ: the seven great sages; *pūrve*: of old; *tathā*: as also; *catvāraḥ manavaḥ*: the four law-givers (*manus*); *jātāḥ*: are born; *mad bhāvāḥ*: from My own process of becoming; *mānasāḥ*: (and) mind; *yeṣāṁ imāḥ*: (and) from these; *prajāḥ*: (all) progeny; *loke*: in the world.

The seven great sages of old, as also the four law-givers, are born from My own process of becoming and mind, and from these all progeny in the world.

7. एतां विभूतिं योगं च मम यो वेत्ति तत्त्वतः ।
सोऽविकम्पेन योगेन युज्यते नात्र संशयः ॥

etāṁ vibhūtiṁ yogaṁ ca mama yo vetti tattvataḥ ।
so 'vikampena yogena yujyate nā ' tra saṁśayaḥ ॥

saḥ yaḥ vetti: he who understands; *tattvataḥ*: according to fundamental principles; *etāṁ mama vibhūtiṁ*: this My unique value; *ca yogaṁ*: and (its) unitive balance; *avikampena yogena*: by non-wavering contemplation; *yujyate*: attains union; *atra na saṁśayaḥ*: here (there is) no (room for) doubt.

He who understands according to fundamental principles My unique value together with its unitive balance, by non-wavering contemplation attains union. In this there is no room for doubt.

8. अहं सर्वस्य प्रभवो मत्तः सर्वं प्रवर्तते ।
इति मत्वा भजन्ते मां बुधा भावसमन्विताः ।।

ahaṁ sarvasya prabhavo mattaḥ sarvaṁ pravartate ।
iti matvā bhajante māṁ budhā bhāvasamanvitāḥ ॥

ahaṁ prabhavaḥ sarvasya: I (am) the Source of all; *mattaḥ*: from Me; *sarvaṁ pravartate*: everything moves outward; *matvā iti*: understanding thus; *budhāḥ bhajante māṁ*: the wise adore Me; *bhāvasamanvitāḥ*: endowed with (the intuition of) pure becoming.

I am the Source of all; from Me everything moves outward; understanding thus, the wise adore Me, endowed with the intuition of pure becoming.

9. मच्चित्ता मद्गतप्राणा बोधयन्तः परस्परम् ।
कथयन्तश्च मां नित्यं तुष्यन्ति च रमन्ति च ।।

maccittā madgataprāṇā bodhayantaḥ parasparam ।
kathayantaś ca māṁ nityaṁ tuṣyanti ca ramanti ca ॥

maccittāḥ: with their relational minds affiliated to Me; *madgata prāṇā*: their life-tendencies penetrating in Me; *bodhayantaḥ*: enlightening; *parasparam*: each other; *ca nityaṁ kathayantaḥ māṁ*: and ever conversing about Me; *tuṣyanti ca*: (they are) content and; *ca ramanti*: and (they) rejoice.

With their relational minds affiliated to Me, their life-tendencies penetrating in Me, enlightening each other and ever conversing about Me, they are content and rejoice.

10. तेषां सततयुक्तानां भजतां प्रीतिपूर्वकम् ।
ददामि बुद्धियोगं तं येन मामुपयान्ति ते ।।

teṣāṁ satatayuktānāṁ bhajatāṁ prītipūrvakam ।
dadāmi buddhiyogaṁ taṁ yena māṃ upayānti te ॥

teṣāṁ: to them; *satatayuktānāṁ*: established in unbroken union; *prīti pūrvakam bhajatāṁ*: with affectionate adoration; *dadāmi taṁ*: (I) grant that (kind of); *buddhi yogaṁ*: unitive understanding; *yena*: by which; *te upayānti mām*: they attain to Me.

To such established in unbroken union with affectionate adoration, I grant that kind of unitive understanding by which they attain to Me.

11. तेषामेवानुकम्पार्थमहमज्ञानजं तमः ।
नाशयाम्यात्मभावस्थो ज्ञानदीपेन भास्वता ।।

teṣām evā 'nukampārtham aham ajñānajaṁ tamaḥ ।
nāśayāmy ātmabhāvastho jñānadīpena bhāsvatā ॥

eva: specifically; *anukampā artham*: because of compassion; *teṣām*: for them; *aham*: I; *ātma bhāvasthaḥ*: abiding as what has become the Self; *nāśayāmi*: destroy; *ajñānajaṁ tamaḥ*: the ignorance born of darkness; *bhāsvatā jñāna dīpena*: by the shining lamp of wisdom.

Specifically because of compassion for them I, abiding as what has become the Self, destroy the ignorance born of darkness by the shining lamp of wisdom.

अर्जुन उवाच –
12. परं ब्रह्म परं धाम पवित्रं परमं भवान् ।
पुरुषं शाश्वतं दिव्यमादिदेवमजं विभुम् ।।

arjuna uvāca –

paraṁ brahma paraṁ dhāma pavitraṁ paramaṁ bhavān ।
puruṣaṁ śāśvataṁ divyam ādidevam ajaṁ vibhum ॥

arjuna uvāca: Arjuna said; *bhavān*: you (are); *paraṁ brahma*: the supreme Absolute; *paraṁ dhāma*: the supreme Abode; *paramaṁ pavitraṁ*: the supreme Purifier; *śāśvataṁ divyam puruṣaṁ*: the eternal divine Person; *ādidevam*: the primal Divinity; *ajaṁ vibhum*: the Unborn, the All-pervading.

13. आहुस्त्वामृषयः सर्वे देवर्षिर्नारदस्तथा ।
असितो देवलो व्यासः स्वयं चैव ब्रवीषि मे ।।

āhus tvām ṛṣayaḥ sarve devarṣir nāradas tathā ।
asito devalo vyāsaḥ svayaṁ cai 'va bravīṣi me ॥

sarve ṛṣayaḥ: all the sages; *āhuḥ tvām*: say (this of) You; *devarṣiḥ nāradaḥ*: the divine sage Nārada; *tathā*: so too; *asitaḥ devalaḥ vyāsaḥ*: Asita, Devala, Vyāsa; *ca svayaṁ eva*: and (You) Yourself even; *bravīṣī me*: say (it) to me.

Arjuna said:

You are the supreme Absolute, the supreme Abode, the supreme Purifier, the eternal divine Person, the primal Divinity, the Unborn, the All-pervading –

all the sages say this of You, the divine sage Nārada, so too Asita, Devala, Vyāsa, and You Yourself confirm it to me.

14. सर्वमेतदृतं मन्ये यन्मां वदसि केशव ।
न हि ते भगवन्व्यक्तिं विदुर्देवा न दानवाः ।।

sarvam etad ṛtaṁ manye yan māṁ vadasi keśava ।
na hi te bhagavan vyaktiṁ vidur devā na dānavāḥ ॥

manye sarvam etat: I believe all this; *yat vadasi māṁ*: which You say to me; *ṛtaṁ*: (is) valid; *keśava*: Oh Kṛṣṇa; *na devāḥ*: neither the divinities; *na hi dānavāḥ*: nor indeed the demons; *bhagavan*: Oh Lord; *viduḥ te*: know Your; *vyaktiṁ*: unique nature.

I believe that all this that You say is valid, Oh Keśava! neither the divinities nor the demons, Oh Lord! know Your unique nature.

15. स्वयमेवात्मनात्मानं वेत्थ त्वं पुरुषोत्तम ।
भूतभावन भूतेश देवदेव जगत्पते ।।

svayam evā 'tmanā 'tmānaṁ vettha tvaṁ puruṣottama ।
bhūtabhāvana bhūteśa devadeva jagatpate ॥

tvaṁ svayam eva: You Yourself indeed; *vettha ātmānam*: know Yourself; *ātmanā*: by Yourself; *puruṣottama*: most high godhead; *bhūta bhāvana bhūteśa*: presiding Principle of elemental expression and of becoming; *devadeva*: Light of Shining Ones; *jagatpate*: Lord of the universe.

You Yourself indeed know Yourself by Yourself, most high godhead, presiding Principle of elemental expression and of becoming, Light of Shining Ones, Lord of the universe.

16. वक्तु मर्हस्यशेषेण दिव्या ह्यात्मविभूतयः ।
याभिर्विभूतिभिर्लोकानिमांस्त्वं व्याप्य तिष्ठसि ।।

vaktum arhasy aśeṣeṇa divyā hy ātmavibhūtayaḥ ।
yābhir vibhūtibhir lokān imāṁs tvaṁ vyāpya tiṣṭhasi ॥

arhasi vaktum: be pleased to tell (me); *aśeṣeṇa*: without omission; *divyāḥ hi*: (of) the divine indeed; *ātma vibhūtayaḥ*: perfections of (Your own) Self; *yābhiḥ*: by which; *vibhūtibhiḥ*: specific expressions; *tvaṁ vyāpya*: You (are) pervading; *imān lokān*: these worlds; *tiṣṭhasi*: (while) remaining (apart).

Be pleased to tell me without omission of the divine perfections of Your own Self, by which specific expressions You pervade these worlds, while remaining apart.

17. कथं विद्यामहं योगिंस्त्वां सदा परिचिन्तयन् ।
केषु केषु च भावेषु चिन्त्योऽसि भगवन्मया ।।

kathaṁ vidyām ahaṁ yogiṁs tvāṁ sadā paricintayan ।
keṣu-keṣu ca bhāveṣu cintyo 'si bhagavan mayā ॥

kathaṁ: how; *sadā paricintayan*: constantly meditating; *tvāṁ*: on You; *ahaṁ vidyām*: shall I know (You); *yogin*: Oh (Mystic) Yogī; *ca keṣu keṣu*: and in what particular; *bhāveṣu*: expressions; *bhagavan*: Oh Blessed One; *asi cintyaḥ*: are (You) to be cognized; *mayā*: by me.

How shall I, constantly meditating on You, know You, Oh Mystic Yogī? In what particular expressions, Oh Blessed One! are You to be cognized by me?

18. विस्तरेणात्मनो योगं विभूतिं च जनार्दन ।
भूयः कथय तृप्तिर्हि शृण्वतो नास्ति मेऽमृतम् ।।

vistareṇā 'tmano yogaṁ vibhūtiṁ ca janārdana ।
bhūyaḥ kathaya tṛptir hi śṛṇvato nā 'sti me 'mṛtam ॥

kathaya: tell (me); *bhūyaḥ vistareṇa*: again in detail; *janārdana*: Oh Kṛṣṇa; *ātmanaḥ*: of Your; *yogaṁ*: balanced perfections; *ca vibhūtiṁ*: and specific expressions; *hi asti me*: indeed (there) is for me; *na tṛptiḥ*: no satiation; *śṛṇvataḥ*: of hearing (your words) *amṛtam*: (of) ambrosial immortality.

Tell me again in detail, Oh Janārdana! of Your balanced perfections and specific expressions, for I am never tired of hearing Your words of ambrosial immortality.

श्रीभगवानुवाच –

19. हन्त ते कथयिष्यामि दिव्या ह्यात्मविभूतयः ।
प्राधान्यतः कुरुश्रेष्ठ नास्त्यन्तो विस्तरस्य मे ।।

śrībhagavān uvāca –

hanta te kathayiṣyāmi divyā hy ātmavibhūtayaḥ ।
prādhānyataḥ kuruśreṣṭha nā 'sty anto vistarasya me ॥

śrībhagavān uvāca: Kṛṣṇa said; *hanta*: Āh!; *kathayiṣyāmi*: I shall recount; *te hi*: to you indeed; *divyāḥ*: the bright and glorious; *ātma vibhūtayaḥ*: values that pertain to Myself; *prādhānyataḥ*: (graded according to their) importance; *kuruśreṣtha*: Oh Arjuna; *asti na antaḥ*: (for there) is no end; *vistarasya*: of the elaboration (of items); *me*: pertaining to Me.

Kṛṣṇa said:

Āh! I shall recount to you the bright, glorious values that pertain to Myself, (graded) according to their importance, Oh Best of the Kurus! for there is no end to the elaboration of items pertaining to Me.

20. अहमात्मा गुडाकेश सर्वभूताशयस्थितः ।
अहमादिश्च मध्यं च भूतानामन्त एव च ।।

aham ātmā guḍākeśa sarvabhūtāśayasthitaḥ ।
aham ādiś ca madhyaṁ ca bhūtānām anta eva ca ॥

aham ātmā: I (am) the soul; *guḍākeśa*: Oh Arjuna; *sarva bhūta āśaya sthitaḥ*: seated in the heart of all beings; *ca aham*: and I (am); *ādiḥ*: the beginning; *ca madhyaṁ*: and the middle; *ca eva antaḥ*: and even the end; *bhūtānām*: of beings.

I am the soul, Oh Guḍākeśa! seated in the heart of all beings; and I am the beginning, and the middle and even the end of beings.

21. आदित्यानामहं विष्णुर्ज्योतिषां रविरंशुमान् ।
मरीचिर्मरुतामस्मि नक्षत्राणामहं शशी ।।

ādityānām ahaṁ viṣṇur jyotiṣāṁ ravir aṁśumān ।
marīcir marutām asmi nakṣatrāṇām śaśī ॥

ādityānām: of the Ādityas (a group of gods); *ahaṁ viṣṇuḥ*: I (am) Viṣṇu; *jyotiṣāṁ*: of luminaries; *aṁśumān raviḥ*: the radiant Sun; *asmi marīciḥ*: (I) am Marīci; *marutām*: of the Maruts (storm gods); *nakṣatrāṇām*: among the stars; *ahaṁ śaśī*: I (am) the Moon

Of the Ādityas I am Viṣṇu, of luminaries the radiant Sun; I am Marīci of the Maruts; among the stars I am the Moon.

22. वेदानां सामवेदोऽस्मि देवानामस्मि वासवः ।
इन्द्रियाणां मनश्चास्मि भूतानामस्मि चेतना ।।

vedānāṁ sāmavedo 'smi devānām asmi vāsavaḥ ।
indriyāṇāṁ manaś cā 'smi bhūtānām asmi cetanā ॥

vedānāṁ: of the Vedas; *asmi sāmavedaḥ*: (I) am the *Sāmaveda*; *devānām*: of the divinities; *asmi vāsavaḥ*: (I) am Indra (Lord of the gods); *indriyāṇāṁ*: in respect of the senses; *asmi manaḥ*: (I) am the Mind; *ca bhūtānām*: and of life-expressions; *asmi cetanā*: (I) am (pure) Intelligence.

Of the Vedas I am the *Sāmaveda*; of the divinities I am Indra; in respect of the senses I am the Mind, and of life-expressions I am pure Intelligence.

23. रुद्राणां शंकरश्चास्मि वित्तेशो यक्षरक्षसाम् ।
वसूनां पावकश्चास्मि मेरुः शिखरिणामहम् ॥

rudrāṇāṁ śaṁkaraś cā 'smi vitteśo yakṣarakṣasām ।
vasūnāṁ pāvakaś cā 'smi meruḥ śikhariṇām aham ॥

ca rudrāṇāṁ: and of the Rudras (a group of gods); *asmi śaṅkaraḥ*: (I) am Śaṅkara (Śiva); *yakṣa rakṣasām*: of the *yakṣa*s and the *rākṣasa*s (spirit beings); *vitteśaḥ*: Vitteśa (Lord of Wealth); *vasūnāṁ*: of the Vasus (eight bright gods); *asmi pāvakaḥ*: (I) am Pāvaka (the purifying elemental Fire); *ca śikhariṇām*: and among heights; *aham meruḥ*: I (am) Meru (mountain at the centre of the world).

Of the Rudras I am Śaṅkara; of the *yakṣa*s and the *rākṣasas*, Vitteśa; of the Vasus I am Pāvaka, and among heights I am Meru.

24. पुरोधसां च मुख्यं मां विद्धि पार्थ बृहस्पतिम् ।
सेनानीनामहं स्कन्दः सरसामस्मि सागरः ॥

purodhasāṁ ca mukhyaṁ māṁ viddhi pārtha bṛhaspatim ।
senānīnām ahaṁ skandaḥ sarasām asmi sāgaraḥ ॥

ca purodhasāṁ: (even in the case) also of the household priests; *pārtha*: Oh Arjuna; *viddhi māṁ*: know Me (to be); *mukhyaṁ*: the chief; *bṛhaspatim*: Bṛhaspati (priest of the gods); *senānīnām*: of the generals; *ahaṁ skandaḥ*: I (am) Skanda (the god of war); *sarasām*: of lakes; *asmi sāgaraḥ*: (I) am the ocean.

Even in the case of the household priests, Oh Pārtha! know Me to be the chief, Bṛhaspati; of the generals I am Skanda; in respect of lakes I correspond to the ocean.

25. महर्षीणां भृगुरहं गिरामस्म्येकमक्षरम् ।
यज्ञानां जपयज्ञोऽस्मि स्थावराणां हिमालयः ॥

maharṣīṇāṁ bhṛgur ahaṁ girām asmy ekam akṣaram ।
yajñānāṁ japayajño'smi sthāvarāṇāṁ himālayaḥ ॥

maharṣīṇāṁ: of the great hermit-sages; *ahaṁ bhṛguḥ*: I (am) Bhṛgu; *girām*: of articulated words; *asmi ekam akṣaram*: (I) am the one-syllable (*AUṀ*); *yajñānāṁ*: of sacrifices; *asmi japa yajñāḥ*: (I) am the sacrifice of silent repetition; *sthāvarāṇāṁ*: of immovables; *himālayaḥ*: (I am) the Himalaya.

Of the great hermit-sages I am Bhṛgu; of articulated words I am the one-syllable (*AUṀ*); of sacrifices I am the sacrifice of silent repetition; of immovables I am the Himalaya.

26. अश्वत्थः सर्ववृक्षाणां देवर्षीणां च नारदः ।
गन्धर्वाणां चित्ररथः सिद्धानां कपिलो मुनिः ।।

aśvatthaḥ sarvavṛkṣāṇāṁ devarṣīṇāṁ ca nāradaḥ ।
gandharvāṇāṁ citrarathaḥ siddhānāṁ kapilo muniḥ ॥

sarva vṛkṣāṇāṁ: of all trees; *aśvatthaḥ*: (I am) *aśvattha* (see XV.1-4); *ca devarṣīṇāṁ*: and of divine sages; *nāradaḥ*: Nārada (messenger between men and gods); *gandharvāṇāṁ*: of *gandharvas* (heavenly beings); *citrarathaḥ*: Citraratha (their chief); *siddhānāṁ*: (and) of those of psycho-physical attainments; *kapilaḥ muniḥ*: Kapila the recluse (founder of Sāṁkhya Philosophy).

Of trees I am *aśvattha*, and of divine sages, Nārada; of *gandharvas*, Citraratha, and of those of psycho-physical attainments, Kapila the recluse.

27. उच्चैःश्रवसमश्वानां विद्धि माममृतोद्भवम् ।
ऐरावतं गजेन्द्राणां नराणां च नराधिपम् ।।

uccaiḥśravasam aśvānāṁ viddhi mām amṛtodbhavam ।
airāvataṁ gajendrāṇāṁ narāṇāṁ ca narādhipam ॥

viddhi mām: know Me; *aśvānāṁ*: among horses; *uccaiḥśravasam*: (to be) Uccaiḥśravas (Indra's horse); *amṛtodbhavam*: born of the ambrosia of immortality; *gajendrāṇāṁ*: of noble elephants; *airāvataṁ*: Airāvata (Indra's elephant); *ca narāṇāṁ*: and of men; *narādhipam*: the king.

Know Me among horses to be Uccaiḥśravas, born of the ambrosia of immortality; of noble elephants, Airāvata, and of men the king.

28. आयुधानामहं वज्रं धेनूनामस्मि कामधुक् ।
प्रजनश्चास्मि कन्दर्पः सर्पाणामस्मि वासुकिः ।।

āyudhānām ahaṁ vajraṁ dhenūnām asmi kāmadhuk ।
prajanaś ca 'smi kandarpaḥ sarpāṇām asmi vāsukiḥ ॥

āyudhānām: of weapons; *ahaṁ vajraṁ*: I (am) the thunderbolt; *dhenūnām*: of cows; *asmi kāmadhuk*: (I) am the milk-yielder of all desires (Kāmadhuk, the heavenly cow); *ca prajanaḥ*: and of progenitors; *asmi kadarpaḥ*: (I) am the god of erotics (Kāma); *sarpāṇām*: of serpents; *asmi vāsukiḥ*: (I) am Vāsuki (their chief).

Of weapons I am the thunderbolt; of cows I am the milk-yielder of all desires; of progenitors I am the god of erotics; of serpents I am Vāsuki.

29. अनन्तश्चास्मि नागानां वरुणो यादसामहम् ।
पितॄणामर्यमा चास्मि यमः संयमतामहम् ।।

anantaś cā 'smi nāgānāṁ varuṇo yādasām aham ।
pitṝṇām aryamā cā 'smi yamaḥ saṁyamatām aham ॥

ca asmi anantaḥ: and (I) am Ananta; *nāgānāṁ*: of Nāgas (snakes); *aham varuṇaḥ*: I (am) Varuṇa; *yādasām*: of the denizens of the deep; *ca pitṝṇām*: and of the ancestors; *asmi aryamā*: am Aryamā (their chief); *aham yamaḥ*: I (am) Yama (god of death); *saṁyamatām*: of controllers.

And I am Ananta of Nāgas; I am Varuṇa of the denizens of the deep, and Aryamā of the ancestors; I am Yama of controllers.

30. प्रह्लादश्चास्मि दैत्यानां कालः कलयतामहम् ।
मृगाणां च मृगेन्द्रोऽहं वैनतेयश्च पक्षिणाम् ।।

prahlādaś cā 'smi daityānāṁ kālaḥ kalayatām aham ।
mṛgāṇāṁ ca mṛgendro 'haṁ vainateyaś ca pakṣiṇām ॥

ca asmi prahlādaḥ: and (I) am Prahlāda (who became a worshipper of Viṣṇu); *daityānāṁ*: of the *daitya*s (enemies of the gods); *kalayatām*: among bases of measurement; *aham kālaḥ*: I (am) time; *ca mṛgāṇāṁ*: and of beasts; *ahaṁ mṛgendraḥ*: I am the lord of beasts (the lion); *ca vainateyaḥ*: and Vainateya (Garuḍa, the eagle which Viṣṇu rides); *pakṣiṇām*: of birds.

And I am Prahlāda of the *daitya*s; among bases of measurement I am time; of beasts I am the lord of beasts; and Vainateya of birds.

31. पवनः पवतामस्मि रामः शस्त्रभृतामहम् ।
झषाणां मकरश्चास्मि स्रोतसामस्मि जाह्नवी ।।

pavanaḥ pavatām asmi rāmaḥ śastrabhṛtām aham ।
jhaṣāṇāṁ makaraś cā 'smi srotasām asmi jāhnavī ॥

pavatām: of purifiers; *asmi pavanaḥ*: (I) am the wind; *aham rāmaḥ*: I am Rāma (hero of the *Rāmāyaṇa*); *śastra bhṛtām*: of bowmen; *jhaṣāṇāṁ*: of fishes; *ca asmi makaraḥ*: I am the *makara* (a mythological fish, noted for its voracity); *srotasām*: of streams; *asmi jāhnavī*: (I) am the Ganges.

Of purifiers I am the wind; I am Rāma of bowmen; of fishes I am the *makara*; of streams I am the Ganges.

32. सर्गाणामादिरन्तश्च मध्यं चैवाहमर्जुन ।
अध्यात्मविद्या विद्यानां वादः प्रवदतामहम् ।।

sargāṇām ādir antaś ca madhyaṁ cai 'vā 'ham arjuna ।
adhyātmavidyā vidyānāṁ vādaḥ pravadatām aham ॥

sargāṇām: (in the structure) of cantos (or chapters); *aham ādiḥ*: I (am) the beginning; *ca antaḥ*: and end; *ca eva madhyaṁ*: and also the middle;

arjuna: Oh Arjuna! *vidyānāṁ*: of the sciences; *adhyātma vidyā*: (I am) the Science of the Self; *aham vadaḥ*: I (am) the dialectic; *pravadatām*: of pre-eminent dialecticians.

(In the structure) of cantos (or chapters) I am the beginning, end, and also the middle, Oh Arjuna; of the sciences I am the Science of the Self; I am the dialectic of pre-eminent dialecticians.

33. अक्षराणामकारोऽस्मि द्वन्द्वः सामासिकस्य च ।
अहमेवाक्षयः कालो धाताहं विश्वतोमुखः ।।

akṣarāṇām akāro 'smi dvandvaḥ sāmāsikasya ca ।
aham evā 'kṣayaḥ kālo dhātā 'haṁ viśtvatomukhaḥ ॥

akṣarāṇām: among syllabic letters; *asmi akāraḥ*: (I) am the letter A; *ca sāmāsikasya*: and of compounds; *dvandvaḥ*: (I am) the paired-compound; *aham eva akṣayaḥ*: *I* (am) also unexpended; *kālaḥ*: time; *aham dhātā*: I (am) the maintainer; *viśvatomukhaḥ*: universally facing.

Among syllabic letters I am the A, of compounds I am the paired-compound; I am also unexpended time; I am the maintainer, universally facing.

34. मृत्युः सर्वहरश्चाहमुद्भवश्च भविष्यताम् ।
कीर्तिः श्रीर्वाक्च नारीणां स्मृतिर्मेधा धृतिः क्षमा ।।

mṛtyuḥ sarvaharaś cā 'ham udbhavaś ca bhaviṣyatām ।
kīrtiḥ śrīr vāk ca nārīnāṁ smṛtir medhā dhṛtiḥ kṣamā ॥

ca aham sarvaharaḥ: and I (am) all-engulfing; *mṛtyuḥ*: death; *ca udbhavaḥ*: and the Source; *bhaviṣyatām*: (throwing up) all things that are to be; *ca nārīṇāṁ*: and of womanly values; *kīrtiḥ śrīḥ*: fame, grace; *vāk smṛtiḥ*: speech, memory; *medhā dhṛtiḥ*: will-power, firmness; *kṣamā*: (and) endurance.

I am all-engulfing death, and the Source throwing up all things that are to be; and of womanly values, fame, grace, speech, memory, will-power, firmness and endurance.

35. बृहत्साम तथा साम्नां गायत्री छन्दसामहम् ।
मासानां मार्गशीर्षोऽहमृतूनां कुसुमाकरः ।।

bṛhatsāma tathā sāmnāṁ gāyatrī chandasām aham ।
māsānāṁ mārgaśīrṣo 'ham ṛtūnāṁ kusumākaraḥ ॥

tathā: likewise; *sāmnāṁ*: of hymns; *bṛhatsāma*: (I am) the *bṛhat-sāma*; *chandasām*: of metres; *aham gāyatrī*: I (am) the Gāyatrī; *māsānāṁ*: of months; *aham mārgaśīrṣaḥ*: I (am) Mārgaśīrṣa (just after harvest); *ṛtūnāṁ*: and of seasons; *kusumākaraḥ*: the flower-abounding.

Likewise, of hymns I am the Bṛhat-sāma; of metres I am the Gāyatrī; of months I am Mārgaśīrṣa, and of seasons the flower-abounding.

36. द्यूतं छलयतामस्मि तेजस्तेजस्विनामहम् ।
जयोऽस्मि व्यवसायोऽस्मि सत्त्वं सत्त्ववतामहम् ।।

dyūtaṁ chalayatām asmi tejas tejasvinām aham ।
jayo 'smi vyavasāyo 'smi sattvaṁ sattvavatām aham ॥

asmi dyūtaṁ: (I) am the chance-risk; *chalayatām*: of (irresponsible) gamblers; *aham tejaḥ*: I (am) the brilliance; *tejasvinām*: of the brilliant (people); *asmi jayaḥ*: (I) am victory; *asmi vyavasāyaḥ*: (I) am decisiveness; *aham sattvaṁ*: I (am) the goodness; *sattvavatām*: of those established in the real.

I am the chance risk of (irresponsible) gamblers; I am the brilliance of the brilliant people; I am victory; I am decisiveness; I am the goodness of those established in the real.

37. वृष्णीनां वासुदेवोऽस्मि पाण्डवानां धनञ्जयः ।
मुनीनामप्यहं व्यासः कवीनामुशना कविः ।।

vṛṣṇināṁ vāsudevo 'smi pāṇḍavānāṁ dhanañjayaḥ ।
munīnām apy ahaṁ vyāsaḥ kavīnām uśanā kaviḥ ॥

vṛṣṇināṁ: of the Vṛṣṇis (Kṛṣṇa's clan); *asmi vāsudevaḥ*: (I) am Vāsudeva (Kṛṣṇa); *pāṇḍavānāṁ*: of the Pāṇḍavas (the sons of Pāṇḍu); *dhanañjayaḥ*: Dhanañjaya (Arjuna); *munīnām api*: of the recluses also; *ahaṁ vyāsaḥ*: I (am) Vyāsa (author of the Bhagavadgītā); *kavīnām*: of the poets; *kaviḥ*: the poet; *uśanā*: Uśanā.

Of the Vṛṣṇis, I am Vāsudeva, of the Pāṇḍavas, Dhanañjaya, of the recluses I am Vyāsa, of the poets, the poet Uśanā.

38. दण्डो दमयतामस्मि नीतिरस्मि जिगीषताम् ।
मौनं चैवास्मि गुह्यानां ज्ञानं ज्ञानवतामहम् ।।

daṇḍo damayātām asmi nītir asmi jigīṣatām ।
maunaṁ cai 'vā 'smi guhyānāṁ jñānaṁ jñānavatām aham ॥

damayatām: of rulers; *asmi daṇḍaḥ*: (I) am the sceptre; *jigīṣatāṁ*: of those who seek victory; *asmi nītiḥ*: (I) am the statesmanship; *ca eva guhyānāṁ*: and also in esoterics; *asmi maunaṁ*: (I) am silence; *jñānavatām*: (and) of knowers; *aham jñānaṁ*: I (am) knowledge.

Of rules I am the sceptre, of those who seek victory I am the statesmanship, in esoterics I am silence, and of knowers I am knowledge.

39. यच्चापि सर्वभूतानां बीजं तदहमर्जुन ।
न तदस्ति विना यत्स्यान्मया भूतं चराचरम् ।।

yac cā 'pi sarvabhūtānāṁ bījaṁ tad aham arjuna ।
na tad asti vinā yat syān mayā bhūtaṁ carācaram ॥

ca api: and further; *yat bījaṁ*: what (is) the seed; *sarva bhūtānāṁ*: of all beings; *tat aham*: that I (am); *arjuna*: Oh Arjuna; *na asti*: nor is (there); *tat bhūtaṁ*: that being; *carācaram*: moving or unmoving; *yat syāt*: which can exist; *vinā mayā*: without Me.

And further, what is the seed of all beings, that I am, Oh Arjuna! nor is there anything moving or unmoving that can exist without Me.

40. नान्तोऽस्ति मम दिव्यानां विभूतीनां परन्तप ।
एष तूद्देशतः प्रोक्तो विभूतेर्विस्तरो मया ।।

nā 'nto 'sti mama divyānāṁ vibhūtīnāṁ paraṁtapa ।
eṣa tū 'ddeśataḥ prokto vibhūter vistaro mayā ॥

asti na antaḥ: (there) is no end; *mama divyānāṁ*: to My divine; *vibhūtīnāṁ*: unique values; *paraṁtapa*: Oh Arjuna; *eṣaḥ proktaḥ*: this (which has been) said; *vibhūteḥ*: (of these) unique values; *tu uddeśataḥ*: (is) but indicatory of; *vistaraḥ mayā*: (their possible extensive) elaboration by me.

There is no end to My divine unique values, Oh Paraṁtapa; what has been said of these unique values is but indicatory of their possible extensive elaboration.

41. यद्यद्विभूतिमत्सत्त्वं श्रीमदूर्जितमेव वा ।
तत्तदेवावगच्छ त्वं मम तेजोंऽशसम्भवम् ।।

yad-yad vibhūtimat sattvaṁ śrīmad ūrjitam eva vā ।
tat-tad evā 'vagaccha tvaṁ mama tejoṁśasaṁbhavam ॥

yat yat: whatever; *sattvaṁ*: entity; *vibhūtimat*: (is) unique in perfected value; *śrīmat*: grace; *vā eva*: or indeed; *ūrjitam*: (in) radical strength; *tvaṁ avagaccha*: you (should) understand; *tat tat eva*: that indeed; *mama tejaḥ aṁśa saṁbhavam*: to have manifested (itself from) a (mere) fraction of My brilliance.

Whatever entity is unique in perfected value, in grace, or in radical strength, understand that to have manifested itself from a mere fractional spark of My brilliance.

42. अथवा बहुनैतेन किं ज्ञातेन तवार्जुन ।
विष्टभ्याहमिदं कृत्स्नमेकांशेन स्थितो जगत् ।।

athavā bahunai 'tena kiṁ jñātena tavā 'rjuna ।
viṣṭabhyā 'ham idaṁ kṛtsnam ekāṁśena sthito jagat ॥

athavā: but; *kiṁ tava*: what (use is there) to you; *arjuna*: Oh Arjuna; *etena bahunā jñātena*: with this pluralistic knowledge; *viṣṭabhya*: supporting; *idaṁ kṛtsnam jagat*: this whole world; *eka aṁśena*: by a single fraction (of Myself); *aham sthitaḥ*: I remain (still as ever).

But what use is there for you, Arjuna, in this pluralistic knowledge? Supporting this whole world by a single fraction of Myself, I remain still as ever.

DIALOGUE

TEACHER: From the first chapter to the ninth chapter there is a progressive lifting of interest from the objective actualities of life to the highly subjective realities of the Self. To leave the teaching of *yoga* in midair after lifting it so high would be an asymmetrical approach. If the first half of the Gītā shows a vertical ascent in theory, with speculation and intuitive flights, in the second half we can see a graded vertical descent until Arjuna and Kṛṣṇa once again stand in the battlefield, duty bound, with each one willing to carry out his role with a perfect understanding of this life and a full acceptance of the contingency of the world of necessary action.

The tenth chapter marks the turning point from theorization to realization of every value in our own lives in terms of the attributes of the Absolute. When truth, kindness, love, peace, beauty, grace, and other such values are conceived in the mind, they are only abstractions. When imperientially and experientially we visualize these values in the psychological and cosmological value-structures, they can be causally related to an activation by the Absolute through its mere numinous presence. When the world outside and corresponding subjective values are thus realized in terms of the Absolute, the value or glory of it can be known as an all-embracing reality.

It is highly necessary that for the purpose of guiding our life we should have realistic conceptions of absolute values, rather than just perceiving them in abstract or subjective terms. Though Kṛṣṇa gives only a few highlights in the scheme of real things, the seeker is offered a wide variety of examples by which the unique glory of the Absolute may be recognized as it penetrates through the commonplace. This is sufficiently explained in the concluding verses of this chapter.

Kṛṣṇa begins the chapter by saying:

> Again, Oh Mighty-Armed! listen to My supreme word, which I, desiring your well-being, shall tell you, so dear and favourably disposed.

STUDENT: *Could it be said that this chapter is a revelation? Is there any special significance in Kṛṣṇa giving an account of his own supreme Self as an absolute structure of values?*

The Absolute is not an object to be known by direct perception. It is not anything previously known in full: it is seen only partially now so that we can understand it with the aid of inference. It does not yield to presumption. Also, it is not realized through any process of elimination. The only way to know the Absolute is by revelation. Kṛṣṇa makes this clear in verse 2:

> Neither the hosts of the gods, nor the great sages know My origin; for I am indeed in every way the source of the gods and the great sages.

If a man speaks very highly of himself we consider him an egotist. Is it permissible for Kṛṣṇa to speak so extravagantly here?

Kṛṣṇa is not bragging or boasting, or saying that he is superior to others. The context to which the Gītā belongs is the confluence of the two cultures of ancient India, namely the Vedic and pre-Vedic civilizations. The source of Vedic wisdom is the belief in the grace of the Shining Ones, or in more down-to-earth terms, the hypostatic values personified and revered as gods by Vedic Aryans. The pre-Aryan wisdom came from the contemplative seers called rishis (*ṛṣis*). Kṛṣṇa is now revaluating both cultures in terms of a more finalized wisdom. He says that the highest notions held or represented by both groups are lopsided, instead recommending values such as:

> Reason, wisdom, non-delusion, patience, truth, self-restraint, calmness, pleasure-pain, becoming and non-becoming, sense of danger and security, non-hurting, balance, contentment, austerity, benevolence, fame-shame, are the various distinct attitudes arising from Me alone.

Why does Kṛṣṇa think negative values also arise from the Absolute?

Our consciousness oscillates between the polarized opposites of pleasure and pain, courage and fear, security and insecurity, and existence and non-existence. By adopting an attitude of sameness, we come to a neutral state in which we can clearly see that pain and pleasure and all such opposites are really two faces of the same coin. The dichotomy, alternations, variance, and ambivalence implied in these moods or attitudes are further clarified:

> The seven great sages of old, as also the four law-givers (*manus*), are born from My own process of becoming and mind, and from these all progeny in the world.

In the Bible there is a reference to the "Mary-type" (contemplative) as contrasted with the "Martha-type" (action oriented). Jesus makes another dichotomous distinction between the realms of God and of Caesar. In the Chinese wisdom-context, we have the pure wisdom contemplation of Lao Tse compared with the worldly-wise socio-political teachings of Confucius. Man has within him these two tendencies right from the very inception. One tendency agrees with the intuitive appreciation of the Absolute, as in the seven sages of the past; the other is in tune with the well-structured and intellectually conceived contracts and constitutions in which the law-givers excel.

Who are the seven sages?

They are differently listed in different books. In the *Mahābhārata*, to which the Gītā belongs, they are Marīci, Atri, Aṅgiras, Pulaha, Kratu, Pulastya, and Vasiṣṭha. According to the *Harivaṁśa* they are Gotama, Bharadvāja, Viśvāmitra, Jamadagni, Kaśyapa, Dakṣa, Pracetas, Bhṛgu, and Nārada.

How do we know the Absolute in order to affiliate with it, and how do we know that we spiritually progress?

Sometimes, we find it most harmonious to express ourselves in our thoughts, words, and actions, and our intuitions and inferences seem to work very well. At other times we find compelling situations of necessity, which leave us no alternative than to orient our thoughts, words, and actions in the direction dictated by this necessity. When both these aspects are unitively conceived, being understood as the way of the Tao, Absolute, or will of God, we are affiliating ourselves to the Absolute. Suppose a person prays: "My Lord, my Father, Omniscient and Omnipotent, All-loving and Glorious, may my words radiate Your joy, and may I be worthy of being used as Your instrument." In such a prayer, every word which is uttered makes a demand upon the consciousness to extend itself to the connotation of each term. At least in principle, the mind has to identify itself with all the qualities attributed to God or the Absolute. This is one way of affiliating ourselves with the Absolute.

Situations presenting themselves to us, without any initiative on our part, and as a result of our most natural and correct behaviour, should be taken as the will of God. That very feeling will give us a sense of our togetherness with God. Even though a situation looks difficult and beyond us, this trust in the Highest will give us new hope and courage, and unsought aid coming from all directions will enhance our trust in God's grace. When this trust and consequential fulfilment increases day by day, we know we are on the right track and we progress. In such a case no one will have any doubt in their mind of what is happening. In the present chapter, Kṛṣṇa reveals to Arjuna the many facets of the Absolute. Arjuna wants to confirm that his inner eyes have now become clear enough to see many other unique values of the Absolute in Kṛṣṇa. Arjuna says:

> You are the supreme Absolute, the supreme Abode, the supreme Purifier, the eternal divine Person, the primal Divinity, the Unborn, the All-pervading –
>
> all the sages say this of You, the divine sages Nārada, so too Asita, Devala, Vyāsa, and You Yourself confirm it to me.
>
> I believe that all this that You say is valid, Oh Keśava! neither the divinities nor the demons, Oh Lord! know Your unique nature.
>
> You Yourself indeed know Yourself by Yourself, most high godhead, presiding Principle of elemental expression and of becoming, Light of Shining Ones, Lord of the universe.

Does Kṛṣṇa teach Arjuna how to meditate on these unique values?

Arjuna himself asks:

> How shall I, constantly meditating on You, know You, Oh Mystic Yogī? In what particular expressions, Oh Blessed One! are You to be cognized by me?
>
> Tell me again in detail, Oh Janardana! of Your balanced perfections and specific expressions, for I am never tired of hearing Your words of ambrosial immortality.

No love or adoption is complete or perfect unless the reciprocity of the counterparts are of equal admiration and sympathy, understanding and dialectical togetherness. In the whole of the ninth chapter and the beginning of the tenth, we have been seeing the great concern of the Guru for his disciple, the initiative taken by Kṛṣṇa out of sheer compassion. In these verses we see how it is reciprocated by an equally strong feeling, deep love, and profound admiration on the part of the disciple. There is nothing that satisfies and rewards the Guru more than to see the bright face and pacified heart of his disciple. A thorn in the disciple's heart is equally annoying to the Guru also. So there has to be an open assurance given by the disciple that he is benefited by the teaching. Arjuna here refers to the wisdom as the ambrosia that gives immortality, and adds further that he will never be satiated. This remark is significant. The love between Guru and disciple is not born of a craving for companionship, nor for the satisfaction of any physiological or psychological urge. It is the coming together of the counterparts of a wisdom situation in which they burn together as a single flame in the fire of the Absolute. In a burning flame the fire is fresh every moment, and it never becomes tired of burning. So this love should not be likened to the sentimental attachment of kith and kin, or of couples where gross indulgence or horizontalization of relations make one soon get on the nerves of the other.

In response to Arjuna's request Kṛṣṇa again recounts his unique values. He says:

> Āh! I shall recount to you the bright, glorious values that pertain to Myself, (graded) according to their importance, Oh Best of the Kurus! for there is no end to the elaboration of items pertaining to Me.

This is followed by a lengthy enumeration of specific, unique, or glorious values that emerge to view in our life as it is actually lived. The unwillingness to reveal the secret of the Absolute given here in the exclamation "Āh!" can be compared to the hesitation of the ghost of Hamlet's father when it was unwillingly compelled to speak about itself. The world of the spirit has a certain hesitation to become the subject of overt, commonplace discussion. One could even say that God Himself likes to remain unseen and untainted by the vulgar gaze of humanity, which belongs to the marketplace. It is at the insistent request of Arjuna that a concession is made here.

Kṛṣṇa further describes himself as the soul seated in the hearts of all beings, and the shining luminaries in the firmament. He verily is the Word of the Guru. Among the articulated words he is *AUṀ*. He is the stability of the mountain. From the vegetative life to the most sublime philosophical vision of the greatest saint, He can be seen shining in different forms and in different modes. From verses 20 through 39, we get a long list of the enumerations of His unique values. He concludes by saying that He is none other than Arjuna himself.

What is the principle by which a unique value is measured?

Kṛṣṇa says:

> Whatever entity is unique in perfected value, in grace, or in radical strength, understand that to have manifested itself from a mere fractional spark of My brilliance.

The human psyche is so representative of the cosmological and psychological richness of the total manifestation that it gains the same status as the Absolute, when it is capable of holding out the three general principles of all unique values: *vibhūtimat*, *śrīmat*, and *ūrjitam*. When this is thought of in terms of an individual, the *vibhūti* can be taken for those rare and unique characteristics of the personality that make a person what they are. Some of these values never get a chance to unfold themselves. To do justice to the *vibhūti*, one has to develop a great inner awareness by which one can make oneself familiar with their own *vibhūti*. *Śrīmat* is a value which can be compared to grace, abundance, harmony, or order. In a haphazard life these inner potentialities get seriously damaged, and so the beauty of life turns into ugliness as one grows up. All children are born beautiful. As they grow up, the horizontal forces of life corrode this spiritual charm and harmony. Hence, one desirous of walking in the spiritual path has to open up his own inner potentials. He should be like an unfailing luminary, lending its light to all who need it. Such a person should be like a reservoir of grace to benefit the whole world. The third quality, *ūrjitam*, stands for vigour and strength, a positive attitude deriving its validity from Truth.

This chapter closes with a verse that is equivalent to the well-known peace invocation where plenitude taken away from plenitude leaves plenitude as a remainder:

> Plenitude is all that is invisible; Plenitude is all that is visible. Plenitude was born out of Plenitude. When Plenitude is absorbed into Plenitude, Plenitude alone remains.

XI

Viśvarūpa-Darśana-Yoga

The Unitive Vision of the Absolute

INTRODUCTION

THE traditionally accepted testimony of valid knowledge arises out of the verticalized harmonization of *śruti*, the a priori Word of the Guru or revelation (*yukti*) reflecting on word-wisdom with sound reason, and *anubhava*, ultimately experiencing the truth of what is heard. What is experimental proof to the scientist is *anubhava* (experience) to the spiritual man. In the Bhagavadgītā the present chapter marks the peak of Arjuna's experience.

From Chapter II, verse 11 on, Arjuna has listened to the word of his God-Guru, and also critically pondered on the deep implication of what he has heard by actively engaging in a dialogue with his Master. In Chapter VII Arjuna was acquainted with the secret of the manifestation of the phenomenal world. Kṛṣṇa instructed him on how the ontologic ground of the concreteness of the physical universe and its psychic counterparts, the mind, intellect and ego, should be seen as only a flux-like elaboration of a small spark of the Absolute. In the same chapter Kṛṣṇa raises a tirade against all conceptualization of the Absolute in terms of anthropomorphic theism. In Chapter VIII Arjuna is further instructed about the cosmic cycles of time and the traditional concepts of eschatology. In Chapter IX Kṛṣṇa further teaches Arjuna the secret of abolishing duality, such as of cause and effect, and of ends and means. This reminds us of the sayings of Jesus Christ in the Gospel according to St. John: "I am the resurrection and the life" (XI:25), and also, "I am the way, the truth and the light" (XIV: 6).

In Chapter X Kṛṣṇa gives a detailed account of several items of His archetypal immanence which have reference to cosmological, mythological, and psychological value-factors. These are given to Arjuna as a graded series of values following sound philosophical principles.

In the present chapter, Arjuna is given the opportunity to express his reaction to Kṛṣṇa's a priori revelation. Arjuna profusely thanks Kṛṣṇa for revealing the highest secret pertaining to the Self. He admits that his confusion is gone. However he is not fully satisfied. In verses 3 and 4 he makes a definite request for a direct vision of Kṛṣṇa's divine form.

In the Bible there are several references to mystical visions, such as those of Enoch, Job, Ezekiel, Daniel, and St. John. Almost all Christian mystics claim mysterious visions. The *Interior Castle* of St. Teresa of Avila more resembles the creative imagination of a good writer than a mystical vision. The Holy Koran was revealed to the prophet Muhammad after a mystical vision. In the *Tibetan Book of the Dead* there are references to the Dharmakāya and Amitābha Buddha.

Although a mystical vision comes like a dream, it is different from a dream in that it is capable of effecting an inner transformation of the recipient of the vision. People of hysterical or neurotic dispositions also have hallucinatory visions. C.G. Jung, in his *Psychology and Religion*, gives the distinctive features of a mystical vision which are different from those of a pathological hallucination.

The rapport between Kṛṣṇa and Arjuna has become complete, and Kṛṣṇa is willing to favour Arjuna with the rare vision of the Absolute. The vision is described in this chapter by Sañjaya, Arjuna, and Kṛṣṇa himself. Sañjaya's description bears a resemblance to the vision of the Supreme One given in the *Ṛgveda*. Arjuna first experiences the cosmic vision very much in conformity with his theistic notion of Viṣṇu as a personal God with several lovable and adorable attributes. Kṛṣṇa grants Arjuna the eye of wisdom to see what was not visible to his naked eyes, and brings the experience to a peak by knocking out of Arjuna the collective memory of the picturesque image of a serene God seated on the throne of the Most High. The Absolute presented in the peak experience is neither good nor evil, and it is beyond all comprehension. As D.T. Suzuki says in *The Essence of Buddhism* (1957: 26):

> It is the most startling event that could ever happen in the realm of human consciousness ... upsetting every form of standardized experience.

A parallel to this in modern science is the impact of the new theories which came like a blast to Albert Einstein. He is quoted in *Philosopher Scientist* (p. 45):

> All my attempts to adapt the theoretical foundation of physics to this (new type of) knowledge failed completely. It was as if the ground had been pulled out from under one, with no firm foundation to be seen anywhere upon which one could have built.

When Arjuna became terrified, he implored Kṛṣṇa to again show him the soothing vision of Viṣṇu. This was not granted, although in the following chapter Kṛṣṇa does approve of the concept of a personal God as a concession to those who are incapable of transcendental experience of the Absolute. In Chapter XIII Kṛṣṇa shows that his real preference is for one to understand the Absolute as a unitive whole by bracketing the knower of the field and the field itself as one.

Between Chapters VII and XI the triple aspects of origination, existence, and dissolution are fully covered. The psychological aspect of the vision in this chapter comes after the revelation of the cosmological and theological aspects. Thus the stage is set for a more thoroughgoing self-analysis by Arjuna so that he can determine his *svadharma* with absolute certitude.

TRANSLATION

अर्जुन उवाच –

1. मदनुग्रहाय परमं गुह्यमध्यात्मसञ्ज्ञितम् ।
यत्त्वयोक्तं वचस्तेन मोहोऽयं विगतो मम ॥

arjuna uvāca –

madanugrahāya paramaṁ guhyam adhyātmasaṁjñitam ।
yat tvayo 'ktaṁ vacas tena moho 'yaṁ vigato mama ॥

arjuna uvāca: Arjuna said; *tena vacaḥ*: by that speech; *yat uktaṁ*: which has been spoken; *tvayā*: by You; *mad anugrahāya*: out of favour for me; *paramaṁ guhyam*: the highest secrect; *adhyātma saṁjñitam*: known as pertaining to the Self; *ayaṁ mama mohaḥ*: this, my confusion; *vigataḥ*: has vanished.

Arjuna said:

By that speech which has been spoken by You out of favour for me – the highest secret known as pertaining to the Self – this, my confusion, has vanished.

2. भवाप्ययौ हि भूतानां श्रुतौ विस्तरशो मया ।
त्वत्तः कमलपत्राक्ष माहात्म्यमपि चाव्ययम् ॥

bhavāpyayau hi bhūtānāṁ śrutau vistaraśo mayā ।
tvattaḥ kamalapatrākṣa māhātmyam api cā 'vyayam ॥

bhavāpyayau hi: the origin and dissolution indeed; *bhūtānāṁ*: of beings; *śrutau mayā*: have been heard by me; *vistaraśaḥ tvattaḥ*: in elaboration from You; *kamala patra akṣa*: Oh Lotus-petal Eyed (Kṛṣṇa); *api ca*: as also; *avyayam māhātmyam*: (Your) unexpended greatness.

The origin and dissolution of beings have been heard by me in elaboration from You, Oh Lotus-petal Eyed! as also Your unexpended greatness.

3. एवमेतद्यथात्थ त्वमात्मानं परमेश्वर ।
द्रष्टुमिच्छामि ते रूपमैश्वरं पुरुषोत्तम ॥

evam etad yathā 'ttha tvam ātmānaṁ parameśvara ।
draṣṭum icchāmi te rūpam aiśvaraṁ puruṣottama ॥

evam etat: so it (is); *yathā tvam āttha*: as You have said; *ātmānaṁ*: Yourself; *parameśvara*: Kṛṣṇa; *icchāmi draṣṭum*: (I) desire to see; *te aiśvaraṁ rūpam*: Your divine Form; *puruṣrottama*: Oh Kṛṣṇa.

So it is as You have said Yourself, Supreme Lord; I desire to see Your divine Form, Oh Supreme Person!

4. मन्यसे यदि तच्छक्यं मया द्रष्टुमिति प्रभो ।
योगेश्वर ततो मे त्वं दर्शयात्मानमव्ययम् ॥

manyase yadi tac chakyaṁ mayā draṣṭum iti prabho ।
yogeśvara tato me tvaṁ darśayā 'tmānam avyayam ॥

yadi manyase: if You think; *tat śakyaṁ*: that (it is) possible; *mayā draṣṭum iti*: for me to see thus; *prabho*: Oh Kṛṣṇa; *tataḥ tvaṁ*: then (do) You; *yogeśvara*: Oh Kṛṣṇa; *darśaya me*: show to me; *ātmānam avyayam*: Yourself, never-decreasing.

If You think that it is possible for me to see it, Oh Powerful One! then do You, Oh Master of Yoga! show me Your never-decreasing Self.

श्रीभगवानुवाच –
5. पश्य मे पार्थ रूपाणि शतशोऽथ सहस्रशः ।
नानाविधानि दिव्यानि नानावर्णाकृतीनि च ॥

śrībhagavān uvaca –

paśya me pārtha rūpāṇi śataśo 'tha sahasraśaḥ ।
nānāvidhāni divyāni nānāvarṇākṛtīni ca ॥

śrībhagavān uvāca: Kṛṣṇa said; *paśya*: behold; *pārtha*: Oh Arjuna; *me rūpāṇi*: My forms; *śataśaḥ atha sahasraśaḥ*: by hundreds and thousands; *nānā vidhāni*: various in kind; *divyāni*: divine; *ca nānā varṇa ākṛtīni*: and of varied colours and shapes.

Kṛṣṇa said:

Behold, Oh Pārtha! My forms, by hundreds and thousands, various in kind, divine, and of varied colours and shapes.

6. पश्यादित्यान्वसून्रुद्रानश्विनौ मरुतस्तथा ।
बहून्यदृष्टपूर्वाणि पश्याश्चर्याणि भारत ॥

paśyā 'dityān vasūn rudrān aśvinau marutas tathā ।
bahūny adṛṣṭapūrvāṇi paśyā 'ścaryāṇi bhārata ॥

paśyā ādityān: behold the Ādityas; *vasūn rudrān*: the Vasus, the Rudras; *aśvinau*: the two Aśvins; *tathā*: (and) also; *marutaḥ*: the Maruts; *paśya bahūni āścaryāṇi*: behold many marvels; *adṛṣṭa pūrvāṇi*: never seen before; *bhārata*: Oh Arjuna.

Behold the Ādityas, the Vasus, the Rudras, the two Aśvins, and also the Maruts; behold many marvels never seen before, Oh Bhārata!

7. इहैकस्थं जगत्कृत्स्नं पश्याद्य सचराचरम् ।
मम देहे गुडाकेश यच्चान्यद्द्रष्टुमिच्छसि ॥

ihai 'kasthaṁ jagat kṛtsnaṁ paśyā 'dya sacarācaram ।
mama dehe guḍākeśa yac cā 'nyad draṣṭum icchasi ॥

adya paśya iha: now behold here; *mama dehe*: in My body; *guḍākeśa*: Oh Arjuna; *kṛtsnaṁ jagat*: the whole world; *sacarācaram*: with the dynamic and the static; *ekasthaṁ*: unitively established; *ca yat anyat*: and whatever else; *icchasi draṣṭum*: (you) desire to see.

Now behold here in My body, Oh Guḍākeśa! the whole world, including the static and the dynamic, unitively established, and whatever else you desire to see.

8. न तु मां शक्यसे द्रष्टुमनेनैव स्वचक्षुषा ।
दिव्यं ददामि ते चक्षुः पश्य मे योगमैश्वरम् ॥

na tu māṁ śakyase draṣṭum anenai 'va svacakṣuṣā ।
divyaṁ dadāmi te cakṣuḥ paśya me yogam aiśvaram ॥

tu na śakyase: but (if) you are unable; *draṣṭum māṁ eva*: to see Me indeed; *anena svacakṣuṣā*: with this (your) own (human) eye; *dadāmi te*: (I) give to you; *divyam cakṣuḥ*: a divine eye; *paśya me*: behold My; *aiśvaram yogam*: sovereign Yoga.

But if you are unable to see Me with this your (human) eye, I give you a divine eye: behold My sovereign Yoga.

सञ्जय उवाच –

9. एवमुक्त्वा ततो राजन्महायोगेश्वरो हरिः ।
दर्शयामास पार्थाय परमं रूपमैश्वरम् ॥

sañjaya uvāca –

evam uktvā tato rājan mahāyogeśvaro hariḥ ।
darśayām āsa pārthāya paramaṁ rūpam aiśvaram ॥

sañjaya uvāca: Sañjaya said; *evam uktvā*: thus having spoken; *tataḥ*: then; *rājan*: Oh King (Dhṛtarāṣṭra); *hariḥ*: Kṛṣṇa; *mahā yogeśvaraḥ*: the great Master of Yoga; *darśayām āsa*: showed; *pārthāya*: to Arjuna; *paramaṁ*: the supreme; *aiśvaram rūpam*: Godly Form.

Sañjaya said:

Having thus spoken, then, Oh King! Hari, the great Master of Yoga showed to Pārtha the supreme Godly Form:

10. अनेकवक्त्रनयनमनेकाद्भुतदर्शनम् ।
अनेकदिव्याभरणं दिव्यानेकोद्यतायुधम् ।।

anekavaktranayanam anekādbhutadarśanam ।
anekadivyābharaṇaṁ divyānekodyatāyudham ॥

aneka vaktra nayanam: with many faces and eyes; *aneka adbhuta darśanam*: with many marvellous aspects; *aneka divya ābharaṇaṁ*: with many divine ornaments; *divya aneka udyata āyudham*: with many divine weapons held aloft.

With many faces and eyes, with many marvellous aspects, with many divine ornaments, with many divine weapons held aloft,

11. दिव्यमाल्याम्बरधरं दिव्यगन्धानुलेपनम् ।
सर्वाश्चर्यमयं देवमनन्तं विश्वतोमुखम् ।।

divyamālyāmbaradharaṁ divyagandhānulepanam ।
sarvāścaryamayaṁ devam anantaṁ viśvatomukham ।

divya mālya ambara dharaṁ: wearing divine garlands and vestures; *divya gandha anulepanam*: anointed with divine perfumes and unguents; *devam*: a God; *sarva āścarya mayam*: made of all marvels; *anantaṁ*: without end; *viśvatomukham*: universally-facing.

wearing divine garlands and vestures, anointed with divine perfumes and unguents, a God representing sheer marvel, without end, universally-facing.

12. दिवि सूर्यसहस्रस्य भवेद्युगपदुत्थिता ।
यदि भाः सदृशी सा स्याद्भासस्तस्य महात्मनः ।।

divi sūryasahasrasya bhaved yugapad utthitā ।
yadi bhāḥ sadṛśī sā syād bhāsas tasya mahātmanaḥ ॥

yadi bhāḥ: if the splendour; *sahasrasya sūrya*: of a thousand suns;

bhavet utthitā yugapat: were to rise together; *divi*: in the sky; *sā syāt sadṛśī*: that might resemble; *bhāsaḥ*: the splendour; *tasya mahātmanaḥ*: of that great Soul.

13. तत्रैकस्थं जगत्कृत्स्नं प्रविभक्तमनेकधा ।
अपश्यद्देवदेवस्य शरीरे पाण्डवस्तदा ।।

tatrai 'kasthaṁ jagat kṛtsnaṁ pravibhaktam anekadhā ।
apaśyad devadevasya śarīre pāṇḍavas tadā ॥

tatra: there; *pāṇḍavaḥ*: Arjuna; *tadā apaśyat*: then beheld; *kṛtsnaṁ jagat*: the whole world; *pravibhaktam anekadhā*: divided into many kinds; *ekasthaṁ*: unitively established; *śarīre*: in the body; *deva devasya*: of the God of gods.

If the splendour of a thousand suns were to rise together in the sky, that might resemble the splendour of that great Soul.

There the Pāṇḍava then beheld the whole world, divided into many kinds, unitively established in the body of the God of gods.

14. ततः स विस्मयाविष्टो हृष्टरोमा धनञ्जयः ।
प्रणम्य शिरसा देवं कृताञ्जलिरभाषत ।।

tataḥ sa vismayāviṣṭo hṛṣṭaromā dhanañjayaḥ ।
praṇamya śirasā devaṁ kṛtāñjalir abhāṣata ॥

tataḥ: then he; *dhanañjayaḥ*: Arjuna; *vismaya āviṣṭaḥ*: struck with amazement; *hṛṣṭaromā*: with his hair standing on end; *praṇamya śirasā*: reverently bowing his head; *devaṁ*: to the God; *kṛtāñjaliḥ*: (and) with joined palms; *abhāṣata*: spoke.

Then he, Dhanañjaya, struck with amazement, with his hair standing on end, reverently bowing his head to the God, and with joined palms, spoke:

अर्जुन उवाच –
15. पश्यामि देवांस्तव देव देहे सर्वांस्तथा भूतविशेषसङ्घान् ।
ब्रह्माणमीशं कमलासनस्थमृषींश्च सर्वानुरगांश्च दिव्यान् ।।

arjuna uvāca –
paśyāmi devāṁs tava deva dehe sarvāṁs tathā bhūtaviśeṣasaṁghān ।
brahmāṇam īśaṁ kamalāsanastham ṛṣīṁś ca sarvān uragāṁś ca divyān ॥

arjuna uvāca: Arjuna said; *paśyāmi devān*: (I) see the gods; *deva*: Oh God; *tava dehe*: in Your body; *tathā sarvān*: and all; *bhūta viśeṣa saṁghān*: specific groups of beings; *brahmāṇam*: Brahmā; *īśaṁ*: the Lord; *kamala āsana sthaṁ*: established on his lotus-seat; *ca sarvān ṛṣīn*: and all seers; *ca divyān uragān*: and divine serpents.

Arjuna said:

I see the gods, Oh God! in Your body, and all specific groups of beings, Brahmā, the Lord, established on his lotus-seat, and all seers and divine serpents.

16. अनेकबाहूदरवक्त्रनेत्रं पश्यामि त्वां सर्वतोऽनन्तरूपम् ।
नान्तं न मध्यं न पुनस्तवादिं पश्यामि विश्वेश्वर विश्वरूप ।।

anekabāhūdaravaktranetraṁ paśyāmi tvāṁ sarvato 'nantarūpam ।
nā 'ntaṁ na madhyaṁ na punas tavā 'diṁ paśyāmi viśveśvara viśvarūpa ॥

paśyāmi tvām: (I) see You; *sarvataḥ*: on every side; *ananta rūpam*: of boundless form; *aneka bāhu udara vaktra netraṁ*: with multitudinous arms, stomachs, faces and eyes; *na antaṁ*: neither (Your) end; *na madhyaṁ*: nor (Your) middle; *na punaḥ*: nor again; *tava ādiṁ*: Your beginning; *paśyāmi*: (do I) see; *viśva īśvara*: O Lord of the Universe! *viśva rūpa*: Oh Universal Form.

I see You on every side, of boundless form, with multitudinous arms, stomachs, faces and eyes; neither Your end, nor Your middle, nor Your beginning do I see, Oh Lord of the Universe, Oh Universal Form!

17. किरीटिनं गदिनं चक्रिणं च तेजोराशिं सर्वतो दीप्तिमन्तम् ।
पश्यामि त्वां दुर्निरीक्ष्यं समन्ताद्दीप्तानलार्कद्युतिमप्रमेयम् ।।

kirīṭinaṁ gadinaṁ cakriṇaṁ ca tejorāśiṁ sarvato dīptimantam ।
paśyāmi tvāṁ durnirīkṣyaṁ samantād dīptānalārkadyutim aprameyam ॥

paśyāmi tvām: (I) behold You; *kirīṭinaṁ*: with diadem; *gadinaṁ ca cakriṇaṁ*: mace and discus; *dīptimantam sarvataḥ*: glowing everywhere; *tejo rāśiṁ*: as a mass of light; *durnirīkṣyaṁ*: hard to look at; *samantāt*: everywhere; *dīpta dyutim anala arka*: blazing (with the) brilliance (of) fire and sun; *aprameyam*: immeasurable.

I behold You with diadem, mace, and discus, glowing everywhere as a mass of light, hard to look at, everywhere blazing like fire and sun, immeasurable.

18. त्वमक्षरं परमं वेदितव्यं त्वमस्य विश्वस्य परं निधानम् ।
त्वमव्ययः शाश्वतधर्मगोप्ता सनातनस्त्वं पुरुषो मतो मे ।।

tvam akṣaraṁ paramaṁ veditavyaṁ tvam asya viśvasya paraṁ nidhānam ।
tvam avyayaḥ śāśvatadharmagoptā sanātanas tvaṁ puruṣu mato me ॥

tvam akṣaraṁ: You (are) the Imperishable; *paramaṁ*: the Supreme; *veditavyaṁ*: (that is) to be known; *tvam paraṁ*: You (are) the ultimate; *nidhānam asya viśvasya*: Basis of this universe; *tvam avyayaḥ*: You (are) the unexpended; *śāśvata goptā dharma*: (and) everlasting Custodian (of natural) law; *tvaṁ sanātanaḥ puruṣaḥ*: You (are) the immemorial Person; *mataḥ me*: believed of me.

You are the Imperishable, the Supreme that is to be known; You are the ultimate Basis of this universe; You are the unexpended and everlasting Custodian of (natural) law; You are the immemorial Person, I believe.

19. अनादिमध्यान्तमनन्तवीर्यमनन्तबाहुं शशिसूर्यनेत्रम् ।
पश्यामि त्वां दीप्तहुताशवक्त्रं स्वतेजसा विश्वमिदं तपन्तम् ॥

anādimadhyāntam anantavīryam anantabāhuṁ śaśīsūryanetram ।
paśyāmi tvāṁ dīptahutāśavaktraṁ svatejasā viśvam idaṁ tapantam ॥

paśyāmi tvām: (I) see You; *anādī madhya antam*: without beginning, middle, (or) end; *ananta vīryam*: of never-ending force; *ananta bāhuṁ*: of numberless arms; *śaśī sūrya netram*: having moon and sun for eyes; *dīpta hutāśa vaktram*: (Your) face like a lit fire (of sacrifice); *tapantam*: burning; *idaṁ viśvam*: this universe; *svatejasā*: with (Your) own radiance.

I see You without beginning, middle or end, of never-ending force, of numberless arms, having moon and sun for eyes, Your face like a lit fire of sacrifice burning this universe with Your own radiance.

20. द्यावापृथिव्योरिदमन्तरं हि व्याप्तं त्वयैकेन दिशश्च सर्वाः ।
दृष्ट्वाद्भुतं रूपमुग्रं तवेदं लोकत्रयं प्रव्यथितं महात्मन् ॥

dyāvāpṛthivyor idam antaraṁ hi vyāptaṁ tvayai 'kena diśaś ca sarvāḥ ।
dṛṣṭvā 'dbhutaṁ rūpam ugraṁ tave 'daṁ lokatrayaṁ pravyathitaṁ mahātman ॥

dyāvā pṛthivyoḥ: of heaven (and) earth; *idam antaraṁ hi*: (and) this intermediate (realm) indeed; *vyāptaṁ tvayā ekena*: (is) pervaded by You alone; *ca sarvāḥ diśaḥ*: (as) also all the quarters (directions); *dṛṣṭvā*: having seen; *idaṁ adbhutaṁ*: this wonderful; *ugraṁ rūpam tava*: terrible form of Yours; *loka trayaṁ*: the three worlds; *prāvyathitaṁ*: (are) in distress; *mahātman*: Oh Kṛṣṇa.

The space between heaven, earth, and the intermediate realm is pervaded by You alone, as also the quarters; having seen this wonderful, terrible form of Yours, the three worlds are in distress, Oh Great Self!

21. अमी हि त्वां सुरसङ्घा विशन्ति केचिद्भीताः प्राञ्जलयो गृणन्ति ।
स्वस्तीत्युक्त्वा महर्षिसिद्धसङ्घा स्तुवन्ति त्वां स्तुतिभिः पुष्कलाभिः ॥

amī hi tvāṁ surasaṁghā viśanti kecid bhītāḥ prāñjalayo gṛṇanti ।
svastī 'ty uktvā maharṣisiddhasaṁghāḥ stuvanti tvāṁ stutibhiḥ puṣkalābhiḥ ॥

amī: those; *sura saṁghāḥ*: hosts of the Suras (gods); *viśanti tvāṁ hi*: enter You indeed; *kecit bhītāḥ*: some in fear (of You); *gṛṇanti prāñjalayaḥ*: mutter with joined palms; *maharṣi siddha saṁghāḥ*: bands of great *ṛṣi*s (seer-sages) and Perfected Ones (*siddhas*); *uktvā iti*: crying thus; *svasti*: May it be well; *stuvanti tvāṁ*: praise You; *puṣkalābhiḥ stutibhiḥ*: with resounding hymns.

22. रुद्रादित्या वसवो ये च साध्या विश्वेऽश्विनौ मरुतश्चोष्मपाश्च ।
गन्धर्वयक्षासुरसिद्धसङ्घा वीक्षन्ते त्वां विस्मिताश्चैव सर्वे ।।

rudrādityā vasavo ye ca sādhyā viśve 'śinau marutaś co 'ṣmapāś ca ।
gandharvayakṣāsurasiddhasaṁghā vīkṣante tvāṁ vismitāś cai 'va sarve ॥

ye rudrāḥ ādityāḥ: these Rudras, Ādityas; *vasavaḥ ca sādhyāḥ*: Vasus and Sādhyas; *viśve ca aśvinau*: Viśvas and the two Aśvins; *marutaḥ ca ūṣmapāḥ*: Maruts and Ūsmapas; *ca eva gandharva yakṣa asura siddha saṁghāḥ*: and even hosts of *gandharvas*, *yakṣa*s, *asura*s, (and) *siddha*s; *sarve vīkṣante tvām*: all gaze at You; *vismitāḥ*: wonderstruck.

Into You enter those hosts of the *sura*s, some in fear of You mutter with joined palms, bands of great *ṛṣi*s and Perfected Ones hail You with the cry "May it be well!" and praise You with resounding hymns.

The Rudras, Ādityas, Vasus and Sādhyas, Viśvas and the two Aśvins, Maruts and Ūṣmapas, hosts of *gandharvas*, *yakṣas*, *asura*s and *siddha*s, all gaze at You, wonderstruck.

23. रूपं महत्ते बहुवक्त्रनेत्रं महाबाहो बहुबाहूरुपादम् ।
बहूदरं बहुदंष्ट्राकरालं दृष्ट्वा लोकाः प्रव्यथितास्तथाहम् ।।

rūpaṁ mahat te bahuvaktranetraṁ mahābāho bahubāhūrupādam ।
bahūdaram bahudaṁṣṭrākarālaṁ dṛṣṭvā lokāḥ pravyathitās tathā 'ham ॥

dṛṣṭvā: seeing; *te mahat rūpaṁ*: Your great form; *bahu vaktra netram*: with many faces and eyes; *mahābāho*: Oh Kṛṣṇa; *bahu bāhu ūru pādam*: of many arms, thighs, and feet; *bahu udaram*: with many stomachs; *bahu daṁṣṭrā karālam*: with many terrible teeth; *lokāḥ pravyathitāḥ*: the worlds are distressed; *tathā aham*: (and) so (am) I.

Seeing Your great form, with many faces and eyes, Oh Mighty-Armed One! of many arms, thighs, and feet, with many stomachs, with many terrible teeth, the worlds are distressed, as also myself.

24. नभःस्पृशं दीप्तमनेकवर्णं व्यात्ताननं दीप्तविशालनेत्रम् ।
दृष्ट्वा हि त्वां प्रव्यथितान्तरात्मा धृतिं न विन्दामि शमं च विष्णो ।।

nabhaḥspṛśaṁ dīptam anekavarṇaṁ vyāttānanaṁ dīptaviśālanetram ।
dṛṣṭvā hi tvāṁ pravyathitāntarātmā dhṛtiṁ na vindāmi śamaṁ ca viṣṇo ॥

dṛṣṭvā tvāṁ: on seeing You; *nabhaḥ spṛśaṁ*: touching the sky; *dīptam aneka varṇaṁ*: shining in many a colour; *vyāttānanaṁ*: with (many) mouths wide open; *dīpta viśāla netram*: with large fiery eyes; *antarātmā hi pravyathita*: (my) inmost self (is) indeed intensely distressed; *vindāmi*: (I) find; *na dhṛtiṁ ca śamaṁ*: neither courage nor control; *viṣṇo*: Oh Viṣṇu (Kṛṣṇa).

25. दंष्ट्राकरालानि च ते मुखानि दृष्ट्वैव कालानलसन्निभानि ।
दिशो न जाने न लभे च शर्म प्रसीद देवेश जगन्निवास ।।

daṁṣṭrākarālāni ca te mukhāni dṛṣṭvai 'va kālānalasaṁnibhāni ।
diśo na jāne na labhe ca śarma prasīda deveśa jagannivāsā ॥

ca dṛṣṭvā eva: and having seen indeed; *te mukhāni*: Your mouths; *daṁṣṭrā karālāni*: fearful with teeth; *saṁnibhāni kāla anala*: like time's (devouring) flames; *na jāne*: (I do) not know; *diśaḥ*: (my) spatial bearings; *ca labhe na śarma*: and find no joy; *prasīda*: be gracious; *deveśa*: Oh Kṛṣṇa; *jagannivāsa*: Container of the world.

On seeing You touching the sky, shining in many a colour, with mouths wide open, with large fiery eyes, my inmost self intensely distressed, I find neither courage nor control, Oh All-pervading One!

Having seen Your mouths fearful with teeth, like time's devouring flames, I lose my spatial bearings and find no joy; be gracious, Oh Lord of gods, Container of the world!

26. अमी च त्वां धृतराष्ट्रस्य पुत्राः सर्वे सहैवावनिपालसङ्घैः ।
भीष्मो द्रोणः सूतपुत्रस्तथासौ सहास्मदीयैरपि योधमुख्यैः ।।

amī ca tvāṁ dhṛtarāṣṭrasya putrāḥ sarve sahai 'vā 'vanipālasaṁghaiḥ ।
bhīṣmo droṇaḥ sūtaputras tathā 'sau sahā 'smadīyair api yodhamukhyaiḥ ॥

ca sarve amī: all these; *tvāṁ*: to You; *putrāḥ dhṛtarāṣṭrasya*: sons of Dhṛtarāṣṭra; *saha eva*: together indeed; *saṁghaiḥ avanipāla*: with hosts of rulers; *bhīṣmaḥ droṇaḥ*: Bhīṣma, Droṇa; *tathā asau*: and that; *sūta putraḥ*: son of a charioteer (Karṇa); *saha api asmadīyaiḥ yodha mukhyaiḥ*: also with our warrior chiefs.

27. वक्त्राणि ते त्वरमाणा विशन्ति दंष्ट्राकरालानि भयानकानि ।
केचिद्विलग्ना दशनान्तरेषु सन्दृश्यन्ते चूर्णितैरुत्तमाङ्गैः ।।

vaktrāṇi te tvaramāṇā viśanti daṁṣṭrākarālāni bhayānakāni ।
kecid vilagnā daśanāntareṣu saṁdṛśyante cūrṇitair uttamāṅgaiḥ ॥

tvaramāṇāḥ: hurriedly enter; *te bhayānakāni vaktrāṇi*: Your fearful mouths; *daṁṣṭrā karālāni*: terrible with teeth; *kecit saṁdṛśyante*: some are found; *vilagnāḥ*: sticking; *antareṣu daśana*: in (the gaps) between the teeth; *uttama aṅgaiḥ*: with (their) heads; *cūrṇitaiḥ*: crushed (to powder).

All these sons of Dhṛtarāṣṭra, with hosts of rulers, Bhīṣma, Droṇa, and that son of a charioteer, with our warrior chiefs,

are rushing into Your fearful mouths, terrible with teeth; some are found sticking in the gaps between the teeth with their heads crushed to powder.

28. यथा नदीनां बहवोऽम्बुवेगाः समुद्रमेवाभिमुखा द्रवन्ति ।
तथा तवामी नरलोकवीरा विशन्ति वक्त्राण्यभिविज्वलन्ति ॥

yathā nadīnāṁ bahavo 'mbuvegāḥ samudram evā 'bhimukhā dravanti ।
tathā tavā 'mī naralokavīrā viśanti vaktrāṇy abhivijvalanti ॥

yathā eva: as indeed; *bahavaḥ ambuvegāḥ nadināṁ*: many (rushing) torrents of rivers; *dravanti abhimukhāḥ samudram*: race toward the ocean; *tathā amī*: so these; *naraloka vīrāḥ*: heroes in the world of men; *viśanti tava*: enter Your; *abhivijvalanti vaktrāṇi*: flaming mouths.

As many rushing torrents of rivers race toward the ocean, so do these heroes in the world of men enter Your flaming mouths.

29. यथा प्रदीप्तं ज्वलनं पतङ्गा विशन्ति नाशाय समृद्धवेगाः ।
तथैव नाशाय विशन्ति लोकास्तवापि वक्त्राणि समृद्धवेगाः ॥

yathā pradīptaṁ jvalanaṁ pataṅgā viśanti nāśāya samṛddhavegāḥ ।
tathai 'va nāśāya viśanti lokās tavā 'pi vaktrāṇi samṛddhavegāḥ ॥

yathā pataṅgāḥ: as moths; *samṛddha vegāḥ*: with great speed; *viśanti*: enter; *pradīptaṁ jvalanaṁ*: a blazing fire; *nāśāya*: to be destroyed; *tathā eva*: so indeed; *lokāḥ api*: (do these) worlds also; *samṛddha vegāḥ*: with great speed; *viśanti*: enter; *tava vaktrāṇi*: Your mouths; *nāśāya*: unto (their) destruction.

As moths speed into a blazing fire to be destroyed, just so do these worlds also speed into Your mouths unto their destruction.

30. लेलिह्यसे ग्रसमानः समन्ताल्लोकान्समग्रान्वदनैर्ज्वलद्भिः ।
तेजोभिरापूर्य जगत्समग्रं भासस्तवोग्राः प्रतपन्ति विष्णो ॥

lelihyase grasamānaḥ samantāl lokān samagrān vadanair jvaladbhiḥ ।
tejobhir āpūrya jagat samagraṁ bhāsas tavo 'grāḥ pratapanti viṣṇo ॥

lelihyase: (You) lick up; *samagrān lokān*: all worlds; *grasamānaḥ*: devouring; *samantāt*: on every side; *jvaladbhiḥ vadanaiḥ*: with (Your) flaming mouths; *āpūrya samagraṁ jagat*: filling the whole world;

tejobhiḥ: with glory; *tava ugrāḥ bhāsaḥ*: Your fierce rays; *pratapanti*: are blazing forth; *viṣṇo*: Oh Viṣṇu (Kṛṣṇa).

You lick up all worlds, devouring on every side with Your flaming mouths, filling the whole world with glory; Your fierce rays are blazing forth, Oh All-pervading One!

31. आख्याहि मे को भवानुग्ररूपो नमोऽस्तु ते देववर प्रसीद ।
विज्ञातुमिच्छामि भवन्तमाद्यं न हि प्रजानामि तव प्रवृत्तिम् ॥

ākhyāhi me ko bhavān ugrarūpo namo 'stu te devavara prasīda ।
vijñātum icchāmi bhavantam ādyaṁ na hi prajānāmi tava pravṛttim ॥

ākhyāhi me: tell to me; *kaḥ bhavān*: who You (are); *ugra rūpaḥ*: (so) fierce in form; *namaḥ astu te*: I bow to You; *devavara*: Oh Kṛṣṇa; *prasīda*: be gracious; *icchāmi vijñātum*: I want to understand; *bhavantam*: You; *ādyam*: Oh Kṛṣṇa; *na hi*: nor indeed; *prajānāmi*: (do) I know; *tava pravṛttim*: Your (positive) continued becoming.

Tell me who You are, so fierce in form; I bow to You, Oh Superior God; be gracious! I want to understand You, Oh Primal One! nor do I know Your positive continued becoming.

श्रीभगवानुवाच –

32. कालोऽस्मि लोकक्षयकृत्प्रवृद्धो लोकान् समाहर्तुमिह प्रवृत्तः ।
ऋतेऽपि त्वां न भविष्यन्ति सर्वे येऽवस्थिताः प्रत्यनीकेषु योधाः ॥

śrībhagavān uvāca –

kālo 'smi lokakṣayakṛt pravṛddho lokān samāhartum iha pravṛttaḥ ।
ṛte 'pi tvāṁ na bhaviṣyanti sarve ye 'vasthitāḥ pratyanīkeṣu yodhāḥ ॥

śrīhagavān uvāca: Kṛṣṇa said; *asmi*: (I) am; *loka kṣaya kṛt*: world destroying; *kālaḥ*: Time; *pravṛddhaḥ*: grown into (hardened) maturity; *pravṛttaḥ iha*: operating here (continuously); *samāhartum lokān*: desolating the worlds; *api ṛte tvāṁ*: even without you; *na sarve*: none; *yodhāḥ ye*: (of) the warriors who; *avasthitaḥ*: (are) standing; *pratyanīkeṣu*: in the opposing armies; *bhaviṣyanti*: shall continue to exist.

33. तस्मात्त्वमुत्तिष्ठ यशो लभस्व जित्वा शत्रून् भुङ्क्ष्व राज्यं समृद्धम् ।
मयैवैते निहताः पूर्वमेव निमित्तमात्रं भव सव्यसाचिन् ॥

tasmāt tvam uttiṣṭha yaśo labhasva jitvā śatrūn bhuṇkṣva rājyaṁ samṛddham ।
mayai 'vai 'te nihatāḥ pūrvam eva nimittamātraṁ bhava savyasācin ॥

tasmāt tvam: therefore (do) you; *uttiṣṭha*: arise; *labhasva yaśaḥ*: (and) gain fame; *jitvā śatrūn*: conquering (your) foes; *bhuṅkṣva rājyaṁ samṛddham*:

enjoy the realm of abundance; *mayā eva*: by Me alone; *ete*: these; *nihatāḥ pūrvam eva*: have been slain already indeed; *bhava nimitta mātraṁ*: be the incidental cause only; *savyasācin*: Oh Arjuna.

34. द्रोणं च भीष्मं च जयद्रथं च कर्णं तथान्यानपि योधवीरान् ।
मया हतांस्त्वं जहि मा व्यथिष्ठा युध्यस्व जेतासि रणे सपत्नान् ।।

droṇaṁ ca bhīṣmaṁ ca jayadrathaṁ ca karṇaṁ tathā 'nyān api yodhavīrān ।
mayā hatāṁs tvaṁ jahi mā vyathiṣṭhā yudhyasva jetāsi raṇe sapatnān ॥

droṇaṁ ca bhīṣmaṁ: Droṇa and Bhīṣma; *ca jayadrathaṁ ca karṇaṁ tathā*: and Jayadratha and Karṇa also; *anyān yodha vīrān api*: other (great) battle-heroes too; *hatān mayā*: are (all) slain by Me; *mā vyathiṣṭhāḥ*: do not be distressed; *jahi yudhyasva*: kill, fight; *tvaṁ jetāsi raṇe*: you shall conquer in battle; *sapatnān*: (your) rival (co-warriors).

Kṛṣṇa said:

I am world-destroying Time, grown into hardened maturity, operating here continuously, desolating the worlds. Even without you, none of the warriors standing in the opposing armies shall continue to exist.

Therefore, arise and gain fame! Conquering your foes, enjoy the realm of abundance. By Me they have already been slain. Be the incidental cause only, Oh Left-handed One!

Droṇa and Bhīṣma, Jayadratha, Karṇa, and other great battle-heroes, are all slain by Me. Do not be distressed. Fight on, you shall conquer in battle your rival co-warriors.

सञ्जय उवाच –

35. एतच्छ्रुत्वा वचनं केशवस्य कृताञ्जलिर्वेपमानः किरीटी ।
नमस्कृत्वा भूय एवाह कृष्णं सगद्गदं भीतभीतः प्रणम्य ।।३५।।

sañjaya uvāca –

etac chrutvā vacanaṁ keśvasya kṛtāñjalir vepamānaḥ kirīṭī ।
namaskṛtvā bhūya evā 'ha kṛṣṇaṁ sagadgadaṁ bhītabhītaḥ praṇamya ॥

sañjaya uvāca: Sañjaya said; *śrutvā*: having heard; *etat vacanaṁ*: that speech; *keśavasya*: of Keśava (Kṛṣṇa); *kirīṭī*: the Diademmed One (Arjuna); *kṛtāñjaliḥ*: with worshipfully joined palms; *vepamānaḥ namaskṛtvā*: trembling, inclining (himself); *bhūyaḥ eva*: again thus; *kṛṣṇam*: to Kṛṣṇa; *sagadgadam*: with (emotional) stuttering; *bhītabhītaḥ*: in sustained fear; *praṇamya*: bowing down; *āha*: spoke.

Sañjaya said:

Having heard that speech of Keśava, the Diademmed One, with worshipfully joined palms, trembling, inclining himself again before Kṛṣṇa, with emotional stuttering, in sustained fear, bowing down, spoke:

अर्जुन उवाच –

36. स्थाने हृषीकेश तव प्रकीर्त्या जगत्प्रहृष्यत्यनुरज्यते च ।
रक्षांसि भीतानि दिशो द्रवन्ति सर्वे नमस्यन्ति च सिद्धसङ्घाः ॥

arjuna uvāca –

sthāne hṛṣikeśa tava prakīrtyā jagat prahṛṣyaty anurajyate ca ।
rakṣāṁsi bhitāni diśo dravanti sarve namasyanti ca siddhasaṁghāḥ ॥

arjuna uvāca: Arjuna said; *hṛṣīkeśa*: Oh Kṛṣṇa; *sthāne*: rightly; *jagat*: the world; *prahṛṣyati ca anurajyate*: rejoices and is delighted; *prakīrtyā tava*: in praising You; *rakṣāṁsi*: demons; *dravanti bhītāni*: fly in fear; *diśaḥ*: to (every) quarter; *ca sarve*: and (that) all; *siddha saṁghāh*: hosts of perfected ones; *namasyanti*: bow (in adoration to You).

Arjuna said:

Oh Hṛṣikeśa, it is but right that the world is delighted in praising You, that demons fly in fear to every quarter, and that all hosts of perfected ones bow in adoration to You.

37. कस्माच्च ते न नमेरन्महात्मन् गरीयसे ब्रह्मणोऽप्यादिकर्त्रे ।
अनन्त देवेश जगन्निवास त्वमक्षरं सदसत्तत्परं यत् ॥

kasmāc ca te na nameran mahātman garīyase brahmaṇo 'py ādikartre ।
ananta deveśa jagannivāsa tvam akṣaraṁ sad asat tatparaṁ yat ॥

ca kasmāt: and why; *na nameran te*: should they not bow to You; *mahātman*: Oh Great Self (Kṛṣṇa); *garīyase*: more venerable; *api brahmaṇaḥ*: even than Brahmā (god of creation); *ādi kartre*: the first maker; *ananta deveśa*: Oh Endless God of gods; *jagannivāsa*: Basis of the Universe; *tvam akṣaraṁ*: You are the Imperishable One; *sat asat*: Existence and Non-Existence; *yat param tat*: (and) what (is) beyond (even) that.

And why should they not bow to You, Oh Great Self! more venerable even than Brahmā, the first maker, Oh Endless God of gods, Basis of the Universe! You are the Imperishable One, Existence and Non-Existence, and what is beyond even that.

38. त्वमादिदेवः पुरुषः पुराणस्त्वमस्य विश्वस्य परं निधानम् ।
वेत्तासि वेद्यं च परं च धाम त्वया ततं विश्वमनन्तरूप ॥

tvam ādidevaḥ puruṣaḥ purāṇas tvam asya viśvasya paraṁ nidhānam ।
vettā 'si vedyaṁ ca paraṁ ca dhāma tvayā tataṁ viśvam anantarūpa ॥

tvam ādi devaḥ: You (are) the first of the gods; *purāṇaḥ puruṣaḥ*: (and) the Ancient Spirit; *tvam paraṁ nidhānam*: You (are) the Supreme Basis; *asya viśvasya*: of this Universe; *asi vettā ca vedyaṁ*: (You) are both the Knower and the Knowable; *paraṁ*: (You are) the (transcendent) Beyond; *ca dhāma*: and the (immanent) Receptacle (here); *viśvam tataṁ tvayā*: the universe is pervaded by You; *ananta rūpa*: Oh One (capable) of Limitless Form.

You are the first of the gods and the Ancient Spirit; You are the Supreme Basis of the Universe; You are both the Knower and the Knowable; You are the (transcendent) Beyond and the (immanent) Receptacle (here); the universe is pervaded by You, Oh One (capable) of Limitless Form!

39. वायुर्यमोऽग्निर्वरुणः शशाङ्कः प्रजापतिस्त्वं प्रपितामहश्च ।
नमो नमस्तेऽस्तु सहस्रकृत्वः पुनश्च भूयोऽपि नमो नमस्ते ।।

vāyur yamo 'gnir varuṇaḥ śaśāṅkaḥ prajāpatis tvaṁ prapitāmahaś ca ।
namo namas te 'stu sahasrakṛtvaḥ punaś ca bhūyo 'pi namo namas te ॥

tvaṁ vāyuḥ: You (are) Vāyu (wind deity); *yamaḥ agniḥ*: Yama (death deity), Agni (fire deity); *varuṇaḥ śaśāṅkaḥ*: Varuṇa (sea deity), Śaśāṅka (lunar deity); *prajāpatiḥ*: Prajāpati (first of progenitors); *ca prapitāmahaḥ*: and the Great-Grandsire; *namaḥ namaḥ*: hail, hail; *te*: to You; *astu sahasra kṛtvaḥ*: may it be a thousand times made; *punar ca bhūyaḥ api*: again and again also; *namaḥ namaḥ te*: hail, hail to You.

You are Vāyu, Yama, Agni, Varuṇa, Śaśāṅka, Prajāpati, and the Great-Grandsire. Hail! Hail to You! A thousand times and again, hail! Hail to You!

40. नमः पुरस्तादथ पृष्ठतस्ते नमोऽस्तु ते सर्वत एव सर्व ।
अनन्तवीर्यामितविक्रमस्त्वं सर्वं समाप्नोषि ततोऽसि सर्वः ।।

namaḥ purastād atha pṛṣṭhatas te namo 'stu te sarvata eva sarva ।
anantavīryāmitavikramas tvaṁ sarvaṁ samāpnoṣi tato 'si sarvaḥ ॥

namaḥ te: prostrations to You; *purastāt atha pṛṣṭhataḥ*: before and after; *namaḥ astu te*: prostrations be to You; *sarvataḥ eva*: on every side also; *sarva*: Oh All; *ananta vīrya*: of endless potency; *amita vikramaḥ*: (and) immeasurable strength; *tvaṁ samāpnoṣi sarvaṁ*: You terminate all; *tataḥ asi sarvaḥ*: then (You) become all.

Prostrations to You before and after; prostrations to You on every side; Oh All, of endless potency and immeasurable strength, You terminate all, then You become all!

41. सखेति मत्वा प्रसभं यदुक्तं हे कृष्ण हे यादव हे सखेति ।
अजानता महिमानं तवेदं मया प्रमादात्प्रणयेन वापि ॥

sakhe 'ti matvā prasabhaṁ yad uktaṁ he kṛṣṇa he yādava he sakhe 'ti ।
ajānatā mahimānaṁ tave 'daṁ mayā pramādāt praṇayena vā 'pi ॥

yat mayā: whatever by me; *uktaṁ*: (was) said; *prasabhaṁ*: rashly; *pramādāt*: from carelessness; *vā api praṇayena*: or even fondness; *iti*: thus; *he kṛṣṇa*: Oh Kṛṣṇa; *he yādava he sakhe*: Oh Yādava, Oh Comrade; *matvā sakhā iti*: thinking of (You as) an intimate thus; *ajānatā*: (and) ignorant; *idaṁ tava mahimānaṁ*: (of) this Your greatness.

42. यच्चावहासार्थमसत्कृतोऽसि विहारशय्यासनभोजनेषु ।
एकोऽथवाप्यच्युत तत्समक्षं तत्क्षामये त्वामहमप्रमेयम् ॥

yac cā 'vahāsārtham asatkṛto 'si vihāraśayyāsanabhojaneṣu ।
eko 'thavā 'py acyuta tatsamakṣaṁ tat kṣāmaye tvām aham aprameyam ॥

ca yat avahāsa artham: and (for) whatever jesting; *asatkṛtaḥ*: irreverence; *asi vihāra śayyā āsana bhojaneṣu*: (I may have shown) to You, (whether) at play, reposing, or seated, or at meals; *ekaḥ*: alone; *athavā api*: or also; *tat samakṣaṁ*: before the eyes; *tat aham kṣāmaye tvām*: that I ask you to forgive; *acyuta*: Oh Kṛṣṇa; *aprameyam*: Oh Unpredicable One.

Whatever I have said rashly from carelessness, or fondness, addressing You as "Oh Kṛṣṇa, Oh Yādava, Oh Comrade", thinking of You as an intimate and ignorant of this Your greatness,

and for whatever jesting irreverence I may have shown You, whether at play, reposing, or seated, or at meals, either when remaining by myself, or when You were present, That I ask you, Oh Acyuta, to forgive, Oh Unpredicable One!

43. पितासि लोकस्य चराचरस्य त्वमस्य पूज्यश्च गुरुर्गरीयान् ।
न त्वत्समोऽस्त्यभ्यधिकः कुतोऽन्यो लोकत्रयेऽप्यप्रतिमप्रभाव ॥

pitā 'si lokasya carācarasya tvam asya pūjyaś ca gurur garīyān ।
na tvatsamo 'sty abhyadhikaḥ kuto 'nyo lokatraye 'py apratimaprabhāva ॥

asi pitā lokasya: (You) are the Father of the world; *cara acarasya*: of the moving and unmoving; *tvam pūjyaḥ*: You (are) to be reverenced; *asya*: of this (world); *ca garīyān guruḥ*: and (are) the supreme Guru; *na asti tvatsamaḥ*: none is Your equal; *kutaḥ*: how (then could there be); *anyaḥ abhyadhikaḥ*: another greater (than You); *api loka traye*: even in the three worlds; *apratima prabhāva*: Oh One of Incomparable Greatness.

You are the Father of the world, of the moving and unmoving; You are to be reverenced by this world, and are the supreme Guru; none is Your equal; how then could there be one greater than You, even in the three worlds, Oh One of Incomparable Greatness!

44. तस्मात्प्रणम्य प्रणिधाय कायं प्रसादये त्वामहमीशमीड्यम् ।
पितेव पुत्रस्य सखेव सख्युः प्रियः प्रियायार्हसि देव सोढुम् ॥

tasmāt praṇamya praṇidhāya kāyaṁ prasādaye tvām aham īśam īḍyam ।
pite 'va putrasya sakhe 'va sakhyuḥ priyaḥ priyāyā 'rhasi deva soḍhum ॥

tasmāt: therefore; *praṇamya*: bowing down; *praṇidhāya kāyaṁ*: (and) prostrating my body; *aham prasādaye tvām*: I seek grace (From) You; *īḍyam īśam*: Oh Adorable Lord; *arhasi deva*: (it is but proper that) You should, Oh God; *soḍhum*: bear with (me); *iva pitā putrasya*: as father to son; *iva sakhā sakhyuḥ*: as friend to friend; *priyaḥ priyāyāḥ*: as lover to beloved.

Therefore bowing down and prostrating my body, I seek Your grace, Oh Adorable Lord! (it is but proper that) You, Oh God! should bear with me, as father to son, as friend to friend, as lover to beloved.

45. अदृष्टपूर्वं हृषितोऽस्मि दृष्ट्वा भयेन च प्रव्यथितं मनो मे ।
तदेव मे दर्शय देवरूपं प्रसीद देवेश जगन्निवास ॥

adṛṣṭapūrvaṁ hṛṣito 'smi dṛṣṭvā bhayena ca pravyathitaṁ mano me ।
tad eva me darśaya deva rūpaṁ prasīda deveśa jagannivāsa ॥

asmi hṛṣitaḥ: (I) am glad; *dṛṣṭvā*: having seen; *adṛṣṭapūrvaṁ*: what has never been seen (by anyone) before; *ca me manaḥ*: and my mind; *pravyathitaṁ bhayena*: (is) troubled with fear; *deva prasīda*: Oh God be pleased; *darśaya me*: to show to me; *tat eva rūpaṁ*: that very form; *deveśa*: Oh God of gods; *jagannivāsa*: Oh Abode of the Universe.

46. किरीटिनं गदिनं चक्रहस्तमिच्छामि त्वां द्रष्टुमहं तथैव ।
तेनैव रूपेण चतुर्भुजेन सहस्रबाहो भव विश्वमूर्ते ॥

kirīṭinaṁ gadinaṁ cakrahastam icchāmi tvāṁ draṣṭum ahaṁ tathai 'va ।
tenai 'va rūpeṇa caturbhujena sahasrabāho bhava viśvamūrte ॥

aham icchāmi draṣṭum tvāṁ: I want to see You; *tathā eva*: even so; *kirīṭinaṁ*: diademed; *gadinaṁ cakra hastam*: with mace (and) discus in (Your) hand; *bhava tena eva*: assume that very; *rūpeṇa caturbhujena*: form with four Arms; *sahasra bāho*: Oh Thousand-Armed; *viśva mūrte*: Oh One of Universal Form.

I am glad having seen what has never been seen by anyone before, and my mind is troubled with fear; Oh God! be pleased to show me that very form, Oh God of gods, Oh Abode of the Universe!

I want to see You even so, diademed, with mace and discus in Your hand; assume that very form with four arms, Oh Thousand-Armed, Oh One of Universal Form!

47. श्रीभगवानुवाच –
मया प्रसन्नेन तवार्जुनेदं रूपं परं दर्शितमात्मयोगात् ।
तेजोमयं विश्वमनन्तमाद्यं यन्मे त्वदन्येन न दृष्टपूर्वम् ।।

śrībhagavān uvāca –

mayā prasannena tavā 'rjune 'daṁ rūpaṁ paraṁ darśitam ātmayogāt ।
tejomayaṁ viśvam anantam ādyaṁ yan me tvadanyena na dṛṣṭapūrvam ॥

śrībhagavān uvāca: Kṛṣṇa said; *mayā prasannena tava*: by My favour to you; *arjuna*: Oh Arjuna; *idaṁ paraṁ rūpaṁ me*: this supreme form of mine; *darśitam*: has been shown; *ātma yogāt*: from the *yoga* pertaining to the Self; *tejomayaṁ*: made up of light; *viśvam anantam ādyaṁ*: universal, endless, primal; *yat na dṛṣta pūrvam*: which (was) never seen before; *anyena*: by any other; *tvat*: than yourself.

Kṛṣṇa said:

By My favour, Oh Arjuna! this supreme form has been shown, by the *yoga* pertaining to the Self, made up of light, universal, endless, primal, never before seen by any other than yourself.

48. न वेदयज्ञाध्ययनैर्न दानैर्न च क्रियाभिर्न तपोभिरुग्रैः ।
एवंरूपः शक्य अहं नृलोके द्रष्टुं त्वदन्येन कुरुप्रवीर ।।

na vedayajñādhyayanair na dānair na ca kriyābhir na tapobhir ugraiḥ ।
evaṁrūpaḥ śakya ahaṁ nṛloke draṣṭuṁ tvadanyena kurupravīra ॥

na veda: neither by the Vedas; *yajña adhyayanaiḥ*: sacrifices, (nor) by study; *na dānaiḥ*: nor by gifts; *na kriyābhiḥ*: nor by ritual; *ca na ugraiḥ tapobhiḥ*: and not by severe austerities; *ahaṁ śakyaḥ draṣṭuṁ*: (can) I possibly be seen; *evaṁ rūpaḥ*: in such a form; *nṛloke*: in the human world; *anyena tvat*: by (anyone) other than you; *kurupravīra*: Oh Arjuna.

Neither by the Vedas, sacrifices, nor by study, nor by gifts, nor by ritual, nor by severe austerities, can I possibly be seen in such a form in the human world, by anyone other than you, Oh Hero of the Kurus!

49. मा ते व्यथा मा च विमूढभावो दृष्ट्वा रूपं घोरमीदृङ्ममेदम् ।
व्यपेतभीः प्रीतमनाः पुनस्त्वं तदेव मे रूपमिदं प्रपश्य ।।

mā te vyathā mā ca vimūḍhabhāvo dṛṣṭvā rūpaṁ ghoram īdṛṅ mame 'dam ।
vyapetabhīḥ prītamanāḥ punas tvaṁ tad eva me rūpam idaṁ prapaśya ॥

te mā vyathā: for you there should not be distress; *ca mā vimūḍha bhāvaḥ*: and do not be confused; *dṛṣṭvā idaṁ*: having seen this; *īdṛk ghoram rūpaṁ*: such a terrible form; *mama*: of Mine; *vyapetabhīḥ*: free from fear; *prītamanāḥ*: mentally comforted; *punar*: again; *tvaṁ prapaśya*: you behold; *tat eva rūpam*: that very form; *me idaṁ*: of Mine (presently) here.

Be not distressed, do not be confused, having seen such a terrible form of Mine; free from fear, mentally comforted, again behold that very form of Mine (presently) here.

सञ्जय उवाच –

50. इत्यर्जुनं वासुदेवस्तथोक्त्वा स्वकं रूपं दर्शयामास भूयः ।
आश्वासयामास च भीतमेनं भूत्वा पुनः सौम्यवपुर्महात्मा ।।

sañjaya uvāca –

ity arjunaṁ vāsudevas tatho 'ktvā svakaṁ rūpaṁ darśayām āsa bhūyaḥ ।
āśvāsayām āsa ca bhītam enaṁ bhūtvā punaḥ saumyavapur mahātmā ॥

sañjaya uvāca: Sañjaya said; *iti uktvā tathā*: thus having spoken in this way; *arjunaṁ*: to Arjuna; *vāsudevaḥ*: Kṛṣṇa; *bhūyaḥ darśayām āsa*: again showed; *svakaṁ rūpaṁ*: (His) own form; *ca mahātmā*: and the Great Self (Kṛṣṇa); *bhūtvā punar*: becoming again; *saumya vapuḥ*: mild in form; *āśvasayām āsa*: consoled; *enaṁ bhītam*: this terrified one.

Sañjaya said:

Having thus spoken to Arjuna, Vāsudeva again showed His own form, and the Great Self, becoming mild in form, consoled him who was terrified.

अर्जुन उवाच –

51. दृष्ट्वेदं मानुषं रूपं तव सौम्यं जनार्दन ।
इदानीमस्मि संवृत्तः सचेताः प्रकृतिं गतः ।।

arjuna uvāca –

dṛṣṭve 'daṁ mānuṣaṁ rūpaṁ tava saumyaṁ janārdana ।
idānīm asmi saṁvṛttaḥ sacetāḥ prakṛtiṁ gataḥ ॥

arjuna uvāca: Arjuna said; *dṛṣṭvā idaṁ*: beholding (again) this; *tava saumyaṁ mānuṣaṁ rūpaṁ*: Your mild human form; *janārdana*: Oh Kṛṣṇa; *asmi idānīm saṁvṛttaḥ*: (I) am now calm; *sacetāḥ*: with the (living) mind; *gataḥ prakṛtiṁ*: restored to its natural state.

Arjuna said:

Beholding again this Your mild human form, Oh Janārdana! I am now calm, with the living mind restored to its natural state.

श्रीभगवानुवाच –

52. सुदुर्दर्शमिदं रूपं दृष्टवानसि यन्मम ।
देवा अप्यस्य रूपस्य नित्यं दर्शनकाङ्क्षिणः ।।

śrībhagavān uvāca –

sudurdarśam idaṁ rūpaṁ dṛṣṭavān asi yan mama ।
devā apy asya rūpasya nityaṁ darśanakāṅkṣiṇaḥ ॥

śrībhagavān uvāca: Kṛṣṇa said; *idaṁ rūpaṁ mama*: this form of Mine; *yat dṛṣṭavān asi*: which you have seen; *sudur darśam*: (is very) hard to see (indeed); *api devāḥ*: even the gods; *nityaṁ*: ever; *kāṅkṣiṇaḥ darśana*: aspire to behold; *asya rūpasya*: of this form.

Kṛṣṇa said:

This form of Mine which you have seen is very hard to see indeed; even the gods ever aspire to behold this form.

53. नाहं वेदैर्न तपसा न दानेन न चेज्यया ।
शक्य एवंविधो द्रष्टुं दृष्टवानसि मां यथा ।।

nā 'haṁ vedair na tapasā na dānena na ce 'jyayā ।
śakya evaṁvidho draṣṭuṁ dṛṣṭavān asi māṁ yathā ॥

na vedaiḥ: not by Vedas; *na tapasā*: nor by austerity; *na dānena*: nor by gifts; *ca na ijyayā*: and not by sacrifice; *śakyaḥ ahaṁ draṣṭuṁ*: can I be seen; *evaṁ vidhaḥ*: in this form; *yathā dṛṣṭavān asi māṁ*: as you have seen Me.

Not by Vedas, nor by austerity, nor by gifts, nor by sacrifice, can I be seen in this form as you have seen Me.

54. भक्त्या त्वनन्यया शक्य अहमेवंविधोऽर्जुन ।
ज्ञातुं द्रष्टुं च तत्त्वेन प्रवेष्टुं च परन्तप ।।

bhaktyā tv ananyayā śakya aham evaṁvidho 'rjuna ।
jñātuṁ draṣṭuṁ ca tattvena praveṣṭuṁ ca paraṁtapa ॥

tu bhaktyā: but by devotion; *ananyayā*: that excludes all else; *arjuna*: Oh Arjuna; *evaṁ vidhaḥ*: in such a way; *aham śakyaḥ jñātuṁ*: I can be known; *draṣṭuṁ*: seen; *ca tattvena*: and in principle; *praveṣṭuṁ ca*: entered into also; *paraṁtapa*: Arjuna.

But by devotion that excludes all else, Oh Arjuna! I can be known, seen, and in principle entered into, Paraṁtapa.

55. मत्कर्मकृन्मत्परमो सद्भक्तः सङ्गवर्जितः ।
निर्वैरः सर्वभूतेषु यः स मामेति पाण्डव ॥

matkarmakṛn matparamo madbhaktaḥ saṅgavarjitaḥ ।
nirvairaḥ sarvabhūteṣu yaḥ sa mām eti pāṇḍava ॥

yaḥ: (he) who; *mat karmakṛt*: does actions that are Mine; *mat paramaḥ*: whose Supreme is Myself; *mat bhaktaḥ*: whose devotion is to Me; *saṅga varjitaḥ*: devoid of attachment; *nirvairaḥ*: free from enmity; *sarva bhūteṣu*: to all beings; *saḥ eti mām*: he reaches Me; *pāṇḍava*: Oh Arjuna

He who does actions that are Mine, whose Supreme is Myself, whose devotion is to Me, devoid of attachment, free from enmity to all beings – he reaches Me, Oh Pāṇḍava.

DIALOGUE

TEACHER: To enter into the spirit of this chapter we should make ourselves familiar with the literary device employed by the author. This chapter is distinctly different from all the others. Here we find three varying descriptions of the vision presented by Kṛṣṇa. Sañjaya again comes in to help the narrative. When a highly mystical or spiritual experience is transpiring between a guru and disciple, or between a seeker and the Absolute, there emerges a silence which is profound and eloquent to the counterparts concerned, while the same may remain obscure or even opaque to others who are physically present. Thus there is the need for an impartial third eye, or witness, to interpret for those who are outside such a mystic presence. It is this role that is assigned to Sañjaya. In his impartial role of reporter he is confined more or less to the cosmological vision revealed to Arjuna. One can easily notice that Sañjaya's description is given in a somewhat cold, matter-of-fact manner. Thereafter we pass on to Arjuna's position. This is presented in a special metre attuned to a note of religious exaltation, characteristic of his present attitude. His vision is coloured more by theology than by cosmology. It ranges from the conventional starting point of a Viṣṇu known to mythology, and goes through various other forms of religious exaggeration and desire, eventually returning to the same conventional picture of a mild and soothing Viṣṇu. The third description is from the voice of Kṛṣṇa himself, which is free from cosmological or theological presuppositions or prejudices. He attributes even a higher value to his own innate spiritual supremacy than that which is implied in the more conditioned visions of the other two.

Even after knowing the supreme truth philosophically and intuitively, one may still feel a degree removed from the actual identity unless one plunges into the flame of a living experience. Hence, Arjuna asks for a vision of the Absolute:

> By that speech which has been spoken by You out of favour for me – the highest secret known as pertaining to the Self – this, my confusion, has vanished.
>
> The origin and dissolution of beings have been heard by me in elaboration from You, Oh Lotus-petal Eyed! as also Your unexpended greatness.
>
> So it is as You have said Yourself, Supreme Lord; I desire to see Your divine form, Oh Supreme Person!
>
> If You think that it is possible for me to see it, Oh Powerful One! then do You, Oh Master of Yoga! show me Your never-decreasing Self.

STUDENT: *Any experience of hearing or seeing is bound to be relative. Does it seem philosophically tenable that one can have an actual seeing or hearing of the Absolute in any empirical sense of the term?*

The actualization of the Absolute might have its limitations and drawbacks in a purely philosophical sense. But philosophy is not limited merely to idealistic abstractions. When we carefully examine the implications of Arjuna's vision as meant by the author, and seen through the direct words of Kṛṣṇa, we will not see defects of religious theophany. When Arjuna is said to have seen the form of Kṛṣṇa, we have to take it that Arjuna sympathizes with Kṛṣṇa to such an extent as to identify himself with him, thus seeing the vision as Kṛṣṇa himself would. What is meant here is not an externalized vision, but an identity which has no inside or outside.

Mysticism presents a vast range of possibilities, extending from quietism and even erotic mysticism, through practical religious works, to the heights of ecstasy and even agony. A disciple's mystical experience initially takes shape along the lines which the Guru suggests or opens up in his or her mind. Similarly, this vision begins with Kṛṣṇa's revelation of his own mystical nature when it is seen through and beyond his localized personality. Kṛṣṇa says:

> Behold, Oh Pārtha! My forms, by hundreds and thousands, various in kind, divine, and of varied colours and shapes.
>
> Behold the Ādityas, the Vasus, the Rudras, the two Aśvins, and also the Maruts; behold many marvels never seen before, Oh Bhārata!
>
> Now behold here in My body, Oh Guḍākeśa! the whole world, including the static and the dynamic, unitively established, and whatever else you desire to see.

> But if you are unable to see Me with this your (human) eye, I give you a divine eye: behold My sovereign Yoga.

If this vision is not seeing in the ordinary sense of the term, could it not be taken for a fantasy? Furthermore, Arjuna is asked to see whatever he is desirous of seeing. Is the actualization of wishful thinking really a spiritual experience? What is this divine eye which Kṛṣṇa offers to Arjuna?

What is objectively divine evidently presupposes its counterpart, which is the capacity of the subject to recognize divinity. The "divine eye" here is this capacity to recognize spiritual values. Mere human eyes are too weak to even see the continuous flow of events in time. They can comprehend only an empirical view of reality consisting of events. A vision of creative becoming is seen only by the yogic eye. Sañjaya reports that Arjuna saw countless faces and eyes, signifying the infinite range of the multifaceted aspects of the Absolute.

This vision further offers another marvel to Arjuna in the instrumental world of divine designs, devices, tools, techniques, and operations. The canopy of the universe of the Absolute is woven of the warp and woof of infinite space, studded with countless stars of unimaginable magnitude and beauty. Its radiant effulgence has the divine fragrance of Truth and Beauty. Its Light is the Light of light, casting no shadow, and there is nothing quantitatively or qualitatively summed up which can be likened to the peerless brightness and thoroughness of the Absolute. Vast is the universe it has projected, and though it has no horizons to limit it, it is finite and meagre in its amplitude when understood as a mere fragmentary phenomenon superimposed on the Infinite. The archetypal projection of the Absolute in terms of the Old-World Hindu mythology seen by Arjuna is described in verses 15 through 20.

Contrary to the normal expectation of the blissful excitement of a vision of God, Arjuna is led to a vision which makes him shudder with dread. A spiritual experience is like an ascent to the mountaintop. One does not know what is there until one gets there. For this reason the experience begins with the fulfilment of what one initially wishes to experience. The element of fantasy cannot be ignored. However this stage changes as one leaves the threshold of preconceived notions. Here is Arjuna's description:

> Into You enter those hosts of the *suras*, some in fear of You mutter with joined palms, bands of great *ṛṣis* and Perfected Ones hail You with the cry "May it be well!" and praise You with resounding hymns.
>
> The Rudras, Ādityas, Vasus and Sādhyas, Viśvas and the two Aśvins, Maruts and Ūṣmapas, hosts of *gandharvas*, *yakṣas*, *asuras* and *siddhas*, all gaze at You, wonderstruck.

Seeing Your great form, with many faces and eyes, Oh Mighty-Armed One! of many arms, thighs, and feet, with many stomachs, with many terrible teeth, the worlds are distressed, as also myself.

On seeing You touching the sky, shining in many a colour, with mouths wide open, with large fiery eyes, my inmost self intensely distressed, I find neither courage nor control, Oh All-pervading One!

Having seen Your mouths fearful with teeth, like time's devouring flames, I lose my spatial bearings and find no joy; be gracious, Oh Lord of gods, Container of the world!

All these sons of Dhṛtarāṣṭra, with hosts of rulers, Bhīṣma, Droṇa, and that son of a charioteer (Karṇa), with our warrior chiefs,

are rushing into Your fearful mouths, terrible with teeth; some are found sticking in the gaps between the teeth with their heads crushed to powder.

As many rushing torrents of rivers race toward the ocean, so do these heroes in the world of men enter Your flaming mouths.

As moths speed into a blazing fire to be destroyed, just so do these worlds also speed into Your mouths unto their destruction.

You lick up all worlds, devouring on every side with Your flaming mouths, filling the whole world with glory; Your fierce rays are blazing forth, Oh All-pervading One!

Tell me who You are, so fierce in form; I bow to You, Oh Superior God; be gracious! I want to understand You, Oh Primal One! nor do I know Your positive continued becoming.

Why is God described almost like a terrible monster in whose mouth everything finds its final extinction? What is the significance of this awful vision?

The vision described here is not of a theological god who can be contrasted with a devil. In an overall picture of the Absolute, the several worlds in which man lives have all to find their respective places. Man lives at once in the past, present, and future. His mind is very often haunted by several hypostatic worlds, both of a cosmological and a psychological nature. Some of the worlds so real to him when he is in a religious frenzy or a mystical exaltation belong to the archetypal imaginations presented in the epics or legendary folklore on which the mind was fed in its formative period. You cannot make a dichotomy of the good and the bad, life and death, and bliss and distress, nor can you eliminate the dark half from the Absolute. The Absolute ceases to be absolute if something else has an existence apart from it. Further, in one sweep in this cosmic vision, the entire range of the imagination of mankind through all ages is to be reviewed and presented as a total whole. All that has been projected on the human mind from time to time is gathered here to be thrown into the fire of a total cessation, so that nothing will be left to mar the purity of the Absolute consciousness described as *sat-cit-ānanda* (existence, subsistence, and the value of immaculate bliss).

In the highest spiritual experience there is an overwhelming awe as one is regressively pulled back into the very womb of his origin and the seed of projection, and the causal seed itself is finally burnt away in the all-consuming fire of wisdom. What remains may appear to be nothingness (*śūnyatā*), but it has a content which is more positive than the positive, and it is counterbalanced by the negation of negation.

The sacrificial fire is supposed to have seven tongues, namely Viśvaruci (the fire that consumes the universe itself); Kālī (the dark, smoky fire that envelops light and produces opacity in place of vision); Karālī (the fierce flames of tremendous dynamism); Manojava (the fire that is invisible and yet radiates its light and warmth to far-flung places); Sphuliṅginī (the fire that bursts out and sparks off into a million stars); Sulohita (the fire that is purple like the blush of life); and Dhūmravarṇa (the translucent fire of smokiness mingled with the beauty and grace of changing colour). These tongues of the Absolute both lick things into shape and lick them out of existence. The fire that creates is also the one that finally consumes everything. The sharp teeth described here are the hard fact and harsh realities, which are as real as blissful revelation or fond affection. When Arjuna is already terror-stricken and asking for the withdrawal of the frightful mystery, Kṛṣṇa reveals to him a still more dreadful picture:

> I am world-destroying Time, grown into hardened maturity, operating here continuously, desolating the worlds. Even without you, none of the warriors standing in the opposing armies shall continue to exist.
>
> Therefore do you arise and gain fame. Conquering your foes, enjoy the realm of abundance. By Me they have already been slain. Be the incidental cause only, Oh Left-handed One!
>
> Droṇa and Bhīṣma, Jayadratha, Karṇa, and other great battle-heroes, are all slain by Me. Do not be distressed. Fight on, you shall conquer in battle your rival co-warriors.

In these words I see a definite incitement to war. How could Kṛṣṇa, who represents the Absolute or God, and thus goodness and the highest of spiritual and ethical values, encourage warfare in which the killing of fellow men is involved?

We should not forget that the whole dialogue began from the point where Arjuna could not decide the right and wrong of his conduct, and tended to become negative. Philosophy offers no cover to hide away from the imperativeness of an actual situation. Throughout the Gītā, which is part of an epic poem, there is a general background of warfare, and Arjuna is still present in the middle of the battlefield where fierce fighting is going on. Whatever is taught should have an actual bearing on the life situation in which it is taught. Arjuna has his own status outside the wisdom situation as one of the Pāṇḍavas, with his moral commitment which is adequately described in a number of chapters of the *Mahābhārata* which come before the commencement of the Gītā. Furthermore, we have noticed that each chapter of the Gītā forms a closed system of its own *darśana* (special vision of reality). The consistency of the statements in each chapter has to be referred to in its own proper frame of reference, and not crossways between two different visions of reality. There is an element of indeterminism running side by side with determinism in the nature of the physical world, as scientists recognize. Newton's laws hold good side by side with Einstein's theories.

The persons who are caught in the imperative urge of becoming have before and around them a force that has to be reckoned with. It is true that the God described in this chapter is not the conventional picture of the all-loving, all-good, benign Father. On the contrary, Kṛṣṇa says definitely that he has come to destroy. We have seen the same Kṛṣṇa as a friend of all beings in Chapter V, and in Chapter IX representing a neutral personality. Further, the Absolute should not be looked upon as an impotent or spent force. It is a virile and radical principle, sometimes evident with a touch of tragic heroism. Creation is both comic and tragic, benign and terrible, when viewed from its own negative or positive side. The necessary and contingent aspects exchange positions, yielding primacy to one or the other, depending on the angle from which reality is viewed. When all the different possible views about the Absolute are put into one living whole as finally given to the intuition of a wise person, that should represent reality, and this is what the Gītā attempts to accomplish.

What does Kṛṣṇa mean by saying that he has already killed Bhīṣma, Droṇa, and others, and Arjuna had to kill them only as an instrument?

This can be looked upon in two ways. First, all objective existence, being subject to change, has no intrinsic existence in the light of the Eternal. Second, evil, being based on something false and non-existent, has no proper being as such. A bad person is already dead. Good people approximate to values that are eternal; bad people, to the extent that they are bad, may in principle be said to have already perished. Gaining fame must be construed here to mean fame based on something real or good, and likewise the realm of abundance mentioned in verse 33 need not necessarily refer to that particular kingdom that Arjuna can legalistically claim. It might refer more generally to the way that leads to a more abundant life.

Incidental cause should also be understood with its logical implications. Taking the familiar example of a potter at his wheel, the clay he uses is the material cause, which is of a fundamental nature. The potter and the wheel could vary according to circumstances. The particular potter does not count, nor the particular pattern of the wheel. These are often distinguished in India as the material cause and the efficient cause, respectively. The potter and wheel are only instrumental or of incidental importance, varying according to circumstances. Arjuna here as a person is therefore just an incidental factor in the larger situation given. He is only being reminded of this verity.

Kṛṣṇa referred to specific names like Bhīṣma and Droṇa. Although they are to be feared, they are by no means the worst examples of bad men ranged against Arjuna's side. Why, therefore, specific references should be made to such good teachers and warriors of worth is a relevant question. They represent superior values in themselves even outside the context of warfare, as we have pointed out early in this work. The spirituality imparted to Arjuna now, being thoroughly absolutist in its character, supersedes every other value, however esteemed it might have been until now, in the anterior context of the Mahābhārata War. Therefore the specific mention of these names must be intended to point out the superiority of the revalued spirituality of Kṛṣṇa, which is now Arjuna's also.

People seem to resort to various techniques to get realization. What special methods did Arjuna adopt to have this very unusual experience of cosmic vision?

Various kinds of physiological and psychic excitement are possible by resorting to methods and techniques. But in truly dedicated spiritual life, one gives up entirely to the grace, never trying to catch the Absolute with bait. Kṛṣṇa says:

> By My favour, Oh Arjuna! this supreme form has been shown, by the *yoga* pertaining to the Self, made up of light, universal, endless, primal, never before seen by any other than yourself.
>
> Neither by the Vedas, sacrifices, nor by study, nor by gifts, nor by ritual, nor by severe austerities, can I possibly be seen in such a form in the human world, by anyone other than you, Oh Hero of the Kurus!
>
> Be not distressed, do not be confused, having seen such a terrible form of Mine; free from fear, mentally comforted, again behold that very form of Mine (presently) here.

This last verse consoles Arjuna, but definitely admits that the terrible form did not fit into the normal human context. There was a harsh and specialized quality which belonged perhaps, according to Kṛṣṇa, to the context of war in which Arjuna was involved. Kṛṣṇa would perhaps have avoided showing this terrible aspect if it had not been for the hard actualities of warfare which made such a vision, though somewhat abnormal, necessary all the same. It is further suggested indirectly that visions and ecstatic states properly belong to the field of abnormal psychology. The reference to the human world in the previous verse would support such a view. The only advice Kṛṣṇa gives in this respect to Arjuna is the following:

> But by devotion that excludes all else, Oh Arjuna! I can be known, seen, and in principle entered into, Paraṁtapa.

The way that will surely succeed, not only in producing the full effect, but also in comprehending the full import of the vision, is here stated without ambiguity. This touches the central doctrine of the Gītā, expressed in various ways throughout the work in the familiar form of "you shall even attain to Me". The attaining referred to has implications of an absolutist nature which it would be wrong to overlook. There is always implied in such instances an identity or unity of a very thorough character, as between the seeker and the wisdom of the Absolute. Such references by no means suggest the weak variety of *bhakti* (devotion) which mostly consists of clashing cymbals, bell-ringings, and parrot-like muttering of *mantras* (sacred syllables). But of course these practices have their justification, in so far as they displace worse practices! True spirituality demands total acceptance of the Absolute, but also whole-hearted participation. Thus something more than a mere vision is promised here by Kṛṣṇa, if Arjuna could establish that particular kind of bipolar affiliation which forms, as we have said, part of the finalized doctrine of the Gītā.

XII

Bhakti-Yoga

Unitive Devotion and Contemplation

INTRODUCTION

Bhakti-Yoga is often described as a discipline of the soft-minded sentimentalist. Those who try to understand Chapter XII as a song of sentimental devotion are sure to miss the most fundamental teaching.

Professor Oliver Lacombe is very much justified in describing the Gītā as a book of *ekāntika bhakti* (one-pointed devotion). This one-pointed devotion has behind it a very subtle philosophical vision and psychological togetherness. In Nārada's *Bhakti-Sūtra*, *bhakti* is defined as "love for the Absolute". The original Sanskrit word is *parama premarūpa* (of the nature of Absolute love). In one sense it is the individual's love for the Absolute, and in another sense it is Absolute love. Equating Absolute love with realization is of cardinal importance to Vedānta.

Both Śaṅkara and Narayana Guru define *bhakti* as continuous realization of the Self. Śaṅkara defines it as *svasvarūpa anusandhāna* (continuous contemplation of one's own true being). Narayana Guru defines it as *ātmānusandhāna* (continuous contemplation of the Self).

Three steps in the pursuit of realization are receiving the Word, pondering the Word, and realizing the Word. These are respectively termed as *śravaṇa*, *manana*, and *nididhyāsana*. The word *anusandhāna* includes in its meaning all three aspects.

The Absolute is not a static reality. It is ever new and ever fresh. An individual who relates himself to the Absolute is to be alert and wakeful, to watch and see the ever new revelation. He should have the intuitive empathy to flow with it and to understand the full meaning and significance of it, as and when it is revealed. He should also have a total sense of identity, which will enable him to live the revelation as the most meaningful and fulfilling experience of life.

When such an experience is equated with love, the very concepts of knowledge and action are thrown into a crucible of unitive fusion. It is this alchemy of non-dual wisdom and mystical identity which is presented in the twelfth chapter entitled *Bhakti-Yoga.*

TRANSLATION

अर्जुन उवाच –

1. एवं सततयुक्ता ये भक्तास्त्वां पर्युपासते ।
ये चाप्यक्षरमव्यक्तं तेषां के योगवित्तमाः ।।

arjuna uvāca –

evaṁ satatayuktā ye bhaktās tvāṁ paryupāsate ।
ye ca'py akṣaram avyaktaṁ teṣāṁ ke yogavittamāḥ ॥

arjuna uvāca: Arjuna said; *bhaktāḥ ye*: (those) devotees who; *prayupāsate tvāṁ*: worship You; *evaṁ satata yuktāḥ*: thus ever unitively; *ca api ye*: and (those) again who; *akṣaram*: (meditate on) the Imperishable; *avyaktaṁ*: (and) the Unmanifested; *teṣāṁ*: of them; *ke yoga vittamāḥ*: which excels in *yoga*-knowledge.

Arjuna said:

Those devotees who worship You, ever unitively, and those again who meditate on the Imperishable and the Unmanifested – of them which excels in *yoga*-knowledge?

श्रीभगवानुवाच –

2. मय्यावेश्य मनो ये मां नित्ययुक्ता उपासते ।
श्रद्धया परयोपेतास्ते मे युक्ततमा मताः ।।

śrībhagavān uvāca –

mayy āveśya mano ye māṁ nityayuktā upāsate ।
śraddhayā parayo 'petās te me yuktatamā matāḥ ॥

śrībhagavān uvāca: Kṛṣṇa said; *ye manaḥ*: (those) who (with) minds; *āveśya mayi*: entered into Me; *nitya yuktāḥ*: ever unitively; *upāsate māṁ*: meditate on Me; *upetāḥ śraddhayā parayā*: with a fervour pertaining to the Supreme; *te matāḥ me*: those according to Me; *yukta tamāḥ*: (are) the most unitively (attuned) in *yoga.*

Kṛṣṇa said:

Those with minds entered into Me, who unitively meditate on Me, with a fervour pertaining to the Supreme – those according to Me are the most unitively attuned in *yoga*.

3. ये त्वक्षरमनिर्देश्यमव्यक्तं पर्युपासते ।
सर्वत्रगमचिन्त्यं च कूटस्थमचलं ध्रुवम् ।।

ye tv akṣaram anirdeśyam avyaktaṁ paryupāsate ।
sarvatragam acintyaṁ ca kūṭasthaṁ acalaṁ dhruvam ॥

tu ye: but (those) who; *paryupāsate*: meditate upon; *akṣaram anirdeśyam*: the Imperishable, the Undefinable; *avyaktaṁ sarvatragam*: the Unmanifested, the All-Pervasive; *ca acintyaṁ*: and the Thought-Transcending; *kūṭastham*: the Firmly-Established; *acalaṁ dhruvam*: the Immobile, the Constant.

4. सन्नियम्येन्द्रियग्रामं सर्वत्र समबुद्धयः ।
ते प्राप्नुवन्ति मामेव सर्वभूतहिते रताः ।।

saṁniyamye 'ndriyagrāmaṁ sarvatra samabuddhayaḥ ।
te prāpnuvanti mām eva sarvabhūtahite ratāḥ ॥

saṁniyamya: having restrained; *indriyagrāmaṁ*: (all) sense-aggregates; *sarvatra samabuddhayaḥ*: (regarding) all (with) equalizing understanding; *ratāḥ*: interested; *sarva bhūta hite*: in the well-being of all creatures; *te prāpnuvanti*: they reach; *mām eva*: Me too.

But those who meditate upon the Imperishable, the Undefinable, the Unmanifested, the All-Pervasive, and the Thought-Transcending, the Firmly-Established, the Immobile, the Constant, having restrained all sense-aggregates, regarding all with equalizing understanding, interested in the well-being of all creatures – they reach Me too.

5. क्लेशोऽधिकतरस्तेषामव्यक्तासक्तचेतसाम् ।
अव्यक्ता हि गतिर्दुःखं देहवद्भिरवाप्यते ।।

kleśo 'dhikataras teṣām avyaktāsaktacetasām ।
avyaktā hi gatir duḥkhaṁ dehavadbhir avāpyate ॥

kleśaḥ teṣām: the difficulty of those; *avyakta āsakta cetasām*: whose relational minds are set on the Unmanifested; *adhikataraḥ*: (is) greater; *hi gatiḥ*: indeed the way; *avyaktāḥ*: (of) the Unmanifested; *duḥkhaṁ*: is very hard; *dehavadbhiḥ avāpyate*: for the embodied to reach.

The difficulty of those whose relational minds are set on the Unmanifested is greater, for the way of the Unmanifested is very hard for the embodied to reach.

6. ये तु सर्वाणि कर्माणि मयि संन्यस्य मत्पराः ।
अनन्येनैव योगेन मां ध्यायन्त उपासते ॥

ye tu sarvāṇi karmāṇi mayi saṁnyasya matparāḥ ।
ananyenai 'va yogena māṁ dhyāyanta upāsate ॥

tu ye upāsate: but (those) who worship (Me); *saṁnyasya sarvāṇi karmāṇi*: renouncing all actions; *mayi*: in Me; *mat parāḥ*: (regarding) Me supreme; *dhyāyantaḥ māṁ*: meditating on Me; *yogena*: by that *yoga*; *ananyena eva*: exclusive of all else.

7. तेषामहं समुद्धर्ता मृत्युसंसारसागरात् ।
भवामि नचिरात्पार्थ मय्यावेशितचेतसाम् ॥

teṣām aham samuddhartā mṛtyusaṁsārasāgarāt ।
bhavāmi nacirāt pārtha mayy āveśitacetasām ॥

teṣām: for them; *āveśita cetasām*: whose minds have entered; *mayi*: into Me; *ahaṁ bhavāmi*: I become; *na cirāt*: ere long; *pārtha*: Oh Arjuna; *samuddhartā*: the saviour; *mṛtyu saṁsāra sāgarāt*: out of the ocean of death and repeated cyclic existences.

But those who worship Me, renouncing all actions in Me, regarding Me supreme, meditating on Me by that *yoga* exclusive of all else,

for them whose minds have entered into Me, I become ere long, Oh Pārtha! the saviour out of the ocean of death and repeated cyclic existences.

8. मय्येव मन आधत्स्व मयि बुद्धिं निवेशय ।
निवसिष्यसि मय्येव अत ऊर्ध्वं न संशयः ॥

mayy eva mana ādhatsva mayi buddhiṁ niveśaya ।
nivasiṣyasi mayy eva ata ūrdhvam na saṁśayaḥ ॥

ādhatsva manaḥ: place (your) mind; *mayi eva*: in Me only; *buddhiṁ niveśaya*: let your higher reason enter; *mayi*: into Me; *nivasiṣyasi ata ūrdhvaṁ na saṁśayaḥ*: you shall without doubt thereafter live; *mayi eva*: in Me alone.

Place your mind in Me only, let your higher reason enter into Me; you shall without doubt thereafter live in Me.

9. अथ चित्तं समाधातुं न शक्नोषि मयि स्थिरम् ।
अभ्यासयोगेन ततो मामिच्छाप्तुं धनञ्जय ॥

atha cittaṁ samādhātuṁ na saknoṣi mayi sthiram ।
abhyāsayogena tato mām icchā 'ptuṁ dhanañjaya ॥

atha na śaknoṣi: if (you) are unable; *samādhātuṁ cittaṁ*: to fix (your) thoughts; *sthiram mayi*: steadily on Me; *tataḥ*: then; *abhyāsa yogena*: by means of unitive ascent (*yoga* of practice) *icchā āptuṁ māṁ*: seek to reach Me; *dhanañjaya*: Oh Arjuna.

If you are unable to fix your thoughts steadily on Me, then by means of unitive ascent seek to reach Me, Oh Dhanañjaya!

10. अभ्यासेऽप्यसमर्थोऽसि मत्कर्मपरमो भव ।
मदर्थमपि कर्माणि कुर्वन्सिद्धिमवाप्स्यसि ॥

abhyāse 'py asamartho 'si matkarmaparamo bhava ।
madartham api karmāṇi kurvan siddhim avāpsyasi ॥

asi asamarthaḥ: (if you) are incapable; *api abhyāse*: even for practice; *bhava*: (then) become; *matkarma paramaḥ*: (one whose every) action belongs to Me, the Supreme; *api kurvan karmāṇi*: even doing works; *mad artham*: for My sake; *avāpsyasi*: you shall attain; *siddhim*: to perfection.

If you happen to be incapable even of practice, then become one whose every action belongs to Me, the Supreme; even doing work for My sake, you shall attain to perfection.

11. अथैतदप्यशक्तोऽसि कर्तुं मद्योगमाश्रितः ।
सर्वकर्मफलत्यागं ततः कुरु यतात्मवान् ॥

athai 'tad apy aśakto 'si kartuṁ madyogam āśritaḥ ।
sarvakarmaphalatyāgaṁ tataḥ kuru yatātmavān ॥

atha asi aśaktaḥ: if (you) are unable; *kartuṁ api etat*: to do even this; *tataḥ*: then; *āśritaḥ*: seeking refuge (for your individuality); *mad yogam*: (in) My unitive (Being); *tyāgaṁ*: renouncing; *phala*: the benefits; *sarva karma*: of all actions; *kuru yatātmavān*: act with controlled self.

If you are unable to do even this, then seek refuge (for your individuality) in My unitive Being, renouncing the benefits of all actions, as one of controlled self.

12. श्रेयो हि ज्ञानमभ्यासाज्ज्ञानाद्ध्यानं विशिष्यते ।
ध्यानात्कर्मफलत्यागस्त्यागाच्छान्तिरनन्तरम् ॥

śreyo hi jñānam abhyāsāj jñānād dhyānaṁ viśiṣyate ।
dhyānāt karmaphalatyāgas tyāgāc chāntir anantaram ॥

śreyaḥ hi: better indeed; *jñānam abhyāsāt*: (is) knowledge than practice; *jñānāt*: than knowledge; *dhyānaṁ viśiṣyate*: meditation is superior; *dhyānāt*: than meditation; *tyāgaḥ karma phala*: renunciation of the benefit of action; *anantaram tyāgāt*: after renunciation; *śāntiḥ*: peace.

Better indeed is knowledge than practice; than knowledge, meditation is superior; than meditation, renunciation of the benefit of action; after renunciation – peace.

13. अद्वेष्टा सर्वभूतानां मैत्रः करुण एव च ।
निर्ममो निरहङ्कारः समदुःखसुखः क्षमी ।।

adveṣṭā sarvabhūtānāṁ maitraḥ karuṇa eva ca ।
nirmamo nirahaṁkāraḥ samaduḥkhasukhaḥ kṣamī ॥

adveṣṭā: (he who has) no hatred; *sarva bhūtānāṁ*: (toward) all creatures; *eva maitraḥ*: (who is) also friendly; *ca karuṇaḥ*: and compassionate; *nir mamaḥ*: (who is) free from possessiveness (mineness); *nir ahaṁkāraḥ*: (and) egoism; *sama duḥkha sukhaḥ*: who is equalized in pain and pleasure; *kṣamī*: (and) forgiving.

14. सन्तुष्टः सततं योगी यतात्मा दृढनिश्चयः ।
मय्यर्पितमनोबुद्धिर्यो मद्भक्तः स मे प्रियः ।।

saṁtuṣṭah satataṁ yogī yatātmā dṛḍhaniścayaḥ ।
mayy arpitamanobuddhir yo madbhaktaḥ sa me priyaḥ ॥

yogī: (such) a unitively-disciplined one; *satataṁ*: (who is) always; *saṁtuṣṭaḥ yatātmā*: contented, self-controlled; *dṛḍha niścayaḥ*: firmly resolved; *arpita mano buddhiḥ*: whose mind and reason are dedicated; *mayi*: in Me; *saḥ yaḥ*: he who (is); *madbhaktaḥ*: My devotee; *priyaḥ me*: (is) dear to Me.

He who has no hatred toward all creatures, who is also friendly and compassionate, who is free from possessiveness, and egoism, who is equalized in pain and pleasure, and forgiving,

such a unitively-disciplined one, who is always contented, self-controlled, firmly resolved, whose mind and reason are dedicated to Me – he, My devotee, is dear to Me.

15. यस्मान्नोद्विजते लोको लोकान्नोद्विजते च यः ।
हर्षामर्षभयोद्वेगैर्मुक्तो यः स च मे प्रियः ।।

yasmān no 'dvijate loko lokān no 'dvijate ca yaḥ ।
harṣāmarṣabhayodvegair mukto yaḥ sa ca me priyaḥ ॥

yasmāt: from whom; *lokaḥ*: the world; *na udvijate*: (is) not disturbed; *ca yaḥ na udvijate*: and who (is) not disturbed; *lokāt*: by the world; *ca yaḥ muktaḥ*: and who (is) free; *harṣa amarṣa bhaya udvegaiḥ*: from exaggerations of joy, hate, and fear; *saḥ priyaḥ me*: he (too is) dear to Me.

He who does not disturb (the peace of) the world and (whose peace) is not disturbed by the world, and who is free from exaggerations of joy, hate, and fear – he too is dear to Me.

16. अनपेक्षः शुचिर्दक्ष उदासीनो गतव्यथः ।
सर्वारम्भपरित्यागी यो मद्भक्तः स मे प्रियः ।।

anapekṣaḥ śucir dakṣa udāsīno gatavyathaḥ ।
sarvārambhaparityāgī yo madbhaktaḥ sa me priyaḥ ॥

yah anapekṣaḥ: (he) who expects no favours; *śuciḥ dakṣaḥ*: (who is) clean, expert; *udāsīnaḥ*: (who) sits unconcerned; *gatavyathaḥ*: carefree; *sarva ārambha parityāgī*: who has relinquished all undertakings; *saḥ mat bhaktaḥ*: he, My devotee; *priyaḥ me*: (is) dear to Me.

He who expects no favours, who is clean, expert, who sits unconcerned, carefree, who has relinquished all undertakings – he, My devotee, is dear to Me.

17. यो न हृष्यति न द्वेष्टि न शोचति न काङ्क्षति ।
शुभाशुभपरित्यागी भक्तिमान्यः स मे प्रियः ।।

yo na hṛṣyati na dveṣṭi na śocati na kāṅkṣati ।
śubhāśubhaparityāgī bhaktimān yaḥ sa me priyaḥ ॥

yaḥ na hṛṣyati: (he) who neither rejoices; *na dveṣṭi na śocati*: nor hates, nor grieves; *na kāṅkṣati*: nor desires; *yaḥ*: (and) who; *śubha aśubha parityāgī*: (has) relinquished (both) the beneficial and the harmful; *saḥ*: such a one; *bhaktimān*: endowed with devotion; *priyaḥ me*: (is) dear to Me.

He who neither rejoices nor hates, nor grieves nor desires, and who has relinquished both the beneficial and the harmful – such a one, endowed with devotion, is dear to Me.

18. समः शत्रौ च मित्रे च तथा मानापमानयोः ।
शीतोष्णसुखदुःखेषु समः सङ्गविवर्जितः ।।

samaḥ śatrau ca mitre ca tathā mānāpamānayoḥ ।
śītoṣṇasukhaduhkheṣu samaḥ saṅgavivarjitaḥ ॥

samaḥ: (he who is) the same; *śatrau ca mitre*: to foe and friend; *ca tathā*: and also; *māne apamānayoh*: in honour and dishonour; *samaḥ*: (who is) the same; *śīta uṣṇa sukha duḥkheṣu*: in cold and heat, in pleasure and pain; *vivarjitaḥ saṅga*: (and who is) free from attachment.

19. तुल्यनिन्दास्तुतिर्मौनी संतुष्टो येन केनचित् ।
अनिकेतः स्थिरमतिर्भक्तिमान्मे प्रियो नरः ।।

tulyanindāstutir maunī saṁtuṣṭo yena kenacit ।
aniketaḥ sthiramatir bhaktimān me priyo naraḥ ॥

nindā stutiḥ tulya: (to whom) censure and praise are equal; *maunī*: (who is) silent (in manner); *saṁtuṣṭah*: content; *yena kenacit*: with anything whatever; *aniketaḥ*: having no (fixed) abode; *sthiramatiḥ*: mentally constant; *naraḥ bhaktimān*: (such) a man of devotion; *priyaḥ me*: (is) dear to Me.

He who is the same to foe and friend, and also in honour and dishonour, who is the same in cold and heat, in pleasure and pain, and who is free from attachment,

to whom censure and praise are equal, who is silent (in manner), content with whatever happens to come, having no fixed abode, mentally constant – such a man of devotion is dear to Me.

20. ये तु धर्म्यामृतमिदं यथोक्तं पर्युपासते ।
श्रद्दधाना मत्परमा भक्तास्तेऽतीव मे प्रियाः ।।

ye tu dharmyāmṛtaṁ idaṁ yathoktaṁ paryupāsate ।
śraddadhānā matparamā bhaktās te 'tīva me priyāḥ ॥

tu ye: but (they) who; *paryāpasate*: cherish devotedly; *idaṁ dharmya amṛtam*: this righteous immortal value; *yathā uktaṁ*: as stated; *śraddha dhānāḥ*: endowed with faith; *mat paramāḥ*: with Me for the Supreme; *te bhaktāḥ*: these devotees; *atīva*: (are) exceedingly; *priyāḥ me*: dear to Me.

But they who cherish devotedly this righteous immortal value, as stated, endowed with faith, with Me for the Supreme – these devotees are exceedingly dear to Me.

DIALOGUE

TEACHER: In the world of devotion two trends are prominent. One is the acceptance of the Absolute as a divine person, hallowed in glory, with whom the devotee can enter into a personal intimacy – almost as in the case of a father and son, mother and child, or the beloved and lover. In the second case, the Absolute is looked upon as the inexpressible experience of an encounter in which personal identity is almost effaced to nothingness. It admits of no name or form. Nothing can be affirmed of it. Nothing can be denied of it. Popularly this is understood as *parā-bhakti* (the devotion of the impersonal).

This chapter begins with Arjuna wanting to know which of these two forms of worship is superior and suited to him. Kṛṣṇa votes definitely for the personal, as far as a *yogī* is concerned. At the same time, he recognizes the superiority of a person capable of accomplishing the more difficult task of contemplating the Absolute in its abstraction, without reducing the reality of it in any manner that affects the relation of the individual with the Absolute in the total situation of supreme devotion.

When the Absolute is conceived impersonally and loved, there has to be a cancelling out of the lover and the beloved in the contiguity of the joy that is lived. It must go beyond pain and pleasure and all sense of duality. This bipolarity is the mystical way, which is not different from that of *yoga* (contemplation). The conditions are not consciously fulfilled by rationalization when the Absolute is thought of impersonally. Take the example of physicists or chemists who are convinced of the inner organic oneness of all in terms of particles or waves, in other words, capable of intellectually reducing everything to an impersonal whole. Yet they do not derive the resultant happiness or perennial wisdom of the Absolutist, who merges with the Total in his state of devotion.

STUDENT: *When Kṛṣṇa is an Absolutist master of* yoga *and contemplative wisdom, how can he tolerate anthropomorphism by recommending a personal deity?*

The Gītā is a Yogaśāstra, a well structured textbook on unitive understanding. Although a merely theistic approach is outside its scope, as we have pointed out, a certain amount of anthropomorphism is admitted into its general scheme. It is a personal Kṛṣṇa who represents the Absolute, and, as the technique of *yoga* implies counterparts, one of which is always a personal devotee, the representation of the Absolute as a person should not be considered altogether inconsistent. Such a position does not, however, amount to theism. It should be treated as part of the inevitable technique in the practice of contemplation of the Absolute.

Here is Arjuna's question:

> Those devotees who worship You, ever unitively, and those again who meditate on the Imperishable and the Unmanifested – of them which excels in *yoga*-knowledge?

Could there be a worshipful meditation or a meditative worship?

Worship of a personal deity is called *upāsanā* in Sanskrit. The term describing meditation is *dhyāna*. Though one is related to the other, these disciplines are treated as different. To understand *upāsanā*, let us take the example of a person who worships an image. An image is made of stone, wood, or metal. The devotee first localizes the Absolute in his own physical being. Then he transfers these points of consciousness, synergically located in the various centres of the body, to the image, thereby psychologically effecting a transference of the divine in him to the image. Thereafter the image, for him, is no longer a mere piece of metal or wood. To the devotee it is perhaps more real and alive than his own being, which articulates through an equally inertial body of bones, blood, flesh, and skin. It is as if the body and the image of the deity are two receptacles containing the same spirit. As a person gets a clear vision of their own face by looking in a mirror, the devotee now sees in the image the otherwise unimaginable Divine. He knows that the Divine is not in any way limited to the image, but it is none the less quite real. To this image he offers mentally and even proto-linguistically, with gestures of the hand, various offerings such as water, light, incense, consecrated food, flowers, and garlands. After receiving the presence of the Divine in a fitting manner, he sings the praises, repeats the divine Name, and views the Divine as master, lord, saviour, teacher, beloved, friend, father, and mother all in one. He delights himself in the company of the Divine. This act of worship is what is called *upāsanā*. For *upāsanā* the mind has to be kept entirely in tune with a subtle resonance coming from the mirror image of the deity, which, as we have said, has its counterpart in the devotee's own thoughts, feelings, and emotions. This inevitably removes all gross sense of duality. All that remains unresolved is the attitude of the lover to the beloved.

Let us take the example of one on the path of contemplation. The aid of an image or picture is not used. This person is likely to adopt either the method of acceptance (affirming everything as belonging to the Absolute), or of denial (denying the visible to be real). If the former is chosen, the contemplative reduces everything to its abstracted existence. Existence is further understood in terms of one's knowledge of it, or of its subsistence. That knowledge is seen as the operation of a value within one's own self. The discursive and the individual reference to value is further referred back to the whole gamut of value systems belonging to the Absolute; thus, the entire existential universe is integrated into a total reality. Naturally in the process, individuality and the personal ego are lost.

If the negative way is chosen, the contemplative takes all pairs of opposites and cancels them out, such as existence and non-existence, cause and effect, being and becoming, attention and non-attention, good and bad, and pleasure and pain. First he negates everything, then he negates negation itself. This brings him to an overwhelming silence which fills him within and without with the being that is as good as non-being. We may say that this is an example of *dhyāna* (meditation). Arjuna wants to know which of these two methods is superior. Both are included in the context of *yoga*, so it is only a matter of choosing between them, and that is what is undertaken here.

Does Kṛṣṇa teach both these methods?

Listen to what Kṛṣṇa says:

> Those with minds entered into Me, who unitively meditate on Me, with a fervor pertaining to the Supreme – those according to Me are the most unitively attuned in *yoga*.
>
> But those who meditate upon the Imperishable, the Undefinable, the Unmanifested, the All-Pervasive, and the Thought-Transcending, the Firmly-Established, the Immobile, the Constant,
>
> having restrained all sense-aggregates, regarding all with equalizing understanding, interested in the well-being of all creatures – they reach Me too.

In Kṛṣṇa's answer we find two important expressions. Although both groups are *yogīs*, what distinguishes the first is that they are "with minds entered into Me". We have already discussed in what sense this entering into is to be understood. It pertains to the condition of a bipolar reciprocity. The other expression distinguishing the first group is the word "faith", which the author takes care to modify at once by the qualification "pertaining to the Supreme". Mere religious devotion to an object will not fulfil the requirement in the mind of the author. This faith has to refer to something beyond. Thus we see that it is, as it were, a two way traffic between the worshipper and the worshipped. This is insisted upon throughout this chapter on devotion and contemplation.

When the idea of a personal God becomes more vague or theoretically superior, there must be compensation through a faith that is more fervent. When faith becomes superior through a better philosophical understanding, the idea at the other pole will gain in definiteness of outline. Therefore, although Kṛṣṇa apparently votes definitely in favour of an affiliation to a personal God, this becomes qualified by other considerations as we proceed in the chapter, until one is left gasping. The true picture of the Absolute intended by the Gītā seems to be one that is neither personal nor altogether impersonal.

In this verse you spoke of, the Absolute is described as the Imperishable, the Undefinable, the All-Pervasive, and Thought-Transcending. In contrast to this, Arjuna stands in the middle of a fierce battle in which bodies perish, every assailant or victim could be separately known, and everything has its changing objective profile. Remaining there, bow in hand, how could he ever attain the Absolute?

It is really difficult. Kṛṣṇa, knows this and says:

> The difficulty of those whose relational minds are set on the Unmanifested

> is greater, for the way of the Unmanifested is very hard for the embodied to reach.

All devotees are human beings first and *yogīs* afterwards, and there are limitations belonging to bodily existence which set a limit on the establishment of effective relations with the Absolute. According to their own temperament, each person has to draw the line between the transcendental and immanent aspects of the Absolute, for their own purposes and constant meditation. For this reason Kṛṣṇa suggests a method to Arjuna which might be more natural to him:

> But those who worship Me, renouncing all actions in Me, regarding Me supreme, meditating on Me by that *yoga* exclusive of all else, for them whose minds have entered into Me, I become ere long, Oh Pārtha! the saviour out of the ocean of death and repeated cyclic existences.
>
> Place your mind in Me only, let your higher reason enter into Me; you shall without doubt thereafter live in Me.

The Gītā's distinction as a philosophical treatise is that it never minimizes the importance of the necessary aspects of life.

If one fails to place his mind unitively in the Absolute, what should he do?

Kṛṣṇa gives several alternatives for those who are less intense in their resolution:

> If you are unable to fix your thoughts steadily on Me, then by means of unitive ascent seek to reach Me, Oh Dhanañjaya!
>
> If you happen to be incapable even of practice, then become one whose every action belongs to Me, the Supreme; even doing work for My sake, you shall attain to perfection.
>
> If you are unable to do even this, then seek refuge (for your individuality) in My unitive Being, renouncing the benefits of all actions, as one of controlled self.
>
> Better indeed is knowledge than practice; than knowledge, meditation is superior; than meditation, renunciation of the benefit of action; after renunciation – peace.

The alternatives given in verses 6 through 11 were based on the factor of easiness. In this last verse (12), a gradation is indicated which is based on superiority. Whether a devotee worships a manifested God in the form of Viṣṇu or Rudra, or whether they are capable of meditating on the abstract notion of the Absolute as the Unmanifested, the final criterion by which all have to be measured is how far their devotion has brought them happiness or peace.

Judging from this normative principle of peace, it is possible to grade all forms of devotional practice or contemplation as is done here. The blind practice of devotion without knowledge can only be inferior to a devotion that is guided by knowledge. It is therefore legitimate that the author has given knowledge primacy over practice. Practice covers quite a variety of items, from *yoga* which is forced, involving severe psychophysical discipline, and ritualistic and religious practices, to restraint of vital forces, like breath, mentioned by Patañjali. Even taking the most respectable connotation of practice here, as indicated in verse 26, there is an artificial and mechanistic effort to be made by the devotee to bring the mind back to the subject of meditation. Unless the interest in the subject is intelligent, the effort to bring the mind back constantly would in most cases be futile. Primacy is therefore given to knowledge.

In turn, knowledge cannot be sustained and focused for a long time uninterruptedly without that element of interest which can give it the flow so often referred to, which distinguishes meditation from mere thought or knowledge. The condition of bipolarity in devotion is better fulfilled in meditation, and therefore it is given primacy over knowledge.

To sustain meditation uniformly and to save it from distractions that might develop at any time one should have the power to eliminate all those factors which are likely to drag the mind into channels of instinctive desires. This implies a certain neutrality with regard to means and ends, which is implied in the phrase "renunciation of the benefits of action", already explained. Whether in the form of such a limited relinquishment of benefit only, or in the form of fuller renunciation, as implied in verses 6 and 7 earlier, the element of the giving up of personal interest goes very far in establishing that final value in spiritual life leading to peace or happiness for the contemplative devotee. Thus renunciation has its place above meditation, because it is by renunciation that peace comes.

Verse 12 brings the subject of devotion further in line with the discipline of *yoga* (contemplation) as understood in other chapters. Devotion or practice in the Gītā is not to be confused with indications in such texts as the *Nārada Bhakti-Sūtra*s and Patañjali's *Yogasūtra*, which would be looked upon as *darśana*s (distinct systematic visions of reality) on their own, with very little in common with the pure contemplation of the Absolute which is implied in this chapter.

Earlier there were definitions and descriptions of a man established in unitive understanding, sthitaprajña; *in* yoga yogārūḍhaḥ; *and of a man stabilized in* Brahman brāhmī sthiti. *Do we get a similar definition of the true devotee?*

Yes. Here is the description of a devotee *par excellence*:

> He who has no hatred toward all creatures, who is also friendly and compassionate, who is free from possessiveness, and egoism, who is equalized in pain and pleasure, and forgiving,
>
> such a unitively-disciplined one, who is always contented, self-controlled, firmly resolved, whose mind and reason are dedicated to Me – he, My devotee, is dear to Me.
>
> He who does not disturb (the peace of) the world and (whose peace) is not disturbed by the world, and who is free from exaggerations of joy, hate, and fear – he too is dear to Me.
>
> He who expects no favours, who is clean, expert, who sits unconcerned, carefree, who has relinquished all undertakings – he, My devotee, is dear to Me.
>
> He who neither rejoices nor hates, nor grieves nor desires, and who has relinquished both the beneficial and the harmful – such a one, endowed with devotion, is dear to Me.
>
> He who is the same to foe and friend, and also in honour and dishonour, who is the same in cold and heat, in pleasure and pain, and who is free from attachment,
>
> to whom censure and praise are equal, who is silent (in manner), content with whatever happens to come, having no fixed abode, mentally constant – such a man of devotion is dear to Me.
>
> But they who cherish devotedly this righteous immortal value, as stated, endowed with faith, with Me for the Supreme – these devotees are exceedingly dear to Me.

The Unmanifested Impersonal could be conceived by some rare devotee as a supreme Value that does not violate the laws of inner coherence that admit the non-duality of the Transcendent Being *in Itself* and *of Itself* as Absolute Existence. Such a devotee is given a superior status to all the other types mentioned here.

XIII

Kṣetra-Kṣetrajña-Vibhāga-Yoga

Unitive Understanding of the Distinction between the Actual and the Perceptual

INTRODUCTION

THE main theme of the twelfth chapter was the cultivation of a possible bipolarity between an individual and the Absolute, which could ultimately lead to the individual's identity with the Absolute. Unfortunately, many hallucinatory malfunctions of the mind easily pass for mystical experiences, and pseudo-*yogīs* and pretentious spiritualists claim the experience of non-dual visions. As *brahma-vidyā* the Gītā is an uncompromising science, not admitting into its scope anything that refutes sound reason. As a Yogaśāstra it attempts to be precise and truthful in comprehending every detail of the perceptual and conceptual world, so that the aspiring *yogī* (spiritual seeker) will not take any false step in advancing toward the final realization of non-dual identity with the Absolute.

In the seventh chapter Kṛṣṇa makes an analysis of the existential constituents of the empirically presented world, and enumerates eight factors: earth, water, fire, air, space, mind, intellect, and ego. He classifies these eight factors under his "lower nature" and differentiates them from his "higher nature". His higher nature is the witnessing consciousness and the unmoved Mover present in all beings, without being contaminated with the imperfections of the individuated being.

Mere abstraction or generalization of the manifold entities of the phenomenal world will not bring the spiritual or mystical experience of becoming undifferentiated from the existential, subsistential, and affective unity of the Ground of all values, or in other words, of becoming one with the Absolute. All distinctions and differences that are relevant in the empirical, interpersonal, transactional, and transubjective worlds are to be clearly understood and appreciated, while transcending every one of them. True transcendence does not cause the least violation of the inner integrity of the empirical nature of the transactional world.

The field of transactional experience is described in Chapter XIII as *kṣetra*, and the spiritual core of the experiencing self is referred to as *kṣetrajña*. Kṛṣṇa compares, contrasts, and integrates the two frames of reference – the immanent and the transcendent – without disturbing the logical relation of the facts of the physical world, with the inner cohesion of an ever-proliferating lower nature constituted of the five elements, and the mental processes of living organisms.

The problem dealt with here is subtle and difficult to comprehend in its fullest sense without going into the intent of each verse with insight and penetration. A very calm, leisurely, and intense meditative pondering on the meaning of each verse is the only way to understand the full significance of this chapter.

TRANSLATION

अर्जुन उवाच –

* प्रकृतिं पुरुषं चैव क्षेत्रं क्षेत्रज्ञम् एव च ।
एतद वेदितुम् इच्छामि ज्ञानं ज्ञेयं च केशव ।।

arjuna uvāca –

prakṛtiṁ puruṣaṁ cai 'va kṣetraṁ kṣetrajñam eva ca ।
etad veditum icchāmi jñānaṁ jñeyaṁ ca keśava ॥

arjuna uvāca: Arjuna said; *prakṛtiṁ ca eva puruṣaṁ*: nature and indeed spirit; *kṣetraṁ ca eva kṣetrajñam*: the field and indeed the knower of the field; *jñānaṁ ca jñeyaṁ*: knowledge (wisdom) and what is to be known; *etat icchāmi veditum*: this (I) should like to know; *keśava*: Oh Kṛṣṇa.

Arjuna said:

Nature and spirit, the field and the knower of the field, knowledge and what is to be known – these I should like to know, Oh Keśava!

श्रीभगवानुवाच –

1. इदं शरीरं कौन्तेय क्षेत्रमित्यभिधीयते ।
एतद्यो वेत्ति तं प्राहुः क्षेत्रज्ञ इति तद्विदः ।।

* Following the example of some other editions, this opening verse is not included in the serial numbering, for the reason that the Gītā traditionally is supposed to consist of 700 verses. This verse added would make 701.

śrībhagavān uvāca –

idaṁ śarīraṁ kaunteya kṣetram ity abhidhīyate ।
etad yo vetti taṁ prāhuḥ kṣetrajña iti tadvidaḥ ॥

śrībhagavān uvāca: Kṛṣṇa said; *idaṁ śarīraṁ*: this body; *kaunteya*: Oh Arjuna; *iti abhidhīyate*: thus is called; *kṣetram*: the field; *etat yaḥ vetti taṁ*: (and) this (one) who knows that; *iti prāhuḥ*: thus (they) call; *tadvidaḥ*: the knower of that; *kṣetrajñaḥ*: the knower of the field.

Kṛṣṇa said:

This body, Oh Kaunteya! is called the field, and he who knows this, thus they call, who know, the knower of the field.

2. क्षेत्रज्ञं चापि मां विद्धि सर्वक्षेत्रेषु भारत ।
क्षेत्रक्षेत्रज्ञयोर्ज्ञानं यत्तज्ज्ञानं मतं मम ।।

kṣetrajñaṁ cā 'pi māṁ viddhi sarvakṣetreṣu bhārata ।
kṣetrakṣetrajñayor jñānaṁ yat taj jñānaṁ mataṁ mama ॥

ca api viddhi māṁ: and also know Me; *kṣetrajñaṁ*: (as) the knower of the field; *sarva kṣetreṣu*: in all fields; *bhārata*: Oh Arjuna; *jñānaṁ yat*: (that) knowledge which (refers to the knowledge); *kṣetra kṣetrajñayoḥ*: of the field and the knower of the field; *tat mama mataṁ*: that, (in) My opinion; *jñānaṁ*: (is) *the* knowledge.

And also know Me as the knower of the field in all fields, Oh Bhārata! that knowledge, which (refers to the knowledge) of the field and the knower of the field, is, in My opinion, *the* knowledge.

3. तत्क्षेत्रं यच्च यादृक्च यद्विकारि यतश्च यत् ।
स च यो यत्प्रभावश्च तत्समासेन मे शृणु ।।

tat kṣetraṁ yac ca yādṛk ca yadvikāri yataś ca yat ।
sa ca yo yatprabhāvaś ca tat samāsena me śṛṇu ॥

tat śṛṇu: that hear; *samāsena me*: in brief from Me; *yat tat kṣetraṁ*: what that field is; *ca yādṛk*: and what (it is) like; *ca yadvikāri*: of what (it is) the modification; *ca yataḥ*: and whence; *ca yat*: and which (it is); *ca yaḥ saḥ*: also what he, (the knower of the field, is); *ca yat prabhāvaḥ*: (and) what (is his) specialized resulting expression.

That hear in brief from Me: what the field is, what it is like, of what it is the modification, and whence, and which (it is), also what he (the knower of the field) is, and what is his specialized resulting expression.

4. ऋषिभिर्बहुधा गीतं छन्दोभिर्विविधैः पृथक् ।
ब्रह्मसूत्रपदैश्चैव हेतुमद्भिर्विनिश्चितैः ।।

ṛṣibhir bahudhā gītaṁ chandobhir vividhaiḥ pṛthak ।
brahmasūtrapadaiś cai 'va hetumadbhir viniścitaiḥ ॥

gītam ṛṣibhiḥ: sung by *ṛṣis* (seers); *bahudhā*: in many ways; *vividhaiḥ pṛthak*: severally (and) distinctly; *chandobhiḥ*: in (different) metres; *ca eva*: and also; *brahma sūtra padaiḥ*: in the aphoristic words of the *Brahmasūtra*; *hetumadbhiḥ*: replete with critical reasonings; *viniścitaiḥ*: (and) positively determined.

Sung by *ṛṣis* in many ways, severally and distinctly in (different) metres, and also in the aphoristic words of the *Brahmasūtra*, replete with critical reasonings and positively determined.

5. महाभूतान्यहङ्कारो बुद्धिरव्यक्तमेव च ।
इन्द्रियाणि दशैकं च पञ्च चेन्द्रियगोचराः ॥

mahābhūtāny ahaṁkāro buddhir avyaktam eva ca ।
indriyāṇi daśai 'kaṁ ca pañca ce 'ndriyagocarāḥ ॥

mahā bhūtāni: the great elements; *ahaṁkāraḥ buddhiḥ*: ego-sense, reason; *ca eva avyaktam*: and also the Unmanifest; *daśa indriyāṇi*: the ten senses; *ca ekaṁ*: and the one (mind); *ca pañca indriyagocarāḥ*: and the five conceptual aspects of the senses.

6. इच्छा द्वेषः सुखं दुःखं सङ्घातश्चेतना धृतिः ।
एतत्क्षेत्रं समासेन सविकारमुदाहृतम् ॥

icchā dveṣaḥ sukhaṁ duḥkhaṁ saṁghātaś cetanā dhṛtiḥ ।
etat kṣetraṁ samāsena savikāram udāhṛtam ॥

icchā dveṣaḥ: wish-dislike; *sukham duḥkhaṁ*: pleasure-pain; *saṃghātaḥ*: the organic aggregation; *cetanā*: vital intelligence; *dhṛtiḥ*: firmness; *etat samāsena kṣetram*: this, in brief, (is) the field; *savikāram udāhṛtam*: with modifications named.

The great elements, ego-sense, reason, and also the Unmanifest, the ten senses, the one mind, and the five conceptual aspects of the senses,

wish–dislike, pleasure–pain, the organic aggregation, vital intelligence, firmness – this, in brief, is the field, with modifications named.

7. अमानित्वमदम्भित्वमहिंसा क्षान्तिरार्जवम् ।
आचार्योपासनं शौचं स्थैर्यमात्मविनिग्रहः ॥

amānitvam adambhitvam ahiṁsā kṣāntir ārjavam ।
ācāryopāsanaṁ śaucaṁ sthairyam ātmavinigrahaḥ ॥

amānitvaṁ: freedom from (conventional) pride; *adambhitvam ahiṁsā*: unpretentiousness, non-hurting; *ksāntiḥ*: (non-retaliating) forbearance; *ārjavam*: straightforwardness; *upāsanaṁ ācārya*: loyal support of the teacher; *śaucaṁ sthairyam*: purity, steadfastness; *ātma vinigrahaḥ*: state of self-withdrawal.

Freedom from conventional pride, unpretentiousness, non-hurting, non-retaliating forbearance, straightforwardness, loyal support of the teacher, purity, steadfastness, state of self-withdrawal,

8. इन्द्रियार्थेषु वैराग्यमनहङ्कार एव च ।
जन्ममृत्युजराव्याधिदुःखदोषानुदर्शनम् ।।

indriyārtheṣu vairāgyam anahaṁkāra eva ca ।
janmamṛtyujarāvyādhiduḥkhadoṣānudarśanam ॥

vairāgyam: detachment; *indriya artheṣu*: in respect of sense-interests; *ca eva anahaṁkāraḥ*: and indeed absence of egoism; *anudarśanam*: insight regarding; *duḥkha doṣa janma*: the pain (and) evil (of) birth; *mṛtyu jarā vyādhi*: death, old age, (and) disease.

detachment in respect of sense-interests, absence of egoism, insight regarding the pain and evil of birth, death, old age, and disease,

9. असक्तिरनभिष्वङ्गः पुत्रदारगृहादिषु ।
नित्यं च समचित्तत्वमिष्टानिष्टोपपत्तिषु ।।

asaktir anabhiṣvaṅgaḥ putradāragṛhādiṣu ।
nityaṁ ca samacittatvam iṣṭāniṣṭopapattiṣu ॥

asaktiḥ: without clinging to; *anabhiṣvaṅgaḥ*: (and) without intensely-involved attachment to; *putra dāra gṛhādiṣu*: (relations such as) son, wife, (and property such as) a house; *ca nityaṁ*: and (having) a constant; *sama cittatvam*: neutral mental attitude; *iṣṭa aniṣṭa upapattiṣu*: (in respect of) desirable (and) undesirable happenings.

without clinging to, and without intensely-involved attachment to, (relations such as) sons, wives, (and property such as) houses, and having a constant neutral mental attitude in respect of desirable and undesirable happenings,

10. मयि चानन्ययोगेन भक्तिरव्यभिचारिणी ।
विविक्तदेशसेवित्वमरतिर्जनसंसदि ।।

mayi cā 'nanyayogena bhaktir avyabhicāriṇī ।
viviktadeśasevitvam aratir janasaṁsadi ॥

bhaktiḥ mayi: devotion to Me; *ananya yogena*: with a *yoga* exclusive of everything other; *ca avyabhicāriṇī*: and never straying from the (direct) path; *sevitvam deśa vivikta*: (preference) to dwell in a place apart; *aratiḥ janasaṁsadi*: distaste for crowded living.

devotion to Me to the exclusion of everything extraneous, and never straying from the direct path, preference to dwell in a place apart, distaste for crowded living,

11. अध्यात्मज्ञाननित्यत्वं तत्त्वज्ञानार्थदर्शनम् ।
एतज्ज्ञानमिति प्रोक्तमज्ञानं यदतोऽन्यथा ॥

adhyātmajñānanityatvaṁ tattvajñānārthadarśanam ।
etaj jñānam iti proktam ajñānaṁ yad ato 'nyathā ॥

adhyātma jñāna nityatvaṁ: everlasting affiliation to the wisdom pertaining to the Self; *tattva jñāna artha darśanam*: insight into the content of philosophical wisdom; *etat proktam*: this is declared; *jñānam*: (to be) wisdom; *iti yat*: thus, whatever; *anyathā ataḥ*: is other than this; *ajñānaṁ*: (is) ignorance.

everlasting affiliation to the wisdom pertaining to the Self, insight into the content of philosophical wisdom – this is declared to be wisdom; whatever is other than this is ignorance.

12. ज्ञेयं यत्तत्प्रवक्ष्यामि यज्ज्ञात्वामृतमश्नुते ।
अनादिमत्परं ब्रह्म न सत्तन्नासदुच्यते ॥

jñeyaṁ yat tat pravakṣyāmi yaj jñātvā 'mṛtam aśnute ।
anādimat paraṁ brahma na sat tan nā 'sad ucyate ॥

pravakṣyāmi: (I) shall declare; *tat yat jñeyaṁ*: that which is to be known; *jñātvā yat*: knowing which; *aśnute amṛtam*: (one) gains immortality; *anādimat*: the beginningless; *paraṁ*: (having Me as its) supreme (culminating factor); *brahma*: the Absolute; *tat ucyate*: that is said to be; *na sat*: neither existence; *na asat*: nor non-existence.

I shall declare that which is to be known, knowing which one gains immortality: the beginningless, having Me as its supreme culminating factor, the Absolute, which is said to be neither existence nor non-existence.

13. सर्वतःपाणिपादं तत्सर्वतोऽक्षिशिरोमुखम् ।
सर्वतःश्रुतिमल्लोके सर्वमावृत्य तिष्ठति ॥

sarvataḥpāṇipādaṁ tat sarvatokṣiśiromukham ।
sarvataḥśrutimal loke sarvam āvṛtya tiṣṭhati ॥

sarvataḥ pāṇi pādaṁ: with hands and feet everywhere; *sarvataḥ akṣi siraḥ mukham*: with eyes and heads and mouths everywhere; *sarvataḥ śrutimat*: with hearing everywhere; *loke*: in the world; *tat tiṣṭhati*: That remains; *āvṛtya sarvam*: enveloping all.

With hands and feet everywhere, with eyes and heads and mouths and hearing everywhere – in the world, That remains, enveloping all.

14. सर्वेन्द्रियगुणाभासं सर्वेन्द्रियविवर्जितम् ।
असक्तं सर्वभृच्चैव निर्गुणं गुणभोक्तृ च ।।

sarvendriyaguṇābhāsaṁ sarvendriyavivarjitam ।
asaktaṁ sarvabhṛc cai 'va nirguṇam guṇabhoktṛ ca ॥

sarva indriya guṇa ābhāsaṁ: shining by the specific characters of all the senses; *sarva indriya vivarjitam*: devoid of all sense (attributes); *asaktaṁ*: unattached; *sarvabhṛt*: supporting all; *nirguṇaṁ*: without qualities; *ca eva*: and yet; *ca guṇabhoktṛ*: also perceiving qualities.

Shining by the specific characters of the senses, devoid of all sense attributes, unattached, supporting all, without qualities, yet perceiving qualities,

15. बहिरन्तश्च भूतानामचरं चरमेव च ।
सूक्ष्मत्वात्तदविज्ञेयं दूरस्थं चान्तिके च तत् ।।

bahir antaś ca bhūtānām acaraṁ caram eva ca ।
sūkṣmatvāt tad avijñeyaṁ dūrasthaṁ cā 'ntike ca tat ॥

bahiḥ ca antaḥ bhūtānām: without and within beings; *acaram ca caram eva*: immobile and mobile too; *sūkṣmatvāt*: because subtle; *tat avijñeyaṁ*: That (is) unknowable; *tat dūrasthaṁ ca antike ca*: That stands far and near also.

without and within beings, immobile and mobile too – because subtle, That is unknowable; That stands far and near also.

16. अविभक्तं च भूतेषु विभक्तमिव च स्थितम् ।
भूतभर्तृ च तज्ज्ञेयं ग्रसिष्णु प्रभविष्णु च ।।

avibhaktaṁ ca bhūteṣu vibhaktam iva ca sthitam ।
bhūtabhartṛ ca taj jñeyaṁ grasiṣṇu prabhaviṣṇu ca ॥

ca avibhaktaṁ: and undivided; *ca sthitam vibhaktam*: and (yet) remaining divided; *iva bhūteṣu*: as it were, in beings; *bhūta bhartṛ*: supporter of existence; *ca tat*: and That; *jñeyaṁ*: which is to be known; *grasiṣṇu ca*: holding back and; *prabhaviṣṇu*: releasing for expansive becoming.

And undivided, yet remaining divided, as it were, in beings, supporter of existence, and That which is to be known, holding back and releasing for expansive becoming,

17. ज्योतिषामपि तज्ज्योतिस्तमसः परमुच्यते ।
ज्ञानं ज्ञेयं ज्ञानगम्यं हृदि सर्वस्य विष्ठितम् ।।

jyotiṣām api taj jyotis tamasaḥ param ucyate ।
jñānaṁ jñeyaṁ jñānagamyaṁ hṛdi sarvasya viṣṭhitaṁ ॥

jyotiḥ api jyotiṣāṁ: the Light even of lights; *tat ucyate param tamasaḥ*: That is said to be beyond darkness; *jñānaṁ jñeyaṁ*: knowledge, the knowable; *jñānagamyaṁ*: and what is to be reached through knowledge; *viṣṭhitam*: particularly located; *hṛdi sarvasya*: in the hearts of everyone.

the Light even of lights – That is said to be beyond darkness: knowledge, the knowable, and what is to be reached through knowledge, particularly located in the hearts of everyone.

18. इति क्षेत्रं तथा ज्ञानं ज्ञेयं चोक्तं समासतः ।
मद्भक्त एतद्विज्ञाय मद्भावायोपपद्यते ।।

iti kṣetraṁ tathā jñānaṁ jñeyaṁ co 'ktaṁ samāsataḥ ।
madbhakta etad vijñāya madbhāvāyo 'papadyate ॥

iti kṣetraṁ: thus the field; *tathā jñānaṁ*: thus wisdom; *ca jñeyaṁ*: and what has to be known; *samāsataḥ uktaṁ*: (have been) briefly told; *madbhaktaḥ*: My devotee; *vijñāya etat*: having known this; *upapadyate madbhāvāya*: attains to My state of being.

Thus, the field, and wisdom, and what has to be known, have been briefly told; My devotee, having known this, attains to My state of being.

19. प्रकृतिं पुरुषं चैव विद्ध्यनादी उभावपि ।
विकारांश्च गुणांश्चैव विद्धि प्रकृतिसम्भवान् ।।

prakṛtiṁ puruṣaṁ cai 'va viddhy anādi ubhāv api ।
vikārāṁś ca guṇāṁś cai 'va viddhi prakṛtisaṁbhavān ॥

viddhi: know (that); *prakṛtiṁ ca eva puruṣaṁ*: nature and indeed spirit; *ubhau*: (are) both; *anādi*: beginningless; *ca viddhi api*: and know also; *vikārān*: (that) modifications; *ca eva guṇān*: and indeed (their) intrinsic modalities; *prakṛti saṁbhavān*: (are) born of nature.

Know that nature and spirit are both beginningless; and know also that modifications and their intrinsic modalities are born of nature.

20. कार्यकारणकर्तृत्वे हेतुः प्रकृतिरुच्यते ।
पुरुषः सुखदुःखानां भोक्तृत्वे हेतुरुच्यते ।।

kārya kāraṇa kartṛtve hetuḥ prakṛtir ucyate ।
puruṣaḥ sukhaduḥkhānāṁ bhoktṛtve hetur ucyate ॥

kārya kāraṇa kartṛtve: in what concerns the agency of cause and effect; *hetuḥ*: the motivating factor; *ucyate prakṛtiḥ*: is said to be nature; *bhoktṛtve*: in the matter of the experiencer; *sukha duḥkhānāṁ*: of pleasure and pain; *hetuḥ ucyate*: the motivating factor is said to be; *puruṣah*: spirit.

In what concerns the agency of cause and effect the motivating factor is said to be nature; in the matter of the experiencer of pleasure and pain the motivating factor is spirit.

21. पुरुषः प्रकृतिस्थो हि भुङ्क्ते प्रकृतिजान्गुणान् ।
कारणं गुणसङ्गोऽस्य सदसद्योनिजन्मसु ।।

puruṣaḥ prakṛtistho hi bhuṅkte prakṛtijān guṇān ।
kāraṇaṁ gunasaṅgo 'sya sadasadyonijanmasu ॥

puruṣaḥ: the spirit; *prakṛtisthaḥ*: seated in nature; *bhuṅkte hi*: appreciates indeed; *guṇān*: the modalities; *prakṛtijān*: born of nature; *guṇasaṅgaḥ*: association with the modalities; *kāraṇaṁ asya*: (is) the cause of this; *sat asat yoni janmasu*: births in good or evil wombs.

The spirit, seated in nature, appreciates the modalities born of nature; association with the modalities is the cause of births in good or evil wombs.

22. उपद्रष्टानुमन्ता च भर्ता भोक्ता महेश्वरः ।
परमात्मेति चाप्युक्तो देहेऽस्मिन्पुरुषः परः ।।

upadraṣṭā 'numantā ca bhartā bhoktā maheśvaraḥ ।
parmātme ti cā 'py ukto dehe 'smin puruṣaḥ paraḥ ॥

upadraṣṭā: Supervisor; *ca anumantā*: and Permitter; *bhartā bhoktā*: Supporter, Experiencer; *maheśvaraḥ*: the Great Lord; *ca api uktaḥ*: and also called; *paramātmā*: the supreme Self; *iti puruṣah paraḥ*: thus (is) the supreme Spirit; *asmin dehe*: in this body.

Supervisor, and Permitter, Supporter, Experiencer, the Great Lord, also called the supreme Self, is the supreme Spirit in the body.

23. य एवं वेत्ति पुरुषं प्रकृतिं च गुणैः सह ।
सर्वथा वर्तमानोऽपि न स भूयोऽभिजायते ।।

ya evaṁ vetti puruṣam prakṛtiṁ ca guṇaih saha ।
sarvathā vartamāno 'pi na sa bhūyo 'bhijāyate ॥

yaḥ evaṁ vetti: (he) who thus knows; *puruṣam ca prakṛtiṁ*: spirit and nature; *saha guṇaiḥ*: together with the intrinsic modalities; *api saḥ*: though he; *vartamānaḥ sarvathā*: (may happen to) be living in whatever way; *na abhijāyate bhūyaḥ*: is not born again.

He who thus knows spirit and nature, together with the intrinsic modalities, though he may happen to be leading any kind of life, is not born again.

24. ध्यानेनात्मनि पश्यन्ति केचिदात्मानमात्मना ।
अन्ये साङ्ख्येन योगेन कर्मयोगेन चापरे ।।

dhyānenā 'tmani paśyanti kecid ātmānam ātmanā ।
anye sāṁkhyena yogena karmayogeṇa cā 'pare ॥

dhyānena: by meditation; *kecit paśyanti*: some behold; *ātmānam*: the Self; *ātmani*: in the Self; *ātmanā*: by the Self; *anye sāṁkhyena yogena*: others by *sāṁkhya-yoga* (unitive reasoning); *ca apare*: and others; *karma yogena*: by *karma-yoga* (action unitively understood).

By meditation some behold the Self in the Self by the Self, others by *sāṁkhya-yoga*, and others by *karma-yoga*.

25. अन्ये त्वेवमजानन्तः श्रुत्वान्येभ्य उपासते ।
तेऽपि चातितरन्त्येव मृत्युं श्रुतिपरायणाः ॥

anye tv evam ajānantaḥ śrutvā 'nyebhya upāsate ।
te 'pi cā 'titaranty eva mṛtyuṁ śrutiparāyaṇāḥ ॥

tu anye: but others; *ajānantaḥ evam*: not knowing thus; *upāsate*: worship; *śrutvā anyebhyaḥ*: having heard from others; *ca te api*: and they also; *atitaranti*: cross beyond; *mṛtyuṁ eva*: death indeed; *śruti parāyaṇāḥ*: depending on hearsay.

But others, not knowing in this way, worship, having heard from others; they also cross beyond death, depending on hearsay.

26. यावत्सञ्जायते किञ्चित्सत्त्वं स्थावरजङ्गमम् ।
क्षेत्रक्षेत्रज्ञसंयोगात्तद्विद्धि भरतर्षभ ॥

yāvat sañjāyate kiñcit sattvaṁ sthāvarajaṅgamam ।
kṣetrakṣetrajñasaṁyogāt tad viddhi bharatarṣabha ॥

kiñcit sattvaṁ: whatever being; *yāvat sañjāyate*: inasmuch as (it) is produced; *sthāvara jaṅgamam*: the unmoving or the moving; *bharatarṣabha*: Oh Arjuna; *viddhi tat*: know that (to be); *kṣetra kṣetrajña saṁyogāt*: from the union of the field and the knower of the field.

Whatever is produced, the unmoving or the moving, Oh Best of Bhāratas! know that to be from the union of the field and the knower of the field.

27. समं सर्वेषु भूतेषु तिष्ठन्तं परमेश्वरम्।
विनश्यत्स्वविनश्यन्तं यः पश्यति स पश्यति ॥

samaṁ sarveṣu bhūteṣu tiṣṭhantaṁ parameśvaram ।
vinaśyatsv avinaśyantaṁ yaḥ paśyati sa paśyati ॥

yaḥ paśyati: (he) who sees; *parameśvaram*: the supreme Lord; *tiṣṭhantaṁ samaṁ*: abiding in (a state of) equality; *sarveṣu bhūteṣu*: in all beings; *vinaśyatsu*: within the perishing; *avinaśyantaṁ*: as the non-perishing; *saḥ paśyati*: he sees.

He who sees the supreme Lord abiding in (a state of) equality in all beings, within the perishing as the non-perishing – he sees.

28. समं पश्यन्हि सर्वत्र समवस्थितमीश्वरम् ।
न हिनस्त्यात्मनात्मानं ततो याति परां गतिम् ।।

samam paśyan hi sarvatra samavasthitam īśvaram ।
na hinasty ātmanā 'tmānaṁ tato yāti parāṁ gatim ॥

paśyan hi: seeing indeed; *īśvaram*: the Lord; *samavasthitam samaṁ sarvatra*: seated equally everywhere; *hinasti na*: (he) destroys not; *ātmānaṁ*: the Self; *ātmanā*: by the Self; *tataḥ*: (and) so; *yāti paraṁ gatim*: (he) attains the supreme goal.

For he who sees the Lord seated equally everywhere, destroys not the Self by the Self; and so he attains the supreme goal.

29. प्रकृत्यैव च कर्माणि क्रियमाणानि सर्वशः ।
यः पश्यति तथात्मानमकर्तारं स पश्यति ।।

prakṛtyai 'va ca karmāṇi kriyamāṇāni sarvaśaḥ ।
yaḥ paśyati tathā 'tmānam akartāraṁ sa paśyati ॥

yaḥ paśyati: (he) who sees; *sarvaśaḥ karmāṇi kriyamāṇāni*: all actions are done; *prakṛtyā eva*: by nature alone; *ca tathā*: and likewise; *ātmānam akartāraṁ*: (that) the Self (is) actionless; *saḥ paśyati*: he (truly) sees.

He who sees that all actions are done by nature alone, and likewise that the Self is actionless – he truly sees.

30. यदा भूतपृथग्भावमेकस्थमनुपश्यति ।
तत एव च विस्तारं ब्रह्म सम्पद्यते तदा ।।

yadā bhūtapṛthagbhāvam ekastham anupaśyati ।
tata eva ca vistāraṁ brahma saṁpadyate tadā ॥

yadā anupaśyati: when (he) perceives; *bhūta pṛthak bhāvam*: the disjunct existence of beings; *ekastham*: established in the One; *ca tataḥ eva*: and from whence also; *vistāraṁ*: (their) expansion; *tadā saṁpadyate*: then (he) becomes; *brahma*: the Absolute.

When he perceives the disjunct existence of beings established in the One, and from whence also their expansion, then he becomes the Absolute.

31. अनादित्वान्निर्गुणत्वात्परमात्मायमव्ययः ।
शरीरस्थोऽपि कौन्तेय न करोति न लिप्यते ।।

anāditvān nirguṇatvāt paramātmā 'yam avyayaḥ ।
śarīrastho 'pi kaunteya na karoti na lipyate ॥

anāditvāt: having no beginning; *nirguṇatvāt*: having no attributes (*guṇas*); *ayam paramātmā*: this supreme Self; *avyayaḥ*: suffers no decrease; *api śarīrasthaḥ*: though dwelling in the body; *kaunteya*: Oh Arjuna; *na karoti*: (it) neither acts; *na lipyate*: nor is (it) tainted.

Having no beginning, having no attributes, this supreme Self suffers no decrease, though dwelling in the body, Oh Son of Kuntī! it neither acts nor is it tainted.

32. यथा सर्वगतं सौक्ष्म्यादाकाशं नोपलिप्यते ।
सर्वत्रावस्थितो देहे तथात्मा नोपलिप्यते ॥

yathā sarvagataṁ saukṣmyād ākāśaṁ no 'palipyate ।
sarvatrā 'vasthito dehe tathā 'tmā no 'palipyate ॥

yathā sarvagataṁ: as the all-pervading; *ākāśaṁ*: (subtle) space-principle; *na upalipyate*: is untarnished; *saukṣmyāt*: by (reason of) its subtlety; *tathā ātmā*: so the Self; *avasthitaḥ sarvatra*: seated everywhere; *dehe*: in the body; *na upalipyate*: is untarnished.

As the all-pervading subtle space-principle is untarnished by reason of its subtlety, so the Self, seated everywhere in the body, is untarnished.

33. यथा प्रकाशयत्येकः कृत्स्नं लोकमिमं रविः ।
क्षेत्रं क्षेत्री तथा कृत्स्नं प्रकाशयति भारत ॥

yathā prakāśayaty ekaḥ kr̥tsnaṁ lokam imaṁ raviḥ ।
kṣetraṁ kṣetrī tathā kr̥tsnaṁ prakāśayati bhārata ॥

yathā ekaḥ raviḥ: as the one sun; *prakāśayati imaṁ*: illumines this; *kr̥tsnaṁ lokam*: whole world; *tathā kṣetrī*: so the Lord of the field; *bhārata*: Oh Arjuna; *prakāśayati kr̥tsnam kṣetram*: illumines all the field.

As the one sun illumines this whole world, so the Lord of the field, Oh Bhārata! illumines all the field.

34. क्षेत्रक्षेत्रज्ञयोरेवमन्तरं ज्ञानचक्षुषा ।
भूतप्रकृतिमोक्षं च ये विदुर्यान्ति ते परम् ॥

kṣetrakṣetrajñayor evam antaraṁ jñānacakṣuṣā ।
bhūtaprakr̥timokṣaṁ ca ye vidur yānti te param ॥

ye: (those) who; *jñāna cakṣuṣā*: by the eye of wisdom; *evam viduḥ*: thus perceive; *antaraṁ*: the difference; *kṣetra kṣetrajñayoḥ*: of the field and the knower of the field; *ca bhūta prakr̥ti mokṣaṁ*: and (its bearing on) elements–nature–emancipation; *te yānti param*: they go to the Supreme.

Those who by the eye of wisdom perceive the difference between the field and the knower of the field, and (its bearing on) elements–nature–emancipation – they go to the Supreme.

DIALOGUE

Teacher: Arjuna begins this chapter with a question which even today baffles authorities in the fields of philosophy and psychology. He asks:

> Nature and spirit, the field and the knower of the field, knowledge and what is to be known – these I should like to know, Oh Keśava!

Student: *Should he have such doubts, even after having a direct cosmic vision and receiving Kṛṣṇa's final lesson on the superior form of devotion?*

Arjuna has already become a wise man in principle, but he has to organize in his own mind a philosophical structure in which everything will find its coordinated placement and function. Kṛṣṇa answers:

> This body, Oh Kaunteya! is called the field, and he who knows this, thus they call, who know, the knower of the field.

The reference to *śarīram* (body) retains a tinge of dualism in its connotation as employed here. This is only tentatively permitted in the present verse, and will be modified in the next. We should not, therefore, take the first definition too literally when it is stated that the body is the "field". There has to be something common between the actual and the perceptual, between the field and the knower of the field, before they can be interrelated unitively. In the next verse, the revised concept of the body as a value is offered:

> And also know Me as the knower of the field in all fields, Oh Bhārata! that knowledge which (refers to the knowledge) of the field and the knower of the field, is, in My opinion, *the* knowledge.

It is commonly understood that knowledge is comprised of our understanding of both subjective and objective aspects. Does this verse imply anything more than that?

Wisdom consists in rightly understanding the relation between the field and the knower of the field, between the actual and the perceptual. Even modern philosophers like Bertrand Russell state that this relation touches one of the most difficult problems in philosophy. The relation is a very elusive one, and lack of understanding of it leads to errors of judgement in almost every department of intelligent human life, many times with disastrous consequences. This chapter itself makes reference to some aspects of this problem in so far as they are conducive to the notion of the Absolute. God does not change or evolve; it is the field that evolves and not the knower of the field. The Gītā employs a parallel or double method in which the necessary and the contingent are discussed side by side. Throughout the text we can see a subtle interplay of these counterparts. Sometimes they complement each other; at other times they may cancel out. In either case the result will be a unitive or contemplative value. The Gītā reasons not in terms of "either/or", but in terms of "this as well as that". In the expression "know Me as the knower of the field in all fields", there is a delicate paradox implied which is inevitable in all truly dialectical forms of reasoning. Here, "the knower of the field" suggests both unity as well as multiplicity. Its field is a multiplicity of bodies. The knower is the same in all these various bodies. Thus unity and multiplicity, the One and the many, are delicately counterpoised or set one against the other in this statement, as if to cancel out both in favour of a truly Absolutist value.

Could there be such a clear-cut dichotomy of the "field" and the "knower" without causing an epistemological violation of the non-dual reality of the Absolute?

The field results from ignorance. Ignorance itself is a conditioning factor. In so far as it is capable of affecting the ordinary person's notion of a pure, unconditioned Absolute, it must remain as a limiting attribute to the Absolute. To lift the notion of the Absolute too far out of the human context would tend to make it a mere abstraction, thereby dissipating its value. It would become a philosophical triviality prejudicial to the cause of wisdom. Still, it is possible for the ordinary human being to find indications in all the valid scriptures of the world of a wide range of human values in the Absolute, which can be understood and adopted without tainting it with mundane considerations. The existential aspects which Kṛṣṇa enumerates below can easily be seen to be different from what are usually termed as existential, physical, or material aspects. Kṛṣṇa says:

> The great elements, ego-sense, reason, and also the Unmanifest, the ten senses, the one mind, and the five conceptual aspects of the senses,
>
> wish–dislike, pleasure–pain, the organic aggregation, vital intelligence, firmness – this, in brief, is the field, with modifications named.

Does the field, the existential categorization given here, correspond to the Sāṁkhyan concept of prakṛti *(nature)?*

We see in these references a great affinity to Sāṁkhyan categories. It is hard to say to what value each of these correspond. The series, starting with *mahābhūtāni* (great elements), refers to ontological realities, such as earth, water, et cetera. This is legitimate because the field has been primarily designated as the decaying body. The reference to the five conceptual aspects of the senses implies the *tanmātra* (thing in itself), of the Sāṁkhyas. They depend on our own consciousness for their reality. The senses themselves represent the windows of consciousness. In between these two extremes, the ontological and the conceptual, factors such as *buddhi* (intelligence) and *ahaṁkāra* (individuality) are placed. All these items so far enumerated may be said to represent the field more directly than their derivations, given as wish–dislike, pleasure–pain, the organic aggregation, vital intelligence, and firmness.

This is evidently very different from the description of nature in earlier chapters. How does Kṛṣṇa categorize the knower?

Kṛṣṇa describes the attributes of the knower as the essence of wisdom:

> Freedom from conventional pride, unpretentiousness, non-hurting, non-retaliating forbearance, straightforwardness, loyal support of the teacher, purity, steadfastness, state of self-withdrawal,
>
> detachment in respect of sense-interests, absence of egoism, insight regarding the pain and evil of birth, death, old age, and disease,
>
> without clinging to, and without intensely-involved attachment to, (relations such as) sons, wives, (and property such as) houses, and having a constant neutral mental attitude in respect of desirable and undesirable happenings,
>
> devotion to Me to the exclusion of everything extraneous, and never straying from the direct path, preference to dwell in a place apart, distaste for crowded living,
>
> everlasting affiliation to the wisdom pertaining to the Self, insight into the content of philosophical wisdom – this is declared to be wisdom; whatever is other than this is ignorance.

In the previous series we saw an integrated organism which constitutes the personal value called the "field", which is the basis for higher virtues to be cultivated or erected. The structural secrets of the field and the knower of the field are to be clearly understood before we proceed further.

Could you please explain that?

We have already seen the field as the basis where higher virtues can be cultivated. The vital intelligence that leads to a personal quality is here called "firmness". It is related to the idea of vigour (*ūrjitam*) in Chapter X. It suggests both stability and strength, and, as a personal quality, marks the furthermost limit to which perfection in the context of the field can attain. Firmness represents the narrow neck of the hour-glass structure of values presented. From the most broad-based of the great elements at the bottom of the lower cone to this pointedly personal virtue of firmness at the central apex is the field. Beyond this we reach up to other personal virtues of a non-social and individualistic character. These are also of the nature of personal virtues, but really belong to the domain of *kṣetrajña* (knower of the field).

After presenting the existential field and its subsistential knower, Kṛṣṇa goes on to that which is neither existential nor non-existential.

> I shall declare that which is to be known, knowing which one gains immortality: the beginningless, having Me as its supreme culminating factor, the Absolute, which is said to be neither existence nor non-existence.
>
> With hands and feet everywhere, with eyes and heads and mouths and hearing everywhere – in the world, That remains, enveloping all.
>
> Shining by the specific characters of the senses, devoid of all sense attributes, unattached, supporting all, without qualities, yet perceiving qualities,
>
> without and within beings, immobile and mobile too – because subtle, That is unknowable; That stands far and near also.
>
> And undivided, yet remaining divided, as it were, in beings, supporter of existence, and That which is to be known, holding back and releasing for expansive becoming,
>
> the Light even of lights – That is said to be beyond darkness: knowledge, the knowable, and what is to be reached through knowledge, particularly located in the hearts of everyone.
>
> Thus the field, and wisdom, and what has to be known, have been briefly told; My devotee, having known this, attains to My state of being.

Does Kṛṣṇa give any precise definition of nature and spirit, prakṛti *and* puruṣa?

He defines nature as the motivating factor that is implied in the agency of cause and effect. Spirit is the motivating factor in the experience of pleasure and pain.

When enjoyment belongs to the ego-sense of the "I" factor, how can it be equated with spirit?

Cause and effect belong to the world of becoming, which is implied in the entire of the phenomenal, whether physical, chemical, biological, or in the abstractions of mathematics and semantics. But the field of pain/pleasure has a direct reference to the conscious recognition of values. *Ānanda* (value) is one of the references of the Absolute. Hence, the two motivating factors of nature and spirit are given the same status. It is the spirit that is made to articulate in nature, appreciating the modalities born of nature.

Does the use of the term "spirit" here refer to the tiny spark of the Absolute that animates all beings, or to the Absolute itself?

The Self is indivisible and One without a second. There is no question of its becoming a spark or attaining any quantitative dimension. Kṛṣṇa says:

> Supervisor, and Permitter, Supporter, Experiencer, the Great Lord, also called the supreme Self, is the supreme Spirit in the body.

The mystery implied in the mode of contact between nature and spirit is hereby clarified. Within the limits of the body the pure Absolute suffers from certain strictures and conditionings. The favourite example in Indian philosophy is of a colourless, transparent crystal placed on red silk, or in contact with a ruby. The colourless apparently becomes coloured. The conditioning factor in this case is the silk or ruby. In Sanskrit this conditioning factor is called *upādhi.* The functions of the seemingly conditioned Absolute given in this verse (22) are:

upadraṣṭā – one who is witnessing one's own negative principle as though it is different from oneself, just as the mind watches its own course.

anumantā – that eternal Presence which sanctions and gives benediction to all permissible and commendable functions or operations of the individual self.

bhartā – the soul and the body are related as husband to wife. *Bhartā* here means the seed that gives fulfilment to the creative dynamism of nature.

bhoktā – the enjoyer. Though the Self has nothing outside it, it attains the status of an enjoyer when it assumes the position of the subject in relation to its own objectivated and phenomenal creation.

maheśvara – the Supreme Lord, who governs all, seated in the hearts of all, as if the One has divided itself into the many.

paramātmā – *ātmā* means the Self, *para* means the Absolute, or the Supreme. Hence, *paramātmā* is the Supreme Self that is mirrored in the conditioning factor of the body. The Self that is mirrored, thereby appearing to be finite and embodied, is called the *jīvātmā.*

puruṣa – spirit. As this spirit is going to be revalued in Chapter XV, where it is raised above the duality of *puruṣa* and *prakṛti,* it is here qualified as *para,* giving the meaning of the all-transcending Supreme.

How do we visualize this Absolute, which resides in us or is mirrored in the conditioning factor called the body?

Some people behold the Self in the Self by meditating on the Self. Others realize the Self through a discipline of the eight-limbed *yoga*. Still others realize the Self by making themselves fully dedicated instruments of the Absolute. The *yoga* of the Gītā implies a certain method of equalization or cancellation of counterparts. It is when two polarized factors are cancelled, one against the other, that we enter into something unitive. Whether in the world of values that might belong to the field of necessary action, or of rational life, or of Self-realization, the final value that emerges from the cancellation of counterparts is the same.

How can the imperishable be seen in the perishable, and the infinite be seen in the finite?

From an image or shadow we can infer the original. For example, however limited and specific is a triangle drawn on paper with points labelled *p–q–r*, from that triangle one can visualize the eternal, non-specific Triangle, which can be equilateral, isosceles, and scalene all at once as well as separately. Kṛṣṇa says:

> He who sees the supreme Lord abiding in (a state of) equality in all beings, within the perishing as the non-perishing – he sees.
>
> For he who sees the Lord seated equally everywhere, destroys not the Self by the Self; and so he attains the supreme goal.
>
> He who sees that all actions are done by nature alone, and likewise that the Self is actionless – he truly sees.
>
> When he perceives the disjunct existence of beings established in the One, and from whence also their expansion, then he becomes the Absolute.

Don't you think the Absolute becomes tainted or coloured by being associated with a body that undergoes various experiences of pain and pleasure, and vice and virtue?

Kṛṣṇa concludes this chapter with a presentation of the Absolute in its full untainted purity and glory:

> Having no beginning, having no attributes (*guṇas*), this supreme Self suffers no decrease, though dwelling in the body, Oh son of Kuntī! it neither acts nor is it tainted.
>
> As the all-pervading subtle space-principle (*ākāśa*) is untarnished by reason of its subtlety, so the Self, seated everywhere in the body, is untarnished.
>
> As the one sun illumines this whole world, so the Lord of the field, Oh Bhārata! illumines all the field.
>
> Those who by the eye of wisdom perceive the difference between the field and the knower of the field, and (its bearing on) elements–nature–emancipation – they go to the Supreme.

In this chapter the most important subject to which the author wanted to direct our attention was the distinction between the field (*kṣetra*) and the knower of field (*kṣetrajña*). In summing up the discussion, the author almost takes the same words out of the contents of verse 2, where it was stated that knowledge itself only amounts to understanding the distinction between these two factors. Standing neutrally between them, linking them into unity, is the enigmatic hyphen (*kṣetra-kṣetrajña*), which is a great mystery, requiring the eye of wisdom to see.

XIV

Guṇatraya-Vibhāga-Yoga

The Unitive Way of Transcending the Three Nature-Modalities

INTRODUCTION

ONE of the paradoxes we come to encounter on the path of realization is that change does not change the Changeless, and that transformation does not transform the beingness of what is transforming. The duality of the subject encountering the object does not cease even after the realization of the non-dual unity of the Self or the Absolute Being. All phenomenal variegations will continue to register their impressions on the senses and the mind as long as our body functions as a healthy organism. Our transactional world is not a hallucinatory fancy. It has as its basis an irreducible nature. For this reason the relevancy of the transactional world will not be obliterated by knowing and envisioning the transcendental, despite the fact that consciousness does not modulate in a transcendent state of mystical absorption.

The theme of the Bhagavadgītā is not of a silent recluse merging into the aloneness of the spirit, but the realization of a man of action who is confronted with the clashing values and conflicting enigmas of a factual world, where necessity bares its teeth even in moments of sublime contemplation. The relevancy of learning, searching, and undergoing discipline comes only in a world of manifested beings with individuated minds.

The two constituent factors of individuation are the articulating spirit and the formalizing matter. Matter is here used in the sense of a primal *thing-in-itself*, which coexists with the spirit as its own negative counterpart. If spirit is defined as "pure beingness, pure awareness, and the meaning of meanings and values", what is termed here as matter is to be described as a medium that can be (1) clear and flawless in its capacity to represent, (2) a kinetically functinning dynamic which can cause grave variations in the presentative operation of the medium, and (3) an inertial veiling that can either obscure or distort the articulation of spirit. This seemingly complicated definition of spirit and matter is given simply in Sanskrit terms as *sat*, *cit*, and *ānanda* in the case of spirit, and *sattva*, *rajas*, and *tamas* with respect to matter.

In the previous chapter the emphasis was given to the pure source of life by affirming its belonging to *sat-cit-ānanda*. In the present chapter it is counterbalanced with a detailed examination of the ontologic basis of the transactional ground of life, giving due attention to both the nature and function of the constituent factors of matter (*prakṛti*). It would be of great advantage to the student to treat Chapters XIII and XIV as complementary, and this will prepare the mind to receive the message of Chapter XV, which presents the overall philosophy of the Gītā in terms of both the acceptance and the transcendence of the Sāṁkhyan duality of *prakṛti* and *puruṣa*.

TRANSLATION

श्रीभगवानुवाच –

1. परं भूयः प्रवक्ष्यामि ज्ञानानां ज्ञानमुत्तमम् ।
यज्ज्ञात्वा मुनयः सर्वे परां सिद्धिमितो गताः ॥

śrībhagavān uvāca –
paraṁ bhūyaḥ pravakṣyāmi jñānānāṁ jñānam uttamam ।
yaj jñātvā munayaḥ sarve parāṁ siddhhim ito gatāḥ ॥

śrībhagavān uvāca: Kṛṣṇa said; *bhūyaḥ pravakṣyāmi*: (I) shall again declare; *paraṁ jñānam*: (that) superior wisdom; *uttamam jñānānāṁ*: the best of (all) wisdom; *jñātvā yat*: knowing which; *sarve munayaḥ*: all sage-recluses (*munis*); *gatāḥ*: have gone; *parāṁ siddhim*: to transcendental perfection; *itaḥ*: from here.

Kṛṣṇa said:

I shall again declare that superior wisdom, the best of all wisdom, by knowing which all sage-recluses have passed to transcendental perfection from here.

2. इदं ज्ञानमुपाश्रित्य मम साधर्म्यमागताः ।
सर्गेऽपि नोपजायन्ते प्रलये न व्यथन्ति च ॥

idaṁ jñānam upāśritya mama sādharmyam āgatāḥ ।
sarge 'pi no 'pajāyante pralaye na vyathanti ca ॥

upāśritya: having resorted to; *idaṁ jñānam*: this wisdom; *ca āgatāḥ*: and having attained to; *sādharmyam*: conformity in (express) features; *mama*: pertaining to Me; *na upajāyante*: (they) are neither born; *sarge*: at creation; *na api vyathanti*: nor are (they) adversely affected; *pralaye*: at dissolution.

Having resorted to this wisdom, and having attained to conformity in (express) features pertaining to Me, they are neither born at creation, nor are they adversely affected at dissolution.

3. मम योनिर्महद्ब्रह्म तस्मिन्गर्भं दधाम्यहम् ।
संभवः सर्वभूतानां ततो भवति भारत ॥

mama yonir mahad brahma tasmin garbhaṁ dadhāmy aham ।
saṁbhavaḥ sarvabhūtānāṁ tato bhavati bhārata ॥

mama yoniḥ: My womb; *mahat brahma*: (is) great Brahmā (Supreme Deity); *tasmin*: in that; *aham dadhāmi garbhaṁ*: I place the germ; *tataḥ bhavati saṁbhavaḥ*: thence is the birth; *sarva bhūtānāṁ*: of all beings; *bhārata*: Oh Arjuna.

My womb is great Brahmā; in that I place the germ; thence is the birth of all beings, Oh Bhārata!

4. सर्वयोनिषु कौन्तेय मूर्तयः सम्भवन्ति याः ।
तासां ब्रह्म महद्योनिरहं बीजप्रदः पिता ॥

sarvayoniṣu kaunteya mūrtayaḥ saṁbhavanti yāḥ ।
tāsāṁ brahma mahad yonir ahaṁ bījapradaḥ pitā ॥

yāḥ murtayaḥ: whatever tangible forms; *saṁbhavanti*: are produced; *sarva yoniṣu*: in all the wombs; *kaunteya*: Oh Arjuna; *mahat brahma*: great Brahmā (Lord of Creation); *tāsāṁ yoniḥ*: (is) their (common) womb; *ahaṁ*: (and) I (am); *bījapradaḥ pitā*: the seed-bestowing Father.

Whatever tangible forms are produced in all the wombs, Oh Son of Kuntī! great Brahmā is their (common) womb, and I am the seed-bestowing Father.

5. सत्त्वं रजस्तम इति गुणाः प्रकृतिसम्भवाः ।
निबध्नन्ति महाबाहो देहे देहिनमव्ययम् ॥

sattvaṁ rajas tama iti guṇāḥ prakṛtisaṁbhavāḥ ।
nibadhnanti mahābāho dehe dehinam avyayam ॥

sattvaṁ: the pure-clear; *rajaḥ*: the affective-active; *tamaḥ*: (and) the inert-dark; *iti prakṛti saṁbhavāḥ*: thus the nature (necessity) born; *guṇāḥ*: modalities; *nibadhnanti*: bind; *mahābāho*: Oh Arjuna; *avyayam*: the imperishable; *dehinam dehe*: embodied One in the body.

The pure-clear, the affective-active, and the inert-dark – these nature-necessity-born modalities bind, Oh Mighty-Armed, the imperishable embodied One!

6. तत्र सत्त्वं निर्मलत्वात्प्रकाशकमनामयम् ।
सुखसङ्गेन बध्नाति ज्ञानसङ्गेन चानघ ॥

tatra sattvaṁ nirmalatvāt prakāśakam anāmayam ।
sukhasaṅgena badhnāti jñānasaṅgena cā 'nagha ॥

tatra: of these; *sattvaṁ*: the pure-clear modality; *nirmalatvāt*: from its purity; *prakāśakam*: causing brightness; *anāmayam*: (and expressing) normal well-being; *badhnāti*: binds; *sukha saṅgena*: by pleasure-conditioning; *ca jñāna saṅgena*: and by knowledge-conditioning; *anagha*: Oh Arjuna.

Of these, the pure-clear modality, from its purity, causing brightness and expressing normal well-being, binds by pleasure-conditioning and by knowledge-conditioning, Oh Sinless One!

7. रजो रागात्मकं विद्धि तृष्णासङ्गसमुद्भवम् ।
तन्निबध्नाति कौन्तेय कर्मसङ्गेन देहिनम् ।।

rajo rāgātmakaṁ viddhi tṛṣṇāsaṅgasamudbhavam ।
tan nibadhnāti kaunteya karmansaṅgena dehinam ॥

viddhi: know; *rajaḥ*: the affective-active modality; *rāgātmakaṁ*: (as being) of the nature of attachment; *samudbhavam tṛṣṇā saṅga*: arising from the thirst (for life and) the adhering tendency; *tat nibadhnāti*: that binds fast; *kaunteya*: Oh Arjuna; *dehinam*: the embodied One; *karma saṅgena*: by action-association.

Know you the affective-active modality as being of the nature of attachment, conditioned by thirst for life and the adhering tendency; it binds fast, Oh Son of Kuntī! the embodied One, by action-association.

8. तमस्त्वज्ञानजं विद्धि मोहनं सर्वदेहिनाम् ।
प्रमादालस्यनिद्राभिस्तन्निबध्नाति भारत ।।

tamas tv ajñānajaṁ viddhi mohanaṁ sarvadehinām ।
pramādālasyanidrābhis tan nibadhnāti bhārata ॥

tu tamaḥ: but the inert-dark modality; *viddhi*: know; *ajñānajaṁ*: (is) born of ignorance; *mohanaṁ sarva dehinām*: deluding all embodied beings; *tat nibadhnāti*: that binds; *bhārata*: Oh Arjuna; *pramāda ālasya nidrābhiḥ*: by delusion, lassitude, and somnolence.

But the inert-dark modality, know you, is born of ignorance, deluding all embodied beings: it binds, Oh Bhārata! by delusion, lassitude, and somnolence.

9. सत्त्वं सुखे सञ्जयति रजः कर्मणि भारत ।
ज्ञानमावृत्य तु तमः प्रमादे सञ्जयत्युत ।।

sattvaṁ sukhe sañjayati rajaḥ karmaṇi bhārata ।
jñānam āvṛtya tu tamaḥ pramāde sañjayaty uta ॥

sattvaṁ: the pure-clear modality; *sañjayati sukhe*: conduces to pleasure; *rajaḥ karmaṇi*: (and) the affective-active modality to action; *bhārata*: Oh Arjuna; *tu tamaḥ*: while the inert-dark modality; *āvṛtya jñānam*: shrouding wisdom; *sañjayati pramāde uta*: conduces to delusion indeed.

The pure-clear modality conduces to pleasure, and the affective-active modality to action, Oh Bhārata! while the inert-dark modality, shrouding wisdom, conduces to delusion.

10. रजस्तमश्चाभिभूय सत्त्वं भवति भारत ।
रजः सत्त्वं तमश्चैव तमः सत्त्वं रजस्तथा ॥

rajas tamaś cā 'bhibhūya sattvaṁ bhavati bhārata ।
rajaḥ sattvaṁ tamaś cai 'va tamaḥ sattvaṁ rajas tathā ॥

sattvaṁ bhavati: (now) the pure-clear modality comes to be; *abhibhūya*: overpowering; *rajaḥ*: the affective-active; *ca tamaḥ*: and the inert-dark; *ca eva rajaḥ*: and indeed the affective-active; *sattvaṁ*: (prevails over) the pure-clear; *tamaḥ*: (and) the inert-dark; *tathā tamaḥ*: likewise the inert-dark; *sattvaṁ*: (over) the pure-clear; *rajaḥ*: (and) the affective-active; *bhārata*: Oh Arjuna.

Now the pure-clear modality dominates, overpowering the affective-active and the inert-dark, and the affective-active prevails over the pure-clear and the inert-dark, likewise the inert-dark over the pure-clear and the affective-active, Oh Bhārata!

11. सर्वद्वारेषु देहेऽस्मिन्प्रकाश उपजायते ।
ज्ञानं यदा तदा विद्याद्विवृद्धं सत्त्वमित्युत ॥

sarvadvāreṣu dehe 'smin prakāśa upajāyate ।
jñānaṁ yadā tadā vidyād vivṛddhaṁ sattvam ity uta ॥

yadā prakāśa: when light; *jñānaṁ*: (which is) wisdom; *upajāyate*: streams forth; *sarva dvāreṣu*: from all the doors; *asmin dehe*: in this body; *tadā vidyāt*: then it may be understood; *sattvam iti*: (that) the pure-clear modality thus; *vivṛddhaṁ uta*: (is) predominant indeed.

When light, which is wisdom, streams forth from all the doors of the body, then it may be understood that the pure-clear modality is predominant.

12. लोभः प्रवृत्तिरारम्भः कर्मणामशमः स्पृहा ।
रजस्येतानि जायन्ते विवृद्धे भरतर्षभ ॥

lobhaḥ pravṛttir ārambhaḥ karmaṇām aśamaḥ spṛhā ।
rajasy etāni jāyante vivṛddhe bharatarṣabha ॥

rajasi vivṛddhe: when the affective-active modality dominates; *etāni jāyante*: these arise; *lobhaḥ pravṛttiḥ*: greed, activity; *ārambhaḥ karmaṇām*: initiation of works; *aśamaḥ spṛhā*: impatience (and) covetousness; *bharatarṣabha*: Oh Arjuna.

When the affective-active modality dominates, there arises greed, activity, initiation of works, impatience, and covetousness, Oh Best of the Bhāratas!

13. अप्रकाशोऽप्रवृत्तिश्च प्रमादो मोह एव च ।
तमस्येतानि जायन्ते विवृद्धे कुरुनन्दन ॥

aprakāśo 'pravṛttiś ca pramādo moha eva ca ।
tamasy etāni jāyante vivṛddhe kurunandana ॥

tamasi vivṛddhe: when the inert-dark modality dominates; *aprakāśaḥ*: dullness; *ca apravṛttiḥ*: and lack of initiative; *mohaḥ*: delusion; *ca eva pramādaḥ*: and indeed infatuation; *etāni jāyante*: these arise; *kurunandana*: Oh Arjuna.

When the inert-dark modality dominates, dullness, lack of initiative, delusion, and infatuation arise, Oh Joy of the Kurus!

14. यदा सत्त्वे प्रवृद्धे तु प्रलयं याति देहभृत् ।
तदोत्तमविदां लोकानमलान्प्रतिपद्यते ॥

yadā sattve pravṛddhe tu pralayaṁ yāti dehabhṛt ।
tado 'ttamavidāṁ lokān amalān pratipadyate ॥

tu dehabhṛt: but (if) the body-bearer; *yāti pralayaṁ*: goes to dissolution; *yadā sattve pravṛddhe*: when the pure-clear modality predominates; *tadā pratipadyate*: then (it) attains to; *amalān lokān*: the pure worlds; *vidām uttama*: of those who understand the best (values).

15. रजसि प्रलयं गत्वा कर्मसङ्गिषु जायते ।
तथा प्रलीनस्तमसि मूढयोनिषु जायते ॥

rajasi pralayaṁ gatvā karmasaṅgiṣu jāyate ।
tathā pralīnas tamasi mūḍhayoniṣu jāyate ॥

gatvā pralayaṁ: having gone to dissolution; *rajasi*: when the affective-active modality (predominates); *jāyate*: (he) is born; *karma saṅgiṣu*: among those attached to action; *tathā*: (and) likewise; *pralīnaḥ*: (if) dissolved; *tamasi*: in (a state of) inert-dark modality; *jāyate*: (he) is born; *mūḍha yoniṣu*: in the wombs of the foolish.

If the body-bearer goes to dissolution when the pure-clear modality predominates, then it attains to the pure worlds of those who understand the best values.

Meeting with dissolution when the affective-active modality predominates, he is born among those attached to action; and likewise if dissolved in a state of inert-dark modality, he is born in the wombs of the foolish.

16. कर्मणः सुकृतस्याहुः सात्त्विकं निर्मलं फलम् ।
रजसस्तु फलं दुःखमज्ञानं तमसः फलम् ॥

karmaṇaḥ sukṛtasyā 'huḥ sāttvikaṁ nirmalaṁ phalam ।
rajasas tu phalaṁ duḥkham ajñānaṁ tamasaḥ phalam ॥

phalam: the benefit; *karmaṇaḥ sukṛtasya*: of good action; *āhuḥ*: is said to be; *sāttvikaṁ*: pure-clear; *nirmalaṁ*: (and) pure; *tu phalaṁ*: while the benefit; *rajasaḥ duḥkham*: of the affective-active modality (is) pain; *ajñānaṁ*: (and) ignorance (is); *phalam tamasaḥ*: the benefit of the inert-dark modality.

The benefit of good action is said to be pure-clear and pure; while the benefit of the affective-active modality is pain; and ignorance is the benefit of the inert-dark modality.

17. सत्त्वात्सञ्जायते ज्ञानं रजसो लोभ एव च ।
प्रमादमोहौ तमसो भवतोऽज्ञानमेव च ॥

sattvāt sañjāyate jñānaṁ rajaso lobha eva ca ।
pramādamohau tamaso bhavato 'jñānam eva ca ॥

sattvāt: from the pure-clear modality; *sañjāyate jñānaṁ*: arises wisdom; *eva ca rajasaḥ*: as also from the affective-active modality; *lobhaḥ*: greed; *pramāda mohau*: both infatuation and delusion; *ca eva ajñānam*: and also ignorance; *bhavataḥ tamasaḥ*: come to be from the inert-dark modality.

From the pure-clear modality arises wisdom, as also from the affective-active modality, greed; both delusion and infatuation, and also ignorance, arise from the inert-dark modality.

18. ऊर्ध्वं गच्छन्ति सत्त्वस्था मध्ये तिष्ठन्ति राजसाः ।
जघन्यगुणवृत्तिस्था अधो गच्छन्ति तामसाः ॥

ūrdhvaṁ gacchanti sattvasthā madhye tiṣṭhanti rājasāḥ ।
jaghanyaguṇavṛttisthā adho gacchanti tāmasāḥ ॥

sattvasthāḥ: those who abide in the pure-clear modality; *gacchanti ūrdhvaṁ*: go upward; *rājasāḥ*: the affective-active; *tiṣṭhanti madhye*: dwell in the middle; *tāmasāḥ*: (and) the inert-dark; *jaghanya guṇa vṛttisthāḥ*: abiding in the function of the lowest modality of nature; *gacchanti adhaḥ*: go downward.

Those who abide in the pure-clear modality go upward; the affective-active dwell in the middle, and the inert-dark, abiding in the function of the lowest modality of nature, go downward.

19. नान्यं गुणेभ्यः कर्तारं यदा द्रष्टानुपश्यति ।
गुणेभ्यश्च परं वेत्ति मद्भावं सोऽधिगच्छति ।।

nā 'nyaṁ guṇebhyaḥ kartāraṁ yadā draṣṭā 'nupaśyati ।
guṇebhyaś cā paraṁ vetti madbhāvaṁ so 'dhigacchati ॥

yadā draṣṭā: when the seer; *anupaśyati na anyaṁ kartāraṁ*: beholds no other agent; *guṇebhyaḥ*: than the modalities of nature; *ca vetti*: and knows; *paraṁ guṇebhyaḥ*: what is beyond the modalities; *saḥ adhigacchati*: he attains to; *mat bhāvaṁ*: My state of being.

When the seer beholds no other agent than the modalities of nature, and knows that which lies beyond the modalities, he attains to My state of being.

20. गुणानेतानतीत्य त्रीन्देही देहसमुद्भवान् ।
जन्ममृत्युजरादुःखैर्विमुक्तोऽमृतमश्नुते ।।

guṇān etān atītya trīn dehī dehasamudbhavān ।
janmamṛtyujarāduḥkhair vimukto 'mṛtam aśnute ॥

dehī: the embodied; *atītya etān*: having transcended these; *trīn guṇān*: three modalities of nature; *deha samudbhavān*: originating in the body; *vimuktaḥ*: (is) freed; *janma mṛtyu jarā duḥkhaiḥ*: from sufferings of birth, death, and old age; *aśnute amṛtam*: (and) attains immortality.

The embodied, having transcended these three modalities of nature, originating in the body, is freed from the sufferings of birth, death, and old age, and enjoys immortality.

अर्जुन उवाच –
21. कैर्लिङ्गैस्त्रीन्गुणानेतानतीतो भवति प्रभो ।
किमाचारः कथं चैतांस्त्रीन्गुणानतिवर्तते ।।

arjuna uvāca –

kair liṅgais trīn guṇān etān atīto bhavati prabho ।
kimācāraḥ kathaṁ cai 'tāṁs trīn guṇān ativartate ॥

ārjuna uvāca: Arjuna said; *kaiḥ liṅgaiḥ*: by what marks; *prabho*: Oh Kṛṣṇa; *atītaḥ*: (does he who) has transcended; *etān trīn guṇān*: these three modalities of nature; *bhavati*: become (recognized); *kim ācāraḥ*: what (is his) conduct; *ca kathaṁ ativartate*: and how does he transcend; *etān trīn guṇān*: these three modalities of nature.

Arjuna said:

By what marks, Oh Master! does he who has transcended those three modalities of nature become recognized? What is his conduct, and how does he transcend those three modalities of nature?

श्रीभगवानुवाच –

22. प्रकाशं च प्रवृत्तिं च मोहमेव च पाण्डव ।
न द्वेष्टि सम्प्रवृत्तानि न निवृत्तानि काङ्क्षति ॥

śrībhagavān uvāca –

prakāśaṁ ca pravṛttiṁ ca moham eva ca pāṇḍava ।
na dveṣṭi saṁpravṛttāni na nivṛttāni kāṅkṣati ॥

śrībhagavān uvāca: Kṛṣṇa said; *prakāśaṁ ca*: light and; *pravṛttiṁ ca*: activity and; *ca moham eva*: also delusion indeed; *saṁpravṛttāni*: when present; *pāṇḍava*: Oh Arjuna; *na dveṣṭi*: (he) is not dissatisfied; *nivṛttāni*: when absent.

Kṛṣṇa said:

Light and activity and delusion: when present, Oh Pāṇḍava! he is not dissatisfied, nor does he hanker for them when absent.

23. उदासीनवदासीनो गुणैर्यो न विचाल्यते ।
गुणा वर्तन्त इत्येव योऽवतिष्ठति नेङ्गते ॥

udāsīnavad āsīno guṇair yo na vicālyate ।
guṇā vartanta ity eva yo 'vatiṣṭhati ne 'ṅgate ॥

yaḥ āsīnaḥ udāsīnavat: (he) who, seated as a neutral; *na vicālyate*: is not moved; *guṇaiḥ*: by the modalities of nature; *guṇāḥ vartante iti eva*: who, (thinking that) the modalities of nature operate in rotation thus indeed; *yaḥ avatiṣṭhati*: who, standing apart; *na iṅgate*: is unmoved.

24. समदुःखसुखः स्वस्थः समलोष्टाश्मकाञ्चनः ।
तुल्यप्रियाप्रियो धीरस्तुल्यनिन्दात्मसंस्तुतिः ॥

samaduḥkhasukhaḥ svasthaḥ samaloṣṭāśmakāñcanaḥ ।
tulyapriyāpriyo dhīras tulyanindātmasaṁstutiḥ ॥

sama duḥkha sukhaḥ: the same in pain and pleasure; *svasthaḥ*: at rest in himself; *sama loṣṭa aśma kāñcanaḥ*: to whom a clod of earth, and a stone, and gold are alike; *dhīraḥ*: firm (in attitude); *tulya priya apriyaḥ*: alike to loved and unloved; *tulya nindā ātma saṁstutiḥ*: who regards his being blamed or praised equally.

24. मानापमानयोस्तुल्यस्तुल्यो मित्रारिपक्षयोः ।
सर्वारम्भपरित्यागी गुणातीतः स उच्यते ।।

mānāpamānayos tulyas tulyo mitrāripakṣayoḥ ।
sarvārambhaparityāgī guṇātītaḥ sa ucyate ॥

tulyaḥ: the same; *māna apamānayoḥ*: in honour and disgrace; *tulyaḥ mitra ari pakṣayoḥ*: taking no sides as between friends or foes; *sarva ārambha parityāgī*: abandoning all initiation of works; *saḥ ucyate*: he is said (to have); *guṇa atītaḥ*: transcended the modalities of nature.

He who, seated as a neutral, is not moved by the modalities of nature, thinking that the modalities of nature operate in rotation, who, standing apart, is unmoved,

the same in pain and pleasure, at rest in himself, to whom a clod of earth, and a stone, and gold are alike, firm in attitude alike to loved and unloved, who regards his being blamed or praised equally,

the same in honour and disgrace, taking no sides as between friends or foes, abandoning all initiation of works – he is said to have transcended the modalities of nature.

26. मां च योऽव्यभिचारेण भक्ति योगेन सेवते ।
स गुणान्समतीत्यैतान्ब्रह्मभूयाय कल्पते ।।

māṁ ca yo 'vyabhicāreṇa bhaktiyogena sevate ।
sa guṇān samatītyai 'tān brahmabhūyāya kalpate ॥

ca yaḥ: (he) also who; *sevate māṁ*: serves Me; *bhakti yogena*: with a *yoga* of devotion; *avyabhicāreṇa*: never deviating from the proper path; *samatītya etān guṇān*: transcending these modalities of nature; *saḥ kalpate*: he is considered fit; *brahma bhūyāya*: for becoming the Absolute.

He also who serves Me with a *yoga* of devotion, never deviating from the proper path, transcending these modalities of nature – he is considered fit for becoming the Absolute.

27. ब्रह्मणो हि प्रतिष्ठाहममृतस्याव्ययस्य च ।
शाश्वतस्य च धर्मस्य सुखस्यैकान्तिकस्य च ।।

brahmaṇo hi pratiṣṭhā 'ham amṛtasyā 'vyayasya ca ।
śāśvatasya ca dharmasya sukhasyai 'kāntikasya ca ॥

hi aham pratiṣṭhā: for I (am) the basis; *brahmaṇaḥ*: of the Absolute; *ca avyayasya*: and the unexpended; *amṛtasya*: nectar of immortality; *ca śāśvatasya*: and the eternal; *dharmasya*: way of right conduct; *ca ekāntikasya sukhasya*: and of lonely final happiness.

For I am the basis of the Absolute, and the unexpended nectar of immortality, and the eternal way of right conduct, and of lonely final happiness.

DIALOGUE

TEACHER: The three *guṇas* (nature modalities), with which this chapter is concerned belong to nature as expressed in the personality or the self. We have learned in the previous chapter that there are two eternal selves, both having an equal status, and it was stated that from the union between these two aspects all creation came to be. Kṛṣṇa repeats this more clearly in verses 3 and 4 of the present chapter:

> My womb is great Brahmā; in that I place the germ; thence is the birth of all beings, Oh Bhārata!
>
> Whatever tangible forms are produced in all the wombs, Oh Son of Kuntī! great Brahmā is their (common) womb, and I am the seed-bestowing Father.

Like positive and negative poles, the father-principle and the mother-principle are to be visualized as belonging to the same Absolute.

STUDENT: Prakṛti *(nature) and* puruṣa *(spirit) are given as dual principles in the Sāṁkhya system. If the same duality is accepted here, how can we say that the Gītā teaches non-dual wisdom?*

In these two verses not only duality, but even multiplicity and plurality are accepted for restructuring. Yet we see how the multiplicity of wombs is abolished in favour of one common womb for all. In the same way, by making the ovum and the sperm complementary, the duality of nature and spirit is also transcended. The process of becoming is examined in more intimate terms in the present chapter. Kṛṣṇa now introduces a full-dress discussion of the three modalities in verse 5:

> The pure-clear (*sattva*), the affective-active (*rajas*), and the inert-dark (*tamas*) – these nature-necessity-born modalities (*guṇas*) bind, Oh Mighty-Armed, the imperishable embodied One!

Does the guṇa *influence the personality to conform to one or another psychological type?*

In the popular mind of the Indian people these three modalities have been closely associated with the four *varṇas* ("colours", or divisions of society). This has led to disastrous consequences. In the Gītā, however, the three modalities are applied not only to discern psychological types and problems of vocational guidance, but also to evaluate the significance of schools of philosophical thought, and to decide the nature of contemplative discipline, and even attitudes in general that one might adopt. The importance of this theory is discussed by Nataraja Guru in his Gītā commentary, and deserves close attention:

> To reduce this theory to a fetish and cling to it too easily as a rule of thumb whenever racial, religious or caste superiority or inferiority is to be discussed has been a bane which has given rise to many forms of injustice and inequality in social, economic and even educational fields, stifling and submerging or suffocating large groups of people in respect of their natural freedom and self-expression. Men like Mahatma Gandhi have fallen under the false spell of such a misinterpreted and misunderstood theory.
>
> Therefore, in entering into the subject of the three nature modalities, we should be quite aware of its full implications and should avoid treating it as the popular mind has done, in too easy a fashion. To treat it as supporting a particular theory of caste, instead of taking it as generally meant to explain subtle deep-seated problems of necessary human life, has been the great error since the time of Manu.
>
> In the first place, the three nature-modalities do not suggest any differentiation within the human species itself, giving rise to any sub-species or race, as many might suppose by the constant use of the word *jāti* (kind, species) in connection with *varṇa*, often taken as the same as "caste" questions. The modalities in nature implied in the *guṇa*s are not such as to make it possible for anyone to separate people physiologically or even scientifically into any watertight groups. Even hereditary, tribal, or clan groupings are not envisaged by the theory as presented in the Gītā.
>
> When we include deeper traits of the personality, to arrive at any such classification, we see in common life that the modalities mentioned here alternate and change over in the same person during the course of his growth or development as an individual, and even from moment to moment in his daily behaviour. Moreover, if we take the case of Arjuna's own kṣatriyahood (warrior status) we find it is true and valid only when the occasion of a righteous or absolutist war is present. Killing would be right for Arjuna at best for a few hours.
>
> Inertia, motion and stability are suggested by the three modalities, and may be said to be at the basis of *tamas* (inert-dark), *rajas* (affective-active) and *sattva* (pure-clear), respectively. They could also be said to express themselves in dullness, alertness and steady intelligence, or as sloth, excitement and contemplative capacity. We could similarly speak of three-gradations based on harmony, or on unitive philosophical insight, or again in terms of affectivity. In fact, this is what the Gītā has attempted in Chapter XVIII, after explaining and defining as completely as possible the origin of these modalities of nature and their field of operation, which is limited to the lower Self.

This theory as applied here contributes one of the grandest positive contributions of Vyāsa to philosophy. He has stated here the rationale of many departments of spiritual life, especially in India, which otherwise would have remained shrouded in a mysterious confusion, favourable to every kind of superstition, in the name of a common belief. By the help of this theory, Vyāsa has succeeded in grading and arranging spiritual life.

The three *guṇa*s (nature modalities) should be viewed dynamically and not statically, as a triple-stranded regulative necessary principle which interferes with the flux of becoming, and above all as something that still pertains to the relative side of life only, without having anything to do with spirituality properly understood. They are normative and not experimentally fixed in character. Above all they have to be understood only in conjunction with the objective counterparts belonging to each, without which they are absurd in themselves. Such is the only sense of II.45, where Arjuna is asked to transcend the three nature modalities and not to cultivate them. We can also see in this chapter, in verse 25, the recommending reference to *guṇātītaḥ* (one who has transcended the three modalities of nature). We have already drawn attention to the fact that the Self is bound to necessity as implied in the word *nibadhnanti* (bind). Anything tending to bind the Self, however, even if the bondage is with a golden thread, cannot be called truly spiritual, because all spirituality implies release or freedom.

Even a person conforming to the highest or the purest modality of the three, the *sattva guṇa*, can lay claim at best only to an exalted form of holiness and not to true spirituality, which is quite another thing. The first qualification of a spiritual person is *anahaṁkāra* (egolessness), which is an attribute belonging properly to the *kṣetrajña* (the perceptual side of life, the "knower of the field", see XIII.7), while simple egoism belongs to the opposite counterpart, the *kṣetra* (the actual, relative, the "field" – as stated in XIII.5). A person conscious of his own holiness to the slightest degree is tainted by *ahaṁkāra* (egoism), revealing his self-sense as belonging to the actual rather than to the perceptual. This field to which the three *guṇa*s belong should therefore be understood to be relativistic in character, and so all the modalities, including the *sattva* (pure-clear), have the tendency of binding rather than releasing. A sāttvic brāhmin would automatically degenerate to the status of an untouchable even if the most superior of the egoisms arising from the *guṇa*s should taint him.

What is sattva? *How does it operate in us?*

The nature of spirit is described as one of Self-founded awareness, which can be analogically compared to a shadowless light that is totally aware of itself. Nature, though not in principle self-luminous, has one aspect which is pure and clear like a transparent medium, and is at the same time capable of mirroring facts without any kind of exaggeration, distortion, or lacuna.

The concept of *prakṛti* (nature) as constituted of three modalities belongs to the philosophy of the Sāṁkhya school. In the Bhagavadgītā we are given a revised and revalued presentation of the theory of the three *guṇa*s. Only by understanding in detail the adoption of the Saṁkhyan theory of the *guṇa*s by Vedānta can one fully appreciate the application of it in the present chapter. In Chapter VII Kṛṣṇa speaks of his two aspects, the vertical (*parā*), and the horizontal (*aparā*).

The Absolute has a negative aspect. It is by this negative principle that the non-differentiated Absolute appears as if it has within it the dichotomy of a vertical and a horizontal. The horizontal aspect produces the phenomenal complex of the five elements which constitute the physical universe, and the three principles of its psychic counterparts, namely the mind, the intellect, and the ego. According to the Sāṁkhyan philosophy, the five physical principles of earth, water, fire, air, and space are only effects. Their corresponding causes are the *tanmātra*s: smell, taste, form touch, and sound. These primary causes are not to be understood as sensory experiences: *tanmātra* means "that which is measured by itself". In this theory a one-to-one correspondence is given for the physical and psychic principles. The two sets indicate the two stages of horizontalization of the Supreme Spirit. At the first level it becomes psychic, and at the second level it becomes physical.

The order of evolution is to be understood in the following way. The Absolute, or Supreme Spirit, is by nature pure and unmodulated consciousness. It has within it no separation. This is what we should always keep in mind when thinking of *puruṣa.* Within this there is a latent potential that is capable of circumlimiting itself to any degree of specificity. This negative aspect is called the "Great Principle" (*mahātattva*). When a division iṣ drawn between spirit and nature, this primary cause of horizontalization, termed here as *mahātattva*, is treated as *prakṛti* (creative energy), in contrast to *puruṣa* (the unmodulated Self). The Great Principle bifurcates consciousness into modes by presenting the spirit in three distinct ways. One is a mirroring of the pure consciousness of the Self, and is named *sattva.*

The Absolute has the triple attributes of existence, consciousness, and tranquillity (which is sometimes qualified as "bliss" or "value"). The reflected image of this Self in the *sattva* can present itself as a miniature version of the Spirit. This primary operation of *sattva* is the starting point of all confusion. It is hard to distinguish between Spirit and its reflection in the sāttvic mode.

The two other modes of the Great Principle are *rajas* and *tamas. Rajas* is a degree more remote from the Spirit than *sattva*. It distorts the mirrored image of the Spirit in the *sattva* by causing positive or negative exaggerations of the existential, subsistential, and value aspects of that image. The third mode, *tamas*, totally veils the image of the Self.

The intellect, which is somewhat similar to the *logos*, is the ground of the operation of the triple principles of *prakṛti*. In other words, we may say that the first circumlimitation that arises in the infinitude of the knowledge of the Self is the individuation of consciousness as a discerning principle. This eventuality, in the otherwise non-eventual consciousness of the Self, is now redesignated as *avyakta* (indistinct). At this stage a special agency is assigned to the differentiating intellect. This agent is called *ahaṁkāra* (ego). When ego assumes the office of operation as an individual, it is provided with a field of operation which is at once a function as well as a process. This functional field is called *manas* (mind). The mind has the potential to know and to act. As the ego is already placed in a field of discernment, and is aided by the triple principles of *sattva*, *rajas*, and *tamas*, the first series of distinctions drawn by it are of a sensory order. At this stage we should bear in mind that in the process of horizontalization we have not yet come to the physical or gross manifestation of the world. This is an early phase in the process of manifestation.

The first evolutes of the Great Principle, now bracketed as the indistinct, are the first five primary norms, already mentioned as the *tanmātra*s. As we proceed from this to the physical plane, we get the five gross physical elements (*mahābhūta*s) and also five physical organs of perception (*indriya*s). Thus there comes a one-to-one correspondence between the power to smell, the concretization of the earth principle, and the organ of smell. The other four corresponding series are: the principle of taste, the concretization of the element water, and the organ of taste; the power to see, the manifestation of the physical reality of fire, and the organ of sight; the power to touch, the physical manifestation of air, and the cutative organ; and lastly the power to hear, the manifestation of ether (*ākāśa*), and the organ of hearing. Now we have a psycho-physical organism operating at the physical level. The very process of horizontalization reveals that the quality of the negative principle of the Absolute, termed in the Gītā as *yoga-māyā*, is to be operative or functional. Thus action becomes the most dominant aspect of negativity. What have evolved from this urge to act are the five organs of action: speech, action, movement, procreation, and excretion. The central pivot of the entire process of manifestation thus rests with that mirror of the Spirit (*sattva*). Kṛṣṇa says:

> Of these, the pure-clear modality (*sattva*), from its purity, causing brightness and expressing normal well-being, binds by pleasure-conditioning and by knowledge-conditioning, Oh Sinless One!

It is further explained that the pure-clear modality (*sattva*) conduces to pleasure. When the pure-clear modality dominates, it overpowers the affective-active (*rajas*) and the inert-dark (*tamas*). When light, which is wisdom, streams forth from all the doors of the body, then it may be understood that the pure-clear modality is predominant. If the body-bearer goes to dissolution when the pure-clear modality predominates, then it attains to the pure worlds of those who understand the best values. The benefit of good action is said to be pure-clear (sattvic). From the pure-clear modality of *sattva* arises wisdom. Those who abide in the *sattva* qualify themselves to have the higher understanding of the transcendental.

What is rajas?

Rajas has been already mentioned as the mode that meddles with the image of the Self mirrored by *sattva*. It is translucent. It sparks off in various kinetic operations, and is highly coloured by emotional fluctuations. Kr̥ṣṇa describes it as follows:

> Know the affective-active modality (*rajas*) as being of the nature of attachment, conditioned by thirst for life and the adhering tendency; it binds fast, Oh Son of Kuntī! the embodied One, by action-association.

It is further said that the affective-active modality (*rajas*) conduces to action. When the affective-active modality predominates, it overpowers the pure-clear (*sattva*) and the inert-dark (*tamas*). When the affective-active modality predominates there arises greed, activity, initiation of works, impatience, and covetousness. When a person with a predominance of *rajas* in him meets with dissolution, he is born among those attached to action. The benefit of the affective-active modality is said to be pain. From it arises greed. Those who abide in the affective-active modality dwell in the middle world of the mediocre.

What is tamas?

Tamas was mentioned above as the mode of the negative tendency, which obscures the image of the Self. It veils, stratifies, crystallizes, and keeps everything in a state of inertia. Compared to the other two aspects, *sattva* and *rajas*, *tamas* is opaque. Kr̥ṣṇa describes it as follows:

> But the inert-dark modality (*tamas*), know you, is born of ignorance, deluding all embodied beings; it binds, Oh Bhārata! by delusion, lassitude, and somnolence.

It is further stated that the inert-dark modality, shrouding wisdom, conduces to delusion. When the inert-dark modality dominates, it overpowers the pure-clear and affective-active modalities. It causes dullness, lack of initiative, delusion, and infatuation. On meeting with dissolution while the inert-dark modality dominates, one is born in the wombs of the foolish. Those who abide in *tamas*, abiding in the function of the lowest modality of nature, are likely to degenerate further into still lower forms of life.

How does knowledge of these three modalities help us in our realization?

When a seer beholds no other agent than the modalities of nature, and becomes sure that the true Self is that which lies beyond the modalities, he is in a state of realization. What is advised is not a mere curbing or taming of the modalities, but a full transcendence of them.

Does Kṛṣṇa describe a person who has transcended the three modalities?

In earlier chapters there were descriptions of:

- a person established in unitive understanding (*sthitaprajña*);
- one who has ascended the peak of the yogic state (*yogārūḍha*);
- one who is established in the Absolute (*brāhmī sthiti*);
- and one who is perfect in devotion (*bhakta*).

Now Kṛṣṇa describes the nature of a person who may be understood as of transcendental mind:

> Light and activity and delusion: when present, Oh Pāṇḍava! he is not dissatisfied, nor does he hanker for them when absent.
>
> He who, seated as a neutral, is not moved by the modalities of nature, thinking that the modalities of nature operate in rotation, who, standing apart, is unmoved,
>
> the same in pain and pleasure, at rest in himself, to whom a clod of earth, and a stone, and gold are alike, firm in attitude alike to loved and unloved, who regards his being blamed or praised equally,
>
> the same in honour and disgrace, taking no sides as between friends or foes, abandoning all initiation of works – he is said to have transcended the modalities of nature.

What happens to a person who has fully transcended his modalities?

He becomes fit to be the Absolute.

Does he become the Absolute by his own effort or understanding, or is it made possible by grace?

This is explained in the last verse of the chapter:

> For I am the basis of the Absolute, and the unexpended nectar of immortality, and the eternal way of right conduct, and of lonely final happiness.

In the previous chapter the Self was clearly distinguished from the non-Self. Also described was how the field of the knower and the knower become intertwined in a snare of confusion when the attributes of the non-Self are mistakenly taken for qualities of the Self. After guiding Arjuna on how to steer past all such misconceptions, Kṛṣṇa favours Arjuna in an even more compassionate manner in the present chapter by going into greater detail on the psycho-dynamics of the modalities which decide the personality structure and motivational forces of the individuated being. The symptomatic description of the three *guṇa*s will help anyone to make a diagnosis of their own personality type.

Although certain genetic fixations are obdurate and come in the way of behavioural correction, the realization that one's true Self is different from what is mirrored in the *sattva* of the individuated self gives hope that one may liberate oneself from the self-posited limitation of the Self which accounts for the "limited-ego" and the "limited non-Self" as Fichte puts it. The existence of the phenomenal world is a borrowed ground from the Absolute. Kṛṣṇa describes Himself as the ontologic basis of the manifested world. The phenomenal manifestation cannot be refuted until one discovers that the existential ground is a mirrored variant of the inconceivable Absolute, which Kṛṣṇa reveals to be His unmanifested aspect. The assumed empirical verity of the phenomenal world, structured out of the five elements, the mind, the intellect, and the ego, presents itself as the object of experience, the process of experiencing, and the resultant end, such as happiness, misery, and delusion. An individuated Self left to itself (himself or herself) can only move toward these ends. *Sattva* leads to happiness, *rajas* to misery, and *tamas* to delusion. Even this happiness provided by *sattva* is only a snare. That is why in the *Īśa Upaniṣad* it says:

> *With a golden vessel*
> *The Real's face is covered o'er;*
> *That do thou, Oh Pūṣan! uncover*
> *For one whose* dharma *it is to see the Real.*

XV

Puruṣottama-Yoga

The Unitive Approach to the Paramount Person

INTRODUCTION

IN Chapter XI Kṛṣṇa gave Arjuna a cosmic vision of the universe. Through the next two chapters Arjuna's agitated mind is renormalized and he is brought to a clear state so that he can comprehend the philosophical implications of his mystical vision. Having known Kṛṣṇa in person as a dear and trusted friend, he was stunned upon seeing the many unaccountable forms – beautiful, awesome, and frightening – emanating from him. He needed reassurance from Kṛṣṇa as to the right form of devotion to the Absolute he should have. In contrast to the overwhelming vision of the Cosmic Person, Arjuna found himself to be a helpless mortal caught in the vortex of cosmic happenings. After that, he had no alternative other than to submit himself to the course of events to which he was led, partly by his own action, dictated by his innate disposition, and partly by the circumstances created by the collective *karma* of the people to whom he belonged. The only bright spot Arjuna saw in the dark foreboding of a suicidal civil war was Kṛṣṇa's love for him. As Kṛṣṇa is no longer a mere friend or kinsman, and Arjuna is convinced of his overlordship as the Supreme Being, he has no hesitation about offering his body, mind, and soul to be used as an instrument of the Divine. However, he needs instruction as to just what this body, mind, and soul are, as well as what the world is.

In Chapter XIII Kṛṣṇa clearly demarcates the division between the knower (*kṣetrajña*) and the field of knowledge (*kṣetra*). Arjuna further learns of the immanence of the Supreme Lord, which is animating all sentient beings as the spark of consciousness enabling all to know, feel, will, and act. The dichotomy outlined in that chapter between the knowing spirit (*puruṣa*), and the field that it illuminates, is re-examined in the present chapter and re-integrated unitively in the one Paramount Person (*puruṣottama*). Also in

Chapter XIII Arjuna learns the secret of action, and how little he has to be concerned with its merits or demerits.

In Chapter XIV Arjuna is further instructed in the dynamics of the *guṇa*s (modalities of nature). Having learned exactly how the three modalities, *sattva*, *rajas*, and *tamas*, are triggered and activated by his own previously acquired hate-desire propensities, Arjuna becomes further qualified to evaluate the exact nature of the transactional and the transcendental.

In the present chapter any asymmetry that might have arisen from the exclusive treatment given to the different aspects of the Absolute in previous chapters is rounded off so that a clear picture of the Absolute may emerge. The duality of the two Persons spoken of before as the Unmanifested and the Manifested are united in the idea of the Paramount Person, referred to as a third possibility. Kṛṣṇa himself describes the teaching of this chapter as a doctrine of the utmost secrecy. It is not a secret in the esoteric sense, but has the nature of a mystery that is to be distilled from the ambiguity of the symbols and allegories through which it is presented. The main symbol is of a fig tree having its roots above and its branches below. This ideogram is apparently adapted from the Upaniṣads. A similar tree is mentioned in the *Kaṭha Upaniṣad* VI.1. Slight variations occur in the *Maitrī Upaniṣad* VI.4, and the *Śvetāśvatara Upaniṣad* III.9 and VI.6. The closest description is the cosmic tree alluded to in the *Kaṭha Upaniṣad*:

> *Its root is above, its branches below –*
> *This eternal fig-tree!*
> *That (root) indeed is the Pure. That is Brahmā.*
> *That indeed is called the Immortal*
> *On it all the worlds do rest,*
> *And no one soever goes beyond it.*[1]

A similar reference to our heavenly origin comes in Plato's Dialogues, *Timaeus* 90A:

> And we should consider that God gave the sovereign part of the human soul to be the divinity of each one, being that part which, as we say, dwells at the top of the body, and inasmuch as we are a plant not of an earthly but of a heavenly growth, raises us from earth to our kindred who are in heaven. And in this we say truly, for the divine power suspends the head and root of us from that place where the generation of the soul first began, and thus makes the whole body upright.[2]

---

[1] Robert Ernest Hume, 1979, *The Thirteen Principal Upanishads*, New York: Oxford University Press, p. 358.

[2] Plato, 1961, *The Collected Dialogues*, ed. Edith Hamilton and Huntington Cairns, (Bollingen Series LXXI), Princeton University Press, p. 1209.

After the fig tree analogy, Kṛṣṇa paradoxically gives the vehement instruction to cut-off the firmly-rooted *aśvattha* (fig tree) with the strong sword of non-attachment. The mystery is heightened by the qualification of its leaves as the *chanda*s (sacred utterances of the Vedas). To the orthodox Indian mind, cutting down the Vedas would be most sacrilegious. As far back as Chapter II, we have seen the Gītā's aversion to the relativistic aspect of Vedic hedonism. Here Kṛṣṇa emphasizes the importance of ridding oneself of every kind of relativistic approach to the Absolute, including even what the Vedas imply. This does not mean that the Gītā is heterodox, which will become evident in the next chapter where there is a return to a form of revised orthodoxy. In verse 24 Arjuna is definitely asked not to disregard the Śāstras (scriptural texts).

If the fig tree symbolizes this world, then its life-giving sap comes from Kṛṣṇa himself, for he says:

> A qualitative unit of Mine, which is eternal, having become life in the world of life, attracts to itself the senses – of which the mind is the sixth – which abide in nature.

The tree has two sets of roots, one above and one below, which bind everyone to the matrix of action. There is no specific reference which implies that the cutting of the roots refers only to the roots below. If we are to understand Kṛṣṇa as asking for both the roots above and below to be cut, it amounts to his saying that he is inviting Arjuna to deny his own manifestation. To one who is aspiring to realization of the Absolute, the elimination of the cause of manifestation is as important as the escape from the bondage of action occasioned by empirical manifestation.

In mystical traditions, grace seems to come only after one completes labours or trials by facing them squarely. An example is the Biblical story of Job, wherein the loathsome Satan hurls misery upon misery on him. Satan does this with the permission of the very God whom Job loves with all his heart and soul. With some justification we can say that, although we find it very trying to face all the trials and tribulations of our life on earth, this world stems from the very God of our own salvation. All through Satan's persistent attack on Job, Job's love for God gave him the immense strength to overcome Satan. It is hard to understand how God's grace comes, sometimes in a concealed manner. Similarly, in Chapter XV, the same God who has manifested as this world, symbolized by the fig tree, is now asking Arjuna to cut its roots above and below with the sword of non-attachment.

In verses 8 and 9 a pointed reference is made to what is usually known as reincarnation. One can easily see that it is a bold departure from the common belief. It is important to note that in verse 8 it is the Lord who is taking a body and leaving it, and not an individual person. In this chapter we get a happy blend of mystical vision and philosophical insight, sung in a rhapsody by Kṛṣṇa alone, without its flow being interrupted by any question arising from Arjuna.

TRANSLATION

श्रीभगवानुवाच –

1. ऊर्ध्वमूलमधःशाखमश्वत्थं प्राहुरव्ययम् ।
छन्दांसि यस्य पर्णानि यस्तं वेद स वेदवित् ।।

śrībhagavān uvāca –

ūrdhvamūlam adhaḥśākham aśvatthaṁ prāhur avyayam ।
chandāṁsi yasya parṇāni yas taṁ veda sa vedavit ॥

śrībhagavān uvāca: Kṛṣṇa said; *prāhuḥ*: (they) speak of; *avyayam aśvatthaṁ*: an unexpended (holy) fig tree; *ūrdhva mūlam*: (with) roots above; *adhaḥ śākham*: (and) branches below; *yasya parṇāni*: whose leaves; *chandāṁsi*: (are) sacred verses; *saḥ yaḥ veda taṁ*: he who knows that; *vedavit*: (is) a Veda-knower.

Kṛṣṇa said:

They speak of an unexpended holy fig tree, with roots above and branches below, whose leaves are sacred verses; he who knows it is a Veda-knower.

2. अधश्चोर्ध्वं प्रसृतास्तस्य शाखा गुणप्रवृद्धा विषयप्रवालाः ।
अधश्च मूलान्यनुसन्ततानि कर्मानुबन्धीनि मनुष्यलोके ।।

adhaś co 'rdhvaṁ prasṛtās śakhā guṇapravṛddhā viṣayapravālāḥ ।
adhaś ca mūlāny anusaṁtatāni karmānubandhīni manuṣyaloke ॥

adhaḥ ca ūrdhvaṁ: below and above; *prasṛtāḥ tasya śākhāḥ*: spread its branches; *guṇa pravṛddhāḥ*: nourished by the modalities of nature; *viṣaya pravālāḥ*: sense-values its buds; *adhaḥ ca*: (and) downward also; *mūlāni anusaṁtatāni*: (there are) roots stretched out; *karma anubandhīni*: which bind to action; *manuṣya loke*: in the world of men.

Below and above spread its branches, nourished by the modalities of nature, sense-values its buds, and downward also there are ramified roots which bind to action in the world of men.

3. न रूपमस्येह तथोपलभ्यते नान्तो न चादिर्न च सम्प्रतिष्ठा ।
अश्वत्थमेनं सुविरूढमूलमसङ्गशस्त्रेण दृढेन छित्त्वा ।।

na rūpam asye 'ha tatho 'palabhyate' nā 'nto na cā 'dir na ca saṁpratiṣṭhā ।
aśvattham enaṁ suvirūḍhamūlam asaṅgaśastreṇa dṛḍhena chittvā ॥

na asya rūpam: nor (is) its form; *iha upalabhyate tathā*: here comprehended thus (as stated); *na antaḥ*: nor (its) end; *na ca ādiḥ*: nor (its) beginning; *na ca saṁpratiṣṭhā*: nor (its) foundation; *chittvā*: having sundered; *enaṁ aśvattham*: this (holy) fig tree; *suvirūdha mūlam*: with strongly-fixed roots; *asaṅga śastreṇa dṛḍhena*: with the weapon of decisive non-attachment.

4. ततः पदं तत्परिमार्गितव्यं यस्मिन्गता न निवर्तन्ति भूयः ।
तमेव चाद्यं पुरुषं प्रपद्ये यतः प्रवृत्तिः प्रसृता पुराणी ॥

tataḥ padaṁ tat parimārgitavyaṁ yasmin gatā na nivartanti bhūyaḥ ।
tam eva cā 'dyaṁ puruṣam prapadye yataḥ pravṛttiḥ prasṛtā purāṇī ॥

tataḥ tat padam: then (alone) that path; *parimārgitavyaṁ*: is to be sought; *gatāḥ yasmin*: treading on which; *na nivartanti bhūyaḥ*: (they) do not return again; *ca eva prapadye*: and indeed (thinking) (I) seek refuge; *tam ādyaṁ purṣaṁ*: in that Primordial Man; *yataḥ purāṇī*: from whom of old; *prasṛtā*: streamed forth; *pravṛttiḥ*: active (relativist) manifestation.

Nor is its form here comprehended thus (as stated), nor its end, nor its beginning, nor its foundation. Having sundered this holy fig tree, with strongly-fixed roots, with the weapon of decisive non-attachment,

then alone that path is to be sought, treading which they do not return again, thinking: "I seek refuge in that Primordial Man from whom of old streamed forth active relativist manifestation".

5. निर्मानमोहा जितसङ्गदोषा अध्यात्मनित्या विनिवृत्तकामाः ।
द्वन्द्वैर्विमुक्ताः सुखदुःखसञ्ज्ञैर्गच्छन्त्यमूढाः पदमव्ययं तत् ॥

nirmānamohā jitasaṅgadoṣā adhyātmanityā vinivṛttakāmāḥ ।
dvandvair vimuktāḥ sukhaduḥkhasaṁjñair gacchanty amūḍhāḥ padam avyayaṁ tat ॥

nirmāna mohāḥ: (those who are) neither proud (nor) deluded; *jita saṅga doṣāḥ*: who have overcome the evil of attachment; *adhyātma nityāḥ*: (who are) ever constant to (that value which pertains to) the Self; *vinivṛtta kāmāḥ*: whose passions are withdrawn; *vimuktāḥ dvandvaiḥ*: (who are) freed (from) the (opposing) dual factors; *sukha duḥkha saṁjñaiḥ*: known as pleasure-pain; *amūḍhāḥ*: (and who are) non-foolish; *gacchanti tat padam*: (they) go (to) that place; *avyayaṁ*: (which knows) no decay.

Those who are neither proud nor deluded, who have overcome the evil of attachment, who are ever constant to that value which pertains to the Self, whose passions are withdrawn, who are beyond the opposing dual factors known as pleasure–pain, and who are non-foolish, wend that way of life which knows no decay.

6. न तद्भासयते सूर्यो न शशाङ्को न पावकः ।
यद्गत्वा न निवर्तन्ते तद्धाम परमं मम ॥

na tad bhāsayate sūryo na śaśāṅko na pāvakaḥ ।
yad gatvā na nivartante tad dhāma paramaṁ mama ॥

sūryaḥ: the sun; *na bhāsayate tat*: does not illumine That; *na śaśāṅkaḥ*: nor the moon; *na pāvakaḥ*: nor the fire; *tat mama*: That (is) My; *paramaṁ dhāma*: supreme abode; *gatvā yat*: having gone to which; *nivartante na*: (they) return not.

The sun does not illumine That, nor the moon, nor the fire; That is My supreme abode, from which, having reached, they return not.

7. ममैवांशो जीवलोके जीवभूतः सनातनः ।
मनःषष्ठानीन्द्रियाणि प्रकृतिस्थानि कर्षति ॥

mamai 'va 'ṁśo jīvaloke jīvabhūtaḥ sanātanaḥ ।
manaḥṣaṣṭhānī 'ndriyāṇi prakṛtisthāni karṣati ॥

eva aṁśaḥ mama: a mere (qualitative) unit of Mine; *sanātanaḥ*: (which is) eternal; *jīva bhūtaḥ*: having become life; *jīva loke*: in the world of life; *karṣati indriyāṇi*: attracts (to itself) the senses; *manaḥ ṣaṣṭhāni*: of which the mind is the sixth; *prakṛtisthāni*: which abide in nature.

A qualitative unit of Mine, which is eternal, having become life in the world of life, attracts to itself the senses – of which the mind is the sixth – which abide in nature.

8. शरीरं यदवाप्नोति यच्चाप्युत्क्रामतीश्वरः ।
गृहीत्वैतानि संयाति वायुर्गन्धानिवाशयात् ॥

śarīraṁ yad avāpnoti yac cā 'py utkrāmatī 'śvaraḥ ।
gṛhītvai 'tāni saṁyāti vāyur gandhān ivā 'śayāt ॥

yat īśvaraḥ: when the Lord; *avāpnoti śarīraṁ*: takes a body; *ca api yat*: and also when; *utkrāmati*: (He) leaves (it); *gṛhītvā etāni*: (He) takes these (mind and senses); *saṁyāti iva vāyuḥ*: (and) goes (even) as the wind; *gandhān*: (gathering) scents; *āśayāt*: from (their) retreats.

When the Lord takes a body, and when He leaves it, He takes these (mind and senses) and goes, even as the wind gathering scents from their retreats.

9. श्रोत्रं चक्षुः स्पर्शनं च रसनं घ्राणमेव च ।
अधिष्ठाय मनश्चायं विषयानुपसेवते ॥

śrotraṁ cakṣuḥ sparśanaṁ ca rasanaṁ ghrāṇam eva ca ।
adhiṣṭhāya manaś cā 'yaṁ viṣayān upasevate ॥

adhiṣṭhāya: presiding over; *śrotraṁ cakṣuḥ*: the ear, the eye; *ca sparśanaṁ rasanaṁ*: and touch, taste; *ca eva ghrāṇam ca manaḥ*: and even smell and (also) the mind; *ayaṁ upasevate*: this (One) avails (himself) of; *viṣayān*: the values relating to the senses.

Presiding over the ear, the eye, touch, taste, smell, and also the mind, this One avails himself of the values relating to the senses.

10. उत्क्रामन्तं स्थितं वापि भुञ्जानं वा गुणान्वितम् ।
विमूढा नानुपश्यन्ति पश्यन्ति ज्ञानचक्षुषः ।।

utkrāmantaṁ sthitaṁ vā 'pi bhuñjānaṁ vā guṇānvitam ।
vimūḍhā nā 'nupaśyanti paśyanti jñānacakṣuṣaḥ ॥

vā api: whether; *utkrāmantaṁ sthitaṁ*: departing, staying; *vā bhuñjānaṁ*: or experiencing; *guṇānvitam*: conditioned (as they are) by the modalities of nature; *vimūḍhāḥ na anupaśyanti*: the foolish cannot see; *jñāna cakṣuṣaḥ*: the wisdom-eyed; *paśyanti*: (can) see.

Whether departing, staying, or experiencing, conditioned as they are by the modalities of nature, the foolish cannot see; the wisdom-eyed can see.

11. यतन्तो योगिनश्चैनं पश्यन्त्यात्मन्यवस्थितम् ।
यतन्तोऽप्यकृतात्मानो नैनं पश्यन्त्यचेतसः ।।

yatanto yoginaś cai 'naṁ paśyanty ātmany avasthitam ।
yatanto 'py akṛtātmāno nai 'naṁ paśyanty acetasaḥ ॥

yoginaḥ yatantaḥ: the *yogīs* striving; *ca paśyanti*: also perceive; *enaṁ*: this (One); *avasthitam ātmani*: established in the Self; *api yatantaḥ*: though striving; *akṛta ātmānaḥ*: (those *yogīs*) of imperfected Self; *acetasaḥ*: lacking wisdom; *na paśyanti enaṁ*: do not see this (One).

The *yogīs*, striving, also perceive this One established in the Self; though striving, those *yogīs* of imperfected Self, lacking wisdom, do not see this One.

12. यदादित्यगतं तेजो जगद्भासयतेऽखिलम् ।
यच्चन्द्रमसि यच्चाग्नौ तत्तेजो विद्धि मामकम् ।।

yad ādityagataṁ tejo jagad bhāsayate 'khilam ।
yac candramasi yac cā 'gnau tat tejo viddhi māmakam ॥

tejaḥ yat: (that) brilliance which; *āditya gataṁ*: reaches the sun; *bhāsayate*: (and) brightens; *akhilam jagat*: the whole world; *yat candramasi*: (that) which is in the moon; *ca yat agnau*: and which is in the fire (too); *tat tejaḥ*: that brilliance; *viddhi māmakam*: know (to be) of Me.

That brilliance which reaches the sun and brightens the whole world, that which is in the moon and the fire too – that brilliance know to be of Me.

13. गामाविश्य च भूतानि धारयाम्यहमोजसा ।
पुष्णामि चौषधीः सर्वाः सोमो भूत्वा रसात्मकः ।।

gām āviśya ca bhūtāni dhārayāmy aham ojasā ।
puṣṇāmi cau 'ṣadhīḥ sarvāḥ somo bhūtvā rasātmakaḥ ॥

āviśya gām: permeating the earth; *aham dhārayāmi*: I sustain; *bhūtāni*: (all) elemental existences; *ojasā*: by (My) vitalizing heat-principle; *ca bhūtvā*: and become; *somaḥ*: Soma (king of herbs of the Vedas); *rasātmakaḥ*: identical with sap (or taste); *ca puṣṇāmi*: (I) also nourish; *sarvāḥ auṣadhīḥ*: all herbs.

Permeating the earth, I sustain all elemental existences by My vitalizing heat-principle, and become Soma, identical with sap (or taste); I also nourish all herbs.

14. अहं वैश्वानरो भूत्वा प्राणिनां देहमाश्रितः ।
प्राणापानसमायुक्तः पचाम्यन्नं चतुर्विधम् ।।

ahaṁ vaiśvānaro bhūtvā prāṇināṁ deham āśritaḥ ।
prāṇāpānasamāyuktaḥ pacāmy annaṁ caturvidham ॥

bhūtvā: having become; *vaiśvānaraḥ*: the fire of life; *āśritaḥ*: (and) resorting to; *deham prāṇināṁ*: the body of living creatures; *prāṇa apāna samāyuktaḥ*: uniting with the ingoing and outgoing vital energies; *ahaṁ pacāmi*: I cook (digest); *catur vidham annaṁ*: the four kinds of food.

Having become the fire of life and resorting to the body of living creatures, uniting with the ingoing and outgoing vital energies, I digest the four kinds of food.

15. सर्वस्य चाहं हृदि सन्निविष्टो मत्तः स्मृतिर्ज्ञानमपोहनं च ।
वेदैश्च सर्वैरहमेव वेद्यो वेदान्तकृद्वेदविदेव चाहम् ।।

sarvasya cā 'haṁ hṛdi saṁniviṣṭo mattaḥ smṛtir jñānam apohanaṁ ca ।
vedaiś ca sarvair aham eva vedyo vedāntakṛd vedavid eva cā 'ham ॥

ca aham: and I (am); *saṁniviṣṭaḥ*: seated; *hṛdi sarvasya*: in the heart of all; *mattaḥ*: from Me; *smṛtiḥ jñānam*: (are) memory, (positive) wisdom; *ca apohanam*: and (its) negative process; *ca aham vedyaḥ*: and I (am) (that which is), to be known; *sarvaiḥ vedaiḥ*: by all the Vedas; *aham eva*: I (am) indeed; *vedānta kṛt*: the Vedānta-maker; *ca vedavit eva*: and the Veda-knower too.

And I am seated in the heart of all; from Me are memory and positive wisdom and its negative process; I am that which is to be known by all the Vedas; I am indeed the Vedānta-maker and the Veda-knower too.

16. द्वाविमौ पुरुषौ लोके क्षरश्चाक्षर एव च ।
क्षरः सर्वाणि भूतानि कूटस्थोऽक्षर उच्यते ॥

dvāv imau puruṣau loke kṣaraś cā 'kṣara eva ca ।
kṣaraḥ sarvāṇi bhūtāni kūṭastho 'kṣara ucyate ॥

imau dvau: there are these two; *puruṣau loke*: Persons in the world; *kṣaraḥ*: the Changing; *ca akṣaraḥ*: and the Changeless; *sarvāṇi bhūtāni*: (comprises) all beings; *ca eva*: and indeed; *kūṭasthaḥ*: the (mysteriously) fixed; *ucyate akṣaraḥ*: is called the Changeless.

There are two Persons in the world, the Changing and the Changeless; the Changing comprises all beings, and the mysteriously-fixed is called the Changeless.

17. उत्तमः पुरुषस्त्वन्यः परमात्मेत्युदाहृतः ।
यो लोकत्रयमाविश्य बिभर्त्यव्यय ईश्वरः ॥

uttamaḥ puruṣas tv anyaḥ paramātme 'ty udāhṛtaḥ ।
yo lokatrayam āviśya bibharty avyaya īśvaraḥ ॥

puruṣaḥ uttamaḥ: (that) Person Paramount; *tu anyaḥ*: however (is) another; *udāhṛtaḥ iti*: called thus; *paramātmā*: the Supreme Self; *avyayaḥ īśvaraḥ*: the eternal Lord; *yaḥ*: who; *āviśya loka trayam*: pervading the three worlds; *bibharti*: sustains (them).

That Person Paramount, however, is another, called the Supreme Self, the eternal Lord, who, pervading the three worlds, sustains them.

18. यस्मात्क्षरमतीतोऽहमक्षरादपि चोत्तमः ।
अतोऽस्मि लोके वेदे च प्रथितः पुरुषोत्तमः ॥

yasmāt kṣaram atīto 'ham akṣarād api co 'ttamaḥ ।
ato 'smi loke vede ca prathitaḥ puruṣottamaḥ ॥

yasmāt aham atītaḥ: because I transcend; *kṣaram*: the Changing; *ca api*: and (am) even; *uttamaḥ akṣarāt*: superior to the Changeless; *ataḥ*: therefore; *loke*: in the world; *ca vede*: and in the Veda; *asmi prathitaḥ*: (I) am celebrated as; *puruṣottamaḥ*: the Paramount Person.

Because I transcend the Changing and am even superior to the Changeless, therefore I am celebrated in the world and in the Veda as the Paramount Person.

19. यो मामेवमसम्मूढो जानाति पुरुषोत्तमम् ।
स सर्वविद्भजति मां सर्वभावेन भारत ।।

yo mām evam asaṁmūḍho jānāti puruṣottamam ।
sa sarvavid bhajati māṁ sarvabhāvena bhārata ॥

yaḥ asaṁmūḍhaḥ: (he) who, undeluded; *evam jānāti mām*: thus knows Me; *puruṣottamam*: the Paramount Person; *saḥ sarvavit*: he, the all-knower; *bhajati māṁ*: adores Me; *sarva bhāvena*: in all aspects; *bhārata*: Oh Arjuna.

He who, undeluded, thus knows Me, the Paramount Person – he, the all-knower, adores Me in all aspects, Oh Bhārata.

20. इति गुह्यतमं शास्त्रमिदमुक्तं मयानघ ।
एतद्बुद्ध्वा बुद्धिमान्स्यात्कृतकृत्यश्च भारत ।।

iti guhyatamaṁ śāstram idam uktaṁ mayā 'nagha ।
etad buddhvā buddhimān syāt kṛtakṛtyaś ca bhārata ॥

iti idam: thus this; *guhya tamaṁ*: most secret; *śāstram*: doctrine; *uktaṁ mayā*: has been taught by Me; *anagha*: Oh Arjuna; *buddhvā etat*: understanding this; *syāt buddhimān*: (one) becomes wise; *ca kṛta kṛtyaḥ*: and one who has done with all works; *bhārata*: Oh Arjuna.

Thus this most secret doctrine has been taught by Me, Oh Sinless One! understanding this, one becomes wise, and one who has done with all works, Oh Bhārata!

DIALOGUE

TEACHER: Sāṁkhya speaks of *puruṣa* and *prakṛti.* This implicit duality is not acceptable to Vedānta. Hence, these notions are revalued to fit a more unitive conception of the Absolute as given in this chapter. Chapter XV also brings in the favourite image of a cosmic tree, which occurs in various other archaic writings. The tree itself is meant to be a mystery, reaching, as it were, from Heaven to Earth. What is more important here is to keep in mind that this mysterious tree is to be cut asunder with a certain severe relentlessness. The tree is equated with the world of the Vedas, and the thought of cutting it down would be sacrilegious in the usual context of orthodoxy. The Gītā's aversion to Vedism on the one side as well as atheistic materialism on the other is evident in numerous places in the text.

STUDENT: *What is the cosmic tree referred to here?*

Kṛṣṇa describes it in verses 1 and 2:

They speak of an unexpended holy fig tree (*aśvattha*), with roots above

> and branches below, whose leaves are sacred verses; he who knows it is a Veda-knower.
>
> Below and above spread its branches, nourished by the modalities of nature, sense-values its buds, and downwards also there are ramified roots which bind to action in the world of men.

The tree is sometimes called the tree of *saṁsāra* (relative existence of a cyclic nature). Inasmuch as the text takes pains to refer in detail to each part of this tree, it would be justifiable to relate each part to some aspects in the domain of *saṁsāra*.

The branches of the tree are said to grow upwards and downwards: the upward-growing branches being values in the context of holiness or ostentatious forms of religion, the downward-growing branches being values tending to be more earthy, or at least based on tangible realities of life.

The branches are said to be nourished by the modalities of nature, the *guṇas*; the upward-growing branches may therefore correspond to the pure-clear (sattvic) tendencies in nature, while the inert-dark (tāmasic) nourishes the more earthy branches, and the affective-active (rājasic), may be said to nourish those branches not specifically mentioned here which radiate horizontally in the mass, as in the world of actions and agents.

The buds or sprouts correspond to the ever-growing interests of man, reaching out to objects that give him pleasure. In the manner in which this picture here is conceived, there is no strict differentiation between the subjective and the objective aspects of any item. Thus the sprout represents both the senses and sense-objects which result in pleasures, interests, or values.

There are also roots that grow downwards, besides the main roots above. These roots have ramifications and may be supposed to keep those interested in ritual or other active forms of spirituality enmeshed and hopelessly caught within their tangle of conflicting interests belonging to each family, tribal, or group tradition. All obligations, taboos, laws and other necessary aspects connected with spiritual or even everyday life-interests may be said to be represented by these multiple tangled spreading roots.

The roots here correspond to necessity, for necessity does not originate above. It belongs to the earth and therefore such roots are below. As we know from other parts of the Gītā, necessity itself is beginningless, and these downward roots are represented as reaching to subtle aspects of the unmanifested reality lying below or beyond the earth, in the same way as the main roots are directed to the transcendental Supreme, which is also unmanifest. Further, the downward roots may be spoken of as referring to retrospective values, such as instinctive respect for ancestral traditions.

Does the tree symbolize a structural correlation of values? Should we take this as an exemplary model to direct our life pattern?

Certainly the tree implies a scheme of structural correlation. It is, altogether, a reference to the relativistic matrix of life which is to be methodically denied in order to arrive at a pure notion of the Absolute. For this the following verses are to be examined:

> Nor is its form here comprehended thus (as stated), nor its end, nor its beginning, nor its foundation. Having sundered this holy fig tree, with strongly-fixed roots, with the weapon of decisive non-attachment,
>
> then alone that path is to be sought, treading which they do not return again, thinking: "I seek refuge in that Primordial Man from whom of old streamed forth active relativist manifestation".

The tree described here is of the order of a comprehensive philosophical vision, referring to the world of relativist interest in all values and in all their bearing and aspects together. In a sense, it covers the whole of the realistic and pragmatic world of relativistic values and actions. In the above verses, Kṛṣṇa recommends a relentless cutting of the roots that keep such a tree firm in cyclic becoming. On one side, man is attached to values belonging to the pure domain of the holy. At the other extreme there is a multiple tangle of minor items of ancestral, tribal, caste, or other instinctive traditional values, which bind the spirit of man just as do the purer religious ideas rooted above. These two thickets of roots are to be torn out by the weapon of non-association or non-attachment. That this weapon has to be decisive suggests that non-attachment must be strong and determined and not lukewarm. One qualifies himself to tread the path of the Absolute only when these conditions have been fulfilled.

The reference here to the Primordial Man from whom the relativistic manifestation is said to have streamed forth is quite interesting. Does this refer to the puruṣa *(spirit) or the puruṣottama (Supreme Spirit), that Kṛṣṇa introduces in his revalued philosophy?*

This Primordial Man is said to be the cause of cyclic becoming. He belongs to a religio-mythical imagery which was current in the Vedic conception. We shall come later to the Supreme Spirit named here as *puruṣottama.* In order to arrive at the notion of the Supreme Spirit, one has to prepare oneself. Kṛṣṇa says:

> Those who are neither proud nor deluded, who have overcome the evil of attachment, who are ever constant to that value which pertains to the Self, whose passions are withdrawn, who are beyond the opposing dual factors known as pleasure-pain, and who are non-foolish, wend that way of life which knows no decay.
>
> The sun does not illumine That, nor the moon, nor the fire; That is My supreme abode, from which, having reached, they return not.

When the Absolute is equated with the Self, we should necessarily see the Absolute in our own selves. Yet in all the references to the Supreme, it seems to be far removed from the world of human habitation and man's natural passions. Just how are we related to the Absolute?

Kṛṣṇa speaks to that as follows:

> A qualitative unit of Mine, which is eternal, having become life in the world of life, attracts to itself the senses – of which the mind is the sixth – which abide in nature.
>
> When the Lord takes a body, and when He leaves it, He takes these (mind and senses) and goes, even as the wind gathering scents from their retreats.

Why is it said here that it is God assuming the body, and that it is he who takes it back and reincurnates?

One of the most important contributions of the Gītā to Indian philosophy is the revalued theory of reincarnation, summarily given in these two verses. Even scholars tend to go wrong in interpreting the Gītā's unique stand on the matter. Every animated being has two aspects, the physical and the spiritual. With regard to the attributes of these two aspects, they are so different that it seems almost impossible to relate one to the other. Matter implied in the physical organism of an animate being has an extension in space and time and is divisible, changing, finite, and different from other organisms. Spirit, on the other hand, has no extension, either in time or space, and it is indivisible and infinite. Every possible union is based on the principle of homogeneity. Matter is described in the Gītā as nature-naturing as well as nature-natured. This is somewhat similar to the famous dictum of Spinoza: *natura naturans–natura naturata.* The one link of homogeneity between spirit and matter is the implied capacity of the three modalities of nature to mirror the light of the intelligence of Spirit in differing degrees, ranging from the most clear, as in the case of the transparent *sattva*, through the coloured and distorted *rajas*, to the veiled and opaque, *tamas.* Every individuated form of life is a circumscription of the light or intelligence of Spirit by a unit of the changing triad of nature. In other words, we can say that it is God who enters the body to make it animate.

From the light the Lord lends to the three modalities constituting the body, there arises the inner organ, which in its turn brings about ego-consciousness, mind, intellect, and the organs of perception and action. In this sense every individuated self is a reflection of the Divine in the physical organism. When a person dies, all that happens is the withdrawal of the circumscribed Spirit back to its original source. When the same is re-projected in matter to again function in accordance with the impressions formed in the previous life (*vāsanās*), it may be called reincarnation.

Life comes from God; life is preserved and governed by God; life returns to God; and life reincarnates from God. So what is essential in life at all times is God alone. Life never undergoes any change in its truest aspect. Limitation, finitude, birth, death, experiences of pain and pleasure, and sin and merit have only a phenomenal status.

That means in essence we are the Divine, yet man is in search of his unknown God. How can we always feel this within us?

God is nearer than our eyes and ears and the throb of our hearts.

Kṛṣṇa says:

> Presiding over the ear, the eye, touch, taste, smell, and also the mind, this One avails himself of the values relating to the senses.
>
> Whether departing, staying, or experiencing, conditioned as they are by the modalities of nature, the foolish cannot see; the wisdom-eyed can see.
>
> The *yogīs*, striving, also perceive this One established in the Self; though striving, those *yogīs* of imperfected Self, lacking wisdom, do not see this One.

Does the Spirit permeate the bodies of the inanimate as well as the animate?

The phenomenal event of the universe has within it the psychological counterpart which experiences the universe, and the cosmological aspect that is experienced. Both are aspects of the same Spirit shining over the kaleidoscopic exuberance of nature's triple principles of *sattva*, *rajas*, and *tamas*. Kṛṣṇa says:

> That brilliance which reaches the sun and brightens the whole world, that which is in the moon and the fire too – that brilliance know to be of Me.
>
> Permeating the earth, I sustain all elemental existences by My vitalizing heat-principle, and become *soma*, identical with sap (or taste); I also nourish all herbs.
>
> Having become the fire of life and resorting to the body of living creatures, uniting with the ingoing and outgoing vital energies, I digest the four kinds of food.

> And I am seated in the heart of all; from Me are memory and positive wisdom and its negative process; I am that which is to be known by all the Vedas; I am indeed the Vedānta-maker and the Veda-knower too.

If Spirit is the animating principle of life, how can you say it undergoes no change?

Every beam of light that issues from the sun is in principle the sun itself. Pure light entering and passing through a prism may show the beam split into a spectrum of colours, but this does not affect the source in the least. So one has to think of two aspects, the Changing and the Changeless. Kṛṣṇa says:

> There are two Persons in the world, the Changing and the Changeless; the Changing comprises all beings, and the mysteriously-fixed is called the Changeless.
>
> That Person Paramount, however, is another, called the Supreme Self, the eternal Lord, who, pervading the three worlds, sustains them.

XVI

Daivāsura-Saṁpad-Vibhāga-Yoga

The Unitive Way of Discriminating between Higher and Lower Values

INTRODUCTION

THE chapters of the Gītā have a symmetrical arrangement, like stones or bricks in an archway. The first and last chapters could be likened to horizontally placed bricks, while the middle ones, nine and ten, are vertically placed, and thus are mainly devoted to the description of divine or absolutist values. The third chapter, which has only a slight vertical tilt when compared to the first, is entitled Karma-Yoga. Although the chapter appears to be meant to discuss action, what we find is a revaluation of action in the light of absolutist wisdom. Action is equated with sacrifice, and Kṛṣṇa himself is referred to as a model for those engaged in action.

The sixteenth chapter, which marks the symmetrical counterpart of the third chapter, discusses the axiology of the Gītā. In this the reader may expect an ethical theory that could be likened to the Ten Commandments, or some glorification of social virtues. However, Vyāsa uses this chapter to bring the natural action of man in line with the epistemological considerations of the main teachings of the Gītā. In that sense we can say that its slant brings the close of the chapter once again to the horizontal actualities of life.

In the Bible (St. Matthew 5:14-16), Jesus says:

> Ye are the light of the world. A city that is set on a hill cannot be hid.
>
> Neither do men light a candle, and put it under a bushel, but on a candlestick: and it giveth light unto all that are in the house.
>
> Let your light so shine before men, that they may see your good works, and glorify your Father which is in heaven.

Here the light of man is treated as a continuation of the divine light. In another passage, Christ says that those who do not walk in the light will stumble and fall in the dark. After elucidating the path of wisdom, and even confiding to Arjuna the most secret teaching of the Absolute, Kṛṣṇa also says that those who do not walk in the light will perish in darkness. Either one knows and is emancipated, or one does not know and tends to become foolish.

Becoming wise or foolish is not accidental. These also have reference to the overall epistemological elucidation of the theory of the Absolute propounded in the Gītā. Kṛṣṇa speaks of his higher and lower natures. His higher nature is the Transcendental, the Unmanifested. What is manifested as his lower nature is qualified as *ekāṁśa* (a tiny fragment). The dynamic used for manifestation is given as the Lord's *yoga-māyā. Māyā* is a negative principle. When it is not understood in conjunction with the Divine, it becomes a delusive principle.

What is prized most highly in the Gītā is an unfailing attention to the Absolute, which runs through every moment of life like a golden thread, giving unity to life and order to the world. This is called *śraddhā.* Chapter XVII is dedicated to presenting a final appraisal of *śraddhā.* In the present chapter we are told that the natural dichotomy between light and darkness, or wisdom and ignorance, is a consequence arising in the lives of people. After repeated exposure to situations requiring discrimination, those who have continually succeeded in giving their best attention to values which go with a superior vision of truth come under the category of the divine. Those who have repeatedly failed fall under the classification of the demonic.

In the opening verse of the first chapter we come across the terms *dharma-kṣetra* and *kuru-kṣetra*, which mean "the field of the *dharma*" and "the field of action". Between Bādarāyaṇa and Jaimini, the main purport of the Vedas is divided into the study of *Brahman* (Absolute), and *dharma* (works of specificatory and obligatory nature). The exposition of *Brahman* comes mainly in the latter part of the Vedas, known as Vedānta or the Upaniṣads. The obligatory actions and rituals of *dharma* come in the Saṁhitās of the Vedas. From the very beginning of the Gītā, Kṛṣṇa is disinclined to popularize this aspect of the Vedas. At least three strong comments are made to deny the worth of the gross rituals to which the Vedas give permission. The only *dharma* that the Gītā teaches is the Upaniṣadic *dharma*, which can be otherwise termed as the *dharma* of all *dharma*s. As elucidated elsewhere, *dharma* is that which sustains the specificatory aspect of the phenomenal world, which is comprised of both our fantasies and our transactions. It can be attributed to *māyā.* Thus we can think of *māyā* as the ground or *dharma* of everything we experience. However, *māyā* cannot be a ground in itself since it has no existence of its own. The only truth that *is*, of which *māyā* is a shadow, is the Absolute. Therefore, the Absolute is to be understood as the *dharma* of the Upaniṣads. Those who realize this cannot confine themselves to action that ensues from the Vedic notion of blind obligation. However, the lower nature of the Absolute, given as *aparā prakṛti* in the seventh chapter, cannot be slighted, even though it is only a fragmentary splinter of the Absolute. We belong to that domain until we free ourselves from our psycho-physical imprisonment. It is here that action becomes necessary. The imperativeness of it is to be understood in conjunction with our oneness with the Divine, to whom the world-perpetuating *māyā* belongs. Just as the world belongs to the all-supporting *Brahman*, which we have termed above as the *dharma* of all *dharma*s, our ground is also not different from this; hence we must conduct our lives in resonance with the truth of this ultimate Ground of all.

The first verse of the sixteenth chapter begins with fearlessness, and the penultimate refers to the need to attain perfection (*siddhi*), happiness (*sukham*), and the Supreme Path (*mokṣa*). The three values of man which ultimately lead him to emancipation are *dharma*, *artha*, and *kāma.* In the popular mind these are thought of as virtue or righteousness, acquisition of wealth, and fulfilment of desires, respectively. In the present context they are to be understood differently. The highest of all attainments is to know that there is nothing to attain, because one is with the Absolute, which lacks nothing. In that sense, *dharma* and *siddhi*, the ground and attainment, are not two. *Artha* is wealth only when wealth becomes meaningful in its instrumentality to make one happy. Happiness exists when one is entirely with oneself and there is not a second to tempt or threaten. One who has realized that one's Self cannot be differentiated from the Absolute finds the highest meaning in that state. The Absolute is adorably precious and there is nothing that can be equated with it. Hence *artha* and *sukham* (meaningful wealth and happiness) are seen in the attainment of one's original state. *Kāma* is usually looked upon as fulfilment of sexual or sensory pleasures. The value of sexual pleasure is a momentary sense of union in which the mating pairs forget all dualities. To that extent it is very valuable. In sensual pleasure, the existentiality of value fills consciousness, and thus for a moment the artificial division between existence, subsistence, and value is sublated. But these are only momentary effects. The highest fulfilment occurs when one transcends all dualities by discovering the imperishable bliss which is one's own nature. In that sense, *kāma* and *mokṣa* (desire and liberation) are identical.

In this chapter Kṛṣṇa refers to three dark shadows which are like negative counterpoints of *siddhi*, *sukham*, and *mokṣa*. These are *kāma* (blind desire) *krodha* (deluding anger) and *lobha* (binding greed). Those who walk in the demonic path are bound to be trapped by these three evil forces, which Kṛṣṇa describes as the three gates of hell.

The virtues enumerated by Kṛṣṇa in the introductory verses are of a diagnostic nature, to identify those who are naturally endowed with divine traits. Because of the particular placement of this chapter in the overall scheme of the Gītā, the emphasis on action is bound to be heavy. From the first half of the book the student will have a good grasp of the harmonious union of knowledge and action, which is presented as the perfect approach to life on earth. In the second half this attitude is further sweetened with *bhakti* (devotion). Action is no longer treated as individual fulfilment of personal desire: it is meant to be for the welfare of the whole world. In the Bible (St. Matthew 16:24-25), Jesus said to his disciples:

> If any man will come after me, let him deny himself,
> and take up his cross, and follow me.
> For whosoever will save his life shall lose it:
> and whosoever will lose his life for my sake shall find it.

The call for action in the present chapter is of the same order. The values implied in it are not religious or ethical, but mystical and contemplative.

In one's path to the Absolute one comes to many crossroads of confusion, where reliance on personal whims and fancies is dangerous. One should have normative notions to guide one's life. The paths that are tried and found beneficial by seers of several generations are recorded in the scriptures of mankind. Kṛṣṇa exhorts Arjuna to prize these revelations as invaluable. In a Science of the Absolute, axiomatic teaching and a priori word wisdom each have their appropriate place.

TRANSLATION

श्रीभगवानुवाच –

1. अभयं सत्त्वसंशुद्धिर्ज्ञानयोगव्यवस्थितिः ।
दानं दमश्च यज्ञश्च स्वाध्यायस्तप आर्जवम् ॥

śrībhagavān uvāca –

abhayaṁ sattvasaṁśuddhir jñānayogavyavasthitiḥ ।
dānaṁ damaś ca yajñaś ca svādhyāyas tapa ārjavam ॥

śrībhagavān uvāca: Kṛṣṇa said; *abhayaṁ*: fearlessness; *sattva saṁśuddiḥ*: transparency to truth; *jñāna-yoga vyavasthitiḥ*: proper affiliation to unitive wisdom; *dānaṁ*: generosity; *damaḥ ca yajñaḥ*: self-restraint and sacrifice; *svādhyāyaḥ*: private perusal of sacred books; *tapaḥ ca ārjavam*: discipline and rectitude.

2. अहिंसा सत्यमक्रोधस्त्यागः शान्तिरपैशुनम् ।
दया भूतेष्वलोलुप्त्वं मार्दवं ह्रीरचापलम् ।।

ahiṁsā satyam akrodhas tyāgaḥ śāntir apaiśunaṁ ।
dayā bhūteṣv aloluptvaṁ mārdavaṁ hrīr acāpalam ॥

ahiṁsā satyam: non-hurting, truth; *akrodhaḥ tyāgaḥ*: non-anger, relinquishment; *śāntiḥ apaiśunaṁ*: calmness, self-integrity; *dayā bhūteṣu*: compassion to beings; *aloluptvaṁ*: non-interest in sense-values; *mārdavaṁ hrīḥ*: gentleness, modesty; *acāpalam*: non-fickleness.

3. तेजः क्षमा धृतिः शौचमद्रोहो नातिमानिता ।
भवन्ति संपदं दैवीमभिजातस्य भारत ।।

tejaḥ kṣamā dhṛtiḥ śaucam adroho nā 'timānitā ।
bhavanti saṁpadaṁ daivīm abhijātasya bhārata ॥

tejaḥ kṣamā: alertness, forgiveness; *dhṛtiḥ śaucam*: fortitude, cleanliness; *adrohaḥ*: absence of malice; *na atimānitā*: absence of excessive respectability; *bhavanti*: (these) are; *daivīm saṁpadaṁ*: the divine (higher) values; *abhijātasya*: of anyone born (for them); *bhārata*: Oh Arjuna.

Kṛṣṇa said:

Fearlessness, transparency to truth, proper affiliation to unitive wisdom, attitude of generous sharing, self-restraint, sacrifice, private perusal of sacred books, discipline, rectitude,

non-hurting, truth, non-anger, relinquishment, calmness, self-integrity, compassion to beings, non-interest in sense-values, gentleness, modesty, non-fickleness,

alertness, forgiveness, fortitude, cleanliness, absence of malice, absence of excessive respectability – these make up the divine (higher) values of anyone, Oh Bhārata! born for them.

4. दम्भो दर्पोऽभिमानश्च क्रोधः पारुष्यमेव च ।
अज्ञानं चाभिजातस्य पार्थ सम्पदमासुरीम् ।।

dambho darpo 'bhimānaś ca krodhaḥ pāruṣyam eva ca ।
ajñānaṁ cā 'bhijātasya pārtha saṁpadam āsurīm ॥

dambhaḥ darpaḥ: pretentiousness, arrogance; *ca abhimānaḥ*: and a sense of self-importance; *krodhaḥ ca pāruṣyam*: anger and harshness; *ca eva ajñānaṁ*: and also ignorance; *pārtha*: Oh Arjuna; *āsurīm saṁpadam*: (these make up) the demonic (lower) values; *abhijātasya*: of anyone born (with them).

Pretentiousness, arrogance, a sense of self-importance, anger, harshness, and also ignorance – these, Oh Pārtha! make up the demonic (lower) values of anyone born with them.

5. दैवी सम्पद्विमोक्षाय निबन्धायासुरी मता ।
मा शुचः सम्पदं दैवीमभिजातोऽसि पाण्डव ॥

daivī saṁpad vimokṣāya nibandhāyā 'surī matā ।
mā śucaḥ saṁpadaṁ daivīm abhijāto 'si pāṇḍava ॥

daivī saṁpat: the divine (higher) values; *matā*: are deemed to be; *vimokṣāya*: for emancipation; *āsurī*: (and) the demonic (lower); *nibandhāya*: for bondage (to necessity); *mā śucaḥ*: do not regret; *pāṇḍava*: Oh Arjuna; *asi abhijātaḥ*: (you) are born (for); *daivīm saṁpadaṁ*: the divine (higher) values.

The divine values are deemed to be for emancipation, and the demonic for bondage to necessity; do not regret, Oh Pāṇḍava! you are born for the divine values.

6. द्वौ भूतसर्गौ लोकेऽस्मिन्दैव आसुर एव च ।
दैवो विस्तरशः प्रोक्त आसुरं पार्थ मे शृणु ॥

dvau bhūtasargau loke 'smin daiva āsura eva ca ।
daivo vistaraśaḥ prokta āsuraṁ pārtha me śṛṇu ॥

dvau: (there are) two; *bhūta sargau*: orders of created beings; *asmin loke*: in this world; *daivaḥ ca eva āsura*: the divine and also the demonic; *daivaḥ*: the divine; *proktaḥ vistaraśaḥ*: have been described at length; *śṛṇu me*: hear from Me; *pārtha*: Oh Arjuna; *āsuraṁ*: of the demonic.

There are two orders of created beings in this world: the divine and the demonic; the divine have been described at length; hear from Me, Oh Partha! of the demonic.

7. प्रवृत्तिं च निवृत्तिं च जना न विदुरासुराः ।
न शौचं नापि चाचारो न सत्यं तेषु विद्यते ॥

pravṛttiṁ ca nivṛttiṁ ca janā na vidur āsurāḥ ।
na śaucaṁ nā 'pi cā 'cāro na satyaṁ teṣu vidyate ॥

āsurāḥ janāḥ: the demonic men; *na viduḥ*: do not know; *pravṛttiṁ ca*: the way of positive action and; *ca nivṛttiṁ*: also the way of negative withdrawal; *teṣu vidyate*: in them (there) is; *na śaucaṁ*: neither cleanliness; *ca api na ācāraḥ*: and also no propriety in conduct; *na satyaṁ*: nor veracity.

The demonic men do not know the way of positive action, nor the way of negative withdrawal; in them is found neither cleanliness, nor propriety in conduct, nor veracity.

8. असत्यमप्रतिष्ठं ते जगदाहुरनीश्वरम् ।
अपरस्परसम्भूतं किमन्यत्कामहैतुकम् ॥

asatyam apratiṣṭhaṁ te jagad āhur anīśvaram ।
aparasparasaṁbhūtaṁ kim anyat kāmahaitukam ॥

te āhuḥ: they say (that); *jagat asatyam*: the world is without true existence; *apratiṣṭhaṁ*: without a basis; *anīśvaram*: without a presiding principle; *aparaspara saṁbhūtaṁ*: not resulting from reciprocal factors (lying beyond immediate vision); *kim anyat*: (as if asking) what (else is there) other than (that); *kāmahaitukam*: caused by lust.

They say that the world is without true existence, without a basis, without a presiding principle, not resulting from reciprocal factors (lying beyond immediate vision), as if asking: "What else is there other than that caused by lust?"

9. एतां दृष्टिमवष्टभ्य नष्टात्मानोऽल्पबुद्धयः ।
प्रभवन्त्युग्रकर्माणः क्षयाय जगतोऽहिताः ॥

etāṁ dṛṣṭim avaṣṭabhya naṣṭātmāno 'lpabuddhayaḥ ।
prabhavanty ugrakarmāṇaḥ kṣayāya jagato 'hitāḥ ॥

avaṣṭabhya: (willfully) holding (to); *etāṁ dṛṣṭim*: this view; *naṣṭātmānaḥ*: these (men) of lost souls; *alpa buddhayaḥ*: of little understanding; *ugra karmāṇaḥ*: of harsh deeds; *prabhavanti*: emerge; *ahitāḥ*: as non-beneficial; *jagataḥ kṣayāya*: (effecting) the world's decline.

Willfully holding to this view, these men of lost souls, of little understanding, of harsh deeds, emerge as non-beneficial, effecting the world's decline.

10. काममाश्रित्य दुष्पूरं दम्भमानमदान्विताः ।
मोहाद्गृहीत्वासद्ग्राहान्प्रवर्तन्तेऽशुचिव्रताः ॥

kāmam āśritya duṣpūraṁ dambhamānamadānvitāḥ ।
mohād gṛhītvā 'sadgrāhān pravartante 'śucivratāḥ ॥

āśritya: holding to; *duṣpūraṁ kāmam*: insatiable desire; *dambha māna mada anvitāḥ*: accompanied by pretentiousness, arrogance, and madness; *gṛhītvā*: (fondly) grasping; *asat grāhān*: false values; *mohāt pravartante*: deludedly (they) act; *aśuci vratāḥ*: (with) unclean resolve.

Holding to insatiable desires, accompanied by pretentiousness, arrogance, and madness, fondly grasping false values deludedly, they act with unclean resolve.

11. चिन्तामपरिमेयां च प्रलयान्तामुपाश्रिताः ।
कामोपभोगपरमा एतावदिति निश्चिताः ।।

cintām aparimeyāṁ ca pralayāntām upāśritāḥ ।
kāmopabhogaparamā etāvad iti nīścitāḥ ॥

ca upāśritāḥ: and engrossed (with); *aparimeyāṁ cintām*: infinite cares; *pralayāntām*: lasting till doomsday; *kāma upabhoga paramāḥ*: for whom desire and enjoyment is the supreme end; *niścitāḥ*: cocksure; *etāvat iti*: that such (is the way).

12. आशापाशशतैर्बद्धाः कामक्रोधपरायणाः ।
ईहन्ते कामभोगार्थमन्यायेनार्थसञ्चयान् ।।

āśāpāśaśatair baddhāḥ kāmakrodhaparāyaṇāḥ ।
īhante kāmabhogārtham anyāyenā 'rthasañcayān ॥

baddhāḥ: bound; *āśā pāśa śataiḥ*: by a hundred cords (consisting) of expectations; *kāma krodha parāyaṇāḥ*: given to lust and anger; *īhante anyāyena*: (they) strive unfairly; *artha sañcayān*: (to) hoard wealth; *kāma bhoga artham*: for the purpose of sensual enjoyment.

Engrossed with infinite cares lasting till doomsday, for whom desire and enjoyment is the supreme end, cocksure that such is the way,

bound by a hundred cords consisting of expectations, given to lust and anger, they strive unfairly to hoard wealth for sensual enjoyment.

13. इदमद्य मया लब्धमिमं प्राप्स्ये मनोरथम् ।
इदमस्तीदमपि मे भविष्यति पुनर्धनम् ।।

idam adya mayā labdham imaṁ prāpsye manoratham ।
idam astī 'dam api me bhaviṣyati punar dhanam ॥

idam adya: this today; *labdham mayā*: has been gained by me; *imaṁ manoratham*: this (particular) end; *prāpsye*: I will get; *idam dhanam asti me*: this wealth is mine; *api idam punaḥ*: and this (wealth) also; *bhaviṣyati*: will be (mine).

14. असौ मया हतः शत्रुर्हनिष्ये चापरानपि ।
ईश्वरोऽहमहं भोगी सिद्धोऽहं बलवान्सुखी ।।

asau mayā hataḥ śatrur haniṣye cā 'parān api ।
īśvaro 'ham ahaṁ bhogī siddho 'haṁ balavān sukhī ॥

asau śatruḥ: that enemy; *hataḥ mayā*: has been killed by me; *ca aparān*: and others; *haniṣye api*: I will also kill; *aham īśvaraḥ*: I (am) the lord; *ahaṁ bhogī*: I (am) the enjoyer; *ahaṁ siddhaḥ*: I (have) satisfied (my ambitions); *balavān sukhī*: (I am) powerful and happy.

15. आढ्योऽभिजनवानस्मि कोऽन्योऽस्ति सदृशो मया ।
यक्ष्ये दास्यामि मोदिष्य इत्यज्ञानविमोहिताः ॥

āḍhyo 'bhijanavān asmi ko 'nyo 'sti sadṛśo mayā ।
yakṣye dāsyāmi modiṣya ity ajñānavimohitāḥ ॥

asmi āḍhyaḥ: (I) am rich; *abhijanavān*: (and) well-born; *kaḥ anyaḥ*: who else; *asti sadṛśaḥ mayā*: is like me; *yakṣye*: I will sacrifice; *dāsyāmi*: I will give; *modiṣye*: I will rejoice; *iti*: thus; *ajñāna vimohitāḥ*: deluded by ignorance.

16. अनेकचित्तविभ्रान्ता मोहजालसमावृताः ।
प्रसक्ताः कामभोगेषु पतन्ति नरकेऽशुचौ ॥

anekacittavibhrāntā mohajālasamāvṛtāḥ ।
prasaktāḥ kāmabhogeṣu patanti narake 'śucau ॥

aneka citta vibhrāntāḥ: maddened by many thoughts; *moha jāla samāvṛtāḥ*: caught within the snare of confusing (values); *prasaktāḥ*: addicted to; *kāma bhogeṣu*: lustful gratifications; *patanti*: (they) fall; *aśucau narake*: into an unclean hell.

"This today has been gained by me; this particular end I will get; this wealth is mine, and that wealth also will be mine;

that enemy has been killed by be; and others I will also kill; I am the lord; I am the enjoyer; I have satisfied my ambitions; I am powerful and happy; I am rich and well-born; who else is like me? I will sacrifice; I will give; I will rejoice" – thus deluded by ignorance,

maddened by many thoughts, caught within the snare of confusing values, addicted to lustful gratifications, they fall into an unclean hell.

17. आत्मसम्भाविताः स्तब्धा धनमानमदान्विताः ।
यजन्ते नामयज्ञैस्ते दम्भेनाविधिपूर्वकम् ॥

ātmasaṁbhāvitāḥ stabdhā dhanamānamadānvitāḥ ।
yajante nāmayajñais te dambhenā 'vidhipūrvakam ॥

ātmasaṁbhāvitāḥ: self-righteous; *stabdhāḥ*: perversely immobile; *dhana māna mada anvitāḥ*: filled with pride and intoxication of wealth; *te yajante dambhena*: they perform sacrifices ostentatiously; *nāma yajñaiḥ*: (which are only) nominal sacrifices; *avidhi pūrvakam*: not conforming to scriptural rules.

Self-righteous, perversely immobile, filled with pride, and intoxication of wealth, they perform sacrifices ostentatiously, which are only nominal sacrifices, not conforming to scriptural rules.

18. अहङ्कारं बलं दर्पं कामं क्रोधं च संश्रिताः ।
मामात्मपरदेहेषु प्रद्विषन्तोऽभ्यसूयकाः ॥

ahaṁkāraṁ balaṁ darpaṁ kāmaṁ krodhaṁ ca saṁśritāḥ ।
mām ātmaparadeheṣu pradviṣanto 'bhyasūyakāḥ ॥

saṁśritāḥ: resorting to; *ahaṁkāraṁ balaṁ*: egoism, force; *darpaṁ kāmaṁ*: insolence, lust; *ca krodhaṁ*: and anger; *abhyasūyakāḥ*: these envious ones; *pradviṣantaḥ mām*: hate Me; *ātma para deheṣu*: in their own and others' bodies.

Resorting to egoism, force, insolence, lust, and anger, these envious ones hate Me in their own and others' bodies.

19. तानहं द्विषतः क्रूरान्संसारेषु नराधमान् ।
क्षिपाम्यजस्रमशुभानासुरीष्वेव योनिषु ॥

tān ahaṁ dviṣataḥ krūrān saṁsāreṣu narādhamān ।
kṣipāmy ajasram aśubhān āsurīṣv eva yoniṣu ॥

tān krūrān dviṣataḥ: these cruel haters; *saṁsāreṣu*: in the world (of cyclic becoming); *narādhamān*: worst of men; *ahaṁ kṣipāmi*: I hurl; *ajasram*: unceasingly; *eva aśubhān yoniṣu*: even into the degraded wombs; *āsurīṣu*: of demons.

20. आसुरीं योनिमापन्ना मूढा जन्मनि जन्मनि ।
मामप्राप्यैव कौन्तेय ततो यान्त्यधमां गतिम् ॥

āsurīṁ yonim āpannā mūḍhā janmani-janmani ।
mām aprāpyai 'va kaunteya tato yānty adhamāṁ gatim ॥

āpannāḥ: attaining; *āsurīṁ yonim*: a demonic womb; *mūḍhāḥ*: deluded; *janmani janmani*: birth after birth; *aprāpya mām eva*: not reaching Me indeed; *kaunteya*: Oh Arjuna; *tataḥ yānti*: then (they) go (to); *adhamāṁ gatim*: the lowest state.

These cruel haters in the world, worst of men, I hurl unceasingly even into the degraded wombs of demons;

attaining a demonic womb, deluded birth after birth, not reaching Me, Oh Son of Kuntī! they go to the lowest state.

21. त्रिविधं नरकस्येदं द्वारं नाशनमात्मनः ।
कामः क्रोधस्तथा लोभस्तस्मादेतत्त्रयं त्यजेत् ॥

trividhaṁ narakasye 'daṁ dvāraṁ nāśanam ātmanaḥ ।
kāmaḥ krodhas tathā lobhas tasmād etat trayaṁ tyajet ॥

trividhaṁ idaṁ: triple (is) this; *narakasya dvāraṁ*: infernal gate; *nāśanam ātmanaḥ*: destructive of the Self; *kāmaḥ*: lust; *krodhaḥ tathā lobhaḥ*: hate and greed; *tasmāt*: therefore; *etat trayaṁ*: these three; *tyajet*: should be avoided.

Triple is the infernal gate, destructive of the Self: lust, hate, and greed; therefore these three should be avoided.

22. एतैर्विमुक्तः कौन्तेय तमोद्वारैस्त्रिभिर्नरः ।
आचरत्यात्मनः श्रेयस्ततो याति परां गतिम् ॥

etair vimuktaḥ kaunteya tamodvārais tribhir naraḥ ।
ācaraty ātmanaḥ śreyas tato yāti parāṁ gatim ॥

naraḥ vimuktaḥ: a man (who has) abandoned; *etaiḥ tribhiḥ*: these three; *tamodvāraiḥ*: gates of darkness; *kaunteya*: Oh Arjuna; *ācarati*: observes; *ātmanaḥ śreyaḥ*: what conduces to his progress; *tataḥ*: (and) thereafter; *yāti parāṁ gatim*: attains to the Supreme Path.

A man who has abandoned these three gates of darkness, Oh Son of Kuntī! observes what conduces to his progress, and thereafter attains to the Supreme Path.

23. यः शास्त्रविधिमुत्सृज्य वर्तते कामकारतः ।
न स सिद्धिमवाप्नोति न सुखं न परां गतिम् ॥

yaḥ śāstravidhim utsṛjya vartate kāmakārataḥ ।
na sa siddhim avāpnoti na sukhaṁ na parāṁ gatim ॥

yaḥ: (he) who; *utsṛjya*: having abandoned; *śāstra vidhim*: the (guiding) principles of scripture; *vartate*: acts; *kāmakārataḥ*: under the promptings of desire; *saḥ na*: he cannot; *avāpnoti siddhim*: attain perfection; *na sukhaṁ*: nor happiness; *na parāṁ gatim*: nor the Supreme Path.

24. तस्माच्छास्त्रं प्रमाणं ते कार्याकार्यव्यवस्थितौ ।
ज्ञात्वा शास्त्रविधानोक्तं कर्म कर्तुमिहार्हसि ॥

tasmāc chāstraṁ pramāṇāṁ te kāryākāryavyavasthitau ।
jñātvā śāstravidhānoktaṁ karma kartum ihā 'rhasi ॥

tasmāt: therefore; *śāstraṁ*: the scripture; *te pramāṇaṁ*: (is) your authority; *kārya akārya vyavasthitau*: in deciding what should and should not be done; *jñātvā*: understanding; *śāstra vidhāna uktaṁ*: what is indicated for guidance in scripture; *arhasi*: you should; *kartum karma iha*: do work here.

He who, having abandoned the guiding principles of scripture, acts under the promptings of desire – he cannot attain perfection, nor happiness, nor the Supreme Path.

Therefore the scripture is your authority in deciding what should and should not be done. Understanding what is indicated for guidance in scripture, you should do work here.

DIALOGUE

TEACHER: This chapter is the second in the series on devices for self-analysis. In Chapter XIV we saw how the three modalities of nature are applied to account for typical personality variations. Here in Chapter XVI a principle of dichotomy is introduced. *Saṁpat* in Sanskrit means anything in possession. We inherit many latent virtues and vices from our family tree as well as from previous lives. Any skill or talent that we inherit could be called a *saṁpat*. If the talent, skill, aptitude, or virtue has a bright, positive value, then it is said to belong to the Divine. It is termed *daivī saṁpat*. *Div* means light. *Daivī* means luminous or bright. This is opposed to *āsura*, which means dark. Kṛṣṇa is going to enumerate values that are bright (*daivī*) and dark (*āsura*). In the enumeration of these values we can see a gradation according to a principle which is neither strictly ethical nor wholly religious, but which arises independently of the epistemological frame of reference of the Gītā itself.

Religion can be static or dynamic. The type of spirituality which the Gītā teaches cannot be lived within the closed walls of a static religion. Similarly there can be morality which is closed or open. The virtues listed below as belonging to Divine manifestation are "open".

This chapter can be said to have reference to the day of judgement. It is not a fixed day on which the soul is summoned to another world. True judgement comes almost every moment, at every pulsation of the brain. There is the all-seeing eye of the Divine which has its own counter-pole in the core of every person's consciousness, operating as their own moral conscience. When our inner conscience and the assent of God fall into one vertical line, our judgement attains the flawless veracity of divine approval.

Let us examine the bright values from verse 1:

- *abhayam* – When a person turns to himself in order to judge whether he is good or bad, the first reaction that may come is fear. Fear is always of the uncertain. If there is no sense of duality there is no fear. One who is in perfect bipolarity with the Absolute has not any thought or word or action which is not in conformity with the divine decree. Hence there is no reason for fear in the fully affiliated mind.
- *sattva saṁśuddhi* – When the transparency of mind is not affected by any kind of emotional crisis, intellectual conflict, or psychotic or other

pathological affectation, it gives a spontaneous expression of its own truthful nature. The body is not luminous. Even the mind has not its own light. The awareness that seeps through the inner organ, the mind, and the senses comes from the self-luminous divine spark of God or Universal Consciousness. When that light brightens up one's inner life and its outer expression, one's being is said to be all pure.

- *jñāna-yoga vyavasthiti* – Life has a sequential flow. In it our consciousness is shifted from one thing to another, or from one context to another. Each situation has its own frame of reference, value structure, and mode of correlation. In other words, each situation is a gestalt. A meditative mind has to see how every gestalt is centrally related to the core of one's own being. One who sees the Divine as the most central reality of their being will naturally see the gestalt, or frame of reference, as belonging to a divine situation in which the individual self has to harmoniously relate itself to the Absolute. The capacity to see everything as aspects of the Divine comes only by the grace of God. Hence, this is specified as the third of the *daivī saṁpat.*
- *dānam* – The joy of life is in sharing it with all. Man likes to share his wealth, the comforts of his home, food, physical skills, intellectual abilities, and even his own peace and harmony, with all fellow beings. This spontaneous offering in love is termed *dānam.* When one gives gifts to others, if it is done as an expression of one's identity with the Self of all, it can be truly called a divine virtue. On the other hand, if one gives gifts to others to show off or as an act of vanity, this is a vexation and has no spiritual value.
- *dama* – The next value in the series is *dama.* The fulfilment of a pursuit, whether spiritual or mundane, is delayed and obstructed by various distractions coming from outside as well as from one's own inner restlessness. There are many evil forces prowling in the unconscious, waiting for an opportunity to take possession of our mind and senses. If a wakeful and vigilant mind can foresee all such destructive forces and ward them off from causing obstruction to the harmonious function of mind, this is an act of *dama.*
- *yajña* – After restraint comes sacrifice. Sacrifice as a ritual is the offering of an oblation into the fire. Whatever is offered in the fire is burned away – nothing remains. Similarly, every action is to be treated as a sacrifice offered to God. To do something good with the anticipation of a reward is not spiritual. One who is always conscious of the Divine within does not enter into any kind of bilateral contract with a profit motive, he just expresses himself through words and actions in the

most spontaneous way. His thoughts, words, and actions are oblations in the fire of his love for God. Such a sacrifice is called *yajña.*

- *svādhyāya* – After *yajña* comes self-instruction. There cannot be any better purpose in life than achieving Self-realization. All states of consciousness are required to be related to the Absolute as a part of one's unbroken contemplation on the nature of the Self. It should be made a part of everyday discipline to spend some time exclusively for self-instruction. This includes reading the scriptures, listening to the instruction of one's own teacher, and also spending at least some time in intense meditation or contemplation. Self-instruction is called *svādhyāya.*
- *tapas* – After *svādhyāya* comes *tapas. Tap* means to burn. When gold is melted in fire it becomes purified. Similarly, the dross of our life leaves us when we undergo purificatory disciplines. There are different kinds of *tapas.* When a man directs his thoughts only through the channels of truth and always feels the presence of the Divine within his own self, he is observing *tapas* of his mind. When a man by habitual choice speaks only truthful words in the sweetest possible manner, with the intention of doing good to all, he is observing a *tapas* of his speech. When a man is physically helpful to others and does not engage his body in any untoward action, he is having a *tapas* of his body. What a man gains through incessant *tapas* is *ārjavam.*
- *ārjavam* – A disciplined mind has neither any fear nor any desire, so there is no need for it to twist or shade truth to suit the convenience of others. A well-disciplined mind remains always upright. Uprightness of the mind is called *ārjavam.* These nine values form the first part of the series of divine virtues given by Kṛṣṇa.

Do you think that these sequences show any kind of correlative structure of the value system termed as daivī saṁpat?

Yes, the sequences show a definite structure. Man is assailed by three kinds of calamities. He is afraid of natural forces, the caprices of society in which he lives, and also of the unknown and unknowable will of God. Confronted by these three factors, man spends at least the earlier part of his life in fear. Thereafter, when he turns to light, or wisdom, the sole purpose of his search is to have release from these threefold calamities. That is why fearlessness is given first place in the enumeration of divine virtues. The instrument for such a search is an unpolluted mind, hence the reference to the purity of the self after the mention of fearlessness. The process of realization implies a conscious appraisal of every situation in terms of a divinely-oriented frame of reference. Giving gifts, imposing a discipline of restraint, offering sacrifice, engaging in self-instruction, and observing *tapas* have reference to a traditionally recognized sequence of discipline enjoined by the schools of Yoga and Vedānta.

What other virtues are given as daivī saṁpat?

Kṛṣṇa continues:

> non-hurting, truth, non-anger, relinquishment, calmness, self-integrity, compassion to beings, non-interest in sense-values, gentleness, modesty, non-fickleness,
>
> alertness, forgiveness, fortitude, cleanliness, absence of malice, absence of excessive respectability – these make up the divine (higher) values of anyone, Oh Bhārata! born for them.

It is hardly to be denied that both good and bad people are found in the world. To speak of them as belonging to different groups by the peculiarity of their birth does not mean that humanity is being summarily divided into sheep and goats depending on some status related to birth. There is a complete theory put forward by the author in great detail, in the light of which these divisions should be understood. It is nowhere suggested in the Gītā that birth is based on heredity. We should understand these distinctions as belonging to type-psychology, based on capacity to appreciate higher and lower values in life, which do not always follow the line of heredity. In fact, Mendel's laws of heredity prove just the opposite. It is commonly known that sons of the same parents can be poles apart in the respective types they represent.

What are the dark qualities?

Kṛṣṇa says:

> Pretentiousness, arrogance, a sense of self-importance, anger, harshness and also ignorance – these, Oh Pārtha! make up the demonic (lower) values of anyone born with them.

Do these higher and lower values come in a mixture, or do we find types conforming exclusively to either group?

Until one becomes all pure and perfect, so as to be able to merge in the Divine, there will not be conformity with the *daivī saṁpat* alone. The divine values are deemed to be for emancipation, and the demonic or lower values for bondage. These are two paths: one of liberation, called *nivṛtti*, and the other of bondage, called *pravṛtti*. When a person is on the path of liberation he will have more and more of the divine qualities manifested in him.

Kṛṣṇa now gives an extensive discourse on the characteristics of people held in bondage. Here are the demonic qualities predominant in them:

> The demonic men do not know the way of positive action, nor the way of negative withdrawal; in them is found neither cleanliness, nor propriety in conduct, nor veracity.
>
> They say that the world is without true existence, without a basis, without a presiding principle, not resulting from reciprocal factors (lying beyond immediate vision), as if asking: "What else is there other than that caused by lust?"
>
> Willfully holding to this view, these men of lost souls, of little understanding, of harsh deeds, emerge as non-beneficial, effecting the world's decline.
>
> Holding to insatiable desires, accompanied by pretentiousness, arrogance, and madness, fondly grasping false values deludedly, they act with unclean resolve.
>
> Engrossed with infinite cares lasting till doomsday, for whom desire and enjoyment is the supreme end, cocksure that such is the way,
>
> bound by a hundred cords consisting of expectations, given to lust and anger, they strive unfairly to hoard wealth for sensual enjoyment.
>
> "This today has been gained by me; this particular end I will get; this wealth is mine, and that wealth also will be mine;
>
> that enemy has been killed by me; and others I will also kill; I am the lord; I am the enjoyer; I have satisfied my ambitions; I am powerful and happy;
>
> I am rich and well-born; who else is like me? I will sacrifice; I will give; I will rejoice" – thus deluded by ignorance,
>
> maddened by many thoughts, caught within the snare of confusing values, addicted to lustful gratifications, they fall into an unclean hell.

What happens to such demonic types?

They enter a regressive involution and go to lower and lower kinds of birth, so that they have to begin again from the zero point.

What paves the way for one to become degraded and demonic?

Lust, hate, and greed are the three gates to the hell of self-destruction. Hence Kṛṣṇa says:

> A man who has abandoned these three gates of darkness, Oh Son of Kuntī! observes what conduces to his progress, and thereafter attains to the Supreme Path.

> He who, having abandoned the guiding principles of scripture, acts under the promptings of desire – he cannot attain perfection, nor happiness, nor the Supreme Path.
>
> Therefore the scripture is your authority in deciding what should and should not be done. Understanding what is indicated for guidance in scripture, you should do work here.

Every man is likely to follow some scripture or other, especially if he is religious-minded. Non-religious people have their own authorities whom they consult, and even atheists swear in the name of some favourite writers. Inasmuch as such writings contribute to the abandonment of the three vices mentioned, and help a person to decide what should and should not be done, such guidance must be acceptable to whatever regional, religious, or traditional background they might belong to. Conformity to scripture as recommended in these last two verses should be understood in this larger and more general sense.

Chapter XVI began with fearlessness as the first-mentioned value, and ended with the triple vices of darkness to be avoided. In the latter, it touched the lowest water-mark of a life of contemplation and recommended reliance on some written authority to save the ordinary man from falling into error, or of degrading himself further spiritually.

This seemingly conservative recommendation will be relieved in the next chapter by the description of a more discriminating way of life involving faithful affiliation to what can be included under religious values, which are not merely ethical. This chapter has prepared us to take one more step into the field of necessary life.

XVII

Śraddhātraya-Vibhāga-Yoga

The Unitive Recognition of the Three Patterns of Faith

INTRODUCTION

In a note jotted down by Karl Marx in 1845 he wrote:

> The question whether human thought achieves objective truth is not a question of theory but a *practical* question.... Dispute over the actuality or non-actuality of any thinking that isolates itself from *praxis* is a purely scholastic question.[1]

The point of reference in this observation is the dynamics of faith and value vision, which have a categorical impact on man's thought and behaviour. Does man spontaneously think and act, or has he within him an inherent or innate essence of the happenings of the past that makes his thoughts and actions compulsive?

Jean-Paul Sartre, in his *Existentialism is a Humanism,* defines existentialism as the *conviction* "that existence precedes essence or ... that one must take subjectivity as his point of departure."[2] According to him, a person is nothing more than how he acts and what he thinks. Nobody disputes a person's existential identification with what they think and do. A more basic question is: What is that compulsive element in a person or his environment which makes it necessary for him to have a conviction? To this we can also add: Why does a man do what he does, and why does he do it how he does it? To answer these fundamental questions, we should carefully consider the claims of social biology, cosmo-sociology, psychology, and the unitive vision of the Upaniṣadic seers.

---

[1] Quoted by Martin Heidegger, 1976, *Basic Writings,* New York: Harper and Row, p. 190.

[2] Jean-Paul Sartre, 1946, *Existentialism is a Humanism,* Paris: Nagel, p. 17.

Social biology brings us to grips with the Darwinian, Lamarckian, and Mendelian theories, as well as the recent developments in genetics. However, Henri Bergson warns us against the mechanical interpretation which has found its way into most of these theories. After carefully considering the theories put forward by neo-Darwinians, neo-Lamarckians and Spencerians, Bergson concludes:

> The neo-Darwinians are probably right, we believe, when they teach that the essential causes of variation are the differences inherent in the germ borne by the individual, and not the experiences or behaviour of the individual in the course of his career. Where we fail to follow these biologists is in regarding the differences inherent in the germ as purely accidental and individual. ... Already, in fact, the theory of *mutations* is modifying Darwinism profoundly on this point.
>
> We ... arrive at a hypothesis like Eimer's, according to which the variations of different characters continue from generation to generation in definite directions. This hypothesis seems plausible to us. ... Where we differ from Eimer is in his claim that combinations of physical and chemical causes are enough to secure the result. We have tried to prove, on the contrary, by the example of the eye of *salamandra maculata*, that if there is "orthogenesis" here, a psychological cause intervenes. ... Certain neo-Lamarckians do indeed resort to a cause of a psychological nature. ... But if this cause is nothing but the conscious effort of the individual, it cannot operate in more than a restricted number of cases. ... So we come back ... to the idea we started from, that of an *original impetus* of life, passing from one generation of germs to the following generation of germs through the developed organisms which bridge the interval between the generations.[3]

Mendelian heredity depends on three fundamental concepts:

> The organism is a mosaic of unit characters capable of separate hereditary transmission.
>
> A unit character may mask a related unit character completely when the potentialities for the development of both are present in the same individual. This principle is called *dominance*, and the masked character is said to be *recessive*.
>
> Unit characters may be segregated during reproduction, regardless of the combinations in which they have been associated.

According to Sir Francis Galton's theory of the *law of ancestral inheritance*, each parent contributes one quarter of the total heritage of the individual, each grandparent one-sixteenth, and so on in a rapidly diminishing percentage. The law indicates a great reduction in the possibility of a hereditary character

[3] Henri Bergson, 1911, *Creative Evolution*, New York: Holt and Co., pp. 85-87.

reappearing after a lapse of generations. His *law of filial regression* says that extreme parents tend to produce offspring less extreme than themselves. This theory favours the pseudo-science of eugenics. The postulates of eugenics were once utilized by Nazi Germany to foster the breeding of a pure race of Aryans, and are still practised in India by caste-minded people.

The cosmo-sociologists uphold a longitudinal view that recognizes evolution through millennia. They see kinship between the present human generation and the primates of the Cenozoic Era, the dinosaurs of the Mesozoic Era, and the microorganisms and bacteria of the Proterozoic Era.

All these studies, at their best, can answer what functions as a hereditary principle, but do not answer why animal behaviour, especially that of man, is purposive. Psychologists like Freud and Jung postulated the theory of libidinal cathexis to account for the motivation of human behaviour. The role that Freud assumed was somewhat similar to that of the Sphinx of Delphi. He combined in himself a thoroughgoing empiricist, an occult symbologist who looked for a secret key in Greek mythology, and a literary critic who interpreted his patients' dreams to decipher neuroses caused by childhood shocks.

Jung enlarged the field of the uncanny by conceiving of the archetypes of the collective unconscious and the transformation of symbols in accordance with the variants of the individual's personal unconscious. On somewhat arbitrary lines, he also propounded his theory of types. It is interesting to note that the first theory of types came from Galen's classification (200 CE) of the four temperaments – choleric, sanguine, phlegmatic, and melancholic – which roughly agree with the Ayurvedic classification of the three *doṣa*s: *vāta*, *pitta* and *kapha*. In Wundt's classical typology, based on Galen's system, melancholic, choleric, sanguine, and phlegmatic roughly correspond to the *varṇa*s of the Gītā: śūdra, kṣatriya, vaiśya, and brāhmaṇa, respectively. Gross and Eysenk's hierarchical hypothesis of type is at best only a statistical speculation. Jung, in his system, postulates extroversion and introversion as the two directions into which the libido may be preferentially directed. This is in agreement with the Indian theory of the dynamics of *kāma* (erotics) in the affairs of men and women. According to Jung, the four fundamental functions of the psyche that decide a person's type are thinking, feeling, sensing, and intuiting. Although he claims to be an empiricist, Jung never bothered to substantiate his types with any experimental data. Kretschmer's classification was mainly made with a view towards categorizing mentally diseased people. He suggested a dimension of personality ranging from one extreme, characterized by schizophrenic disorder, to another, characterized by manic-depressive disorder.

It is obvious that all these theories are only cases of brilliant speculation, although some of them are partially supported by experimental or anecdotal data, and hence have a pseudo-scientific acceptability. The Upaniṣadic approach to the evaluation of personality comprises within it psychology, cosmology, and theology. The exposition of personality traits elaborately dealt with in the Gītā throws light on the "what", "how", and "why" of behavioural patterns.

According to the Gītā, the universe is presided over and operated upon by an all-embracing Intelligence that enjoins upon everything a co-partnership in its creation. This creation is an eternal process of purposive and meaningful transformation. Although we do not know the exact purpose of the rose bush that brings beautiful flowers of gentle fragrance year after year, or the pretty butterfly that flutters by, only to die in a few days, we have no doubt in our minds that our one purpose in life is to seek happiness. The seventh chapter of the *Chāndogya Upaniṣad*, when read in reverse order, takes us from our final goal to the initial promptings of life. It can be somewhat summarized as follows:

> We are happy when we do not envisage death, disease, and old age feebleness. The highest of happiness is devoid of any ego boundary that separates the Self from any imaginary other. There is nothing like discovering and regaining the lost Self. One who is fully realized has the Self to meditate on, has the Self to breathe, and has only the Self to desire. He is ever in adoration of the Self; the vast expanse in which he lives and moves about is also the Self. His food and drink are from the Self, and his strength, knowledge, absorption, memory, imagination, mind, word, name, *mantra*, and action are all derived from the Self. To such a person, what is above and below and in all directions is nothing but the Self. His knowledge, enjoyment, sport, and consummation of love are all with the Self. He is his own Lord. His fulfilment is not limited by any place. He is never enslaved by a second. He sees himself in all and says, "I am above and below, in the East and the West, in the North and the South. I am this very universe. It is the happiness of the Self that I see as cows and horses, elephants and jewellery, attendants, and my spouse. There is no separation. This happiness is great." It is known as *bhūmā*. One who knows *bhūmā* knows nothing else. There is no happiness in relativistic pleasures because they have a termination. When pleasure terminates, its absence becomes painful and one is assailed by desires. Only true happiness gives one the feeling, "I have fully lived and achieved what I aspired for". To have such realization one should become fully committed. A person is totally committed when he has a purpose to achieve and his heart, soul, and mind are all yoked to it. Such kind of

> commitment is called *niṣṭhā*. Commitment is possible only when there is a natural arousal of interest. One cannot commit oneself disinterestedly. When the interest is absolute, it is called *śraddhā*. *Śraddhā* comes only when one's aspiration becomes identified with one's passionate knowledge. Knowledge of a pleasing item has a magical power to capture one's mind and induce a desire to possess its object. Right knowledge of right value attracts the mind in the right direction, and wrong knowledge of wrong value lures it away to the wrong path.[4]

How do we know which is the right path? To avoid such a question, Kṛṣṇa exhorts Arjuna in the very last verse of the previous chapter to put his trust in the scriptural injunctions. What is given above is the scriptural injunction on *śraddhā*. In the final chapter, Kṛṣṇa reiterates that Arjuna's egoism would become detrimental to his wisdom if he were to disregard the underlying laws of the world order to which he is subjected and of which he is expected to be a promoter. Nataraja Guru, in his commentary on this, says as follows:

> We have thus two factors: the ego of Arjuna on the one hand, and the necessary action that he is impelled to do by a conspiracy of natural circumstances on the other hand. The action is outward, and the ego of Arjuna belongs to an inner philosophical order. The whole problem of the Gītā is to make these two factors come together unitively without leading to absurdities in life.[5]

The conspiracy of natural circumstances Nataraja Guru is referring to appears in verse 2 of the present chapter, in which Kṛṣṇa says:

> The faith of the embodied is of three kinds, born of their proper nature (*svabhāvajā*): the pure-clear (*sattva*), the affective-active (*rajas*), and the inert-dark (*tamas*).

Although the prime cause of the universe is homogeneous, undivided, and single, its manifestation as the universe begins with an initial dichotomy of an ontological law that governs its own teleological operation. Out of these come the intentionality of creation and the endless proliferation of the above-mentioned modalities of nature. Hence, all types and classifications within the system are to be studied in the light of the specific qualities of the modes that go into the creation of everything. In the present chapter Arjuna wants to know the influence of these modes in the lives of those who are not conversant with the dictates of scriptural injunction. All people everywhere have their own hoary traditions of word-wisdom. Even scientists

---

[4] *Chāndogya Upaniṣad*, chapter 7, sections 18-26.

[5] Nataraja Guru, 2008, *The Bhagavad Gita*, 2nd impression New Delhi: D.K. Printworld, pp. 632-33.

and politicians who think they have nothing to do with revelations or a priori teaching, have their articles of faith and universally acclaimed theories which they honour as laws or conventions. In the special case of Arjuna, his scriptural background is the Vedas and its final teaching that comes in the Upaniṣads, known as Vedānta. Both Vedas and Vedānta are commonly referred to as *śruti* – what is heard.

In Chapters II and XV, Kṛṣṇa explicitly asked Arjuna to go beyond the Vedic injunctions which are of a relativistic order. The spirit of heterodoxy that one may read into those passages is corrected by effecting a revaluation in the present chapter, where the scripture is given its rightful place as a correct norm to decide what is right and wrong in one's action. The Gītā also agrees with the existentialist position that a man is what he knows and what he does. In every man the prime light of his consciousness comes from the Lord, who is without blemish. The cloud of unknowing belongs to nature. Nature comprises within itself both heredity and environment. By bringing the mind into a bipolar relationship with the Absolute, one can correct both the hereditary and environmental flaws.

TRANSLATION

अर्जुन उवाच –

1. ये शास्त्रविधिमुत्सृज्य यजन्ते श्रद्धयान्विताः ।
तेषां निष्ठा तु का कृष्ण सत्त्वमाहो रजस्तमः ।।

arjuna uvāca –

ye śāstravidhim utsṛjya yajante śraddhayā 'nvitāḥ ।
teṣāṁ niṣṭhā tu kā kṛṣṇa sattvam āho rajas tamaḥ ॥

arjuna uvāca: Arjuna said; *tu kā*: but what (is); *niṣṭhā*: the status (in faith); *kṛṣṇa*: Oh Kṛṣṇa; *teṣāṁ ye*: of those who; *utsṛjya*: discarding; *śāstra vidhim*: scriptural injunctions; *yajante*: sacrifice; *śraddhayā anvitāḥ*: with faith; *āho*: is it; *sattvam*: pure-clear; *rajaḥ*: affective-active; *tamaḥ*: (or) intert-dark.

Arjuna said:

What is the status in faith, Oh Kṛṣṇa! of those who, discarding scriptural injunctions, sacrifice with faith: pure-clear, affective-active, or inert-dark?

श्रीभगवानुवाच –

2. त्रिविधा भवति श्रद्धा देहिनां सा स्वभावजा ।
सात्त्विकी राजसी चैव तामसी चेति तां शृणु ।।

śrībhagavān uvāca –

trividhā bhavati śraddhā dehināṁ sā svabhāvajā ।
sāttvikī rājasī cai 'va tāmasī ce 'ti tāṁ śṛṇu ॥

śrībhagavān uvāca: Kṛṣṇa said; *śraddhā dehināṁ*: the faith of the embodied; *bhavati trividhā*: is of three kinds; *sā svabhāvajā*: that (is) born of (their) own nature; *sāttvikī*: the pure-clear; *rājasī*: the affective-active; *ca eva tāmasī*: and indeed the inert-dark, *ca iti śṛṇu tāṁ*: and so hear that.

Kṛṣṇa said:

The faith of the embodied is of three kinds, born of their proper nature: the pure-clear, the affective-active, and the inert-dark. About it hear:

3. सत्त्वानुरूपा सर्वस्य श्रद्धा भवति भारत ।
श्रद्धामयोऽयं पुरुषो यो यच्छ्रद्धः स एव सः ।।

sattvānurūpā sarvasya śraddhā bhavati bhārata ।
śraddhāmayo 'yaṁ puruṣo yo yacchraddhaḥ sa eva saḥ ॥

bhavati śraddhā: the faith; *sarvasya*: of everyone (is); *anurūpā sattva*: shaped according to (their) true nature; *bhārata*: Oh Arjuna; *puruṣaḥ*: man; *śraddhā mayaḥ ayaṁ*: (is) made of this, (his) faith; *yat śraddhaḥ yaḥ*: what faith he (has); *eva saḥ*: even that; *saḥ*: he (is).

The faith of everyone is shaped according to their true nature, Oh Bhārata! man is made of his faith; of what faith a man is, even that he is.

4. यजन्ते सात्त्विका देवान्यक्षरक्षांसि राजसाः ।
प्रेतान्भूतगणांश्चान्ये यजन्ते तामसा जनाः ।।

yajante sāttvikā devān yakṣarakṣāṁsi rājasāḥ ।
pretān bhūtagaṇaṁś cā 'nye yajante tāmasā janāḥ ॥

sāttvikāḥ janāḥ: the pure-clear men; *yajante devān*: worship the divinities; *rājasāḥ*: the active-passionate; *yakṣa*: the gods of eating and wealth; *rakṣāṁsi*: (and) the gods of ferocity and violence; *anye tāmasāḥ*: the others, the inert-dark; *yajante*: worship; *pretān*: the spirits of the dead; *ca bhūta gaṇān*: and the host of elemental beings.

Pure-clear men worship the divinities; the active-passionate, the gods of eating and wealth, and the gods of ferocity and violence; the others, the inert-dark, worship the spirits of the dead, and the hosts of elemental beings.

5. अशास्त्रविहितं घोरं तप्यन्ते ये तपो जनाः ।
दम्भाहङ्कारसंयुक्ताः कामरागबलान्विताः ।।

aśāstravihitaṁ ghoraṁ tapyante ye tapo janāḥ ।
dambhāhaṁkārasaṁyuktāḥ kāmarāgabalānvitāḥ ॥

janāḥ ye: (those) men who; *tapyante*: practise; *ghoraṁ tapaḥ*: terrible austerities; *aśāstra vihitaṁ*: not enjoined by the scripture; *dambha ahaṁkāra saṁyuktāḥ*: given to hypocrisy and egoism; *kāma rāga bala anvitāḥ*: along with lust, passion, and power.

6. कर्शयन्तः शरीरस्थं भूतग्राममचेतसः ।
मां चैवान्तःशरीरस्थं तान्विद्ध्यासुरनिश्चयान् ॥

karśayantaḥ śarīrasthaṁ bhūtagrāmam acetasaḥ ।
māṁ cai 'vā 'ntaḥśarīrasthaṁ tān viddhy āsuraniścayān ॥

acetasaḥ: unthinking; *karśayantaḥ*: torturing; *bhūta grāmam*: all the organs; *śarīrasthaṁ*: of the body; *ca eva māṁ*: and thus (harassing) Me; *antaḥ śarīrasthaṁ*: seated in the body; *viddhi tān*: know them (to be); *āsura niścayān*: of demonic resolves.

Those men who practise terrible austerities not enjoined by the scripture, given to hypocrisy and egoism, lust, passion, and power,

torturing all the organs of the body and harassing Me, seated in the body – know them to be of demonic resolves.

7. आहारस्त्वपि सर्वस्य त्रिविधो भवति प्रियः ।
यज्ञस्तपस्तथा दानं तेषां भेदमिमं शृणु ॥

āhāras tv api sarvasya trividho bhavati priyaḥ ।
yajñas tapas tathā dānaṁ teṣāṁ bhedam imaṁ śṛṇu ॥

tu api āhāraḥ: and even the food; *bhavati priyaḥ*: (which) is dear; *sarvasya*: to everyone; *trividhaḥ*: (is) of three kinds; *tathā yajñaḥ*: (as) also the sacrifices; *tapaḥ dānaṁ*: austerities (and) gifts; *śṛṇu*: hear (you); *imaṁ bhedam teṣāṁ*: of this distinction (between) them.

Even the food which is dear to everyone is of three kinds, as also the sacrifices, austerities, and gifts. Hear you of the distinction between them.

8. आयुःसत्त्वबलारोग्यसुखप्रीतिविवर्धनाः ।
रस्याः स्निग्धाः स्थिरा हृद्या आहाराः सात्त्विकप्रियाः ॥

āyuḥsattvabalārogyasukhaprītivivardhanāḥ ।
rasyāḥ snigdhāḥ sthirā hṛdyā āhārāḥ sāttvikapriyāḥ ॥

āhāraḥ: the foods; *vivardhanāḥ*: which promote; *āyuḥ sattva*: life, vitality; *bala ārogya*: strength, health; *sukha prīti*: joy (and) cheerfulness; *rasyāḥ*: (and which are in themselves) tasty; *snigdhāḥ sthirāḥ*: rich, substantial; *hṛdyāḥ*: (and) appealing; *sāttvika priyāḥ*: (are) dear to the pure-clear (types).

The foods which promote life, vitality, strength, health, joy and cheerfulness, and which are (in themselves) tasty, rich, substantial, and appealing, are dear to the pure-clear types.

9. कट्वम्ललवणात्युष्णतीक्ष्णरूक्षविदाहिनः ।
आहारा राजसस्येष्टा दुःखशोकामयप्रदाः ।।

kaṭvamlalavaṇātyuṣṇatīkṣṇarūkṣavidāhinaḥ ।
āhārā rājasasye 'ṣṭā duḥkhaśokāmayapradāḥ ॥

āhārāḥ: foods; *kaṭu*: (that are) strongly-flavoured; *amla lavaṇa*: sour, saline; *atyuṣṇa tīkṣṇa*: excessively hot, pungent; *rūkṣa vidāhinaḥ*: hardened (and) burning; *iṣṭāḥ*: (are) liked; *rājasasya*: by the active-passionate; *duḥkha śoka āmaya pradāḥ*: (and are) producers of pain, unhappiness, and indisposition.

Foods that are strongly-flavoured, sour, saline, excessively hot, pungent, hardened, and burning, are liked by the active-passionate, and are producers of pain, unhappiness, and indisposition.

10. यातयामं गतरसं पूति पर्युषितं च यत् ।
उच्छिष्टमपि चामेध्यं भोजनं तामसप्रियम् ।।

yātayāmaṁ gatarasaṁ pūti paryuṣitaṁ ca yat ।
ucchiṣṭam api cā 'medhyaṁ bhojanaṁ tāmasapriyam ॥

ca yat: and (that) which (is); *yātayāmaṁ*: left over; *gatarasaṁ*: (which has) lost its taste; *pūti paryuṣitaṁ*: (which is) putrid, stale; *ucchiṣṭam*: (which is) refuse; *ca api*: and also; *amedhyaṁ*: unfit for consumption; *bhojanaṁ*: (such) alimentary items; *tāmasa priyam*: (are) welcome to the inert-dark (types).

That which is left over, which has lost its taste, which is putrid, stale, which is refuse, and unfit for consumption – such alimentary items are welcome to the inert-dark types.

11. अफलाकाङ्क्षिभिर्यज्ञो विधिदृष्टो य इज्यते ।
यष्टव्यमेवेति मनः समाधाय स सात्त्विकः ।।

aphalākāṅkṣibhir yajño vidhidṛṣṭo ya ijyate ।
yaṣṭavyam eve 'ti manaḥ samādhāya sa sāttvikaḥ ॥

saḥ yajñaḥ: that sacrifice; *sāttvikaḥ*: (is) pure-clear; *yaḥ ijyate*: which is offered; *aphala ākāṅkṣibhiḥ*: by those desiring no gain; *vidhi dṛṣṭaḥ*: (having) injunctional recognition; *iti manaḥ*: thus on the mind; *samādhāya eva*: having become tranquil indeed; *yaṣṭavyam*: (by saying to themselves): (this is) to be sacrificed.

That sacrifice is pure-clear which is offered by those desiring no gain, having injunctional recognition on the mind, having become tranquil by saying to themselves that sacrifice is necessary.

12. अभिसन्धाय तु फलं दम्भार्थमपि चैव यत् ।
इज्यते भरतश्रेष्ठ तं यज्ञं विद्धि राजसम् ।।

abhisaṁdhāya tu phalaṁ dambhārtham api cai 'va yat ।
ijyate bharataśreṣṭha taṁ yajñaṁ viddhi rājasam ॥

tu yat ijyate: but (that sacrifice) which is offered; *abhisaṁdhāya phalaṁ*: with expectation of return; *ca eva dambhārtham*: or even for egoistic show; *viddhi*: know; *bharataśreṣṭha*: Oh Arjuna; *taṁ yajñaṁ*: that sacrifice (to be); *rājasam*: active-passionate.

That sacrifice which is offered with expectation of return, or for egoistic show, Oh Best of Bhāratas! – know that sacrifice to be active-passionate.

13. विधिहीनमसृष्टान्नं मन्त्रहीनमदक्षिणम् ।
श्रद्धाविरहितं यज्ञं तामसं परिचक्षते ।।

vidhihīnam asṛṣṭānnaṁ mantrahīnam adakṣiṇam ।
śraddhāvirahitaṁ yajñaṁ tāmasaṁ paricakṣate ॥

yajñaṁ: the sacrifice; *vidhihīnam*: which does not conform to scriptural rules; *asṛṣṭa annaṁ*: without food distribution; *mantra hīnam*: without sacred chants; *adakṣiṇam*: (and) without token gifts meant for the Guru; *śraddhā virahitaṁ*: (and) devoid of faith; *paricakṣate*: they declare (to be); *tāmasaṁ*: inert-dark.

The sacrifice which does not conform to scriptural rules, without food distribution, without sacred chants and token gifts meant for the Guru, and devoid of faith, they declare to be inert-dark.

14. देवद्विजगुरुप्राज्ञपूजनं शौचमार्जवम् ।
ब्रह्मचर्यमहिंसा च शारीरं तप उच्यते ।।

devadvijagurruprājñapūjanaṁ śaucam ārjavam ।
brahmacaryam ahiṁsā ca śārīraṁ tapa ucyate ॥

pūjanaṁ: worship offered to; *deva dvija*: the gods, wisdom-initiates; *guru prājña*: spiritual teachers, (and) the wise (generally); *śaucam ārjavam*: cleanliness, straightforwardness; *brahmacaryam*: the chaste ways of a wisdom-novice; *ca ahiṁsā*: and non-hurting; *ucyate*: are said (to constitute); *tapaḥ śārīraṁ*: austerity of the body.

Worship offered to the gods, to wisdom-initiates, to spiritual teachers, and the wise (generally), cleanliness, straightforwardness, the chaste ways of a wisdom-novice, and non-hurting, are said to constitute austerity of the body.

15. अनुद्वेगकरं वाक्यं सत्यं प्रियहितं च यत् ।
स्वाध्यायाभ्यसनं चैव वाङ्मयं तप उच्यते ॥

anudvegakaraṁ vākyaṁ satyaṁ priyahitaṁ ca yat ।
svādhyāyābhyasanaṁ cai 'va vāṅmayaṁ tapa ucyate ॥

anudvegakaraṁ vākyaṁ: inoffensive speech; *yat satyaṁ*: which (is) truthful; *priya ca hitaṁ*: pleasant and beneficial; *ca eva svādhyāya abhyasanaṁ*: and indeed contemplative self-study; *ucyate*: are named; *tapaḥ vāṅmayaṁ*: the austerity of speech.

Inoffensive speech, which is truthful, pleasant, and beneficial, and contemplative self-study, are named the austerity of speech.

16. मनःप्रसादः सौम्यत्वं मौनमात्मविनिग्रहः ।
भावसंशुद्धिरित्येतत्तपो मानसमुच्यते ॥

manaḥprasādaḥ saumyatvaṁ maunam ātmavinigrahaḥ ।
bhāvasaṁśuddhir ity etat tapo mānasam ucyate ॥

manaḥ prasādaḥ: mental happiness; *saumyatvaṁ maunam*: gentleness, silence; *ātma vinigrahaḥ*: self-restraint; *bhāva saṁśuddhiḥ*: an imagination of creative transparency; *iti etat ucyate*: thus, this (is) named; *tapaḥ mānasam*: the austerity of the mind.

Mental happiness, gentleness, silence, self-restraint, an imagination of creative transparency, are named the austerity of the mind.

17. श्रद्धया परया तप्तं तपस्तत्त्रिविधं नरैः ।
अफलाकाङ्क्षिभिर्युक्तै : सात्त्विकं परिचक्षते ॥

śraddhayā parayā taptaṁ tapas tat trividhaṁ naraiḥ ।
aphalākāṅkṣibhir yuktaiḥ sāttvikaṁ paricakṣate ॥

tat trividhaṁ tapaḥ: this threefold austerity; *taptaṁ*: practised; *parayā śraddhayā*: with transcendent faith; *yuktaiḥ naraiḥ*: by unitively balanced men; *aphala ākāṅkṣibhiḥ*: without desire of gain; *paricakṣate*: (is) named; *sāttvikaṁ*: pure-clear.

This threefold austerity, practised with transcendent faith by unitively balanced men, without desire of gain, is named pure-clear.

18. सत्कारमानपूजार्थं तपो दम्भेन चैव यत् ।
क्रियते तदिह प्रोक्तं राजसं चलमध्रुवम् ॥

satkāramānapūjārthaṁ tapo dambhena cai 'va yat ।
kriyate tad iha proktaṁ rājasaṁ calam adhruvam ॥

tat tapaḥ: that austerity; *yat kriyate*: which is practised; *satkāra māna pūjā arthaṁ*: for gaining respect, honour, reverence; *ca eva dambhena iha*: and even for the sake of show here; *proktaṁ*: (is) named; *rājasaṁ*: active-passionate; *calam adhruvam*: (it is) changeful and insecure.

That austerity which is practised for gaining respect, honour, reverence, and for the sake of show, is named active-passionate, changeful and insecure.

19. मूढग्राहेणात्मनो यत्पीडया क्रियते तपः ।
परस्योत्सादनार्थं वा तत्तामसमुदाहृतम् ।।

mūḍhagrāhe ṇā 'tmano yat pīḍayā kriyate tapaḥ ।
parasyo 'tsādanārthaṁ vā tat tāmasam udāhṛtam ॥

tat tapaḥ: that austerity; *yat kriyate*: which is practised; *mūḍha grāheṇa*: out of foolish obstinacy; *ātmanaḥ pīḍayā*: with self-torture; *vā arthaṁ utsādana parasya*: or (with) the aim of the detriment of another; *udāhṛtam*: is named; *tāmasam*: inert-dark.

That austerity which is practised out of foolish obstinacy, with self-torture, or for the detriment of another, is named inert-dark.

20. दातव्यमिति यद्दानं दीयतेऽनुपकारिणे ।
देशे काले च पात्रे च तद्दानं सात्त्विकं स्मृतम् ।।

dātavyam iti yad dānaṁ dīyate 'nupakāriṇe ।
deśe kāle ca pātre ca tad dānaṁ sāttvikaṁ smṛtam ॥

dānaṁ yat iti: (that) gift which thus; *dātavyam*: (clearly) ought to be made; *dīyate*: given; *anupakāriṇe*: to one from whom no return is expected; *deśe ca kāle*: in (the right) place and time; *ca pātre*: and to a deserving person; *tat dānaṁ*: that gift; *smṛtaṁ*: is remembered (as); *sāttvikaṁ*: pure-clear.

That gift which clearly ought to be made, given to one from whom no return is expected, in the right place and time, and to a deserving person – that gift is pure-clear.

21. यत्तु प्रत्युपकारार्थं फलमुद्दिश्य वा पुनः ।
दीयते च परिक्लिष्टं तद्दानं राजसं स्मृतम् ।।

yat tu pratyupakārārthaṁ phalam uddiśya vā punaḥ ।
dīyate ca parikliṣṭaṁ tad dānaṁ rājasaṁ smṛtam ॥

tu yat dīyate: but what (is) given; *pratyupakārārthaṁ*: with the view to return benefit; *vā punaḥ*: or again; *phalam uddiśya*: with gain in view; *ca parikliṣṭaṁ*: and reluctantly; *tat dānaṁ*: that gift; *smṛtam*: is remembered (to be); *rājasaṁ*: active-passionate.

And what is given with a view to return benefit, or with gain in view, reluctantly – that gift is held to be active-passionate.

22. अदेशकाले यद्दानमपात्रेभ्यश्च दीयते ।
असत्कृतमवज्ञातं तत्तामसमुदाहृतम् ॥

adeśakāle yad dānam apātrebhyaś ca dīyate ।
asatkṛtam avajñātaṁ tat tāmasam udāhṛtam ॥

dānam: the gift; *yat dīyate*: which is given; *adeśa kāle*: at a wrong place or time; *asatkṛtam*: disdainfully; *ca avajñātaṁ*: and patronizingly; *apātrebhyaḥ*: to persons unfit (to receive it); *tat udāhṛtam*: that (is) said to be; *tāmsam*: inert-dark.

The gift that is given at a wrong place or time, disdainfully, and patronizingly, to persons unfit to receive it, affords an example of the inert-dark.

23. ॐ तत्सदिति निर्देशो ब्रह्मणस्त्रिविधः स्मृतः ।
ब्राह्मणास्तेन वेदाश्च यज्ञाश्च विहिताः पुरा ॥

auṁ tat sad iti nirdeśo brahmaṇas trividhaḥ smṛtaḥ ।
brāhmaṇās tena vedāś ca yajñāś ca vihitāḥ purā ॥

auṁ tat sat: *auṁ tat sat* (Absolute Word, That is Real); *iti trividhaḥ*: so (this), threefold; *smṛtaḥ*: is remembered; *nirdeśaḥ*: (as) designating; *brahmaṇaḥ*: the Absolute; *brāhmaṇāḥ*: the (scriptures called) Brāhmaṇas; *vedāḥ ca*: the Vedas and; *yajñāḥ ca*: sacrifices also; *tena vihitāḥ*: by this were prescribed; *purā*: of old.

Auṁ tat sat: this, threefold, has been known in the past as designating the Absolute. The (scriptures called) Brāhmaṇas, the Vedas, and sacrifices also, by this were prescribed of old.

24. तस्मादोमित्युदाहृत्य यज्ञदानतमःक्रियाः ।
प्रवर्तन्ते विधानोक्ताः सततं ब्रह्मवादिनाम् ॥

tasmād aum iti udāhṛtya yajñadānatapaḥkriyāḥ ।
pravartante vidhānoktāḥ satataṁ brahmavādinām ॥

tasmāt udāhṛtya iti: therefore, uttering thus; *aum*: *auṁ* (Absolute Word); *yajña dāna*: sacrifice, giving; *tapaḥ*: austerity; *kriyāḥ vidhāna uktāḥ*: (and) action enjoined by scriptural ordinance; *satataṁ*: always; *pravartante*: begin; *brahma vādinām*: for those who represent the doctrine of the Absolute.

Therefore, uttering *auṁ*, sacrifice, giving, austerity, and action enjoined by scriptural ordinance always begin for those who represent the doctrine of the Absolute.

25. तदित्यनभिसन्धाय फलं यज्ञतपःक्रियाः ।
दानक्रियाश्च विविधाः क्रियन्ते मोक्षकाङ्क्षिभिः ॥

tad iti anabhisaṁdhāya phalaṁ yajñatapaḥkriyāḥ ।
dānakriyāś ca vividhāḥ kriyante mokṣakāṅkṣibhiḥ ॥

tat: (with) *tat* (That); *iti anabhisaṁdhāya*: thus excluding; *phalaṁ*: (all) values of gain; *yajña tapaḥ kriyāḥ*: acts of sacrifice and austerity; *ca dāna kriyāḥ*: (as) also acts of giving; *vividhāḥ*: of various kinds; *kriyante*: are performed; *mokṣa kāṅkṣibhiḥ*: by those who desire liberation.

With *tat*, excluding all values of gain, acts of sacrifice and austerity, as also acts of giving, of various kinds, are performed by those who desire liberation.

26. सद्भावे साधुभावे च सदित्येतत्प्रयुज्यते ।
प्रशस्ते कर्मणि तथा सच्छब्दः पार्थ युज्यते ॥

sadbhāve sādhubhāve ca sad ity etat prayujyate ।
praśaste karmaṇi tathā sacchabdaḥ pārtha yujyate ॥

etat: this (term); *sat*: *sat* (the Real); *iti prayujyate*: thus is used; *sat bhāve*: in the sense of existence; *ca sādhubhāve*: and in the sense of goodness; *tathā*: likewise; *pārtha*: Oh Arjuna; *praśaste karmaṇi*: to all laudable actions; *śabdaḥ sat*: the word *sat*; *yujyate*: is (usually) applied.

This term *sat* is used in the sense of existence, and of goodness; and likewise, Oh Pārtha! to all laudable actions, the expression *sat* is usually applied.

27. यज्ञे तपसि दाने च स्थितिः सदिति चोच्यते ।
कर्म चैव तदर्थीयं सदित्येवाभिधीयते ॥

yajñe tapasi dāne ca sthitiḥ sad iti co 'cyate ।
karma cai 'va tadarthīyaṁ sad ity evā 'bhidhīyate ॥

sthitiḥ yajñe: steadiness in sacrifice; *tapasi ca dāne*: austerity and giving; *ca ucyate iti*: also is called thus; *sat*: *sat* (good and existing); *ca eva karma*: and so also action; *tadarthīyaṁ*: so intended; *iti eva abhidhīyate sat*: thus indeed is called *sat*.

Steady loyalty in sacrifice, austerity, and giving is also called *sat*, and so also action so intended is called *sat*.

28. अश्रद्धया हुतं दत्तं तपस्तप्तं कृतं च यत् ।
असदित्युच्यते पार्थ न च तत्प्रेत्य नो इह ॥

aśraddhayā hutaṁ dattaṁ tapas taptaṁ kṛtaṁ ca yat ।
asad ity ucyate pārtha na ca tat pretya no iha ॥

yat hutaṁ: whatever (is) sacrificed; *dattaṁ kr̥taṁ*: given, (or) done; *ca tapaḥ*: and (whatever) austerity; *taptaṁ*: is gone through; *aśraddhayā*: without faith; *iti ucyate*: thus is called; *asat*: *asat* (non-existent, no good); *pārtha*: Oh Arjuna; *tat na*: that (is) nothing; *naḥ iha*: to us here; *pretya*: (or) hereafter.

Whatever is sacrificed, given, or done, and whatever austerity is gone through without faith, is called *asat*, Oh Pārtha! it has no value here or hereafter.

DIALOGUE

Teacher: The three modalities of nature, *sattva*, *rajas*, and *tamas*, were introduced in the fourteenth chapter as innate principles operating in all manifested beings. In the present chapter they are reintroduced in terms of their functional actualities. To realize the Absolute the aspirant was asked to sever the roots of the tree of life originating from above as well as from action here. Even when these roots are cut-off by wisdom, they will persist in a phenomenal sense as long as the body lives. Hence, it is essential for us to see how these modalities operate in our everyday life and condition or colour our personality. This chapter takes us far deeper into the structural details of our persona and its function. Each *guṇa* has its symptom for the recognition of its operation. This chapter introduces us to a symptomatic diagnosis of the psychological type to which each of us truly belongs.

Student: *If this chapter is dealing with the functional operations of the* guṇas, *why is it not called the* Unitive Recognition of the Three Patterns of Modalities, *instead of the* Three Patterns of Faith?

What is translated here as "faith" is *śraddhā* in the original Sanskrit. Faith is not an, appropriate word to bring out the entire connotation of the term *śraddhā*. *Śraddhā* means one-pointed attention, perfect bipolarity, total acceptance, pure devotion, ardent faith, full sympathy, unconditional appreciation, and an attitude of loving regard which is continuous and consistent, like the unbroken flow of oil. In the present chapter, wherever we use the word "faith", it should be understood to have the same meaning as *śraddhā*. Just as the tree is known by its fruit, a man is known by his faith.

Why do you say that a man is known by his faith?

The objective world is manifested out of the perishable aspect of the existential phenomena superimposed on the pure existence of the Absolute by its own negative principle of nescience. Faith is an identity of one's own self on the existential level, whether with a transient or a perennial value.

The faith of a person is expressed by his life interests and what might be called his pattern of behaviour. There might even be conformity to patterns of behaviour based on the faith belonging to groups that behave according to some common single pattern. Even a person's attraction to certain types of food can reveal the pattern of interest in life. The chapter closes with a special reference to one of the most important philosophical formulae of Vedānta, *auṁ tat sat*.

At the outset, Arjuna once again takes the initiative and puts a general question to Kṛṣṇa that has specific reference to his personal life. Arjuna asks:

> What is the status in faith, Oh Kṛṣṇa, of those who, discarding scriptural injunctions, sacrifice with faith: pure-clear (*sattva*), affective-active (*rajas*), or inert-dark (*tamas*)?

The majority of people who are sincere and pursuing some discipline with great faith are not strictly guided by any systematized canonical scripture. Arjuna himself was not following any special Vedic injunction.

Therefore he wished to know whether his own faith was in order.

But why does he make a reference to the three modalities?

From the earlier reference to the modalities he learned to diagnose interests in terms of *guṇa*s. He wanted to apply the same normative notions in understanding his own self. Kṛṣṇa replies:

> The faith of the embodied is of three kinds, born of their proper nature: the pure-clear (*sattva*), the affective-active (*rajas*), and the inert-dark (*tamas*). About it hear:
>
> The faith of everyone is shaped according to their true nature, Oh Bhārata; man is made of his faith; of what faith a man is, even that he is.

A man holds a form of faith dear to him because it corresponds with a subtle and essential aspect of his nature. This may be called his true nature, as distinguished from a nature pretended or artificially assumed. When it is stated that a man is made of his faith, and of what faith a man is, he *is* that, there is a reference to faith as an objective counterpart of man's subjective nature. It is just like saying that a tree is known by its fruits. Kṛṣṇa shows Arjuna how the operation of modalities can be applied in a number of cases, such as worship, food, sacrifice, penance, and gifts.

How does he distinguish types of worship in terms of the three modalities?

Kṛṣṇa says:

> Pure-clear (sāttvic) men worship the divinities; the active-passionate

(rājasic), the gods of eating and wealth, and the gods of ferocity and violence; the others, the inert-dark (tāmasic), worship the spirits of the dead, and the hosts of elemental beings.

Those men who practise terrible austerities not enjoined by the scripture, given to hypocrisy and egoism, lust, passion, and power,

torturing all the organs of the body and harassing Me, seated in the body – know them to be of demonic resolves.

How do we understand the quality of our own devotion in the present sociocultural set-up? Gods, demigods, and devils no longer have any place in our understanding.

The original Sanskrit term *devān* means any value that has the dignity, brightness, beauty, and magnificence associated with the Divine, or the Absolute. We have among us many who can go beyond the limitations of their sensual interest and personal motives to the appreciation of higher meditative and contemplative values in the fields of philosophy and science, in art and literature, and in interpersonal and trans-subjective experiences. The devotion to the numinous implied in higher values is characterized here as sāttvic devotion. *Yakṣa*s symbolize indulgence in sensual pleasures. In people who are hunting for the pleasures of the body, and who are fond of overspecializing in hedonistic values, there is a clear case of rājasic pursuit. Another aspect of the active-passionate approach can be seen in the gross and aggressive applications of the instruments of coercion. In the case of the inert-dark types, they dabble in all kinds of questionable pursuits, such as witchcraft, black magic, and other puerile forms of distorted devotion to negative forces.

Some people resort to severe penances and mortification of the body. Is this of much value in spirituality?

According to the Gītā, those who practise terrible austerities not enjoined by scriptures, given to hypocrisy and egoism, lust, passion, and power are torturing all the organs of the body. They not only violate the harmony of their physical, mental, and spiritual well-being, but also unconsciously show great disregard to the Divine that is enshrined in every heart. Their penance and mortification are demonic.

How do we diagnose our personality type by detecting special interest in the kind of food we prefer?

Each temperament has its corresponding food. As we can tell something of the character of a person by the company he keeps or his dress, it is possible to distinguish different temperaments on the basis of the food each prefers. Kṛṣṇa says:

> The foods which promote life, vitality, strength, health, joy and cheerfulness, and which are (in themselves) tasty, rich, substantial, and appealing, are dear to the pure-clear (sāttvic) types.
>
> Foods that are strongly-flavoured, sour, saline, excessively hot, pungent, hardened, and burning, are liked by the active-passionate (rājasic), and are producers of pain, unhappiness, and indisposition.
>
> That which is left over, which has lost its taste, which is putrid, stale, which is refuse, and unfit for consumption – such alimentary items are welcome to the inert-dark (tāmasic) types.

Only a clear-minded, refined person, capable of enjoying a good dinner as it ought to be enjoyed, can choose those items which are tasty, rich, substantial, and appealing, which have good effects, and can enjoy them properly, as in the case of sāttvic types. Active people like certain foods selected not on the basis of their beneficial effects, but mainly on the basis of pampering to taste. This can cause pain and unhappiness and even indisposition. In the case of tāmasic types there is no choice on the part of the eater. The items are conditioned by necessity and may even verge on being poisonous.

How do you decide types in terms of the sacrifices performed?

Three kinds of sacrifice are mentioned in this chapter. The main distinction between good and bad sacrifices lies in the fact that while the good one does not have any immediate result in view, the bad one is definitely prompted by motives of gain. Kṛṣṇa says:

> That sacrifice is pure-clear (sāttvic) which is offered by those desiring no gain, having injunctional recognition on the mind, having become tranquil by saying to themselves that sacrifice is necessary.
>
> That sacrifice which is offered with expectation of return, or for egoistic show, Oh Best of Bhāratas – know that sacrifice to be active-passionate (rājasic).
>
> The sacrifice which does not conform to scriptural rules, without food distribution, without sacred chants and token gifts meant for the Guru, and devoid of faith, they declare to be inert-dark (tāmasic).

What austerities are recommended to be pure?

Kṛṣṇa says:

> Worship offered to the gods, to wisdom-initiates, to spiritual teachers, and the wise (generally), cleanliness, straightforwardness, the chaste ways of a wisdom-novice, and non-hurting, are said to constitute austerity of the body.

> Inoffensive speech, which is truthful, pleasant, and beneficial, and contemplative self-study, are named the austerity of speech.
>
> Mental happiness, gentleness, silence, self-restraint, an imagination of creative transparency, are named the austerity of the mind.
>
> This threefold austerity, practised with transcendent faith by unitively balanced men, without desire of gain, is named pure-clear (sāttvic).
>
> That austerity which is practised for gaining respect, honour, reverence, and for the sake of show, is named active-passionate (rājasic), changeful and insecure.
>
> That austerity which is practised out of foolish obstinacy, with self-torture, or for the detriment of another, is named inert-dark (tāmasic).

The guiding principles in all these verses have been mentioned already in speaking of sacrifices.

Giving gifts or alms is considered a virtue in certain religions. For instance, the Koran recommends that one-tenth of one's income should be distributed as gifts. What does Kṛṣṇa recommend?

The act of giving becomes noble or ignoble in accordance with the attitude in which it is given. Hence, Kṛṣṇa says:

> That gift which clearly ought to be made, given to one from whom no return is expected, in the right place and time, and to a deserving person – that gift is pure-clear (sāttvic).
>
> And what is given with a view to return benefit, or with gain in view, reluctantly – that gift is held to be active-passionate (rājasic).
>
> The gift that is given at a wrong place or time, disdainfully, and patronizingly, to persons unfit to receive it, affords an example of the inert-dark (tāmasic).

Promiscuous gift-giving into which no study of the situation enters, and gifts made disdainfully and patronizingly, ignoring the suitability of place and occasion, are described here. Having referred to three kinds of faith corresponding to three types of persons who adopt such faiths, Kṛṣṇa next speaks of three aspects of the Absolute given in one of the great formulae: *auṁ tat sat*. He says:

> *Auṁ tat sat*: this, threefold, has been known in the past as designating the Absolute. The (scriptures called) Brāhmaṇas, the Vedas, and sacrifices also, by this were prescribed of old.
>
> Therefore, uttering *auṁ*, sacrifice, giving, austerity, and action enjoined by scriptural ordinance always begin for those who represent the doctrine of the Absolute.

> With *tat*, excluding all values of gain, acts of sacrifice and austerity, as also acts of giving, of various kinds, are performed by those who desire liberation.
>
> This term *sat* is used in the sense of existence, and of goodness; and likewise, Oh Pārtha! to all laudable actions, the expression *sat* is usually applied.
>
> Steady loyalty in sacrifice, austerity, and giving is also called *sat*, and so also action so intended is called *sat*.

Constancy or continued affiliation to what constitutes the faith-value of sacrifice, austerity, and gift-bestowing, which are the three items dealt with in this chapter, is itself a spiritual value. The person who is thus steady and loyal to the outward values represents in himself a certain high value. Conversely, if we should swing to the objective side of the situation implied in an act of faith, inasmuch as all these acts refer to the value of the Absolute through what is connoted by the word *tat* (That), the status of the crude actions themselves can in principle be equated to the Absolute itself, and thus become both existent and good, *sat*, as stated in verse 27.

Thus the four rungs of the ladder of values, the lowest referring to action, the next to existence and goodness at once, the next to that which is the passionless goal of liberation, and the fourth and highest, which consists of the pure wisdom-value of the Absolute as the word *auṁ*, are seen as a series with each enjoying an equal status vertically. The crudest form of this outward necessary aspect of spirituality is seen in the context of warfare, from which background the Gītā discussion emerged and to which it returns in Chapter XVIII. From an ontological discussion of values we pass on, in the next chapter, to a teleological discussion centring around action as a keyword. Necessary action alone brings us finally to the scene of warfare, fitting philosophy correctly into the context of inevitability in life.

XVIII

Saṁnyāsa-Yoga

The Unitive Way in Behaviour Patterns

INTRODUCTION

As we have said, the structural symmetry of the eighteen chapters of the Gītā can be compared to an arch. In that kind of an arrangement, the first and last chapters rest on the horizontal actualities of life, while the ninth and tenth chapters have reference to pure and vertical values. As we proceed from Chapter I to Chapter IX, we can see a gradual and steady verticalization of the discussion in which the arguments can be said to be of a dialectically ascending order. From Chapter XI on, a dialectical descent becomes evident; there is gradual horizontalization and increasing stress on the action side of life.

The Gītā story of Arjuna begins in the first chapter with Arjuna throwing away his bow and arrows, and sitting in the chariot unable to make up his mind whether to fight or not. The idea which is uppermost in his mind in that chapter and the beginning of the second is to renounce the horrible action that is obligatory for a warrior, in favour of living the pious life of a mendicant (*saṁnyāsī*). The Gītā's eighteenth chapter concludes with a final consideration of the relevancy of *saṁnyāsa* in the life of a man of action, and by bringing Arjuna's attitude toward his duty to the logical conclusion of its inevitability. We once again see Arjuna standing firm in his chariot with his bow held high and his mind determined to uphold truth and justice.

In this concluding chapter there is an overall recapitulation of the teaching given in the previous seventeen chapters. Vyāsa uses the first chapter as a cathartic device for Arjuna to state his case by himself. All the questions he raises here are given due attention by Kṛṣṇa throughout the rest of the discourse. In the introduction to the first chapter we have already mentioned the importance of carefully examining the nature of Arjuna's conflict.

In the second chapter, *yoga* was first presented as two distinct schools of Sāṁkhya and Yoga. To those who are familiar with the *darśana*s (systems) of the Sāṁkhya of Kapila and the Yoga of Patañjali, their treatment in this chapter would not seem to be in conformity with the orthodox conceptions of them. In the Gītā Dhyānam, which is given at the beginning of this text, the Gītā is described as the cream of the teachings of the Upaniṣads. One of the oldest Upaniṣads is the *Īśāvāsya Upaniṣad*, which has a venerable place in both Veda and Vedānta. The opening *mantra*s allude to two models of perfection. The first is that of the wise man living in absolute freedom, who sees nothing but his non-differentiation with the Absolute. The second model, which is given as an alternative to the first, is that of the man of action who stands firm in his station of life as one fully committed to the maintenance of the world order to which he belongs, as an integral functionary of its smooth flow. These two models figure in the Gītā as Sāṁkhya and Yoga respectively, and are otherwise called *jñāna-yoga* (unitive understanding of wisdom) and *karma-yoga* (being established in unitive action). Unitive understanding of wisdom is the same as knowing the truth of the Self, by which one attains to immortality. This is the promise which Kṛṣṇa gives in verse fifteen of Chapter II.

The role of the Bhagavadgītā as a book of revaluation is evident in the second chapter itself when Kṛṣṇa says that only uninformed people will think of the path of wisdom and the path of action as separate. Throughout the Gītā Kṛṣṇa is revaluing and restating the place of action in life. Unitive action is mentioned in verse 51 of Chapter II as action performed without any clinging to the gratification of its rewarding consequence; this is considered to be efficacious in purifying the mind of its dross of anxiety and anticipation. It is the duality of ends and means that makes a person conscious of the past, present, and future as distinct and separate entities. When life flows as smoothly as a river which has no cleavage, one transcends time. That way, action performed with the right poise of mind and steadfastness in wisdom is not different from the life of the renunciate, so far as its worth in terms of immortality is concerned.

The disciplines of unitive understanding and unitive action are once again covered in Chapter III. The complex character of *karma* is further elucidated. Distinctions between proper action, wrong action, and inaction, as well as the method by which all necessary actions can be treated as a form of sacrifice, are also expounded upon.

In the fourth chapter the primacy of wisdom is again stressed. The actions of a wise man are explained to Arjuna. The role of a Guru, and the hierarchical relationship between Guru and disciple are given as the means for the continuation of wisdom through the ages. Divine intervention in order to restore wisdom whenever it fails is also revealed in this chapter. On hearing the superiority of wisdom, Arjuna is again tempted to leave the field of horrid action to follow the path of the contemplative.

In Chapter V Kṛṣṇa explains the imperativeness of action, proving to Arjuna that he cannot deliberately cut himself off from the path of action after having resorted to the role of a warrior as one committed to the duty of upholding social righteousness. However, in the same chapter Kṛṣṇa advises him on how to tread the path of realization despite being caught in a web of necessary action.

Saṁnyāsa is revalued in the sixth chapter. Although a man of realization, whose Self is fully established in the Absolute, has no action to perform, people like Arjuna who continue to be in the throes of the transactional world should cultivate relinquishment of the awards of action rather than a total renunciation of action. Arjuna receives instruction for disciplining the mind, and also comes to understand how the course of action continues unbroken through several lives as a vertical counterpart of *dharma.*

In the seventh chapter Arjuna is told how rare it is for a person to turn to the path of wisdom. This world, constituted of the five elements and experienced by the mind, intellect, and ego, is revealed to be the manifestation of a fragment of the Absolute. Kṛṣṇa calls this aspect his lower form.

In the eighth chapter Kṛṣṇa explains the nature of the Absolute, the Self, action, sacrifice, and the world of matter and spirit.

Values pertaining to the Self as the Absolute are revealed to Arjuna in Chapter IX. The final teaching of the Gītā is also presented here as *ananya bhakti*, devotion to the Absolute to the exclusion of everything else.

In the tenth chapter the origin of the world and all beings, as well as the unfolding potentials in individuated beings, are seen as primarily emerging from the Absolute. After a short discourse on the characteristics of unitive understanding and the efficacy of devotion, Kṛṣṇa instructs Arjuna how he, as the Absolute, can be seen as the essential value (*vibhūti*) at different levels of manifestation.

In the eleventh chapter Arjuna receives the cosmic vision of the Absolute as all-devouring Time.

In the twelfth chapter *bhakti-yoga* (union with the Absolute through devotion) is briefly described.

A distinction between the field and its knower is made in Chapter XIII. Apart from the constituent factors of the field, the essentials of knowledge and what is to be known are also explained.

The fourteenth chapter is a diagnostic study of *sattva*, *rajas* and *tamas*.

The fifteenth chapter is a philosophical counterpart to Chapter XI. Instead of a cosmic vision, unitive understanding of the cosmic Person is presented, in which the manifesting Person, the unmanifesting Person, and manifested Nature are all shown to be integral aspects of the Paramount Person.

In the sixteenth chapter the bright and dark ambivalent forces that seem to operate in all and which can even tend to become pathological are given, as in a descriptive psychology.

The operational dynamics of *sattva*, *rajas*, and *tamas*, mentioned in the fourteenth chapter, are once again considered for a more thoroughgoing symptomatic study in Chapter XVII.

The questions raised by Arjuna in the first and subsequent chapters, and the various topics discussed in the sixteen chapters from the second to the seventeenth, are taken up in the eighteenth chapter for review and revision. This chapter is very important as it resolves for all time the true *svadharma* of Arjuna. The revaluation of *saṁnyāsa* as *tyāga*, the relinquishment of attachment to the rewards of action, is among the main contributions of the Gītā. According to Nataraja Guru, the stress given to necessary action distinguishes this chapter from the rest. We are incorporating here part of his introduction to Chapter XVIII, which cannot be put in any better terms:

> Action has to be unitively understood in the context of wisdom. In other words, wisdom values have to infuse, regulate and modify necessary action in such a way that the sublimation of the spirit of the actor may take place. They may thus help to lead him in his spiritual progress from the lowest of levels in which he is caught in confusion and necessity, up to the clear heights of a wisdom which is both pure and practical. The height of wisdom itself need not necessarily be considered to fall outside the scope of thought as an activity which the actor is capable of, in other words, thought itself could be included in the highest values belonging to the context of action and inseparable from the actor.
>
> We have noticed how, in the immediately preceding chapters, more and more positive, objective and overt aspects of life were successively treated as the counterparts of the contemplative implied in the Gītā. Faith, as an outward value to which individuals may be attached, was discussed in Chapter XVII. In the present chapter we take one step more in the same direction of objectivity and the overtness of the value implied, which is here action as a counterpart of the actor. Action does not refer to items of activity but to action that conforms to certain patterns of behaviour.
>
> What gives unity to the present chapter, therefore, is this notion of action

conceived globally as consisting of types or patterns of behaviour on the part of the actor, who in turn is the contemplative aspirant of the Gītā. Action thus conceived includes such items as thought, opinion, and philosophy itself. A man's ideas about life can regulate his behaviour, while the pattern of behaviour he consciously adopts can have repercussions on his thought. In this way action (*karma*) in its modified or extended sense becomes a counterpart of the actor. The same truth can be stated in terms of knowledge, by considering the knower instead of the actor. Between what is knowable and the knower, an interplay of relationship is possible, resulting in the supreme absolutist value called knowledge or wisdom. The delicate methodological and epistemological considerations entering into the discussion here have to be carefully noticed.

In verse 20 of this chapter there is reference to sāttvic (pure) knowledge. Again in verse 30 there is reference to sāttvic reason as a form of thought-functioning. What such a thought accomplishes is to distinguish between ambivalent values, such as bondage and liberation. From these instances it would be clear that action as intended in this chapter has a very extended, generalized, and global sense. Knowledge results from the interaction of the knower and the knowable, as implied in the first line of verse 18. However, in the second line of the same verse it is implied that action and actor are counterparts where the faculties of the mind are involved. These two sets of triple factors are seen rearranged in a slightly different way in the very next verse, 19. Action and actor are the counterparts now, and knowledge takes the place of the emergent value implied between them. Arjuna being a contemplative aspirant for wisdom in the field of battle, we can think also of fighter, battle, and absolute victory as the triple factors involved in the chapter, after the same pattern as the two triple sets mentioned in verses 18 and 19.

A careful reading of verses 18 and 19 reveals what at first sight seems an unwarranted interposing of actual factors for those belonging to the perceptual. The triple set of verse 19 which consists of knowledge, action, and actor is derived from the two distinct sets of the previous verse, the former of which belongs to the perceptual (*kṣetrajña*) order, while the latter belongs to the actual (*kṣetra*). When we notice that both actual and perceptual were brought progressively closer and more unitively together even in the previous chapter (XVII) it is easy to concede that in this next and final chapter the author has the express intention of synthesizing as completely as possible, so that the requirements of theoretical knowledge and the actualities of the battlefield may come under one inclusive view with a revalued notion of the Absolute.

The internal structure of this chapter has other incompatibilities which, however, on closer examination also become justifiable. We find that the chapter starts with a very definite doubt in regard to the difference between

> *saṁnyāsa* (renunciation) and *tyāga* (relinquishment of benefit-motivation in active life). Renunciation is a pattern of behaviour belonging to the contemplative context of spirituality based on a rationalistic and anti-ritualistic outlook. *Tyāga* (relinquishment) is the revised version of the same as recommended in the Gītā (V.4) by which only benefit-motivation in action is to be avoided, actions as such being held permissible and even necessary in normal life. That some sort of action is inevitable to a living being is clearly laid down in verse 11.
>
> Besides *saṁnyāsa* as a global or unitive form of action belonging to a contemplative pattern of behaviour, there are various other patterns of behaviour equally important for the contemplative to understand in the revised light of the epistemology and methodology of the Gītā. This epistemology is discussed in detail between verses 13 and 19. After this has been done the chapter passes in review various forms of contemplative behaviour under sacrifice, gift, austerity, and under knowledge, action, and actor. Bravery and happiness are derivative virtues or values of the action context which are also discussed before the types of actor, such as the brāhmin, kṣatriya, vaiśya and śūdra are discussed in the Gītā (and by no means the same as these signify in the code of Manu, for example).
>
> We have pointed out earlier that the latter half of the Gītā has the purpose of referring to the personality of Arjuna in the actual battlefield, not as a mere philosophical abstraction, but with all his actual peculiarities, as when one would distinguish a Peter from a Paul. This task has been progressively accomplished from the beginning of Chapter XIV. The necessary basis of absolutist life was discussed there in relation to nature and its three modalities. Positive and negative values were made clear by the end of Chapter XVI, after effecting a synthesis in the Paramount Person of Chapter XV. In Chapter XVII types of faith as a counterpart of the faithful aspirant to wisdom were synthetically reviewed and subjected to revaluation. With the discussion of bravery and happiness as forming the value counterparts of an active contemplative, the Gītā now comes finally to close grips with the actualities of the situation. Arjuna is threatened with spiritual destruction in verse 58. He has to do or die. Such is the imperative nature implicit in the situation. The philosophy of obligation and necessity is preached to Arjuna only till the end of verse 62, where he is allowed to act as he likes. The style becomes contemplative again after this verse and retains the tone in which the Gītā has been conceived as a whole. In verse 66 Arjuna is asked to abandon altogether all obligatory duties, in unequivocal language. Without suffering a whit in the apodictic realism of outlook, the Gītā comes to the culminating final verse in which values such as justice and fair-play are referred to, in verse 78, as belonging to the contemplative context.

As *karma* (action) has a character of inevitability, nobody, according to this chapter, can be called a true *saṁnyāsin* (total renouncer). The possibility of an exception to this rule by which all beings are committed to some act or other is, on the whole, discountenanced, although such a possibility has been given sufficient recognition in other chapters. For example, III.17, IV.20 and V.8 mention the possibility of keeping aloof from action. Only in verse 49 of the present chapter is there a passing reference to a *saṁnyāsin* (renouncer) and that merely as a possible ideal to be reached.

As far as this chapter is concerned, therefore, it would not be wrong to generalize by saying that it tends to discredit *saṁnyāsa* (renunciation) in favour of *tyāga* (relinquishment).

TRANSLATION

अर्जुन उवाच –

1. संन्यासस्य महाबाहो तत्त्वमिच्छामि वेदितुम् ।
त्यागस्य च हृषीकेश पृथक्केशिनिषूदन ।।

arjuna uvāca –

saṁnyāsasya mahābāho tattvam icchāmi veditum ।
tyāgasya ca hṛsīkeśa pṛthak keśinisūdana ॥

arjuna uvāca: Arjuna said; *icchāmi veditum*: (I) desire to know; *mahābāho*: Oh Kṛṣṇa; *tattvam*: the truth; *saṁnyāsasya*: of renunciation; *ca tyāgasya*: (as) also of relinquishment; *hṛṣikeśa*: Oh Kṛṣṇa; *pṛthak*: each distinctly; *keśinisūdana*: Oh Kṛṣṇa

Arjuna said:

I desire to know, Oh Mighty-Armed! the truth of renunciation as also of relinquishment, Oh Hṛṣīkeśa! each distinctly, Oh Keśinisūdana!

श्रीभगवानुवाच –

2. काम्यानां कर्मणां न्यासं संन्यासं कवयो विदुः ।
सर्वकर्मफलत्यागं प्राहुस्त्यागं विचक्षणाः ।।

śrībhagavān uvāca –

kāmyānāṁ karmaṇāṁ nyāsaṁ saṁnyāsaṁ kavayo viduḥ ।
sarvakarmaphalatyāgaṁ prāhus tyāgaṁ vicakṣaṇāḥ ॥

śrībhagavān uvāca: Kṛṣṇa said; *kavayaḥ viduḥ*: bards (of old) understood; *saṁnyāsaṁ*: (by) renunciation; *nyāsaṁ*: the renunciation; *kāmyānāṁ karmaṇāṁ*: of desire-prompted action; *tyāgaṁ*: the relinquishing (of); *phala*: the benefit; *sarva karma*: (of) all actions; *vicakṣaṇāḥ*: those with insight; *prāhuḥ*: declare; *tyāgaṁ*: (to be) relinquishment.

Kṛṣṇa said:

Bards of old understood by *saṁnyāsa* (renunciation) of desire-prompted action; the relinquishing of the benefit of all actions, those with insight declare to be *tyāga*.

3. त्याज्यं दोषवदित्येके कर्म प्राहुर्मनीषिणः ।
यज्ञदानतपःकर्म न त्याज्यमिति चापरे ॥

tyājyaṁ doṣavad ity eke karma prāhur manīṣiṇaḥ ।
yajñadānatapaḥkarma na tyājyam iti cā 'pare ॥

karma: action; *tyājyaṁ*: should be given up; *doṣavat*: (as) an evil; *iti prāhuḥ*: thus declare; *eke manīṣiṇaḥ*: some rationalists; *ca apare iti*: and others say thus; *yajña dāna tapaḥ karma*: acts of sacrifice, giving, and austerity; *na tyājyam*: should not be abandoned.

"Action should be given up as an evil", declare some rationalists: others say that "acts of sacrifice, giving, and austerity should not be abandoned".

4. निश्चयं शृणु मे तत्र त्यागे भरतसत्तम ।
त्यागो हि पुरुषव्याघ्र त्रिविधः सम्प्रकीर्तितः ॥

niścayaṁ śṛṇu me tatra tyāge bharatasattama ।
tyāgo hi puruṣavyāghra trividhaḥ saṁprakīrtitaḥ ॥

śṛṇu tatra: hear now; *bharatasattama*: Oh Arjuna; *me niścayaṁ*: My settled conclusion; *tyāge*: about relinquishment; *tyāgaḥ hi*: relinquishment indeed; *puruṣavyāghra*: Oh Arjuna; *saṁprakīrtitaḥ*: has been well known; *trividhaḥ*: (as) of three kinds.

5. यज्ञदानतपःकर्म न त्याज्यं कार्यमेव तत् ।
यज्ञो दानं तपश्चैव पावनानि मनीषिणाम् ॥

yajñadānatapaḥkarma na tyājyaṁ kāryam eva tat ।
yajño dānaṁ tapaś cai 'va pāvanāni manīṣiṇām ॥

yajña dāna tapaḥ karma: acts of sacrifice, gift and austerity; *na tyājyaṁ*: should not be relinquished; *tat kāryam eva*: that should indeed be observed; *yajñaḥ*: sacrifice; *dānaṁ*: gift; *ca tapaḥ*: and austerity; *eva pāvanāni*: (are) indeed the purifiers; *manīṣiṇām*: of rational men.

6. एतान्यपि तु कर्मणि सङ्गं त्यक्त्वा फलानि च ।
कर्तव्यानीति मे पार्थ निश्चितं मतमुत्तमम् ॥

etāny api tu karmāṇi saṅgaṁ tyaktvā phalāni ca ।
kartavyānī 'ti me pārtha niścitaṁ matam uttamam ॥

tu api: but even; *etāni karmāṇi*: these actions; *kartavyāni*: should be done; *tyaktvā saṅgaṁ*: leaving out attachment; *ca phalāni*: and (desire for) result; *pārtha*: Oh Arjuna; *iti me*: thus (is) My; *niścitaṁ uttamam*: decided (and) best; *matam*: conviction.

Hear now from Me, Oh Best of the Bhāratas! the settled conclusion about relinquishment; relinquishment indeed, Oh Best of Men! has been well known as of three kinds:

The acts of sacrifice, gift, and austerity should not be relinquished, each should indeed be observed; sacrifice, gift, and austerity are the purifiers of rational men;

but even these actions should be done leaving out, attachment and desire for result; this, Oh Pārtha! is My decided and best conviction.

7. नियतस्य तु संन्यासः कर्मणो नोपपद्यते ।
मोहात्तस्य परित्यागस्तामसः परिकीर्तितः ।।

niyatasya tu saṁnyāsaḥ karmaṇo no 'papadyate ।
mohāt tasya parityāgas tāmasaḥ parikīrtitaḥ ॥

tu saṁnyāsaḥ: verily the renunciation; *niyatasya karmaṇaḥ*: of necessary, inevitable action; *na upapadyate*: does not arise; *parityāgaḥ tasya*: the renunciation of such; *mohāt*: through delusion; *parikīrtitaḥ*: is said to be; *tāmasaḥ*: inert-dark.

Verily, the renunciation of necessary inevitable action does not arise; the renunciation of such through delusion is said to be inert-dark.

8. दुःखमित्येव यत्कर्म कायक्लेशभयात्त्यजेत् ।
स कृत्वा राजसं त्यागं नैव त्यागफलं लभेत् ।।

duḥkham ity eva yat karma kāyakleśabhayāt tyajet ।
sa kṛtvā rājasam tyāgaṁ nai 'va tyāgaphalaṁ labhet ॥

saḥ: he (who); *kāya kleśa bhayāt*: from fear of bodily trouble; *tyajet karma*: relinquishes action; *yat eva duḥkham*: which (is) merely painful; *iti rājasaṁ kṛtvā*: thus wilfully (with *rajas*) doing; *tyāgaṁ*: relinquishment; *eva na labhet*: (he) indeed should not get; *tyāga phalaṁ*: the (legitimate) benefit of relinquishment.

He who, from fear of bodily trouble, relinquishes action, considering it painful, thus wilfully relinquishing, does not get the (legitimate) benefit of relinquishment.

9. कार्यमित्येव यत्कर्म नियतं क्रियतेऽर्जुन ।
सङ्गं त्यक्त्वा फलं चैव स त्यागः सात्त्विको मतः ।।

kāryaṁ ity eva yat karma niyataṁ kriyate 'rjuna ।
saṅgaṁ tyaktvā phalam cai 'va sa tyāgaḥ sāttviko mataḥ ॥

karma niyataṁ: necessary action; *yat kriyate*: which is done; *arjuna*: Oh Arjuna; *iti eva kāryam*: thus indeed (recognizing its) imperative character; *tyaktvā saṅgaṁ*: relinquishing attachment; *ca eva phalaṁ*: and indeed benefit; *saḥ tyāgaḥ*: that relinquishment; *mataḥ*: is considered; *sāttvikaḥ*: pure.

When necessary action is done, Oh Arjuna, recognizing its imperative character, relinquishing attachment and benefit, such relinquishment is considered pure.

10. न द्वेष्ट्यकुशलं कर्म कुशले नानुषज्जते ।
त्यागी सत्त्वसमाविष्टो मेधावी छिन्नसंशयः ।।

na dveṣṭy akuśalaṁ karma kuśale nā 'nuṣajjate ।
tyāgī sattvasamāviṣṭo medhāvī chinnasaṁśayaḥ ॥

tyāgī: the relinquisher; *samāviṣṭaḥ sattva*: pervaded with purity; *medhāvī*: (of) strong intelligence; *chinna saṁśayaḥ*: (and of) sundered doubts; *dveṣṭi na*: hates not; *akuśalaṁ karma*: unpleasant action; *na anuṣajjate*: nor is (he) attached; *kuśale*: to pleasant (ones).

The relinquisher pervaded with purity, of strong intelligence, and of sundered doubts, hates not unpleasant action, nor is he attached to pleasant ones.

11. न हि देहभृता शक्यं त्यक्तुं कर्माण्यशेषतः ।
यस्तु कर्मफलत्यागी स त्यागीत्यभिधीयते ।।

na hi dehabhṛtā śakyaṁ tyaktuṁ karmāṇy aśeṣataḥ ।
yas tu karmaphalatyāgī sa tyāgī 'ty abhidhīyate ॥

na hi: nor indeed; *śakyaṁ*: (is it) possible; *dehabhṛtā*: for an embodied one; *aśeṣataḥ tyaktuṁ*: to completely relinquish; *karmāṇi*: actions; *saḥ yaḥ*: he who; *karma phala tyāgī*: (is) a relinquisher of the benefit of action; *tu abhidhīyate iti*: verily is called thus; *tyāgī*: a relinquisher.

Nor indeed is it possible for an embodied one to completely relinquish action; he who relinquishes the benefit of action is verily called a relinquisher.

12. अनिष्टमिष्टं मिश्रं च त्रिविधं कर्मणः फलम् ।
भवत्यत्यागिनां प्रेत्य न तु संन्यासिनां क्वचित् ।।

aniṣṭam iṣṭaṁ miśraṁ ca trividhaṁ karmaṇaḥ phalam ।
bhavaty atyāgināṁ pretya na tu saṁnyāsināṁ kvacit ॥

iṣṭaṁ aniṣṭam: pleasant, unpleasant; *ca miśraṁ phalam*: and mixed benefits; *karmaṇaḥ*: of action; *trividhaṁ bhavati*: (these) three accrue; *pretya*: (in the spiritual progress) beyond; *atyāgināṁ*: of a non-relinquisher; *tu na kvacit*: but none whatever; *saṁnyāsināṁ*: of renouncers.

Pleasant, unpleasant, and mixed benefits accrue in the spiritual progress beyond of a non-relinquisher, but none anywhere to renouncers.

13. पञ्चैतानि महाबाहो कारणानि निबोध मे ।
सांख्ये कृतान्ते प्रोक्तानि सिद्धये सर्वकर्मणाम् ।।

pañcai 'tāni mahābāho kāraṇāni nibodha me ।
sāṁkhye kṛtānte proktāni siddhaye sarvakarmaṇām ॥

mahābāho: Oh Arjuna; *nibodha me*: learn from Me; *etāni pañca kāraṇāni*: these five causes; *siddhaye*: for the accomplishment; *sarva karmaṇām*: of all actions; *proktāni*: (as) stated; *sāṁkhye*: in the Sāṁkhya; *kṛtānte*: at the end of (the age called) Kṛta.

14. अधिष्ठानं तथा कर्ता करणं च पृथग्विधम् ।
विविधाश्च पृथक्चेष्टा दैवं चैवात्र पञ्चमम् ।।

adhiṣṭhānaṁ tathā kartā karaṇaṁ ca pṛthagvidham ।
vividhāś ca pṛthakceṣṭā daivaṁ cai 'va 'tra pañcamam ॥

adhiṣṭhānaṁ: the basis; *tathā kartā*: and actor; *ca pṛthak vidham*: and (also) the various kinds (of); *karaṇaṁ*: (mental) instruments; *pṛthak ca vividhāḥ*: the several and varied; *ceṣṭāḥ*: movements (activities); *ca eva atra*: and indeed here; *pañcaman*: fifth; *daivaṁ*: the divine (factor).

15. शरीरवाङ्मनोभिर्यत्कर्म प्रारभते नरः ।
न्याय्यं वा विपरीतं वा पञ्चैते तस्य हेतवः ।।

śarīravāṅmanobhir yat karma prārabhate naraḥ ।
nyāyyaṁ vā viparītaṁ vā pañcai 'te tasya hetavaḥ ॥

yat karma: whatever action; *naraḥ prārabhate*: a man undertakes; *śarīra vāk manobhiḥ*: by the body, speech, and mind; *vā nyāyyaṁ*: either justifiable; *vā viparītaṁ*: or the opposite; *ete pañca*: these five; *tasya hetavaḥ*: (are) its causes.

Oh Mighty-Armed! learn from Me these five causes for the accomplishment of all actions, as stated in the Sāṁkhya at the end of the age called Kṛta:

The basis and actor, and also the various mental instruments, the several and varied movements, and fifth, the divine factor;

whatever action a man undertakes by the body, speech, and mind, justifiable or the opposite – these five are its causes.

16. तत्रैवं सति कर्तारमात्मानं केवलं तु यः ।
पश्यत्यकृतबुद्धित्वान्न स पश्यति दुर्मतिः ।।

tatrai 'vaṁ sati kartāraṁ ātmānaṁ kevalam tu yaḥ ।
paśyaty akṛtabuddhitvān na sa paśyati durmatiḥ ॥

tatra evaṁ sati: now, such being the case; *durmatiḥ yaḥ*: (the man) of perverted mind who; *akṛta buddhitvāt*: because of unfinished intelligence; *paśyati ātmānaṁ*: sees himself; *kevalaṁ kartāram*: (as) the isolated agent of action; *saḥ na paśyati tu*: he does not see indeed.

Now, such being the case, the man of perverted mind who, because of unfinished intelligence, looks upon himself as the isolated agent of action – he does not see indeed.

17. यस्य नाहङ्कृतो भावो बुद्धिर्यस्य न लिप्यते ।
हत्वापि स इमाँल्लोकान्न हन्ति न निबध्यते ।।

yasya nā 'haṁkṛto bhāvo buddhir yasya na lipyate ।
hatvā 'pi sa imāṁl lokān na hanti na nibadhyate ॥

yasya: of he who (is); *na bhāvaḥ*: free from the state (of); *ahaṁ kṛtaḥ*: ego-sense ("I am the doer"); *yasya buddhiḥ*: whose intelligence; *na lipyate*: is unaffected; *api saḥ hatvā*: though he kills; *imān lokān*: these people; *na hanti*: (he) neither kills; *na nibadhyate*: nor is bound.

He who is free from ego-sense, whose intelligence is unaffected, though he kills these people – he neither kills nor is bound.

18. ज्ञानं ज्ञेयं परिज्ञाता त्रिविधा कर्मचोदना ।
करणं कर्म कर्तेति त्रिविधः कर्मसङ्ग्रहः ।।

jñānaṁ jñeyaṁ parijñātā trividhā karmacodanā ।
karaṇaṁ karma karte 'ti trividhaḥ karmasaṁgrahaḥ ॥

jñānaṁ jñeyaṁ: knowledge, the knowable; *parijñātā*: (and) the knower; *trividhā*: (are) the threefold; *karmacodanā*: incentive to action; *karaṇaṁ*: the (mental) instrument; *karma kartā*: the action, (and) the actor; *iti trividhaḥ*: thus, the threefold; *karma saṁgrahaḥ*: aggregate-base of action.

Knowledge, the knowable, and the knower are the threefold incentive to action; the mental instrument, the action, and the actor are the threefold aggregate-base of action.

19. ज्ञानं कर्म च कर्ता च त्रिधैव गुणभेदतः ।
प्रोच्यते गुणसङ्ख्याने यथावच्छृणु तान्यपि ।।

jñānaṁ karma ca kartā ca tridhai 'va guṇabhedataḥ ।
procyate guṇasaṁkhyāne yathāvac chṛṇu tāny api ॥

eva jñānaṁ: even knowledge; *ca karma*: and action; *ca kartā*: and actor; *procyate*: are said; *guṇa bhedataḥ*: according to modality-difference; *guṇa saṁkhyāne*: in their enumeration according to the modalities; *tridhā*: (to be) of three kinds; *śṛṇu*: hear (you); *tāni api yathāvat*: of them even (as they are) actually.

Even knowledge, action, and actor are said, according to modality-difference, by way of their enumeration according to the modalities, to be of three kinds; hear you of them as they are actually.

20. सर्वभूतेषु येनैकं भावमव्ययमीक्षते ।
अविभक्तं विभक्तेषु तज्ज्ञानं विद्धि सात्त्विकम् ।।

sarvabhūteṣu yenai 'kaṁ bhāvam avyayam īkṣate ।
avibhaktaṁ vibhakteṣu taj jñānaṁ viddhi sāttvikam ॥

yena: (that) by which; *ekaṁ*: the one; *avyayam bhāvam*: unexpended Being; *īkṣate*: is seen; *sarva bhūteṣu*: in all beings; *avibhaktaṁ*: undivided; *vibhakteṣu*: in the divided; *viddhi*: know; *tat jñānaṁ*: that knowledge; *sāttvikam*: (to be) pure.

That by which the one unexpended Being is seen in all beings, undivided in the divided – know that knowledge to be pure.

21. पृथक्त्वेन तु यज्ज्ञानं नानाभावान्पृथग्विधान् ।
वेत्ति सर्वेषु भूतेषु तज्ज्ञानं विद्धि राजसम् ।।

pṛthaktvena tu yaj jñānaṁ nānābhāvān pṛthagvidhān ।
vetti sarveṣu bhūteṣu taj jñānaṁ viddhi rājasam ॥

tu jñānaṁ: but the knowledge; *yat vetti*: which knows; *nānā bhāvān*: multiple existences; *sarveṣu bhūteṣu*: of all beings; *pṛthagvidhān*: with the different kinds; *pṛthaktvena*: (because) of separateness as distinct; *viddhi tat jñānaṁ*: know that knowledge; *rājasam*: (to be) affectively-pragmatic.

The knowledge which sees a multiplicity of beings as distinct in the different kinds, because of separateness – know that knowledge to be effectively-pragmatic.

22. यत्तु कृत्स्नवदेकस्मिन्कार्ये सक्तमहैतुकम् ।
अतत्त्वार्थवदल्पं च तत्तामसमुदाहृतम् ।।

yat tu kṛtsnavad ekasmin kārye saktam ahaitukam ।
atattvārthavad alpaṁ ca tat tāmasam udāhṛtam ॥

tu yat saktam: but (that) which clings; *ekasmin kārye*: to one effect; *kṛtsnavat*: as if it were the whole; *ahaitukam*: without reason;

atattvārthavat: without meaning, based on any principle; *ca alpaṁ*: and insignificant; *tat udāhṛtam*: that is called; *tāmasam*: the inert-dark.

But that which clings to one single effect as if it were the whole, without reason, without meaning, based on any principle, and insignificant – that is called the inert-dark.

23. नियतं सङ्गरहितमरागद्वेषतः कृतम् ।
अफलप्रेप्सुना कर्म यत्तत्सात्त्विकमुच्यते ।।

niyataṁ saṅgarahitam arāgadveṣataḥ kṛtam ।
aphalaprepsunā karma yat tat sāttvikam ucyate ॥

karma: an action; *yat niyataṁ*: which (is) obligatory; *kṛtam saṅga rahitam*: performed without attachment; *arāga dveṣataḥ*: without affection or disregard; *aphala prepsunā*: by (one) not benefit-motivated; *tat ucyate*: that is called; *sāttvikam*: pure.

24. यत्तु कामेप्सुना कर्म साहङ्कारेण वा पुनः ।
क्रियते बहुलायासं तद्राजसमुदाहृतम् ।।

yat to kāmepsunā karma sāhaṁkāreṇa vā punaḥ ।
kriyate bahulāyāsaṁ tad rājasam udāhṛtam ॥

tu tat karma: but that action; *yat kriyate*: which (is) done; *bahula āyāsaṁ*: (with) great strain; *kāma īpsunā*: by one desire-prompted; *vā punaḥ*: or again; *sāhaṁkāreṇa*: together with egoism; *udāhṛtam*: is called; *rājasam*: affective-passionate.

25. अनुबन्धं क्षयं हिंसामनवेक्ष्य च पौरुषम् ।
मोहादारभ्यते कर्म यत्तत्तामसमुच्यते ।।

anubandhaṁ kṣayaṁ hiṁsām anapekṣya ca pauruṣam ।
mohād ārabhyate karma yat tat tāmasam ucyate ॥

karma yat: the action which (is); *ārabhyate*: undertaken; *mohāt*: from confusion (of values); *anapekṣya anubandhaṁ*: disregarding consequences; *kṣayaṁ hiṁsām*: loss (or) injury; *ca pauruṣam*: and human limitations; *tat ucyate tāmasam*: that is called dark.

An action which is obligatory, performed without attachment, without affection or disregard, by one not benefit-motivated – that is called pure.

But that action done with great strain, by one desire-prompted, or possessed of egoism, is called affective-passionate.

The action undertaken from confusion (of values), disregarding consequences, loss or injury, and human limitations – that is called dark.

26. मुक्त सङ्गोऽनहंवादी धृत्युत्साहसमन्वितः ।
सिद्ध्यसिद्ध्योर्निर्विकारः कर्ता सात्त्विक उच्यते ॥

muktasaṅgo 'nahaṁvādī dhṛtyutsāhasamanvitaḥ ।
siddhyasiddhyor nirvikāraḥ kartā sāttvika ucyate ॥

kartā: the actor; *muktasaṅgaḥ*: free from attachment; *anahaṁvādī*: who avoids references to himself in the first person ("not I speaking"); *dhṛti utsāha samanvitaḥ*: endowed with firmness and zeal; *nirvikāraḥ*: unmoved; *siddhi asiddhyoḥ*: in success or failure; *ucyate sāttvikaḥ*: is called pure.

27. रागी कर्मफलप्रेप्सुर्लुब्धो हिंसात्मकोऽशुचिः ।
हर्षशोकान्वितः कर्ता राजसः परिकीर्तितः ॥

rāgī karmaphalaprepsur lubdho hiṁsātmako 'śuciḥ ।
harṣaśokānvitaḥ kartā rājasaḥ parikīrtitaḥ ॥

kartā rāgī: the actor, passionate; *karma phala prepsuḥ*: desiring benefits of action; *lubdhaḥ hiṁsātmakaḥ*: greedy, violent-natured; *aśuciḥ*: maladjusted; *harṣa śoka anvitaḥ*: with (moods of) exaltation and depression; *parikīrtitaḥ rājasaḥ*: is called affective-passionate.

28. अयुक्तः प्राकृतः स्तब्धः शठो नैकृतिकोऽलसः ।
विषादी दीर्घसूत्री च कर्ता तामस उच्यते ॥

ayuktaḥ prākṛtaḥ stabdhaḥ śaṭho naikṛtiko 'lasaḥ ।
viṣādi dīrghasūtrī ca kartā tāmasa ucyate ॥

kartā: the actor; *ayuktaḥ*: (who is a) misfit; *prakṛtaḥ stabdhaḥ*: crude, stubborn; *śaṭhaḥ naikṛtikaḥ*: deceitful, malicious; *alasaḥ viṣādī*: lazy, despondent; *ca dīrghasūtrī*: and procrastinating; *ucyate tamasaḥ*: is called dark.

The actor, free from attachment, who avoids references to himself in the first person, endowed with firmness and zeal, unmoved by success or failure, is called pure.

The actor, passionate, prompted by desire for benefits, greedy, violent-natured, maladjusted, with moods of exaltation and depression, is called affective-passionate.

The actor who is a misfit, crude, stubborn, deceitful, malicious, lazy, despondent, and procrastinating, is called dark.

29. बुद्धेर्भेदं धृतेश्चैव गुणतस्त्रिविधं शृणु ।
प्रोच्यमानमशेषेण पृथक्त्वेन धनञ्जय ॥

buddher bhedaṁ dhṛteś cai 'va guṇatas trividhaṁ śṛṇu ।
procyamānam aśeṣeṇa pṛthaktvena dhanañjaya ॥

śṛṇu: hear (now); *trividhaṁ bhedaṁ*: the threefold difference; *buddheḥ*: of reason; *ca dhṛteḥ eva*: and of firmness also; *guṇataḥ*: according to the modalities of nature; *dhanañjaya*: Oh Arjuna; *procyamānam*: (to be) set forth; *aśeṣeṇa pṛthaktvena*: fully (and) severally.

Hear now the threefold difference of reason and firmness also, according to the modalities of nature, Oh Winner of Wealth! to be set forth fully and severally.

30. प्रवृत्तिं च निवृत्तिं च कार्याकार्ये भयाभये ।
बन्धं मोक्षं च या वेत्ति बुद्धिः सा पार्थ सात्त्विकी ॥

pravṛttiṁ ca nivṛttiṁ ca kāryākārye bhayābhaye ।
bandhaṁ mokṣaṁ ca yā vetti buddhiḥ sā pārtha sāttvikī ॥

sā buddhiḥ: that reason; *yā vetti*: which knows; *pravṛttiṁ ca*: the positive way of action and; *ca nivṛttiṁ*: also the negative way of inaction; *kārya akārye*: what ought to be done (and) what ought not to be done; *bhaya abhaye*: what is to be feared (and) what is not to be feared; *bandhaṁ*: the binding; *ca mokṣaṁ*: and the liberating (actions); *pārtha*: Oh Arjuna; *sāttvikī*: (is) pure.

That reason which knows the positive way of action and the negative way of inaction, what ought to be done and what ought not to be done, what is to be feared and what is not to be feared, the binding and the liberating actions, Oh Pārtha! is pure.

31. यया धर्ममधर्मं च कार्यं चाकार्यमेव च ।
अयथावत्प्रजानाति बुद्धिः सा पार्थ राजसी ॥

yayā dharmaṁ adharmaṁ ca kāryaṁ cā 'kāryam eva ca ।
ayathāvat prajānāti buddhiḥ sā pārtha rājasī ॥

buddhiḥ: (that) reason; *yayā*: by which (one) understands; *dharmam ca adharmaṁ*: right and wrong; *kāryaṁ ca*: the permissible and; *ca eva akāryam*: also indeed the banned; *ayathāvat*: in a sense incompatible with reality; *pārtha*: Oh Arjuna; *sā rājasī*: that (is) affective-passionate.

That reason which takes right and wrong, the permissible and the banned, in a sense incompatible with reality – that, Oh Pārtha! is affective-passionate.

32. अधर्मं धर्ममिति या मन्यते तमसावृता ।
सर्वार्थान्विपरीतांश्च बुद्धिः सा पार्थ तामसी ॥

adharmaṁ dharmam iti yā manyate tamasā 'vṛtā ।
sarvārthān viparītāṁś ca buddhiḥ sa pārtha tāmasī ॥

sā buddhiḥ: that reason; *āvṛtā tamasā*: enveloped by darkness; *yā manyate iti*: which regards in this way; *adharmaṁ dharmam*: wrong (as) right; *ca sarvārthān*: and (sees) all values; *viparītān*: pervertedly; *pārtha*: Oh Arjuna; *tāmasī*: (is) dark.

That reason enveloped in darkness, which regards wrong as right, and sees all values pervertedly, Oh Pārtha! is dark.

33. धृत्या यया धारयते मनःप्राणेन्द्रियक्रियाः ।
योगेनाव्यभिचारिण्या धृतिः सा पार्थ सात्त्विकी ।।

dhṛtyā yayā dhārayate manaḥprāṇendriyakriyāḥ ।
yogenā 'vyabhicāriṇyā dhṛtiḥ sā pārtha sāttvikī ॥

dhṛtyā yayā: the firmness by which; *manaḥ prāṇa indriya kriyāḥ*: the activities of mind, vital functions, and the senses; *pārtha*: Oh Arjuna; *dhārayate*: are kept; *avyabhicāriṇyā*: from deflecting (from the true path); *yogena*: by *yoga*; *sā dhṛtiḥ*: that firmness; *sāttvikī*: (is) pure.

34. यया तु धर्मकामार्थान्धृत्या धारयतेऽर्जुन ।
प्रसङ्गेन फलाकाङ्क्षी धृतिः सा पार्थ राजसी ।।

yayā tu dharmakāmārthān dhṛtyā dhārayate 'rjuna ।
prasaṅgena phalākāṅkṣī dhṛtiḥ sā pārtha rājasī ॥

tu dhṛtya yayā: but the firmness by which; *dhārayate*: (one) holds fast to; *dharma kāma arthān*: duty, pleasures, and wealth; *arjuna*: Oh Arjuna; *prasaṅgena phalākāṅkṣī*: with attachment, desirous of the result (of each, when the occasion presents itself); *sā dhṛtiḥ*: that firmness; *pārtha*: Oh Arjuna; *rājasī*: (is) affective-passionate.

35. यया स्वप्नं भयं शोकं विषादं मदमेव च ।
न विमुञ्चति दुर्मेधा धृतिः सा पार्थ तामसी ।।

yayā svapnaṁ bhayaṁ śokaṁ viṣādaṁ madam eva ca ।
na vimuñcati durmedhā dhṛtiḥ sā pārtha tāmasī ॥

yayā: (that) by which; *durmedhā*: a stupid man; *na vimuñcati*: does not give up; *svapnaṁ bhayaṁ*: sleep, fear; *śokaṁ viṣādaṁ*: grief, despondency; *ca eva madam*: and indeed wantonness; *sā dhṛtiḥ*: that firmness; *pārtha*: Oh Arjuna; *tāmasī*: (is) dark.

The firmness by which the activities of mind, vital functions, and the senses, Oh Pārtha! are kept from deflecting (from the true path) by *yoga*, is pure.

But the firmness by which one holds fast, Oh Arjuna! to duty, and pleasures, and wealth, desirous of the result of each, when the occasion presents itself – that firmness, Oh Pārtha, is affective-passionate.

That by which a stupid man does not give up sleep, fear, grief, despondency and wantonness – that firmness, Oh Pārtha, is dark.

36. सुखं त्विदानीं त्रिविधं शृणु मे भरतर्षभ ।
अभ्यासाद्रमते यत्र दुःखान्तं च निगच्छति ॥

sukhaṁ tv idānīṁ trividhaṁ śṛṇu me bharatarṣabha ।
abhyāsād ramate yatra duḥkhāntaṁ ca nigacchati ॥

tu idānīṁ: and now; *śṛṇu me*: hear from me; *bharatarṣabha*: Oh Arjuna; *trividhaṁ sukhaṁ*: the three kinds of happiness; *yatra*: in which; *abhyāsāt*: from practice; *ramate*: (one) rejoices; *ca nigacchati*: and (in which he) reaches; *duḥkha antam*: the end of pain.

37. यत्तदग्रे विषमिव परिणामेऽमृतोपमम् ।
तत्सुखं सात्त्विकं प्रोक्तमात्मबुद्धिप्रसादजम् ॥

yat tad agre viṣam iva pariṇāme 'mṛtopamam ।
tat sukhaṁ sāttvikaṁ proktam ātmabuddhiprasādajam ॥

tat sukhaṁ: that happiness; *yat iva viṣam*: which (is) like gall; *agre*: at first; *amṛta upamam*: ambrosial; *pariṇāme*: at the end; *ātma buddhi prasādajam*: born of lucid self-understanding; *tat proktam sāttvikaṁ*: that is called pure.

38. विषयेन्द्रियसंयोगाद्यत्तदग्रेऽमृतोपमम् ।
परिणामे विषमिव तत्सुखं राजसं स्मृतम् ॥

viṣayendriyasaṁyogād yat tad agre 'mṛtopamam ।
pariṇāme viṣam iva tat sukhaṁ rājasaṁ smṛtam ॥

tat sukhaṁ: that happiness; *viṣaya indriya saṁyogāt*: arising out of contact of senses with objects; *yat agre*: which at first (is); *amṛta upamam*: like ambrosia; *pariṇāme*: at the end; *iva viṣam*: like gall; *tat smṛtam*: that is remembered (as); *rājasam*: affective-passionate.

39. यदग्रे चानुबन्धे च सुखं मोहनमात्मनः ।
निद्रालस्यप्रमादोत्थं तत्तामसमुदाहृतम् ॥

yad agre cā 'nubandhe ca sukhaṁ mohanam ātmanaḥ ।
nidrālasyapramādotthaṁ tat tāmasam udāhṛtam ॥

tat sukhaṁ: that happiness; *yat agre ca*: which at first and; *ca anubandhe*: also in after-effects; *mohanam ātmanaḥ*: (is) self-confounding; *nidrā ālasya pramāda utthaṁ*: arising from sleep, lassitude, and listlessness; *udāhṛtam tāmasam*: is called dark.

And now hear from Me, Oh Best of the Bhāratas! the three kinds of happiness, in which one by practice rejoices, and in which he reaches the end of pain;

that happiness which is like gall at first, ambrosial at the end, born of lucid self-understanding, is called pure;

that happiness arising out of contact of the senses with objects, at first like ambrosia, at the end like gall, is called affective-passionate;

that happiness which at first and in after-effects is self-confounding, arising from sleep, lassitude, and listlessness, is called dark.

40. न तदस्ति पृथिव्यां वा दिवि देवेषु वा पुनः ।
सत्त्वं प्रकृतिजैर्मुक्तं यदेभिः स्यात्त्रिभिर्गुणैः ॥

na tad asti pṛthivyāṁ vā divi deveṣu vā punaḥ ।
sattvaṁ prakṛtijair muktaṁ yad ebhiḥ syāt tribhir guṇaiḥ ॥

asti na: (there) is not; *tat sattvaṁ*: that entity; *vā pṛthivyāṁ*: either on earth; *vā punaḥ divi*: or again in heaven; *deveṣu*: among the (Vedic) divinities; *yat syāt muktaṁ*: which could be free; *ebhiḥ tribhiḥ guṇaiḥ*: from these three modalities; *prakṛtijaiḥ*: born from nature.

There is no entity either on earth or in heaven, among the Vedic divinities, that could be free from these three modalities born from nature.

41. ब्राह्मणक्षत्रियविशां शूद्राणां च परन्तप ।
कर्माणि प्रविभक्तानि स्वभावप्रभवैर्गुणैः ॥

brāhmaṇakṣatriyaviśāṁ śūdrāṇāṁ ca parantapa ।
karmāṇi pravibhaktāni svabhāvaprabhavair guṇaiḥ ॥

brāhmaṇa: brāhmins (quiet contemplatives); *kṣatriya*: kṣatriyas (active contemplatives); *viśāṁ*: vaiśyas (men of affairs); *ca śūdrāṇāṁ*: and of śūdras (proletarians); *parantapa*: Oh Arjuna; *karmāṇi*: actions; *pravibhaktāni*: (are) separately assigned; *guṇaiḥ*: in conformity with the modalities; *svabhāva prabhavaiḥ*: arising from their own nature.

Of brāhmins, kṣatriyas, vaiśyas and śūdras, Oh Conqueror of the Foe! vocations are separately assigned in conformity with the modalities arising from their own nature.

42. शमो दमस्तपः शौचं क्षान्तिरार्जवमेव च ।
ज्ञानं विज्ञानमास्तिक्यं ब्रह्मकर्म स्वभावजम् ॥

śamo damas tapaḥ śaucaṁ kṣāntir ārjavam eva ca ।
jñānaṁ vijñānam āstikyaṁ brahmakarma svabhāvajam ॥

śamaḥ damaḥ: calmness, self-restraint; *tapaḥ śaucaṁ*: austerity, purity; *kṣāntiḥ*: forgiveness; *ca eva ārjavam*: and indeed straightforwardness;

jñānaṁ vijñānam: (pure) wisdom, applied wisdom; *āstikyaṁ*: belief; *brahma karma*: (these are the items of) activity of the brāhmin; *svabhāvajam*: born of (his) own nature.

Calmness, self-restraint, austerity, purity, forgiveness, and straightforwardness, pure wisdom, applied wisdom, belief: these are the items of activity of the brāhmin, born of his own nature.

43. शौर्यं तेजो धृतिर्दाक्ष्यं युद्धे चाप्यपलायनम् ।
दानमीश्वरभावश्च क्षात्रं कर्म स्वभावजम् ।।

śauryaṁ tejo dhṛtir dākṣyaṁ yuddhe cā 'py apalāyanam ।
dānam īśvarabhāvaś ca kṣātraṁ karma svabhāvajam ॥

śauryaṁ tejaḥ: prowess, brightness; *dhṛtiḥ*: firmness; *dākṣyaṁ*: skill in fighting; *ca api apalāyanam yuddhe*: and also never-absconding in battle; *dānam*: generosity; *ca īśvarabhāvaḥ*: and dignity of mien; *kṣātraṁ karma*: (refer to the pattern of) activity of the kṣatriya; *svabhāvajam*: born of his own nature.

Prowess, brightness, firmness, skill, and also never-absconding, generosity, and dignity of mien, refer to the pattern of activity of the kṣatriya, born of his own nature.

44. कृषिगौरक्ष्यवाणिज्यं वैश्यकर्म स्वभावजम् ।
परिचर्यात्मकं कर्म शूद्रस्यापि स्वभावजम् ।।

kṛṣigaurakṣyavāṇijyaṁ vaiśyakarma svabhāvajam ।
paricaryātmakaṁ karma śūdrasyā 'pi svabhāvajam ॥

kṛṣi gaurakṣya vāṇijyaṁ: ploughing, tending cattle, and trade; *vaiśya karma*: (are the items of) vocation of the *vaiśya*; *svabhāvajam*: born of his own nature; *karma*: work; *paricaryā ātmakaṁ*: of the nature of (menial) service; *api*: (is) likewise; *śūdrasya svabhāvajaṁ*: born of the śūdra's own nature.

Ploughing, tending cattle, and trade are the items of vocation of the vaiśya, born of his own nature; work of the nature of menial service is likewise born of the śūdra's own nature.

45. स्वे स्वे कर्मण्यभिरत: संसिद्धिं लभते नर: ।
स्वकर्मनिरत: सिद्धिं यथा विन्दति तच्छृणु ।।

sve-sve karmaṇy abhirataḥ saṁsiddhiṁ labhate naraḥ ।
svakarmanirataḥ siddhiṁ yathā vindati tac chṛṇu ॥

sve sve abhirataḥ karmaṇi: each engaged in (his) own action; *naraḥ labhate*: man reaches; *saṁsiddhiṁ*: perfection (in practical *yoga*); *yathā*:

how; *sva karma nirataḥ*: devoted to his own occupation; *vindati siddhiṁ*: (he) attains (such) perfection; *tat śṛṇu*: that (do) hear.

Devoted each to his own occupation, man reaches perfection (in practical *yoga*); how, devoted to his own occupation, he attains such perfection – that do hear.

46. यतः प्रवृत्तिर्भूतानां येन सर्वमिदं ततम् ।
स्वकर्मणा तमभ्यर्च्य सिद्धिं विन्दति मानवः ॥

yataḥ pravṛttir bhūtānāṁ yena sarvam idaṁ tatam ।
svakarmaṇā tam abhyarcya siddhiṁ vindati mānavaḥ ॥

yataḥ: (he) from whom; *bhūtānāṁ pravṛttiḥ*: (all) existences come forth; *yena*: (and) by whom; *sarvam idaṁ*: all this; *tatam*: is pervaded; *abhyarcya tam*: (by) offering worship to Him; *sva karmaṇā*: with his own occupation; *mānavaḥ vindati siddhiṁ*: man wins perfection.

He from whom all existences come forth, and by whom all this is pervaded – by offering worship to Him with his own occupation, man wins perfection.

47. श्रेयान्स्वधर्मो विगुणः परधर्मात्स्वनुष्ठितात् ।
स्वभावनियतं कर्म कुर्वन्नाप्नोति किल्बिषम् ॥

śreyān svadharmo viguṇaḥ paradharmāt svanuṣṭhitāt ।
svabhāvaniyataṁ karma kurvan nā 'pnoti kilbiṣam ॥

śreyān: better (is); *svadharmaḥ*: one's own duty; *viguṇaḥ*: (though) inferior; *para dharmāt*: than the duty of another; *su anuṣṭhitāt*: well-performed; *kurvan karma*: doing the action; *niyataṁ svabhāva*: determined by his own nature; *āpnoti*: (one) incurs; *na kilbiṣam*: no sin.

Better is one's own duty, though inferior, than the duty of another well-performed. One doing the duty determined by his own nature incurs no sin.

48. सहजं कर्म कौन्तेय सदोषमपि न त्यजेत् ।
सर्वारम्भा हि दोषेण धूमेनाग्निरिवावृताः ॥

sahajaṁ karma kaunteya sadoṣam api na tyajet ।
sarvārambhā hi doṣeṇa dhūmenā 'gnir ivā 'vṛtāḥ ॥

karma: duty; *sahajaṁ*: (naturally) belonging (to one) by birth; *kaunteya*: Oh Arjuna; *api sadoṣam*: though accompanied by defects; *na tyajet*: ought not to be abandoned; *sarva ārambhāḥ hi*: all undertakings indeed; *āvṛtāḥ*: are enveloped; *doṣeṇa*: with defects; *iva agniḥ dhūmena*: as fire by smoke.

Duty naturally belonging to one by birth, Oh Son of Kuntī! though accompanied by defects, ought not to be abandoned; all undertakings are enveloped with defects, as fire by smoke.

49. असक्तबुद्धिः सर्वत्र जितात्मा विगतस्पृहः ।
नैष्कर्म्यसिद्धिं परमां संन्यासेनाधिगच्छति ॥

asaktabuddhiḥ sarvatra jitātmā vigataspṛhaḥ ।
naiṣkarmyasiddhiṁ paramāṁ saṁnyāsenā 'dhigacchati ॥

asakta buddhiḥ: (he) whose reason is unattached; *sarvatra*: in all situations; *jitātmā*: whose Self has been won over; *vigata spṛhaḥ*: whose desire has gone; *saṁnyāsena*: by renunciation; *adhigacchati*: (he) reaches; *paramāṁ siddhiṁ*: the supreme perfection; *naiṣkarmya*: (of) transcending action.

He whose reason is unattached in all situations, whose Self has been won over, from whom desire has gone, by renunciation reaches the supreme perfection of transcending action.

50. सिद्धिं प्राप्तो यथा ब्रह्म तथाप्नोति निबोध मे ।
समासेनैव कौन्तेय निष्ठा ज्ञानस्य या परा ॥

siddhiṁ prāpto yathā brahma tathā 'pnoti nibodha me ।
samāsenai 'va kaunteya niṣṭhā jñānasya yā parā ॥

yathā prāptaḥ: how (he who has) ascended; *siddhiṁ*: to perfection; *tathā āpnoti*: thereby obtains; *brahma*: the Absolute; *ya parā*: which (is) the supreme; *niṣṭhā jñānasya*: consummation of wisdom; *nibodha me eva*: learn from Me indeed; *kaunteya*: Oh Arjuna; *samāsena*: in brief.

How he who has ascended to perfection thereby obtains the Absolute, that supreme consummation of wisdom – that do you learn from Me, Oh Son of Kuntī! in brief.

51. बुद्ध्या विशुद्धया युक्तो धृत्यात्मानं नियम्य च ।
शब्दादीन्विषयांस्त्यक्त्वा रागद्वेषौ व्युदस्य च ॥

buddhyā viśuddhayā yukto dhṛtyā 'tmānaṁ niyamya ca ।
śabdādīn viṣayāṁs tyaktvā rāgadveṣau vyudasya ca ॥

yuktaḥ viśuddhayā buddhyā: endowed with pure reason; *ca niyamya ātmānaṁ*: and restraining the Self; *dhṛtyā*: with firmness; *tyaktvā*: detaching (oneself from); *śabdā ādīn*: sound and other; *viṣayān*: sense-objects; *ca vyudasya*: and casting out; *rāga dveṣau*: liking and disliking.

52. विविक्तसेवी लघ्वाशी यतवाक्कायमानसः ।
ध्यानयोगपरो नित्यं वैराग्यं समुपाश्रितः ॥

viviktasevī laghvāśī yatavākkāyamānasaḥ ।
dhyānayogaparo nityaṁ vairāgyaṁ samupāśritaḥ ॥

sevī vivikta: dwelling in solitude; *laghvāśī*: frugal in diet; *yata vāk kāya mānasaḥ*: controlling speech, body, and mind; *nityaṁ*: ever; *dhyāna-yoga paraḥ*: for whom meditative contemplation is highest; *samupāśritaḥ vairāgyaṁ*: resorting to dispassion.

53. अहङ्कारं बलं दर्पं कामं क्रोधं परिग्रहम् ।
विमुच्य निर्ममः शान्तो ब्रह्मभूयाय कल्पते ॥

ahaṁkāraṁ balaṁ darpaṁ kāmaṁ krodhaṁ parigraham ।
vimucya nirmamaḥ śānto brahmabhūyāya kalpate ॥

vimucya: relinquishing; *ahaṁkāraṁ balaṁ*: egoism, power; *darpaṁ kāmaṁ*: arrogance, desire; *krodhaṁ parigraham*: anger, possessiveness; *nirmamaḥ*: free from ownership; *śāntaḥ*: (and) tranquil; *kalpate*: (he) is worthy; *brahma bhūyāya*: of becoming the Absolute.

Endowed with pure reason, restraining the Self with firmness, detaching oneself from sound and other sense-objects, and casting out liking and disliking,

dwelling in solitude, frugal in diet, controlling speech, body, and mind, ever in meditative contemplation, resorting to dispassion,

relinquishing egoism, power, arrogance, desire, anger, and possessiveness, free from ownership, and tranquil – he is worthy of becoming the Absolute.

54. ब्रह्मभूतः प्रसन्नात्मा न शोचति न काङ्क्षति ।
समः सर्वेषु भूतेषु मद्भक्तिं लभते पराम् ॥

brahmabhūtaḥ prasannātmā na śocati na kāṅkṣati ।
samaḥ sarveṣu bhūteṣu madbhaktiṁ labhate parāṁ ॥

brahma bhūtaḥ: becoming the Absolute; *prasanna ātmā*: blissfully serene in the Self; *na śocati*: (he) neither despairs; *na kāṅkṣati*: nor hankers; *samaḥ*: equal-minded; *sarveṣu bhūteṣu*: toward all beings; *labhate*: (he) attains; *madbhaktiṁ*: a devotion to Me; *parāṁ*: supreme (in character).

Becoming the Absolute, blissfully serene in the Self, he neither despairs nor hankers; equal-minded toward all beings, he attains a devotion to Me supreme in character.

55. भक्त्या मामभिजानाति यावान्यश्चास्मि तत्त्वतः ।
ततो मां तत्त्वतो ज्ञात्वा विशते तदनन्तरम् ॥

bhaktyā mām abhijānāti yāvān yaś cā 'smi tattvataḥ ।
tato māṁ tattvato jñātvā viśate tadanantaram ॥

bhaktyā: through devotion; *abhijānāti mām*: (he) comes to know Me; *yāvān*: how far (comprehensible); *asmi*: (I) am; *ca yaḥ*: and who; *tattvataḥ*: in accord with first principles; *tataḥ*: then; *jñātvā māṁ*: having known Me; *tattvataḥ*: philosophically; *tat anantaram*: (he) immediately; *viśate*: enters into (Me).

Through devotion he comes to know Me, how far comprehensible I am and who, in accord with first principles; then, having known Me philosophically, he immediately enters into Me.

56. सर्वकर्माण्यपि सदा कुर्वाणो मद्व्यपाश्रयः ।
मत्प्रसादादवाप्नोति शाश्वतं पदमव्ययम् ॥

sarvakarmāṇy api sadā kurvāṇo madvyapāśrayaḥ ।
matprasādād avāpnoti śāśvataṁ padam avyayam ॥

api sadā: although still continuing; *kurvāṇaḥ sarva karmāṇi*: to do all actions (in life); *mat vyapāśrayaḥ*: treating Me as his refuge; *mat prasādāt*: from My grace; *avāpnoti*: (he) obtains; *śāśvataṁ*: the everlasting; *avyayam padam*: undiminishing status.

Although still continuing to do all actions in life, treating Me as his refuge, by My grace he obtains the everlasting undiminishing status.

57. चेतसा सर्वकर्माणि मयि संन्यस्य मत्परः ।
बुद्धियोगमुपाश्रित्य मच्चित्तः सततं भव ॥

cetasā sarvakarmāṇi mayi saṁnyasya matparaḥ ।
buddhiyogam upāśritya maccittaḥ satataṁ bhava ॥

cetasā saṁnyasya: mentally renouncing; *sarva karmāṇi*: all actions; *mayi*: into Me; *matparaḥ*: (regarding) Me as the Supreme; *upāśritya*: resorting to; *buddhi yogam*: unitive understanding; *mat cittaḥ satataṁ bhava*: having Me wholly filling your (relational) consciousness.

Mentally renouncing all actions into Me, regarding Me as the Supreme, resorting to unitive understanding, having Me wholly filling your relational consciousness,

58. मच्चित्तः सर्वदुर्गाणि मत्प्रसादात्तरिष्यसि ।
अथ चेत्त्वमहंकारान्न श्रोष्यसि विनङ्क्ष्यसि ॥

maccittaḥ sarvadurgāṇi matprasādāt tariṣyasi ।
atha cet tvam ahaṁkārān na śroṣyasi vinaṅkṣyasi ॥

mat cittaḥ: (thus with) consciousness filled with Me; *tariṣyasi*: (you) will overcome; *sarva durgāṇi*: all obstacles; *matprasādāt*: by My grace;

atha cet: but if; *ahaṁkārāt*: from egoism; *tvam na śroṣyasi*: you will not listen; *vinaṅkṣyasi*: (you) shall come to ruin.

(thus with) consciousness filled with Me, you will overcome all obstacles by My grace, but if, from egoism, you will not listen, you shall come to ruin.

59. यदहङ्कारमाश्रित्य न योत्स्य इति मन्यसे ।
मिथ्यैष व्यवसायस्ते प्रकृतिस्त्वां नियोक्ष्यति ।।

yad ahaṁkāram āśritya na yotsya iti manyase ।
mithyai 'ṣa vyavasāyas te prakṛtis tvāṁ niyokṣyati ॥

yat: if; *āśritya ahaṁkāram*: resorting to egoism; *manyase iti*: (you) think thus; *na yotsya*: (I) will not fight; *mithyā eṣaḥ*: absurd (is) this; *te vyavasāyaḥ*: your resolution; *prakṛtiḥ niyokṣyati tvāṁ*: nature will compel you.

If, resorting to egoism, you think, "I will not fight", absurd is this, your resolution. Nature will compel you.

60. स्वभावजेन कौन्तेय निबद्धः स्वेन कर्मणा ।
कर्तुं नेच्छसि यन्मोहात्करिष्यस्यवशोऽपि तत् ।।

svabhāvajena kaunteya nibaddhaḥ svena karmaṇā ।
kartuṁ ne 'cchasi yan mohāt kariṣyāsy avaśo 'pi tat ॥

yat mohāt: (that) which through confusion; *na icchasi kartuṁ*: you do not like to do; *kaunteya*: Oh Arjuna; *kariṣyasi api tat*: (you) shall do even that; *avaśaḥ*: helplessly; *nibaddhaḥ*: bound; *svena svabhāvajena karmaṇā*: by your own nature-born action.

That which, through confusion, you do not like to do, Oh Son of Kuntī! – you shall do that very thing, helplessly, bound by your own nature-born action.

61. ईश्वरः सर्वभूतानां हृद्देशेऽर्जुन तिष्ठति ।
भ्रामयन्सर्वभूतानि यन्त्रारूढानि मायया ।।

īśvaraḥ sarvabhūtānāṁ hṛddeśe 'rjuna tiṣṭhati ।
bhrāmayan sarvabhūtāni yantrārūḍhāni mayayā ॥

īśvaraḥ tiṣṭhati: the Lord dwells; *hṛddeśe*: in the heart-region; *sarva bhūtānāṁ*: of all beings; *arjuna*: Oh Arjuna; *bhrāmayan sarva bhūtāni*: causing all beings to revolve; *māyayā*: through the principle of appearance (*māyā*); *yantra ārūḍhāni*: (as if) mounted on a machine.

The Lord dwells in the heart-region of all beings, Oh Arjuna, causing all beings to revolve through the principle of appearance, as if mounted on a machine.

62. तमेव शरणं गच्छ सर्वभावेन भारत ।
तत्प्रसादात्परां शान्तिं स्थानं प्राप्स्यसि शाश्वतम् ॥

tam eva śaraṇaṁ gaccha sarvabhāvena bhārata ।
tatprasādāt parāṁ śāntiṁ sthānaṁ prāpsyasi śāśvatam ॥

śaraṇaṁ gaccha: seek refuge; *tam eva*: in Him alone; *sarva bhāvena*: in all ways; *bhārata*: Oh Arjuna; *tat prasādāt*: from that grace; *prāpsyasi*: (you) shall obtain; *śāntiṁ sthānaṁ*: the peaceful abode; *parāṁ śāśvatam*: supreme, everlasting.

Seek refuge in Him alone in all ways, Oh Bhārata; by His grace you shall obtain the peaceful abode, supreme, everlasting.

63. इति ते ज्ञानमाख्यातं गुह्याद्गुह्यतरं मया ।
विमृश्यैतदशेषेण यथेच्छसि तथा कुरु ॥

iti te jñānam ākhyātaṁ guhyād guhyataraṁ mayā ।
vimṛśyai 'tad aśeṣena yathe 'cchasi tathā kuru ॥

iti jñānam: thus wisdom; *guhyataraṁ*: more secret; *guhyāt*: than (all that is) secret; *ākhyātaṁ te*: has been declared to you; *mayā*: by me; *vimṛśya etat*: (critically) scrutinizing (all) this; *aśeṣeṇa*: omitting nothing; *tathā kuru*: so do; *yathā icchasi*: as (you) like.

Thus has wisdom more secret than all that is secret been declared to you by Me; critically scrutinizing all, omitting nothing, do as you like.

64. सर्वगुह्यतमं भूयः शृणु मे परमं वचः ।
इष्टोऽसि मे दृढमिति ततो वक्ष्यामि ते हितम् ॥

sarvaguhyatamaṁ bhūyaḥ śṛṇu me paramaṁ vacaḥ ।
iṣṭo 'si me dṛḍham iti tato vakṣyāmi te hitam ॥

śṛṇu bhūyaḥ: listen again; *me paramaṁ vacaḥ*: to My supreme word; *sarva guhya tamaṁ*: the most secret of all; *iti asi dṛḍham*: because (you) are greatly; *iṣṭaḥ me*: beloved of Me; *tataḥ vakṣyāmi te*: therefore (I) will tell to you; *hitam*: what is for your good.

Listen again to My supreme word, the most secret of all; because you are greatly beloved of Me, I will tell you what is for your good.

65. मन्मना भव मद्भक्तो मद्याजी मां नमस्कुरु ।
मामेवैष्यसि सत्यं ते प्रतिजाने प्रियोऽसि मे ॥

manmanā bhava madbhakto madyājī māṁ namaskuru ।
māṁ evai 'ṣyasi satyaṁ te pratijāne priyo 'si me ॥

bhava manmanā: become one in mind with Me; *madbhaktaḥ*: (be) devoted to Me; *madyājī*: sacrifice to Me; *namaskuru māṁ*: bow down to Me; *eṣyasi mām*: (you) shall come to Me; *eva*: alone; *pratijāne te*: (I) promise you; *satyaṁ*: (in) truth; *asi priyaḥ me*: (you) are dear to Me.

Become one in mind with Me; be devoted to Me; sacrifice to Me; bow down to Me; you shall come to Me alone; I promise you, in truth, you are dear to Me.

66. सर्वधर्मान्परित्यज्य मामेकं शरणं व्रज ।
अहं त्वा सर्वपापेभ्यो मोक्षयिष्यामि मा शुचः ॥

sarvadharmān parityajya mām ekaṁ śaraṇaṁ vraja ।
ahaṁ tvā sarvapāpebhyo mokṣayiṣyāmi mā śucaḥ ॥

parityajya: abandoning; *sarva dharmān*: all duties; *vraja śaraṇaṁ*: take refuge; *mām ekaṁ*: in Me, the One; *ahaṁ mokṣayiṣyāmi tvā*: I shall absolve you; *sarva pāpebhyaḥ*: from all sins; *ma śucaḥ*: do not despair.

Abandoning all duties, come to Me, the One, for refuge; I shall absolve you from all sins; do not despair.

67. इदं ते नातपस्काय नाभक्ताय कदाचन ।
न चाशुश्रूषवे वाच्यं न च मां योऽभ्यसूयति ॥

idaṁ te nā 'tapaskāya nā 'bhaktāya kadācana ।
na cā 'śuśrūṣave vācyaṁ na ca māṁ yo 'bhyasūyati ॥

idaṁ na vācyaṁ: this is never to be spoken (about); *te*: by you; *atapaskāya*: to one (spiritually) undisciplined; *na kadācana*: nor at any time; *abhaktāya*: to one devoid of devotion; *na ca aśuśrūṣave*: nor to one indisposed to listen; *na ca*: nor; *yaḥ abhyasūyati māṁ*: to one who denies Me.

This is never to be spoken about by you to one spiritually undisciplined, nor to one devoid of devotion, nor to one indisposed to listen, nor to one who denies Me.

68. य इमं परमं गुह्यं मद्भक्तेष्वभिधास्यति ।
भक्तिं मयि परां कृत्वा मामेवैष्यत्यसंशयः ॥

ya idaṁ paramaṁ guhyaṁ madbhakteṣv abhidhāsyati ।
bhaktiṁ mayi parāṁ kṛtvā mām evai 'ṣyaty asaṁśayaḥ ॥

yaḥ abhidhāsyati: (he) who gives; *idaṁ paramaṁ guhyaṁ*: this supreme secret; *madbhakteṣu*: to My devotees; *kṛtvā mayi*: (thereby) doing for Me; *parāṁ bhaktiṁ*: supreme devotion; *eṣyati asaṁśayaḥ*: shall doubtless come; *mām eva*: to Me alone.

He who gives this supreme secret to My devotee, thereby doing for Me supreme devotion, shall doubtless come to Me.

69. न च तस्मान्मनुष्येषु कश्चिन्मे प्रियकृत्तमः ।
भविता न च मे तस्मादन्यः प्रियतरो भुवि ।।

na ca tasmān manuṣyeṣu kaścin me priyakṛttamaḥ ।
bhavitā na ca me tasmād anyaḥ priyataro bhuvi ॥

na ca: nor (is there); *tasmāt*: besides such a one; *manuṣyeṣu*: among men; *kaścit me*: any to me; *priya kṛttamaḥ*: (who is the highest) performer of dear acts; *na ca bhavitā me*: nor shall there be for Me; *anyaḥ*: another; *priyataraḥ tasmāt*: dearer than this one; *bhuvi*: on earth.

Nor is there besides such a one, among men, any who is the highest performer of dear acts, nor shall there be for Me another dearer on earth.

70. अध्येष्यते च य इमं धर्म्यं संवादमावयोः ।
ज्ञानयज्ञेन तेनाहमिष्टः स्यामिति मे मतिः ।।

adhyeṣyate ca ya imaṁ dharmyaṁ saṁvādam āvayoḥ ।
jñānayajñena tenā 'ham iṣṭaḥ syām iti me matiḥ ॥

ca yaḥ: and (he) who; *adhyeṣyate*: will study; *imaṁ saṁvādam*: this dialogue; *āvayoḥ*: of ours; *dharmyaṁ*: conducive to righteousness; *tena*: by him (in effect); *aham syām*: I shall have been; *iṣṭaḥ*: worshipped; *jñāna yajñena*: through the wisdom-sacrifice; *iti me matiḥ*: such (is) my thought.

And he who will study this dialogue of ours, conducive to righteousness, by him (in effect) I shall have been worshipped through the wisdom-sacrifice; so I hold.

71. श्रद्धावाननसूयश्च शृणुयादपि यो नरः ।
सोऽपि मुक्तः शुभाँल्लोकान्प्राप्नुयात्पुण्यकर्मणाम् ।।

śraddhāvān anasūyaś ca śṛṇuyād api yo naraḥ ।
so 'pi muktaḥ śubhāṁl lokān prāpnuyāt puṇyakarmaṇām ॥

api naraḥ yaḥ: even the man who; *śṛṇuyāt*: may (merely) happen to hear; *śraddhāvān*: endowed with faith; *ca anasūyaḥ*: and uncarping; *api saḥ*: even he; *muktaḥ*: liberated; *prāpnuyāt*: shall attain to; *śubhān lokān*: the good worlds; *puṇya karmaṇām*: of those (who perform) meritorious deeds.

And the man who may merely happen to hear, endowed with faith, and uncarping – even he, liberated, shall attain to the good worlds of those who perform meritorious deeds.

72. कच्चिदेतच्छ्रुतं पार्थ त्वयैकाग्रेण चेतसा ।
कच्चिदज्ञानसंमोहः प्रणष्टस्ते धनञ्जय ।।

kaccid etac chrutaṁ pārtha tvayai 'kāgreṇa cetasā ।
kaccid ajñānasaṁmohaḥ pranaṣṭas te dhanañjaya ॥

kaccit etat: has this; *śrutaṁ tvayā*: been heard by you; *pārtha*: Oh Arjuna; *ekāgreṇa cetasā*: with one-pointed mind; *dhanañjaya*: Oh Arjuna; *kaccit te*: has your; *saṁmohaḥ ajñāna*: delusion of ignorance; *pranaṣṭaḥ*: been destroyed.

Has it been heard by you, Oh Pārtha, with one-pointed mind? Oh Winner of Wealth! has your delusion of ignorance been destroyed?

अर्जुन उवाच –

73. नष्टो मोहः स्मृतिर्लब्धा त्वत्प्रसादान्मयाच्युत ।
स्थितोऽस्मि गतसन्देहः करिष्ये वचनं तव ।।

arjuna uvāca –

naṣṭo mohaḥ smṛtir labdhā tvatprasādān mayā 'cyuta ।
sthito 'smi gatasaṁdehaḥ kariṣye vacanaṁ tava ॥

arjuna uvāca: Arjuna said; *naṭṣaḥ mohaḥ*: gone (is) (my) delusion; *smṛtiḥ*: (and) Self-recognition; *labdhā mayā*: has been gained by me; *tvat prasādāt*: through Your grace; *acyuta*: Oh Kṛṣṇa; *asmi sthitaḥ*: (I) am (properly) established; *gata saṁdehaḥ*: with doubts gone; *kariṣye*: I shall carry out; *tava vacanaṁ*: Your word.

Arjuna said:

Gone is my delusion, and Self-recognition has been gained by me through Your grace, Oh Acyuta! I am properly established, with doubts gone; I shall carry out Your word.

सञ्जय उवाच –

74. इत्यहं वासुदेवस्य पार्थस्य च महात्मनः ।
संवादमिममश्रौषमद्भुतं रोमहर्षणम् ।।

sañjaya uvāca –
ity ahaṁ vāsudevasya pārthasya mahātmanaḥ ।
saṁvādam imam aśrauṣam adbhutaṁ romaharṣaṇam ॥

sañjaya uvāca: Sañjaya said; *iti aham aśrauṣam*: thus have I heard; *imam adbhutaṁ saṁvādam*: this wonderful dialogue; *vāsudevasya*: of Kṛṣṇa; *ca mahātmanaḥ pārthasya*: and of the high-souled Arjuna; *roma harṣaṇam*: causing (my) hair to stand on end.

Sañjaya said:

Thus have I heard this wonderful dialogue between Vāsudeva and the high-souled Pārtha, causing my hair to stand on end.

75. व्यासप्रसादाच्छ्रुतवानेतद्गुह्यमहं परम् ।
योगं योगेश्वरात्कृष्णात्साक्षात्कथयतः स्वयम् ।।

vyāsaprasādāc chrutavān etad guhyam ahaṁ param ।
yogaṁ yogeśvarāt kṛṣṇāt sākṣāt kathayataḥ svayam ॥

vyāsa prasādāt: by the grace of Vyāsa; *ahaṁ śrutavān*: I heard; *etat param*: this supreme; *guhyam yogaṁ*: (and most) secret *yoga*; *kathayataḥ*: spoken; *kṛṣṇāt svayam*: by Kṛṣṇa Himself; *yogeśvarāt*: the Lord of Yoga; *sākṣāt*: as immediately given to my senses.

By the grace of Vyāsa I heard this supreme and most secret *yoga*, spoken by Kṛṣṇa Himself, the Lord of Yoga, as immediately given to my senses.

76. राजन्संस्मृत्य संस्मृत्य संवादमिममद्भुतम् ।
केशवार्जुनयोः पुण्यं हृष्यामि च मुहुर्मुहुः ।।

rājan saṁsmṛtya-saṁsmṛtya saṁvādam imam adbhutam ।
keśavārjunayoḥ puṇyaṁ hṛṣyāmi ca muhur-muhuḥ ॥

rājan: Oh King (Dhṛtarāṣṭra); *saṁsmṛtya saṁsmṛtya*: (as I) remember and remember; *imam adbhutam*: this marvellous; *puṇyaṁ saṁvādam*: (and) sacred dialogue; *keśava arjunayoḥ*: of Kṛṣṇa and Arjuna; *hṛṣyāmi*: (I) rejoice; *ca muhuḥ muhuḥ*: over and over again.

Oh King! as I remember and remember this marvellous and sacred dialogue between Keśava and Arjuna, I rejoice over and over again.

77. तच्च संस्मृत्य संस्मृत्य रूपमत्यद्भुतं हरेः ।
विस्मयो मे महान् राजन्हृष्यामि च पुनः पुनः ।।

tac ca saṁsmṛtya-saṁsmṛtya rūpam atyadbhutaṁ hareḥ ।
vismayo me mahān rājan hṛṣyāmi ca punaḥ-punaḥ ॥

saṁsmṛtya saṁsmṛtya: (as I) remember and remember; *ca tat*: that; *atyadbhutam rūpam*: most marvellous form; *hareḥ*: of Kṛṣṇa; *mahān me vismayaḥ*: great (is) my astonishment; *rājan*: Oh King; *ca hṛṣyāmi*: and (I) rejoice; *punaḥ punaḥ*: over and over again.

As I remember and remember that most marvellous form of Hari, great is my astonishment, Oh King, and I rejoice over and over again.

78. यत्र योगेश्वरः कृष्णो यत्र पार्थो धनुर्धरः ।
तत्र श्रीर्विजयो भूतिर्ध्रुवा नीतिर्मतिर्मम ।।

yatra yogeśvaraḥ kṛṣṇo yatra pārtho dhanurdharaḥ ।
tatra śrīr vijayo bhūtir dhruvā nītir matir mama ॥

yatra: where (there is); *kṛṣṇaḥ*: Kṛṣṇa; *yogeśvaraḥ*: the Lord of Yoga;

yatra: where (there is); *pārthaḥ*: Arjuna; *dhanurdharaḥ*: the Archer; *tatra*: there (will be); *śrīḥ vījayaḥ*: prosperity, victory; *bhūtiḥ*: progress; *dhruvā nītiḥ*: (and) well-established justice; *mama matiḥ*: (such is) my (Sañjaya's) belief.

Where there is Kṛṣṇa, the Lord of Yoga, where there is Pārtha, the Archer, there will be prosperity, victory, progress, and well-established justice: such is my belief.

DIALOGUE

STUDENT: *This chapter begins with Arjuna's desire to know the truth of renunciation as distinct from relinquishment. I thought his passing reference to the innocent life of a mendicant, given in verse five of Chapter II, was only a sentimental outburst. It seems he still has wishful thinking about* saṁnyāsa, *even at the close of the Gītā discourse. Why is he so enamoured with* saṁnyāsa?

TEACHER: It would be surprising if Arjuna did not give thought to renunciation after having full recourse to wisdom at the feet of the greatest of all teachers. The very realization of your true Self automatically brings a renunciation of all claims to the possession of things or any agency of action. According to the tradition of India, the last stage of life is that of a *saṁnyāsin*. Such being the case, it is not surprising that Arjuna is alive to the idea of the hoary tradition of *saṁnyāsa*. However, he is now given an alternative to the total renunciation of action, that of the relinquishment of any personal reward accruing from one's action. Both by temperament and training Arjuna is a man of action. In spite of the insight he has into the futility of transient life on earth, he sees an incompatibility in making a sudden swing from his role of a warrior to that of a silent contemplative. In his mind he has almost resolved to adopt the pattern of relinquishment suggested by Kṛṣṇa. As he still has a chance to make this point clear, he is asking Kṛṣṇa for a final clarification. Kṛṣṇa gives his definition of *saṁnyāsa* and *tyāga* in verse 2:

> Bards of old understood by *saṁnyāsa* (renunciation) of desire-prompted action; the relinquishing of the benefit of all actions, those with insight declare to be *tyāga*.

Renunciation is defined here as the giving up of kāmya-karma. Kāmya-karma *is usually understood as performing burnt sacrifice according to Vedic injunctions and other such rituals by which one can please the gods, but in the present translation it looks as if all desire-prompted actions are covered by the term.*

If we look upon the Gītā as a special scripture only of the Hindus of India, there is a relevancy in understanding *kāmya-karma* as pertaining to Vedic rituals. It is true that in the Indian tradition a *saṁnyāsī* is not obligated to perform any ritual. This narrow view of *saṁnyāsa* has already been discarded in verse 4 of Chapter III. It is better to take *kāmya-karma* in its literal sense, "desire-prompted action", than to limit it to Vedic rituals.

With these definitions, is Kṛṣṇa equating saṁnyāsa *with* tyāga? *Should we take both as the same*?

That would be an oversimplification. We should give due attention to the two separate terms Kṛṣṇa is using in defining *saṁnyāsa* and *tyāga*. In the definition given of *saṁnyāsa, kāmyānāṁ karmāṇām nyāsaṁ*, the renunciation is of action and not of its reward, whereas in the definition of *tyāga, sarvakarmaphalatyāgaṁ*, it is a relinquishment only of the benefit of all actions. The moral issues of justice and parity arise from action that is done without any desire for its benefit. All actions are supposed to be subjected to cause and effect. It is well known in the world that a man performing good actions should reap good results, and one who does evil should be punished by the evil consequences of his actions. If the good man is performing virtuous action with a sense of resignation, and is not benefited by his meritorious actions, then we will not see any parity between cause and effect. We will have to say that the world order has no justice in it. Kant, in his *Ethics*, assigns to God the function of apportioning justice to each person according to their actions, even when the person is willing to forego any merit. A *saṁnyāsī* has no action, and therefore the question of the benefit of action does not arise. The *tyāgī* performs action, but is not benefit-motivated. Hence, the question of benefit does arise in his case.

Wasn't this question previously discussed?

Yes. In the fourth chapter, verse 19, we saw the wise man whose action has been reduced to nothing in the fire of wisdom. In verse 20 we saw the man who relinquishes attachment to the benefit of works, and is ever happy and independent. Although he is engaged in work, in principle he does nothing at all.

I think the distinction between saṁnyāsa *and* tyāga *has already been brought to a minimum in Chapter IV.*

I agree with you. From verse 21 to 24 of Chapter IV, the action of a wise person is treated only as an autonomous function. What is important is the attitude, not the action. In verse 24, everything coming within the scope of action is relegated to the Absolute. In verses 8 and 9 of Chapter V, all bodily functions, while being performed, are treated as cancelled if the performer firmly believes, "I do nothing at all".

In verse 3 of the present chapter Kṛṣṇa says:

> "Action should be given up as an evil", declare some rationalists; others say that "acts of sacrifice, giving, and austerity should not be abandoned".

Who are these rationalists? Who are the people who insist on sacrifice, alms, and austerity?

The first opinion is held by the Sāṁkhyans. According to them, the object of life, namely cessation of pain, cannot be achieved by means of any course of action, and they therefore conclude that one should renounce all action. The Pūrva-Mīmāṁsins insist on action.

Why does Kṛṣṇa quote these contradictory opinions of two schools?

These two schools of thought represent two typical attitudes of human beings. Even modern thinkers like Jung look upon introversion and extroversion as two typical modes with which to classify personality types. Kṛṣṇa was a great revaluator. Like the Buddha, who taught the golden Middle Path, Kṛṣṇa always tried to normalize the value-visions of people by giving positive content to the lives of those tending to become negative, and pacifying those who were likely to become aggresive. In the next three verses he gives his own decided opinion:

> Hear now from Me, Oh Best of the Bhāratas! the settled conclusion about relinquishment (*tyāga*); relinquishment indeed, Oh Best of Men! has been well known as of three kinds:
>
> The acts of sacrifice, gift, and austerity should not be relinquished, each should indeed be observed; sacrifice, gift, and austerity are the purifiers of rational men;
>
> but even these actions should be done leaving out attachment and desire for result; this, Oh Pārtha! is My decided and best conviction.

Why, at the close of verse 6, does Kṛṣṇa say, "This is My decided and best conviction"?

You will find such expressions in the words of all great teachers who have taken upon themselves the responsibility to correct the opinions of previous teachers or the conventions of an established tradition. In the New Testament, again and again we come across such statements by Jesus Christ. When he is about to give his own conclusive correction of a previous teaching, he begins by saying, "Verily, verily I say unto you".

Yajña (*sacrifice*), dāna (*giving gifts*) *and* tapas (*austerity*) *are well known to be part of Indian religious life. When Kṛṣṇa agrees with the Pūrva-Mīmāṁsā people that sacrifice, gifts, and austerity should not be relinquished, how do people of other countries and traditions look upon such an instruction?*

The revaluation in which the Gītā is interested has a parallel in modern psychology. The word *psyche* originally came from the Greeks. They had a concept of the psyche which was afterwards lost to the world. In the Medieval Period it came to mean anything connected with the mind. When psychology was conceived in modern days, people like Wundt thought of it as the determinants of behaviour. Afterwards, when behaviourism and physiological psychology began looking upon the mind as an epiphenomenon or by-product of organized neural functioning, the reference to mind was even considered absurd by people like Watson. An alternative stress which became popular in Europe was depth psychology. Freud, Adler, Rank, and Jung are considered to be the exponents of depth psychology. The pioneer among them, Freud, made a return to the legends of the Greek people who first coined the word "psyche". Even now, the Western scientist is not fully reconciled to the idea of relating empirical events of life to mysterious functions which are said to be taking place in the unconscious, and which are analogous to Greek myths, as in the case of the Oedipus and Electra complexes. The role that the myths play in generating the collective unconscious that is spoken of by psychologists like Jung, almost as an article of faith, is a very vital factor in psychoanalysis and analytical psychology. In the same way, the Vedic hymns and the protolinguistic references to geometrical diagrams (*maṇḍala*s), rituals, and sacred formulae given in the Vedic texts play a vital role in understanding the cosmology and psychology dealt with in the Bhagavadgītā.

The first term of reference given here is *yajña* (sacrifice). Sacrifice as a pious act or a hoary practice was not confined to India. It is a concept before which even great conquerors have stood bewildered, confused, and helpless. It is glorified even in the present day in several transfigured forms. Even the word "God", which is universally accepted as a term for the Supreme Being, whose grace is evoked through prayers, incantations, and worship, is derived from the Hebrew term, *hod*, itself derived from the Sanskrit term, *hut*, which is connected with *āhuti* (offering oblation with fire to the deities). A priest is called *purohit*. Thus, some of our deep articles of faith lie buried in the words we use, like fire concealed by ashes. Although it is possible for man to reject myth and mythical language and live on a rational foundation, by that very act he rips himself away from the roots from which his individuation has arisen. This amounts to spiritual suicide.

Although the mysterious nature of compulsion that is often asserted by the collective mind can sometimes spell great evil, as in the sacrifice of

Iphigenia by her father Agamemnon, we cannot shut our eyes to forces that act on our psyches. There is always the danger of charlatans thriving in such a field of mystery and ambiguity. In the Gītā, Kṛṣṇa wants to preserve the rich legacy of the cosmic consciousness of mankind on the one hand, and on the other to safeguard the individual consciousness from being smothered by the brute collective will of people steeped in ignorance. He accepts traditional practices by highlighting how they can become spiritually meaningful, and rejects them when they become morally deviant.

What are the three kinds of relinquishment which Kṛṣṇa speaks of?

The first relinquishment he speaks of is the renunciation of action. The second is the relinquishment of the benefit of action, and the third is the renunciation of one's identification with the agency of action.

If the highest form of realization is one's identification with the Absolute, how could there be any relevancy at all for admitting action?

When we speak of renunciation of action, relinquishment of the benefit of action, and renunciation of the agency of action, there has to be a person to whom we can attribute these things. Such a person is called *kartā* (actor). The agency of action is the *dharma* in him. When that *dharma* is denied, there is no actor. There is only the Self. We have already seen that the individuation of a person is superimposed on the Self by ignorance. It is the ego that brings identification with individuation, and it is again the same ego that causes the notion of one's being an actor. It is by lack of discrimination that one attributes individuation and action to the Self. The problem arising from this is to regain the power of proper discrimination.

Clarity of vision is referred to in verse 5 as resulting from the purification of the rational mind. The method given for that purification is the performance of action without benefit-motive. What is meant here by purification is the removal of ignorance by which one thinks of oneself as a person. Where there is no personal identification, the question of action does not arise at all. This consequence, the total identification with the Absolute, as in the great dictum *aham brahmāsmi* (I am the Absolute), is truly to be understood as *saṁnyāsa*. Thus, in actuality *saṁnyāsa* is not an alternative to *tyāga*. It is the final result that comes as a consequence of true wisdom. All that remains to be discussed is the kind or nature of relinquishment, which depends on the attitude of the person whose ego continues to be functional as individuated consciousness.

If the relinquishment of benefit is tyāga, *how could there be any difference between one person's relinquishment and that of another?*

We have seen from the previous chapter how one's disposition is influenced by the primacy of any one of the three *guṇas*, which dominate individuated consciousness from time to time. For instance, in verse 7 the renunciation of the inert-dark type of person is given:

> Verily, the renunciation of necessary inevitable action does not arise; the renunciation of such through delusion is said to be inert-dark (tāmasic).

In the original Sanskrit, Kṛṣṇa says, niyatasya tu saṁnyāsaḥ karmaṇaḥ na upapadyate. *It is translated here as "necessary inevitable action* (niyatasya karmaṇaḥ), *the renunciation of which* (tu saṁnyāsaḥ) *does not arise* (na upapadyate)". *How do you decide which action is* niyatam (*inevitable*)?

That which is required varies from person to person. What is inevitable for one can be of no consequence in the life of another. No science can classify or categorize the action that is relevant in the case of each person. The Gītā therefore leaves it entirely up to the individual to decide his own mandatory action.

Even then, can't there be a general indication by which one can decide what is mandatory?

Yes, of course. If the omission of a certain action is bound to bring misery to oneself and others, and will not in any way promote happiness, that action should be known as truly obligatory.

If it is truly obligatory, how could a person ever renounce it?

That is exactly what is brought out by this verse. A man of inert-dark disposition is likely to be subject to delusion (*moha*). Out of the five *kleśas* (obstructions to *yoga*), *avidyā* (ignorance) is given as the primary cause. The same is said to manifest as *ālasya* (torpor), *pramāda* (delusion), and *nidrā* (sleep). If a man is physically weak and cannot rise from his bed, he will not perform what needs to be done, even though he may be fully conscious that the omission of the action will only deteriorate his state still further. In another state, although such a person is aware that he has to do some inevitable action to avoid misery, because of his delusion he does not know how to go about it. In either case the consequence is inaction where action is called for, which further darkens the mind and brings additional misery.

Is there any justification in calling one's omission a saṁnyāsa, *especially when one does not even know what he is doing?*

The word *saṁnyāsa* is used in the present context only because of its semantic affinity to the non-performance of action, and not in the sense of a calculated spiritual attitude adopted by a person.

A totally ignorant person does not desire to perform anything. He has no benefit-motive, and he does not even think that he has an agency of action. Is he not as good as a fully realized person, who also renounces action, relinquishes motives, and gives up the agency of action?

There is only one difference between a totally ignorant person and an absolutely wise person. The former is continuously miserable, while the latter is always in a state of unbroken happiness.

How do the other forms of kleśa, *such as* asmitā (*egoism*), rāga (*attachment*), dveṣa (*repulsion*) *and* abhiniveśa (*clinging to life and fear of death*), *come in the way of relinquishment?*

In all these aspects except *dveṣa* (hatred) there are both bright and dark dispositions. The dark dispositions are born of *rajas*. This is given in verse 8:

> He who, from fear of bodily trouble, relinquishes action, considering it painful, thus wilfully (with *rajas*) relinquishing does not get the (legitimate) benefit of relinquishment.

The tāmasic *person does not do any action, and this* rājasic *person is also blamed for not performing action. What differentiates one from the other?*

The man of *tamas* is steeped in ignorance. He is oblivious to what is to be done. In the case of the man of *rajas*, he is fully conscious of his responsibility. The symptoms given here are more or less those of a neurotic person. Psychologists describe it as a "flight into sickness":

> An escape, to a greater or less extent subconscious, from a reality that can be neither mastered nor endured, into a state of sickness that frees the sufferer from all responsibility. An incapacity mechanism then comes into operation, and the subject shuts himself off from the world and experiences feelings of resignation and inferiority and other neurotic complications.[1]

Relinquishment of the benefit-motive is recommended by Kṛṣṇa, but in verse 8 he says the man of rajas-tyāga *does not get the legitimate benefit of relinquishment. When it is not good to be benefit-motivated, should one become mindful of the benefit of relinquishment?*

Performance of action without benefit-motive is recommended for the purification of the mind. Ultimately, that should enable a person to be rid of his false identification with the ego. In an indirect way, this verse says

---

[1] H.J. Eysenck (ed.), 1972, *Encyclopedia of Psychology*, New York: Herder and Herder, vol. I, p. 379.

that the high state of *karma-saṁnyāsa* is not obtained by mere omission of action, because of the intensification of the egoistic consciousness of one who is assailed by the fear of misery. Mere benefit-motive is different from the highest of all benefits, one's own liberation.

What is the result of relinquishment?

As has already been explained, it is the recovery of the natural state of consciousness through purging the mind of its various conditionings and colourations. This ultimately leads to real *saṁnyāsa*, the concept of which is going to be restated in verse 49 of this chapter.

It seems there is no common ground between verse 9 and the previous two verses, because the tāmasic and rājasic people are relinquishers of action, while the ninth verse refers to a performer of action:

> When necessary action is done, Oh Arjuna! recognizing its imperative character, relinquishing attachment and benefit, such relinquishment is considered pure (sāttvic).

The common ground here is the consequence of an attitude. Verses 7 to 9 constitute a set wherein the *guṇa*s (modalities of nature) are referred to in an inverse order.

When someone performs action it is a positive gesture. Why should it be thought of in terms of renunciation?

True renunciation is *saṁnyāsa.* The very word implies properly giving up. In the individuation of the Self there is the accretion of ego, with which the individuated consciousness begins to identify. It is a false identification. But the ego is riveted to the Self with interests that are born of incipient memories (*vāsanā*s). Incipient memories, which perpetuate bondage to chains of action, are almost an undetectable factor. They present themselves only as the sense of pain and pleasure the ego experiences, and the consequent desire and hatred which motivate the functioning of the ego. Liberation is nothing short of the emancipation of consciousness from its identification with this ego.

This is the problematic situation of every embodied person. Embodiment is not an isolated incident: the entire world is an aggregate of bodies. There is an inner law which is regulating the formation and dissolution of bodies. What the individual can do as a first step of release is resign the body to doing the functions that are natural to the order to which it belongs. Hence the reference to the term *niyatam.* The imperative (*nitya*), optional (*niyata*), and incidental (*naimittika*) aspects of action were all described in detail elsewhere. In the present context, the word *niyata* is to be understood as what is natural in a situational sense. The renunciation which is relevant to this verse is the avoidance of attachment and the non-desire for the benefits of action.

When action is described as imperative, how is it possible to ever renounce it?

Action is imperative only in the case of embodied beings who are conscious of their bodily functions. Verses 10, 11, and 12 speak to your question:

> The relinquisher, pervaded with purity (*sattva*), of strong intelligence, and of sundered doubts, hates not unpleasant action, nor is he attached to pleasant ones.
>
> Nor indeed is it possible for an embodied one to completely relinquish action; he who relinquishes the benefit of action is verily called a relinquisher.
>
> Pleasant, unpleasant, and mixed benefits accrue in the spiritual progress beyond of a non-relinquisher (*atyāgī*), but none anywhere to renouncers (*saṁnyāsināḥ*).

In the *Yoga-Vāsiṣṭha* there is reference to *brahmavit varīya* and *brahmavit variṣṭha*. The state of *brahmavit varīya* was already described in verses 22 through 26 of Chapter XIV, where such a person was labelled *guṇātīta*, transcendent over the *guṇas*. *Brahmavit variṣṭha* is totally oblivious to any modification of consciousness. Such a person is defined in the Nirvāṇa Darśana of Narayana Guru's *Darśana Mālā*:

> *He who by himself does not know anything,*
> *And even when made to know knows not –*
> *Such a one, always void of activity,*
> *The most elect, is the Absolute alone in itself.*[2]

What is the relevancy of the reference to the action of a man of sattva *in the above-given verses?*

We have mentioned elsewhere that Arjuna's thoughts of *saṁnyāsa* in Chapter II were not mere wishful thinking. By his attention and inquiry he has already proved beyond doubt that the main goal before him is neither victory in war nor the possession of a kingdom, but the welfare of his soul. The *saṁnyāsa* there referred to as *bhaikṣacarya* (living by begging) has been a traditionally accepted means in India to secure the liberation of the soul. However noble this intention may be, Arjuna has yet to prove his immunity to sensory and emotional provocations. In spite of having

---

[2] Nataraja Guru (tr.), 1977, *An Anthology of the Poems of Narayana Guru*, Somanahalli Gurukula Institute of Esthetic Values, p. 76.

the rare experience of a cosmic vision, the vestiges of his ego have not left him completely. As Nataraja Guru mentions in his commentary on verse 12, he neither conforms to the natural man nor yet to the ideal man. The purification Kṛṣṇa prescribes for such a person is to flush the ego with *sattva* so that the dross of *rajas* and *tamas* can be first removed. This will prepare him for the true *saṁnyāsa* (which is neither social nor conventional) that he has been secretly aspiring for. Kṛṣṇa is respectful of wishes, and he does not ridicule the earnestness of any person. This is evident from his own words in verse 21, Chapter VII:

> By whichever (particular) form such and such a devotee with faith wishes to worship, each to his own faith I confirm.

Verse 12 says, "But none anywhere to renouncers (saṁnyāsināḥ)*". The* saṁnyāsin *is here compared with* atyāgī (*a non-relinquisher*). *In what sense should we understand the* saṁnyāsin *here? Is he one who relinquishes his attachment and desire for the benefit of his actions, or one who has renounced all actions?*

The main point of reference in this verse is action. Where there is no action, there is no relevancy in speaking of the benefit of action. If a *saṁnyāsī* is to be included in this, he should be one in whose life action has some appropriate place. We have seen the possibility of renouncing action, relinquishing the benefit of action, and renouncing the egoistic identification with the agency of action. Although we have come all the way to the eighteenth chapter, the venue of the Gītā teaching continues to be a battlefield, and Arjuna is still facing the necessity of action which in his case comes under the category of *niyatam* (enjoined). In verse 33 of Chapter XI Kṛṣṇa made it clear to him that he has no agency of action independently willed by himself, and that he was acting only as an instrument of the Divine. If that lesson has gone home, Arjuna should be considered as a *saṁnyāsī* who has renounced his agency of action. It is not evident from his own words that he has come to such a state. His indifference to victory and the gains of war was already made explicit in verse 32 of Chapter I. In the present verse Arjuna is to be considered as a relinquisher of the benefit of action.

If Arjuna has not attained the status of an absolute renouncer, why does Kṛṣṇa bring in the question of saṁnyāsa *at all?*

We have already mentioned that Arjuna's ulterior interest is his spiritual progress (*niḥśreyas*). The traditional belief of India associates this with the conventional model of *saṁnyāsa*, the path of the contemplative wayfarer. In Kṛṣṇa's revaluation he places a man fully engaged in the transactions of life on a par with the wisest of all contemplatives if he is capable of effecting a proper bipolarity with the Absolute. As the eighteenth chapter is a dialectical counterpart of the first, two main apprehensions which Arjuna had at the outset are now conclusively revised. The first is his fear of the guilt which might follow from the killing of his relatives, even though they are standing before him as shameless aggressors and grabbers of wealth. This fear can only be resolved by discussing the relation between an action and its inevitable result. The second consideration is the feasibility of changing his lifestyle from a warrior to a contemplative mendicant. So it is appropriate that in this verse Kṛṣṇa is bringing his focus to action and a state of mind which is equivalent to the attitude of a full-fledged *saṁnyāsin*.

It seems to me that action is a responsible function. How can the performer of it relinquish his responsibility for its consequences? This attitude allows even superstitious brutes who are caught in the snares of hallucination to perform atrocities, such as the sacrifice of their own son or daughter, while holding the firm conviction that it is the will of God, not their own will, which is responsible. As an example, in the book of Genesis, held sacred by the Jews, Christians, and Muslims, we read, "And it came to pass after these things, that God did tempt Abraham, and said unto him, Abraham: and he said, Behold, here I am. And he said, Take now thy son, thine only son Isaac, whom thou lovest, and get thee into the land of Moriah; and offer him there for a burnt offering upon one of the mountains which I will tell thee of" (22:1-2).

According to the story, Abraham resolved to carry out this decree. How do we know the authenticity of God's will when we can be fooled by our own hallucinations? Is God a person with whom we can interact, or is it only an abstraction? If God is an abstraction, how do we surrender our will and action to that? How can we expect an abstraction to bear the responsibility for our own actions, especially when they involve violence such as fratricide?

There is an incompatibility between the freedom of man's will to act on his own choice and the fateful determinism which is often attributed to the omnipotency of an omniscient God. If a man is acting on his own, he is the agent of his action and there is no justification in thinking that the benefit of his action be resigned to God. If the action is always enjoined by an omnipotent God, it would be impossible for anyone to do anything which has the slightest taint of evil, since God is believed to be always good and perfect.

In Chapter VII Kṛṣṇa says, in verse 5, that it is by his non-transcendental nature that the phenomenal world is sustained. In verse 7 he says that everything is united in him as if strung as a classified series of precious beads on a string. In verse 19 he says it is very rare to find a person who sees the Absolute as the indwelling immortal, Vāsudeva, in all beings. In Chapter IX, verse 4, he says:

> By Me all this world is pervaded, My form unmanifested; all beings have existence in Me and I do not have existence in them.

In Chapter XIII Kṛṣṇa asks Arjuna to know him as the knower of the field in all fields and even as the knowledge of both the field and the knower of the field. The Absolute introduced in the Bhagavadgītā, which Kṛṣṇa speaks of in both the first and third person, does not always square with the God spoken of in theistic religions. The total and independent Absolute is One, without a second, and nothing falls outside its scope. At the same time the individual with relative existence, who is entirely a dependent factor, has a course of action necessitated by his own personal history. The complexity of this action is either resolved or further confounded by the wisdom or ignorance that the individual gains through understanding or failing to understand the nature of his own individuation. There is no freedom for a dependent being until it finds itself in total identification with the independence of the Absolute. Kṛṣṇa is not asking Arjuna for a surrender in the sense in which religious people think of it: as a virtue to be cultivated. The attachment to one's ego-identity as actor and clinging to the benefit of action are born of a partial understanding of one's placement in the world. Kṛṣṇa's stress is on having total understanding. In the next three verses he is going to give the fivefold aspects of every action performed by man:

> Oh Mighty-Armed! learn from Me these five causes for the accomplishment of all actions, as stated in the Sāṁkhya at the end of the age called Kṛta:
>
> The basis and actor, and also the various mental instruments, the several and varied movements, and, fifth, the divine factor;
>
> whatever action a man undertakes by the body, speech, and mind, justifiable or the opposite – these five are its causes.

Why is sāṁkhye kṛtānte proktāni *translated as "in the Sāṁkhya at the end of the age called Kṛta", instead of "in the wisdom that comes when action ceases"?*

The translation of the verses adopted in this work are of Nataraja Guru. In his commentary the Guru says:

> Regarding *kṛtānta* (the end of the first or golden age called Kṛta), which can also be interpreted as "end of action", we find the former meaning more acceptable, as the Gītā makes historical references, such as to Manu in IV.1, etc. Here it refers to the time of Kapila, the Sāṁkhya exponent.

However, we think that *kṛtānta* can be translated as "end of action" when we look at the word Sāṁkhya as used hitherto in Chapters II, III, V, and XIII. The word occurs in verse 39 of Chapter II, and Franklin Edgerton, Radhakrishnan and Nataraja Guru all agree that the Sāṁkhya given in this verse is not the same as the Sāṁkhya system known to us from Kapila's time. In verse 3 of Chapter III, *jñāna-yoga* (unitive way of wisdom) is identified as the Sāṁkhya discipline recognized by the Gītā. In verses 4 and 5 of Chapter V, the doctrinal difference between Sāṁkhya and Yoga is negated. In Nataraja Guru's commentary on verse 24 of Chapter XIII he recognizes Sāṁkhya as the teaching which implies the equalizing principle given in verse 48 of Chapter II.

Please explain to me the five aspects of action dealt with in these three verses.

Kṛṣṇa is giving here five interrelated factors that are to be taken into consideration in understanding any action. If we schematically show them, then *adhiṣṭhāna* (ground) is to be placed at the negative pole of the vertical axis. At the positive pole is *daiva* (God). On the horizontal axis, *karaṇa* (instruments of action) are to be placed on the minus side, and on the plus side, *ceṣṭāḥ* (behavioural expressions). *Kartā* (actor) is to be placed at the centre where the two axes intercept. Although *adhiṣṭhāna* is given as the alpha and *daiva* is given as the omega, they are to be understood as aspects of one and the same reality. In different schools of Vedānta *adhiṣṭhāna* is explained differently. According to the non-dualistic school of Śaṅkara, it is the true ground on which phenomenality is superimposed. The true ground of all being is none other than the Absolute. The Absolute is defined as *sat* (pure existence), *cit* (self-luminous knowledge) and *ānanda* (norm of all values). The negative principle of the Absolute, variously called *prakṛti, pradhāna, avidyā,* or *māyā,* causes the individuation of separate beings through an act of superimposition. As a result of this superimposition, the pure state of the Absolute is obscured by *sattva, rajas* and *tamas* (three modalities of nature). In the individual the *adhiṣṭhāna* does not remain in its pure state, so it is to be taken along with *adhyāsa* (superimposition). Although the individual is a transient phase and has no existence of its own, the urge to be is always there due to the individual's participation in the existence of the eternal ground. Similarly, the pure knowledge or self-luminosity of the universal Self lends its light to illumine the mind and senses of the individual, even when they are distorted and disfigured by the intervention of the three *guṇa*s. The obscuration or mirroring of the Self's blissful being by the individuated mind gives the individual the dual experiences of pain and pleasure, or love and hatred. The *adhiṣṭhāna* becomes a breeding ground for incipient memories. In short, the individual self, with its entire history of formation through long periods of time, and with the latent impressions that are processed, ingested, and registered as *vāsanās*, is to be treated as the *adhiṣṭhāna* that is spoken of here.

The school of Rāmānuja, that of qualified non-dualism, holds that the world is not superimposed on its ground. The only ground of everything is God. The universe with its variegated forms is an expression of the Divine.

According to Madhva, the individual self is a dependent factor in relation to God. In spite of the differences between these three schools, there is agreement that the only ground is the Absolute. The *adhiṣṭhāna* can also be understood in terms of cosmo-sociology as the laws of nature that govern the physical, chemical, biological, and psychological aspects of life. In terms of bio-sociology, the ground is one's genetic heredity.

From the universal ground our attention is directed to *kartā* (actor). The central locus of the actor is the I-consciousness, which assumes the role of the knower, the enjoyer, and the doer. It is in this living centre of consciousness that the external and internal, and the subject and object are linked. The orientation of the individual's life is secured again and again by the ego's agency as the knower, doer, or enjoyer.

The individual lives in an objective world of time and space, and a subjective world of various sensory and mental impressions. A person experiences only to the extent his mind and senses permit. All latent skills in the instrument of the body and mind can be developed, however the body–mind complex allows only a few coordinations to each individual. Thus there is a limit to the skills or talents that may be developed. Very rarely do we find a genius like Leonardo da Vinci who is born with multiple skills and can develop them. For most people the body–mind instrument they possess is only equipped to function in a single field, and they become misfits when placed in a different life situation.

Kartā (actor) is to be understood in this context as the superimposed ego whose intelligence, power to foresee and act, and normative notion of happiness are all derived from the ground which is basically the universal Self, *sat-cit-ānanda* (pure existence, knowledge, and value) while its individualistic colouration has come from its incipient memories, modulated by the negativity of the *sattva, rajas*, and *tamas* of nature. This aspect is recognized in Western psychology as the *unconscious disposition to act.* Sir Karl R. Popper, in *The Self and Its Brain*, writes:

> Our unconscious knowledge can well be described as a set of dispositions to act, or to behave, or to expect. ... Our unconscious dispositions are certainly very important for our selves. Much that contributes to the unity of the self, and, more especially, to its temporal continuity, seems to be unconscious.

> There is a kind of memory – the ability to recall what has happened to us in the immediate past – which is, like all latent memory, unconscious, but can be recalled into consciousness. We usually "know" in considerable detail what we have done and experienced a minute ago, in the sense that we know how to recall it into consciousness *if we so wish*. It is this unconscious disposition which gives a self its continuity from moment to moment, in its normal state of wakefulness.
>
> ... There are at least two kinds of unconscious dispositional states:
>
> 1. Dispositions to recall to consciousness (which may or may not lead to conscious action);
> 2. Dispositions to behave unconsciously.
>
> It seems that both of these bear heavily on the self. The first kind is most important in what we may describe as the memory which produces the potential continuity of the self or the continuity-producing memory.[3]

Further stress on this memory and the dispositions of the agent (*kartā*) comes in the reference to *karaṇa* (instruments). Although *karaṇa* means literally an instrument, in Vedānta it refers to the individual's intentionality, orientational memory, decision making, and adherence–avoidance dispositions. The actor being an embodied person, he or she functions within the delimited field of the *universe of physical entities*. The physical world is known to be a continuous flux of process in which forces interact. As a conscious as well as physical being, the person has mental states. These mental states can be influenced by rational scientific understanding, rational–irrational social demands, and a-rational myths. If a person has no prior conceptual image of a word, the mere hearing or seeing of it won't make any sense. If a person does not have an innate disposition, such as an ear for music, he or she cannot become a musician. Thus the *karaṇa* goes a long way in determining the scope, meaning, and quality of action. *Karaṇa* is constituted of *manas*, *buddhi*, *citta*, and *ahaṁkāra*, which each have their own formations, scope, and peculiarities that decide what question a mind can ask, what motive it is bound to promote, how right or wrong a decision will be, what association of memory can be recalled, and how one is affected by any incident, subjective or objective.

One swallow does not make a summer, and, in the same way, you cannot deduce the complexities of a person's behavioural pattern from a single example of behaviour. An outburst of emotion may come as a catharsis after a long period of repression. We tend to show compassion and sympathy

---

[3] Karl R. Popper, 1977, *The Self and Its Brain*, Berlin: Springer International, pp. 130-31.

to those whom we love, and hatred to those whom we despise. Only a lengthy follow-up through time and a careful consideration of several samples of behaviour will reveal the character of a person. That is why behaviour in this verse is qualified as *vividhāś ca pṛthakceṣṭā* (variegated and separate items of behaviour).

Daiva, translated here as "the divine factor", is to be understood teleologically. As in Aristotle's conception, everything progresses towards perfection. God as the Ground is both the principle and stuff of creation; God as the manifested Word is the process and individuation of things and beings; God as teleologic perfection is the end result that is constantly being approached and approximated but never fully accomplished. This idea is partly shared by Socrates:

> "When I was young, Cebes, I had an extraordinary passion for that branch of learning which is called natural science. I thought it would be marvellous to know the causes for which each thing comes and ceases and continues to be. I was constantly veering to and fro, puzzling primarily over this sort of question. Is it when heat and cold produce fermentation, as some have said, that living creatures are bred? Is it with the blood that we think, or with the air or the fire that is in us? Or is it none of these, but the brain that supplies our senses of hearing and sight and smell, and from these that memory and opinion arise, and from memory and opinion, when established, that knowledge comes? Then again I would consider how these faculties are lost, and study celestial and terrestrial phenomena, until at last I came to the conclusion that I was uniquely unfitted for this form of inquiry. I will give you a sufficient indication of what I mean. I had understood some things plainly before, in my own and other people's estimation, but now I was so befogged by these speculations that I unlearned even what I had thought I knew, especially about the cause of growth in human beings. Previously I had thought that it was quite obviously due to eating and drinking – that when, from the food which we consume, flesh is added to flesh and bone to bone, and when in the same way the other parts of the body are augmented by their appropriate particles, the bulk which was small is now large, and in this way the small man becomes a big one. That is what I used to believe – reasonably, don't you think?
>
> "Yes, I do," said Cebes.
>
> "Consider a little further. I had been content to think, when I saw a tall man standing beside a short one, that he was taller by a head, and similarly in the case of horses. And it seemed to me even more obvious that ten is more than eight because it contains two more, and that two feet is bigger than one because it exceeds by half its own length."
>
> "And what do you believe about them now?" asked Cebes.

> "Why, upon my word, that I am very far from supposing that I know the explanation of any of these things."[4]

Daiva literally means "the Source and embodiment of light; the knowledge that guides every creature". God is the final cause in everything. When a potter makes a pot, he has in mind an idea of the pot which he is trying to fashion out of clay. He almost approximates his idea. Throughout the process of creation, it is this idea that helps him to make the *upādāna*, pulling or fashioning out of the clay the appropriate form that distinguishes a pot from everything else. In the present verse *daiva* (God), is also to be understood as a situational overlordship of each life context, a mysterious conjuring of natural benevolence, which assembles all favourable chance factors to promote the success of an endeavour and, from within, to provide the agent with the right intuition to proceed in the right manner. In this sense, God is a constant companion, a bestower of Grace, a dependable counsellor in times of need, and a source of inspiration and encouragement, particularly in times of adversity.

In verse 15, mentation is also treated as action. There are many unconscious urges that come into the mind, and many emotional states that are present in spite of all precautions taken to not get agitated. Should we say that these autonomous functions are also actions?

In Chapter XIII all these are relegated to the field (*kṣetra*). That is why in the next verse the correction of the confusion between the attributes of *kṣetra* and *kṣetrajña* (knower of the field) is reiterated. Verse 16 reads:

> Now, such being the case, the man of perverted mind who, because of unfinished intelligence, looks upon himself as the isolated agent of action – he does not see indeed.

Who is a durmati (*man of perverted mind*)?

Although *durmati* is translated here as "man of perverted mind", *mati* is the same as *buddhi*, which means intellect. *Buddhi* (intellect) is that special aspect of consciousness originating from *puruṣa* (pure Spirit). It becomes conjoined with mind, which is an evolute of the ego, acted upon by the three *guṇas*: *sattva*, *rajas*, and *tamas*. This conjunction of intelligence and mind works for the good when the mind becomes subservient to intelligence. On the other hand, when intelligence becomes a tool in the hands of the mind, which is already vitiated by the colourations of past impressions, it loses its efficacy to release the lower self from bondage and

---

[4] Plato, 1961, *Dialogues*, ed. Edith Hamilton and Huntington Cairns, Princeton: Bollingen, p. 78.

becomes *durmati* (perverted intelligence). In this state the individual, who is helplessly caught in the imperativeness of action and cannot recognize it as merely belonging to the field, mistakes it for the action of the Self.

Why is the intelligence of such a person qualified as akṛta buddhi (*unfinished intelligence*)?

The proper function of *buddhi* (intelligence), is to discern right from wrong, the Self from the non-Self, and the eternal from the transient. If *buddhi* fails to do this it is *akṛta buddhi* (unfinished intelligence).

Some people, like John Locke, think that when a child is born it comes into the world with a mind as blank as a clean slate, a tabula rasa. If this is true, the power to discern must come as an acquired or learned skill. Also, the scope to train intelligence being unlimited, shouldn't all people be considered to have unfinished intelligence?

This is not the view of present-day scientists and psychologists. Sir Karl Popper writes:

> This idea [of *tabula rasa*] is not merely mistaken, but grotesquely mistaken: we have only to remember the ten thousand million neurons of our cerebral cortex, some of them (the cortical pyramidal cells) each with an "estimated total of ten thousand" synaptic links. These may be said to represent the material traces of our inherited and almost entirely unconscious knowledge, selected by evolution. Although there is really no method of comparing the two (this is so in general with the nature *versus* nurture problem) I should be intuitively inclined to say that the huge amount of information we can acquire in a lifetime through our senses is small compared with the amount of this inherited background of potentialities.[5]

What is referred to as "inherited and almost entirely unconscious knowledge" is treated by the Vedāntin as superconsciousness coming from the Ground, *sat-cit-ānanda.* It is the continuation of life. It reaches its teleologic goal only when the awareness of the individual is brought to its final fruition of total emancipation. Until this is achieved it is *akṛta buddhi.*

Verse 17 contradicts the very definition of a wise man. It says:

> He who is free from ego-sense, whose intelligence is unaffected, though he kills these people – he neither kills nor is bound.

Isn't a wise person fully committed to ahiṁsā?

This question has already been discussed in Chapter II, verses 18 and 19:

> These bodies (however) of the everlasting indestructible and undefinable

[5] Popper, 1977, op. cit., p. 121.

> embodied One are spoken of as having an end. Therefore go on with the battle, Oh Bhārata!
>
> He who thinks of This as the killer, and he who thinks of This as killed – both these know not. This does not kill, is not killed.

We have made it explicit on several occasions that there is a paradox lurking in the very heart of the Absolute. Our minds work both analytically and synthetically. When they operate synthetically they are endowed with a unitive vision of seeing everything as one. In that vision there cannot be any differentiation, such as the killer and the killed. In contrast to that transcendental vision, everything in the transactional world has the status of mere appearance. The appearance that is relevant to the context of a battlefield is the imagery of people killing each other. Kṛṣṇa is not making a case for the wise man to kill. He only says that if it appears to a dull-headed person that a wise man is killing or that a wise man is being killed, that judgement has no real validity.

A wise man is not a species by himself. Every embodied person has his or her imperative actions to perform. The nature of the action depends very much on one's placement in society. If a man is invested with the authority of the state to function as a judge, it becomes imperative for him to listen to arguments and act upon the findings of his jury within the frame of reference of a legislated law. If the law decrees capital punishment, in one sense we can establish that the judge is directly connected with the killing of a person by the state, but when the same action is judged as part of the operation of a whole system, he cannot be accused of becoming violent. The natural role assigned to Arjuna is that of a warrior. Everyone expects him to kill unless he is being killed. Kṛṣṇa is only revealing to Arjuna that even in such a context a man can raise himself to the status of a wise person.

What is the relationship between knowledge and action?

That depends on the kind of knowledge one possesses. The relationship between the two at the transactional level is given in verse 18:

> Knowledge, the knowable, and the knower are the threefold incentive to action; the mental instrument, the action, and the actor are the threefold aggregate-base of action.

In Chapter IV, verse 33, it is said, sarvaṁ karma akhilaṁ pārtha jñāne parisamāpyate (*All actions, Oh Pārtha! have their culmination in wisdom*). *How can Kṛṣṇa now say that knowledge is an incentive to action?*

Here we have to consider the frame of reference to which the present verse belongs. In Chapter IV Kṛṣṇa was employing an ascending, dialectic to raise Arjuna's mind from the dismay caused by, gross action to a pure state of identification with the mind of the Absolute, as it were. In the present chapter Kṛṣṇa is employing a descending dialectic. Arjuna is once again brought down to touch the harsh world of transactional reality. This does not contradict or compromise the position of a truly wise man.

What is the difference between karmacodanā (*incentive to action*) *and* karma-saṁgraha (*aggregate-base of action*)?

Knowledge, the knowable, and the knower are described here as the incentive for action. Some commentators interpret *jñāna* (knowledge) as the instrument of knowledge. This is not correct because *karaṇa* (instrument of knowledge) is listed with the aggregate-base of action. However, knowledge should be taken here as ensembles of ideas that come constantly to one's mind as memories of the past and allied possibilities of the future. An engineer has in his mind a plan of a bridge, road, or building before he starts his construction work. Even the pursuit of knowledge is a big incentive for action. The secret of the shimmering planets of the heavens is an invitation to scientists to work hard and make ingenious devices, like the Explorer, which are fired into outer space to orbit Mars or Venus. Man wants to know anything which is knowable. *Parijñātā* is to be taken as one who is satisfied only when he or she makes a thorough search of whatever is to be known. Hence *parijñātā* stands for a quality of the knower, like curiosity or the irrepressible desire to know. Thus, the transactional knower is a potential actor. Even though *codanā* means mandatory, in the present context it is to be understood as that which induces.

After considering the primary cause of action, the instrumentality of its execution is shown as the bona fide factor which is an aggregate of the person who deliberates action by willing it, the *kartā*, the employment of his or her mind, intellect, memory, and ego, *karaṇa*, and the inevitable consequence of performance, which is action (*karma*). The first set visualizes action and the second set executes it. Between the transactional knower and the doer most of us live our lives.

Are not knowledge, the knower, and the doer basically the Self?

There is a difference between the ground of truth and its mistaken identity.

What do you mean by mistaken identity?

Without the self-luminous consciousness of the Self nothing is known, but when its light undergoes modification, due to the intercepting mind born of nature, the same knowledge and sense of agency, knower and actor, become modulated and typified. Kṛṣṇa says:

Even knowledge, action, and actor are said, according to modality-difference, by way of their enumeration according to the modalities, to be of three kinds; hear you of them as they are actually.

That by which the one unexpended Being is seen in all beings, undivided in the divided – know that knowledge to be pure (sāttvic).

The knowledge which sees a multiplicity of beings as distinct in the different kinds, because of separateness – know that knowledge to be affectively-pragmatic (rājasic).

But that which clings to one single effect as if it were the whole, without reason, without meaning, based on any principle, and insignificant – that is called the inert-dark (tāmasic).

Is there any knowledge that is absolutely unconditioned?

When knowledge is free of any conditioning, it is the Self. When it is reflected by the mind, it becomes conditional to the state of mind. The mind necessarily is of the three modalities.

Isn't the Absolute beyond the triple modalities? Kṛṣṇa is seeing the one unexpended Being in all beings, so it looks like his knowledge is conditioned by sattva.

We have already seen that the Absolute has a pure, unmanifested state, and a lower, manifested state. In the manifested state, it becomes inclusive of the modalities. The state of *sattva* is pure and clear. Hence, sāttvic knowledge is the closest approximation to the knowledge of the Absolute.

In our transactional world everything is classified, and we treat individual objects as distinctly separate from each other. Should we say that our transactional knowledge is entirely rājasic?

The very basis of classification is a unitive notion. Even when a botanist classifies plant life and recognizes individual plants, he is conscious of the biological unity of the entire vegetative world. Thus, analytic notions as well as synthetic notions are operating with integral harmony. Here the rājasic colouration is very advantageous in understanding the complex world of name and form. In scientific understanding, *sattva* is ruling *rajas*.

When does conditional knowledge become detrimental to happiness?

When one clings to a single effect as if it were the whole.

Isn't wholehearted devotion to a single interest recommended as a virtue, even being looked upon as a state of yoga?

What is extolled as a virtue is the unitive understanding of the Absolute as an invariable reality, even though there is seeming change. One-pointedness, which is recognized as *yoga*, comes only when the knower and the known become identified as one. Such a state cannot be taken for tāmasic indulgence. The definition of *tamas* given in verse 22 leaves no room for any misunderstanding.

Can you give me an example of pure tamas?

When a person is under the spell of any mind-blowing drug and becomes apprehensive about its effect, yet cannot lift his mind out of the situation, he is in a state of *tamas.*

What about a religious or social fanatic who is exaggerating a part as if it were the whole?

That is a case where tāmasic conditioning is infused with rājasic passion. We get a clear picture of the effect of *sattva, rajas,* and *tamas* in action in verses 23 through 25:

> An action which is obligatory, performed without attachment, without affection or disregard, by one not benefit-motivated – that is called pure (sāttvic).
>
> But that action done with great strain, by one desire-prompted, or possessed of egoism, is called affective-passionate (rājasic).
>
> The action undertaken from confusion (of values), disregarding consequences, loss or injury, and human limitations – that is called dark (tāmasic).

Isn't obligatory action a result of one's false identification with the body? How can a realized person recognize anything as obligatory?

The bodily state is not an individual creation. Although there is an implied ignorance in recognizing the formal and nominal modalities of things, that ignorance is part and parcel of a universal nescience. Through realization one sees the universal Being in all as unexpended. At the same time, one recognizes the empirical nature of the flux, in which one's individual consciousness has manifested, as being centralized around an I-consciousness that is giving orientation to all functions of the mind. Because of this contingency, the individual recognizes the transactional verity of the world to which embodied beings belong. It is this recognition that makes certain actions obligatory to any embodied being. In this respect, obligation does not necessarily imply any social compulsion, as the term might otherwise convey. The evaluation of action should go hand in hand with the evaluation of the actor. The three kinds of actors are given in verses 26, 27, and 28:

> The actor, free from attachment, who avoids references to himself in the first person, endowed with firmness and zeal, unmoved by success or failure, is called pure (sāttvic).

> The actor, passionate, prompted by desire for benefits, greedy, violent-natured, maladjusted, with moods of exaltation and depression, is called affective-passionate (rājasic).
>
> The actor who is a misfit, crude, stubborn, deceitful, malicious, lazy, despondent, and procrastinating, is called dark (tāmasic).

When we apply the above-mentioned definitions of the three categories of actors to the case of Arjuna as we saw him in the first chapter, we cannot place him under any of these classifications.

It is true that Arjuna was not free of his ego-sense in the first chapter, but he did show evidence of being firm in his resolve to not do an action which he did not understand. Success and failure did not mean anything to him. These are given here as elements of *sattva.* Although he was not prompted by desire and could not be described as greedy, violent-natured, or maladjusted, he was definitely in a mood of depression, which is given in verse 27 as being indicative of *rajas.* It is agreed that he was not crude, deceitful, malicious, or lazy, but he was certainly despondent and procrastinating, which are signs of *tamas.* Thus there was a mixed influence of all three *guṇa*s in him.

Does the obligatory quality of Arjuna's action arise from the fact that he is a kṣatriya?

Both the obligatory nature of his action and his status as a kṣatriya arise from his natural placement in the order of things and the contiguity of events that have gone into the formation of his life. It is a consistency in character that decides a psychological type such as a kṣatriya. The action that is recommended to Arjuna in the Bhagavadgītā does not violate the characteristic function of a warrior. However, the Gītā binds action to Arjuna as a spontaneous expression of a contemplative in a special placement. A resolve for war implies a firmness that can be right or wrong. Arjuna belongs to a war situation. Hence, the dynamics of action are described next, in verses 33 through 35:

> The firmness by which the activities of mind, vital functions, and the senses, Oh Pārtha! are kept from deflecting (from the true path) by *yoga*, is pure (sāttvic).
>
> But the firmness by which one holds fast, Oh Arjuna! to duty, and pleasures, and wealth, desirous of the result of each, when the occasion presents itself – that firmness, Oh Pārtha! is affective-passionate (rājasic).
>
> That by which a stupid man does not give up sleep, fear, grief, despondency, and wantonness – that firmness, Oh Pārtha! is dark (tāmasic).

Why is firmness called the dynamics of action?

Every action implies an attempt to actualize an envisioned value. In verse 14, five factors were given for the accomplishment of any action. Two of these were the actor and the various mental instruments. There is a basis of action, indicated in the same verse as *adhiṣṭhāna*, which is to be understood both as the psycho-sociological formation of the individual and his placement in a particular context in which action becomes either imperative or optional. It is the individual's recognition of the impelling need for action that initiates action in him. In every deliberated action, the mind, organs of perception, and organs of action are all to be harmonized to function as one single force until the action is completed. The purposive inner cohesion which attunes the mind senses, and action to the performance of a singled-out motivational endeavour is described here as firmness. That is why it is called the dynamics of action.

Is Arjuna's firmness sāttvic *or* rājasic?

Kṛṣṇa is not telling Arjuna what he is, he is only giving a symptomatic description of firmness that is evidenced in the actions of people of different modalities. The firmness indicated in verse 33 is to be understood in the context of *yoga*. A contemplative has his mind and senses under control and does not allow them to deflect from the path of realization. In realization there is a here and now aspect and also the achievement of an eternal present. The vision of the eternal present comes from the admission of knowledge into the infinitude of the Self. The actualization of such an experience has reference to what is going on in the here and now. The firmness of the actor's attitude should be understood both in the light of his envisioning as well as his performing.

In Chapter II, verse 31, Kṛṣṇa specifically points out that it is Arjuna's svadharma *to fight. He does not conceal the fact that he is classifying Arjuna as a kṣatriya, as he explicitly states this in verse 32 of the same chapter. Further, in verse 35 of Chapter III, Kṛṣṇa says:*

> Better is activity rightly conforming to one's own nature though lacking in superior quality than activity foreign to one's own nature although it may be well done (otherwise). (Even) death by the performance of what fits one properly has merit. Activity foreign to oneself is fraught with danger.

From this it is clear that Kṛṣṇa attaches the highest importance to the performance of dharma. *However, in the above-cited verses,* dharma *is relegated to the category of the rājasic modality. Does this mean that Kṛṣṇa considers Arjuna only as a rājasic person?*

Much water has flowed over the dam between Chapter III and Chapter

XVIII. Arjuna is now fully instructed in all aspects of *yoga*, and there is no reason why one should believe that he has not become a well-disciplined contemplative. The incentive for Kr̥ṣṇa to instruct Arjuna arose from the fact that Arjuna asked for the highest goal of life rather than victory in war. Although his princely birth and outward conformity to a mode of life can be easily categorized as that of a kṣatriya, his contemplative qualities far outweigh the characteristics of a rājasic person. A king is looked upon as a "defender of the faith". From this it follows that he is duty-bound. At the close of this chapter Arjuna is shown as being prepared to perform his duty. Nataraja Guru says of this in his commentary:

> Whether Arjuna, as a person admitted to the order of those who possess high or divine endowments, when he finally consents to obey Kr̥ṣṇa in verse 73 of this chapter, does so in conformity with what verse 33 implies or with the implications of verse 34, or perhaps with *both*, is left an open question.

The nature of an action can be judged from its motivational cause and also from the kind of satisfaction that ensues from it. Kr̥ṣṇa now presents the three kinds of happiness that accompany action:

> that happiness which is like gall at first, ambrosial at the end, born of lucid self-understanding, is called pure (sāttvic);
>
> that happiness arising out of contact of the senses with objects, at first like ambrosia, at the end like gall, is called affective-passionate (rājasic);
>
> that happiness which at first and in after-effects is self-confounding, arising from sleep, lassitude, and listlessness, is called dark (tāmasic).

What is the kind of satisfaction that Arjuna seeks?

In verse 7 of Chapter II, when Arjuna asked Kr̥ṣṇa about his discipleship, his intention was to purge his mind of the evil of a disposition which confounded his mind in regard to what was right for him to do. He wanted to learn from Kr̥ṣṇa what was definitely meritorious. Further, he took refuge in Kr̥ṣṇa to be disciplined. The happiness that ensues from *yoga* is given in verse 23 of Chapter VI as "disaffiliation from the context of suffering". In fact, this is exactly what Arjuna is seeking.

When Kr̥ṣṇa suggested to Arjuna that he act in conformity with his *svadharma*, it appeared to Arjuna as a bitter commandment. That is why he complained in verses 1 and 2 of Chapter III that Kr̥ṣṇa was only confusing his reason, which was already confounded, by enjoining him to a ghastly action. However, in the present chapter he is once again taking a resolve to act out his role, perceiving that the joy of a warrior need not necessarily be opposed to the happiness of a contemplative.

The discernment of psychological types based on the interplay of moods is given in verses 41 through 49. Verse 40 introduces this important section:

> There is no entity either on earth or in heaven, among the Vedic divinities, that could be free from these three modalities born from nature.

Why does Kṛṣṇa make such a sweeping remark? It is hard to believe that there is no entity at all, either in earth or in heaven, which could be free from the triple modalities of nature. After all, in Chapter XIV Kṛṣṇa spoke of that which lies beyond the modalities and of transcending them.

We have already shown that the structural requirement of this chapter is to bring Arjuna once again to the world of horizontal facts. Apart from recapitulating the entire discussion of the first seventeen chapters, Chapter XVIII also serves as a perfect counterpart of the first chapter. The problem raised by Arjuna in Chapter I, verses 40 through 45, should be carefully re-read in order to understand the implications of what Kṛṣṇa says here in verses 40 through 49. In Arjuna's presentation of *dharma*, he treats it as a closed hereditary nature of man, which is vocationally oriented with a sociological exclusiveness. It has religious sanctions. Arjuna's concept of *kula-dharma* is clannish, of *jāti-dharma* is tribalistic, and of *varṇa* is racial. Thus he was maintaining a prejudice that was of the worst form of caste-ism. Śrī Kṛṣṇa did not give any attention to Arjuna's caste apprehensions, except by making a passing reference (Chap. IV, v. 13) to the origin of *varṇa* as his instrumentality. The triad of the Absolute (*sat-cit-ānanda*) and the triad of nature (*sattva*, *rajas* and *tamas*) are complementary aspects of the Absolute, referring respectively to its positive and negative aspects. The former unifies and the latter differentiates. Although action is a universal function, the role played by each actor is different. Thus, the uniqueness of the actor looms large when one enters into the field of action. If *Brahman* is the basis of all knowledge, *dharma* is the basis of all action.

In man, both these aspects come together from opposite sides. He belongs at once to earth and to heaven. From the side of earth he has his gross body, and from the side of heaven his animating intelligence. When these two aspects are bracketed, they come under the category of the manifested aspect of the Absolute. Kṛṣṇa wants Arjuna to know that within the range of that manifestation there is no entity which is free of the influence of the three *guṇas*. He makes specific reference to that which belongs to earth (*pṛthivyam*) and to the *devas* of heaven (*divi*). The word *pṛthivī* is derived from *prathate*, which means "that which is flat". This refers to the horizontality of life, the mundaneness of the world of gross necessity. The words *dyov* (heaven) and *deva* (shining one) are taken from the root *div*, which means light. This represents our vertical nature. The uniqueness or characteristic differentiation of a person is to be understood both vertically and horizontally.

Kr̥ṣṇa is speaking to Arjuna on the battlefield, where arrows are flying and a fierce battle is raging. Arjuna's main question at the beginning of the Gītā was to know what right action he should do. Hence, it is most appropriate that the Gītā should close with its focus on *satkarma* (good or true action).

Since each person is unique, what justification is there for making a fourfold division?

Historically, man is prone to adhere to stratified classes. Such classification has both a rational and an irrational basis. When the stress is on the irrational the result is bigotry and fanaticism, which push people to the absurdity of mutual exclusion or apartheid. The remedy to this social ill is to turn one's attention to the rational basis. The fourfold division does not imply any social stratification. It is only one way of looking at the general typology to which one belongs. For instance, C.G. Jung, in his study of types, makes a broad division of people into introverts and extroverts. It is not difficult to understand that some people are active by temperament while others tend to brood and are withdrawn. Jung further classifies the extroverts into extrovert–extroverts and extrovert–introverts. This is again not difficult to understand. There are people who live as if they have no inner life at all, constantly needing to relate themselves with others. The only meaning in their lives is self-expression. This is an extreme case of double extroversion. The more moderate ones are the extrovert–introverts. In the same way we can understand the divisions of introvert–introvert and introvert–extrovert. The four *varṇa*s spoken of in the Gītā are recognized by Plato as the philosopher, the soldier, the man of affairs, and the servant. In a modern society we have people belonging to holy orders, military service, business, and wage-earning groups.

Then how did a psychological type become the basis of the exclusive caste system in India?

India had a culture and tradition of its own before the advent of the Aryans. The people of those days were generally of a quiet, contemplative nature when compared to the aggressive immigrants. When there are clashes between two groups of people there always comes the closing in of ranks. Thus the Aryan immigrants and the natives became two stratified groups. The ritual that was symbolic of Aryan unity was Agnihotra (burnt sacrifice) and therefore priestcraft was central to them. Also in group clashes there are always some defectors from one side to the other. The natives who were admitted into the camp of the Aryans were those who could help them with their defence, supplies, and menial services. People who go into such services seek the satisfaction that is natural to their temperament. Thus the psychological types first became vocational groups, and then the vocational groups stratified into a hierarchy of classes. This was further solidified by the old world custom of clothing everything in religious sanctions. Manu even described these fourfold classes as a divine creation in the *Manusmṛti*:

> But in order to protect this universe He the most resplendent one, assigned separate (duties and) occupations to those who sprang from the arms, thighs and feet.
>
> To brāhmins He assigned teaching and studying (of the Veda), sacrificing for their own benefit and for others, giving and accepting (of alms).
>
> The kṣatriya He commanded to protect the people, to bestow gifts, to offer sacrifices, to study (the Veda) and to abstain from attaching himself to sensual pleasures.
>
> The vaiśya to tend cattle, to bestow gifts, to study (the Veda), to trade, to lend money and to cultivate land.
>
> One occupation only the Lord prescribed to the śūdra, to serve meekly even these (other) three castes.[6]

The absurd mixing of the psychological type with sociological classification became the greatest scourge of Indian culture. In one way or another similar divisions and class superiority are practised shamelessly throughout the world. A man should be understood by what he does in conformity with his inner temperament rather than by birth or social pedigree.

Next Kṛṣṇa gives his delineation of the four psychological types in verses 41 through 45:

> Of brāhmins, kṣatriyas, vaiśyas, and śūdras, Oh Conqueror of the Foe! vocations are separately assigned in conformity with the modalities arising from their own nature.
>
> Calmness, self-restraint, austerity, purity, forgiveness, and straightforwardness, pure wisdom, applied wisdom, belief: these are the items of activity of the brāhmin, born of his own nature.
>
> Prowess, brightness, firmness, skill, and also never-absconding, generosity, and dignity of mien, refer to the pattern of activity of the kṣatriya, born of his own nature.
>
> Ploughing, tending cattle, and trade are the items of vocation of the vaiśya, born of his own nature; work of the nature of menial service is likewise born of the śūdra's own nature.

---

[6] *The Laws of Manu*, tr. G. Buhler, S.B.E., Oxford, 1886, I.87-91.

Devoted each to his own occupation, man reaches perfection (in practical *yoga*); how, devoted to his own occupation, he attains such perfection – that do hear.

If varṇa *is not caste, why does* Manusmṛti *speak of brāhmins, kṣatriyas, vaiśyas, and śūdras as separate classes?*

A *smṛti* does not have the canonical validity of a *śruti. Manusmṛti* is especially responsible for many iniquities and atrocities that were practised by the Indian people in the name of *varṇa.* For instance, in Chapter VIII of the *Manusmṛti* it says:

> A brāhmin may confidently seize the goods of (his) śūdra (slave) for that (slave) can have no property, his master may take his possessions.[7]

And again in Chapter X it says:

> No collection of wealth must be made by a śūdra, even though he is able (to do it): for a śūdra who has acquired wealth gives pain to brahmins.[8]

Many Indian scholars even pretend that there are no such references in the sacred books of the Hindus. To correct this iniquity Narayana Guru wrote a critique of caste thousands of years later:

A Critique of Caste

(*Jāti-Mīmāṁsā*)

I

Man's humanity marks out the human kind
Even as bovinity proclaims a cow.
Brahminhood and such are not thus-wise;
None do see this truth, alas!

II

One of kind, one of faith, and one in God is man;
Of one womb, of one form; difference herein none.

III

Within a species, is it not, that offspring truly breed?
The community of man thus viewed, to a single caste belongs.

---

[7] *The Laws of Manu*, Ch. VIII.

[8] Ibid., Ch. X.

IV

Of the human species is even a brahmin born, as is the Pariah too,
Where is difference then in caste as between man and man?

V

In bygone days of a Pariah woman the great sage Parāśara was born,
As even he of Vedic-aphorism fame of a virgin of the fisher-folk.[9]

If the four varṇas *are an extension of the three* guṇas, *how do they correspond to them? When the Gītā could have limited it to three varṇas, corresponding to three guṇas, why are there four?*

Actually we should think of five psychological types rather than four. The true counterpart of the śūdra is not the brāhmin, it is the *saṁnyāsin*. A true *saṁnyāsin* transcends the influence of all three *guṇas*. In that sense he is a *guṇātīta*. A careful look at the characteristics of the brāhmin and the kṣatriya given in verses 42 and 43 will reveal to us that there is not an exact correspondence between the nature-modalities and the colourations of the psyche. We can say that the qualities of a brāhmin, such as calmness, self-restraint, and the like, are evidently of a sāttvic nature. But he also engages in activities (*pravṛtti*). Action is born of *rajas*. The *saṁnyāsin*, on the other hand, has the same qualities as the brāhmin, the only difference being that he has no incentive to act. So we can say that in a brāhmin's life, *sattva* dominates *rajas*.

In verse 43, the kṣatriya is described as having prowess, firmness, and skill, and as one who does not abscond from his position. These qualities are easily recognizable as born of *rajas*, but qualities like brightness, generosity, and love for God are evidently sāttvic. So we can say that in a kṣatriya, *sattva* is counterbalanced by *rajas*. The vaiśya's main vocation is given in verse 44 as farming, trade, and commerce. In a life of that kind there is an incentive to become greedy and to want to hoard, as can be seen in the bourgeois attitude of those who are engaged in high-level business. In a vaiśya's case, *rajas* rules his passions and *sattva* has only a weak voice that comes to him as a corrective prick to his conscience.

The śudra's peculiarity, as given in this verse, is his *fait accompli* to live in servility. This is definitely all *tamas*. However, as such a person is constantly engaged in action, he cannot be said to be in a state of total inertia. In order to perform whatever service he is rendering, he has to be active. So in his case it is *tamas* using *rajas* as a tool. From the classification it is evident

[9] Nataraja Guru (tr.), 2019, *An Anthology of the Poems of Narayana Guru*, p. 77, Varkala: Narayana Gurukula.

that the first two, the brahmin and the kṣatriya, have a contemplative disposition, while the other two have no such inclination.

In verse 45 there is a definite injunction given to each person to stick to his occupational category.

That is a misreading of this verse. Most people think that Arjuna is apt to fight because he is a kṣatriya, but the fact is that he is called a kṣatriya because he fights. Although Droṇa was born of a brāhmin and was referred to as *dvijottama*, the best among brāhmins, by Duryodhana in Chapter I, verse 7, in the *Mahābhārata* he was never given the reverence due to a real brāhmin, such as Vasiṣṭha. Parāśara, born of a pariah woman, Vyāsa, born of a fisherwoman, and Vāśvamitra, who was a king in his youthful days, are all venerated as the best of brāhmins. From this it is evident that it is not one's birth that decides one's vocation. It is one's temperament and attitude which open up a value-vision. When one's vocation provides for progressive advancement toward one's goal of perfection, that is to be understood as one's *svadharma.* It is not the occupation that matters, but how one consecrates it as his own personal dedication to the Absolute. Kṛṣṇa says:

> He from whom all existences come forth, and by whom all this is pervaded – by offering worship to Him with his own occupation, man wins perfection.
>
> Better is one's own duty, though inferior, than the duty of another well-performed. One doing the duty determined by his own nature incurs no sin.

Why should we bring in the idea of the all-pervading God in such a simple matter as choosing one's vocation?

The situation of the Gītā teaching is a complex one. An earnest spiritual seeker offers himself to be disciplined by a wisdom-teacher. The teacher, prior to being acclaimed as a Guru, was only a comrade and relative of the seeker. Afterwards, the seeker realizes as a disciple that his Guru is none other than the Supreme God. Even after realizing that God is standing by him as a faithful servant, a charioteer, the disciple has a serious role to play outside the wisdom-context as part of his social commitment. This commitment requires him to fight in the battlefield and to kill his own teachers and intimate relatives. At the beginning of the Gītā this man speaks like a conscientious objector to war. The entire teaching of the Gītā is oriented toward accomplishing two ends. One is to make this man fight. The other is to help him to actualize the highest good in his life, God-realization. Needless to say, his vocation comes in the way of his concept of the contemplative. So, the reference to vocation here is not a mere matter of guidance. It is intrinsically connected with this man's highest realization. That is why Kṛṣṇa is relating the vocation of Arjuna to the very Source of all manifestation.

Each person's relationship with the Absolute is analogous to the part played by each organ of the body. The brain is fulfilling a very important function in discerning truth. Although the feet are incapable of performing such a complex function, that does not minimize their importance. They serve the body in their own unique way. Similarly, each person settles into a certain pattern of self-expression that is most natural to them. In the *Mahābhārata* there is the story of an anchorite, a housewife, and a butcher. In his spiritual pride the anchorite thought that his path was superior to others' for obtaining realization, but he realized that he was sorely mistaken. A simple housewife and a butcher proved to have unsurpassed wisdom in just being true to their own way of life, which enabled them to establish perfect bipolarity with the Absolute.

The Absolute is not a person or a thing. It is well expressed in verse 46 as "He from whom all existences come forth, and by which all this is pervaded". The third person singular, "He", used here is to be understood as a poetic device. In bipolar relationship, man seeks a personified counterpart so that he as the seeker can get into a relationship which has the warmth of sentiments. There is no harm in referring to the Absolute as "He" or "She".

God-realization is not the exclusive privilege of any chosen people. The eskimo in the Arctic regions and the Negro of tropical Africa have as much need and ability to realize God as a Protestant American or someone from Israel or Indochina. The Gītā does not want to accept the theory of God's chosen people. There are as many ways of realizing God as there are people. The only condition is to establish an absolute bipolarity which puts the individual at ease in working out his or her course of life in a meaningful way.

How can a well-performed duty be inferior to one's own ill-performed duty?

Part of the misunderstanding of verse 47 comes from the limitations of the English translation, into which it is difficult to bring words like *śreyān*, *svadharma*, *paradharma*, *svabhāvaniyatam*, and *kilbiṣam*. The intention of the verse is not to restrict a person from doing what they want to do. Unfortunately, such a reading was made of its meaning by *paṇḍit*s in India, either for reasons of prejudice or vested interest. The main point to notice here is the differences between *svadharma* and *paradharma*. Duty is a very narrow connotation of *dharma*. Those intrinsic qualities of a person which are unique, making them what they are, are *svadharma*. *Paradharma* refers to the qualities that do not belong to that person. Nataraja Guru, in his commentary on this verse, cites the examples of a fish out of water, a sheep in wolf's clothing, a jackdaw in peacock's feathers, painting the lily, and making a gift of stolen goods as examples for understanding *paradharma*. The situation which the Gītā wants to correct is any departure or deviation from one's own Self that can severely hamper the integrity of the personality. The promulgators of the caste system in India always tried to bind a son to the trade of his father, and so equal opportunity to acquire training in the field of one's preference was discouraged. The present verse was always misquoted to make vocational opportunities rigid and exclusive. If one correctly understands what *svadharma* and *paradharma* are, such a mistake can be easily avoided. The true spirit of this verse may be better appreciated if it is read in the light of verses 5 and 6 of Chapter XVII, which allude to egoistic people who have no respect for the harmony of the laws that govern the world as a whole and the individual's personality.

The term *svabhāvaniyatam* means the potential, the urge, the ability, and the limit that are naturally inherent in a person. When one's action or self-expression is in perfect conformity with these factors, we can say that their actions are *svabhāvaniyatam*. As such a natural function is sure to bring coherence and integrity to one's personality, that person is sure to have a very high sense of satisfaction. This is what the Gītā wants to teach, not any imposition or limiting of a person's free choice of vocation.

The state of harmony and wholesomeness which one gains through one's best expression is referred to here as *śreyān*, which means "most satisfactorily befitting". The word *kilbiṣam* is compounded of *kelayati* (indulging, as in a sport) and *viṣayeṣvati* (in objects of interest). It is translated in verse 47 as "sin". The sin spoken of here has not even the remotest resemblance to the Christian concept. Its significance is one of epistemological import. A true artist, when he gives himself wholeheartedly to his performance, experiences a oneness which is neither inside nor outside. Like that, in unitive action the purpose of acting ceases to be an extraneous goal in the future, which separates a person from their happiness. Instead, happiness prevails all through. The "sin" spoken of here is only a potential frustration or regret that is likely to be produced by a certain course of action.

What is most important in verses 46 and 47 is to understand the meaning of one's vocation in one's own contemplative life. Here, in the last chapter of the Gītā, Kṛṣṇa is effecting a fusion of the two halves of Arjuna's personality. One half is enmeshed in contemplative discipline, while the other half is to be attuned to a programme of rigorous action belonging to a warrior who is placed in a war situation. A secret of this fusion was already suggested by Kṛṣṇa when he advised Arjuna to meditate on him and also fight, in verse 7, Chapter VIII.

The relevancy of action belongs to one's bodily state. The embodied being is a creation of nature. Everything in nature is guided by the three *guṇas*, so it is unlikely that there will be any action which is totally free of defects. In other words, there is no course of action which can be entirely pleasure-giving. The desire to avoid a course of action because of the strain and hardship it might cause the doer has already been indicated as a sign of the overpowering influence of *rajas* and *tamas*. To help a person to approximate their action to the requirements of *sattva*, verse 48 is given:

> Duty naturally belonging to one by birth, Oh Son of Kuntī! though accompanied by defects, ought not to be abandoned; all undertakings are enveloped with defects, as fire by smoke.

Isn't this verse trying to perpetuate vocation-oriented caste?

The insistence here is not on any hereditary vocation belonging to the family, but on what comes naturally to a person. This is to be read in the light of Chapter XIII, verses 7 through 11, which gives the model of a wise man. These verses reflect an attitude of general neutrality toward happenings, and of devotion to the Absolute. In verse 39 of Chapter III, *karma* is described as the eternal enemy of the wise. It comes in the form of desire. That desire is compared to the fire that burns without satiation, and as the smoke that envelops wisdom.

What is translated here as "duty belonging to one by birth" is *sahajam-karma* in the original Sanskrit. *Sahajam* literally means congenital. Our potentials are genetic. There is scope for enlarging and developing these potentials into skills with education and training. However, development is also restricted by these same inherent genetic factors. *Karma* is only an outward expression of what is potential. The genetic theory of the Gītā is not mechanistic. Apart from the physiologic or biologic structuring of the genes, which come from a family tree, the Gītā also takes into account the continuation of a personality trait from a previous life. The concept of previous lives is also quite different from the popular belief of a linear continuation of an ego-unit from one embodied life to another. As seen here, death marks the return of the essence of a person into *Īśvara*, the creative energy of perpetual becoming. Birth marks the re-emergence of that essence as restructured by the cosmic creative intelligence. As a result of this, we may find a genius born to parents of mediocre ability, or a dull-headed offspring to a genius. The social set-up of the environment in which any person is born does not indicate their natural or inherent abilities or aptitudes. Thus we can say with confidence that this verse does not support the claims of the class proponents at all.

You have mentioned the saṁnyāsin *as the counterpart of the śūdra. To what pattern of life does he conform?*

A *saṁnyāsin* is called *varṇātīta* (one whose psyche is freed of all colourations), and *guṇātīta* (one who has successfully transcended all three modalities of nature). Kṛṣṇa describes him in verses 49 through 55 as follows:

> He whose reason is unattached in all situations, whose Self has been won over, from whom desire has gone, by renunciation (*saṁnyāsa*) reaches the supreme perfection of transcending action.
>
> How he who has ascended to perfection thereby obtains the Absolute, that supreme consummation of wisdom – that do you learn from Me, Oh Son of Kuntī! in brief.
>
> Endowed with pure reason, restraining the Self with firmness, detaching oneself from sound and other sense-objects, and casting out liking and disliking,
>
> dwelling in solitude, frugal in diet, controlling speech, body, and mind, ever in meditative contemplation, resorting to dispassion,
>
> relinquishing egoism, power, arrogance, desire, anger, and possessiveness, free from ownership, and tranquil – he is worthy of becoming the Absolute.
>
> Becoming the Absolute, blissfully serene in the Self, he neither despairs nor hankers; equal-minded toward all beings, he attains a devotion to Me supreme in character.
>
> Through devotion he comes to know Me, how far comprehensible I am and who, in accord with first principles; then, having known Me philosophically, he immediately enters into Me.

Then isn't saṁnyāsa *a total renunciation of action after all? Verse 49 seems to indicate this as* naiṣkarmya siddhi.

Naiṣkarmya siddhi is not the same as inaction, which is called *akarma*. *Akarma* indicates only omission of action due to laziness or incapacity. There is no need to glorify inaction, but the attainment of *naiṣkarmya* is given a very high place in this verse. *Karma* originates from incipient memories. When incipient memories are burned in the fire of wisdom, the relevancy of action for the fulfilment of any desire does not occur at all. Only when a person attains that state can we say that they have achieved *naiṣkarmya*. The *saṁnyāsa* mentioned in verse 49 is not the deliberate giving up of action, but the natural cessation of the need to act that comes to a person who has nothing to push away in hatred and nothing to achieve for the gratification of desire.

How does one come to that state?

Three conditions are given in this verse: a reason that is unattached in situations, a Self that has been won over, and having desire gone.

What is asakta buddhi?

Ego is the link between *buddhi* (intellect) and the consolidated memory of the individual (*citta*) which is intimately connected with the incipient memories of the past. When the ego is employing reason, the identification of the ego and the intellect is so close that one fails to distinguish between the two. In such a state, the intellect becomes concerned with the promotion of one incipient memory after another. This is called *saṅga* or *sakti* (attachment). *Buddhi* is the true light of the Self. When it attains its freedom from bondage with ego and memory, it is called *asakta buddhi* (unattached intelligence). Mind is too feeble to know the Absolute. Only intellect can comprehend it. That is why Kr̥ṣṇa insists on freeing the intellect from the entanglements of the mind.

How does one become a jitātmā?

Kr̥ṣṇa describes this in verses 51 through 53.

Are these verses instructions for practice?

If you read these verses carefully, you can see that they are not items to perform, but are indications of an attitude of elimination, such as deciding "not this, not this" (*neti-neti*). It is a withdrawal of the self into the peace which is in one's Self. These verses give the characteristics of a *saṁnyāsin*.

Is it necessary to turn away from the beauty of nature and the sound of its music, to live as a recluse, frugal in diet, to become dear to God?

Kr̥ṣṇa is not instructing Arjuna to conform to the pattern of the *saṁnyāsin*, he is only describing the model. By comparing himself with that model, Arjuna can easily see that he is not of that type. The only requirement for being established in the Absolute is to have absolute devotion to the Supreme. Real devotion makes one blissfully serene in the Self. Thereafter one does not despair or hanker. He becomes equal-minded toward all beings.

If saṁnyāsa *is not an outward mode but an inner attitude of consistent sameness, can we not say that Arjuna has that quality and is therefore qualified for* naiṣkarmya siddhi?

Naiṣkarmya siddhi means total cessation of the prompting of incipient memories. That happens only when there are no latent urges. Even when one regulates his action with the conscious thought that he is acting only as an instrument, the incentive to act is there. The complete cessation of the incentive to act is the same as the highest state of liberation. A person in this state does not find himself carried away by any force of circumstance. In the case of Arjuna, even at this stage he does not feel free to not fight or to walk away from the battlefield. It is probably true that Arjuna is free of desires, but he has not yet come to the state which is described in verse 50 as the supreme consummation of wisdom (*niṣṭhā jñānasya yā parā*).

In the eleventh chapter Arjuna was said to have had a cosmic vision of the Lord. Could this not be taken as the supreme consummation of wisdom?

In verse 50, ascending to perfection is given as a condition for the supreme consummation of wisdom. The Absolute alone is perfect. Nobody attains perfection without becoming fully identified with the Absolute. There is no dispute that Arjuna had the psychic experience of an unusual vision of several awesome forms. All forms are constituted of limbs. Structured bodies are subject to evolution and change. If Arjuna saw only forms, that vision was of the lower realm of impressions. *Vidyā* and *avidyā* (conceptual knowledge of God and ignorance of God) come under the category of *māyā*. Thus, the highest consummation of wisdom cannot be a formal vision.

In the tenth chapter Kṛṣṇa himself describes to Arjuna how the Absolute has become all manifestations. In verse 41 he specifically states:

> Whatever entity is unique in perfected value, in grace or in radical strength understand that to have manifested itself from a (mere fractional) spark of My brilliance.

In the verse immediately following that one Kṛṣṇa questions Arjuna about the use of such pluralistic knowledge. The tenth chapter ends with Kṛṣṇa saying that the entire manifested world is a projection of a single fraction of the Absolute. To have a psychic experience of a fraction of a fraction does not give anyone the title of perfection.

Even if it is only a fraction of the Absolute which becomes manifest, the Absolute is absolute. Therefore the Absolute can be with form and without form.

When a person sees the stump of a tree in moonlight as a ghost, it is evident that the ghost has no substance. If it is argued that by a fragment of the tree the ghost came into existence, you are trying to establish the existence of two entities, that is, the tree and the ghost. When you see the ghost you have no idea of the tree. When you see the tree, there is not even the slightest trace of the ghost in it. Again, when you look at it from a distance, your timidity may suggest a ghost to your mind. If you want others to believe that what you experience is a confection of ghost and tree, that is far-fetched. Out there in the moonlight the tree alone is. The ghost is in your mind.

Perception is universally accepted as a valid testimony of knowledge: "Seeing is believing". Arjuna's vision was more than seeing. ...

It is undisputed that perception has a primary place among the forms of valid methodology. That does not assure us that one can measure the truth of anything with perception. You speak of the universal validity of perception.

Do you see "the universal" with an act of perception? You have already brought in inference. Perception has to be supported by reason, and reason ultimately rests on the axiomatic acceptance of imperceptible universals. Most of the universals which guide our reasoning come to us as a priori knowledge, as when a scientist is taking a stand to continue the search of his predecessor. He does not do this by experimentally reaching the validity of all the postulates put forward from the time of Democritus to de Broglie. He takes for granted the truth of what is said in the physics textbooks. This is the same as a religious person putting his faith in the authority of the scriptures. Kṛṣṇa alludes to this truth in verse 2 of Chapter IX, verse 4 of Chapter XIII, and verse 24 of Chapter XVI.

One can look at a building from a certain angle: that is perception. Then he presumes that the building has an interior and other sides: that is inference. But he does not know the architect of the building, nor what prompted him to design it, without asking a knowledgeable person. In this way, one can understand the physical world and its functioning with the aid of perception and inference. However, these methods are not helpful in understanding the Absolute, which is invisible and not limited by any forms.

What faculty is there in us with which we can comprehend the truth that transcends form, spatial extension, and temporal duration? The absolutists always speak of the Absolute as transcendental.

Nobody speaks here of knowing the Absolute. We are concerned only with knowing the truth of the world that is presented to our senses and mind. A well-disciplined and instructed mind is capable of recognizing the transient nature of the world that our senses present to us. One of the primary requisites for a seeker of truth is to have the power to discern the eternal from the transient. The transactional validity of perceptible things belongs to the world of cause and effect. In Chapter IX which is qualified as containing the crowning secret of the Gītā, Kṛṣṇa discloses to Arjuna that the Supreme cannot be known by knowing any of the constituent parts of the world. In verses 4 and 5 of that chapter, Kṛṣṇa says:

> By Me all this world is pervaded, My form unmanifested; all beings have existence in Me and I do not have existence in them.
>
> And further, beings do not exist in Me; behold My status as a divine mystery; further, Myself remaining that urge behind beings, I bear them but do dot exist in them either.

The key to resolving paradoxes in the path of knowledge is not discursive reasoning, but wisdom engendered by the deep love that one experiences in one's bipolarity with the Absolute. This was already indicated in verse 55. Perfecting oneself through love is further elaborated from verse 56 to 63:

> Although still continuing to do all actions in life, treating Me as his refuge, by My grace he obtains the everlasting undiminishing status.
>
> Mentally renouncing all actions into Me, regarding Me as the Supreme, resorting to unitive understanding, having Me wholly filling your relational consciousness,
>
> (thus with) consciousness filled with Me, you will overcome all obstacles by My grace, but if, from egoism, you will not listen, you shall come to ruin.
>
> If, resorting to egoism, you think, "I will not fight", absurd is this, your resolution. Nature will compel you.
>
> That which, through confusion, you do not like to do, Oh Son of Kuntī! – you shall do that very thing, helplessly, bound by your own nature-born action.
>
> The Lord dwells in the heart-region of all beings, Oh Arjuna! causing all beings to revolve through the principle of appearance (*māyā*), as if mounted on a machine.
>
> Seek refuge in Him alone in all ways, Oh Bhārata! by His grace you shall obtain the peaceful abode, supreme, everlasting.
>
> Thus has wisdom more secret than all that is secret been declared to you by Me; critically scrutinizing all, omitting nothing, do as you like.

How does love substitute for reasoning?

In Bergson's *Introduction to Metaphysics*, he speaks of knowing a thing from outside by going around it and examining it from a series of viewpoints, and also knowing a thing by entering into it and being it. The former kind of knowledge is relativistic, the latter absolutist. Love is like an alchemy. The intimacy of love corrodes the dividing line between Self and non-Self. Like a river flowing into an ocean and merging with it, the limit of consciousness of the finite Self becomes absorbed into the limitless expanse of universal appreciation. In Patañjali's *Yogasūtra, saṁyama* is suggested as a method to effect the perfection of spiritual absorption. *Saṁyama* is the bringing together of concentration, the uninterrupted flow of consciousness, and spiritual absorption. The method suggested for this is to kindle interest in a value such as love, especially love for God (*īśvara praṇidhāna*) and to continue the flow of consciousness in the same direction by repeatedly going over the same theme of love until one becomes absorbed in it. A similar discipline is suggested by the Buddhists, combining *maitrī* (fellowship), *karuṇā* (compassion), and *mudita* (serene cheerfulness). Sometimes the place of serene cheerfulness is given to *prajña* (right understanding).

A botanist examining a flower to derive detailed information about its calyx, petals, ovary, and mode of pollination is different from a lover, moved by its beauty, offering it as a precious token of love to his beloved. The kind of knowledge recommended here is not the punditry of a scholar but the intimations of immortality that grow between man and God. Although the devotion spoken of in verse 55 as the instrument to know God is given only as *bhakti*, we should qualify it with the word *parām*, with which verse 54 closes. *Parā-bhakti* is absolute devotion. It is also known as *ekāntika bhakti* (one-pointed love).

Why does Kṛṣṇa speak like the angry Jehovah of the Old Testament in verse 59, right after very compassionately assuring Arjuna of his grace in verse 58?

Kṛṣṇa is not trying to exact from Arjuna any personal glorification of his supremacy as God. In verses 59 through 61 he is pointing out to Arjuna the imperativeness of action. Kant's categorical imperative, based on a priori reasoning, comes nearest to the idea of the demand that necessity makes. Kṛṣṇa categorizes necessity in verse 59 as nature (*prakṛti*) in verse 60 as Arjuna's own active nature (*svabhāvajena svena karmaṇā*) and in verse 61 as the Lord who dwells in the heart-region of all beings (*īśvaraḥ sarvabhūtānāṁ hṛddeśe tiṣṭhati*).

Does the Gītā recognize man's free will?

Man's personality is caught between his free will and the force of necessity. It would be fatal not to recognize one or the other. As early as verse 48 of Chapter II, Kṛṣṇa advised Arjuna to take a neutral stand between these two and to cultivate a sameness of vision.

In verse 1 of Chapter IX, Kṛṣṇa admits the egolessness of Arjuna. Why does he now think that Arjuna might become negative, asserting his ego?

Kṛṣṇa never admitted anywhere that Arjuna had become absolutely egoless.

He only recognized the latter's trust in him and his reciprocal love for Arjuna. Nataraja Guru mentions in his commentary that the reference to egoism in verses 58 and 59 has a special meaning as related to *yoga* on the one hand, and to the supreme force of absolute necessity in verse 61 on the other.

When Kṛṣṇa himself is the Lord, why does he speak of Īśvara *in the third person?*

The *Īśvara* spoken of in verse 61 refers to the Absolute as having all the possible implications of the categorical imperative. One should notice the difference in the wording between verse 58 and verse 62, which in essence are referring to the same kind of one-pointed devotion to the Absolute. The personal aspect of God or Guru in verse 58 indicates the stress is on intimate bipolar relationship, while the impersonal and universal control of an overall principle given in verse 62 puts the stress on the imperativeness of guarding one's self against erring in the domain of necessity.

That means that Arjuna has to give his implicit obedience to his Guru and to God.

The nature of Arjuna's free will is explicitly stated in verse 63. Kṛṣṇa is not asking for any obedience. He only expects Arjuna to give deserving attention to every word that transpires by way of teaching. Kṛṣṇa even asks Arjuna to be critical in scrutinizing his word. Finally, he says, "Do as you like". After stating the harshness of necessity, Kṛṣṇa imparts to Arjuna the final teaching of the Gītā, which was previously given in Chapter IX:

> Listen again to My supreme word, the most secret of all; because you are greatly beloved of Me, I will tell you what is for your good.
>
> Become one in mind with Me; be devoted to Me; sacrifice to Me; bow down to Me; you shall come to Me alone; I promise you, in truth, you are dear to Me.
>
> Abandoning all duties, come to Me, the One, for refuge; I shall absolve you from all sins; do not despair.

Why does Kṛṣṇa qualify his teaching as the supreme word and the most secret of all?

Me paramaṁ vacaḥ (my supreme word) is given in the singular. This corresponds to what St. John describes in the beginning of his Gospel as the Word of God, which is with God and is also identical with Him. The word that is listened to from the mouth of one's Master is called *śruti*. *Śruti* and *upaniṣad* are the same. The word *upaniṣad* can be interpreted in several ways. In one sense it means sitting at the feet of a great one and listening with devotion to the secret of the supreme word. In another sense it is receiving the light of the Absolute that will dispel in a flash the darkness of ignorance, accrued through a million lives. Again, it is the most secret of all teachings which only an initiate who has established a bipolarity of the highest order understands. All these meanings are relevant in this context.

In the *Bṛhadāraṇyaka Upaniṣad* it is said:

> Whoever thus knows "I am *Brahman*!" becomes this All; even the gods have not power to prevent his becoming thus, for he becomes their self (*ātman*).
>
> So whoever worships another divinity (than this Self), thinking "He is one and I another", he knows not. He is like a sacrificial animal for the gods.[10]

Verticalizing one's self-awareness is one of the greatest secrets of the Upaniṣads. The first step in it is to identify one's mind with an absolutist vision and attitude. In the *Chāndogya Upaniṣad* 3.18.1, it says, "One should reverence the mind as *Brāhman*."[11] When Kṛṣṇa says, "Become one in mind with Me", he is calling Arjuna's attention to the difference in their attitudes. Even though Kṛṣṇa and Arjuna were both placed in the same situation, Arjuna became filled with a great sense of guilt and was very agitated. Kṛṣṇa, on the other hand, stood there smiling with an even mind. These two minds are, respectively, one subjected to relativistic influence and the other free of all taints of relativism. Kṛṣṇa's mind has a transparency. He sees the past, the present, and the future all at once, and all happenings as phenomenal becoming. For Arjuna to gain the same state of mind, Kṛṣṇa asks him to be his *bhakta. Bhakti* is meditating on the true nature of one's own Self. Becoming Kṛṣṇa's *bhakta* means for Arjuna to accept him as his very Self and for him to bring his thoughts as close as possible to Kṛṣṇa's. There is imitation in adoration. To live a Christian life one should imitate Christ. To follow Kṛṣṇa one should be filled with Kṛṣṇa-consciousness. This is best achieved when one thinks that all one's doings are a sacrifice to consecrate oneself to the Absolute. Absolute bipolarity does not permit fickleness or distraction of any sort. When Jehovah says he is a jealous God and cannot tolerate his lover turning to anyone else, it may sound harsh and fanatical. Yet in bipolar relationship there has to be an absolute primacy given to one's counterpart. One cannot serve two masters at once. In verse 66 Kṛṣṇa even asks Arjuna to abandon all his duties so that he can take total refuge in the Absolute.

When we began the study of the Gītā we were told in the very first verse that it was going to revalue both dharma *and* karma. *Why does Kṛṣṇa now ask Arjuna to abandon all* dharmas? *Arjuna's very fear in the opening chapter was of losing* dharma.

---

[10] Robert Ernest Hume (tr.), 1979, *The Thirteen Principal Upanishads*, New York: Oxford University Press, pp. 83-84.

[11] Ibid., p. 213.

The word *dharma* can be understood in a theological sense as one's religion, and in an epistemological sense as the root cause of the phenomenal experience of distinguishing Self from non-Self, and of making distinctions such as this and that, based on name, form, time, space, motion, structure, and functions. When *dharma* is taken as one's religion this final teaching of Kṛṣṇa may sound like heresy. Religion is supposed to inculcate and safeguard the highest moral norms and ethical principles. Asking one to discard it may appear like giving permission to become licentious. What Kṛṣṇa actually suggests is not a regression from *dharma* to *adharma*, it is a progression to transcending *dharma*. Through seventeen chapters Kṛṣṇa has taught Arjuna how to purify himself of alt taints of *adharma*, transgressions of law. Now he wants to reveal to him man's final freedom.

The greatest promise of the Upaniṣads is *tarati śokam ātmavit* (knower of the Self crosses over all sorrows) (*Chāndogya Upaniṣad* 7.1.3). The Gītā's final teaching, in verse 66 of Chapter XVIII, should be understood in the light of the very first words that Kṛṣṇa uttered in his role as Guru in verse 11, Chapter II:

> You are sorry for those with whom sorrow is unreasonable. You speak in terms of reason too. Veritable philosophers are not affected in regard to those whose breath has gone and those whose breath has not gone.

Sorrow has relevancy only in the world of separate individuals. Individuation is based on the structuring of specific properties. When one moves from the specific to the general, distinguishing marks disappear. A man living as a member of his family has to make several distinctions, such as father, mother, grandparents, brother, sister, daughter, and son. But one who has no family does not have to bother about any of these relationships. What is important in the family set-up will appear to the non-family man as a tyranny of sentiments. A *saṁnyāsin* goes beyond society's norms of good and bad and all kinds of classifications, because his wisdom is established in the knowledge of *Brahman*. That knowledge also implies his transcendence of *dharma*. The *ātman* that is to be known is the same as knowing the Tao. In the *Māṇḍūkya Upaniṣad*, verse 7, the Self or the Absolute is described as:

> Not inwardly cognitive (*antaḥ-prajña*), not outwardly cognitive (*bahiḥ-prajña*), not both-wise cognitive (*ubhayataḥ-prajña*), not a cognition-mass (*prajñāna-ghana*), not cognitive (*prajña*), not non-cognitive (*aprajña*), unseen (*adṛṣṭa*), with which there can be no dealing (*a-vyavahārya*), ungraspable (*a-grāhya*), having no distinctive mark (*alakṣaṇa*), non-thinkable (*acintya*), that cannot be designated (*a-vyapadeśya*), the essence of the assurance of which is the state of being one with the Self (*ekātmya-pratyayasāra*), the cessation of

> development (*prapañcopaśama*), tranquil (*śānta*), benign (*śiva*), without a second (*advaita*) – (such) they think is the fourth. He is the Self (*Ātman*). He should be discerned.[12]

In the above definition of the Absolute we do not find anything tangible for the mind to grasp. This discourse does not seem to resemble the precise definitions and descriptions given in books of science.

All books of wisdom can take us only to the furthest limit of concepts. After many scholarly discourses in the *Chāndogya Upaniṣad*, the following story is given to illustrate the need to go beyond everything studied by way of science or art:

> Nārada, one of the ancient sages, once went to obtain wisdom from the great seer Sanatkumāra. He said, "Sir, please teach me". On hearing that, Sanatkumāra said, "Tell me what you know. If your knowledge is wanting, I shall instruct you". Then Nārada said, "Sir, I know *Ṛkveda*, *Yajurveda*, *Sāmaveda*, and the fourth one, *Atharva*. I know also epics and mythology. I am also instructed in grammar, eschatology, astronomy, theology, economics, logic, ethics, rhetoric, knowledge of metaphysics, physics, the art of archery, and prediction. All these I know. But sir, my knowledge is only of a scholar. I have heard that a knower of the Self crosses over sorrows. I am still afflicted with sorrows, so my knowledge is only theoretical." On hearing this, Sanatkumāra said, "What you said you know is non-knowledge. You are only familiar with the discursive connotations of names." – 7.1.1-3

Going beyond name and form implies the true secret of *yoga*. In the Yoga Darśana of Narayana Guru's *Darśana Mālā* the Guru says:

That which always unites the mind
With the reasoning Self, and also gets united with it,
And which is in the form of restraint,
That is praised as Yoga.[13]

In this verse, Narayana Guru speaks of a union that is coming from two sides. It is a complementary function, as in the coming together of a bolt and a nut. On the bolt are the threads. Their complementary grooves are on the nut. There has to be a correspondence between the thread and the groove. There also has to be the application of a progressive, gentle force of turning the bolt or the nut in the right direction. This does not mean forcing one's way, but rather submitting to the requirements of the situation. Thus, the final union has in it both a positive and a negative attitude

---

[12] Robert Ernest Hume, 1979, op. cit., p. 392.

[13] Nataraja Guru (tr.), 2019, *Anthology of Poem of Narayana Guru*, Varkala: Narayana Gurukula, p. 72.

which cancel out the pairs of opposites. Leaving all *dharma* is negative, and taking refuge in the Absolute is positive. Both these are happening simultaneously. In the highest sense nothing is happening. It is only like waking up from a dream. No effort is needed to leave the persons, things, and situations of the dream when consciousness emerges from it to the wakeful state. Similarly, when one recognizes the universality of Being, the several demands and peculiarities of the individuated persona vanish like mist in the sunlight.

Hmmm. What is the significance of verses 67 to 71?

Please read them.

Alright:

> This is never to be spoken about by you to one spiritually undisciplined, nor to one devoid of devotion, nor to one indisposed to listen, nor to one who denies Me.
>
> He who gives this supreme secret to My devotee, thereby doing for Me supreme devotion, shall doubtless come to Me.
>
> Nor is there besides such a one, among men, any who is the highest performer of dear acts, nor shall there be for Me another dearer on earth.
>
> And he who will study this dialogue of ours, conducive to righteousness, by him (in effect) I shall have been worshipped through the wisdom-sacrifice; so I hold.
>
> And the man who may merely happen to hear, endowed with faith, and uncarping – even he, liberated, shall attain to the good worlds of those who perform meritorious deeds.

It is a tradition in Sanskrit classics to give at the end of a book all the good that accrues from the learning of it. The author also uses a literary device, to add as an afterthought certain do's and don'ts. Kṛṣṇa's teaching terminates with verse 66. The verses which follow are put in Kṛṣṇa's mouth only to emphasize the authenticity of the teaching, giving it the stamp of a genuine revelation. Similarly, verse 72 is only added to make sure that the Gītā is brought to a logical conclusion:

> Has it been heard by you, Oh Pārtha! with one-pointed mind? Oh Winner of Wealth! has your delusion of ignorance been destroyed?

This verse marks the counterpart of verse 7, Chapter II, in which Arjuna surrendered himself to Kṛṣṇa as his disciple, complaining that he had become confused and had lost the memory of right and wrong. Verse 73 is Arjuna's acknowledgement of the Gītā teaching:

> Gone is my delusion, and Self-recognition has been gained by me through Your grace, Oh Acyuta! I am properly established, with doubts gone; I shall carry out Your word.

What is the significance of verse 74? I will read it also:

> Sañjaya said:
>
> Thus have I heard this wonderful dialogue between Vāsudeva and the high-souled Pārtha, causing my hair to stand on end.

In the Introduction we spoke of the device of using three curtains. Now that the drama is over, the dropped curtain device is applied as the heroes disappear from the stage.

By the grace of Vyāsa I heard this supreme and most secret *yoga*, spoken by Kṛṣṇa himself, the Lord of Yoga, as immediately given to my senses.

In verse 75 we see the author of the Gītā putting his signature, assuming the humble role of a compiler. He does not want to take credit for the teachings of Kṛṣṇa, although in the wisdom-context there is no difference between Kṛṣṇa and Vyāsa.

The last three verses are to express the gratitude of the listener and to glorify Kṛṣṇa both as *yogī* and *Īśvara*:

> Oh King! as I remember and remember this marvellous and sacred dialogue between Keśava and Arjuna, I rejoice over and over again.
>
> As I remember and remember that most marvellous form of Hari, great is my astonishment, Oh King! and I rejoice over and over again.
>
> Where there is Kṛṣṇa, the Lord of Yoga, where there is Pārtha, the Archer, there will be prosperity, victory, progress, and well-established justice: such is my belief.

AUṀ TAT SAT

Index